The Russian Nanny, Real and Imagined

The Russian Nanny, Real and Imagined:

History, Culture, Mythology

Steven A. Grant

Washington, DC

Copyright © 2012 by Steven A. Grant
New Academia Publishing 2012

All rights reserved. No part of this book may be reproduced or transmitted in any form or by any means, electronic or mechanical, including photocopying, recording, or by any information storage and retrieval system.

Printed in the United States of America

Library of Congress Control Number: 2012938727
ISBN 978-0-9855698-1-5 paperback (alk. paper)
ISBN 978-0-9855698-2-2.hardcover (alk. paper)

New Academia Publishing
PO Box 27420, Washington, DC 20038-7420
info@newacademia.com - www.newacademia.com

For Sharon and Elliot

Contents

Introduction	1
1. The Celebrated Case of Pushkin's Nanny	15
2. Russian Nannies Before Pushkin	39
3. Socio-Cultural Background for the Modern Nanny	55
4. The Classic, Pre-Emancipation Nanny	81
5. The Everyday Life of (Mostly) Ordinary Women	109
6. Post-Emancipation and Post-1917 Nannies	149
7. Significance of the Nanny in the Child's Life	187
8. The Long Literary Career of the Nanny	215
9. To Mythologize or Not? Nanny's Role in Creative Lives	245
10. Nanny as Symbol	289
Concluding Thoughts	307
Endnotes	311
Bibliography	436
Index	479

List of Illustrations

Bas-relief, allegedly of Arina Rodionovna by Iakov Seriakov (1840s?)	16
Dmitrii Beliukin, *Alexander Pushkin at Arina Rodionovna's in Mikhailovskoe* (1985)	21
Memorial in Pskov, Russia: *Pushkin and Peasant* (i.e., Arina), Oleg Komov, sculptor/M. Konstantinov, architect (1983)	35
Konstantin Makovskii, *Nanny of Ivan the Terrible* (1880)	41
Aleksei Venetsianov, *Wet-nurse with Child* (1830)	61
Pavel Fedotov, *Domnushka, Nanny in the Zhdanovich Family* (1846/47)	66
Vasilii Vereshchagin, sketch of his nanny Anna (ca. 1890?)	72
Aleksei Venetsianov, *Portrait of the Panaev Children with Their Nanny* (1841)	84
Pavel Fedotov, *Vasia and Nanny/Vasia and Kitty* (1848/49)	119
Nanny of Sergei Pankeev, Freud's "Wolf-Man," ca. 1890s?	146
Pankeev children, Anna and Sergei	147
Nanny Pasha, Chernov Andreev family, ca. 1907	155
Leon Bakst, *Portrait of Sergei Diagilev* (1906)	163
Nikolai Ge, *Pushchin Visiting Pushkin at Mikhailovskoe* (1875)	222
Aleksei Venetsianov, *Old Nanny in Peasant Head-dress* (1829?)	248
Ivan Goncharov's nanny Annushka (ca. 1867)	250
Nikolai Ge, *My Nanny* (1867)	273
Pskov Memorial to Pushkin and Arina (1983)	297

Permissions/Thanks to:

Iurii Kiselev, Cover photo and other pictures of the Pskov Pushkin-Arina Memorial

State Russian Museum, St. Petersburg © 2012: Makovskii, *Nanny of Ivan the Terrible;* Venetsianov, *Old Nanny;* Bakst, *Diagilev;* Fedotov, *Domnushka* and *Vasia and Nanny*

Tret'iakov Gallery, Moscow (Venetsianov, *Panaev Children* and *Wet-nurse;* Ge, *My Nanny*)

RIA Novosti: visualrian (Ge, *Pushchin Visit* and Beliukin, *Pushkin at Arina's*)

I.A. Goncharov Museum, Ul'ianovsk, Russia (Photo of Goncharov's nanny)

Photo of Nanny Pasha reproduced by permission of Olga Andreyev Carlisle

Photos of Pankeev family nanny and children from Manuscripts Division, Library of Congress

David M. Bethea, for his translation of Khodasevich's poem to his wet-nurse/nanny

Introduction

She is ubiquitous in modern Russian history and culture: the Russian nanny.[1] In life histories, novels, stories, plays, musical compositions, and paintings, this figure appears – sometimes unexpectedly, sometimes incongruously, but continuously. Usually remembered fondly, lovingly, sometimes as saintly, the Russian nanny casts a shadow – or is it a spell? – over a broad swath of the Russian past.

From its title, this study might seem to have a narrow focus. How much can one say about child caretakers? The answer is: more than one might think at first blush. Far from being narrow, this subject opens up vistas on Russia and its history from several viewpoints. As we shall see, Russian nannies are claimed to have (a) changed the course of Russian history, (b) contributed greatly to the development of Russian language and literature, and (c) played a fairly significant role in the evolution of Russian national music.[2]

This book is principally about women, women in the occupation (or calling) of caring for small children, and about ideas or myths surrounding both individual nannies and nannies in the abstract. Its two major themes are thus reality and constructed reality. It examines how a figure that fell all too easily into a near caricature still retained tremendous emotional power and specificity in the lives of so many Russians, especially creative writers and artists. Secondarily, the book concerns the limits of autobiography and biography, the conscious and unconscious manipulation of memory, and the autobiographical fallacy. An important subtext that recurs frequently is that of intellectuals seeking to (super) impose their own notions, values, and ideals upon others to satisfy their personal needs and desires.

To anticipate a bit of what follows, it might surprise the reader to learn that "the Russian nanny" was not always a serf or former serf, nor even a peasant; she served not just in noble households; she was far from always old and wrinkled or ethnic Russian; and she – was sometimes a he! That being said, however, the focus of the book is on what I call the "classic Russian nanny," familiar to most readers: a peasant woman, often born before emancipation of the serfs (1861), working in a noble family.[3]

Like Caesar's Gaul, my book is tripartite. One part concerns real-life nannies, the role(s) they played in and the impact they had on their charges' lives – mostly in childhood. This story of real-life caretakers is documented in all kinds of ego-documents and illustrated in a great deal of fiction. Another part explores the ways in which the idea and myths of the nanny played out in Russia, in history and culture, particularly in literature but also in other spheres of art. This section demonstrates that not-so-real stories about many of these caretakers have grown in Russian culture to the point of taking on a life of their own. The final part is a discussion of how and why the nanny figure, in Russia as elsewhere, became a cultural phenomenon and symbol.

Origins

The genesis of this book came from the pure pleasure of reading memoirs and autobiographies over the past 40 years or more. I was originally struck by how often sundry important or interesting people in nineteenth-century Russia made reference to their nannies. This fact in itself is not surprising; after all, nannies played a central role in the infancy of most people of the upper classes in that society, as in most European societies of the time. Yet it was still a curiosity. The more I looked into the subject, the "curiouser and curiouser" things seemed, as Alice would say. Nannies became an obsession. What you now hold in your hands is the fruit of this obsession.

Ambivalence and Ambiguity

A key recurring subtheme throughout the following pages is that of ambivalence. One continually finds feelings of ambivalence with regard to nearly all aspects of childcare: in attitudes toward servants and caretakers, in opinions of the best kind of *vospitanie*[4] or upbringing to give a child. Ambiguities, ironies, paradoxes, and contradictions will show up over and over again in the analyses which follow. Let me highlight three kinds of ambivalence, all of which are important for grasping why nannies could become a matter of attention and moment. These are relations between the peasantry and upper classes, the relationship between masters and servants, and the treatment of women.[5] Village life, peasant customs and rituals, folklore and folkways might seem familiar to other social groups in Russia, especially before the eighteenth century. But increasingly after 1700, these things could all seem as foreign to the life of the manor house as another country. For economic and political reasons these two worlds have historically been forced into almost constant contact. While the interests of each sphere can sometimes overlap or even coincide, they are not the same in the best of circumstances. In the worst case, as with the institution of serfdom, those interests can diverge drastically. Suspicion and distrust are the frequent result; ambivalent feelings are usually a given.

In almost exactly the same way as for peasants, the relations of "master and man" have always been full of ambiguities. Existing in closest proximity, each side of this relationship is forced to deal with the other: to accommodate, resist, absorb, and otherwise interact with personalities and personages dissimilar in social status and economic circumstances. Masters and servants could respectively be objects of respect, admiration, affection, and even love while simultaneously being objects of disapprobation, scorn, dislike, or hatred. Suspicion, one of the other, was perhaps not always paramount, but it usually lurked just beneath the surface of many master-servant relationships.[6] In this limited sense, the oft-expressed sentiment – from both ends of the relationship – of the closeness of master and servant, of servants (especially nannies) being (like) "members of the family" rings somewhat false. It is as if both sides were trying to convince themselves of the claim's truth; they sometimes "protest too much." It seems this was in part a shibboleth designed to ward off the ever-present threat of disharmony within a very small community.[7]

Everything about women in the centuries under discussion was surrounded by ambiguity. Every view of womanhood embodied ambivalence. This was true of women of high and low social status, educated and uneducated, young and old. Even if every generalization risks contradiction by counter-example and exception, the following points seem "safe" and relevant. The values of society and of women tended to coincide, and positive qualities seen in women mirrored what was perceived as best in life at the time. Thus, in medieval and early modern times there are famous examples of noble women humble, obedient, and submissive; loyal and steadfast; resourceful and energetic; strong-willed; and of high moral character.[8] At the same time, the generic picture of women included such negative traits as being superstitious, irrational, overly emotional, ignorant, and flighty – no matter if the latter contradicted the former qualities. The purveying of such images in the written word and on the stage, from altars and classrooms, served well the purposes of a male-dominated, hierarchical world.

Because a Russian nanny was most often peasant, servant, and female, ambivalence colored nearly all aspects of what most pre- and post-emancipation nannies were and did. The qualities which noble masters genuinely admired in female peasant servants – their "simplicity," directness, genuineness, lack of pretension, "open" natures, steadfastness and loyalty, commonsense, and so on – often were or were seen as the obverse of a social currency the reverse of which were deceitfulness and guile, boorishness, laziness, stubbornness, recalcitrance, ignorance, superstition, and prejudice.

In short, a complex set of expectations and attitudes toward the nanny were at work throughout modern Russian history, and these undoubtedly shaped the portrayal of the nanny to a large degree in memoirs, literature, and culture more generally.

The Problem of Stereotypes and Other Biases

One issue addressed herein with respect to both the memoir record and literature is that of stereotypes. Throughout much of modern Russian culture, the nanny represented a stereotype of one kind or another. I believe I've come to grips fairly successfully with some of these stereotypes in various chapters that follow.

Female Stereotyping and the Issue of Gender.[9] Most nanny stereotyping revolves around aspects of gender. Notions of nannies clearly reflect more general ideas about women current at the time. Ideas about gender changed only slowly if at all throughout this story. We can assume without much fear of contradiction that the vast majority of authors and memoirists of the eighteenth and nineteenth centuries were unconscious and unabashed "sexists," firmly believing in the existence of major differences between the genders, and that they found certain traits far more in evidence in one sex than the other. Thus, when autobiographers from 1700 to at least 1900 constantly use the terms "dedication," "devotion," and "deep attachment" (*posviashchenie, predannost', priviazannost'*) in describing their nannies, one's guard should be up. These descriptors often enough mutate in print into extreme forms of selflessness, self-sacrifice or self-abnegation (*samootverzhennost', samopozhertvovanie, samootrechenie*). All remind one of what is usually called "maternal instinct" or "mother love"– characteristics uncomfortably close to being stereotypical not just for nannies and mothers, but for women as a whole.[10] Such blanket descriptors nearly always fail the sniff test, and we would be well-advised to use extreme caution with memoirs and other sources that speak in such terms of females generally or nannies in particular.

At the same time, however, differences between the sexes can be acknowledged and even celebrated. For all their stereotypicality, some traits nonetheless seem to me to have been a real part of the makeup of many, even most nannies. A feminist writer might disagree with my assessment, might link my view to a gender bias. However, these characteristics of nannies are recorded not just by male memoirists but equally or more by female autobiographers.

By custom and religion, in the village or town, women in medieval and early modern Russian society were destined mostly for marriage and child-bearing. By law they preserved some few rights, especially to property, but bore more burdens and responsibilities than privileges. Patriarchy and Orthodoxy set the tone in all things gender-related. For the vast majority of females, career choices beyond the home were nearly nonexistent, with the exception of the calling of nun (and, much later, writer or poet). Even though this changed somewhat in the eighteenth century, if only at the highest levels of society, the opening up of public life for the well-born remained circumscribed if not short-lived. Individual self-realization outside the family was an aspiration of or possibility for few young women (and virtually nonexistent for females of the peasantry, merchantry, and clergy) until well into the nineteenth century. Violence against women was, if not endemic, no stranger in peasant homes and probably many merchant families as well.

By the end of the eighteenth and for about half the nineteenth century, secular bourgeois values (emanating largely from West Europe) served mostly to reinforce the more traditional values which kept women out of public life and focused on private/family life. This seemingly static situation, never completely uniform, was changing through time, due in part to better educational opportunities for women. None of this seemed to affect peasant women – the bulk of nannies – until late in the nineteenth century.

It would be difficult to fix accurate dates for any specific changes in the outlook or treatment of women, low and high. One senses that between about 1750 and 1850 inner turmoil and societal evolution had greatly altered some aspects of distaff life. Some women of the middle and upper classes aspired to and achieved satisfying, nontraditional careers. Strangely enough, as working women, the position of nannies – in life and the public imagination – varied but little through the years. Subordinate by definition, yet with a power all her own due to her caretaking, a nanny enjoyed a kind of freedom even though she was – like all women – constrained by being female. Perhaps it was not until the larger issue of peasant emancipation was fully addressed that the question of female emancipation could take a more central place. If so, this pattern would repeat itself after 1917, when feminists nearly all subordinated (or forsook) their aims in support of the "greater" political revolution.

In works of literature women of all social stations long appeared conventionally: pure and innocent (the peasant girl Liza in Karamzin's sentimental tale, Tat'iana in Pushkin's *Onegin*), or aggressive-demonic, often harridan-like (Madam Prostakova in Fonvizin's *Minor*, the family matriarch in Aksakov's *Family Chronicle*, some Dostoevskii heroines). Plot lines involving women were yawningly predictable: a girl might be seduced and abandoned, pursued and won, but without a male counterweight she had little gravity. Except in ego-documents and poetry, even women writers were slow to break this mold. Yet by the second half of the nineteenth century, if not before, male and female authors can be seen to introduce a more nuanced treatment of women characters. To be virtuous might still seem paramount in women high and low, but new definitions of female virtue began to emerge. Stereotypes like the long-suffering peasant woman, the constricted and neglected provincial gentry or merchant woman, the empty-feeling high-society woman remained staples of fiction and stage, but new kinds of women – more independent and autonomous – also appeared.

In the twentieth century, which dawned with great promise for Russian women, especially from the village and lower strata of society, one hoped for better but "all turned out as usual." 1917 did not so much raise all women to a higher level equal to that of men but instead, in good Shigalevan fashion, tended to lower women *and men* to a common, meaner level. A surprising exception to this rule, in some ways, was a child's nanny. The status of and regard for these women never seemed to dim noticeably, the demand for them did not diminish, and their hold on the public's imagination remained strong well into the last century.

Slanted History. Patently nonobjective historical writing is an unfortunate constant in the world. No matter how high-minded the purpose, it will always diminish the value of historical study. In the mid-twentieth century professional historians coined a felicitous phrase for one kind of such writing. The enterprise was called "the search for a usable past." What does this formulation mean? Typically, it refers to people who were single-mindedly seeking out in the past of their own ethnic, national, gender, what-have-you group only those elements which served to raise the stature of that group. This practice of paying attention to limited parts of the historical record, particularly widespread in the past among nationalistic writers of less-developed countries, sometimes gave disproportionate, often undeserved prominence to the chosen elements.

Claims of "redressing" the historical balance or simply shedding light on hitherto neglected or unknown facts might justify the practice. But such intentional distortion of the past frequently requires its own rebalancing in turn, and certainly leads to ambiguities in the historical record. This endeavor of combing through the past selectively is similar to what Russian writers of the eighteenth or nineteenth century engaged in while writing their novels, stories, and plays – or autobiographies. But beyond how this applied to the building of Russian national consciousness in this period, it applies as well in a more narrow sense. Many authors, for example, were in search of a usable past with regard to the peasantry.[11] In their search, often of their own personal histories, it was natural that many would light on personages from their childhood, including a well-remembered peasant caretaker.

Women's History. How does this study fit into the larger picture of women's studies in Russia? As working women, nannies are a part of labor history and gender studies. This book is nearly a prosopography for a subset of female servants. Were all nannies of peasant origin, it might claim to be more of a contribution to village studies. Many nannies provide a glimpse into female social mobility in Russia, as women from lower social strata moved upward into higher positions in their world. To play devil's advocate briefly, one might even claim that these women enjoyed some advantages over their more educated or more privileged sisters. They were able to find employment outside the parental home at a much earlier period; the seeming majority developed a very clear sense of identity and self-worth; most took evident pride in their work.

The Background Against Which My Story Unfolds

What makes the subject of the nanny so appealing for me is that in looking at several centuries of Russian history, nannies help shed light on some important social, cultural, political, and intellectual developments. If the skeptical reader is now thinking that this work sounds like a Stoppardian take on Hamlet, I plead guilty. There is a "Rosencrantz-and-Guildenstern" quality in what follows. But that is not necessarily a negative; I believe it adds to the fun of the research, using relatively unimportant figures to explore larger themes.

There are some subjects in history which can never be done justice. There are topics for which a beginning can never be pinpointed, others which are too encompassing, too vague, or too complex to be nailed down in truly satisfactory fashion. It is a daunting yet somehow invigorating fact that the background for this book includes not one or two but many such themes and subjects. The very mention of them sets the mind racing. In the general history of the last half millennium, such themes include modernization, nationalism, and secularism. In sociocultural history, similar subjects with great resonance include the Enlightenment, Classicism, Romanticism, modernism, feminism. More narrowly, all the following subjects also figure in my story: family dynamics; the development of a recognizably national language and culture in Russia, coupled with the search for a national identity; education, particularly private; the rise and decline of the Russian nobility; socio-economic class differences (what Marxian scholars would doubtless call "class conflict") and master-servant relations; the system of serfdom and its fate, especially just before and then in the decades after 1861; the spread of radical and revolutionary ideas; the "watershed" of 1917 and the problem of change and continuity.[12]

Sources, Lines of Inquiry, Methodology

The vast majority of my sources are personal documents like autobiographies and memoirs (I've read nearly 1000), less often letters or diaries (all "ego-documents" in current parlance). These sources are a hybrid of factual record and literature. To paraphrase Winston Churchill's oft-quoted observation about forms of government, autobiographies and memoirs are the worst form of historical source material – except for all the others. Memoir literature is an indispensable source, among the most valuable the historian has, for two reasons. First, they offer factual material that can be found nowhere else. Second, and often more important, they provide undoubted evidence of the psychological, emotional, and mental states of those composing them, if not at the time of some occurrence in the life, at least at the time of composition of the autobiography. I am particularly interested in the extent to which reality has been distorted or misrepresented, intentionally or otherwise, and – as previously noted – in the autobiographical fallacy. In most cases, if trying to pin down some significant point in an argument, I try to cite more than one source that at least purports to draw a true picture of life. To illustrate these points, however, I frequently appeal to fictional sources as well.

One major line of inquiry which informs the bulk of this work is: what is the relationship between historical reality and works of art or culture which deal with a rather narrow subject, Russian nannies. How did the reality affect the art? It will readily be seen in what follows that there is a great mythology – or better, a set of various myths – that has attached itself to Russian nannies. These myths arise and then resonate among many people for very specific reasons, most of which I try to explain. I hope to show that scholars have not always been as careful as they might in dealing with aspects of these myths. Along the way, the reader will also learn about some of the main promulgators of these nanny myths in the nineteenth century – such leading cultural figures as Pëtr Bartenev, Vladimir Stasov, Ivan Aksakov, and Fëdor Dostoevskii.

In following these lines of inquiry, I often start by trying to break down generalizations and what is "common knowledge." This book takes as its motto "the devil is in the details," because therein lie all the important differences. The major point of several chapters, if not of the entire book, is that more is lost than gained by generalizing. Not that these kinds of summarizing statements and ideas are always wrong – far from it. But it is most often the exceptions, the outliers, and the "special cases" that have proven most interesting to me. By the accumulation of detail upon detail, I believe that a clearer picture of reality emerges, one that might not fit exactly the broader picture commonly held and for that reason seems to add depth and balance and sharper color to a more inclusive but generalized picture.

About dates I have tried to be scrupulous; some may even find it annoying that I so often insert the lifetimes of most of those mentioned in the text. However, long experience with secondary sources has taught me that primary sources are too often misused for the simple reason that they relate to a time period other than that about which the author is speaking. The reader's forbearance is therefore asked. And when I cite a source which is clearly not from the time under discussion, I have tried to signal this anomaly and comment on why this use may be appropriate.

I am critical of some colleagues in these pages, but not overly so I hope. I often call them to task for making unwarranted generalizations, or adhering to myths that fail one or another acid test, and, most often, for accepting works of fiction as documentation for the author's actual life. In doing so, I'm all too aware that some of my own analyses and conclusions may not withstand the scrutiny of those more expert than I. My peccadilloes will doubtless prove fodder for this book's readers and reviewers. The reader should therefore keep in mind – as I have tried – the musing of Jane Austen's Mr. Bennet: "For what do we live, but to make sport for our neighbors, and laugh at them in our turn?"

Finally, there is an abundance of quotations in this book, more, perhaps, than most scholarly works permit. Paraphrasing and summary might have done as well, but I have been guided by the fact that my primary sources – autobiographies and memoirs – are works of literature and, yes, imaginative recreation. Some, like Herzen's *My Past and Thoughts*, are masterpieces of world literature. Many, many more have been written by renowned authors of fiction or prose. To rob them of speaking directly, in words often too poignant, limpid, or pointed to replicate, seemed a shame.

A Note on Caretaker and Other Terminology

Before getting into the heart of this study, it would be well to pause for a short vocabulary lesson. Throughout this book, the English word "nanny" is used to translate several different Russian words, most of them just variations of the same thing. The basic word for a nanny in Russian is either *niánia* or *nián'ka*. (The diminutive-affectionate versions of *niania* include *niániushka* and *niánechka*.[13]) Its usage can be traced well back past the eighteenth century, as we will see. Its etymology is not exactly clear, but similar words for "mother," "aunt," "wet-nurse," and "nanny" occur in many Indo-European languages.[14] More importantly, as Marina Warner notes, the "n" sound is one of the first a child is capable of; the repetitive "n" sound is thus a most natural early part of an infant's speech.[15]

In addition to *niania* there were several other terms by which a nanny might be called. First, the words *mámushka* and *mámka* were frequent substitutes. Originally these words – forms of those meaning simply "mother," "*mat'*" or "*mama*" – were used to mean a "wet-nurse" or "a supervisory/senior nanny." But by the seventeenth century they were used increasingly to mean as well the same thing as "*niania*." Given the various connotations of "*mamushka*" and "*mamka*," I've decided that the best translation must be "mammy," the more so in that it is virtually obligatory, from the Russian folk tradition, that the word rhyme almost exactly with "nanny."

Two borrowings from other languages were also frequently employed to designate a nanny or a governess if she was of foreign origin or not peasant-born: the French *bonne* (either in the original or in its Russian form of *bónna*); and the German *fraülein* (nearly always in the Russian *fréilein*). The latter is merely a short form of the German word for a nursery-maid or nursery-governess, *Kinderfraülein* (cf. the similar terms *Kinderfrau*, *Kindermädchen*, and *Kinderpflegerin*, all used more or less interchangeably).[16] There was a clear distinction implied in the use of the term *bonna* or *bonne*: this word was apparently used only for a woman who was literate.[17] I know of no instances in which a Russian peasant woman (often one step removed from the village) was called a "*bonna*" or "*freilein*." A *bonne* thus differed from a peasant nanny in ways which had nothing to do with ethnic origin or country of birth: most Russian peasant women until the twentieth century were illiterate and therefore incapable of being *bonnes*; and a *bonne* – unlike virtually all Russian peasant nannies – was capable of becoming a governess and rearing her charge intellectually as well as physically and behaviorally.

A nanny was engaged in *vospitanie* (upbringing) rather than *obrazovanie* (more formal education). I leave the first word (and derivatives, like *vospitatel'nitsa* – upbringer) untranslated in nearly all cases, as the connotations in Russian are rich. *Vospitanie* involved behavior more than mental activity – training the moral character of a child as much as its mind. A nanny's master, before 1861 in particular, was often a *pomeshchik* (fem. *pomeshchitsa*) – a serfowner and proprietor of a country estate. Again, no single English word is a good equivalent.

Acknowledgments

I would like to thank the following individuals who have been kind enough to share with me their thoughts and knowledge on a variety of topics or rendered particular assistance in obtaining needed materials: the staff of the European Reading Room of the Library of Congress (including Grant Harris, Angela Cannon, Harry Leich, Ken Nyirady, Regina Frackowiak, Helen Fedor, Predrag Pajic, Erika Spencer, and Mark Brown) – my home away from home; Mary Fleming Zirin, Edward L. Keenan, Marina Meehan and Kristen Regina of the Hillwood Museum, Malcolm H. Brown, Liudmila Taimasova, Anita Kondoyanidi, Anton Fedyashin, Alissa Klots, Nancy Shields Kollmann, Helen Sullivan and the staff of the Slavic Reference Service at the University of Illinois at Urbana-Champaign, June Farris, Michael David-Fox, Svetlana Mangutova of the Russian National Library in St. Petersburg, Natalia Baschmakoff of the Academy of Finland, Iurii Nikolaevich Kiselev of the Pskov State Museum, Viktoriia Kadochnikova of the State Russian Museum in St. Petersburg, Christine Worobec, Kate Pickering Antonova, Sergei Antonov, Caryl Emerson, Jussi Wacklin, David Goldfrank, Melissa Stockdale, Marjorie Mandelstam Balzer, Richard Taruskin, Viktor Belopolskii, Aleksandr Lokshin, Barbara Alpern Engel, Andrei Pliguzov, Carolyn Pouncy, Thomas C. Owen, and the two anonymous reviewers for New Academia.

I owe a very special debt to Barbara Evans Newman, Katie Trumpener, Katharina Kucher, Max J. Okenfuss, Catriona Kelly, Kevin Bartig, Gerald Newman, Ned Keenan, Greg Guroff, Vladimir Frumkin, Mary Zirin, and especially my son Elliot T. Grant for reading either the entire draft manuscript or sections of it and offering invaluable advice, counsel, and encouragement. The late Richard Stites, enormously missed, provided much needed moral support when the book was taking shape.

1

The Celebrated Case of Pushkin's Nanny

The most famous Russian nanny of all is a peasant woman named Arina Rodionovna (1758-1828), renowned as the nanny of the poet Aleksandr Pushkin (1799-1837).[1] She has become legendary – even mythic – for many reasons. The seeds of the legend were planted during Pushkin's own lifetime, aided by the writer himself (though unconsciously). He "immortalized" Arina – and her counterparts – in various works, in particular his masterpiece, the novel in verse *Evgenii Onegin*.[2] But the legend grew to mythical proportions in the years following his death, thanks largely to the efforts of Pushkin friends and biographers. The myth continued to grow in later years, aided and abetted by romanticizing memoirists as well as by peasant-sympathetic Slavophile, *narodnik* and especially Soviet writers. It has become so ingrained in the public's imagination as to be a force in Russian life and culture.[3]

Pushkin was not the first Russian nobleman to have a peasant nanny; his was not the first literary depiction of a Russian nanny. Why begin our story *in medias res*? First, because everything about Pushkin and his nanny is a cautionary tale, one that sets the proper tone for the rest of my study. Too many have been led astray about this poet by "facts" that turn out to be illusionary.[4] Second, because Pushkin marks a watershed for the Russian nanny in both fiction and history. Few images in Russian literature have had the incredible afterlife of the devoted nanny of Pushkin's *Onegin*. In giving us this portrayal he was just a part of a much larger peasant-

Bas-relief, allegedly of Arina Rodionovna by Iakov Seriakov (1840s?)

sympathetic movement that would shortly encompass not only literature but much of society. He would change, perhaps forever, the image of the nanny for most Russian readers and writers. Third, Pushkin's *oeuvre* and biography raise most of the fundamental issues examined in this book. Was Arina a typical Russian nanny? What was her life like? Did Pushkin portray her accurately – *or at all* – in *Onegin* or other works? Can we say anything more about the relationship between Pushkin's having had a nanny and his *oeuvre*? Was she an inspiration for him?

For some time, in thinking about this one nanny, I felt her legend-myth to be a kind of aberration. But it happens that there are broader contexts for this seemingly unique phenomenon. In the first place, similar legendary nannies exist in other cultures, most notably in the British Isles, though none reached the cult status of Arina. In the second place, nanny figures elsewhere played about the same symbolic role as Arina. However, in one sense it seems that Russians in the nineteenth century managed to anticipate – one of the rare times this has happened culturally – a development that came somewhat later in Western Europe. They took the magic of childhood, a rather unoriginal idea by Pushkin's time, and for the first time that I'm aware associated it with one figure of childhood, a caretaker. The analogy is far from perfect, but it is not a huge stretch to see in the almost preternatural qualities invested in Arina a harbinger of later magical nannies like J.M. Barrie's anthropomorphized Nana, P.L. Travers's Mary Poppins, and Christianna Brand's Nurse[maid] Matilda (Nanny McPhee).

Elements of the Arina Myth Are Many and Varied

What I am describing here as a myth goes something like this: Aleksandr Pushkin, arguably the greatest of Russian writers, grew up speaking and writing mostly French. Largely under the influence of his illiterate, kindhearted and loving Russian nanny, Arina, and the vivid fairy tales she spun for him, he began to pay closer attention to his native tongue and its potential as a literary language. She sang him folk songs and introduced him to peasant folkways, which – along with the tales – further inflamed his imagination and inspired him in his writings. She was the primary early Muse of the poet. As with most myths, the real story of Arina is not without some basis in fact; her cult was not fashioned entirely out of whole cloth.

All Pushkin specialists in Russia and abroad are aware of the Arina phenomenon.[5] Not all, however, will agree with my interpretation of the facts of the matter. Debate over the merits of one or another part of this myth is ongoing, and this chapter will hardly settle all arguments once and for all.[6] To some, my retelling of the story will seem like beating a dead horse. But the exercise is not futile, for several reasons. First, even though the broad outlines of this story are fairly well known, I introduce source-based evidence not previously cited. Second, no matter how many times some elements of the story are disproved, they remain in popular consciousness in Russia and even in otherwise solid works of scholarship in the West and in Russia. I hope to dispel forever a few of these dubious elements. Third, the story of the nanny in Russian history and culture cannot be understood properly without a thorough rehearsal of the story of Arina Rodionovna, including her myth.[7]

The following passage from a standard earlier biography of the poet conveys the flavor and essence of the Arina myth quite well:

> Arina occupied a special position in the household - a familiar type of house serf whose earthy wisdom, severe virtues, and unfailing loyalty were a bulwark against a variety of disintegrating influences common among Russian noble families of the time. She performed the most menial tasks with a simple dignity. And in her sturdy nature she united goodness with querulousness and infinite patience with a pretended severity. She was the guiding genius of the children, but clumsy little Sasha [Pushkin] was her favorite, perhaps for the obvious reason that he was nobody else's. Like many old peasant women, Arina's strong memory was stocked with fascinating tales drawn from the rich storehouse of Russian folklore.[8]

According to Ernest J. Simmons, Pushkin cherished his memories of nights spent with his nanny. "Arina Rodionovna awoke and fostered in him a love for the folklore of his native land which was to inspire some of his greatest poems."[9] Not only was his nanny Pushkin's childhood guide and practically his only "friend" in those early years, assert Tatiana Wolff and countless others, but she was also pivotal in the later, crucial years of his development as a poet. In his exile at Mikhailovskoe in 1824-26, according to this view, Arina was Pushkin's Muse, audience, and supplier of essential source material.[10] The poet Vladislav Khodasevich, in his otherwise discerning study of Pushkin, fully embraces the legend-myth of Arina's being Pushkin's Muse.[11] And for virtually all Russians schooled in Soviet times, the "fact" of Arina's role in Pushkin's life is a given: " Pushkin's nanny['s] *influence on the formation of the poet's character was enormous.*"[12]

These are the basic lines of the Arina myth. Over past decades, several skeptics have pointed out numerous flaws in the myth,[13] yet it lingers on in works of contemporary writers and the Russian popular imagination.[14] We must now look more closely at the woman herself to see whether the legend, much less the myth, can stand up to closer scrutiny.

What Is Known About Pushkin's Nanny in His Childhood and up to 1824

Hard, indisputable facts about Pushkin's nanny are few. There are official written records that help us learn about her. Much of what is said or written by individuals, however, depends on the unreliable memories of people recalling events of decades earlier. The following exposition contains what I feel comfortable presenting as factual.

Arina Rodionovna was the serf of Pushkin's maternal grandmother, Mariia Alekseevna Gannibal (née Pushkina; 1745-1818). Born about 1758, the daughter of Rodion Iakovlev and Luker'ia Kirillovna, she married a fellow villager named Fëdor Matveev in 1781.[15] The couple had four children; the family lived at the Gannibal estate of Kobrino until at least the death of Fëdor Matveev in the mid- to late 1790s. In about 1799, Mariia Alekseevna sold Kobrino and acquired another estate called Zakharovo, where the young Pushkin spent his early summers. At that time Mariia Alekseevna offered her serf Arina and at least one of the children their freedom, but Arina declined to accept the offer. Instead, she left her own children and moved in with the Pushkins in Moscow, as nanny primarily for Ol'ga Sergeevna (1797-1868) but soon also for her younger brothers, Sasha (the future poet) and Lev Sergeevich (1805-1852).[16] In the Pushkin household, as in many well-off gentry families, there was more than one nanny to look after children.

That is pretty much what we know of "Pushkin's nanny," Arina Rodionovna, until he left for school. Arina stayed on with the poet's parents after he had left for the Lyceum at Tsarskoe Selo in 1812, the year of Napoleon's invasion. We learn nothing more about her until Pushkin's return to Mikhailovskoe in 1824. Whether he gave any thought at all to Arina in the pre-Mikhailovskoe-exile period (from 1812 to 1824) is unknown. By the evidence of his letters to his family, of which a few survive, and of his literary output, he probably did not.[17]

The Mikhailovskoe Exile and After

All the poet's writings involving Arina are associated with his re-acquaintance with her during the years 1824 and after. This is the one period in the poet's life when Arina indisputably played an important role, during his lonely exile at the family estate of Mikhailovskoe (near Pskov, in northwest Russia). Given exaggerated claims of how dear the old woman was to him in his teen years, it is perhaps of minor interest that he noted his arrival at Mikhailovskoe in August 1824 with the very laconic "arrivé à Michailovsky" and nothing more – not a word, for instance, about who was there to greet him.[18]

His first allusion to Arina, in a letter of 4 December 1824 to his parents, is brief and inconsequential.[19] But in a letter dated 9 December 1824 to Dmitrii M. Shvarts he wrote: "My isolation is complete – idleness has triumphed…in the evening I listen to the fairy tales of my nanny, the original of Tat'iana's nanny; it seems you saw her once; she's my only friend – and only with her am I not bored."[20] This missive signaled something of greater import. It begins a period when Pushkin did feel close to Arina and she figures in his letters and other writings. (See below)

By this time Arina was approaching the end of her life. After spending the two years of his exile with the poet, she had remained at the Mikhailovskoe estate when he returned to Moscow in 1826. But not for long. In 1827 she too went to Moscow, to live with Pushkin's sister Ol'ga, her reputed favorite among the three children. She had minor contact with the poet in her last two years, none of it apparently in person. Her stay with Ol'ga was not a long one; she died in July 1828.[21]

Origins of the Legend I: What Pushkin Wrote and Did Not Write

It is not difficult to establish how the Arina legend arose. We need look no further than, on the one hand, the writings of the poet and his friends and, on the other, early biographies of Pushkin. We will not, however, always find what we seek.

Pushkin's Early Poems – No Mention of Arina. Any number of scholars both Russian/Soviet and Western, will insist that Pushkin

Dmitrii Beliukin, *Alexander Pushkin at Arina Rodionovna's in Mikhailovskoe* (1985)

wrote at least two poems about his nanny in his teen years. They have been quoted *ad nauseam* by Arina devotees to prove his devotion to her at the time, and by biographers looking too hard for information about the young boy. Yet the definitive work on Pushkin's early poems argues that neither "The Hamlet" (*Gorodok*, written in 1814-1815) nor "A Dream" (*Son*; Apr-Dec 1816) are about Arina. The *starushka* (old woman) in the first poem and endearment *mamushka* in the second both refer to Pushkin's grandmother, Mariia Gannibal, and not to Arina.[22]

Pushkin Letters and Poems about Arina. It is indisputable that between late 1824 and fall 1835 Pushkin actually did write about his nanny Arina – in nine separate letters to family and friends and in three poems or poem fragments. The epistles are quite mundane, typical of "the familiar letter" of the day,[23] and offer no grounds for later mythmaking.

In 1825, still at Mikhailovskoe, Pushkin wrote "A Winter's Evening" (*Zimnii vecher*). It probably helped create Arina's legend by its repeated publication between 1829 and 1833. (The poem was even set to music by a Pushkin Lyceum friend, the composer and baritone Mikhail Iakovlev [1798-1868], and published in this form several times in 1835.[24]) This poem does indeed celebrate Arina Rodionovna, not as his caretaker in childhood but as the boon companion of his otherwise solitary drinking bouts. Amidst the roar and whine of a winter's storm, the poet calls out to Arina, in a repeated refrain, to drink up: Let's drink, dear friend/Of my poor youth,/Let's drink from sorrow; where's the tankard?/It will make the heart more merry.

In 1826, a year after writing this first poem involving Arina, the poet composed some lines which began: Friend of my difficult days,/My decrepit old dear!/Alone in the piny backwoods/For a long, long time you've been awaiting me./By the window in your lit-up garret you/Grieve, as if keeping watch,/And the knitting needles in your wrinkled hands/Slow by the minute.[25] These few lines seem heartfelt, unsentimental, and to the point. They are probably the purest expression of some affection for the old woman *at that time*. They clearly reflect the thoughts he put in the December 1824 letter to Shvarts cited above.

There is no need to extend them back or forward in time, however, to make them an expression of how he felt about her before 1824 or after his exile. Without his urbane friends and able to spend only so much time visiting more lively neighboring estates, Pushkin was doubtless feeling a little sorry for himself by the end of his exile (in September 1826). His gratitude toward a major companion at the Mikhailovskoe estate was natural; the rueful tone of the piece speaks volumes.[26]

Finally, in September 1835, on the occasion of a return visit to the place of his youthful exile, Pushkin penned the verses known by their first line as "… Once Again I Visited" [*Vnov' ia posetil*]. In the following lines the poet evokes the memory of Arina, at this time dead for over seven years: Here's the exile's little home,/Where I lived with my poor nanny./The old woman is no more – beyond the wall/I no longer hear her heavy tread,/Nor [the sound of] her laborious patrol.[27] This is no lament for a lost "Muse" but a sad remembrance of an erstwhile friend of unhappier days.

These three poems compose the sum total of all direct references to Arina in Pushkin's poetry. None of them says a word about the poet's relationship to Arina (or any nanny) in his childhood; none of them even hints at some "influence" she had on him as a writer.

Origins of the Legend II: What Others Wrote and Did Not Write

The Major Impetus of Iazykov's Poems. The story of Pushkin's nanny might have withered at this point were it not for the hands of others. The poet's good friend and fellow poet, Nikolai Iazykov (1803-1846), wrote not one but *two* poems in Arina Rodionovna's honor. The first, dated 17 May 1827 and called "To A.S. Pushkin's Nanny,"[28] sang her praises in a most conventional way. As the "hostess" at Mikhailovskoe during Pushkin's exile, she welcomed Iazykov, fed the two friends, and entertained them with tales of bygone days.[29]

A number of ironies surround Iazykov's first poem. To begin with, he was in fact celebrating more his comradeship with Pushkin and their mutual friend A.N. Vul'f than he was the old woman who joined in their carouses at Mikhailovskoe. Second, the ostensible recipient of his "epistle" was illiterate. Third, Iazykov had apparently been so little impressed by the real woman he was nominally praising that he couldn't remember her name a few years after meeting her; and fourth – the 1827 poem was actually a jest among the three amigos. When he sent off the draft of the poem "To P[ushkin]'s Nanny" to Vul'f, he wrote: "This is the promised missive to the nanny (so far as I recall, her name is Vasil'evna); this is a versified joke, the fruit of meditation of the heart and mind – accept it with a smile, my friend!"[30]

Then in 1830 Iazykov did something even Pushkin did not do: he wrote a poem about the death of Aleksandr Sergeevich's nanny. This second work devoted to Arina – "On the Death of A. S. Pushkin's Nanny" (1830) is longer than Iazykov's first poem and reveals more about her personally.

He again roundly praises the dead woman's generosity with food and drink:

My pirovali. Ne dichilas'	We feasted. Unstinting were
Ty nashei doli - i poroi	You with our portions– and at times
K svoei vesne perenosilas'	Got carried away to your own springtime
Razgoriachennoiu mechtoi;	By [your] flushed dream;
Liubila slushat' nashi khory,	You loved to hear our songs,
Zhivye zvuki chuzhdykh stran	The vivid sounds of foreign lands,
Rechei napory i otpory	The ebb and flow of speeches
I zvon stakana ob stakan!	And the sound of glass against glass!
Sadis'-ka, dobraia starushka,	Sit yourself down, dear old lady,
I s nami brazhnichat' davai![31]	And tie one on with us!

The salient points about Iazykov's two poems devoted to Arina are: first, many people tended to remember his works more than Pushkin's own poems about Arina; and second, readers remembered not so much what was said about Arina as just the fact that she had been sung about by Pushkin's friend. In a sense, whatever "renown" she had in the first years following Pushkin's death in 1837 was probably owed as much to Iazykov as to Pushkin.

Watershed 1850s and End of Serfdom. While I intend to explore this idea more fully in Chapter 10, a few words are in order here about the time period in which the Arina myth arose. It is hardly by chance that a peasant nanny commanded such interest and respect just when the end of serfdom was in view (if not yet fully decided).

Serfowners and nobles more generally, the intelligentsia, and the government were all coming to grips with the situation of the unfree peasantry by the 1850s. Master-serf relations were of paramount importance for society. In a short span the country's world situation and internal order would be shaken to the core, by the Crimean War and the Great Reforms. Feelings of tranquility, assurance, and security that members of the upper social strata may have felt in the first half of the century following the great victory over Napoleon were dissipated rapidly in the course of the 1850s. At the same time, however, the promise of a brighter future loomed. It was in this atmosphere of uncertainty, trepidation, and hope that the legend of one noble's childhood caretaker apparently offered some form of comfort and inspiration.

Earliest Biographies, Beginning of Pushkin Idolatry. The earliest posthumous sketches of Pushkin's life – not full-blown biographies at all – either skip lightly over the poet's childhood and boyhood or fail to touch on them at all. None mention his nanny.[32] Similarly, an 1838 biographical essay by Pushkin's friend, the Russian literature professor Pëtr Pletnev, mostly omits his childhood and thus any reference to his nanny at that time. However, he makes the following statement about Pushkin's exile at Mikhailovskoe: "In his solitude the poet's frequent interlocutor was an old woman, his nanny, touchingly celebrated [*vospetaia*] in Iazykov's verses."[33]

The poet's literary reputation remained high after his death, yet it appears that in the eyes of his closest friends and admirers Pushkin's luster was not what they would have liked. In 1851 the Pushkin cottage industry was heating up as the poet-translator Nikolai Berg visited the village of Zakharovo outside Moscow and there encountered Arina's daughter Mar'ia. Her disjointed, confused recollections of the Pushkin family sparked public interest in the "celebrated nanny" [*znamenitaia niania*], whom Aleksandr Sergeevich had "glorified" [*proslavil*] in his verses.[34]

The literary scholar Pavel Annenkov was preparing the first "complete" edition of Pushkin's works and a major biography, but the historian Pëtr Bartenev preceded him by almost two years with a life of Pushkin.

Bartenev and His Connections. At this juncture we must take a close look at Bartenev (1829-1912), publisher of *Russkii arkhiv*. He is my candidate for the person most responsible for the Pushkin-Arina myth. While attending university in Moscow in 1847-51, Bartenev became friends with the poet Iazykov. Through Iazykov, Bartenev met Aleksei Khomiakov and other leading Slavophiles (Khomiakov was married to Iazykov's sister).[35] By early 1853 Bartenev was a fixture in the Moscow salon of Avdot'ia Elagina, half-sister of Zhukovskii and the mother of Pëtr and Ivan Kireevskii, two of the foremost Slavophiles. The Elagins became like his own family, Bartenev reports.[36]

Bartenev's close connections with Iazykov and many prominent Slavophiles suggest the strong likelihood that talk of Pushkin and his peasant nanny might have been a favorite subject at the very time he wrote about the poet's life. At the very least, it would have been difficult for Bartenev to escape the influence of the generally peasant-centric and -sympathetic Slavophiles.[37] Most likely, Pëtr Bartenev had an ideological axe to grind in his writings about Pushkin.[38]

In November 1853 Bartenev published a milestone in Pushkiniana called "Pushkin's Clan and Childhood."[39] In this sketch, the Slavophile author makes the following claim: "Historical and family traditions [*predaniia*] from his grandmother and folk ones from the nanny, Arina Rodionovna – who knew songs, fairy tales, [and folk] beliefs very well and poured forth sayings and proverbs – early made an impression on the soul of the future poet and were not lost on it, despite the fact that all his formal education was completely foreign." A year later, Bartenev's "Aleksandr Sergeevich Pushkin. Materials for his Biography" appeared. In it he elaborated on his earlier claim:

> Mar'ia Alekseevna [the poet's grandmother]...spoke only Russian ... She was, without doubt, the first *vospitatel'nitsa*

of the future poet... This good grandmother was also Aleksandr Sergeevich's first teacher. She taught him to read and write Russian.

Fortunately Pushkin's nanny was a true representative of Russian nannies. The *famous* Arina Rodionovna, exalted by Iazykov, masterfully recounted fairy tales, poured forth sayings and proverbs, knew folk beliefs and *indisputably had a great influence on her nurseling*, destroyed later by neither foreign governors nor a *vospitanie* at the Tsarskoe Selo Lyceum.[40]

Bartenev performed some sleight of hand or at least played fast and loose with his facts in these pieces. He clearly seems to imply that Arina's fame lies in being Pushkin's childhood nanny, when she allegedly plied him with folktales and lore. He asserted but in no way demonstrated that Arina had influenced Pushkin.

Pavel Annenkov's Biography. Like Bartenev, Pavel Annenkov was peasant-sympathetic. Quite independent of Bartenev (and, in fact, in rivalry with him), this writer-scholar had been gathering Pushkin material for some time when he began publishing his edition of the poet's "complete works" in 1855. In a biographical sketch for this edition, he says of "the nanny common for all the young Pushkins, the renowned [*znamenitaia*] Arina Rodionovna" that she "nannied the whole new generation of this family." He then more or less repeats Bartenev's claims: "*What touching relations with her had the second of her nurselings – who glorified her name throughout Rus – is known to everyone.*"[41]

Speaking about the Mikhailovskoe exile at a later point in his essay, Annenkov says that Pushkin's nanny did the most to put the poet in touch with peasant life: "Arina Rodionovna was the intermediary, as is well known, in his relations with the Russian fairy-tale world, his guide in learning the beliefs, customs, and the very ways of the people [peasants], with which he approaches the creation even of poetry. Aleksandr Sergeevich would speak of his nanny as his final preceptor, and would say that he was much obligated to this teacher for correcting the deficiencies of his primary, French *vospitanie*."[42] That last sentence would seem to provide solid evidence for the more questionable claims of Annenkov and Bartenev regarding Arina. But it was not Annenkov's final word on the subject.

How much Annenkov was influenced by Bartenev is hard to judge, but the earlier Pushkin biography had seemingly created notions about Pushkin's nanny that Annenkov, even if he thought differently, may have found it difficult to counter.[43]

The Legend Builds

Dostoevskii's 1863 "Winter Notes," Ivan Aksakov's 1880 Speech. Within a short time the legends about Arina had not only gained a foothold, they had increased in traction to the point where the unfounded claims of Bartenev and Annenkov were accepted by many public figures. Fëdor Dostoevskii almost apotheosized Arina in his 1863 travel piece "Winter Notes on Summer Impressions":

> Not our nannies and mammies have protected us from being reborn [as typical Europeans], have they. In fact, you know it's sad and ludicrous to think that had it not been for Arina Rodionovna, Pushkin's nanny, perhaps we would not have had Pushkin. This is nonsense, isn't it? But if it's not nonsense? What if in fact it is not nonsense? Today, people are taking many Russian children to France to be reared; what if they took some other Pushkin thither and he didn't have there either Arina Rodionovna or [the sound of] Russian speech from birth?[44]

By the time of the 1880 unveiling of a statue marking the eightieth anniversary of Pushkin's birth, the facts of the poet and his nanny had become completely overshadowed by the demophilic rendering of reality. The leading Slavophile Ivan Aksakov gave a speech in which Arina received more than her due. He repeated the by-now familiar claim that the poet had been all but destroyed by his "French upbringing" and by French literature as well as by the "distractions and temptations" of high society. And how was the true Russian individual preserved in the face of all these dangers? How could there be preserved "the artist with such a Russian bent of mind and soul, with such a profound sympathy for the poetry of the people – in song, in fairy tale, and in life?"

> The superficial explanation for this phenomenon must be sought, primarily, in the village impressions of childhood and in his relationship to [his] *nanny*. But a nanny and childhood impressions of the village were hidden away in those days in the memories of almost every inveterate denier of Russian nationality, so that this Russian-life characteristic of Pushkin's poetry seems ipso facto to his moral credit and an original peculiarity. In fact, from adolescence right up to the grave this brilliant, celebrated poet…felt no shame for all that has to do with the common people, to confess in wondrous verses his tender attachment not to his mother …but to his *"mamushka,"* to his "nanny," and with deeply sincere gratitude to honor in her his first Muse. …Thus here is who's the first inspirer, the first Muse of this great artist and first truly Russian poet; it's the nanny, this simple Russian village *baba*! Precisely having fallen onto the breast of an earth-mother, thirstily he drank up in her tales the pure strains of the people's speech and spirit! May she, this nanny, retain eternal thankful memory in the person of Russian society! It's impermissible here not to make mention of this nanny in Pushkin's own verses, in which his soul's Russian strings ring forth …[45]

He goes on to quote from the poem "A Dream," which does not pertain to Arina, as we have seen, as well as from the poems in which the poet did refer to Arina. It seems we owe to Aksakov a large part of the myth that Arina was Pushkin's first Muse.

A Re-Examination of the Legend

Annenkov's "Recantation." By this time, however, something very unusual had occurred – mostly unmarked or ignored by those deeply involved in the great mythmaking enterprise and later scholars. Pavel Annenkov actually had had the grace and good sense to recant his earlier excesses with respect to Arina. In late 1873 he began publishing a series of articles about the young Pushkin. He had learned a great deal since 1855. In this rendering of the writer's childhood nearly every detail and interpretation differs from what Annenkov had said earlier.

Now, it is grandmother Mar'ia Alekseevna who is the "famous" [*izvestnaia*] one, not the nanny. Annenkov lauds the "simplicity, clarity, and precision" of her speech, later so praised by Pushkin and his friend [Baron Anton] Del'vig. ..." He says not one word about Arina Rodionovna at this stage of Pushkin's life, but notes the lad's "unpleasantnesses" with his governesses and the fact that his parents didn't understand him. The biggest influence on the child is now his father's library – the key factor that stimulated his imagination – and his being allowed to follow his own "passions" in his reading.[46]

As if to emphasize how clearly he wanted to divorce his current views from his past stance, his conclusion to this first article in the series concerns an event which earlier would have undoubtedly involved Arina but here does not. He tells his readers that he can now clarify the cryptic note in Pushkin's planned autobiography about the Iusupov Gardens, an earthquake and the child's nanny. Annenkov proceeds to relate the tale using only the word "*niania*" and never mentioning Arina Rodionovna.[47]

The capstone of this revisionist Annenkov comes in the final installment. He discusses how, during his Mikhailovskoe exile, Pushkin threw himself into collecting Russian folk songs and sayings and into the study of Russian history (in part under Shakespeare's influence). He marvels that Pushkin wrote his innovative "Comedy about Tsar Boris" in just one year, 1825. He claims, in short, that Pushkin's work took on a whole new direction at this time.[48] Then comes his almost backhanded *mea culpa*:

> After all that's been said it's rather difficult to imagine how biographers of Pushkin [read Bartenev et al. but also himself!] – due to the words of our poet himself but understood by them much too narrowly – make his nanny, Arina Rodionovna, out to be a participant in Pushkin's development and even to be the guiding force of this development. This is one of those misunderstandings which come out of the

sphere of "biographical prejudices".... The idea of this tradition is that allegedly the good but none-too-bright [literally, "limited"] old woman, Arina Rodionovna, played something like the role of unconscious, mystical stimulator in the life of her nurseling and opened up for him the realm of folk creativity, thanks to her own knowledge of Russian fairy tales, songs, and traditions. Arina Rodionovna was truly a faithful and diligent intermediary in acquainting Pushkin with some examples and motifs of folk imagination, but, of course, [it was] not her weak and feeble hand [that] pointed out to the poet that path on which he now found himself: here there were pointers of a different kind and order altogether.[49]

More Problems With the Legend

Arina's Influence on the Child Pushkin. What should we make of Bartenev's and Annenkov's (early) claim of the "huge influence" Arina had on the young boy? It is at best an exaggeration, at worst a fabrication. Any notion of a moral influence is best left to biographical speculators and other wishful thinkers. I can speak only to the idea of creative-artistic and linguistic influence. The very young Sasha Pushkin probably did accustom his ears to something of the *flavor* and nuances of *ordinary* (read peasant) Russian from a nanny, Ul'iana or Arina. This would be some small basis for fame for her were the claim not so consistently overblown. Originally, Bartenev rightly notes that the person who most championed his native tongue was his grandmother, Mariia Alekseevna; she tutored both Aleksandr and Ol'ga. To her should likely go the lion's share of the credit for Pushkin's beautiful Russian.[50]

It was also his grandmother – not his nanny – who kindled in Pushkin his interest in historical subjects, with her tales of her (and his) family's illustrious past and of Russia's bygone days. Similarly, his love of fairy tales, folklore, and so on can only partly be attributed to the *early* influence of any nanny. As even a Soviet scholar – at the height of Stalinist enforced patriotism and demotism – admits, Pushkin's great interest in and study of his country's history and folkways came later than his childhood, in the teens (his and the nation's), while he was at the Lyceum. It progressed rapidly when he encountered fellow lovers of the past and people much interested in "ordinary" (i.e., lower-class) people, peasants, and non-Russian ethnic groups. This was particularly true of the poet's "southern exile," which preceded the Mikhailovskoe exile.[51] While it is probably the case that a nanny – Ul'iana or Arina – and her tales played some role in firing the future poet's imagination and stirring what would later develop into recognizable "Romantic" traits, Arina's significance in Pushkin's childhood is generally overstated and oversimplified.

Arina His Muse for Onegin *or Other Works?* By late 1824 the poet appears to have had a revelation, and it takes no great leap in logic to conclude that Arina's presence at Mikhailovskoe had much to do with this epiphany. Primed after his sojourn in the south and acquaintance with many peasant-sympathetic nobles – and all his prior interest in Russian and family history – to look at rural folk in a new light, he was likely intrigued by this peasant woman he came into contact with daily. But *pace* Pushkin's claim in his letter to Shvarts, Arina was not exactly the inspiration for Filippovna.[52] While the Larins' nanny may – *in the final version* – have been modeled partly on Arina, she is not a carbon copy of the Pushkins' nanny. She is an amalgam of Arina and other peasant women.

In writing or re-writing and polishing the stanzas of the third chapter of his magnum opus in the autumn of 1824, he must have realized what a powerful literary creation he had before him. So beginning with the nannies in both *Onegin* and the play *Boris Godunov* (started and finished at Mikhailovskoe) there comes a small torrent of allusions to nannies in his creative work and to Arina in his letters. If one chooses to call her a Muse for this reason, so be it, though it is not a term I would use. Her mere presence almost certainly abetted the creation of some of Pushkin's most well-known characters. It's also true that the poet recorded directly from Arina several folktales. However, as noted above, it is an exaggeration to impute Pushkin's interest in these subjects to Arina. Equally clear is the fact that he gathered material from many different peasants in the Mikhailovskoe area, not just from Arina. Despite the efforts of many to extoll her prowess as a storyteller, one must take all these claims *cum grano salis*. There is no record I'm aware of which describes firsthand, *contemporaneously*, her storytelling abilities. (Only years later did Pushkin's sister Ol'ga make such assertions in her reminiscences of childhood.)

Arina the Person. Despite portraits of Arina that border on hagiography, we should probably accept the judgment of Pushkin's nephew Lev Pavlishchev (1834-1915) that she was "a person semiliterate and in absolutely no way remarkable in [her] essence."[53] We know that she liked to imbibe from testimony of Pushkin's Mikhailovskoe neighbors the Osipovs, who also found her "estimable."[54]

For those more inclined than I to read facts into fiction, much about Arina might also be made of several nanny characters in Pushkin's works from the late 1820s through spring 1832.[55] But only his unfinished novel *Dubrovskii* (1832-33), an exciting Robin Hood-like tale, might possibly shed light on Arina.[56] Dubrovskii's nanny Egorovna is "a stupid old woman" in his eyes (when she's nursing his dying father); she resists his direct orders on occasion; and when she objects to his burning down the family home, he tells her to shut up in no uncertain terms. If this was indeed revealing of any secret thoughts the poet harbored about Arina, many an Arina devotee should be horrified. But based on family accounts, elements of Egorovna do match up with the real nanny: Arina was not a particularly submissive or meek person.

At Mikhailovskoe, Arina did become important to Pushkin, as discussed in a preceding section. Her presence became the dearer to him as his family deserted him a few short months after his arrival, when they learned the truth behind his return "home." Arina became almost his sole companion in this forced isolation. There are some indications of a warmth between them that had been (re)kindled.[57] Yet even at this time, one should not exaggerate the closeness of their relationship. Despite her entreaty that he visit her, Pushkin apparently never saw Arina again before her death, two years later – and this is when she was living in the same city as he. As noted, Arina's favorite by some accounts was Ol'ga Sergeevna, her first charge.[58] This is corroborated in part by the fact that Arina went to live with Ol'ga's family in the 1820s and stayed there – apart from the two-year hiatus at Mikhailovskoe with Pushkin – until she breathed her last in July 1828.

Some Thoughts on the Myth and Cult

A Part of Russian Culture... The legend, and then the myth, of Arina spread so quickly among cultured Russians that within a very short time references to Pushkin entered their everyday discourse and thoughts. Two examples are Lermontov and Goncharov. When the former wrote, in 1830, that it was a shame he had not had a Russian nanny from whom to hear Russian folktales (see Chapter 9), it was likely a reference to Pushkin's literary creation rather than to Arina directly. (Some people even misquote Lermontov by including Pushkin's name in his "aphorism": "...a Russian nanny, like Pushkin.") In an 1855 letter to E.V. Tolstaia, Ivan Goncharov included a humorous remark that presupposed his interlocutor knew without question what his reference to "Tat'iana" meant: "You (and others in this circumstance) [isolated in the country with no one to talk with] begin to speak with inanimate objects, at first with the desk, then with the stove, and so forth. Tat'iana talked with animate ones also, with a *nanny*: it's good if someone has a nanny [to talk with], but someone who has none can exchange a couple words with even a *fly*."[59]

The philosopher-belletrist Apollon Grigor'ev (1822-1864) referred to Arina Rodionovna in 1859 in glowing terms that also assume she already occupied a prominent place in Russian consciousness.[60] Ivan Grevs (1860-1941), one of Russia's premier cultural historians, says that, in having a peasant nanny

> I was thus not deprived in my early childhood of the influence of a spiritual image characteristic for our Russian gentry pedagogical days of old – an image to which already Pushkin had given an immortality – which typically entered into Russian literature and realistically introduced a trait of uniqueness into the life of children of the pre-reform privileged class, often tying – through the budding love for a nanny – a bond with the people and its poetry.[61]

The Celebrated Case of Pushkin's Nanny

Memorial in Pskov, Russia: *Pushkin and Peasant (i.e., Arina)*, Oleg Komov, sculptor/M. Konstantinov, architect (1983)

...With Echoes in European Culture. While the status of Arina Rodionovna in Russia is unparalleled by any similar nanny cult elsewhere, there are yet many comparable examples in modern European literature. Facts, legends, and myths about nannies and their influence are associated in Britain alone with such writers as Lord Byron, Charles Dickens, Robert Louis Stevenson, and Emily Brontë, as well as with such public figures as Winston Churchill and Lord Curzon.[62] Heinrich Heine's nanny has attracted similar attention.

The Myth Mars Much Pushkin Study. The legend-myth of Arina becomes a cautionary tale for scholars.[63] Examined through the prism of Pushkin's nanny, one finds that after thousands of books and articles and some 175 years of study, the poet's life is still, on paper, full of distortions, errors, and misunderstandings. Pre-revolutionary writers – early on, friends or acquaintances of the poet himself; later, ideologues of various stripes – often had ulterior motives in writing about Pushkin. Most seem to have been either in need of glorifying and thus exaggerating some aspect of his life and *oeuvre*, or on a quest for what has been called "a usable past." They tried to stick him in one "camp" or another: with the Slavophiles or other patriots, with the peasant-sympathetic and *narodnik*-inclined, certainly with the radicals or revolutionaries.

After the revolution some of these trends naturally disappeared, but others were magnified. If only Soviet-era Russian writers had not been so constrained by an official party line or so bound by their own democratic yearnings, the near-hagiography which surrounds Arina would not be so prevalent as it is.[64] If only later scholars in the West had paid closer attention to their predecessors, most of the misinformation and mistakes that have crept into even fairly recent work would not be there.

The Myth's Impact on Later Russian Writing

One of the hypotheses of this book is that educated – especially well-born – Russians after Pushkin drew upon his writings as a model when they examined their own lives or wrote poetry and fiction. I am arguing, in fact, that what Andrew Wachtel claims Tolstoi did for all of (literary) childhood,[65] Pushkin did for this one aspect of childhood. As a result, hundreds of autobiographies and memoirs include an almost obligatory appearance of a beloved family nanny, often playing an allegedly large role in the author's life. Similarly, Pushkin's nannies in prose, plays, and poems – and the myth attached directly to Arina – influenced subsequent literary presentations of nannies and inspired litterateurs.[66]

There is no absolute proof of the first assertion, but it is based on more than just impressions. I have tried to make a fairly systematic survey of the genre of memoir literature spanning two and a half centuries. I cannot claim to have read all autobiographies extant, but I have read a reasonably large proportion of them, especially those that might be expected to discuss their authors' early years. Of the thousands of such life stories available, I've read well over 900. While the sample is not representative in the strict statistical sense, I am convinced that sheer numbers alone permit me to draw an important conclusion and am further convinced that a reading of all memoirs of childhood would not significantly alter this conclusion.

The next two paragraphs speak first of autobiographies and then of other genres, but not of the hybrid quasi-autobiographical writing.[67] After Pushkin, the treatment of nannies in conventional autobiographies and memoirs differed in no basic way from their treatment in quasi-autobiographies (or in fiction). Nannies exhibited the same traits, same behavior, the same language and thoughts in both genres.

The Findings for Memoirs. I've perused 143 autobiographies or memoirs of men and women who were born before 1800. Just 30 of these works mention a specific nanny who cared for the author in infancy and/or childhood.[68] Of these 30, however, a mere six autobiographers wrote their life histories before Pushkin wrote about Tat'iana's nanny.[69] All the rest produced their life histories *after* the appearance of "Filippovna." Thus, roughly four percent of the autobiographers who produced such histories without the stimulus of Pushkin's character even thought to mention their nannies.

Sixty-four of 127 autobiographers I've read born between 1800 and 1825 – *all of whose life histories were written and published after October 1827* (when the third chapter of *Onegin* appeared) – mention their own nannies or a nanny in their family (e.g., their own children's nanny). That is half the total.

One hundred fourteen of 190 autobiographies I've read of individuals born between 1826 and 1861– 60 percent – include at least a mention of such a nanny. Of 233 autobiographies I've looked at by authors born between 1862 and 1900, 140 (again 60 percent) note a nanny – but already these nanny figures are becoming more generic in memoirs.

Finally, and perhaps most surprising, I've read 111 autobiographies or memoirs of people born after 1900; of these, fully 79 (over 70 percent) discuss a family nanny, usually their own. (For those born after the revolution, the proportion falls to something more than half.) I believe these figures are unarguable[70] and that they point to just one conclusion: the almost compulsory inclusion of the figure of a highly revered, often nearly saintly, usually peasant nanny in Russian autobiographies and memoirs begins with the belletristic writings of Aleksandr Pushkin, which many readers apparently took to be largely autobiographical.[71]

Concerning Literature and Literary Criticism. The *fact* that Pushkin wrote of nannies, including Arina, had an impact on subsequent

Russian literature, as we'll see in a later chapter. The *myth* of Arina influenced other Russian writers even more directly. One prime example is the poet Vladislav Khodasevich (1886-1939), who, in various essays on Pushkin's poetry, not only accepted that Arina was Pushkin's muse (before Mikhailovskoe) but then "imitated" Pushkin by writing a major poem devoted to his own wet-nurse-nanny as his inspiration in Russian culture.

In direct line, the poet Evgenii Rein (b. 1935) then imitated both earlier poets by writing about his nanny, leaving no doubt as to his model by quoting Khodasevich in an epigraph. Similarly, Marina Tsvetaeva (1892-1941) accepted most of the mythology of Arina and exalted her supposed role in Pushkin's life in more than one of her essays on the poet.[72]

Concluding Thoughts

Those who read this chapter carefully and with unbiased eyes will, I trust, come to agree with most, if not all my arguments. They will appreciate that the Arina cult is an artifact based not so much on the reality of Pushkin's life as on the dreams and needs of many others, pre- and post-1917. First Pëtr Bartenev, then other Slavophiles and nationalists (like Aksakov and Dostoevskii) took up the championing of the nanny. Thinking (only) allegorically, they were little concerned with the subject matter of my next few chapters – the mundane world of working women.

In addition, the excessive praise of Arina and the raising of her to cult status cannot be seen as a positive thing for this individual and other women like her. It is in reality a putdown of Arina, as she is viewed as almost nothing except in juxtaposition with a male, Pushkin. This is a variation of the same phenomenon analyzed by Barbara Heldt with respect to female heroines in nineteenth-century Russian literature.[73] Arina, other nannies, and women in general were rarely seen as independent, autonomous actors, worthwhile in and of themselves.

2

Russian Nannies Before Pushkin

The Nanny in Russian History

Long before there were kindergartens and daycare centers for children, there were nannies. I don't know exactly when a nanny first appears in Russian historical records or in Russian literature.[1] I've unearthed one account from early Russian history, which is doubtless apocryphal. Zoe Palaeologa, niece of the last Byzantine emperor before the Ottoman conquest, allegedly had a Russian nanny named Evdokiia in Rome in the 1460s. This nanny purportedly introduced her charge to the Russian language and acquainted the princess with her own Russian homeland.[2] Zoe went on to marry Ivan III of Muscovy as the Grand Princess Sophia. I include this likely fairy tale because it is the very stuff of which this book is made – the myths and legends surrounding nannies. These tales form a part of the Russian historical imagination. At the very least, they figure in what many Russians would *like* to be a part of their national traditions and history.

The most authoritative dictionary of early Russian shows conclusively that in Kievan Rus' the word *"kormilitsa"* designated nannies and wet-nurses alike and was in use in the earliest centuries. For some time, this was probably the only word in widespread usage, and its employment for wet-nurses alone appears to have arisen only after an alternative term for nanny arose. That word, *"nian'ka"* – and its various formations/diminutives, denoting a nanny and seemingly not a wet-nurse – was in circulation by at least the sixteenth century.[3]

In this chapter we will look at three aspects of nannies in Russian history before about 1825, based on three different kinds of sources. First, we'll examine nannies of some historical significance, looking at official records. Second, we'll discuss nannies on a more personal level, among noble families, based on memoir literature. Third, we'll talk about nannies and their role more generally, citing views of social commentators and critics.

Documented Early Royal Nannies. At a time when family really meant something – when Muscovite politics was clan politics[4] – nannies played a small but crucial role in Russian political life. Supervisory Russian nannies were not from the peasantry; their subordinates often were. Those at the top were important in two ways. First, the appointment of a woman to tend the royal offspring was both a sign and a confirmation of prominence for her and her family. (One could liken this form of political signaling to Kremlin-watching in the twentieth century: the closer one stood to, say, Stalin, the more favored he was.) Second, a woman placed in such a position could easily advance both her own and her family's fortunes.

A prime example of this phenomenon is the *boiarynia* Princess Agrafena Cheliadnina (d. after 1540?), sister of Prince Ivan Telepnev-Obolenskii (d. 1538). Her husband, the boiar and *dvoretskii* (palace administrator) Vasilii Cheliadnin (d. 1518), was a descendant of German ancestors who had moved east and served Russian grand princes for well over a century, placing them among the most favored of clans. Sophia-Zoe's son Grand Prince Vasilii Ivanovich (Vasilii III) appointed Agrafena the nanny of his infant son Ivan, the future tsar known to history as Ivan the Terrible. According to one source, as he was dying Vasilii instructed this nanny to budge "not an inch" from her nursling. Once Vasilii's widow, Elena Glinskaia (d. 1538), took over the reins of power, Agrafena and her brother assumed positions of enormous power at court, second only to the sovereign and *her* brother Mikhail Glinskii.

The extraordinary success of the Telepnev-Obolenskiis was due in part to Ivan Fedorovich's abilities – he was a courageous and very able warrior – but mostly to the fact that the tsarevich was deeply attached to his nanny. Elena Glinskaia showered Agrafena with wealth and land.[5]

Konstantin Makovskii, *Nanny of Ivan the Terrible* (1880) oil on canvas[6]

Another early reference to a royal nanny is in Ruslan Skrynnikov's slight monograph on "Ivan the Terrible" (Ivan Groznyi). Most of the issue from Groznyi's first marriage (in 1547), to Anastasiia Romanovna (Zakharina), died young, as did their mother. While the heir Dmitrii was still an infant, his parents reportedly traveled with him to the Kirillov Monastery. On the return journey, he perished in what Skrynnikov calls "an absurd accident." According to him, the nanny (*niania*), supported by two boiars, was holding the child in her arms. When the boat carrying the royal party came to shore, the procession stepped onto the gangplank, but the board flipped over and all were thrown into the water. The child fell from the nanny's hands, was immediately fished from the water, but was already dead.[7]

Skrynnikov offers no substantiation for his facts, but others have investigated Dmitrii's untimely end. In a 1994 article the historian Isolde Thyrêt gives the following, much fuller account of the tsarevich's demise and the possible role of his nanny in his death:

> Dmitrii Ivanovich was born in October 1552. The circumstances of his death in June 1553 are controversial. The Nikon chronicle simply mentions Dmitrii's death on the way back from the royal couple's pilgrimage to Kirillov ([*Polnoe sobranie russkikh letopisei*], 13, pt. 1:232). According to the *vita* of St. Nikita of Pereslavl, Dmitrii died from an illness on this trip (*ibid.* 21, pt. 2:651). Kurbskii connects the tsarevich's death with a crossing of the river Sheksna... According to Isaac Massa, the baby slipped out of his mother's hands into the water when she tried to hand the tsarevich to her husband. ... In his *Vremennik*, Ivan Timofeev maintains that a nursemaid accidentally dropped the baby into the water.[8]

By a rather remarkable coincidence, another tsarevich named Dmitrii (b. 1582), the half-brother of the preceding heir, also died under cloudy circumstances involving his nanny. An investigation into his death revealed that in all likelihood he had mortally wounded himself with a knife while playing in the company or presence of several other people, one of whom was his wet-nurse, Orina.[9] (Orina, doubtless Dmitrii's wet-nurse earlier, would have been his nanny by his age of 9.) Dmitrii, an epileptic and recently weakened by an unspecified illness, either fainted – or, running, tripped – and fell on the knife he was carrying.[10]

Some Noble-Family Nannies Before Pushkin

In the late seventeenth century, correspondence between family members might include frequent mentions of a nanny, a practice that continued right through the nineteenth century. For example, the final paragraph of a letter from a certain Agaf'ia Krovkova (identified as a relative) to Princess Paraskov'ia Khovanskaia reads "Mammy [*mamushka*] Dolmatovna and nanny [*nianiushka*] Larivonovna and all the boiar ladies wish for long life with the favor of their lords!"[11] In another missive from Krovkova to the princess she offers greetings to all in the household. She then specifically asks if the Khovanskaia nanny Larivonovna is still alive – "our faithful secret emissary." In one letter Krovkova "addresses" the nanny: "*Nianiushka*, you've forgotten me, you don't write about your health!"[12] It's far from certain that these mammies and nannies were of the peasantry; they could well have been from a higher social stratum.

One early historical nanny shows up not in an autobiography, but in biographical material. She is of added consequence because she foreshadows many later nannies, all of them tending the children of political exiles. In the early 1740s, Count Ioann-Ernst Minikh (1708-1788) was a high court official, newly married, and seemingly destined for as distinguished a career as his father, a fieldmarshal invited to Russia by Peter the Great. But after the death of Catherine I, the father got involved in political intrigues. The innocent son also fell under suspicion when Peter's daughter Elizabeth came to the throne in fall 1741. He was arrested; tried and convicted of "state crimes"; deprived of all his ranks, honors, and property; and sent into exile in Vologda, accompanied by his family.[13] According to documents from the Ministry of Foreign Affairs archives, dated 26 May 1743, the traveling party included:

Minikh and wife	2
Their child with its wet-nurse	2
Children's nanny	1
Maids	3
Male servants	5
Total	13

So nannies were already leaving traces long before 1800.[14] The only questions are how widespread the institution was, and how far down the social order it extended. There are no adequate records, unfortunately, which would permit quantitative answers to these questions. Census data for Moscow for these periods, for example, although very detailed – providing information about masters and many servants – fail to note the occupations of females.[15] (This is doubtless due to the intent of the surveys, which appears to have been to record potential military personnel.)

It's a fairly safe assumption that the great spread of the occupation of nanny can most likely be tied to two phenomena. The first was the rising fortunes of the gentry service class. The second was the corollary rise of the institution of serfdom, especially from the late seventeenth century.

The First Memoir Evidence. At the heart of this book lie ego-documents (mostly autobiographies and memoirs). In the first chapter I explained how Pushkin marked a watershed in the writing of such documents so far as Russian nannies are concerned. A detailed discussion of the pre-Pushkin works in these genres – and how they differed from those post-Pushkin – was deferred to this chapter. They demonstrate that the social origins of nannies were shifting as the older high nobility (*boiarstvo*) confronted a rising gentry (*dvorianstvo*). More importantly, they also document the start of the post-Pushkin trend to mix factuality with invention when discussing childhood caretakers.

In Chapter 1 I also noted finding just six writers before 1827 who mentioned in their memoirs that they had had a nanny in childhood. Significantly, hardly any were effusive or expansive about these women. The earliest such mention of a nanny I'm aware of is in the autobiography of Matvei Artamonovich Murav'ev (b. 1711), written presumably in the 1770s, after he had retired. Murav'ev had been a military engineer, reaching the rank of major-general.[16] As he recalls: *We had an old woman named Ul'iana as a nanny, who used to say: "Children, now children, I'm cooking something very hot, so don't take a bite."*[17] (Italics in original.) This is the entire single passage where he refers to her existence.

Other autobiographers who wrote before 1827 were somewhat more informative about their respective nannies, but they were still mostly matter-of-fact. The agronomist, scholar, and memoirist Andrei Bolotov (1738-1833) tells us that his grandmother midwived his birth and was his first nanny. About a relative he showed emotion: "[Grandmother] was a good woman; a devout old lady, an honest old woman...fine in all respects and I, as a young boy, loved her very much and often shed tears over her, because she was my nanny [*mamka*]..."[18] He later acquired another nanny it appears. Describing events of the early 1750s, he notes dryly that "My industriousness and eagerness to be writing was so great that I would sometimes sit scribbling for hours on end, and my old nanny, almost alone keeping me unbroken company and growing tired from sitting over her distaff in the corner next to the stove, would often have to remind me that it was time for supper and that it was already long past midnight."[19]

Dmitrii Mertvago (1760-1824) describes in his memoirs what might be called the first of many "heroic" nannies. During the Pugachëv revolt his family had to flee their estate in Simbirsk province, but his father was caught and killed by the rebels. Mother and sons escape briefly but are again caught. The family nanny saves one of his younger brothers, at the cost of a hand.[20] *We never learn the fate of this nanny or even her name.*

Prince Ivan Dolgorukov (1764-1823) and Fëdor Pecherin (1773-1835) are transitional authors; the former is perhaps the first autobiographer to describe some of the emotions that nannies evoked in their charges and their families. In 1788 he wrote of the time – about a decade and a half earlier, in 1772 – when he was eight and lost his governess, a Frenchwoman named Madam Constantin, and was turned over to male tutors to complete his *vospitanie*. It was sad to see Madam depart, but "it was twice as sad to stop spending the night in the same room with my nanny [*mamushka*] Mar'ia

Karpovna, who often fed me honeyed gingerbread and, with the weakness inherent to women, sometimes let me be completely unfettered. But I could still see her in time free from lessons; she remained living in our home."[21] By 1818, when he extrapolated from his earlier work a "calendar" of events and people important in his life, he had more to say about his nanny:

> Mar'ia Karpovna. Widow of free-peasant status [*svobodnogo sostoianiia*]. She was taken into our home as a wet-nurse-nanny, looked after me all during my childhood, grew old in our home and died in it, when I was already married and had children. A good woman, assiduous and adept at her calling [*prilezhnaia i sposobnaia k svoemu zvaniiu*]. She loved me excessively [*chrezvychaino*]. I will never forget her tender ministrations [*popecheniia*] over me. She coddled and raised all of us in father's house, and it's impossible for any of us to forget her. Eternal memory to our good and revered *mamushka*.[22]

About the same time, in 1816, Pecherin writes: "But when I was left alone in the village in childhood, the nanny Afaf'ia was given responsibility for all of my care."[23] In a footnote, he adds: "She was part of my mother's dowry, the nanny of all the children, [then] the housekeeper [*kaznacheia*]. She died unmarried in Moscow, at more than 50 years of age. My mother received this news – in the village in the summer of 1792 – with great sorrow [*priskorbie*]. Her services will not be forgotten by us."[24]

These five examples of memoirs and autobiographies might well have begun the "craze for nannies" in personal histories that I attribute to Pushkin's writings of the 1820s and 1830s except for one fact: None of these autobiographies was published in their authors' lifetimes. Indeed, all were published long after Pushkin's death. And that brings us to the sixth and last of these memoirs.

The Special Case of Anna Labzina. Written about 1810 but not published for another nine decades, the autobiography of Anna Labzina (1758-1828) stands apart from the other five examples already discussed. Her account is in many ways the most important of the six in the development of the genre. But at the same time, it is the most problematic and puzzling. To put it succinctly, the narrative is almost complete melodrama.[25] She used as models such earlier works as the *Life of Avvakum written by himself* and even John Bunyan's novel *The Pilgrim's Progress*. In short, Labzina chose not so much to write about reality as to produce an autohagiography, "canonizing" herself, her father, her mother, and her nanny.[26]

She set the tone right from the beginning, with an early deathbed scene in which her dying father, among other things, commends Labzina's moral upbringing to her nanny as a substitute for himself and even her mother in some ways.[27] Then throughout her narrative, Labzina's nanny – never named! – plays the role of protector, moral preceptor, confidante, and companion.[28] She is full of sage advice and words of spiritual wisdom. In Labzina's reconstruction, the nanny arouses the wrath of Anna's husband, Aleksandr Karamyshev (1744-1791), as she is the antithesis of all that he stands for in the book. Made out to be nearly the Devil himself in Labzina's mind, if not in actuality, Karamyshev represents Western rationalism, secularism, sensuality, and "free-thinking." The nanny – and Labzina – represent Russian spirituality, religion, denial of the flesh, meekness, and modesty. With the sensibility of a medieval morality play, the memoirs depict a struggle between Good and Evil which can and must end in only way: the triumph of virtue over sin, of wife over husband.[29] In sum, we learn precious little about real-life Russian nannies from Labzina, even though her nanny plays a major role in her autobiography.[30]

What I am arguing in this section is nothing surprising, given the literary nature of life histories. But it bears emphasis: practically from the beginning, when autobiographers wrote about their childhood and youth, the desire to record the dry facts of those years was almost simultaneously mixed with emotional tinges and even – in one case – the temptation to invent or create a preconceived scenario for various actors to play. For nannies, this process took full flight after Pushkin's death.

A Later Royal Nanny

By the end of the eighteenth century, royal nannies were mostly not homegrown. One of the first beneficiaries of a British nanny was the Grand Prince Nikolai Pavlovich, the future Nicholas I.[31] Unfortunately, in his own memoirs, Nicholas does not speak of his nanny. Happily, his major biographers do.[32] Nikolai Pavlovich was born in late June 1796; his grandmother Catherine died shortly thereafter. Before her death in November, however, she made known her wishes for her third grandson's upbringing; she had already selected a nanny for him.

> ...and it must be acknowledged that the empress's choice was superb. It was an Englishwoman, or more precisely, a Scottish lady, Evgeniia Vasil'evna Laion [Jane Lyon; 1771-1842], the daughter of a master artisan...one of many artists invited to Russia by the empress. During the first seven years of the grand prince's life, she was his sole guiding force; she was always proud of the fact that although a Britisher [*anglichanka*], she was the first to teach him to say the "Our Father" and "Hail Mary," the first also to teach him how to hold his fingers to make the sign of the cross. Nikolai Pavlovich was ardently attached to his *nanny-lioness*, as he called her (Lion, a pun of the Emperor Nicholas himself).
>
> Baron M. A. Korf hypothesizes that in the first years of the grand prince's life, when all feelings, impressions, antipathies are formed by the child unconsciously, there existed a most profound kinship of natures between him and his nanny; at the same time, the heroic, chivalrously noble, strong and open character of this nanny-lioness must inevitably have influenced the character formation of the future Russian autocrat.[33]

Here we have two intriguing pieces of evidence about the future Emperor, who is usually painted in rather austere colors. As a child, he apparently had a sense of humor and a playful side; and a close student of his life believes that his nanny had a strong, seemingly unique influence on his character. Her own character, meanwhile, was admirable, if not impeccable: "In fact, the character of Miss Lyon was bold, decisive, noble. She was very quick-tempered, but, like the majority of quick-tempered people, uncommonly kind. Her attachment to the most august pupil entrusted to her tutelage rose to a passion in her, to a fanaticism, which she preserved to the end of her life."[34]

An unpleasant incident in her life may even have had a considerable influence on one aspect of Nicholas I's domestic/foreign policy. Again according to Shil'der:[35]

> The future nanny of Nikolai Pavlovich was by chance in Warsaw in 1794 and spent a difficult seven months of internment with some Russian fine ladies. The prisoners were at last freed by Suvorov after the storming of Prague. In later years the Emperor Nicholas would more than once recount how he had inherited his hatred for Poles from his nanny, and that this feeling had taken root in him from the time of the stories which he heard from her in the first years of his life, about the horrors and cruelties which occurred in Warsaw in 1794

Such a simplistic explanation for Nicholas's Polish policy would not normally pass muster, at least not by itself. But the nanny's stories and the feelings they elicited in the young boy could well have fed into the other reasons for the tsar's decisions. His later recollections might also demonstrate that he had not completely lost his childhood sense of humor.

Ambivalence about the Nanny's Role Starts Early

Nannies and the Vospitanie of Children – Eighteenth Century. In the course of the eighteenth century, if indeed not long before, child-rearing became an enterprise of great moment for all Europeans, including Russians. By century's end it was a truism that, as Aleksandr Radishchev would say in his essay "On Man, His Mortality and Immortality" (1792), "upbringing decides everything" [*vospitanie delaet vse*].[36]

For our purposes, one of the key elements in eighteenth-century thinking about a good *vospitanie* was concern about how children of the upper class, the nobility, would interact with their social inferiors. Nikolai Novikov (1744-1818) – the journalist, publisher, satirist, Freemason, and proselytizer of Enlightenment ideals and values – could warn parents against allowing contact between their children and the uneducated without necessarily making this a condemnation of an entire socio-economic group. Nonetheless, in a sweeping and rather vague phrase, he asked rhetorically "is it not very dangerous to leave children frequently and for long periods under the supervision and in the company of *people who have a mind that is coarse and full of mistaken ideas [zabluzhdeniia] and prejudices?*"[37] The words seem to refer to servants, including nannies. Yet further on, he urges these same parents:

> *Try to instill in them* [your children] *a sincere love of and goodwill toward all people, without distinction of material standing, religion, ethnicity or lot in life.* Teach them to respect as brothers all men, low and eminent, poor and rich; to acknowledge [all] people as human beings, that is, as rational creatures with immortal souls, and their external circumstances as things of chance.[38]

Thus even the most enlightened of men, such as Novikov, were either ambivalent or had misgivings about what transpired in home *vospitanie*. Another example is Aleksandr Bestuzhev (1761-1810), the father of four sons who became Decembrists: Nikolai (1791-1855); Aleksandr (1797-1837), the widely popular author who wrote under the pseudonym "Marlinskii"; Mikhail (1800-1871); and the youngest, Pëtr (d. 1840). Their political views from early childhood were to a large extent formed by the very progressive ideas of their father: he was "democratic," anti-serfdom, and critical of what he considered the dissolute life of much of the gentry. Bestuzhev *père* was also a leading theoretician of pedagogy, who tried to put his ideas into practice with his sons.[39]

Like Novikov, the senior Bestuzhev was a product of Enlightenment ideas of the eighteenth century, especially of its latter part. In 1798 he and a colleague of Radishchev named I. I. Pnin began publishing an anti-serfdom progressive monthly, the *Sankt-Peterburgskii Zhurnal*. In its first few issues, Bestuzhev began to publish his thoughts on the raising of children. Called simply "On [Children's] Upbringing" (in the January and February issues; its title and scope expanded and altered later), the tract speaks of the need for moral education. In it Bestuzhev tries to draw from personal experience; he puts great faith in the power of education to transform people. In these ways he differs little from Novikov and indeed the French *philosophes*. However, on one key point he departed from Novikov's careful ambiguity about the lower classes. In his first chapter, on "private *vospitanie*," Bestuzhev "reproaches parents for the fact that in the first months of life of an infant the parents do not pay the necessary attention to its *vospitanie*, entrusting it to a wet-nurse and nanny [*nian'ka*], who fill 'the minds of their nurselings with their own fears, misconceptions, faults and stupidities'."[40]

When nannies told fairy tales to little children, the reaction throughout the period covered here – from roughly 1700 well into the twentieth century – was not uniformly positive. Children and parents, educators and psychologists, might think of this as the most innocent and pleasant of activities, with beneficial aspects for the child and its future development. Fairy tales, for instance, arguably stimulated the imaginations, aspirations, and moral sensitivities of the little ones. At the same time, however, there were toddlers who became overly frightened by some folktales and afterward regretted listening to them, while many adults fulminated against such stories as inclining immature minds toward the impractical, the fantastic, the silly, or the darker sides of life.

Berezaiskii. An author little remembered today, Vladimir Berezaiskii was very well-known to his contemporaries.[41] In 1798, he published his most famous book, *Anecdotes of the Old Poshekhonians*, a cautionary tale aimed largely against all sorts of "old wives tales."[42] Written in the fashionable epistolary form, the book recounts local folklore and folk "wisdom" allegedly current among the residents of the region.[43] This short book deserves to be better known; it is a gem, important to us for its lengthy preface dedicated to "Nannies and Mammies" (*nianiushkam i mamushkam*). Its apostrophe to nannies is a model of rhetorical irony, full of sly humor. In it he highlights what most educated Russians of his and the next century would consider one of the worst traits of nannies. Being peasant women, they were imbued with the "superstitions," beliefs, and folk traditions of their social estate. Berezaiskii pooh-

poohed the idea that dreams, nightmares, and fortune-tellers could reveal anything about the future or the supernatural world, ridiculing sorcerers, witches, and the like. He derides nannies' "spells, palms, roots, pendants, sprinklings" and all sorts of nanny (peasant) medicinal aids, but praises nannies' knowledge of various fairy-tale goblins, demons, and changelings.

Berezaiskii was doubtless poking fun, by extension, at countless other Russians, men and women, high born as well as low, who believed in most of these same things. How much of this "folk wisdom" was silly nonsense, based on ignorance, and how much was actually of some merit is sometimes hard to judge. But there is little doubt of what our author thought of it. He was almost totally dismissive of these absurdities. To some well-born Russians, but especially to educators and the better-educated, it was a matter of no small concern that peasant nannies would pass on to their charges these folk beliefs and thereby stunt or ruin the young ones' mental and emotional development. Peasant nannies' alleged superstitions are the subject of admonitions from well-meaning educators throughout the eighteenth and nineteenth centuries.

Preceptors of the Early Nineteenth Century. This ambiguity about nannies and other caretakers on the part of self-appointed pedagogs *if not necessarily of parents* would continue right into the next century and beyond.[44] The best-known doctor-writer of the day, Kondratii Grum, was both wary and laudatory of nannies.[45] The poetaster, sentimental proser, and publisher Prince Pëtr Shalikov (1767/68-1852) wrote often on the subject of raising children in the pages of his *Fine Ladies' Journal* (*Damskii zhurnal*). On the one hand, he would rhapsodize about all the females in a child's life, including the nanny:

> Only women make up the unbroken chain of our *love*, and for this reason the sweetest part of our life: in childhood [*mladenchestvo*] we *love* mother, wet-nurse, nanny...in all... periods of life we *love women*...here is the real source, here is the natural basis of men's eternal devotion to women, our first benefactresses, demanding for that all our thanks.[46]

On the other he warned of the "dangers" that arose from low-born, uneducated servants. Bad influences lurked around many corners. As Gitta Hammarberg has shown,[47] Shalikov's true colors were not as a real "champion" of women, especially female writers. He was condescending toward reading matter for women, and he associated them with what is "unimportant."

A contributor to Shalikov's journal writes in a vein similar but slightly different from Shalikov about the primary importance of home *vospitanie*. "Many *vospitateli*," the anonymous contributor says, "reject home *vospitanie*, basing themselves on the following reasons. 'First,' they say, 'at home children are surrounded by coarse people, the uneducated, i.e., by service people.' But does this [possible danger] not proceed from the negligence of the parents?"

> ...the father and the mother cannot have as much knowledge [and] as much time as to be able to provide a complete education [*obrazovanie*] for their children, and so they frequently put up with the ignorance of hired preceptors. One would agree that in this last respect parents sometimes resemble those buying books by their covers; but this occurs due to their own lack of knowledge; yet if the choice of preceptors is a good one, then it's easy to make up for the other deficiencies.[48]

He then notes a problem associated with a nanny – though one not confined to her alone. "One can't refrain from mentioning still another barbaric custom of nannies and even mothers themselves, i.e., *to frighten* children."[49]

Warming to the subject of caretakers, the author tells parents that they must not only prepare themselves for the "difficult task of *vospitanie*," they must also prepare those who will assist them. Wet-nurses, he agrees with Rousseau, are employed mostly out of "delicacy and due to fashionable ailments."

> But family concerns, unforeseeable circumstances and unavoidable preoccupations demand that one have a nanny. This person is a second mother, which is why one must give her a certain amount of education [*obrazovanie*]

in order that she be capable of taking upon herself such an important responsibility. I'm not talking about our teaching her to write, to read – no, the education of nanny consists in this: you free her mind of crude prejudices, purge her speech of coarse expressions, school her in decorous and noble deportment, and finally, have her learn by heart a few short moral stories with which she will occupy the child at the youngest age and which will replace foolish fairy tales.[50]

What satirists of the eighteenth century were urging with humor and a great deal more subtlety, the moral preachers of the nineteenth century were doing with seriousness and directness. After all, the *Damskii zhurnal* contributor would say, one wouldn't think of entrusting a fine jewel to any but the most skilled artisan to work with. Why then would parents entrust their most precious treasures, their children, to anyone lacking the finer feelings and good sense? "The father and mother...cannot always be with their children; *but the nanny is with them constantly. She is the primary shaper of the mind and the heart.*"[51]

Conclusion

Nannies played a prominent role in Russian life, mostly in highly born families, for many centuries before the nineteenth. As servants and (most often) peasants, they occupied an ambiguous place in the thinking of masters/employers, social commentators, intellectuals, and creative minds. Serfdom no doubt colored some of this thinking. In the nineteenth century, the peasant question became the foremost social and economic issue that government and society sought to resolve. As this was happening, first peasant nannies and then nannies more generally began to engage the public's attention in wholly new ways. The following four chapters tell the story of the women who became this focus of attention.

3

Socio-Cultural Background for the Modern Nanny

How Many Nannies Were There?

The answer to this question is of interest but hard to determine. Certainly it was the expectation that a young married couple, likely to have children, would find themselves in the situation which the Count describes as married life in Aleksei Pisemskii's *One Thousand Souls* (1858): "All your money will have gone on births, christenings, wet nurses, dry nurses... Family life is a whirlpool, a bottomless pit for money."[1] As a rule of thumb, therefore, one might just note that most families of middle or above status who were blessed with children probably had a nanny of some kind – and leave it at that. But for those with a quantitative bent, the following remarks may prove useful.

For what I call "the classic Russian nanny" – a peasant woman caring for children in a noble household in the mid-nineteenth century[2] – there seem two possible ways to estimate numbers: "from the bottom up," starting with a count of serfs, and "from the top down," beginning with a count of noble families. Neither works well.[3] Standard sources on the nineteenth-century serf population say that in late serfdom, the number of household serfs (*dvorovye liudi*) equaled 1,467,378 souls *of both sexes* – an average of about seven serfs per noble family, with no way to tell how many of the seven were caretakers.[4]

Averages are very problematic, however; not all noble families owned serfs. In the wealthiest households, there would often be two to four nannies (a supervisory nanny and one or more under-nannies). At the same time, not all noble households one might expect to have nannies had any.[5] In poorer noble homes a peasant nanny might also be lacking.

A "top-down" method is little better. Throughout the eighteenth and nineteenth centuries the number of hereditary nobles continually increased, often quite rapidly.[6] Family size of noble households and even the number of households in the eighteenth century is difficult to ascertain. Seymour Becker calculates that average noble family size in the second half of the nineteenth century was about 4.5 persons, with the number of hereditary nobles rising (not unilinearly) from roughly 610,000-626,000 in 1858 to about 1,170,000 in 1912.[7]

One could hazard a guess that in the middle of the nineteenth century, *among noble households alone,* there were probably at least 100,000 "classic nannies" in Russia. How much that number fluctuated before and after emancipation is uncertain.[8]

The first nationwide Russian census of 1897 provides more concrete data in the form of occupational tables for some of the largest cities (not the country as a whole). "Domestic servitors" (*Domashnie sluzhashchie*) was the rubric for housekeepers, female companions [*kompan'onki*], readers [*lektrisy*], nannies and governesses and so on.[9] The following table shows the agglomerations for this subcategory for three major cities.

Domestic Servitors in Select Cities, 1897[10]

City	Female	Male
Moscow and environs	2,211	0
St. Petersburg and environs	3,075	40
Odessa and environs	639	16
Totals	5,925	56

We can obtain a slightly clearer picture for the second capital from the Moscow city census of 1902, which includes, for the occupational listing "White-collar workers and servants in nonindustrial occupations," a subcategory comprising all children's caretakers ("*diad'ki, bonny, nian'ki i podnian'ki, kormilitsy i proch. prisluga pri detiakh*"). Here the total number of females in such positions came to 10,407 for the city proper and to an additional 331 females in the environs ("suburbs"). There were just three males so employed, all in the city proper.[11]

Social Origins of Nannies – and The Families They Served

In the "traditional" or stereotypical image, the nanny is a peasant serf in her noble master's household. If not limited to serfs, this description matches my definition of the "classic" nanny (see following chapter). The image based on serfage naturally needs some adjustment after 1861 – if not immediately after that date, at least down the road. But the image must be altered even before emancipation – and in two important ways. First, while the majority of pre-emancipation nannies came from the Russian peasantry, there were many exceptions to that rule. Second, a large number of non-noble families employed nannies.[12]

Nonpeasant Nannies. Among wealthy – or at least fairly well-off – noble families, the lead caretaker was often foreign. (This did not, of course, preclude the presence of peasant subnannies.) Nannies, not just tutors, governesses, and governors, often came from abroad – primarily from Germany, France, Switzerland, and England – to tend little Russian children. (Of course, "German" nannies often originated in Russia as well – in the Baltic lands.)

Prince Mikhail Buturlin (1807-1876) formulated in his memoirs an intriguing rule of thumb concerning foreign nannies. His belief was that among the highest nobility, British nannies were preferred over other European counterparts; French, Swiss, and German nannies would be found more often among middle and lower levels of the gentry.[13] The observation seems valid from my own readings. Among aristocratic Russian families like Buturlin's own, the Obolenskiis, and the Tolstois, a British nanny was the norm. In fact, perhaps the best "proof" of this "theorem" is the fact that the ruling Romanov family had recourse almost exclusively to British women as supervisory nannies for their children from about the last third of the eighteenth century.[14]

The desirability of having a British nanny may have been based on her snob appeal and "the sincerest form of flattery" with respect to the royals. But since British nannies came dear, it may have been mostly the aristocrats who could afford them. Yet another reason for hiring a British nanny, however, is suggested by the memoirist Nadezhda Mandel'shtam (1899-1980). Her father Iakov Khazin, a Jewish lawyer, was an Anglomane. Mandel'shtam writes: "They sent away for English women to be my nanny – typically the daughters of pastors. "They respect children," father would say.... In the child they see an individual"...[*V rebenke oni vidiat cheloveka...*].[15] Another prime reason to hire a foreigner was for the child to learn the nanny's language. Naturally, the hiring of foreign nannies triggered many nationalistic – even chauvinistic – reactions, just as it did with foreign governesses in the eighteenth century.

But foreigners are not the only nonpeasant exceptions. Nannies frequently came from the nonserf Russian population as well – usually from the urban and mercantile ranks, less often from provincial or clergy families – more than ever after 1861, but before then in many cases.[16] The least-known type of nonpeasant nanny – but of which there were probably more than a few – was that of noble origin. Liudmila Vrangel' (née Elpat'evskaia; 1877-1969) says of her nanny Vera Andreevna that no one knew exactly who she was. She left them every spring to return to Moscow and spent months away from their home. But she implies a noble origin when she adds: "I only know that she was in a lively correspondence with Ivan Turgenev's brother, Nikolai Sergeevich, who then lived in Moscow."[17]

The question naturally arises: Did a different social background lead to different nanny practices or the imparting of different cultural values? Autobiographers offer little or no direct evidence that it did. One gets the feeling that, *mutatis mutandis*, clerical and lower merchant families raised children much like peasant offspring and therefore produced nannies with experiences and cultural values similar to peasant nannies. Before 1861, serfdom might be expected to have affected nannies' thinking and behavior, but again there is a lack of strong testimony that it influenced their child caretaking unduly or in a particular way. Nor was there an apparent chasm between nannies from an urban as opposed to a rural background.

Nonnoble Households. Most, if not nearly all, of the great merchant families retained nannies for their children. Unfortunately, the memoir literature is sparse for earlier periods, but for the post-emancipation period there is more. I'm making an assumption that what was true in the later period was probably so for the earlier one.

We have at least partial confirmation, for the first half of the nineteenth century, in the memoirs of the Romantic novelist Ivan Lazhechnikov (1792-1869) and the journalist Anna Volkova (née Vishniakova; 1847-1910) as well as her uncle, Nikolai Petrovich.[18] The social historian Natal'ia Pushkareva, who focuses on women's issues, is convinced that nearly all better-off upper- and petit-bourgeois (merchant) families [*kupecheskie i meshchanskie semi*] had hired servants, including nannies.[19] Al'bin Konechnyi agrees: "In the majority of merchant families the children or *prizhivalki* [hangers-on] from among relatives would help with the household work; therefore servants often consisted only of a nanny and a cook ...who lived in the home and frequently sat at the table with the whole family."[20]

In the second half of the nineteenth century, a prominent mercantile family without a nanny would have been the exception.[21] Among lesser merchant families, the institution was certainly widespread, if not universal.[22] By the nineteenth century, if not before, middle- and upper-class Jewish families like the Mandel'shtams and Pasternaks also employed Russian peasant nannies, despite legal obstacles to the practice. The great attraction for Jewish families of hiring ethnic Russian nannies was usually linguistic: their babies heard everyday Russian from birth.[23]

The situation with families of the lesser officialdom, intelligentsia, clergy, and professional classes is less clear. It seems that a fairly substantial proportion – possibly a plurality, possibly a majority – of these nongentry families also had hired nannies for their children.[24] The five children of the minor government bureaucrat [*truzhenik-chinovnik*] Fëdor Levakovskii (1833-1898) had neither wet-nurses nor nannies, "left to our own devices, *like thousands of others like us.*" Their situation was unlike that of the offspring of the low-level Petersburg official Mikhail Skabichevskii, father of the literary critic Aleksandr (1838-1911), who did employ a nanny.[25]

As I stated in the Introduction, I don't intend to expend much ink on peasant households. But two points are germane to this study. First, the vast majority of nannies in low and middling peasant homes were peasant, but not women. Girls – the older siblings of the infants and toddlers – were the caretakers of choice, usually left to their own devices while both parents were off in the fields.[26] The tragic consequences of leaving so many babies in the hands of little more than babes themselves have been spelled out in graphic detail by Ariadna Tyrkova-Williams.[27] Yet the alternative was worse, as Semën Kanatchikov (1879-1940), born of middling peasants, relates of his first years: "the pigs didn't eat me up, the cow didn't butt me, I didn't drown in a puddle, and didn't die from some sort of infection as *thousands of peasant children – left without supervision during summer harvest time – perished in those days.*"[28] Second, the peasant-serf intelligentsia and kulaks often hired their own "outside" nannies.[29]

The Life Cycle of the Nanny

Entrance into Service. While far from typical, a fair proportion of Russian peasant women became nannies after first being the wet-nurse of their future charge. The important thing to note is that an extremely strong bond usually formed between wet-nurse and nurseling. Therefore, if the nanny had begun her service in that capacity, one can assume that this bond carried over undiminished when the wet-nurse became the child's nanny. It certainly provided a sound foundation to the pair's ongoing relationship. It's of interest that even under serfdom, *with some masters*, a nanny might be allowed "familial rights" vis-à-vis the masters. Thus, Ekaterina Raevskaia (née Bibikova; 1817-1900) writes that her wet-nurse, "a beautiful, healthy peasant woman, Fevron'ia Vasilev'na, from the Bibikovs' Kolomenskoe estate," was "transformed" into her nanny when she was two. This woman was "so smart that mama was sorry to part with her; only at the request of her husband did they let her go back to the village."[30]

Not all nannies, however, began their service in this way. The majority were probably selected otherwise. Putting aside the case when a nanny was ready at hand from the same employment with

Aleksei Venetsianov, *Wet-nurse with child* (1830) oil on canvas

one or more older children, the career of a nanny would begin in one of several ways. Most commonly, pre- and post-1861, the *pomeshchik*-master – or more likely, his wife, the *pomeshchitsa* (mistress of the estate) – would look nearby for a suitable candidate. Closest to hand were the household staff (*dvorovye liudi*). Countless nannies thus moved from the ranks of maids-of-all-work (*gornichnye*) or other generic service women (*devki, sennye devushki*) to being nannies. Somewhat further afield, peasant women from among the estate's villagers could also be enlisted as nannies.

A third way nannies came to a gentry household was from outside the ranks of the landowner's peasants (serfs pre-1861) entirely. Some of these women came upon the strong recommendation of a relative or friend. Indeed, practices then are fully reminiscent of present-day circumstances, when acquaintances pass on to others the names of their favorite cleaning services and automobile mechanics. While many of these "outsiders" would still be serfs, or at least Russian peasants, a sizeable number were not, as we have just seen. Vladimir Taneev (1840-1921) recalls that his parents, for a then princely sum, hired a very good nanny for him.[31]

During the eighteenth and first half of the nineteenth century, there appears to have been a fourth way of finding a nanny – advertising the position. This was typically used to find a foreign-born nanny. However, after emancipation in 1861 especially, there was a common new way to seek a nanny: through the services of an employment office (see Chapter 6).

Career Trajectories. A nanny's work began when an infant was either first born, alongside the wet-nurse or as the wet-nurse, or at least when the babe was weaned. She remained the primary caretaker until the child was about 6 or 7.[32] It is virtually a given in the memoir literature that when the time comes for the child to part with its nanny, usually to move to the care of others, the "loss" of the nanny becomes one of the most traumatic memories of the writer. For some, it marks the "end of childhood"; for others, it becomes almost like a death in the family.[33]

Once in the family, a nanny tended to follow one of two basic "career paths," at least until the turn of the twentieth century. Each path branched off in various directions. It is impossible to quantify this aspect of the story; perhaps about half of nannies traced each of the two basic paths.

The first path was for the nanny to remain a nanny throughout her life. Her nominal career with any one child would naturally span only about a half dozen years. The youngster generally passed – wholly or mostly – to other hands by age 7.[34] Among "lifelong" nannies, some stayed with their original family, continuing to nanny for the younger siblings of their original nurseling until the parents stopped procreating or the nanny got too old to continue. Such nannies might, however, go to live with, and nanny for, their former nurselings after the latter married. Others remained nannies but not in their original households. "Many years later I was glad to meet my nurse again," writes Nikolai Charykov (1855-1930), "...By that time she was, of course, free, but had returned to the Kankrin family, becoming the nurse of the Countess's eldest grandson...."[35]

If the nanny followed this first path, moreover, it was typical that she might also become, at least for a time, essentially a companion for an adolescent girl.[36] Russian literature is rife with examples of nannies who survived into deep old age but continued to play a pivotal role in their former charges' lives. (Chapter 7)

A fine example of the path a "career nanny" might take is that of Aleksandra Bychkova, Svetlana Allilueva's beloved "Granny." She "went to work as a household servant [on the estate where she was born] when she was thirteen years old. Before the Revolution my nurse's entire life was spent with this family.... She worked for them as maid, housekeeper, cook and, finally, as a nurse[maid]. She also spent a long time [post-1917] in the household of Nikolai Yevreinov, a well-known theatre director and critic, looking after his son."[37] When the Evreinovs emigrated, "Granny" returned to her village for a time, but could not bear living outside a city. She came to Moscow in the 1920s, working first for the Samarin family, then the Malkins, whence Stalin's wife lured her to their home.

The memoir literature provides many examples of multigenerational nannies. The string probably stopped at two generations in most instances. This was the case, for example, with both the historian Dmitrii Likhachev (1906-1999) and the writer Lidiia Avilova (1864-1943).[38] Vera Figner's (1852-1942) nanny, Natal'ia Makar'evna, on the other hand, nannied three generations of the family, as did

– apparently – the nanny-turned-house manager Varvara in Iurii Miroliubov's household in the 1890s.[39] But for longevity in the profession, none would appear to top Evgeniia Fraser's (1905-2002) Shalovchikha, who had a hand in caring for four generations of the family.[40] The reverse situation, where one family provided more than one generation of nannies, was nowhere near as widespread, though it did occur. Nanny Elizaveta Il'inichna was formerly the maid of the mother of Anna Lelong (b. 1841). Nanny had only one daughter, Aleftina, subsequently given her freedom "for her services as a nanny" and married off to a merchant in Zaraisk.[41] In 1904 the artist Mstislav Dobuzhinskii traveled to Tambov with his wife, two young children, and their nanny, Veta (Elizaveta), "the niece of my own nanny Mar'ia Osipovna...."[42]

The second basic career path for the peasant nanny was to continue gainful employment in a different capacity. Many became a different kind of servant within the original household. Typically, especially after emancipation, if they were physically fit and possessed good sense and economic "smarts," they became a housekeeper – *kliuchnitsa* (literally, the keeper of the keys) or *ekonomka*.[43] Otherwise, they might become maids, linen-keepers, or some other sort of servant. Rarely did they leave domestic service entirely, but those who did might become agricultural or factory workers, find work in town shops, or engage in other wage-earning pursuits.

An excellent illustration of a career trajectory for a nanny of the second type was Matrësha, nanny for the little brother of Nikolai Findeizen (1868-1928), the music scholar and critic. "She was a glorious [*slavnaia*], intelligent, delicate girl" who, "at the start of the Russo-Turkish War [of 1877-78]...went to the Bulgarian front as a nurse and returned with her nerves shattered but as glorious as before. Mama did not lose track of her and, many years later...glorious Matrësha turned out to be our first housekeeper [*domopravitel'nitsa*]...."[44]

Exceedingly rare (perhaps unique?) was the case where a serf nanny was actually sold to another family, as in the family of Stanislav Okreits (b. 1836). The financially troubled father did not know that his wife had sold the woman for a mere 30 rubles.[45] An unusual case, but probably not unique, is that of a woman in the household of Iurii Miroliubov (1892-1970), an émigré scholar.

In our family there lived an ancient old woman – Varvara, whom everyone called "Granny" ["Praba"] or "Great-granny" ["Prabushka"]. She was near ninety years old when I was five.... Great-grandfather treated her with affection and even gave her her freedom, but she herself did not want to abandon the family and got so used to things that she became the lady of the house [*povelitel'nitsa*]. My father obeyed her unconditionally till he turned grey. Mother esteemed her, and the servitors [*sluzhashchie*] dignified her with either "Great-granny" or "Mistress" ["*barynia*"]. She was in fact the mistress, because she directed everything...[46]

Similar advancement through careers was reached by two former nannies in the Unkovskii family, both named Tat'iana, in the post-emancipation years. The first, Tat'iana Alekseevna, was the former nanny of Aleksandra Unkovskaia's Uncle Sasha. She became the keeper of the keys (i.e., housekeeper) in her grandmother's home but had the added privilege of occasionally advising grandmother. The second, Tat'iana Nikitishna, former nanny of her Uncle Mitia, "helped [the grandmother] with her prayers" – but her stature was even higher. On the grandmother's estate and in the village of Ivanovskoe as a whole, Tat'iana Nikitishna played the role of "a holy elder [*starets*]." "...each could come to her for advice and for comfort; she knew what to say to whom and what to advise because she loved everyone and wished good to everyone..." She even, contrary to the pleas and tears of her mother, encouraged the sixteen-year-old daughter of the mistress to enter a convent, which she did.[47]

Longevity and Mortality of the Nanny. One forms an impression from memoirs and fiction that many nannies lived to a ripe old age. That is why, to anticipate an argument I make in Chapter 7, it seems nannies may have been a presence in their former charges' lives for such a long time. I would speculate that, as compared with the birth mother, the nanny might have been disproportionately more of a presence in the child's later life for the following reason. Given the fairly high fertility rates for women in the eighteenth and nineteenth centuries, but the comparatively low life expectancy, a

Pavel Fedotov, *Domnushka, nanny in the Zhdanovich family* (1846/47) pencil

rather substantial proportion of families were deprived of wives and mothers by the time the children reached middle age. (I'm speaking of both noble and peasant families.) The very fact of giving frequent birth apparently tended to undermine the health, not to mention bring on the death in childbirth, of many middle-class and high-born women.[48] While this theory/hypothesis has been challenged in some recent demographic literature, it appears to hold up fairly well.[49]

Any woman who remained unmarried and/or stopped having children in a "suspended" marriage – as was the case with the bulk of nannies – probably had somewhat higher odds of surviving longer than the average married bourgeois or noble woman giving birth at frequent intervals. If these calculations are reasonable, then children blessed with a nanny had cause to expect that at least one of their two maternal figures would be around for their adulthood, to provide love and comfort when needed. In many cases, that figure would have been the nanny.

The Aged Nanny. Among these women, the late stages of life could become particularly trying or painful. If they stayed in the masters'/employers' home until their death, they might remain figures of veneration and affection; but they might also become objects of indifference or even contempt. That the moral dilemma of what to do with aging servants was not lost on society can be seen in many works of both fiction and nonfiction. (The royal family, it should come as no surprise, faced the same problem of what to do with aging nannies, governesses, and other servants as other noble families had.[50]) One autobiographer speaks movingly of the situation that was all too common: "Not always, however, did the nanny's charges repay her with the same love, and it happened that they forgot about her, and the poor old woman, shunted aside, would sadly while away her life, given up to the masters, far from them. This type of nanny, which did not quite disappear even after the end of serfdom, is well known and not only noted but even praised in our literature."[51]

Even without the devastating turn of events where she lost the regard of her masters and her former charge(s), however, the old nanny's lot was often far from enviable. All the shortcomings of character that might have been overlooked or even rationalized at an earlier stage could easily now make her an object of pity, dislike, or even derision. If the ties of affection weakened, or if the family's financial situation took a turn for the worse, such nannies could end up in the almshouse. Three examples of the last development are an alleged under-nanny of Pushkin; Ol'ga Matveevna, the nanny of Nikolai Malevskii-Malevich (1855-after 1912); and Aksin'ia Makarovna Durnova, beloved nanny of Mariia Frederiks (b. 1832).[52] The "almshouse ending" was all too typical of fiction by second-rank writers, as the temptation to sentimentalize such figures as an old lackey or an old nanny was almost irresistible. This maudlin, or at least sentimentalized approach shows up, for example, in the stories of Tat'iana Shchepkina-Kupernik (1874-1952) and Elizaveta Militsyna (1869-1930), both born – perhaps not coincidentally – after emancipation.[53] Similarly, in Dostoevskii's short fable of the "Little Boy at Christ's New Year's Party," there is an 80-year-old woman dying, abandoned and alone, in squalid quarters, who once made her living as a nanny.[54]

Another example of seeming callousness toward a "faithful" older retainer is the nanny of Natal'ia Mamontova (b. 1903), step-daughter of Russia's "last tsar," the Grand Duke Mikhail Aleksandrovich. In 1905, at age 2, she assures readers in her autobiography, her nanny was "far the most important factor in my life." The nanny's devotion "was limitless" and "she spoilt me." In 1918, when the family's fortunes had taken a drastic turn for the worse, most of their staff was "liquidated" (that is, sent back to their village), and "it was decided to pension off Nyanya. I was sorry to see her go, but it was a relief, as she was an extra mouth to feed and was completely useless, all she did was grumble and pray."[55]

However, not all former nannies who left "their families" were neglected. We have excellent testimony that many former nurselings maintained regular or loving relationships with their childhood nannies. This was easiest, of course, if the "retired" nanny had remained within the household of the nurseling's parents or if the nanny had transferred to the nurseling's family – to continue work as a nanny, to perform other services – say, as a housekeeper, or to enjoy a well-earned retirement. But even nannies who were living apart from the original family or the nurseling's "successor family" were often still in the thoughts of their former charges. For example, from their respective exiles, both the artist Mstislav Dobuzhinskii and Aleksandr Herzen would send money back to Russia (through appropriately difficult-to-trace channels) to help their nannies survive in their declining years. The poet Blok continued to see his favorite nanny socially for many years after she had ceased to be his caretaker and, like the two preceding figures, offered her material help. After nanny Ekaterina Chuprova left the family of Prince Georgii L'vov (1861-1925), all the children retained "sweet memories of her" and "later, upon finishing secondary school, I sought her out in Moscow. She was very poor [*bedstvovala*], with small children; I went to some trouble [*vykhlopotal*] to get free tuition for her son Kolia at the Polivanov Gymnasium."[56]

If the masters did not take care of the former nanny directly, others associated with the family might. This was the case, for example, with Liudmila Vrangel's old nanny. "In the end, the footman, Nikita, a very able serf and mother's favorite, got married and settled in the village. He took in our old nanny Ustia, to live out her life in his clean spacious two-room hut with a cherry orchard and vegetable garden where all was cozy and pristine in the Little Russian fashion."[57]

The Ambiguities of Age. One can't leave the subject of life cycles without saying something about age more generally. The stereotype image of a Russian peasant nanny is that of an old woman, often one who's been in the family for a generation or two. Yet even these women had to have been young at some point. What was the average age of a Russian nanny? That mean age is a figure impossible to calculate and unimportant. From much evidence we can say with confidence that the stereotype old nanny is far from the norm. While it satisfied the esthetic preferences of belletrists to write of older nannies, memoirists document the existence of a multitude of younger nannies, many mere girls. And yet there is more to it than that.

Obviously, from the standpoint of little children, most adults seem ancient, whatever their age. The writer Vera Zhelikhovskaia (1835-1896) recalls that she tried unsuccessfully at times to imagine her nanny as a young person or even as a child. Did she gambol, laugh, misbehave? Or was she always as she was "now"? She had to have been young once but it doesn't seem possible to Zhelikhovskaia. "And will I some day be grey, an old woman like nanny?"[58] Olga Chernov Andreev mused, "As far as I remember, Nyanya never mentioned her age, and when she was still young, counted herself among the 'old folks'."[59] Several memoirists comment ironically on the disparity between what they thought was their nanny's age and what it was in truth. "Old" is always a relative term.[60]

Circumstances and the nannies themselves, moreover, conspired to keep their true age something of a mystery. The children, out of innocent and irritating inquisitiveness, would constantly ply their nannies with questions about their age or otherwise try to ascertain this elusive benchmark. Such queries would elicit a spectrum of responses. For example, Prince Dmitrii Obolenskii (b. 1918) and his brother Ivan found their British nanny's age "strangely indeterminate." They made "frequent and indiscreet attempts" to satisfy their curiosity by searching for Miss Clegg's passport. "To our repeated and intemperate question 'Nanny, how old are you?' she would simulate anger and rebuke us for rudeness." From the earliest time Vera Figner could remember, her nanny already seemed old to her. When asked about her age, the nanny would always answer: "Seventh decade coming." She repeated the same stock phrase when she was near death – her reply never altered. Many nannies, moreover, were fully ignorant of their own ages. Dorothy Russell's peasant nanny, reunited with her in Paris after the revolution, made her first question of her former nurseling "How old are you? Because I only know my age by your age."[61]

The writer Mikhail Osorgin (pseud. of Il'in; 1878-1942) discusses another factor lending confusion to the question – the difference between real age and psychological age. In his quasi-autobiographical novel *My Sister's Story* he says: "Our tiny world was not divided into grown-ups and children. Nurse, for instance, could not possibly have been classed among the grown-ups: she was very old, yet belonged nevertheless to the children's world – lived on our interests, knew all my sister's dolls by name, spoke our children's language, and shared in our games and secrets."[62] Yet another aspect of how the mind can play tricks on this issue of age is revealed, inadvertently, by an evocative phrase in the memoirs of

Zinaida Gippius (1869-1945), a preeminent poet of the Silver Age: "I grew up all alone [*odna*]. *All with the same, eternal nanny, Dar'ia Pavlovna*, and then with countless governesses, who did not get along with me very well [*kotoryia so mnoiu malo uzhivalis'*]."⁶³

So perhaps the stereotype is not that far wrong after all. In literature – but in real life to a certain extent also – a nanny was both ageless and ages-old. This image befits the sense of time in villages. In the anthropologists' pet phrasing, peasants view time not as an "arrow" but as a "cycle" – tied forever to changing but ever-repeating seasons of work and reproduction.⁶⁴

The Cost of a Nanny, The Price of Service

The Issue of Compensation. One can assume that foreign women who came to Russia to be nannies were always paid a salary for their work. This was true for the eighteenth century right through the twentieth. It was no less true for foreign women already in Russia in some other capacity who then became nannies. A classic example of the last kind was Anna Fedorovna Varch, a German woman who had been employed as a linen-keeper at – but then let go by – the Smol'nyi Institute. In 1787 Prince Ivan Dolgorukov and his wife, who was pregnant with their first child, were both deeply involved in searching out a first-rate nanny. When Varch came for an interview, they hired her on the spot, as the princess had herself been educated at Smolnyi and knew Varch well. Her salary was 70 rubles a year. By the time she had raised all ten of the Dolgorukov offspring her wages had more than doubled, to 150 rubles a year "and we would have increased them [beyond that], but she never mentioned it." This good German woman died in 1817. Her employer does not know or does not mention what happened to whatever property she had accumulated in her over quarter century of service with his family.⁶⁵

But what about the classic peasant nannies: early on, did their being serfs mean their labor was uncompensated? Strangely enough, it did not. While it might seem a contradiction in terms, serf nannies and other domestics were not always unpaid workers. This is a subject for a discussion of which I've searched in vain in the literature; none of the standard Western works on serfdom appear

Vasilii Vereshchagin, *Sketch of his nanny Anna*, ca. 1890? pencil

to discuss salaries or wages of the house serfs, at least not at any length.[66] Not just serf nannies but many other serfs received salaries from their own masters: wet-nurses; estate managers and overseers; highly skilled artisans, craftsmen, and artists; even lowly footmen.[67] The most prosaic way in which a serf nanny received pay, however, was when the peasant woman was on *obrok* (paying quitrent to a master) and went to work for a different master. Such was the case in the 1850s, for example, with the nanny in the family of the future humorist Nikolai Leikin (1841-1906). The serf of another *pomeshchik*, on *obrok*, she sent her salary back to her master.[68] But in other cases also it appears that serf nannies obtained compensation in money or in kind (the *mesiachina*). Pushkin's household debts in the 1830s include expenses for nanny services. In addition, of course, serfs might receive sums of money from their masters simply as gifts.

Nonserf peasant nannies were probably always salaried. For example, the nanny of Nikolai Bunakov (1837-1904), Ekaterina Denisovna Khlopova, was from a freed serf family and "lived with us on hire."[69] As noted previously, in 1843, when little Volodia Taneev was three years old, the family hired Pelageia Ivanovna to care for him. "She was celebrated in town as the best nanny. They hired her for the huge sum in those prices of 5 assignat rubles a month." It's not made clear, however, what the social origin of Pelageia Ivanovna was, though "Pelageia" was generally a name reserved for peasant or other lower-class women. Ekaterina Novoselova (b. 1837) also had a hired nanny of unspecified social origin in the late 1830s and 40s ("up to the age of 5"), although the family had serfs on their estate.[70]

Memoir accounts are full of instances of nannies maintaining savings of various amounts. The Dostoevskii family (nonpeasant) nanny Alena Frolovna managed to save a tidy sum from her salary. M. P. Bibikov's nanny was paid an unspecified amount of money each month.[71] The nanny of the revolutionary Vera Figner (1852-1942) received one and a half rubles per month, or, in her reckoning, three assignat rubles a month.[72] In the 1860s and 1870s the services of a good post-emancipation nanny were still comparatively low-paid. The critic and radical writer N. V. Shelgunov and his wife hired a woman to be "on the road" with them – they were in political exile at the time – for 100 rubles (but it's not clear if this salary was for an entire year or a shorter period of time).

The following table shows what nanny wages might be in various historical periods. In the eighteenth century and much of the nineteenth, room and board virtually always accompanied monetary wages. To give some idea of what these wages signified, I include some other workers' and professionals' salaries for selected time periods – pay that did not include room and board.[73] (R = ruble; assignat rubles have been converted to silver/coin rubles.)

Table of Nannies' Wages[1]

Time Period	Nanny Salary	Other Salaries
1780s	70 R/yr*	
ca. 1800	up to 150 R/yr*	ca. 550 R/yr for senior teacher in Nizhnii Novgorod (post-1804)
1820s	ca. 225 R/yr**	
1840s	ca. 215 R/yr** (considered a "huge" sum, for the "best nanny" in town)	ca. 184 R/yr in money + 107 R/yr in kind or ca. 290 R/yr for a Urals iron-smith with 4 children; ca. 204 R/yr total for Urals carpenter with 4 children
1850s	18-48 R/yr**	ca. 200-250 R/yr for an industrial worker; ca. 6/mo for an agricultural worker
1890s	96-120 R/yr plus "certain privileges" for women of varying educational levels	ca. 200 R/yr for an industrial worker; ca. 13 R/mo for an agricultural agricultural worker
1900	144-180 R/yr on average, but up to 300 R/yr for a highly qualified woman	ca. 240-280 R/yr for an industrial worker; ca. 18 R/mo for an agricultural worker
1905	480 R/yr	260-310 R/yr for an industrial worker

*for an educated *bonne*   **for a little- or uneducated, middle- or lower-class woman/peasant

[1]*Sources*: Dolgorukov, *Kapishche moego serdtsa*, p. 63; Andrei Dostoevskii, "Iz 'Vospominanii'," in *F. M. Dostoevskii v vospominaniiakh sovremennikov*, Vol. I, ed. by V. V. Grigorenko et al. (Moscow: Khudozhestvennaia literatura, 1964), p. 42; ; Taneev, *Detstvo*, p. 56; Figner, *Zapechatlennyi trud*. I, pp. 61-62; Leikin, *Moi vospominaniia*, pp. 10, 12; Svetlov, *Peterburgskaia zhizn'*, p. 63; Kelly, *Children's World*, p. 304; Rustemeyer, *Dienstboten*, pp. 197ff; Mikhail Nazimov, "V provintsii i v Moskve s 1812 po 1828 god. Iz vospominanii starozhila," *RV*, Vol. 124, No. 7 (July 1876), pp. 97-98; Nancy Baster, "Some Early Family Budget Studies of Russian Workers," *American Slavic and East European Review*, Vol. 17, No. 4 (Dec. 1958), Table 1, p. 469, p. 477; Mironov, *Blagosostoianie naseleniia*, Table X.8, p. 520 and Table X.12, p. 526

The Price of Service. One aspect of nannies' lives sometimes noted by memoirists but, understandably, seldom dwelt on – especially for the pre-emancipation period – was the enormous personal cost these women paid in order to shepherd gentry children through their formative years. Household staff, serf or not, often bore the brunt of their masters' displeasure, verbal or even physical abuse. As will be seen further in the following section of this chapter, which talks about nannies' personal lives, many faced forced separation from husbands and families. Most examples I can cite come from a later period, as a conspiracy of silence mostly ruled among memoirists for the era of serfdom.

Memorable with regard to the issue of "price" was Avdot'ia, called Dunia, the nanny of young Ol'ga Berggol'ts (1910-1975). Dunia was born and raised in the village of Guzhovo in Pskov province, a three- or four-night trip. Evenings, particularly when the other adults were away, Dunia "would fill [*zavodila*] the whole apartment with a 'long' thin voice, as if crying" about her "native parts" and a younger brother she yearned to see. She would pour tears. When the children would finally start to howl themselves, Dunia would rush to comfort them, asking why they should be in tears. "Now what's with you? You've nothing to cry about, you've got a papa and mama..." "But why are you crying yourself?" "Just so. I have no mama. No papa. I'm an orphan. I was remembering Guzhovo."[74] The lingering, palpable sense of loss and pain over her separation from her beloved village seemed never to leave Dunia.

A very similar picture emerges from Nikolai Astrov's autobiography. From within their Moscow apartment, the family can hear the whistles of the trains from the Kursk Station, which always remind nanny Akulina of her home village in the Tula region, where she'd been a serf. She cuts off remembrance of the village "with not quite a sigh, not quite a repressed sob." "Our nanny did not like to talk about the village. She would say that now she was 'a person on her own' [*"otrezannyi lomot'*," literally a "cut-off slice," but figuratively someone once dependent but now standing on their own feet] and that she could not go back to the village [*ei vozvrashchat'sia v derevniu nekuda*]. Nanny would sigh and tears would fall from her eyes."[75] These scenes often border on bathos, but that doesn't mean they must be completely discounted.

Nor do they contradict the fact that many nannies *were* able to travel (see Chapter 5); they simply demonstrate one of the potential personal costs a nanny might face. This price for service was shared by pre- and post-emancipation nannies.[76]

The Happy Slave. Despite the foregoing examples, which could be repeated *ad nauseum*, there remains the anomalous yet nearly universal attempt in the memoir literature to prove that almost all serfs, but especially the nannies, were content with their lives.[77] Pushkin's Arina Rodionovna spurned the gift of her manumission at the turn of the nineteenth century. But she was not alone. Grigorii Filipson (1809-1883), a general and senator, remembers that his nanny Avdot'ia Nazarovna, who had been his mother's childhood playmate, was gifted to his mother and then given to his mother in her dowry. Avdot'ia had been given her freedom [*otpusknaia*] by his mother (in the 1820s or 30s?), "but she would not even think of leaving us."[78] As he prepared to free his serfs in 1856, Leo Tolstoi had many discussions with village elders and other thoughtful peasants, and he found that many were reluctant to see the end of the old system. Yet he makes it rather clear in his diary that peasant hesitancy nearly always stemmed from their suspicions of being deceived and manipulated by the master.[79]

For memoirists not tone-deaf to the moral implications of serfdom, a more realistic and nuanced picture could emerge. The author and activist Mariia/Mar'ia Tsebrikova (1835-1917) noted that her father maintained that a serf with a "good" master was better off than a free peasant, even though she observed many abuses of the system among her acquaintances.

> Our Ol'ga [the family's only serf] was always envious of the free peasants – more for the sake of the honor of being free, however, because she lived no worse than the nonserf servants, with whom, in accord with the mores of the times, they didn't stand on ceremony…. Allowed to marry and leave five years before the emancipation, she maintained relations with us, like toward "those she'd nannied," and when she found herself unemployed, she and her husband would live with us. Everything which had formerly in life

been difficult, in a life at the master's beck and call, had not changed, but there had appeared a consciousness: I want – I'll leave, but not for my whole life. This feeling of a serf I understood poorly at that time.[80]

The irreducible fact remains that, especially for the serf woman but for her liberated successors also, *there was always a price to pay for being others' nanny.*

Family and Personal Life of Nannies Apart from or Outside the Masters' Household

"All the love, all the devotion of her kind heart, nanny gave to our family. She did not have a life of her own: her joy and grief were exclusively bound with our life." So said the educator Elizaveta Vodovozova (1844-1923) about her own nanny.[81] However embroidered her remembrance, the pedagog captured an essential aspect of a caretaker's life. Nannying for a master's family in pre-emancipation days was far from conducive to a happy family life of her own for a village woman. Peasant nannies were sometimes single women – never married or widowed – but probably more often were married (perforce, if they entered service first as a wet-nurse). If with a husband, the nanny would generally have one or more children as well. This situation could and did create all sorts of difficulties.

The most obvious problem that arose for a nanny watching others' children but with children of her own was how to divide her attention, time, and love between the separate families. Sadly, this was rarely an issue for long. In reality, the nanny would virtually abandon her own children for those of her masters. Even if her husband and children lived in the village in which the masters' estate was located, she rarely would have much time to spend with them. This does not mean that she stopped loving her own offspring, merely that her physical presence was demanded entirely in one place – the home of the lord (*barin*). Vera Ziloti (née Tret'iakova; 1866-1940) – wife of the pianist-composer-conductor Alexander Ziloti (Siloti; 1863-1945) – writes: "I recall – Nanny Tania …had a daughter Sasha somewhere; I understood that Nanny Tania loved us both; she often cried, I was so sorry for her and I loved my Nanny Tania all the more."[82]

Worse fates abounded. M. Bibikov recalls of his nanny: "She had at one time her own children and grandchildren, but God took them all away from her: one died in infancy, one was killed in the war, and one, her favorite grandson, disappeared without a trace in the Moscow fire."[83]

In some cases, a fortunate nanny might have wholly or partly raised her own brood before assuming the duties of nanny for the *barin*. If so, however, she almost certainly again lost daily contact with both husband and children and might have only a few precious items in her possession to remind her of what had once been hers more immediately. "Respectful and deferential was our attitude toward nanny's only photograph," says Ekaterina Olitskaia (1899-1974). "It was taken of nanny surrounded by her family. Already no longer young, she sat in her constant blue cap in the center of a large family group. Twenty-two of her sons surrounded nanny. What did I, a young girl, understand? But 22 sons inspired in me a blissful respect for nanny."[84] In his fictional autobiography, the novel *Under a New Sickle* (Pod novom serpom), the Symbolist poet and critic Konstantin Bal'mont (1867-1942) writes of a rather indifferent mother recalling that the nanny had a son of her own. The nanny responds:

> "My goodness, you've remembered well, little mother. This was so long ago. There was one little son, one there was. And they took him off for a soldier when the English and French and Turks came to fight in the Crimea. There he, the poor little one, laid down his head, not to blame for anything. If only I'd seen him. If he'd died here, I'd be able to visit his grave, pray over him, bring flowers to his grave. But there, on a faraway shore, no one grieved and no one feels sorry [about him]."[85]

As time wore on, the nanny might tend to see less of her husband and even lose track of him. But if the nanny had never been married, she would frequently remain single her entire life.

Post-1861, and especially after the ten-year transitional period, one could expect for many of the newer generation of nannies an altered family situation as compared with their serf predecessors. But my reading of the sources suggests that no major upheaval occurred. As with field-working former serfs, the situation for household staff, including nannies, seems to have changed little, at least until the end of the 1800s. For those who launched a career in childcare after emancipation, the future probably looked more uncertain than it had for generations of earlier nannies. But their career still did not often allow for a full family life of their own so long as they remained in service as nannies.[86]

Conclusion

A nanny's life was not necessarily an easy one, but it was a full life. Nearly all the caretakers I've read about were women secure in knowing who they were and cognizant of making a real contribution to their community. As revealed in these pages, nannies were relatively autonomous beings, gainfully employed, doing important work. That makes them something of an exception in pre-emancipation days, when woman's lot was often lacking in one or more of these respects.

The following two chapters fill out in much greater detail the nature of nannies' lives.

4

The Classic, Pre-Emancipation Nanny

In the previous chapter I introduced little-known details about nonpeasant nannies and nonnoble households. From this point on, I will limit the discussion mostly to the noble household and largely (but not exclusively) to peasant nannies.[1] The reason for doing so is simple: the essence of my story concerns women born in Russia, *whose native tongue was Russian*. "The gentry nest" (Turgenev's famous coinage) is of greatest interest from the cultural and mythologizing standpoints; we have by far more information about nannies in such families than about caretakers in the homes of other social groups. But in any case, the situation with child caregivers in the bulk of noble households – those of the low and middling gentry – was, by memoir testimony, very close to that in most intelligentsia, middling and high merchant, and better-off clerical families. By the same token, nonpeasant nannies, not entirely missing in the remainder of these pages, were most often indistinguishable from their peasant counterparts.

Stereotype and Reality[2]

The Familiar Picture. Anyone familiar with Russian history, and particularly with the Russian gentry of the nineteenth century, probably already has a fairly good idea of what a nanny under the old regime was. In the first place, Russian nannies show up in most memoirs and in a great deal of fiction. Secondly, the topic of the Russian nanny has not gone unstudied; not only does Jessica Tovrov discuss nannies at some length in her monograph on Russian noble families, but others, such as Angela Rustemeyer, Natal'ia Pushkareva, Priscilla Roosevelt, and Orlando Figes, also devote space to the nanny (and the wet-nurse) in their own studies of Russian life and culture. These authors have much of the story right. But they tend to deal in stereotypes of goodness and devotion, don't tell the whole story, and often make assertions that are arguable, unsatisfying, or plain wrong.[3]

Some Russian memoirists make the same mistake, speaking of "typical" nannies.[4] For every nanny that "fit the mold," there were probably as many that did not, bearing only partial or passing resemblance to it. While I will try to avoid too many generalizations in discussing nannies, I need to begin with a generalization that I hope is unarguable. In all that follows, the reader should keep in mind that a nanny was first and foremost a servant. Despite the claim about most nannies – indeed many servants – being "members of the family," they were still in a position of subservience. Their stature might as often be a reflection of the worth or standing of their masters as of their own intrinsic merits. They had duties and responsibilities more than rights and privileges.

In what follows, I want to add more to the familiar picture, to flesh out this image that most readers will have long held. While I will be adding corroborative detail in some cases, I will offer evidence that does not support, or even contradicts, this picture as well. Despite Rustemeyer's warning that it would be hopeless to try to extract an accurate picture of Russian nannies from the memoir literature, I believe it is possible to do so. What I hope to accomplish, however, is almost the reverse of her admonition: to demonstrate that, far from providing a uniformly idealized picture of nannies, the memoir literature actually helps to disprove that image.

The More Ambiguous Reality. It is actually rather difficult to find universal characteristics in Russian nannies. Individual caretakers had their own strengths and weaknesses, to be sure, as will be laid out in what follows. Far from being an *uncomplicated*, straightforward figure, the nanny embodied a panoply of qualities. This leads me to stress once again my major subtext: nannies are surrounded by ambiguity.⁵ A nanny's behavior might sometimes be laudatory, exemplary, judicious, and selfless; this very same nanny might equally be querulous, spiteful, intemperate, or silly. On the one hand, she was a necessary helpmate in the noble household, the mother's indispensable assistant in all things pertaining to the children, at least up to their age of about 6 or 7. On the other hand, she was most often an "ignorant" member of an "inferior" social class, unschooled and unlettered.

How could upper- or even middle-class Russians be expected to reconcile these contradictory aspects of their peasant caretakers? No wonder adults were so often ambivalent about children's nannies in general and even about their own children's nannies (though their children seldom shared this ambivalence). The reader will recall from Chapter 2 the reservations of Nikolai Novikov, Pëtr Shalikov, Kondratii Grum, and others about well-brought-up children's associating with "undesirable" people. Yet many of these same adults, when writing their memoirs, would usually paint their *own* nannies from childhood in almost uniformly positive colors.

One of the best guides to understanding the position of nannies under the old regime is, therefore, not memoirists but publicists. They often have their fingers on the social pulse, and, while not unerring, the best of such writers usually provide a reasonably accurate picture of the society of their times. In 1858 a teacher-pedagog by training, Feliks Toll' (1823-1867), examined the situation of Russian nannies in the *Journal for Education*.⁶ He stressed the importance of his subject by insisting that the influence of a child's nanny lasts its whole life. (p. 443) Assuming the viewpoint of most parents, Toll' said that "with a clear conscience," most Russian mothers entrust their child "to the unimpeded influence of a mentally defective, ignorant peasant woman who is indifferent toward her job." Such a woman carries out her "duties" excellently: for her own benefit or amusement, she teaches the child how to lie and steal, develops all its baser instincts, accustoms it to being spoiled, submits to its whims and willfulness, yet when unobserved abuses the child both orally and physically. (p. 447) For Toll', "the position of nanny is always vilified."

But who is to blame for this? The lower class, from which nannies overwhelmingly come? No, it's the parents who are to blame. (pp. 448-50) They must exercise much greater care in the selection of their caretakers; they must insist on a mature woman, not younger than about 20 but preferably older, perhaps a widow, who has great stores of patience, is healthy, even-tempered, even phlegmatic, restrained. The nanny must be mentally and morally

Aleksei Venetsianov, *Portrait of the Panaev Children with Their Nanny* (1841) oil on canvas

"educated"; she must have empathy; she should be able to sing well. Above all, the nanny must have a real love for children. (pp. 454-58)

How was Russia to provide such a pool of child caretakers? First, society had to act: schools for the training of nannies should be established. Second, "girls and widows from better families" had to be recruited, women able to teach children properly. Since most of these recruits would be poor, material incentives had to be offered to induce them to enter a profession where all too often the poor behavior or treatment of the employer excluded the prospect of employment for most women from a "delicate" background. (pp. 459-61) This harsh view of nannying just before emancipation is eye-opening; the author most likely reflected abolitionist sentiment and his own self-interest.[7]

Peasant Attitudes. Not just the nobility and middle classes but even the peasants themselves had mixed feelings about nannies. The collective folk wisdom of centuries, well-known to upper and lower classes alike, was not all that admiring of the nanny. Not every reference among folk sayings, proverbs, and maxims to nannies is pejorative; still, many references reflect a wariness of nannies and how they went about their work.[8] My best guess, however, is that these pearls of folk wisdom originated in observations about how young peasant girls tended village children rather than a master's (see the preceding chapter).

The best-known reference to nannies in all of Russian folk culture is this axiom: *U semi nianek (mamok) ditia bez glazu (glaza).* Every collector of Russian proverbs seems to have noted it.[9] Literally meaning "With seven nannies there's no eye on the child," it comes close to the old saw that "too many cooks spoil the broth." There appear to be two readings for "eye" in this case. It might mean the child lacks supervision, but it also implies a more dire consequence: the child could lose an eye. While the above saying is the most famous, there are many others which are similar. All are variations on the "too many cooks" adage, many mentioning the likely loss of other body parts (nose, head). There's even the more generic *"Detkam ne porcha – igrushka, a porcha – khudaia prisluzhka"* (A toy doesn't spoil children, but a poor servant does), which certainly encompassed nannies.

Family Member? An age-old cliché of nannies (and other household servants) is that they are "members of the family."[10] Not just the masters (explicitly) but many nannies (secondhand, usually implicitly) expressed this feeling about belonging to one family. Yet I confess to an inner schizophrenia on this matter. As noted in the Introduction, this claim has long seemed to me just a rationalization, with respect to the masters in particular. It reminds one of the claim, equally frequent in memoirs, that while serfdom might have been a terrible institution, the memoirist's own father and mother were caring, much-loved serfowners; and that, whatever the plight of other serfs, their own serfs were well taken care of. One part of me says both master and servant had good reasons to exaggerate the degree of intimacy in their relationship – to try to smooth over an otherwise quite unequal relationship, and the gulf separating the two was too large to be bridged.[11] This part of me argues the standard claim is not to be taken literally; that gratitude, love and affection, condescension, nostalgia, and a host of other emotions and factors have transmuted what was obviously a close relationship into something loftier and more significant. The other part of me says that at some point it's best to suspend disbelief, to accept more or less at face value what legions of memoirists, in Russia and worldwide, have said – that they truly believe they felt no difference between how they viewed their nanny and their other blood kin.

What arguments vie in support of one side or the other of this issue? I don't recall ever reading that a nanny was included in a master's will, yet many were buried alongside the masters in a family burial spot. Countless nannies lived on in "their" families after their charges were grown, some to the end of their days. At least to the middle of the nineteenth century (and before), it was commonplace for young men – and probably young women – when away from home, to include in their letters back to family warm greetings not only for parents and siblings but also for their nannies (and *diad'ki*). Nannies became duennas for teenage girls, companions for the girls' mothers, or just "fixtures" within the household, no longer performing any real service. Perhaps these women really were absorbed into the family in some sense.

Yet the nanny always knew "her place" and rarely overstepped the boundaries of nonfamily propriety. Most nannies ate supper apart from the family, often in their own rooms, not at table with the other adults; yet this was often their own choice, despite the standing invitation of the masters to join them. Nannies were seldom included in social events at home, much less in larger society, unless it was just to parade the little ones out; but regular visitors to some noble homes apparently spent significant time chatting with the family nanny. One can more readily accept the claim of "family membership" in some limited situations – for example, the absence of one or another parent, particularly through death. But that is far from the case in most instances where the claim is made.[12]

Ivan Goncharov (1812-1891) and Leo Tolstoi (1828-1910) both comment without sentimentality on their servants of mid-century. Goncharov's man Matvei, an odd mix of fierce pride and humble subservience, was his master's "friend": "Yes, friend, because in him there were the traits – albeit slave-like...which remained from serfage – of a lively devotion to me and to my interests, material of course. Other interests were beyond his comprehension, and he could not enter into them."[13] Tolstoi's nanny Tat'iana Filippovna "was one of those touching beings from the peasantry who live so intimately with the families of their charges that all the interests of the former transfer to the latter and *they represent for their own families only the possibility of getting something out of them and inheriting a little wherewithal*..."[14] It may be, therefore, that the model that pertained in many cases was of a nanny that was indeed alienated from her roots and who clung to the master's family in lieu of her own blood kin. Whether she felt neither fish nor fowl in such cases, or felt wholly absorbed by the family in which she worked, remains a moot point. In the end I can't find sufficient reason to reject out of hand this notion that the nannies were in some way members of the families they served; but the jury remains out, in my mind, as to exactly what that notion comprehended.

Defining the Nanny by Personal Characteristics

The most common traits of character, personality, and behavior of the classic nanny are discussed in separate sections below. Russian peasant nannies tended to be religious/pious, earnest, single-minded (in their concern and devotion for their charges) – but also "superstitious," unlettered, and socially conservative (even proud of "their" status). Their faults, while not all as generic as the few just listed, tended to fall into recognizable patterns and will be examined subsequently. We will begin with the more positive attributes.

A. Positive Traits[15]

Religiosity. If one part of the nanny's makeup could be called a "true" stereotype – an archetype even – it was her religiosity. Almost every nanny described in the memoir literature is called "pious," "devout," or very religiously inclined.[16] A constantly recurring image of the child going to sleep is that of saying prayers with the nanny (and sometimes with a parent) and then observing the nanny before the icons saying her own prayers. These rituals could seemingly last for hours, at least in the mind's eye of the child. A nanny's religiosity – much more than the parents' practices, it appears obvious – was an integral part of children's lives in ways far beyond night-time prayers. The prolific historian Sergei Solov'ëv's (1820-1879) old nanny "possessed a fine, pure character: she was extremely pious/devout [*sil'no nabozhna*]."[17]

But any discussion of peasant and nanny religiosity begs a major question: of what did this religiosity consist? Most would assume that the nannies believed in and practiced Russian Orthodoxy; they would be right, up to a point. The more discerning would guess that for many of the nannies their Orthodoxy came along with a smaller or larger admixture of village beliefs and other articles of faith. The importance of religious belief is what needs stressing here; the content of belief is discussed in somewhat more detail in a subsection below entitled "Beliefs, 'Superstitions,' and Odd Practices" and more substantially in Chapter 10.

Meekness and Patience. A corollary of religiosity might be the oft-noted meek temperament of a caretaker, her humbleness. But this is an excellent example of where the stereotype could be most misleading: it was often difficult to determine whether patience was a quality of the nanny or a demand of the masters. Under serfdom in particular but even later, with freely hired servants, the relationship of underlings to "superiors" was always problematic. No household staff or servant "family members" were exempt from the pressures exerted by the master and mistress. So what at first glance might appear to be a personal quality could have been "institutional" caution.

Tat'iana Passek (1810-1889), for instance, was perhaps astute enough to note the difference. She writes about one of her neighbors who had a young grandson. When the child was sitting in the arms of his pock-marked nanny Aksin'ia, he would get the urge to scratch her face, and he howled if she did not let him. The mistress would be beside herself, get angry, and shout: "It's a great misfortune that the child will flay [*poderet*] your ugly, pock-marked mug." The child flayed the mug, and the nanny, daring neither to complain nor to resist, said, *to please the mistress*, "Flail away, little father, flail away to your heart's content."[18]

There seems little doubt that, whether they were extremely meek and patient or not, most serf nannies had to endure endless trials and tribulations. As Nikolai Mamaev (1815-1885) – a provincial official, then zemstvo board member and jurist – recalled, when he was nearing seven he faced a milestone in his young life: "Ever closer approaches the time of my studies. My nanny, observing my pranks [*shalosti*] and unable to stop them, more and more often repeats: 'Just you wait a little! Soon the little bull is going to be roped and tied!' By 'little bull' she meant me, and by 'rope' – my studies..."[19] One highborn lady rued how she treated her nanny, though whatever qualms she felt appear to have easily dissipated. She confesses to being completely spoiled.

> Even father, at all the complaints and bad reports about me of my nanny, would say: 'Leave my little smarty-pants [*vostrushka*] alone, let [her] romp' – and the smarty-pants, emboldened by the lack of punishment, would torture her sweet nanny, the eighty-year-old Anna Melent'evna, with disobedience, new outbursts of anger [*rezvosti*] and ever more frequent teasing and calling her a 'tattletale.' Children seldom understand the cruelty of their treatment of nannies, and grasp it when it's already too late, when there's no possibility of smoothing out the past."

She adds, however, "despite the reproaches of my conscience over my sweet nanny, nothing will erase or replace for me the joyful recollections of childhood..."[20]

While most nannies probably were patient, some were less so. Far from self-effacing, peasant nannies could often be officious, interfering, and querulous. Quite unlike the nearly hagiographic portrait in memoirs and belles-lettres, many a fictional and nonfictional nanny was overbearing, demanding, "pushy."[21] As documented in a later section, moreover, some nannies were not especially humble but proud, in their own way.

Earnestness and Seriousness vs. Lightheartedness. While not necessary counterparts to their religiosity, nannies were generally earnest and serious. Indeed, the memoir literature reveals few examples of Russian nannies with a highly developed sense of humor.[22] Photographic evidence might illustrate this general seriousness of "the classic nanny" save for two points. First, the daguerreotype did not come along until 1839, late in the pre-emancipation period. Thus there are few, if any, pictures of nannies from the time I am focusing on here. Second, most people of the period had the same unsmiling facial expressions, the primitive conditions of photography leading to most subjects' faces looking stiff and stern. Still, I've seen dozens of photos of nannies from the nineteenth and twentieth centuries, posing by themselves or with their charges, and in only one can I recall a smile on the nanny's face. While not always a grimace, the expression is virtually never anything but a half-frown.[23] As for portraits in prose, Erazm/Erast Stogov (1797-1880) recalled his nanny Praskov'ia as "a sere, tall, serious-minded old woman." Anna Lelong's (b. 1841) nanny was "always serious, very pious."

As with all anecdotal evidence, can one counter-example overturn all the examples heretofore introduced? Nikolai Bunakov (1837-1904), says that his "merry" nanny was "the very prototype of a Russian nanny."[24] Notwithstanding Bunakov's assertion, I would lay odds that most peasant nannies of the pre-emancipation era – particularly the older and the foreign ones – were not that gay or merry. And unlike the comic foils seen in eighteenth-century works of fiction or stage comedies of manners (Chapter 8), almost none was to be laughed at either.

That is why it is all the more refreshing when an imaginative, inventive, laughing – or more rarely, a humorous – nanny unexpectedly appears in works of autobiography. Nikolai Rusanov (1859-1939), populist-terrorist and writer, had what seems to be the antithesis of the vast majority of pious nannies, a woman slightly irreligious and jocular: "My favorite older nanny...expressed great skepticism with regard to the existence of hell, giggling [*khikhikaia*] and slyly winking with her kindly, faded eyes: 'Yes, my dears, they say it'll be boiling there; they'll heat up the frying pan, like we do with oil for blini, and make you sinners lick it with your tongue... One skin will come off like a mitten, and in its place a new one will grow for your ongoing torture...That's the way things will be in that world'."[25]

The "father of Russian physiology," Ivan Sechenov (1829-1905), portrays a slyly humorous nanny who slept in his room. "Going to bed, I would often move over to her bed for the sake of [hearing] fairy tales," he says. One can picture this Scheherazade-nanny, tired and desirous of cutting short the session, finding a strategy to appease her importuner:

> ...when I kept her from sleep, demanding repetitions of the tales, she...would begin the tale of how a certain tsar, planning to build a palace out of bone, sent an order out throughout his kingdom to gather bones and place them in water for soaking. With these words she would fall silent, and when I would ask what happened next, I received in reply: 'There's nothing more to tell, little father – the bones are still steeping, they're not cleaned up,' with which, according to her words, I was satisfied.[26]

Single-mindedness in Concern and Love for Their Charges and in Fulfilling Their Duty. About another trait of Russian nannies there is little disagreement in the sources. With few exceptions, peasant nannies in noble households were loving and affectionate, with a single-mindedness of purpose in caring for their nurselings. In countless autobiographies this characteristic comes to the fore; it is one of the rare cases where the stereotype may need little revision. Certainly every good nanny always had one quality: the ability to empathize with her nurselings. Some of the best testimony to this nearly universal feature comes not from Russians themselves but from foreigners.[27] We have a mountain of testimony about this attribute of so many nannies. Among the numerous memoirists who claim an extraordinary degree of devotion or love on the part of their nannies are Nikolai Bunakov (1837-1904) and Elizaveta Vodovozova (1844-1923).[28] So despite the disclaimer, I will accede to the likelihood that not all these recollections are faulty and that a large proportion of nannies at least were probably very loving and dedicated caretakers.

Could anything be harmful in the constant devotion of a nanny? Perhaps, if it was too suffocating. The well-known literary critic Aleksandr Skabichevskii (1838-1911) certainly found reason to regret his nanny's dedication when he was a young man. When he entered secondary school in 1848, at age 10, he was a sheltered "mama's boy."

> A very special grief for me consisted in the fact that they would not let me go to the *gimnaziia* alone but only in the company of my dear nanny [*nianiushka*] Katerina Nikitishna, who accompanied me to the *gimnaziia*, carrying my bag, and then came for me at the conclusion of classes. This circumstance conclusively discredited me in the eyes of my classmates and was the reason for the most merciless mockery on their part. It got to the point that I myself received the nickname "*nianiushka*," and my classmates stopped calling me by my surname.
>
> At class change, "they'd tease me in chorus: '*nianiushka! nianiushka! nianiushka!*'... This pained me so much I began to beg my parents with tears in my eyes not to send dear nanny for me any longer. But for a long time all my entreaties were in vain. Katerina Nikitishna, very attached to me and fearful that someone might offend me on the way, continued to come for me even against the will of her masters...."[29]

Convictions, Social and Political. Most serf nannies tended to be very conservative, socially and politically – according to the testimony of their masters. We have almost no records to this effect from nannies themselves. To a large degree, they may have either assimilated the values and attitudes of the masters or at least made a prudent show of doing so. Whether out of inner conviction, self-interest, discretion, or for "protective camouflage" is immaterial; in most cases, nannies absorbed much or all of their "politics" not just from the village of their origins, but also from the big house. They tended to love the tsar and the royal family; they felt enough a part of the families they served to associate themselves with the traditions, honor, reputation, and standing of "their" family.

It's useful, however, to introduce a few counter-examples to the norm. While not themselves rebellious or "revolutionary" in any way, some of these nannies yet associated themselves with oppositional political figures. For example, nannies were a great concern for political exiles; many of the Decembrists sent to Siberia wrote letters home to family members in European Russia full of pleas for help finding such caretakers. They met with varying degrees of success.[30] Other nannies' convictions may have influenced their charges to become politically oppositional. Thus, Aleksandr Herzen says that his nanny Vera Artamonovna, "wanting to wound me grievously for some mischief, would say to me: 'Give it some time – you'll grow up, you'll be just such a lord as the others.' This insulted me horribly. The old woman can be content – *such a one as the others* at least I did not become."[31]

A few nannies were more open in defying political authority, Natal'ia Tuchkova-Ogareva's (1829-1913) being a case in point. Tuchkova was the wife of the poet-radical Nikolai Ogarev and then, after the death of Aleksandr Herzen's wife Natal'ia, Herzen's common-law wife. In the late, repressive years of Nicholas I, both her father and husband came under suspicion and the surveillance of government spies. The police arrested both, took them to the capital, but soon released them. Throughout the family's ordeal, Tuchkova's nanny, Fekla Egorovna, was with them, trying to bolster their spirits and sustain their hopes. Back home, they made the nanny their accomplice. Deciding to hide all writings about the Decembrists and any other "bad" books, they found an unlikely spot to cache them "in the springs of an upstairs couch." "For a week, the old nanny helped us transfer our treasures during the nights." But her mother was still so agitated that the police would somehow find all the compromising material that finally Ogarev says they had to get rid of it all. "For a whole week Fekla Egorovna carried the books and papers back down at night and burned them in the large stoves."[32]

B. Negative Traits

There's no doubt a large number of Russian peasant nannies were sweet, kindly, perhaps bordering on saintly, leaving aside the issue of their competence. A sizable (but not endless) stream of these paragons could be paraded forth from the pages of gentry memoirs; all border on cliché. More importantly, they all amount only to anecdotes, which can never prove an argument. I can find nearly as much anecdotal evidence to show the opposite, so the best antidote to all the treacle one encounters in some gentry memoirs is a closer analysis of the evidence.[33] In every case two questions are begged: (1) is the adult *misremembering* the childhood? and (2) is the adult *misrepresenting* the past? One suspects that the convention of venerating nannies in the decades immediately following Pushkin's "discovery" of Arina Rodionovna led to a kind of conspiracy of silence. Memoir writers in many cases either overlooked or ignored the foibles of their nannies. But the nannies surely had them.

Ignorance and Illiteracy. A clear weakness found among many peasant nannies, universally noted, was the "ignorance and superstition" allegedly endemic to peasant villages, from early times through at least the late nineteenth century. Ignorance in nannies meant they were most often illiterate. One expert on Russian women's history notes that in the middle of the eighteenth century "the underprivileged classes were not thought to have a right to education. Only serf girls who worked in noble households instead of in agriculture could expect to be educated..."[34]

Catherine II and Ivan Betskii's *Institutions and Regulations for the Upbringing and Education of Young People of Both Sexes in Russia*[35] spoke about educating household "slaves" who could then work as wet-nurses and nannies and not pass on their own ignorant superstitions, "silly tales" or moral vices ("perfidy," "coarseness," "wildness," "loose morals") to their charges. I've found virtually no examples of would-be nannies who took advantage of this supposed opportunity to better themselves.[36] Among hundreds of pre-1861 peasant nannies I've read about, the number who could read and write can be counted on the fingers of both hands (though more there undoubtedly were).[37]

In practical terms this deficiency made little difference to the toddlers in their care. But the fact of illiteracy made for two important differences. First, it meant that the peasant nanny culture remained the oral culture that had existed for hundreds of years – *a point critical to the emergence of the nanny as a symbol*;[38] second, it eliminated any possibility of a certain kind of "social mobility" for the nanny – she could never, for example, become the governess of the children she tended.[39]

The typical peasant nanny's lack of a proper education might also lead to a problem not often discussed by memoirists[40] (or scholars): who was the child to believe when parental wisdom and admonitions contradicted nanny's "superstitions" and truisms? This could be a real moral dilemma for many children. The focus of differences was seemingly not behavior or values; even more rarely was it about politics. It was about "what was so" and what not.

Ironically, illiteracy did not always prevent a nanny from approximating literate skills: "I was four years old when my sweet nanny taught me how to pronounce in order the letters of the Russian alphabet," recalls Senator Grigorii Filipson (1809-1883). "She herself was illiterate and only knew how to name the letters from memory and in order: *az, buki, vedi*, and so on. From this time begins my education [*obrazovanie*] – unsystematic, sporadic, by rather wild methods, and sometimes without any method."[41]

This circumstance of general illiteracy – which actually extended well beyond the emancipation – led to what I consider a classic set-piece in both gentry memoirs and literature. We can call this the "letter-writing scene." "Nanny Arina...seldom showed up any more in our nursery; and if she did appear, it was only out of old habit or to have one of us write a letter in her name to her dear [son] Iashen'ka."[42] Of course, in the early eighteenth century, the gap between master and man had not been great in this respect, just as with regard to "superstitions." Mikhail Dmitriev (1796-1866) reminded the readers of his memoirs that "noble lords and ladies were almost all illiterate" in that period. In the "entire village" of Ivashevka, some twelve versts from his family's estate, "there were many young gentry boys and girls, and...there was only one literate person, a household serf of one of the lords...who wrote letters for everyone to husbands and relatives when they were absent."[43]

Beliefs, "Superstitions," and Odd Practices. As for that other major charge against peasant nannies – their irrational, superstitious way of thinking – conventional and "expert" wisdom was alike in believing it to be so. What is missing in that assessment, and in much of the memoir literature, however, is another side of this coin. Women – and men – of all social estates and "classes" during the seventeenth through twentieth centuries (often? sometimes?) shared, to a certain degree, this body of "knowledge" and belief in signs, omens, fortune-telling, and other forms of "superstition." Therefore, to single out nannies is in most ways misleading. To what extent superstition distinguished a peasant nanny and low culture in general from the noble estate and high culture is, it must be stressed, a matter of degree and circumstance, not of kind.[44]

Yet even this caveat begs an important question: to what extent do condemnations by outsiders of peasant "superstition" reflect as much or more the hubris of intellectuals and modernizers than the reality of village life? Are a social group's coping mechanisms (for survival, for moving ahead in life) by definition backward and unsuitable merely because they don't coincide with the thinking of their *soi-disant* "betters"?[45] Without falling into a kind of overdone cultural relativism, one can still point out that "where you stand depends upon where you sit." "Modernization" did not occupy a particularly high place on the agenda of Russian villagers – nor many of their masters – before emancipation (or after). "Rational" planning did not necessarily appear the same to a peasant as to a village outsider, nor was it always the most productive approach in any case.

Be that as it may, it is peasant women we are focusing on in this section. Theirs is a world in many ways beyond their control, and therefore various forms of magic and religion play a central role in their worldview and belief system.[46] A complete catalog of peasant beliefs, superstitions, and practices would be superfluous here. There exist many great compendia of these ideas and ways.[47] To set the stage for what follows, one can cite the recollections of the protean author and critic Prince Apollon Grigor'ev (1822-1864), one chapter of whose superb memoirs is entitled "The World of Superstition":

> Superstition and legends surrounded my childhood, as they do the childhood of every little nobleman whether of great or small means, surrounded by a large or small number of servants and at times left completely in their care. The servants...all came from the country.... When relatives arrived from the country, several members of the extensive servant staff there came with them and added fire to my superstitious, or rather, fantastic inclinations, with new stories....

Herewith some of the best examples of peasant-nanny wisdom that I've found in autobiographical works. They concern both the great mysteries of life and death and the most trivial quotidian events – and myriad subjects in between.

As one might expect, a great number of nanny beliefs concerned matters of health and sickness. In the Obolenskii household of her mother's childhood, described by Ekaterina Sabaneeva (1829-1889), the older sisters were "sickly" and remained confined in their own rooms for large portions of the day. Why? In part because of "nanny nonsense," according to one observer. "What absurd superstitions were inculcated in them by the wet-nurses and nannies! – fortune-telling, divination, fear of the evil eye – all this powerfully disturbed their nerves." "Even the oldest, Kat'ia, who reasoned her way out of these absurdities, still had hysteric fits, was afraid of thunder, spiders, and frogs."[49]

Savvatii Sychugov (1841-1902), a village priest's son who became a zemstvo doctor, had a grandfather who fought peasant superstition all his life – and his grandson's. But it was hard to fight the "nanny's influence," which "could not help but tell on me"; "among other superstitions she instilled in me a kind of unreasoning fear of the dark and especially of ghosts. I believed, for example, that the souls of the just send up little flames from their graves but that sinners pursue the living at night, and so on."⁵⁰ Ol'ga Kornilova (b. ca. 1840), believed, from her nanny's stories, that her mother's soul would remain on earth for six weeks after she died. She would ply the adults with queries about where her mama's soul was at the time – perhaps in a peasant hut nearby, where she could visit it.⁵¹

"I early began to struggle with the superstitious feelings imparted to me by the 'horror stories' of the nannies about the portraits which came down out of their frames at night, about the *rusalki* who danced by the light of the moon, beginning at midnight right up until the cock's first crow...," the *narodnik*-turned-scientist Nikolai Morozov (1854-1946) tells us early in his autobiography. Here again is that side of peasant thinking noted by so many Russian pedagogs as a reason to keep young ones away from servants, even (especially?) nannies. To "temper" himself, Morozov would deliberately test his nerves by going out at night all by himself to the scariest of places – say, to a cemetery – and within the house, with just a candle, to "stare down" those ancestors' pictures that threatened to descend from the wall.

> "If you see an apparition at night," nanny warned me, "run away without turning your head and do not turn around for anything, whatever you may hear behind you!"
> "And if I look back?
> "Then that's the end of everything! It will jump on you and suffocate you!"⁵²

The world of nature was an equally rich repository of peasant beliefs. Tat'iana Passek (1810-1889) details the elaborate views of her nanny Katerina Petrovna. In summers filled with thunderstorms and showers, she would ask her nanny what the thundering and shining (lightning) were; the nanny would answer, crossing herself, that it was the Prophet Elijah traveling across the sky in his fiery chariot. Other signals – and she had one for everything – included a nearly complete "farmer's almanac" of such signs: if she couldn't see small stars in a clear sky, she prepared in summer for a storm, in winter for a frost; starry nights in January foretold for her a good harvest of peas and apples; a storm on Annunciation Sunday announced the same for nuts; frost – for milk-agaric. When the cat licked its tail, Katerina Petrovna said, expect rain; cleaned her face with her paw – fine weather; scratched the wall – a snowstorm; rolled herself up into a ball – a frost; lay down belly up – a warming trend.[53] In the same vein, Morozov's nanny Tat'iana once carried him outdoors to show him the northern lights, which she called "the pillars of fire." She told him this phenomenon occurs before a frost. "Another time they carried me out to show me a large comet, and nanny said that this was a harbinger of war."[54]

War and "history" indeed had their place in peasant beliefs, which often looked backward. But at the heart of nanny beliefs – and the faith many masters placed in them – was the supposed ability to predict the future. "I remember, although dimly, the time when my parents lived in the home of a priest," says the historian-ethnographer and Moscow University professor Ivan Snegirev (1793-1868) of his memories about the year 1803.

> Being just ten years old, I grew terribly angry and argued with nanny, when she repeated the folk prophecy that "Moscow will be taken for 40 hours." But I heard this very same thing not just from nanny but also from my grandmother, Anna Ivanovna Kondrat'eva. Like the voice crying in the African deserts, the people carry within themselves dark traditions and predictions, in which are concealed truths which are unsealed in the future, and not infrequently what seems to us unrealizable occurs.[55]

Peasant superstitions ran the gamut from the sublime (death and dying, nature) to the more ridiculous. If the chickens got in a squabble by the window or a spark flew up out of the burning stove, Tat'iana Passek's nanny "began to prepare for the arrival of guests. And sure enough, by dinnertime, someone would show up."[56]

C. Other Nanny Foibles

Pride. While the faults of nannies might be many, they were mostly minor. Of the seven deadly sins, only one was fairly common to nannies – pride.[57] This was rarely in themselves; they took the most pride in "their" families. There were exceptions. The Dostoevskii family nanny, Alena Frolovna was of petit-bourgeois origins, not a serf, "and was very proud of this title, saying that she was not from the common people."[58] (Thus, she was proud of *not* being a peasant, the one thing that most commended itself to most nanny hagiographers.) Another nanny born about 1802, who witnessed Napoleon's entry and retreat from Moscow, modestly exulted in the mere fact of her own longevity.[59] Undoubted legions of pre-emancipation nannies took pride in their nurselings, but we lack the evidence: most earlier autobiographers were seemingly reticent to admit how admired they were as children.

More to the point, however, many peasant nannies were downright snobs, sometimes worse (at least openly) than their masters. Prime examples of this "failing" are the nannies of aristocrats and well-to-do merchants. Matrena Efremovna took Count Fëdor Tolstoi into her arms as nanny on the day he was born "and parted with him [only] when she died, at 90 years of age," says the count's daughter. The nanny often and vociferously voiced her disapproval for the boy's nonaristocratic passion for drawing, career choice of artist, and marriage clearly "beneath" him. Daughter Mar'ia's (1817-1898) nanny Aksin'ia Dmitrievna, was of similar, prideful views.[60]

But the one who stands out most in this regard was Fedos'ia Stepanovna, the Trubetskoi nanny, who entered service in the 1850s. "We children remained her only joy and her only pride," Prince Evgenii Trubetskoi would recall later. "With this devotion was joined in her a familial pride in us which was absent in ourselves. In her consciousness she was 'not a simple nanny, [but] the Trubetskoi nanny'– she gave herself the epithets 'ancestral and hereditary'." She had put on her grave memorial: "Nanny of the Trubetskois."[61]

Anger. Contrary to the cliché nanny who was always mild and sweet-tempered, real-life nannies could often lose their temper or be out of sorts. Real rage or great anger was, however, rare. It is interesting that such wrath is the only one of the mortal sins not always motivated by selfishness or self-interest. The dearth of truly wrathful nannies is thus of a piece with their much-vaunted selflessness and humility. When one did express anger, it was generally so mild as to be still loving and forgiving. The nanny Anna Larionovna of the painter Vasilii Vereshchagin (1842-1904) was no paragon of equanimity. He loved her "not because she didn't get angry and didn't scold [us]; on the contrary, she grumbled and scolded us often." But, he adds, "her dissatisfaction always passed quickly and left no traces."[62]

Among other memoirists who recorded angry outbursts from their nannies were Nikolai Davydov (1848-1920), a jurist and writer, whose Parasha wakened him one morning with her angry yelling, and Aleksandra Shchepkina (1824-1917), who had one nanny (among several) who was often angry and "was a harmful influence on the children and treated them roughly."[63]

The cause for ire in most cases, however, was not her charge but someone else; the usual culprit was a governess or other servant, especially a servant who insulted her nurseling (as in the case of little Sonia Kovalevskaia [b. 1850]).[64] And then the nanny displayed more indignation than anger. M. E. Vasil'eva's unnamed nanny of the immediate pre-reform years was "horribly quick-tempered, and once she was set off, she would forget herself completely and was even ready to pick a fight." Uniquely in my reading, she even came to physical blows with a member of the nobility, the aunt of the new mistress of the house.[65]

As revealing as the fact that they occasionally lost their tempers was perhaps the way in which some nannies handled such episodes afterward. In the old-fashioned Brianchaninov family, for example, the nanny Efimovna was reportedly more demanding of herself than of those she supervised. In the evening, this blind old nanny "prayed aloud, long and tearfully" that God would forgive her for having once gotten angry and slapping her little mistress. "Having daily before her eyes [sic] the beating of children [by others], this pure soul reckoned herself at fault for a single, probably very light tap!"[66] She may be just a bit too Christian to be believed.

Meanness. It's difficult to find a truly evil nanny in memoirs or fiction. That does not mean, however, that some nannies did not perform – perhaps for reasons not totally despicable – acts that were truly deplorable. The closest example of "evil" I've uncovered is Aleksandr Borovkov's nanny. In the 1790s she was in sore need of some cash to free the man she loved from prison. She had her own moral standards: "My nanny did not engage in thievery, and would not even think of such a dishonorable thing, but she came up with what to her lights was a less shameful means [of obtaining money] – to sell me secretly to the Don Cossacks who in those days often traveled to Moscow on such business." She took little Sasha out for a walk one day and sold him. Luckily, the incident had a happy ending, at least for the boy: acquaintances chanced upon the nanny, childless but loaded with money, and brought her home, where she promptly confessed to all. The police, informed of the transaction, quickly found the Cossacks, with the boy, arrested them and turned them over to the courts. Not so fortunate was the nanny. They sold her at public auction to the very group of Cossacks she'd dealt with. "In those days," Borovkov informs his readers, "people had a poor understanding" of the Cossacks and would sell them people as a form of punishment, "to set an example."[67]

In addition to his well-known nanny Vera Artamonovna, Aleksandr Herzen had many other nannies. As his "cousin" Tat'iana Passek relates, a wet-nurse-nanny named Iudina from her own household (the Kuchins) later became part of the Iakovlev (Herzen) household. "She was as explosive and egotistic as Vera A. was quiet and simple-souled. She was soon relieved of her duties. They found that, putting him to bed, in order to calm him, she pinched, hit and threatened him that if he made a sound she'd do worse than that; he would cry softly and fall asleep."[68]

Alcohol. Another frequently mentioned weakness of nannies – but mostly after emancipation – was that of Arina Rodionovna, tippling. The famous doctor-pedagog Nikolai Pirogov (1810-1881), for example, had such a one.[69] Now these few nannies may have been the exceptions which prove the rule. One doubts, in any case, that there were large numbers of problem drinkers among children's nannies at any period. It's difficult to judge, moreover, how many of the tipplers were tipsy or actually drunk during the time when they were "on the job," at work minding the children.

Some were, but it seems more likely that most did their drinking in their spare time, away from their charges. Those with a minor drinking habit may have allowed the habit to get worse once their charges grew up and no longer needed their care.

Defining the Nanny in Physical Terms

Dress. A Russian wet-nurse was almost universally distinguished by her "national" costume, especially elaborate headwear called a *kokoshnik*. The nanny had no such well-defined dress before emancipation, with the exception of one item: nearly universal was a kerchief or bandanna tightly bound around her tresses, tied beneath the chin, or a cap [*chepets*], usually white. As Mikhail Os[s]orgin puts it in his novel *My Sister's Story* (1931): "[Nanny] never took off her kerchief and nobody had ever seen her bareheaded." Sofiia Buksgevden says all peasant women "rigidly adhered to the tenets of St. Paul, and always wore a handkerchief or some kind of covering on their heads" but her wet-nurse clarifies the reason: "I am a married woman. No man must see me with uncovered hair. Your mother is a lady: that is different."[70]

Aside from the top of the body, however, the dress of a nanny probably did not diverge far from that of the wet-nurse. The "sarafan ensemble" became widespread in Russia at the turn of the eighteenth century, displacing earlier costumes. It was especially typical of the northern and central regions, whence it spread into other regions of the country. In the eighteenth century it was already associated with the Russian national costume. The sarafan was worn by both peasant and urban women of the merchant and petty-bourgeois social strata. On occasion, the nanny or wet-nurse would also don a *kofta*, a short woman's jacket that did not come down to the waist, typically red. A plain skirt (*iubka*) might also be worn.

For Tat'iana's nanny in *Eugene Onegin*, a kerchief over her hair and a long padded jacket (*telogreika*) or "wool dress" were typical wear. Other nannies of the eighteenth through twentieth centuries commonly wore a skirt (*iubka*) or sarafan, often a cotton or calico print blouse (*sitsevaia koftochka*), possibly an apron (*fartuk*), and sturdy bast shoes or slippers (*tufli*) – but boots for outdoors.

Commonly, nannies in full dress were rather shapeless. Dmitrii Likhachev (1906-1999) says at six he

> discovered for the first time, to my surprise, that women have legs. The skirts they wore were so long that usually only the shoe was visible. And here, in the mornings, behind the screen, when [nanny] Katerinushka got up, there would appear two legs in thick stockings of different color (the stocking was all the same not visible under the skirt). I looked at these varicolored stockings down to the ankles which had appeared before me, and I was amazed.[71]

An exception to the general rule of thumb was the "hybrid" Stepanida in Baroness Buksgevden's household. Earlier her brother's wet-nurse, Stepanida was for several years a nursery-maid. She continued to wear the "resplendent national dress of the wet nurse: a pale blue silk or wool sarafan according to the season, trimmed with gold braid. Outdoors, she wore over it the quilted, broad-skirted *shougay* [coat] and on her head, the high *kokoshnik* embroidered with pearls. She discarded this in the house. Rows of amber beads wound round her neck."[72]

Sartorial information about nannies is provided in some detail by Ekaterina Sabaneeva (1829-1889). She describes several different nannies' dress: "Nanny Savishna...always went about in a slightly shabby (*zatrapeznyi*) blue linen sarafan and a white *katsaveika* [short, fur-trimmed, warm jacket] with narrow sleeves, and tied a dark kerchief on her head in the fashion of older women...."[73] The nanny of her grandparents wore a blue *katsaveika* with white collar and a cap with a broad flounce. Finally, the wet-nurses (*mamushki*) and nannies of a princess entering the Sabaneev family dressed "in bright silken sarafans, sleeveless jackets with fur trim, in brocaded *povoiniki* and *sborniki*...." The *povoinik* is the traditional headdress of a married Russian woman; worn under the kerchief, it came in two basic styles, with a brim or as a beanie-style skullcap, and with a band. Both styles had some embellishment, such as embroidery, at the front, which could be covered with the kerchief or left uncovered. It encircled the head and was tied in the back. Tightfitting, so that no hair slipped out, the cap was usually made of either fine soft linen (or other light fabric) among the peasantry. (The nobility, however, would make the basic cap like a thick net woven from gold, silver, or silk thread; it was then called a *voloshnik*.) The *sbornik* was a kind of small *kokoshnik*, generally with gathers (*sborki*) at the back.[74]

For special occasions, such as major Church holidays, the nanny would also have a more formal outfit. On a somewhat more morbid note, moreover, nannies did tend to have other items of clothing worth mention. More than one memoirist (or belletrist) notes having seen, lovingly preserved, usually in her trunk, the clothing in which a nanny would be laid to rest. In Tèffi's poignant tale "An Enserfed Soul," the old nanny – who "had been dying for ten years already" – on a sunny spring day decides to air out her burial outfit [*smertnaia odezhda*]: "a yellowed linen blouse [*rubakha*], embroidered slippers, pale blue waist sash [*poiasok*] woven for the requiem prayers [*tainyi za upokoinoiu molitvoi*], and a Cypress cross."[75]

It does appear that after emancipation, some standardization of costume began to appear among the newer generation of nannies. While not quite a uniform, in the style of, say, British nannies from the mid-nineteenth century on, the dress of younger nannies in photos of the second half of the nineteenth and early twentieth centuries typically includes a white apron or white overskirt. However, older nannies in this period still manifest a variety of dress and headgear (or lack of headcover); in other words, they apparently continued to wear what they had worn as nannies before 1861.[76]

Trunks and Their Significance.[77] If a dress code was not *de rigeur* for all nannies, another possession was pretty much a *sine qua non* and came close to defining them.[78] Memoir after memoir mentions this precious piece of property: a large, usually iron-bound trunk (*sunduk*). In fact, a chest was a possession so dear that one nanny would not allow herself to be saved from the Neva's flooding in 1824 until her trunk had first been secured from the water.[79] Stuffed with items of all sorts, including memorabilia of her life, the nanny's trunk told as much about her as any book could. It was a source of almost endless awe and delight for her little nurselings as well. As one memoirist would recall, decades afterwards: "When nanny opened the trunk, we dashed as fast as we could to look, although we'd seen everything contained therein a hundred times."[80]

Why this fascination with an object that generally lay motionless, in one fixed place? "In a significantly large number of cases, the supreme ecstasies of childhood arise out of contact with the inanimate," says Richard Coe, echoing ideas that we will explore further in Chapter 5. A memoirist tries "to re-endow" the inanimate thing "with the magical powers which, for the child, it once possessed – magical not in the sense of wands and wizardry, but in the sense that pure existence in itself is magical and miraculous..."[81] Numerous autobiographies confirm Gaston Bachelard's view that a casket or trunk "contains the things that are *unforgettable*."[82]

In a few cases, a heightened focus on the nanny's trunk might stem from a kind of self-interest, as with Liudmila Vrangel' (1877-1969). Her nanny would travel back to her home village every year, and when she returned, "as in a fairy tale," she would take from her "magic chest" an array of dolls and gift the children with them. The presents kept them occupied for weeks. Similarly, the poet Vladislav Khodasevich (1886-1939) says his nanny "always kept for me in a cherished trunk covered in white tin-plate either a Vyazemsky gingerbread or a mint gingerbread horse." The most blatant case of self-interest I've found, however, is from the other side of the caretaker-child divide: Lev Tikhomirov's (1852-1923) nanny Agrafena "pinched" any number of items from her masters and stored the pelf in her ever-locked trunk.[83]

But these examples are far from the essence of the allures of a nanny's trunk. No, what made the children "cling like flies" to the lid of the nanny's trunk, in Ekaterina Olitskaia's memorable phrase, were things not destined for their own hands. To start with, "the entire lid of the trunk on the inside" would often be "pasted over with little pictures": of "dolls in smart dresses, and images of various animals, and simply beautiful candy wrappers." Another example: "In the middle [of the lid was glued the picture of] a large horse and rider in a dark green uniform and tricorn hat." This picture "was the center around which were grouped all the rest, primarily from candy." And, in an apt simile: "One [picture] was glued on another, the old ones hidden by the new, like geological strata."[84]

Yet the lid was barely the beginning. The belletrist Vladimir Tikhonov (1857-1914) captures in his autobiography, in exquisite detail, the totality of the experience, the seemingly infinite charms of the "voluminous" [ob"emistyi] trunk's insides: "Ah, what a fascination was this trunk of nanny's! In later years I hardly ever experienced such complete pleasure, in touring various museums and art galleries, as in those glorious days when dear nanny Fevron'ia Stepanovna allowed me to rummage in her trunk." The lock's keyhole made "soft, pretty notes," the lid held a famous colored *lubok* (folk-art picture) showing the mice burying the cat.

> How fine was the aroma from this trunk! And no wonder: in it indeed were kept both the smoky candles and the "brain" pomade, and the sperm-oil soap [*spermatsetovoe mylo*], and a soap – particularly beloved by dear nanny – green, cucumberish; and a little bottle of "ambergris fragrance" ["*ambre*"], and a vial with scents of "jasmine," and in a long drawer on the side lay a small bag with benjamin and several small crosses of cypress, tiny icons, and rosary beads. What a fine bouquet all of this made I cannot now convey.

As Tikhonov puts it, nanny Fev'ronia had "a more striking array of things in her trunk than the Hungarian traveling salesmen" who came around plying their trade for the females of the household. She had saved a piece of dark-blue velvet that was "a remnant from a dress of your mama" (who had died when he was just three) and would tell him that "for some reason I felt it necessary every time to kiss this remnant gratefully (*blagogoveino*)." She had his baby booties, worn even before she herself had entered their service, and her own Sunday-go-to-meeting dress (*paradnoe plat'e*), which again smells wonderful. Next, there was a wax apple, an entire box of Easter eggs, a few of which have "panoramas" – "I inevitably look through the little glassine aperture and see Christ rising from the grave." Then there were artificial flowers, his own tiny baby pants ("the first you ever wore" says nanny), a plait of his baby hair; another lock of hair (but nanny won't say whose – it looks by the color like it might be his father's). Another wooden box with a movable lid came next, in which were gregory-powder and some other golden powder from "Dr. Potto" that tasted bitter but actually helped to reduce fever. Next, a beautiful piece of embroidery and two daguerrotypes, one of him at age three and a half, the other of his father. Something that put them both in a melancholy mood: a pair of his mother's gloves that retain the fragrance of her hands.[85]

All told, they spend an hour or two going through this veritable treasure chest; everything in the trunk is taken out and lovingly examined. He's sad when they have to put it all away, but she reassures him that when they again have some leisure time, they can look at it all once more. He can't wait to see "nanny's riches" again.[86] Tikhonov's vivid depiction of this scene seems to have inspired another writer to borrow it wholesale for a work of fiction published just three years after Tikhonov's account.[87]

Most poignantly of all, as noted earlier, the nanny's trunk usually held her burial outfit, lovingly preserved for its proper time.

Conclusion

Even though women from nearly all social estates became nannies, and some served in homes other than those of the gentry, the most common – and by far the most famous – kind of nanny was a peasant nanny in a noble household. This is the figure, almost exclusively, that has been the preserve of historians ever since the mid-nineteenth century, the figure that stirred the imaginations of countless intellectuals, creative artists, and memoirists. The task of this chapter has been to penetrate the Romantic fog surrounding such women and to portray them as accurately and fully as the sources permit.

5

The Everyday Life of (Mostly) Ordinary Women

The Spaces of the Nanny's and Children's World: The House as Physical Space and the House as "Home"

One of the first things that strikes a reader of gentry childhood memoirs is the physical environment the children – and nanny – inhabited. Rare is the Russian autobiographer of the nineteenth and twentieth centuries who does not pause for a description, often in loving detail, of his or her childhood home. Although sometimes the noble family made do with an "apartment" or "apartments" in the city, being well-off or wealthy meant having one's own house. Most often, it meant having at least two homes: one in town and the other in the countryside – *v derevne*. A minority lived in one or the other year-round; the majority made regular, seasonal shifts in residence. The trek between the two abodes, out to country estate in May or June and then back to urban domicile in August or September, was an inevitable part of the family life-cycle, pictured in countless life histories.[1]

I don't intend here a complete analysis of these gentry houses, what Gaston Bachelard would call a "topoanalysis."[2] My remarks concern mostly the country estates – a summer or year-round residence – and the *osobniaki* (detached town houses) of the middle and higher gentry, though they pertain almost equally to the homes of the wealthiest nobles – even to those living in palaces – and of a good part of the most prosperous merchants.

Divisions of the Home

Within the child's immediate world of the house itself, in better-off families, there tended to be a well-defined division of space. By far the most common arrangement was one that placed the children's world quite apart from that of their parents. Typically this meant a "vertical" division of the home. As in the venerable BBC television series "Upstairs, Downstairs," one part of the household lived on top, the other below. The norm was for the children to be up above, on the second floor or "mezzanine." Anna Lelong (b. 1841) recalls that she couldn't wait to leave the upper floor; she used to rise early "and run downstairs from the second floor."[3]

Marina Tsvetaeva confirms that throughout nearly all gentry (modern) times, this was the rule in effect. Her grandfather Ilovaiskii's Old Pimen abode was "the only home in my memory... where *the parents* lived up above and *the children* below. Both at Three-Pond [the Tsvetaev home] and in all homes similar to it – the children's sphere was the cramped, low-ceiled but hot and bright upper level, the parental – the main, roomy but empty and cold lower level," she writes. "The children found refuge from the parents upstairs. But [in the Ilovaiskii home] the children were cast down by the parents to the nether world... Obviously, the old ways of Old Pimen were more ancient than those of gentry times."[4]

The feeling of separation, apartness, felt by children is only partly physical. The translator-writer Evgeniia Gertsyk (1875-1944) found there was a kind of psychological division inherent in the physical separation of her early home. "Life is divided by a bold line into 'the above' and 'the below.' Below – this is guests or the family which has gotten on each other's nerves... Above are verses, books, letters to selected people, one's own, dreams, dashing around, lollygagging."[5]

Stairways and Attics. The most wonderful part of this up-down arrangement, at least for some, was apparently the stairs themselves. Their verticality emphasized much about the space of the house. Literary theorists have turned their attention to aspects of this physical phenomenon. Mikhail Bakhtin, for example, talks about the chronotope of the threshold, and its related chronotopes – the staircase, front hall and corridor, street and square – where crisis events occur: falls, resurrections, renewals, epiphanies, decisions.[6]

Russians born in the second half of the nineteenth century continually recall staircases as special, "magical," secret, romantic, and wondrous.[7] Marina Tsvetaeva's "Poem of the Staircase" (1926, never completed) appears to deal in part with relations between parents and children, separated as in her own family by the staircase. She wrote that she was seeking "a unifying principle, tying together "all the floors," all the fates of the people populating [the different floors]."[8]

For Gaston Bachelard, an attic or other secluded place of "tranquil solitude" allows one to be alone, even bored – a very important part of the association of a house with dreaming. At least three Russian authors share Bachelard's love of the attic. The estate of A. Kupreianova's mother had a "special place" for her – one like "a magical fairytale, the embodiment of a dream"; a broad staircase led up to the second floor and to attics full of secrets. "Oh how mysterious were these low, dark attics! With what surprising histories did my imagination fill them! And who knows how many true stories they were witness to?" The cultural historian Nikolai Antsiferov (1889-1958) found "an endless land of childhood wonders and treasures" up above an attic in a tower. Vadim Andreev (b. 1903) also discovered "a new world – the attics of the house" at an early age. These spaces inaugurate a big change in his life – he takes books up into the attic to read.[9]

Nonvertical Separation. More rarely, physical separation was not vertical but horizontal and more complete. In some cases, the children and their caretaker(s) were removed to another wing of a large house. These separate living quarters could be more like a different house than a mere extension of the main building. Nikolai Morozov (1854-1946) lived until he was about 8 in such a side wing, along with his sisters and all their caretakers, due to the fact that his father's marriage to a freed serf was not recognized by the Church. But the children's nursery – at least then but perhaps earlier as well – was apparently located on the first floor of the main building.[10] The "anarchist prince," Pëtr Kropotkin (1842-1921), says that when his mother was dying, "we children...were removed from the big house to a small side house in the courtyard." "So we remained... in this little house, in the hands of [their German bonne] Madame

Burman and [their Russian nanny] Uliana."[11] Then, again a little later on, during "the early years of my childhood we occupied with M[onsieur] Poulain one of the separate houses entirely by ourselves," seeing little of their father.[12]

The division by generations, moreover, was not the only sort of physical division that might pertain. At least two others are found in the memoir literature: one by gender, the other by class. The Nizhegorod *pomeshchik* and writer Ianuarii Neverov (1810-1893) observed close at hand a particularly strict arrangement of the first kind in the home of a landowner, Pëtr Koshkarov. Never married, Koshkarov yet had a family, several children with his mistress, a soldier's widow, with all of whom he shared the house. "The lord of the manor's entire house was divided into two halves – the men's and the women's," Neverov writes. "The first consisted of the entrance hall, a huge hall; a buffet, billiard room, sitting room [*divannaia*], and the so-called *fraternal* room [*bratskaia* komnata – for his sons]... All these rooms were very spacious, and guests who spent the night were put in these..." Into the second, women's half of the house, no male servant nor family member nor guest was allowed.[13]

The Nursery

The size, layout, and furnishings of the nursery varied considerably among the nobility. Some memoirists recall a very large room, others, quarters so cramped as to be unhealthy. A few note that there were two nurseries, not one. Many observed that the room was often warm, even overheated and stifling. Many nurseries lacked a *fortochka* (small window over the door) to let in a fresh breeze. The room had a definite "air" about it in any case, both literally and figuratively. Often stale or even foul, quite unhealthy in the view of some pedagogs, it also breathed a sense of freedom. As the protean writer Mar'ia Tsebrikova (1835-1917) observed about this epicenter of the child's life: "our nursery was a dark room, narrow and deep, with one huge Dutch window facing north;" she notes that many, if not most parents "would cram children into the smallest and most uncomfortable room, furthest away from the main part..."[14] Yet it was large and the "best room in the house" for Irina Konkevicha (b. 1903) – where her seriously ill half-brother was tended.[15]

This space could be – often was – both a refuge and a place of exile for children in unhappy homes but a place of regretted remove from parents in happy, loving homes. In one authority's words, any nursery "could be a little heaven of cosy security or a place of torment, according to the character and temper of the nurses [nannies] who presided over them."[16] Quite aside from its distance from oppressive or unloving parents, a nursery had other attributes which gave it a feel not unlike the spaces where servants gathered. It often offered spiritual comfort of the most needed kind. However, while it was a place of happy memory for the vast majority of those recalling their childhoods, it was not universally such. One note of (minor) dissent came from the poet-artist Elena Guro (1877-1913), whose nursery, "separated from the domains of the adults," was "boring" and whose wallpaper was especially boring or irritating.[17]

Some memoirists note that the nursery lingered not only in their minds but in their senses as well. Thus, the renowned mathematician Sophie Kovalevskaia (1850-1891): "No sooner do I think of our nursery than, by an inevitable association of ideas, I begin to be aware of a peculiar odor – a mixture of incense, olive-oil, May balsam, and the smoke of tallow-candles." Needless to say, this aroma owes its existence almost entirely to a nanny – Sophie's and others would often set up their prayer icons and oil lamp in a corner of the nursery. Writing in the 1880s, Kovalevskaia continues that it had been a long time since she'd met with that "peculiar odor." Not only abroad but even in St. Petersburg and Moscow "it is now very rarely to be encountered. But two years ago, when I was visiting some of my country acquaintants, I went into their nursery, and that familiar smell immediately surged to meet me, and evoked a whole series of long-forgotten memories and emotions."[18]

For the youngest children, the nursery would probably contain at most a small bed or two or three, a large bed for the nanny (though she sometimes had her own bedroom next door), perhaps a dresser or two, the aforementioned icons, and a space for play. At a later age, the room might also hold a small desk or two where the youngsters could do their studies and reading – though again there might be a separate "classroom" (*klassnaia*) for this purpose. At an even older age, the children would usually abandon the nursery for a grown-up's bedroom, but not always. By choice, Kovalevskaia's older sister Anna (1843-1887), a leading French Communard in 1870, remained in the nursery with her younger sister well into her teens.[19]

One of the best explanations of the nursery's enduring appeal is offered by Prince Evgenii Trubetskoi (1863-1920), the philosopher. In March 1917, as shells flew overhead and revolutionary crowds milled in the streets, he wrote that "in moments of spiritual exhaustion, at times I also want achingly to be in the nursery, where it was once so bright, so comforting, and everything was so full of loved ones and loving ones." Pondering these feelings, he concluded: "What is this nostalgic yearning for the nursery which I'm experiencing? Is this a manifestation of spiritual weakness? No. This is a different, extremely complex feeling. Not an escape from the present but the seeking of a source of support for the present, as all is shifting and uncertain. The past is known and comforting."[20]

The Maids Room, Servants Hall, and Kitchen

Equally well-known was the third sort of division, the one between master and man, that meant a great deal for the psyches of some privileged children growing up in a society with almost perfect pitch for class distinctions. Virtually all the great houses, and most of the lesser homes as well, included servants halls – one for women (the maids room or *devich'ia*) and one for both men and women (the *liudskaia*) – and the one indispensable room of the home, the kitchen.

As a rule, parents tried at all costs to keep their children out of the places where the servants congregated, for a variety of reasons. Of course, this made such spots "forbidden fruit" and all the more inviting for the children. Three of the best descriptions of the nearly irresistible allures of the *devich'ia* and of its significance in the lives of the young *barchonok* or *barchuk* (master's son) and *baryshnia* (master's daughter) are to be found in the memoirs of the writer Apollon Grigor'ev (1822-1864), the poet Afanasii Fet (1820-1892), and Aleksandr Herzen (1812-1870). They were preceded in literature – autobiographical fiction – by Sergei Aksakov (1791-1859), who noted how "much more cheerful" the children found the maids room than the other rooms in which they spent time.[21]

Grigor'ev says, probably referring to Aksakov: "A certain great writer has already had something good to say in favor of the so-called servant hall and attitudes toward it, when he described his childhood years in his memoirs." Grigor'ev is careful to caveat his remarks by referring to some "bad features" of associating with the servants, but "there was also a good side, even a sacred side, to that acquaintance with the common people, even with its spoiled elements." "I owe much, much to you in my development, disorderly, dissolute, selfish servants hall." Citing just one example: "Few or no folk songs are foreign to me..." "This is where I heard even more wonderful stories – I was passing most of my time in the kitchen with the peasants."[22]

But even more significant than the above-discussed aspects of the servants' rooms was their remembered effect on the children's civic and moral development. Herzen, who felt oppressed by his rather domineering father, is even more compelling in his tribute to the servants' quarters:

> The antechamber and maids room comprised the only vital pleasure which remained for me. Here I had absolute liberty; I took sides of the ones against the others, judged and disposed of their affairs alongside my friends, knew all their secrets and never chattered in the sitting room about the secrets of the anteroom...Children in general love servants; parents forbid them to fraternize with them, especially in Russia; children don't listen to them, because it's boring in the sitting room but merry in the maids room. In this case, as in a thousand others, the parents do not know what they're doing. I cannot imagine that our anteroom was more harmful for children than our 'tea-room' or 'sitting room'. In the anteroom children adopt coarse expressions and bad manners, it is true; but in the sitting room they take in coarse ideas and bad feelings.[23]

Girls too felt the magnet and the pathos of the servants' company. The Riazan *pomeshchitsa* Anna Lelong describes how, as a little girl, she would enter the maids room, where they were all at their spinning, and her nanny was knitting stockings: "I listen to their stories about the everyday life of our people [*narod*] under the serfdom of those times. [About]...how cruelly many landowners treated their peasants, especially the house serfs...And here, as a young girl, I became acquainted with our people through these stories, fell in love with [the people], came to understand all of their hatred for their masters and never condemned them for this." The note of self-congratulation is slightly off-putting, as is the unqualified final assertion in the following: "In [the maids room] lively conversation was going on, there was sometimes laughter and singing; they sat and spun flax on distaffs all winter evenings and how merry and good it seemed to me in their midst; and they were always glad at our coming."[24]

In similar fashion, higher up the social scale, Princess Elizaveta L'vova (b. 1853) remembers the maids room as "a real world" which "belonged to me." "They loved, entertained, and pampered me in the maids room," she felt. "Nanny did not permit my open friendship with the girls, and if, during the day, I happened to find my way from the nursery to the maids room, she would take me by the hand and, leading me back to the nursery, would say in a strict voice: 'Well, just what are you going to the maids room for, my little dove! That's not a place for you, my angel!'" "But I would think: 'Why is there no place for me there? It's much better than here in the boring nursery, where even nanny herself is bored! But *there* there's such charms! There is everything gay in the world!'" Yet what was tabu during the day was permitted under cover of darkness. Nanny would steal away to the maids room, warm herself by the stove, and "I, of course, would follow nanny, and she would not drive me away."[25]

One final note about the servants' quarter: While the basic division I've stressed here is the socio-economic one, that between master and man (child and servant), there was another division embedded within this one. The child's world was so often separated from the world of adults that the maids room must have also served as a kind of bridge between the two domains. The *devich'ia* or the *liudskaia* could provide at the very least a window into the world of grown-ups and perhaps even partial entrée into it.

What did a Nanny Do? The Day's Agenda

Early Routine Chores. The child's day began in the nursery. As noted, nanny slept either in the nursery, in her own bed, or in a room adjacent to the nursery. She would awaken her charges and get them washed and dressed, usually between 7 and 9 AM (there seems no unanimity about the time of rising). But first things first. Sof'ia Skalon (née Kapnist; 1797-1861) would lie and observe as, "rising with the sun, our nanny prayed for a long time before the icon of the saintly martyrs Antoniia and Feodosiia, which hung in a corner of our room, and bowed down to the earth with zeal and with great tenderness; then she got us up and dressed us."[26]

Nannies would typically serve the children a small breakfast, by themselves, consisting generally of tea, bread, jam, kasha, or the like. The next major responsibility was to make sure that the children were taken in to say good morning to the parents when the latter awoke in good time, often late in the morning (unless the breadwinner had official or professional duties). This ritual – of handkissing and expressions of filial love – might take place in the parents' bedroom or dressing room, in the mother's (usually separate) boudoir, or in the father's study.

Other (Noncaretaking) Duties. The nanny's morning routine could range far beyond her occupations with her charges. As a rule, the fewer the number of household servants, the greater the number of additional tasks that might fall on the shoulders of the children's caretaker. The writer Lev Uspenskii (1900-1978) recalls that "it was nanny who, every day in the morning, fixed the lamps in the house – poured kerosene into the reservoirs, cut off the burnt wicks evenly, if necessary put in new ones. Then she'd place them all around, on special hanging devices. She saw this as an important prerogative of hers."[27] In a Nadezhda Tèffi story, when the narrator remembers her childhood, it's her nanny who lights the lamp that turns the entire house into a sort of beacon or lighthouse lamp to beckon and lead her home.[28]

As nannies were often *primus inter pares* among the servants, their responsibilities might also include supervising, even disciplining, the maids or household staff. While the other household staff generally showed affectionate deference to the nanny, and in fact might be good friends with her, this was not always the case. Thus, Andrei Leskov (1866-1953) remembers his father's nanny, Anna Stepanovna, "as a heavily wrinkled, withered old lady with lips respectfully shut tight in the presence of 'the masters,' which eagerly opened up for tireless rebukes and sermonizing addressed to all the younger servants who knew no respite or mercy from her, who didn't want to live in the same house with her."[29] Sophie Kovalevskaia recounts an incident when her father in effect put her nanny to spy on her fellow servants in order to find a thief assumed to be in their midst. The nanny turned out to be a very good detective.[30]

Play. If the children were too young to play on their own, the nanny would play with them. She might cut out paper dolls or other creatures for a small child. With older children she might engage in games of hide-and-seek, or blindman's buff (*zhmurki*), "vulture and chickens," rolling hoops, or "playing at horses" (apparently a variation of what Americans call "piggyback riding").[31] Mikhail Osorgin's nanny Evdokiia Petrovna taught him card games. Sof'ia Lavrent'eva (1836-1918) played "noisy games," like blindman's buff, skip-rope, "cat and mouse," "colors" (*kraski*), and one with the tantalizing name "toilette entire" (*ves' tualet*). In a game called "the road," they lined up chairs to be a sleigh.[32] Even at ninety-plus years of age, the little old nanny of the Briuni family (fans of J.F. Cooper) would be sat down in the children's "wigwam" and made to enact the role of "mother" or "sister" of Uncas and Chingachgook.[33]

In a delicious story called "Hide and Seek" (*Priatki*; 1898), the author Fëdor Sologub (1863-1927) describes how such innocent play might begin. "When Lelechka was still quite small, but had already learned to distinguish between her mother and her nanny, she would sometimes, sitting in her nanny's arms, make a sudden roguish grimace, and hide her laughing face in the nanny's shoulder. Then she would look out with a sly glance...When Lelechka's mother, on coming in, saw how lovely the child looked when she was hiding, she herself began to play hide and seek with her tiny daughter."[34]

For older children, "play" might literally mean "a play" – playing at theater – in many households, especially the wealthier

The Everyday Life of (Mostly) Ordinary Women 119

Pavel Fedotov, *Vasia and Nanny/Vasia and Kitty* (1848/49) pencil
"Nanny, which Vasia do you love more, me or the kitty?"[35]

and more cultivated. Among memoirists mentioning that their nannies became either willing or impressed spectators at their children's amateur theatrics are Benois, Kropotkin, and Mikhail A. Chekhov. The last case is perhaps the most interesting, in that the nephew of the great writer actually became a professional actor. He writes:

> My mother and old nanny were the first viewers of my "home spectacles." I would gather clothes from the whole house: father's jacket, nanny's skirts and jackets, hats both male and female, umbrellas, galoshes – everything that fell to hand, and would begin improvising without a preliminary plan, without an aim. I would take up the first item of clothing that came to hand, put it on, and – wearing it – would feel *who I was*. The improvisations were humorous or serious depending on the costumes.
>
> But, whatever I depicted, nanny's reaction was always the same: she would come out with a long, whistling laugh, which turned into tears.
>
> "Ours, ours!" she'd say, wiping her eyes with the hem of her skirt.
>
> Nanny never, to the end of her days, came to grips with the notion [*ne usvoila mysli o tom, chto*] that I had grown up. She reacted exactly the same way to my performances [*igra*] when she saw me on the stage at MkhAT.[36]

The one thing a typical peasant nanny did *not* do was to discipline her charges, at least severely. Usually parental disapproval or sanction was invoked against an unruly or disobedient child; rarely did nanny apply corporal punishment and then only lightly. As Elizaveta Fen (pseud. of Lydia Jackson; née Lidiia Zhiburtovich;1899-1983) says about her second nanny: "Aniuta was only a nursemaid [sic]; she was not a long-established nanny, whose status in the family would have been much higher, although never as dictatorial as it apparently was in comparable families in Edwardian England. In Russia, nannies or nursemaids were not permitted to punish their charges: they had to report their misbehaviour to the parents."[37] This last is, however, an exaggeration, as the section on "anger" in the preceding chapter showed.

Most other memoirists, of this late period but also of earlier ones, testify to a similar situation in their families. This may explain, in some cases, the difference in affect felt for the nanny and the mother or particularly the father. In a child's often skewed reckoning of what "love" means, it might frequently confuse lack of punishment for love. It certainly added to the "fear" factor earlier generations tend to mention concerning their fathers. Yet in many cases (probably not most), this could apparently be a passive, "fear of the unknown," rather than – as much as? – a feeling based on active grounds of experience.

Strolls and Walks

One of the most famous walks in Russian history has been noted earlier in passing, that of Pushkin with his nanny Ul'iana, when they encountered a rather churlish Paul I. They were not alone in the activity, even if they were singled out on this occasion. For reasons of health primarily, but perhaps in some cases with the ulterior parental motive of removing an unwanted distraction, nearly all families prescribed or encouraged for their children outdoor walks with the nanny, *diad'ka*, governess, or governor. Whatever the time of year or the weather, in the city or the countryside, one could find children out on these peregrinations. The *sine qua non* of a stroll for a British nanny and baby – the perambulator or pram – was rarely to be seen in the land of the tsars before the second half of the nineteenth century.[38] The Russian child therefore typically negotiated the terrain on foot from a rather young age. The length (duration and distance) of the walk – and to some extent the destination – were largely a function of age.

This physical exercise was to such an extent *de rigeur* throughout the nineteenth century (and possibly before) – as well as prescribed and urged by child-care specialists – that one is taken aback by the educator Elizaveta Vodovozova (1844-1923) when she asserts that children as late as the 1840s had to breathe foul air most of the year, *"since no one then had any idea that a daily walk in fresh air is a necessary condition for their correct physical development."*[39] But the strolls had more than exercise as an aim, or at least, they accomplished more than that in hindsight. "The long walks around [St. Petersburg] done 'for health' at first with nanny and then with the teacher [*vospitatel'nitsa*] Yuliia Mikhailovna [Gedda] forever linked us intimately with Peterburg, they forced us to feel its peculiarities and beauty as something inseparable from us ourselves."[40]

With few exceptions, our memoirists have very clear, specific memories of these strolls. We can learn the routes they took, the things and people they saw, the diverse purposes, varied destinations, and lasting memories of these strolls from dozens of sources. The great detail that most of these authors provide about their childhood haunts is not surprising, given that they probably retraced these same routes hundreds if not thousands of times in childhood and often again in later life. Still, it is remarkable how some can recall – or at least appear to recall – so many nuances of their adventures. (The writer Andrei Belyi [1880-1934] tries to present this kind of information through the still-fresh eyes of the child, not the reminiscing adult, in his fictional memoirs *Kotik Letaev*.) In more than one case, in fact, the memoirist's very first memory of life is of being out on a walk with his or her nanny.[41]

Normally a source of great pleasure for the children, these walks were not universally enjoyed. A late dissenting voice recalls that, after the mid-day meal, the Rozanov children were quickly dressed and sent off for a walk, in any weather. "I disliked these walks very much – especially in winter; my hands and feet froze, particularly when they made us go ice-skating. But it didn't even enter my mind to disobey."[42]

There was a division of labor between Herzen's *two* nannies: his Russian nanny "Vera Artamonovna dressed me, put me to bed and bathed me," while his German nanny "Mme. Proveau took me for walks and spoke with me in German." Tat'iana Chernavina (b. 1887) notes that the joy evoked by her walks – usually in mid-afternoon – involved a trade-off. She would rush to the nursery and endure in silence her nanny's dressing her up in warm underclothes, leggings, felt boots, a fur coat, and fur cap. Normally, she would have protested over each of "these heavy, hateful things" – but not when it meant she could go out.[43] In fact, some children took such pleasure in their walks, that deprivation of them – along with meals – was a form of punishment.[44]

Sof'ia Skalon was an infant at the end of the eighteenth century, during which the Western world appeared to rediscover, along with the Romantics, the wonderful world of nature. She recalls that her nanny, at the children's behest and as a reward for their obedience, would hurry into the forest with them "to gather – if this was autumn, the forest apples, pears, and plums which had fallen among the leaves and which she would put up in preserves during the winter."

> Oh! what a joy this was for us, with what ecstasy we rustled the leaves under our feet and flew between the trees and the bushes! How often our kind nanny, without the means to look after both of us at once, for her own peace of mind tied our hands together with a kerchief; then we had to run together out of necessity, and this seemed to us still more gay. In spring and summer we took the very same walks, but instead of fruits we sometimes gathered pale blue snowdrops, fragrant violets, [and] lilies of the valley, and sometimes whole bouquets of hyacinth, narcissuses and roses and carried them to our mother, when we went in to say good morning to her.[45]

There was often a large difference between being out on a walk with the nanny and being out with another adult. Mikhail Bakunin (1814-1876) with his father, the village doctor Savvatii Sychugov (1841-1902) with his grandfather, and the ethnographer Vera Kharuzina (1866-1931) with her governess would all take walks that turned into miniature tutorials, often about nature.[46] Lidiia Chukovskaia (1907-1996) had similar recollections which illustrate the difference between strolling with her nanny and strolling with her very imaginative father, the children's author Kornei Chukovskii (1882-1969). When living in Finland, if they ran out of food and had to go to town for more, they'd set off in a group [*vsei oravoi*] along the Great Road. "...and although the road was most ordinary, still if we were walking not with nanny Tonia but with [father], anything might happen during these two-versts-long peregrinations! What he couldn't dream up!"[47] On these walks Chukovskii loved to engage in nonsensical play, both physical and rhetorical, to the great joy of his offspring.

Strolling with a nanny could be an adventure of a different sort, as negligent nannies frequently, if unintentionally, endangered their little charges while out on walks. They as often performed life-saving acts of heroism. The writer Tat'iana Shchepkina-Kupernik (1874-1952) recalls the time when her inattentive nanny "lost me on the Tsepnoi Bridge." The tired child thought she was dogging her nanny's footsteps, but when she caught up with this woman and grabbed her sleeve – calling out "Nanny!"– she got a shock. "I remember the panicky terror that seized me when there turned around to me a strange face! How long all this lasted I don't know, but a frightened nanny ran up to me and began to beg me 'not to tell mama'..."[48]

Through no fault of her own, the eighty-year-old nanny Shalovchikha allowed a graver danger to her five-year-old nurseling Ghermosha when they went out for a walk in the garden on a fine spring day. No snow remained on the ground but "the pond shimmered like a white saucer under a thin layer of snow and ice." Suddenly Ghermosha broke away and jumped onto the pond's inviting surface; the ice broke and he fell through. "Never hesitating, the old woman threw herself after him." She grabbed the child and dragged him to the bank. "From there, holding the half-conscious child to her breast, she ran stumbling and weeping to the house where, refusing all assistance to herself, she did not rest until she saw her charge revived, warm and safe in bed." Both recovered, none the worse for wear.[49]

Besides the sensory and esthetic pleasures from the children's viewpoint, or the didactic and utilitarian ones from the caretaker's and parents' standpoint, there was much else that played a role in the seemingly simple act of taking walks. These strolls might, for example, foster a sense of social consciousness, even in the quite young. The poet Osip Mandel'shtam (1891-1938), in his fictionalized autobiography *The Noise of Time*, ascribes to walks with his nanny his strong sense of the militarism or militarization of St. Petersburg in the 1890s. The city with its endless processions, military parades, martial buildings and statuary, and "progresses" of the royal family seemed to remove him from his own middle-class, Jewish life. So, he comments, it's not his "fault" that he spent his childhood "under the sign of the most real militarism"; he "blames" his nanny and the city itself.[50]

The authorities frequently paraded prisoners bound for Siberia through the city of Viatka, where the painter Arkadii Rylov (1870-1939) grew up. He hints at a political subtext in his walks with his nanny: "Once our nanny took me for a walk to the [town] square, to the scaffold, surrounded by soldiers and a crowd of the curious. I remember how a woman with a pale face, whom the executioner led to the column, dropped to the ground in a faint..."[51] Some nannies were even forbidden to take their nurselings to their own friends or various peasant haunts.[52]

In the two capital cities, there were clearly favored places or areas whither nannies and governesses took their charges on walks. Many memoirists are so explicit and detailed in their descriptions of their strolls that one is tempted, as it were, to pull out that incomparable guide, the 1914 *Baedecker*'s, and follow along in those tiny footsteps of long ago. In Moscow, the top general attractions were apparently the vicinity of the Kremlin, and along Tver Boulevard, a "radial" leading down to Red Square, where "the zenith" was the renowned Eliseev's food store (the Soviet Gastronom No. 1). The Obolenskii family's governess, Madame Stadler, however, refused to take them walking in the Aleksandrovsk Gardens or out on Tver Boulevard – "Children are put on show there," she'd say, "it gives rise to vanity in them." So they would stroll – spring and autumn, in good weather – around the Maidens' Field (*Devich'e pole*) or even to Vagan'kovsk Cemetery.[53]

In St. Petersburg, the embankments of the Neva River probably drew the most young strollers (as probably older ones as well), though Nevskii Prospekt, the Summer Garden, and the garden of the Tauride Palace were also very popular.[54] In good weather, the poet Blok was out for a walk in the morning, then again in mid-afternoon. Most often, they took him to the sunny University Embankment; and in the spring and fall, they went to the university's botanical garden.[55] In bad weather, the destination might shift slightly. The famous jurist Anatolii Koni (1844-1927) notes in his memoirs of St. Petersburg that there was an open gallery with columns that led from a palace by the Anichkov Bridge out onto Nevskii which was the favorite place "for nannies' walks with children when the climate was unfavorable."[56]

But in many cases, one's own neighborhood was still closest

to the heart. Pëtr Kropotkin (1842-1921) lovingly describes what he considered the "most typical part of Moscow" – the *Staraia koniushennaia* (Old Equerries' Quarter), a "labyrinth of clean, quiet, winding streets and lanes which lies at the back of the Kremlin, between two great radial streets, the Arbat and the Prechistenka." Homes of wood, in gay colors, mostly one-story, line the streets – no shops allowed in what he likens to Paris's Saint-Germain. "In the morning nobody was seen in the streets. About mid-day the children made their appearance under the guidance of French tutors and German nurses [nannies] who took them out for a walk on the snow-covered boulevards."[57]

The Lessons Nannies Teach, Usually Intended, Sometimes Not

Everyday Things. Formal lessons came to noble children from parents, governesses, governors, the occasional *diad'ka*, and tutors. Peasant nannies were virtually never charged with the role of educator. Yet in Chapter 4 we saw how folkways were an inherent part of the classic nanny's ways and also glimpsed something of the impact of these ways on the nurselings. To pursue this point a bit further, let us turn to some of the things that memoirists recall "learning" from their nannies, aside from "superstitions." Nannies naturally imparted a variety of pearls of wisdom drawn from their own and village life more generally, none more vivid than "vocabulary lessons." For example, Ol'ga Kornilova (b. ca. 1840?) recalls learning the expression *razfufyzhen* – "all gussied up" – from her nanny Verushka.[58] The Soviet writer Iurii Libedinskii (1898-1959) "inherited" his sister's old nanny when his first nanny, a Ukrainian German girl named Tereza, left their employ. "I would ask questions, she would answer; I would talk, she would listen, correct, and talk herself." This nanny sang Russian cradle songs "which had remained in [folk] memory for ages." One involved a "nasty stepmother" (*machekha liuta*):

Ona bila kota,	She'd beat the cat,
Kolotila kota,	She'd whip the cat,
Kak skhvatila kota	How she'd grab the cat
Poperek zhivota,	By the tummy,

Kak udarila kota	How she'd slam the cat
Ob mat' syru zemliu...	Down on the damp mother earth…

The ill-starred fate of the cat evoked in me not so much sleep as anxious ruminations:

"Nan [*Nian'*], why did she do this to him?"

"Who knows? In a word – nasty … it means she doesn't know restraint on her malice!"

Thus a word, a new word, enters my world. And when the coachman Dmitrii, coming into the kitchen from the courtyard and shaking the icicles from his beard and mustache, says: "Boy, the cold is nasty!" it's at once understood how powerful a chill is whipping through the courtyard.[59]

Lidiia Ivanova (1896-1985), daughter of a poet, learned about "how one was expected to behave in the village" from her nanny Ol'ga Petrovna.[60] She was somewhat surprised to find that "etiquette was of the most complicated kind, far more complex than our urban rules of behavior: how to enter a home, how to cross oneself before the icons, how to bow to those present and in what order …."

Nannies also dispensed all the conventional wisdom about life and love, such as what one must do with a broken heart. When Tat'iana Bers's sister Sonia (Tolstoi's future wife) "lost" a puppy love to his military service in the capital and was extremely sad over his departure, "Nanny Vera Ivanovna would say: 'It's a common thing, an affair of youth, little mother; time will pass, like the water flows away.'" Tat'iana observes that the nanny could foresee this flow of time because of her "old-time sensibility." When another servant with a nearby room tells them one evening of a young girl who fell in love with a married man with a family who then abandoned his wife and kids for her love, nanny says "Well, God will not send happiness to such a homebreaker."[61]

As further evidence of nanny pedagogy, here's an interchange between Nikolai Morozov (1854-1946) and his nanny. He always wanted to know the answer to questions about the whys and wherefores of things, "but I almost never received answers to [these questions] from father or mother or anyone else in their retinue."

Many of these questions remained fixed in his mind when nearing 60, even though they arose in childhood.

> "What is gold made of?" – I once asked my old nanny Tat'iana, who at the time seemed to me incomparably wiser than mother and father...
> "Out of gold," she replied.
> "And silver?"
> "Out of silver."
> "But then how is it bread is made out of flour?"
> "Bread *is* made of flour," she responded, just as imperturbably.
> "How did the sun come about?" I inquired another time, most likely quite a bit later.
> "God created it."
> "But who created God?"
> "No one. He has existed and will exist eternally."

He soon stopped posing such questions to nanny since he had come to understand that she could not explain them to him – indeed, no one could in some cases. His "independent frame of mind" eventually prepared him for a life in science.[62]

Lessons in Ethics. But of all the lessons imparted, the most important were probably moral. Mikhail Lermontov's German nanny (*bonna*), Khristina Remer, came to him the day he was born. Thereafter, she was "inseparable from him." One of the poet's closest confidants wrote later that Remer was a very principled woman, who insisted that her charge love those around him, even the serfs. If one can overlook the obvious mythologizing tendency, there is probably – or may be – a kernel of truth in what this author has to say about Lermontov and his nanny.[63]

The reverse occurred with the zemstvo doctor Savvatii Sychugov (1841-1902), son of a village priest: a slightly hypocritical nanny caused him to rethink his moral values. "Nanny, who loved me to distraction [*bezumno*], during a fasting time brought me some thick sweet cream and began urging me to eat, but *on the sly* ["*potikhon'ku*"]. I of course ate it up, but the words 'on the sly' stuck in my head...There began to torment me the consciousness that I had acted badly, since I'd eaten secretively, in the manner of a thief, so to speak." His grandfather, also a village priest, confirms his misgivings when he confesses his infraction. The nanny received a light reprimand and he got a lesson in morals.[64]

Nanny Says. Nannies all over the world have a store of pet expressions that they repeat endlessly to their charges.[65] Often used in disciplinary situations, sometimes humorous, they are usually pithy and to the point. Herewith a grab bag of remembered folk expressions and/or pearls of wisdom from Russian nannies; many are well-known idiomatic expressions, probably employed more often by peasants and other nonnobles than by higher social strata. "We are all sinners; wheresoever you have trod, there you have sinned." (The children decided this meant that any footstep murdered all the microorganisms living there.)[66] "A toddler takes a tumble and has an angel for a pillow!" and "It's a sin to talk when you're eating God's gift. Eat with a prayer, blessing yourself! Don't drop crumbs all around yourself – it's a sin!"[67] Also at meals: "You're at the table, not outdoors" and "Sit smooth as honey, don't get excited!"[68] "A lion among sheep but a sheep among lions."[69]

In fiction too nannies repeated such sayings; these are almost certainly "taken from life." Thus, the nanny Natal'ia, the protagonist of Ivan Bunin's story "Sukhodol'," tells a child she can't live away from their estate of Sukhodol': "Where the needle goes, the thread must follow." "Where you're born, there's your home," she explains.[70] Just the opposite of most nannies, however, was Praskov'ia Nikifrovna (Pasha), Ol'ga Andreeva's beloved nanny. As previously noted, she sprinkled her speech with endlessly varied proverbs and *"she never repeated any of her sayings, always coming up with another with a slightly different meaning."*[71]

Nanny as Bard[72] and Storyteller

Storyteller and Audience. In *The Republic,* Plato reports a dialog between Socrates and several young men about how to establish a just state. "You know," Socrates says, addressing Adeimantus, "that we begin by telling children stories which, though not wholly destitute of truth, are in the main fictitious; and these stories are told them when they are not of an age to learn gymnastics [i.e., very young]." He advocates establishing censorship for fiction writers and making "*mothers and nurses* [nannies – *paramana*] *tell their children the authorized [tales] only.*"[73] Two millenia after Plato and Socrates raised the issue of what children should and should not hear and see, it was still of concern to parents in Russia and elsewhere. (It remains an issue today, especially with respect to television, movies, comic books, and other popular-culture outlets.[74]) In a world before electronic media, entertainment as well as a mass of information – and misinformation – passed from mouth to eager ears in the form of folk and fairy tales.[75]

Virtually all of our memoirists make clear that nannies, with the fairy tales and other stories they told, left one nearly universal impression on their charges: a feeling of rapture. What makes the nanny-storyteller's role so critical is that the process she is involved in is, in Marshall McLuhan's famous terminology, "cool." The telling of a fairy tale is an interactive process. The listener, according to Bettelheim, helps shape the story by reacting to the teller's choice of words, plot twists, and characterizations.[76]

Not every family could boast a proper storyteller, especially not a nanny-storyteller, though many great estates had a full complement of semi- or fully professional entertainers.[77] Quite often, in fact, another member of the family circle was the primary storyteller.[78]

Content of the Tales. As for content, the sources all agree that what they heard could be neatly divided into three or four general categories: (1) fairy tales proper, with magical or supernatural elements, full of daring or innocent heroes, brave and beautiful maidens, anthropomorphic animals, scary villains or monsters, seemingly unsolvable puzzles or insurmountable problems to resolve and overcome, and invariably happy endings;[79] (2) tales of their homeland's (mythical) past; (3) "horror stories," designed to raise goose bumps and scare the little ones nearly to death; and (4) family history.

In the late 1860s the Russian poet and playwright Nikolai Pushkarev (b. ca. 1840) cleverly summed up his impressions from listening to folktales in childhood in his poem "National fairy tales."[79a] It's difficult to judge both what the stimulus for this effort might have been – political resentments, personal pique? – and whether to place him in the "anti-fairy-tale" ranks or not. He appears not to be attacking the tales themselves but the national traits they seem to reveal.

> Three nannies of three nations: a German woman with airs,
> A Parisian *mamselle* as lively as quicksilver,
> And a peasant woman – of my own homeland –
> Rocked my cradle.
> Three nannies of three nations, all of different mettle,
> Developed my mind in the earliest years –
> Three nannies of three nations different fairy tales
> Would babble to me in three tongues...
> And in later years, with maturity
> I understood that fairy tales are not the ravings of old women,
> That in fairy tales are told, fully and entirely,
> A people's morals and spirit.

The point of all nations' fairy tales is to show how to find happiness, says Pushkarev – e.g., the French through love, the Germans by ratiocination. "The traditions and facts of my native land," however, are "absurd and pettily banal, like Russian idleness, And crude, like our peasant is crude." The heroes of Russian fairy tales are "*knaves, fools, scoundrels*"

> And their sense: that if, enticed by rest,
> You want to be happy in your native land,
> Be born not smart, be born not a hero,
> Be born *an idler, a fool...*

Since the actual stories are widely available in both Russian and English (see endnote 75), more specific plot summaries are unnecessary. But as a cultural phenomenon related to peasant nannies, the tales deserve some more comment. For children, these tales were ideal, as the very language – peasant language – was so appealing to young ears. One quintessential aspect of village speech was its rhyming and rhythmical qualities.[80] Every child knows in its heart that a bear must be fuzzy-wuzzy, and one can't have a *Zhar-ptitsa* without a *Tsar-devitsa*! It's why so many peasant tales include rhyming references to *"nianki i mamki"* and *"nianushki i mamushki"* – a conjunction endlessly repeated in high culture as well, in fiction and memoirs. As Marina Tsvetaeva once observed, "Children without their own rhymes don't exist..."[81]

Another prototypical and reassuring quality of folktales is repetition, repetition, repetition. In West European or American fairy tales, there's always "Once upon a time" and "happily ever after." There are familiar, but still scary, evil witches and benign, loving fairy godmothers. In Russian fairy tales, some phrases and characters are the same as in the West, but many are quite different. *"Zhil-byl kogda-to,"* the opening of many a Russian tale, is the almost exact equivalent of "Once upon a time." Russian folk heroes must often go to the far ends of the earth in their quests, in which case they travel to the equivalents of "Never-never-land" and "far distant realms": *"Za trideviat' zemel', v trideviatoe tsarstvo, v tridesiatoe gosudarstvo."* Thus, Vera Figner (1852-1942) remembers her nanny's knowing just a few tales, endlessly repeated. "To tell the truth, I remember only one: the evil stepmother-queen turns her unloved stepson into a goat, the father unknowingly orders the goat to be killed for a feast, but Alenushka, the prince's sister, saves her brother, breaking the stepmother's spell at the decisive moment, when "the copper cooking cauldrons are a-boil, they're sharpening up the knives of steel." "But how well nanny told this tale! Wondrously well! You'd never tire of hearing it. It must have been just for the sake of the melody of this old voice which sounded with such unusual sincerity and innocence."[82]

An Implied Cultural Significance of Fairy Tales. In his penetrating study of life on the Russian country estate in the nineteenth century, Vasilii Shchukin discusses the myth of the "gentry nest" as "an oasis of beauty, nobility, freedom, and love." This myth, which arrived with Romanticism, "actively influenced the formation of a self-consciousness of the Russian intelligentsia, and later became an essential part of the national consciousness of every Russian." Shchukin explores what he considers two different ways of life on Russian manors, "two complexes of ethical and esthetic norms," and calls these the European and the "quasi-Asiatic" [*para-Aziatskie*] types.[83]

Thus, he contrasts the worlds of Tiutchev, Fet, Sluchevskii, Tolstoi, and especially Turgenev, on the one hand, with that of Goncharov, on the other: the Turgenev "nest" vs. Oblomovka. The latter is "quasi-Asiatic." One big difference between the two, argues Shchukin, is that Oblomovka preserves the spirit of old-time fables, the fairy tales told by the nanny. Life is timeless at the Oblomov estate; there is no fear of death. At "European" manor houses, "foreign governors and tutors play a large role, but at Oblomovka there is only a Russian nanny and her fairy tales. At Turgenevan estates, truly religious people are met with, but residents of Oblomovka are just superstitious and fatalistic. People have to sit the fourteen-year-old little Il'ia down forcibly with a book, while you can't tear Turgenev heroes away from reading."

Children who had an accomplished storyteller as a nanny were fortunate; those who had as nanny not only a good storyteller but a fine singer as well were doubly blessed. One such beneficiary of these two skills was Sergei Bulgakov, "Father Sergii" (1871-1944), "the greatest religious genius" of the twentieth century in the view of Nikita Struve. Bulgakov was so taken with the "gifts of love and poetry" that his nanny Zinaida bestowed on him that he remained grateful to her his whole life. She was "a remarkable storyteller about her own life, of life under serfdom. She also sang to us her songs from this past, and this singing settled into [*lozhilos'*] the soul like the music of life." The phrase he found to describe his nanny stands out among all the many accounts cited in these pages: "She would tell about the serf theater, about her own past life. *And it was as if she herself did not exist; she was a force of nature, an elemental force of Russian affection, pity, love for us* [*I sama ona kak budto ne sushchestvovala, ona byla stikhiei, stikhiei russkoi laski, zhalosti, liubvi k nam*]."[84]

Nanny as Thrush

The Singers and the Listeners. Vera Figner remembers her nanny as having a "glorious, melodic voice" but never, ever singing a song. Hers was the exception to the rule. Sergei Aksakov (1791-1859) loved to listen to the singing of the peasants, including his nannies ("it always raised me to rapture"), but his mother did not like the songs. Stepanida Iakovlevna, wet-nurse to Baroness Sofiia Buksgevden's brother in the 1880s and later their nursery maid, sang from morning to night, at the top of her voice. She had a lovely voice; by herself in the sewing-room, she'd sing in that "peculiar, high-pitched tone of peasant women" songs of the Volga region. The composer Iurii Arnol'd (1811-1898) first heard Russian folk songs from his nanny and under-nanny.[85]

Anna Chertkova (1859-1927), wife of the Tolstoyans leader Vladimir Chertkov, remembers her nanny's having a "soft, melodic voice."

> She never sang loudly but, when putting us to bed, she sang in a quiet, tender voice her own slightly sad, intimate little songs. Having put us to bed, she would light the lamp, so that it would become semi-dark in the room, and would begin to clear away things, to clean up the room, all the while continuing to sing. And we became accustomed to falling asleep to her singing.
>
> Perhaps, from the point of view of contemporary upbringing [*vospitanie*], this is not rational, but it probably seemed to us boring and melancholy without nanny's songs, which caressed us so tenderly and quietly lulled us to sleep.
>
> And I remember that for a long time afterward I thought that no one could sing as well as nanny used to.[86]

All of the above memoirists, and many more, related nothing out of the ordinary about their nannies' singing. In fact, their reports are usually trite and bland. For a more revealing and perhaps more honest presentation on the subject, we must turn to the military man-turned-writer Aleksandr Vereshchagin (1850-1909), brother of the famous artist Vasilii Vereshchagin. A very early memory: in the nursery, he's building houses out of playing cards at a table. At the other end of the room is the children's old nanny Anna Larionovna with his sister Masha, whom she's singing to sleep. There is heard, in "a gentle and melancholy voice, as she nods her head in time, the familiar song:

The Everyday Life of (Mostly) Ordinary Women 135

"Out in the yard the lamb doth sleep,
And quietly it lies.
Bye-bye; now, slumber on,
And open not thine eyes."

I remember very well how, at the words, "Out in the yard the lamb doth sleep, and quietly it lies," I glance out at the yard, and my eyes seek the spot where that lamb is lying. If nurse sang it, it means that there must be a lamb lying somewhere, and, not finding it, I turn to nurse and ask, "Nurse, where is the lamb lying in the yard?"

Nurse raises herself a little from the small bed, turns towards me [and] makes an angry motion with her head to me, signifying that I am not to make a noise, and then proceeds with her lay, in the same soothing tone: –

"And when thou art a big girl grown,
Thou'lt walk in silk attire.
Bye-bye; now, slumber on
And open not thine eyes."[87]

Now this nanny is a bit more true-to-life: she gets a little cross with him for disturbing her singing. We're also told earlier that she has a weakness for tobacco (her bandana covered with snuff stains). At least in his naïve view, moreover, she is somehow guilty of lying, or at least of stretching the truth.

The Content. What would the nanny have sung to her young charges, and when? Nanny songs appear to fall into three basic types, mostly as forms of play: (1) songs purely for entertainment, for "fun"; (2) songs which accompanied certain activities, including the nanny's work or chores; and (3) lullabies, nominally to help the child fall asleep.[88] (Rarely designed to teach, the song process might still turn out to be educational.[89])

The Russian equivalent of the entertainment ditty "This little piggy..." is this song:

Soroka-vorovka,	A thieving magpie
Kashu varila,	Cooked up some porridge,
Na porog skakala,	Hopped to the doorway,
Gostei sklikala,	Called his guests together,

Gosti na dvor,	The guests to the courtyard,
Kasha na stol.	The porridge to the table.

Then, as the nanny bends each toe of the child in turn, from big to little, both repeat as many times as they want:

Etomu kashki,	A bit of gruel for this one,
Etomu brazhki,	A bit of home brew for this one,
Etomu vintsa,	A sip of wine for this one,
Etomu pivtsa,	A sip of beer for this one,
Etomu net nichego:	But not a thing for this one:
Potomu chto mal,	Because it's so small,
Krup ne dral,	Didn't thresh the groats,
Za vodoi ne khodil,	Didn't go for water,
Kashu ne varil.	Didn't cook the porridge.

The nanny would also sing a song when playing with her charge(s). While singing this one, the nanny rocks the child in her arms, tosses it up, or dandles it:

Tiutiushki, tiutiushki,	Rock-a-bye, rock-a-bye,
Ovsianye lepeshki,	Cookies out of oatmeal,
Pshenichnyi pirozhok,	A patty out of wheat,
Na oparushke meshen,	Mixed on the leavened dough,
Vysokokhon'ko vzoshel.	Has risen up so high.

In another playful song, the child sits on the nanny's lap; she takes it by the hands and, while singing, spreads them apart. After a time, the child is supposed to begin doing the motions by itself:

Tiaten'ke – sazhen',	For auntie -- a *sazhen'* [two meters],
Mamen'ke – sazhen',	For mommie – a *sazhen',*
Dedyshke – sazhen',	For grampa – a *sazhen',*
Babushke – sazhen',	For gramma -- a *sazhen',*
Brattsu – sazhen',	For baby brother -- a *sazhen',*
Sestritse – sazhen',	For little sister -- a *sazhen',*
A Koliushen'ke –	But for little Nicky,
Bol'shuiu, nabol'shuiu.	More, the biggest.

An example of a ditty accompanying one of the nanny's many tasks is the following, sung while dousing the child with water, bathing it:

S gusia voda,	Water from the goose,
S tebia khudoba.	Will keep you nice and loose [literally, thin].

Of lullabies there were a myriad. Most were variations of one like this:

Spi, ditia moe, usni!	Sleep, my babe, now go to sleep!
Ugomon tebia voz'mi!	May the sandman you now keep!
Baiu, baiushki, baiu!	Hush-a-bye, now hush-a-bye!
Kolotushek nadaiu!	I'll rattle you a lullaby!
Kolotushek dvadtsat' piat',	Rattles, twenty-five, abound
Tak pokrepche budesh' spat'.	So you'll sleep a bit more sound.

A variant on the same theme (with a little "proselytizing" thrown in?) is this cradle song:

Vyrostish velik,	You'll grow up big
v zolote khodit',	And walk in gold,
nianushek i mamushek	Your nannies and mammies
v barkhate vodit'.[90]	In velvet enfold.

But Marina Warner reminds us that lullabies are not always what they seem. As it happens, lullabies have multiple functions. "Lullabies, an ancient form of poetry, are sung all over the world to settle infants to sleep, to banish the fear of the dark in older babies and children, and to ease the drop into oblivion against which babies often seem to struggle so hard," Warner writes. "But while this primary function defines lullabies, the songs also calm the mother or caregivers and make the daily struggle bearable."[91]

Lullabies are not simply about sleep. They include foreshadowings of what may come in the baby's life; they try to "ward off dangers" and "forestall harm to the child"; "they explicitly attempt to keep the bogeyman or bogeywoman from the home...these songs mourn future memories, not past events. The effect can be very bitter..." Lullabies can thus "resemble charms and magical wishes: spelling out what might happen in order to bind it is witchcraft." The magic may either make the forecast come true or avert it. "Worries about children, as most parents know, proliferate along these magical axes of prevention and cure." The "measure of a lullaby echoes the regular intake and exhalation of breath and, by extension, the rocking of a cradle," notes Warner, but "the habitual mood of the melody is melancholy." "The minor third dominates lullabies..." They almost sound like keening, "so plaintive are the tunes." In oral, largely female tradition, "these apparently naïve and uncomplicated songs of reassurance touch on complex anxieties. Lullabies often situate the child – and those who care for it – in a perspective of life's risks; their thoughts surprisingly wander into zones of suspicion, aggression, violence and fear."[92]

So contrary to our normal expectation, there can be truly disturbing contents in lullabies, songs that we typically think of as being "lulling"and soporific. As Warner says, "lullabies often threaten the infant directly, the infuriated singer of a cradle song summoning the monster or bogeyman to work on her behalf. It is often the baby, not the barbarian at the gates [or the wolf at the door], who is the target of the threat. This kind of lullaby conjures the terrors of the night, not always to silence them, but to flourish them." An example she cites is Lermontov's "Cossack Lullaby."[93]

An equally apt example from the world of music rather than literature is Modest Musorgskii's "Cradle Song"(1865). "This is no cosy lullaby," writes David Brown, "[the early note scheme] conjures unease at the opening" and "the concluding invocation to angel-guarded sleep" is "opposed by the restless alternation [of other notes]...in the accompaniment. Weariness underlies the gentleness of *Cradle Song*." The text of Musorgskii's composition he took from A. N. Ostrovskii's play "The Voevoda," which shows "the tension between reassuring crib-side musings and bleak reality" for any peasant baby.[94]

There are several additional functions of the cradle song. The lullaby may express longings and wishes of the singer. The dreams of the mother or nanny are typically "simple" – "an end to want and toil, an increase in comforts."[95] Or, as the historical novelist

Pavel Mel'nikov (pseud. Andrei Pecherskii; 1818-1883) put it at the beginning of his 1871 opus *In the Forests*, "But not everyone is wealthy [*v zolote khodit'* – literally, goes about in gold], carries silver in his hands, even though wet-nurses and nannies sing to every Russian such a fate when he is still lying in the cradle." (One is reminded of Eliza's near-lullaby "Wouldn't it be Loverly?" in *My Fair Lady*.) The songs can serve to divert a real threat to an imagined or less dangerous one, a way to protect the baby, and as a kind of tocsin, calling for greater vigilance against any possible threat. Language acquisition occurs through lullabies: babies must acquire "sequences of sounds, like tunes, before grasping single syllables or words."[96]

For their great variety and flexibility of content, lullabies were a favorite genre for all kinds of thinkers to mimic. Russian radicals of the nineteenth century were particularly fond of penning lullabies that reflected their egalitarian, communitarian, and other ideals. The poets Nikolai Nekrasov (in 1846) and Nikolai Ogarev (1871) each composed a variant on the traditional lullaby for the purpose of criticizing social injustice. (See Chapter 8)

Import and Significance. Musicologists have written volumes about folk songs and the creativity to be found in the music and words of Russian peasants. The gist of it all, for me, comes down to two major points. First, the collective wisdom of ages of rural life is expressed in Russian peasants' songs; and second, without formal musical training of any kind, peasants have created remarkably original rhythms, cadences, melodies, and harmonizations in their music.[97] Aside from my treatment of one aspect of this theme in Chapter 9 I have little original to say on the topic. As pertains to nannies and singing, however, I will quote from a (self-taught) student of the subject. The mythographer-folklorist Iurii Miroliubov's essay "The Role of Old Nannies in the Family" argues (mistakenly): "If we compare the content of our Russian songs with those of the West, there's nothing similar... There, songs as such are no longer in the people. The people sing what's been composed for them by urban musicians. But the Russian song is itself 'from the land' and comes from the land to the heart. In it there's a strength which is not in other songs. And it's no accident that a dear old family nanny teaches the songs. She herself is 'from the land'."[98]

At End of Day

Our preceding discussion of lullabies leads naturally to this section. After a day full of activities, whether lively play or walks or storytelling, the time for sleep inevitably came. While bedtimes varied, the rituals of bedtime were usually very similar. For older youngsters, nanny generally got them undressed, had them say their prayers, tucked them in, and retired to her own bed, either in the nursery with the children or in an adjoining room of her own. A fairy tale or lullaby usually helped the drowsy child(ren) drop off to sleep. In the case of infants or tiny toddlers, the nanny would likely rock the babe for a time, probably while crooning a cradle song, then put the tot down in the crib or small bed. At least, that was the hopeful scenario in each case.

Children sometimes had a hard time falling asleep, keeping the nanny awake, making her sing or perhaps insisting on other soothing and petting. Memoirists rarely mention the opposite possibility – of the nanny keeping the children awake. One memorable account of troubled night-times is the anonymous mid-nineteenth century memories of "N," who nightly was "in fear of one thing, that nanny not start in snoring again!"[99] Barely does nanny's head touch the pillow when it begins. "In her loud and variegated snoring I hear the voices of sinners being tortured in hell." "I know there's only one way to make all of hell fall silent: this is to close nanny's mouth with my hand, or to pinch her nose. But in order to do this I have to stretch my hand out from under the covers, and the devils might grab it!" Children being what they are, there were also many occasions when a nanny had to earn her keep (and lose some sleep) over a colicky, uncooperative, misbehaving, recalcitrant, or perhaps mildly insomniac child.[100]

Leisure Time and Time by Herself, Away from the Children

All nannies are clearly kin to Dickens's Madame LaFarge: when not occupied with their charges, nannies knit. One would be hard-pressed to find in the memoir literature an exception to the rule that eighteenth- and nineteenth-century nannies kept their needles in motion a good deal of the time, producing stockings and mittens and other garments to clothe themselves and those in their households. Ol'ga Zhigalova's alter-ego in her autobiographical fiction, Tania, once entered the nursery as her nanny sat knitting. She moved closer to watch as the needles flew like rapiers, "as if in a duel."[101] Such activity was close to a necessity, not a pastime, especially in the countryside. But of course it could not consume all the nanny's free time.

When not busy with their charges, nannies often did housework. Several memoirists note that their nannies were tasked with cleaning chores – dishes, furniture, laundry – particularly in households without a large contingent of servants. In some urban households, they also did the shopping, or at least part of it. Like maids, nannies often lit the samovar for tea, lit and extinguished lamps around the house morning and night, and performed other similar labors. Nannies might take a major hand in some kinds of cooking and food preparation. For example, they often engaged in putting up preserves and other forms of "canning" or the making of sweets. They darned and mended – stockings, clothes, bed linens, and so on.

In an age before mass media there was no television or radio to occupy what free time a peasant nanny might find or make for herself. Being nearly always illiterate (at least until the end of the nineteenth century), she could not read books, magazines, or other printed matter. So most nannies at their leisure betook themselves to the kitchen or the maids room to engage in conversation – the censorious would say in idle chatter or gossip – with her fellow servants, quite often knitting at the same time. This was one more way in which the oral culture of the village made itself felt in the lords' manors.[102] The reverse held as well: nannies and other servants loved to gather round as one of the estate owner's family read aloud, from Bible or secular fiction.

Among themselves and frequently with their mistresses as well (but also at times with the children present), nannies and other female servants loved to engage in fortune-telling. There were methods of divining future spouses, major events, and more mundane occurrences. Some involved tea dregs; others, thrown shoes; still others, water in various forms. As Elizaveta Fen (1899-1983) recalls, her nanny Aniuta "was addicted to fortune-telling in and out of season. When in my parents' absence she kept me company, she would often bring out a dilapidated book, called *The Oracle*, which had a number of diagrams, mostly of circles divided into sections. Each section had a number and a name of some Greek or Roman god or goddess printed on it. You questioned the oracle by rolling a pellet of bread and dropping it on to the circle, then you looked up the prophecy in the book under the number and name of the goddess or god printed on the section on to which the pellet happened to roll."[103]

Yet when larger companionship was not to be had, or no pressing needs had to be met, some other activity would pass the time, usually around the house. Nikolai Astrov's nanny and his brother's wet-nurse apparently spent many minutes, if not hours, gazing out the window at the happenings on their street and in the courtyard of the Surveying Institute.[104] "In her free time [nanny] Avdot'ia's favorite pastime was to sort through the things in the basket" which lay under her bed, notes Ol'ga Berggol'ts (1910-1975). This "round, woven basket" contained "pretty material in rose and butterfly colors and, the main thing, a surprising kerchief: on one side gold, on the other – silver!"[105] In similar fashion, nannies spent a great deal of time rummaging in their trunks, as noted previously.

An activity of a completely different kind also occupied a fair number of nannies: travel. By this I mean not just short jaunts to pay social visits or back to a nearby village – all of which happened with some regularity – but also much longer trips, away from the family. Even before emancipation, for instance, many nannies – like most Orthodox women – were pilgrims to holy sites, a practice which only grew as transportation became easier with better roads and the coming of the railroad.[106] Serfowning families often paid for nannies' travel, though it's difficult to say if this was the rule or not.[107] The historian Sergei Solov'ëv's nanny was constantly on pilgrimages (though it's not clear whether this was during her years as nanny or before).[108] The anonymous author of childhood memoirs who signed herself N had a nanny who traveled to the Solovetsk Monastery and almost capsized in a boat on the White Sea; she – as most nannies – brought back presents for "her family."[109]

Both female and male nannies (*diad'ki*) participated in such travel. In Ivan Shmelëv's (1873-1950) quasi-autobiographical *Pilgrimage* (1930-31), little Vania's father is upset with his *diad'ka*

Gorkin because the latter wants to go on a pilgrimage during Petrovki, the busiest time of harvest. But the two soon reconcile and Gorkin is allowed to go, along with several other servants and workers, to the Troitse-Sergeev Monastery, a trip that will last four days one-way.[110] Among the fellow pilgrims is the pious Domna Parfenovna, Vania's former nanny.[111] In pure fiction as well, nannies made pilgrimages. A central character of Avdot'ia Panaeva's (1819-1893) *Romance in the Petersburg Demimonde* of 1863, the nanny Palageia vows to herself to walk all the way to Kiev on foot to atone for her imagined sins.[112]

The motivation for the pilgrimages naturally varied. In Chapter 4 we saw how strong a component religion was in most peasant nannies' personal lives. Thus "spiritual renewal" was probably the most common purpose and self-motivated. But in some cases, the pilgrimages were not voluntary or self-initiated, and many nannies no doubt included prayers for the wellbeing of their masters or employers as reasons for going. Zinaida Zhemchuzhnaia (née Volkova; 1887-1961) notes that when her mother fell gravely ill, her nanny Annushka and some other women set off to Verkhotur'e on a pilgrimage, "and they sent us with them. When we returned after a week, mama was not at home."[113] (Her mother soon died.)

The intention in this travel was usually to come back to the family, of course, but that was not always the case. Tat'iana Passek (1810-1889) remembered a woman named Mar'ia Ivanovna Iudina, a Pole from Kremenchug, who eventually became a nanny for her "cousin" Sasha (Aleksandr Herzen). After several years she left their home; for a long time she would go on pilgrimages (*khodila po bogomol'iam*). She ended her life in a monastery.[114] Exactly the same thing occurred with the nanny of Boris Pavlov (pseud. Pylin; 1906-1920). Born simultaneously with the appearance of Halley's Comet, he recalls: "This was the year that our nanny, who had lived in our family many years and whom we loved very much, left us. Nanny traveled to her village on foot, intending on the way to visit, as she said, the 'Holy Ones.' She disappeared on the road and never made it to her village. Mama supposed that she went into a monastery. She dropped in and remained to live out her life among her Holy Ones."[115] While the literature does not indicate that such an alternative retirement was a frequent choice, it must have been

Sexual Life

Most nannies pretty much lived a celibate life, whether married or not. As discussed in a previous chapter, if they had been married before entering service as a child's caretaker, the bulk of these women gave up any pretense of normal married life, leaving their own family (husband, children) and own home to live in the big house of the master. They saw their own family irregularly thereafter. *They stopped having children.* At a certain age, older nannies were, *ipso facto*, by and large free of the entanglements of sexual encounters. Of more interest is the subject of sex with regard to younger women and the never-married. (There is another aspect of the question of sexuality which deserves – and has received – much attention: prostitution. But this topic is better treated in my next chapter.)

There are few if any Freudian overtones in what (male) autobiographers say about their nannies in childhood, especially in the days of serfdom.[116] This lacuna might be explained in part as a function of hypocrisy or a Victorian-like straitlacedness and reticence to discuss intimate details of one's life. It is equally likely, however, that there was indeed a kind of general abstinence observed when it came to very young children's caretakers.

Unlike with governesses (not peasants of course), there is little hanky-panky between pre-emancipation masters and their children's nannies recorded in the memoir literature. The landowner Fëdor Panov, married to a former lady-in-waiting at court, is an exception (though the source is somewhat suspect). As supposedly related by a serf woman who was herself a nanny,[117] Panov's wife was sickly and not in good mental health. The couple's daughter "begins to notice that [her father] is beginning to tempt her young nanny." The father marries off the daughter to a neighbor, the serf-narrator's master. Once rid of his daughter, Panov pursues her "modest nanny, his own serf girl, who resisted for a long time but, in the end, submitted to his authority and power." The story has a somewhat unexpected ending. The adulterous master and the nanny have a son named Pëtr. "She [the nanny] was a good, kind, sweet, honest woman. Panov freed her whole family and built a hotel for them in Iaroslavl'. And when his mentally ill wife died, he declared that his son Pëtr was his legal heir."[118] The arts critic Vladimir Stasov (1824-1906) protested vigorously to Milii Balakirev in the early 1860s when his common-law wife accused him of straying with his daughter's married nanny.[119]

There are also few references to sex between nannies and nonmembers of the manor house. Aleksandr Borovkov (1788-1856) began keeping notes for an autobiography shortly after Pushkin published Chapter 3 of *Onegin*. The timing is significant: it was late enough that Pushkin probably affected his inclusion of many anecdotes about his nannies, but early enough that the near-sanctity of the theme was not yet established. Hence he could touch upon aspects of his nannies' lives that were seldom written about by his contemporaries and would become almost tabu in the following decades – sex and sinfulness. "I was three years old and there looked after me my own old maid [*pozhilaia devka*], who comported herself very well; however, she could not overcome a feminine weakness: she had a lover..."[120]

Unusually, Nikolai Davydov (1848-1920) not only mentions a romance (an "affair of the heart") between his young future nanny and an unknown swain but actually discusses sexual relations on *pomeshchik* estates under serfdom. He speaks about such liaisons between masters and servants (not specifically nannies, however), noting that these relations were "frequent." More significantly, he says, the family of the girl or woman involved did not always object – they usually "got something out of it." This was more often the case with a widow or young unmarried girl. It was different with a wife – in such cases protests were more frequent; the outcome could be divorce, separation, or "reconciliation" with a monetary bribe.[121]

As for nannies' involvement in sexual affairs not their own, however, it is a different story, at least in fiction (see Chapter 8). The general ribaldry and sexual license of the last third of the eighteenth century extended to the portrayal of at least one nanny, in Aleksandr Izmailov's *Evgenii* (1799), and it seems likely that was not an exception which proved a rule. Once again, if it was not Pushkin and his work alone that marked a major watershed here,

Nanny of Sergei Pankeev, Freud's "Wolf-Man" (ca. 1890s?)

it was at least a combination of his writings and others'. If only for a time, the first half of the nineteenth century apparently wrought a pronounced change in the treatment (i.e., the *nontreatment*) of this theme in literature.

While not quite asexual, nannies – even young nannies – almost never show up as erotic figures in memoirs. It is almost as if the only way that nannies could be so selflessly devoted to their charges was if they were desexed. Catriona Kelly notes, however, that a commentator in the twentieth century thought it necessary to watch out for nannies who might resort to masturbation to help put their nurselings to sleep; perhaps this was a concern of longstanding.[122] True, many nannies had children (i.e., from their pre-nanny days), usually known to their charges. But questions of a sexual nature directed toward nannies were virtually never inspired by the activity of the nanny. Instead, a younger sibling's arrival was the common precipitant of sexual inquiry. Nannies' responses ranged from the typically and universally disingenuous – about storks or cabbage leaves – to the somewhat more serious and better-informed.

The Everyday Life of (Mostly) Ordinary Women 147

Pankeev children, Anna and Sergei

Asexual or not, one Russian nanny precipitated the most famous case study of Sigmund Freud. A young Russian named Sergei Pankeev, near psychosis, came to see Freud in 1910, telling the doctor an elaborate childhood dream involving white wolves sitting silently in trees observing him. The events precipitating the dream included sexual play with his older sister and then self-exposure to his nanny. Freud "displaced" the sexual content of the dream to the boy's parents' having intercourse and Pankeev's presumed Oedipus Complex. The significance of Pankeev's dream – he became known as "the Wolf-Man" – lies in its being the first in which Freud had to address the fundamental issue of his work – whether dreams and memories were always based on reality or whether they could be based on imaginary or wished-for events that never happened.[123]

Conclusion

As in Chapter 4, I've tried in this chapter to eliminate too much sentimentality when describing the lives and work of nannies. There was hardly anything extraordinary in the usual routine of children's caretakers. If the masters/employers were reasonably fair and responsible parents, there was not much that was burdensome or demanding in the job. If the nanny was also fair and responsible, the children's lives were also not unduly burdened, especially when the caretaker had at least a modicum of care and love for her charges. Not every childhood was "golden" as lived; how it was remembered (or imagined) is the stuff of subsequent chapters.

6

Post-Emancipation and Post-1917 Nannies

February 1861

As might be expected, the watershed events of the mid-nineteenth century in Russia – the emancipation of the serfs and ensuing wide-ranging reforms of local and central government – did not leave the situation of Russian nannies untouched. The most obvious change that occurred was, of course, the elimination of a huge pool of un-free labor that had for at least two centuries been tapped for child caretakers.[1] But in fact there was no drastic alteration in the situation. Just as the situation of the serfs in general shifted only gradually, through a sometimes long, painful period of transition,[2] so too was there no overnight change within the lordly manor with respect to the family's child caretakers.

By the testimony of many *pomeshchiki*, peasants tended to receive the news of their long-awaited emancipation with little joy or celebration. When the emancipation act was read aloud to one group of serfs, including *dvorovye*, one among them was outraged at hearing that household serfs were to remain in obedience to their masters for two years. This man shouted out: "To hell with this piece of paper! Two years – as if I'd actually obey that!" Others in the crowd remained silent.[3] In part the general lack of enthusiasm on the part of the freed was because the terms of their "freedom" were such that they remained bound in most respects, unable to leave their villages and communes except with extraordinary effort and considerable financial output.

Most peasants took some time to adjust to the new order that was going to emerge very slowly. Farming peasants were also less than thrilled by the amount of land they were to receive and the long years of so-called redemption of that land that lay before them. For the vast majority of rural dwellers, the transition to some semblance of independence and autonomy would last at least ten years, a sizable portion of any life in those days. But for the first two years, the *status quo* was virtually frozen, as masters and serfs negotiated the terms of the colossal land transfer.

Dvorovye (Household) Serfs. Change inside the manor house often came slowly as well. In his belletristic autobiography, the writer Vladimir Korolenko (1853-1921) recalled that, when the rumors of emancipation began, "in our kitchen, insofar as I can recall, they expected nothing good – perhaps, because its staff was, to a certain degree, aristocratic." The cook and maids were *"pani"* (ladies).[4] A separate edict was promulgated in 1861 regarding just the household serfs. They received no farmland whatever nor any house-and-garden plot – somewhat understandable, given the fact that few household males were likely capable of taking on the work of real farmers and husbandry-men. One wonders how many males were prepared to take up a hardscrabble life of subsistence farming, given the less physically demanding life they had grown used to over the decades. N. Shatilov recalled that "the emancipation of the peasants did not produce any change whatever in the method of running the farm; it passed, one can say, completely unnoticed; *not even one member of the household serf staff left us.*"[5]

Females, including the nannies, might have had even less reason to want a land allotment unless they could see a way to turn it into income-producing private property. (Perhaps some would have looked on a land share as a kind of "dowry" for a future spouse.) Similar to the field workers, *dvorovye liudi* were obliged to remain working for their masters for the first two years – a proviso with some small justification for the agrarian serfs but none for the *dvorovye*, who had no charters (*ustavnye gramoty*) to negotiate with their masters as the allotment-receiving serfs did.

The mandated two years of continued subservience (service) to the former master was a *de facto* prolongation of serfage but could, at the estate owner's discretion, be reduced. About the only concession made to the household serfs was that, if they were on *obrok*, the *pomeshchik* did not have the right to revoke it or to increase the *obrok*. Pëtr Zaionchkovskii's judgment on the effects of the emancipation for the *dvorovye* is harsh: "At the expiration of the two-year period, all household serfs were freed by the *pomeshchik* without receiving either a land allotment or any kind of compensation, regardless of the length of their service with the *pomeshchik*. Thus, household serfs [who were] sick and the aged, unable to work, were literally thrown out onto the street," he writes. The emancipation statute "envisioned the creation of a certain fund 'for the care of the aged, the decrepit, those suffering spiritual and bodily ailments and minors with no living parent' (art. 33) by means of a tax assessment of one ruble on the household serfs themselves."[6] Zaionchkovskii's conclusion may be overly condemnatory. Since *dvorovye* serfs were given no arable land at emancipation, they did find themselves in a far from enviable position. But as for being thrown to the wolves, that eventuality was unlikely. Most received a bit of land on which to take up residence.

At the L'vov family estate, one Anna Il'inichna, a coachman's widow, "was the only one of the former household staff who remained on our estate. All the household servants [*dvorovye*] received house plots [*usad'by*] without an allotment of field land. Some of them settled down on their house plots, some scattered into the world, went into town; but Anna Il'inichna was very old and childless; she had no place to go and [so] remained with us."[7] The opposite of the L'vov situation occurred at Sergeevka, the estate of Boris Glinskii's relatives, the Sergeevs. There, for a dozen years after emancipation, the number of household staff grew rapidly, the former serfs demanding both room and board in addition to wages (as "freely hired labor") yet doing little or no work. Only when the masters got into financial difficulties did the now "spoiled" servants look for other employment; but when they told prospective employers where they'd come from, almost no one would hire these "dissolute" freeloaders. Then came a larger blow. In the cholera epidemic of 1873, at least a dozen went to the grave – a plot of land, Glinskii notes ironically, much smaller than they and their ancestors had long dreamed of.[8]

Not many *dvorovye* were enterprising or skilled enough to cut all ties with their former lords and strike out on their own. Some of the younger *dvorovye* did just that, especially if they had not been long employed in the manor house. But among older, especially female, serfs there were fewer who did so. Instead, by mutual agreement, the majority seem to have stayed put – working in the same capacities as before, but now as hired servants. Whether most worked out a full-blown compensation system with their *pomeshchiki* is doubtful, especially among those long in service. Some form of room-and-board with a little extra rather than full money wages may have been the norm.[9] In a material sense, life was no doubt more uncertain for many, if not most, hired caretakers than it had been before emancipation. Vera Kharuzina's former wet-nurse would constantly complain to her about the scarcity of goods she experienced in the 1860s as compared to their satiety pre-1861. She also felt the pinch of inflation, as her wages seemed more and more inadequate to provide for her needs.[10] The situation would have been similar for hired nannies at this time.

Aftermath of Emancipation: The New Practicalities

The Getting of Nannies. After emancipation, the majority of nannies appear to have just kept on doing what they did before. From the memoir literature it's obvious that the gentry maintained their standard of living as best they could. For those with much income at all, this meant retaining the services of nannies and other child caretakers. As the system of serfdom receded, however, it meant that a ready-made source for child caretakers would dry up. Both the birthing of children and the demand for nannies were naturally undiminished. Was a capitalistic "market" now to replace serfdom in providing for much noble childcare? Would the nanny labor force change much? Although as we have seen, a fair number of nannies had been hired employees, not serfs, even before emancipation, these had been overwhelmingly foreign *bonnes* or nonpeasants. That situation would evolve in the years after 1861. Two consequences of the change were inevitable. First, new ways of locating and hiring nannies would be increasingly needed. Second, the professionalization of the occupation would be expected, sooner or later, by some if not all prospective employers.[11]

The highly personalized – largely intra- and inter-family – pre-emancipation system of finding nannies began to yield to new methods rather quickly. By the 1880s, if not before, the capitals at least saw a flourishing new business. Osip Mandel'shtam (1891-1938), in the fictive autobiography *The Noise of Time* (1925), recalls that in St. Petersburg

> the renowned office [of Kopanygin and Co.] for the hiring of cooks, nannies [*bonny*] and governesses on Vladimir Street, whither they often dragged me, resembled a true slave market. They trundled out in turn [all] those hoping to obtain a position. The fine ladies would sniff them up and down and demand references. The reference of a completely unknown lady, especially of a general's wife, was considered sufficiently weighty; but it sometimes happened that the creature led out for sale, having scrutinized the prospective purchaser, would snort in her face and turn on her heel. Then the negotiatrix in the trade of these bondmaids would run out, make her apologies, and talk about the decline of manners.[12]

Mandel'shtam further notes the existence of noncommercial (or at least less commercial) "employment offices" as well, often run by different religious organizations. For example, at the Catholic Church of St. Catherine on Nevskii Prospekt in St. Petersburg a "venerable little old man – Father Antoine Lagrange" – rendered a service to many in the upper strata of society. "Among the responsibilities of this Reverend lay that of recommending poor young French girls as nannies [*bonny*] for children in respectable homes. Fine ladies [*damy*] came to Father Lagrange for advice straightaway with their purchases in Gostinnyi Dvor [the huge market which still stands today]." The poet's eye for detail caught all the nuances of the situation. The "decrepit" old man would stroll out in his cassock and "joke affectionately with the children with unctuous Catholic jokes, seasoned with French wit." "A Father Lagrange recommendation was very highly valued," he observes.[13]

"Old-time residents of Moscow," wrote the satirist Nikolai Leskov in the 1890s, "will recall the British colony and the [so-called] 'Scott House' on Leont'evskii Lane." Such Muscovites "know that in this old house there was always a selection of English girls who occupied positions of *vospitatel'nitsy*. And these were always very moral individuals, sometimes very well-educated, and always strictly religious." From the Scott House, the girls went forth "to positions throughout Russia, primarily to those provinces where the four sons of 'old Scott' (Iakov Iakovlevich [i.e., James]) were employed managing the large pomeshchik *estates* of the Naryshkins and the Perovskiis." Word-of-mouth was of course still a major factor in hiring: "Neighbors would ask them [the Scott sons] to recommend *reliable* 'English girls' and would receive precisely what they asked for." The religious affiliation of the girls was apparently of little moment to their employers, an interesting detail given the great importance of Orthodoxy for most pre-emancipation nannies. In fact, says Leskov, "among them were both Methodists and Quakers. Neither the recommenders nor the hirers assumed any sort of difference between them."[14]

Vera Kharuzina's (1866-1931) beloved nanny Dunechka (Evdokiia Nikolaevna Antonova, née Zaitseva; d. 1926) came into service from a very different social institution. The ethnographer says that she "never found out who Dunechka was" at the time she came to them, and later was reticent to ask. "I know that she was brought up in an orphanage...[and] remanded to the home of our grandmother" as a young girl; "and here..she was taught to work – as tirelessly, as conscientiously, as grandmother and her sisters...worked." From the grandmother's home Dunechka then came to the Kharuzin household.[15] Also from an orphanage and then a foster home came Praskov'ia Nikifrovna, the nanny of Olga Chernov Andreev (b. 1903). "She had never known her parents... the government offered small rewards to peasant families who selected children from orphanages and brought them up in their own homes."[16]

Still another common method of hiring blossomed after 1861. Advertising for the services of a nanny, which had been used for decades with respect to finding foreign-born women, was now increasingly used for "homegrown" nannies. A primary example was the just-mentioned Praskov'ia Nikifrovna.[17] In January 1905, a typical issue of the 12-page daily *New Times* (Novoe vremia)

Nanny Pasha, Chernov Andreev family, ca. 1907

newspaper carried 7 pages of want ads (1,788 in total). The greatest demand for household help was for a maid-of-all-work – *odnaia prisluga* (287 ads in just the one issue). Next in order came ads for simple housemaids (*gornichnye* – 210), cooks (*kukharki* – 188), and then nannies (57). Just twelve families were looking for a *bonne*.[18]

The transition for those in service was marked by Prince Evgenii Trubetskoi (1863-1920), the philosopher, publicist, and social activist. Growing up immediately after the emancipation, he could sense the changes that were afoot within his own household. "New was the entire spirit, new was the whole content, but together with that, among the people surrounding us were many of the old types, who by their very contrast set off the new and gave it unusual relief."[19]

Increasingly after 1861, a new type of nanny emerged: the "homegrown" hired caretaker, the object of a spate of new educational initiatives. The new nannies were not always peasants, far from old, and no longer assumed to be illiterate. Even young girls from the villages might be able to read and write quite well, as Sergei Solov'ëv (1885-1942), the grandson of the historian, notes about his nanny Tania, from a village very near Moscow.[20]

By the time of the revolution representatives of the new breed of nanny could be found all over Russia. Now sometimes literate or soon to become so, young village girls thronged to the cities after 1917. Their dream was to find either domestic work of some kind (preferable to factory work) or another line of work which would permit them to better their social standing. Their aspirations were nothing like those of the classic nanny; determined not to remain in service for long, they used the nanny position as more a stepping stone for personal advancement than a permanent posting. A perfect example of this new kind of nanny is Elena Bonner's Niura, discussed again in the following chapter.

Advice Book for the Would-Be Nanny. A little book of instructions for how to be a nanny appeared in the year 1863. The purported author of *A Handbook for Nannies. Precepts on How to Tend and Bring up Small Children*[21] was "an old, experienced woman," writing "just for nannies" in a new age, but echoing complaints and charges that had been leveled against nannies for a century or more. Given the timing of its appearance, it is a social document of some significance, worthy of extended citation and discussion.

There are eerie echoes of the eighteenth-century satirist Vasilii Berezaiskii here, but without his tongue-in-cheek drollness.[22] The scolding tone is apparently meant to be taken in all seriousness. (It may be noted that this kind of excited discussion of the "servant problem" did not abate in the course of the next two decades. Nikolai Leskov alludes to the same phenomenon in his 1887 articles on "Domestic Help."[23]) One can see the legacy of just-ending serfdom in nearly everything the anonymous author of the handbook says. For example, the author makes no assumptions about the social milieu in which a nanny may find employment. "She" says that the conditions of service can vary greatly: the nanny may have to tend one child or several, may work for a rich family or for one of modest means, and may have help or have to do all the work for herself. The family's mother may be at home or out working; the family may be from the gentry or that of a tradesman. The rules of caretaking, of course, stay the same for all these varied situations. The health and character of the child are held equally dear in all different families, and they develop in accord with the same rules. (p. 11)

The anonymous author early points out that the qualities demanded of a nanny are not just a loving heart and good intentions; a nanny must have an irreproachable character and strong will to both be and do good. (pp. 7-9) From this point on, the book becomes almost completely hortatory, offering both practical advice every nanny should have and the reasoning behind this advice, and touches on not just the essentials but also the trivial, even minutiae. Everything from how to dress herself, to when to put children to bed, to how to bathe, dress, and carry them is grist for "her" advice. Sound medical advice is interspersed: never give the child medicine at one's own discretion, without advice of a doctor; always examine the child's stool, as its color is an indication of various ailments (this in the midst of instructions on toilet training); don't ever sleep with the child in the same bed – one bad turn could suffocate the babe. (pp. 13-16, 36, 53-54, 56, 133)

The booklet concludes with a series of moral platitudes and admonitions, reminding the potential nanny of her own frailties and bad habits which must be overcome. But the effort will be worth it, the aspiring caretaker is assured. "When [the mother] sees that you can do [the job], she'll respect and value you. The longer you live with them, the more they'll love you – you'll become a member of the family." But mostly, "you'll earn the full, pure and most sincere love of your dear charges; you'll become necessary to them on all occasions of their young lives. No satisfaction, no joy, no family holiday will go by without their recalling you and having you share in it. And if grief or a bad turn in life comes to you, your now grown-up charges will offer help, solace, and comfort, as they remember in their hearts the sacrifices, labors, and cares of their dear nanny." (pp. 135-36) In a fittingly trite ending, the author quotes from Pushkin's poem "To Nanny."[24]

Nannies in the "Practical New Gentry Family." Valentina Veremenko posits that in the two decades following emancipation, primarily under the impact of the "new winds" blowing and of material problems, three types of intrafamily relations emerged. Alongside the still dominant "old gentry family" there were the "new ideal gentry family" and the "new practical gentry family."[25] The gentry wife increasingly had to work to help support the family, either taking on the family's domestic chores, working for wages at home, or finding employment outside the home. "Husbands ever more frequently expressed to their wives the impossibility of maintaining several servants, as a rule proposing she limit herself to one female, who would simultaneously fulfill the functions of cook, maid, and nanny," says Veremenko. The "help wanted" ads in daily and weekly newspapers overwhelmingly sought such a servant who would work "alone"and for low pay. A "servant of quality" was expensive and always had a "specialty"; if hired as cook or nanny, she would perform that job only. But women who agreed to work "alone," cheaply, were generally not very bright and couldn't perform all the household chores simultaneously. In the upshot, only two viable solutions to the "servant problem" emerged: either a "specialist servant" – usually a cook or nanny – was hired or a woman already hired to work alone was made to expand her duties, with in each case the gentry wife taking up the undelegated duties.[26]

From the middle to the end of the century and beyond, ideas about parenting, childhood, and upbringing were evolving. There is some evidence that middle- and upper-class parents, if not more loving, were often more permissive with their children.[27] If so, this could not fail to influence nanny-child relations in such families. The use of corporal punishment by parents, usually the father, was a staple of eighteenth-century male autobiographies; it is mentioned noticeably less as the nineteenth century wore on. Perhaps for these reasons, among others, nannies in autobiographies and literature were portrayed as disciplinarians more frequently in the 1880s-90s than in earlier works. Toward 1900 memoirists seemed to feel less need to portray their nannies as all-forgiving and ever-sweet, the aura of Pushkin and Arina no doubt diminishing with time.

Education and Training Schools for Nannies

When servants were no longer bound peasants, their character took on even more importance than before, as can be seen in the *Knizhka nianek* summarized above. The servants' educational accomplishments were of greater concern as well. What was true of servants in general was especially true of the caretakers of children. Reflecting the anxieties that existed for centuries, post-reform social activists undertook new programs to improve the preparation of nannies on a much grander scale than in the past. While pre-reform peasant nannies were nearly all illiterate, they rarely seemed to be concerned with this deficiency. Post-reform peasant nannies apparently did care and strongly regretted this inability, as evidenced by the caretakers of Ariadna Tyrkova-Vil'iams, Ol'ga Berggol'ts, and many others.

In 1876 Fëdor Dostoevskii visited the Foundling Home (*Vospitatel'nyi dom*) in St. Petersburg. He was greatly impressed with what he saw, including "a group of adolescent girls of perhaps sixteen and seventeen, alumni of the Home, preparing themselves to be nannies and trying to round out their education: they already know something, they've read Turgenev, they have a clear gaze and speak with you very nicely."[28] But he was more impressed with the staff of the Home. The female supervisors "have such a tender air (not just put on for our visit) – such serene, kind, and intelligent faces. Some seem to have a real education."[29]

His implied criticism of the young girls preparing to become nannies seems to be that, though well-intentioned, they were not – like the supervisors – very well-educated. He goes on to muse, moreover, about when and how the current foundlings will learn that they are somehow below others in society, that they are merely tolerated in society from a sense of humanity but are not the equals of their betters. He concludes that they certainly will not pick up these feelings from their nannies and wet-nurses.

In 1877 the "Home of the Kazan Mother of God for the Training of Russian Nannies" (*Priiut vo imia Kazanskoi Materi dlia vospitaniia russkikh nianek*) opened in St. Petersburg. Its primary aim was to prepare girls for this profession while they were still young, malleable, and unspoiled. Only girls whose character showed that they were suitable to be nannies were supposed to be admitted. Those lacking the desired qualities as a nanny but might otherwise become useful servants were referred to the attached school for maids. "The institution [for nannies] was in principle reserved for girls of the Orthodox faith; the non-Orthodox could be accepted only at the price of converting...or with the express consent of the founder of the home and the priests who looked after the pupils."[30]

These future nannies were instructed in "reading, writing, the Gospels, [and] arithmetic"; they were expected as well to attain "a general understanding of history, geography, natural sciences, and geometry." In addition, "singing, drawing, embroidery [or needlepoint], knitting, cutting out clothes [from patterns], washing and ironing, gymnastics, food preparation and other subjects" were "in their learning plan." "After the conclusion of four grades the pupils whom the directors of the home judged qualified received a suitable certificate to work as 'nannies'."

The "St. Petersburg Fröbel Society" also undertook the training of qualified nannies. Unlike the Home of the Mother of Kazan, based on the Orthodox faith, the Society's training was based on the teachings of the German pedagog who lent his name to the group. With the view that an ideal mother would want not some kind of total replacement but rather an expert helper for her children, the Society concentrated on producing girls well-versed in "rational childrearing." They took public school graduates fourteen years and older and sought to place their own graduates mostly with middle-class families. By the turn of the century, the most apt graduates were receiving the comparatively high salary of 12-15 rubles a month. The school had as many as 37 pupils by 1911. In its statutes, the Society stressed the "blameless conduct" of the nannies it produced; the directors made it "their duty to supervise strictly the behavior and morals of the young girls, so far as was possible, and to make inquiries at admission without fail about the family from which the girl came."

In 1905, concern for extremely high infant mortality rates in Russia (the highest in Europe, along with Romania and parts of the Austro-Hungarian Empire) led to the establishment in Tsarskoe Selo of the School for Children's Medical Nurses and the Home for Children named for the Empress Alexandra Fedorovna. As part of the school's program, a course of studies was also inaugurated to produce up-to-date, well-educated children's nannies (*bonny*). The training was to last for two years and encompass both the theoretical and practical preparation of nannies.[31] This school was probably modeled in part on the famous Norland School for nannies in Britain.

According to Marcelline Hutton, by the end of the century, over a third of female domestic workers were literate; whether the rate for nannies was that high is debatable.[32] In 1904 a "simple" peasant woman of about 40 arrived from a northwest province to nanny young Prince Andrei Kurakin (b.1903); she was able to read and write (barely) – and to teach him to do the same.[33]

Changing Times – Changing Attitudes?

Various writers offer differing testimony as to whether the attitudes and behavior of and toward nannies changed after 1861. Most love to engage in the irresistible temptation to compare the present with "the good (or bad) old days." Inevitably, the sources are contradictory: was it better then, or now? Russian-born Lou Andreas-Salomé (1861-1937)[34] offers insight as to whether emancipation brought an evolution in attitudes of nannies toward their charges. She writes: "My nurse was deeply attached to me. ...Russian nannies have a reputation for total devotion to children which no biological mother can surpass (although their reputation for educating them is less impressive). Many descendants of former serfs were to be found among these nurses, and they still retained a sense of servitude, but now transformed, as it were, into a more pleasant and less literal form of attachment."[35]

The ultra-conservative publicist Iosif Kolyshko (1861-1938) offers a view different from most:

> Ask any healthy village woman, kindhearted and merry – do you want to be a nanny, or a dishwasher? She will choose the latter, even if you add on another 3 rubles a month for nannying and promise there'll be absolutely nothing to do except look after the children.
>
> In every woman who has not lost the hope and faith in her own maternity, there is hidden a kind of fear of being responsible for the children of someone else and an understandable miserliness over using up her store of love, strength, and inspiration which can be needed for her own [children].[36]

Confusingly, in the transition of the 1860s and 1870s at least, pre-emancipation serf nannies (now either salaried or not) mingled with nannies never enserfed – in homes where most of the servants were now becoming fully salaried. Prince Dmitrii Obolenskii (1822-1881), comparing his nanny of the 1820s to caretakers he observed in the 1870s, says "we had a nanny, Sekletiniia Vasil'evna, a most kind woman, who belonged to that type of Russian nannies *who are already disappearing*, leaving in their stead a kind of half-educated madams with pretenses and inordinate caprices."[37] The radical-turned-scientist Nikolai Morozov (1854-1946) would concur. In a letter of 20-27 August 1900, he wrote to his mother: "In our time, especially in the cities, there are no longer to be found such nannies as can occupy the awakening imagination of children with hundreds of different fairy tales, and meanwhile the imagination demands sustenance." Writing in the late 1930s about the upbringing of his close friend Sergei Diagilev in the 1870s, Serge Lifar claims that the latter's nanny, Avdot'ia Adrianovna – Dunia – "represented a type of nurse which has now vanished entirely."[38]

The feeling of all three that such old-style nannies were completely disappearing is misplaced. In a rather too sweeping indictment, Nikolai Leskov – who could be very dyspeptic in observing his fellow humans – would write in 1887: "If you know the olden days and want to speak the truth, then the morals of Russian servants were always very bad. Indeed, in the old days they were even much worse than today." Depite "devoted people of olden days" – among nannies, housekeepers, and valets, they were "exceptional or, at least, rather rare phenomena."[39]

As for nannies' personal qualities, *plus ça change*...Perusing a few selected autobiographies might convince the casual reader that most nannies at the turn of the century remained almost saintly in their demeanor and behavior,[40] as well as devoted and loving caretakers.[41] Still, Vsevolod Rozhdestvennskii (1895-1977) says his peasant nanny Lizaveta Kaliazina had "nothing noteworthy about her – neither in appearance nor in spiritual qualities";[42] the Soviet writer Iurii Libedinskii (1898-1959) wondered if his nanny was "deeply religious."[43] Yet Orthodoxy was as important for many nannies as before 1861.[44] (There are strong grounds for believing that religiosity remained a constant in nannies even after Great

Post-Emancipation and Post-1917 Nannies 163

Leon Bakst, *Portrait of Sergei Diagilev* (1906) oil on canvas. Nanny Dunia in background

October. Of course, the concept had a much different connotation for Soviet-era writers than for pre-revolutionary ones.)

The moral quality of nannies may or may not have deteriorated after emancipation. As noted, it appears from some memoir evidence that women who'd never been serfs physically punished their charges more than pre-1861 nannies. There is little doubt, moreover, that character flaws and moral weaknesses in nannies are mentioned more frequently in autobiographies of those born after 1861 than before; the "Pushkin effect" might have begun to wane, or stark reality might have become more intrusive. In any case, the mention of gossip, eavesdropping, snooping, nagging, sanctimonious hypocrisy, lack of fairness, and other failings multiply by the end of the nineteenth century. Vadim Andreev's (1903-1976) nanny Pasha was "sly, deceitful, and malicious."[45] Nannies remained both serious and earnest,[46] but also – perhaps increasingly – jolly and humorous.[47] There may have been more use of alcohol among nannies after 1861 than before, if the number of mentions in memoirs counts.[48] Complaints about nannies remain remarkably constant over the course of centuries, as previously noted: employers complained of their carelessness and neglect, disobedience to what was expected or ordered, and occasional placing of their own interests above the child's.[49]

The more or less pious, docile, humble, and conservative (politically and socially) nanny of pre-emancipation days – the classic peasant nanny – had not disappeared by the turn of the century, in reality or in people's thinking. But she was evolving, along with society's concepts of gender, family, and politics. Would she soon become just one more disgruntled, underpaid and underappreciated proletarian?

Olga Andreev relates that in the early 1900s all her father Viktor's Socialist Revolutionary (SR) friends loved and trusted her nanny Pasha. "Sometimes they asked her to hide compromising papers such as the minutes of a meeting or some illegal pamphlet. Nyanya would slip these behind her icon case." Andreev alludes in her book to a photo from the family's Paris exile in 1908-09 of four "revolutionary nannies" – including those of the Kamenevs, Steklovs, and Avksentevs– "each holding her small charge in front of her."[50]

Angela Rustemeyer has found evidence of the involvement of nannies in the "First Russian Revolution." On 7 November 1905, many servants, including young housemaids, ladies' maids, and even old nannies, marched and demonstrated in St. Petersburg in front of city employment offices. They were demanding, among other things, that the price (apparently 25 percent of their first month's wages) the bureaus charged to find them positions be lowered.[51]

The Problem of Prostitution

In the relatively well-ordered society that existed under serfdom, the problem of sex and the nanny in gentry homes was largely confined to the (occasionally? more frequent?) predatory master of the house, who claimed the *droit de seigneur* with many of his servants. Perhaps unsurprisingly, there is very little evidence that the masters indulged or attempted to indulge their passions with their children's nannies. After emancipation and with the rise of the freely employed nanny, the situation changed considerably. Both Andrei Belyi, in his quasi-autobiographical novel *Kotik Letaev* (1915-16), and Osip Mandel'shtam in *The Noise of Time* (1925) hint at sexual inclinations and the sexuality of their nannies.

In pre-revolutionary Russia gaining a "yellow ticket" (*zheltyi bilet* – carried by prostitutes in place of a regular passport) was often a voluntary act; prostitution was legal. The profession was regulated by the police, and the alternative passport carried important medical information about the holder. Angela Rustemeyer devotes many pages in her study of household servants from 1861-1917 to the subject of prostitution and how nannies became, willy-nilly, involved in the "oldest profession." As early as 1871, in a study about the rise of syphilis in the capitals, a certain M. Kuznetsov wrote: "Maids, *nannies*, cooks, and female servants as a whole...have prostituted themselves without losing their jobs, for the cheapest of prices, and being very little choosy for what the future would bring; cheap material for a dress, a pair of shoes, a bit of cloth or a similar trifle suffices with the female servant to enter into a bad relationship for many months or longer..."[52]

The girls were not always or not only to blame. They were often young, fresh from the countryside, and especially vulnerable. If they had no acquaintances in town, were the least bit friendly to passers by on the street, or simply inquired about service employment in a neighborhood, they might become a target of seduction. But not all were innocent. They could be "in the labor market" and recruited by pimps. "The history of the prostitute Stepanova," Rustemeyer informs us, "began with the fourteen-year-old's being offered – after her arrival at Nikol'skaia Square in Petersburg from a village in the province of Novgorod – a position as nanny."[53] Nothing said here should imply that a disproportionate share of nannies and maids prostituted themselves. Yet the sex trade can be seen as a small but not insignificant part of "the servant problem."

1917: The Watershed that Wasn't?

I originally intended to end this book with the events of 1917. I had thought that the nanny as an institution had been predicated almost entirely on another social institution – the nobility as a class – which passed from the scene after Great October (only to reappear in the reborn Russia of the 1990s). Were that indeed the case, one could expect nannies to pretty much disappear also. This was actually what happened with the *diad'ka*.[54] But as with much else in Russian history, the year 1917 turned out to be not as significant a disconnect for nannies as I had imagined.

Although at first blush society seemed to change dramatically within a reasonably short span of time, at closer look there were obvious continuities as well. Some changes took longer to play out than others. Definitive alteration was often postponed until the end of the 1920s or even the late 1930s, when Stalin was more firmly in charge, and top-down, mandated change was the rule. For many years after the revolutions of 1917 a nanny remained a fixture in Russian homes, but – due to exigencies – among fewer families than before.[55] In fact, some of the most interesting history of the Russian nanny occurs after the October Revolution. Many memorable nannies either remain on the scene or appear in a new light in the tumultuous days that followed the overthrow of the Romanovs. Did the stereotype of the "classic nanny" change after the revolution? Some would say that the idealized image of the nanny remained mostly or exclusively with the gentry emigration. Not so. Women that became nannies after 1917 were like their sisters of the later nineteenth century in most ways – social origin, motivation, and certainly function. Although literate, the Bruzhes family caretaker of the late teens and 1920s was otherwise of a piece with her pre-emancipation sisters.

> In our house there lived a nanny. She was precisely what a nanny should be. She raised my female, then my male cousin...looked after me, and then brought up my brother Iura. And after that she nannied the daughter of that same female cousin. And she died in their family as kin. The nanny's name was Evdokiia – nanny Dunia Karaseva....At one time she had had a fiancé, a soldier. He was killed in the first world war. And nanny remained an old maid. We children, whom she reared, were her "personal life."[56]

Instead of her own room, however, nanny Dunia had to sleep in a small space behind the kitchen with little Iura, in a communal apartment holding three families. She could not be broken of her habit of addressing her employers as "master" or "lord" (*barin*), "mistress" (*barynia*), and "young mistress" (*baryshnia*). She had a "full voice" in all family matters, and chided young Alla for wanting to become an artist – well-bred girls did not get their hands all "dirty" with paint.

If I had to suggest one aspect of the nanny's life that changed after 1917 – though perhaps for far from every one – it might be that the social and existential gulfs which separated most nannies from their masters and then employers in the past were diminished in two important ways after the revolutions. First, "class" differences were greatly reduced in many cases; in the 1920s, gentry and upper-middle-class families, whether merchant or intelligentsia, resembled lower-class families much more than they had in the decades before 1917. Second, and perhaps more meaningful, the life experiences of employer and nanny had probably become more similar after 1917 than ever before. Deprivation, hunger, need, physical pain and suffering, uncertainty, and submission to arbitrary or unexpected harassment from above were phenomena all too common for peasant women in the past. They became better known to gentry and bourgeois women in the Soviet period.

Getting Through the Revolution: the Nanny as Anchor of Salvation. Some noble families were actually "saved" by the nanny – or other former servants – during the upheavals of 1917-1920. In a few cases, this involved hiding the targets of popular anger from those seeking to harm them.[57] More often it was the nanny's connections with her home village and its food supply that was paramount. Marina Tsvetaeva's case is a classic example: in 1918-19 one or both of her daughters had to be sent from Moscow to live with their former nanny Nadia in the village to escape hunger and disease.[58] The decision to assist the former masters could not have been an easy one for some nannies, given the prejudices of the times. Elena Skriabina (1906-1996) relates in her memoirs how in 1925 her husband decided to send her and her mother back to their old family estate in the village "where my nanny was living in her own home." When they arrived:

> Nanny recounted to us what persecution she had been submitted to in the first years after the revolution because she had been a servant of the *pomeshchiki* and allegedly hiding things belonging to us which they were in vain seeking from her. Nanny had taken nothing from us for safekeeping, but they didn't believe this and threw her in prison, where she had to serve two months. Her nephew, a prominent communist, who had returned from the front, interceded for her and got her out of jail. In the horrible conditions prevailing in those days in houses of detention, she...had gotten typhus and barely survived it. During these years she had lost her aged father and was living with her mother, engaged in simple farming and a rather large fruit orchard. People put nanny in the ranks of well-to-do peasants, because she had a cow, a calf, two piglets and some chickens. Vasia, her nephew, was her faithful and constant defender, and now she was living quite at ease [*spokoino*]; she was not even afraid to invite us [to live with her] for the summer.[59]

Besides harboring and helping feed the *"byvshie"* (literally, "the former ones" or "have-beens," a term applied mostly to the tsarist nobility after October), nannies could save their former charges in other ways. Sophia Wacznadze (b. 1908) was twice rescued by her former caretakers, a Russian nanny and a British governess.[60] Count Nikolai Tolstoi-Miloslavskii (b. 1935) similarly recounts how he owes his existence to his father's British nanny, Lucy Stark. She saved his father Dmitrii, smuggling him out to England on her passport as her own illegitimate son, in 1920.[61] Prince Andrei Kurakin (b. 1903) devotes many pages in his memoirs to describing how his beloved nanny acted as guardian angel for him and his mother in 1919-20. She brought him food in prison, did her utmost to get them released from arrest, and in general stood by them steadfastly until they left the country.[62] Similarly, Baron Mikhail Budberg (b. ca. 1906) was aided by his nanny and especially her son, who became an important commissar in Petrograd, until he could finally flee the country in the early 1920s.[63]

The First Decade: What Becomes of the Family and Servants?

In the early post-revolution days, especially once the civil war ground to an end, and through much of the 1920s, a kind of dualistic thinking gripped many Russians. Radical utopianism combined with the strongest kind of anti-bourgeois (not to mention anti-noble) sentiment within the Bolshevik party ranks and some strata of society. The first strand of thinking was almost perfectly alien to Lenin's mentality (despite his tactical 1917 pamphlet *State and Revolution*), but the second strand mirrored a hallmark of his thought. In fact, it is the consistent element that comes as close to defining Leninism as any other – his deep-seated suspicion and resentment of his own social stratum – the lower nobility and professional classes. Indeed, Lenin appears to have truly despised the entire middle class, for both personal and ideological reasons. He had very much taken to heart the theoretical underpinnings of the 1898 Russian Social Democratic Labor Party (RSDLP) program, penned largely by Pëtr Struve. It reinforced his own desire to avoid any reason for aligning with the bourgeoisie. Almost inevitably, two prime targets of the new regime became the "bourgeois" family and most forms of the master-servant relationship.[64]

The Family and Childcare. In the best of all possible communist worlds, to paraphrase Richard Pipes, the more utopian Soviet leaders and educators would have liked, after October 1917, to abolish the institution of the family. They would have the (would-be proletarian) state take charge of children from the day they were born, "removing them from their parents and placing them in communal nurseries. This was partly to free women for productive work[65] but also and mainly for purposes of conditioning and indoctrination." Private, individual childcare provided by a family nanny would have been consigned to the "dustbin of history."

> The wife of Zinov'ev, Zlata Lilina, an official of the Commissariat of Enlightenment, insisted that it was best for children to be removed from their homes: "Is not parental love to a large extent love harmful to the child?...The [bourgeois] family is individualistic and egoistic and the child raised by it is, for the most part, antisocial, filled with egoistic strivings...Raising children is not the private task of parents, but the task of society."[66]

She was not alone; other radical spokespersons, all arguing essentially that childrearing should and would be taken over by the state – so as to free up the men and women who otherwise would be saddled with the chore – included Inessa Armand, Pëtr Stuchka, Evgenii Preobrazhenskii, and especially Aleksandra Kollontai.[67] In hindsight, these ideas reflect what Isaiah Berlin has called "the mixture of utopian faith and brutal disregard for civilized morality" that characterized so many early Bolshevik policies.[68]

By October 1918, there was a new law on marriage, the family and guardianship which took a few tentative steps toward greater public involvement in the care of children. A key provision, envisioning the demise of the family, was a prohibition against adoption. As one historian says, "the Bolsheviks attached little importance to the powerful emotional bonds between parents and their children. They assumed that most of the necessary care for children, even infants, could be relegated to paid, public employees."[69]

This faction of the party and these attitudes, however, were not in the majority. The government, unsurprisingly, was forced to retreat in its efforts to socialize childrearing. From the world and civil wars, and the 1921 famine, thousands and thousands of homeless children – the *besprizornye* or *besprizorniki* – roamed the countryside in the early 1920s. A 1922 estimate put as many as 7.5 million children as dying and starving. State homes for children were under-resourced and overflowing throughout the decade of the 1920s.[70] Childcare was such a problem that Soviet novelists began taking up the theme; examples are Kollontai's *Vasilisa Malygina* and Fëdor Gladkov's *Cement*.[71] A 1926 decree reversed the 1918 taboo on adoption – peasant families in particular were urged to adopt children from state institutions; a new statute on marriage, family and guardianship became law in January 1927. It could not, of course, resolve all the conflicts between the needs of real life and the more libertarian-utopian Bolshevik views. But the family was "resurrected" to look after children at "almost no cost to the state."

In the end, it was not ideology that most affected post-revolutionary childcare. It was something more basic – and more "Marxian": economics. Public, state-run childcare facilities – though promised by Soviet labor legislation – simply lacked resources and funding. Russia had fewer than 30 public nurseries in 1917, just 500 by 1923. But more than half the nation's daycare centers and homes for single mothers closed their doors between just 1922 and 1923, and their numbers diminished nearly as rapidly in the next two years. For most working women, therefore, social (public) care of their children was not an option. But, receiving low wages, they had no money for hired caretakers. The most common solution, of course, was to rely on family members for help. Both older members – like grandmothers – and younger girls engaged in this sort of "kin care." Elena Dolgikh (née Grebenkina; 1910-after 1998) is one of countless examples of the latter; she became the nanny of her aunt's newborn baby in the mid-1920s.[72]

Another partial solution to the lack of childcare was unusual. Due to the acute shortage of kindergartens around 1930, four-and-a-half-year-old Dmitrii Priemskii was sent off to a "German group, as they were called in those days." There had always been a large number of Germans in the capital; although assimilated, they maintained their native tongue and many of their traditional ways. Some of these Germans ran the equivalent of kindergartens in their homes after the 1917 revolutions; parents paid them a small sum to mind their children. Priemskii's group, with some half dozen children of both sexes, was led by three sisters. The youngsters were able to pick up a smattering of German rather quickly.[73]

Servants, Including Nannies. 1917 provided a jolt to most better-off families that few recovered from fully. A standard of living that had previously been enviable suddenly became pitiable. It was a given that the "exploitation of man by man," as practiced in bourgeois (read tsarist) society, was anathema. What then should happen to the master-servant relationship? The new Soviet regime had to look with suspicion on the use of servants; but was there any justification for their continued employment? Yes. Elites are elites, no matter how revolutionary, and their time is valuable, not to be wasted on nonproductive (or at least less productive) labor. Besides, the new Bolshevik leaders could not be accused of exploitation; they were in the vanguard of the formerly exploited. So they almost immediately gave in to the use of "privileges."[74] Ekaterina Katukova (b. 1913) has perhaps put it better than anyone:

> Privilege is a preferential right to some kind of advantage. [*Privilegiia – eto preimushchestvennoe pravo no razlichnogo roda l'goty.*]
> The Great October Revolution liquidated all privileged estates [*sosloviia*]. The estates were liquidated, but the preferential right to advantages remained, but only for the elect [*dlia izbrannykh*].[75]

Most of the top communist party officials, including Stalin and Zinov'ev (he with the otherwise radical wife), took on servants.[76] Perhaps an even better example was the family of Elena Bonner (b. 1923), later married to the Soviet Union's most famous dissident, Andrei Sakharov. Bonner's stepfather was Gevork Alikhanov, a fairly prominent party figure in the 1920s and early 30s. Briefly "exiled" to Chita between 1924 and 1926 because of a rift with the Leningrad party boss Zinov'ev, the family had a cook and nanny there. And when Kirov took over Leningrad in 1926 and the family returned, geographically and politically, they had no trouble finding servants – and a new nanny for little Elena – in that city.[77] In fact, her family was never without a whole series of nannies and nanny-*domrabotnitsy* (domestic workers). Seeing so many top party officials with servants, in fact, was one of the first "disturbing" elements of the new regime that alienated Emma Goldman.[78]

Property distinctions were blurred. Public servants were entitled to certain amenities, deemed necessary for the public good. "Public" cars and domiciles – which were of course private in all but name (a bit like "public" schools in modern Britain) – were at the disposal of many; so were vacation spots, dachas, and food (at least the access to it). Servants were a slightly less visible perk that were almost a necessity for the hardest working members of society. But in place of the vile, bourgeois *exploitation* of man by man, there was now the benign, comradely *employment* of man by man. Somewhat strangely but refreshingly, the terminology did not immediately change just to make the practice more acceptable from a Marxian point of view.

In later years, the favored term for a household servant, including nannies, was "*domrabotnitsa*."[79] But in the city censuses of the 1920s, the old designations still appear. Thus, the Leningrad census of 15 March 1923 listed the main groups of occupations as workers, servants [*prisluga*], clerks [*sluzhashchie*], army and navy personnel, people of "free professions," owners or managers [*khoziaeva*], those helping members of a family, and "other" (including "*rentiers*" [!], beggars, prostitutes, and so on).[80] Among self-employed females (no males were so designated), there were a total of 500 women working as nannies and wet-nurses – nearly two-thirds in the age brackets older than 50 and younger than 20. An additional 7 males and 5 females were not working independently as child caretakers.[81] The total number of domestic servants – the occupational category which presumably included both nannies and wet-nurses – in Leningrad rose from 3,057 in 1923 to 25,312 in 1926, and in Moscow from 14,335 to 42,217.[82] In the help-wanted ads which ran regularly in *Woman Peasant and Worker* (*Krestianka i rabotnitsa*) in the late 1920s, would-be employers always used the familiar term "nanny" (*niania* or *nian'ka*). In the course of the 1930s, a staff of domestic workers would become known as "service personnel," "to avoid the old bourgeois word 'servants'."[83]

Whereas in the 1930s, as we shall see, employers had something to fear from their employees, in the 1920s the pattern was much the reverse: employees often felt the kind of abuse that serfs endured. One authority on the subject in this period, Rebecca Spagnolo, has studied the archives of three major unions that included domestic workers and finds that employers often did all they could to "sabotage" their employees – to keep them out of unions, to avoid "costly wage books, employment contracts, quotas for work clothes, fixed wage scales, mandatory time off, and paid holidays." She adds that "The employer's most benign tactic was simply to ignore the new protective regulations in the hope that the domestic would remain blissfully unaware." Or they might deceive the worker about putting in union applications that then were "conveniently lost" or "rejected." Or employers might keep their domestics so busy they had no time to attend union meetings. They might also misinform the domestic about what would happen to her if she tried to assert her rights. Finally, if all else failed to keep workers "in line," "threats of summary dismissal and even violence" were sometimes used.[84]

Despite the undoubted continuity in the employment of domestics, some findings of Catriona Kelly about hired help seem to show a different picture. If hypocrisy is indeed an homage vice pays to virtue – as La Rochefoucauld would have it – then the Bolsheviks were merely placing a pretty fig leaf over their private practices. As Kelly says: "As for domestic service, that might as well never have existed so far as Soviet advice literature was concerned. There were no articles in *Sovetskaya zhenshchina* advising professional women on how to cope with uppity *domrabotnitsy*, or even evoking the indebtedness of prominent scientists to their trusty nannies (rather, prominent professional women always emphasized that they were also exemplary housewives). Still less were there pamphlets telling peasant women how to become exemplary *domrabotnitsy*."[85]

The communist party attempted in this and many other ways to mask the deferral of socialism in NEP and later the "great retreat" (N. Timasheff's provocative catch-phrase) of the 1930s.[86] Yet Kelly may be off the mark when she writes that "The readers of *Krest'yanka* and *Rabotnitsa* were never encouraged to consider domestic service as a career possibility: the only work that was assigned value in mass-market magazines of this kind was work for public institutions."[87] In fact, the editorial board may never have promoted such service directly, but, as noted, they consciously accepted help-wanted ads for nannies and similar domestics. Meantime, the state was doing its best to provide more help for families. A new legal code on marriage, the family and guardianship in 1926-27 had greatly increased the number of divorces in the country; women were entering the work force in much greater numbers from at least the mid-20s. After a diminution till the mid-1920s, there was a huge increase in state childcare facilities by the late 20s: twenty-fold between 1928 and 1934 – from 257,000 to 5,143,400; daycare centers increased twelvefold – from 2,132 in 1927-28 to 25,700 in 1934-35.[88]

Yet, as Orlando Figes notes: "Nannies were employed by many urban families, especially in households where both parents worked. There was an almost limitless supply of nannies from the countryside, particularly after 1928, when millions of peasants fled into the cities to escape collectivization, and they brought with them the customs and beliefs of the peasantry."[89] In families where the wife worked, which was true of many Party families, nannies became almost a necessity, says Figes. "Ironically the most senior Bolsheviks tended to employ the most expensive nannies, who generally held reactionary opinions." Indeed, in these families, like Stalin's own, a nanny might even embody values quite contrary to those of the household head. "In 1925," writes Fruma Treivas (1905-after 1993), "I began to work at the publishing house of *Molodaia Gvardiia*...and my child was with a nanny."[90] Treivas's husband was then arrested, sent away to prison, but by 1928 returned to Moscow and a high post. (She herself worked at *Pionerskaia pravda*.) In 1932, despite the earlier blotch on his record, "We enjoyed, as people say now, privileges," including a domestic worker/nanny.[91]

Like Treivas, the parents of the future nuclear engineer and Soviet State Laureate Dmitrii Priemskii (b. 1927) found a private nanny for their boy in these years. But unlike so many pre-revolutionary memoirists, Priemskii had no sentimental effusions in mind when he noted this fact: "As for my *vospitanie* as a person, one can say with assurance that no one particularly occupied theirself with me. The first couple of years nanny Niusha, as I called her, looked after me, but from the age of 10, mother...and I would set off for school simultaneously, and thereafter I was left on my own, often until late at night."[92] The village-born partisan Inessa Konstantinova (1924-1944), presumably a peasant and thus something of an anomaly, notes in her diary that she was "spoiled by a nanny."[93]

Fashions change, as do governments, and a positive aspect of "life with nanny" in earlier centuries became less desirable for some parents in the twentieth. In the mid-1920s, one housewife employing a nanny lodged a complaint with the domestic workers union. Her nanny took her child to church, despite her explicit prohibition. "I made it a condition [in the hiring contract] that the nanny never go to church with the child. But she deceived me for an entire year. Later, her own friends told me that she would go to mass and to vespers with my little girl and would look in on funerals... Instead of running around in the fresh air, in the sun, my child stood for hours in the stuffiness and the damp."[94]

One mildly unexpected source of nannies came with the crackdown on religion of the 1920s and the closing of many monasteries and convents (nunneries). Residents of these second religious institutions included women from both the nobility and the lower classes; sometimes the peasant women were servants who went on serving their mistresses when the noblewoman entered the convent. Some of these convent residents were former nannies, as we saw in Chapter 4. Even some nuns without previous experience as nannies took up the calling. Two beneficiaries of these events were Elena Bonner, whose mother hired a former nun as housekeeper/caretaker, and Irina Golitsyna. The latter writes that, soon after the birth of her daughter in early 1927, her husband Nicky's "old nanny came to live with us – the convent where she lived with his aunt [Valentina], the Mother Superior, had been closed down by the Bolsheviks and robbed. The nuns had been exiled to South Russia and Nanny had been told to leave Moscow. It was a joy and a relief to have her with us; a real nanny, who could be called part of the family, as she had been with Nicky's family since her early youth."[95]

The Changing Standards of the 1930s and 1940s

Material conditions in the 1930s were hardly ideal for the vast majority of Soviet citizens. Even ignoring the horrors of the countryside, where a virtual genocide (regime-induced famine and "liquidization of the kulaks as a class") claimed the lives of millions, life was difficult. But that was not the worst of it. As Andrei Sakharov (1921-1989) puts it: "I grew up in an era marked by tragedy, cruelty, and terror, but it was more complicated than that. Many elements interacted to produce an extraordinary atmosphere," he writes, "the persisting revolutionary élan; hope for the future; fanaticism; all-pervasive propaganda; enormous social and psychological changes; a mass exodus of people from the countryside; and, of course, the hunger, malice, envy, fear, ignorance, and demoralization brought about by the seemingly endless war, the brutality, murder, and violence. It was in these circumstances that there arose what official Soviet jargon euphemistically terms the 'cult of personality'."[96]

Lives and families were destroyed; lives and families went on. The Jewish poet Evgenii Rein (b. 1935) gained a nanny thanks to the losses she suffered.

> ...I was brought up by my nanny, a plain peasant woman of great mind, who was from the same village as Pushkin's famous nanny Arina, near St. Petersburg. Her fate was really remarkable. During the NEP, many peasants began to prosper. The nanny's family kept a village pub, if I'm not mistaken. They had horses and cows, hired workers. But in 1929 they were dispossessed as kulaks. Her husband was sent to a forced labor camp, but she managed to flee to Leningrad and became a domestic servant at my parents' flat long before my birth.[97]

After more than a few trials during World War II – and the loss of her husband and two of three children, to prison, the camps, and death – the nanny returned to Rein's family and stayed with them until her death. He buried her. Rein was somehow surprised by what she told him of the horrors perpetrated on her family:

> "What is amazing, she had a very bright mind and wonderful intuition. I was 10 when she told me about Stalin and since then I have added nothing more to my knowledge about him."

"Truly amazing... And what did she tell you?"
"She said he was a scoundrel who ruined the peasants, a murderer and paranoiac."[98]

In 1932 the Soviet government proposed suspending bread and sugar rations of unemployed housewives, a measure designed primarily to get them to move into industrial production jobs. This was a "cruel" step, according to Marcelline Hutton, given the lack of child care facilities at the time. In these years there were only urban kindergarten spaces for about a half million children, but there were 4-5 million working women. "With the number of nannies declining from 500,000 in 1929 to 200,000 in 1935, child care remained inadequate."[99] The satirist Mikhail Zoshchenko confirms the dearth of nannies in a very funny tale of 1931.[100] Still, if you were a famous writer with comparatively large earnings, life was rather good; you would have as many servants in the home as family members – including a nanny and cook.[101]

In the course of the 1930s things seem to have changed somewhat: "the sharp decline among Russian and European servants from 1890 to 1925 leveled off in the 1930s." In the USSR there were 475,000 women in domestic service in the 1920s but more than 511,000 in the 1930s, Hutton shows in a table. However, her sources reveal some potential problems with her figures. The 1937 Soviet census gives a figure of 511,853 for *domrabotnitsy*; but the all-union census of 1939 "hid domestic servants by listing them with other categories." By the late 1930s, however, domestic service declined again, and women working outside the home had even less support for childcare duties and other family needs. One economist in 1939 estimated the number of domestic workers at just 170,000.[102] "Whereas trade unions encouraged factories to provide child care for working women," says Hutton, "government institutions, which also employed large numbers of professional women, balked at doing so. Consequently, many career women continued hiring nannies. As domestic service declined in the late 1930s, career women enjoyed even less support with family responsibilities."

In June 1936 yet another new law on marriage and the family, plus a decree outlawing abortion, aimed at strengthening the

Soviet family. In it "the most revolutionary provisions of the 1918 and 1926 Codes were all eradicated." It prescribed an increase in the number of childcare institutions and similar maternal support. Unrestrained sexual license had been found wanting, as Richard Pipes notes, because it was acceptable neither to most young people nor to the authorities. Traditional values prevailed.[103] Nannies continued to be in high demand, especially among career women, high Party families, and the intelligentsia. Valentina Bogdan (b. ca. 1910?) graduated from college in the early 1930s and moved to Rostov with her husband Sergei, who took up a teaching post at a local university. She was eager to begin a career in research, but once she started working, the family finances got tighter and their child needed a caretaker.[104] She provides a detailed description of the process of hiring a nanny in this period, one full of nuances and revelations. (p. 394) "On Sunday night I went to the railway station to meet [my daughter] Natasha and her nanny, Davydovna."

> The next day I went to the local trade union office to register the nanny. They asked me a lot of questions to determine whether I really needed her services. Then Davydovna and I were asked to sign a contract, which listed our mutual obligations. I was responsible for paying her salary (thirty rubles a month), providing her with housing and work clothes (one dress and one pair of shoes a year), giving her one day a week off, allowing her to attend trade union meetings, and guaranteeing her a two-week paid vacation every year, at my convenience. Her responsibilities included taking care of my child and cleaning the apartment. In fact, she did less than that. She was very slow, and soon the apartment got so dirty that I was forced to hire extra help to do the big weekly cleaning. (p. 395)

It is remarkable how similar the situation in the 1930s was to that with the nobility and foreign governors-*diad'ki* in the eighteenth century, and how different from that of the classic nannies of the nineteenth century in the nanny's being literate. (p. 415) But the really fascinating aspect of Bogdan's story is what it says about the atomization and politicization of society during high Stalinism at the time the Terror is being launched:

Our nanny Davydovna loved all kinds of meetings and rallies, and, according to our contract, I had to let her attend them all. Her meetings took place in the evening, and she usually found out about them from our janitor, who belonged to the same union.

One day she returned from her meeting very excited and immediately told me everything that had been said there. I did not particularly encourage talk about these meetings – I had had enough of my own – but the following words made me sit up and pay attention:

"Today we had an especially important meeting. You know how many enemies of the people they've been discovering recently, so at today's meeting they told us how we maids and nannies could help the Soviet state fight its enemies." (p. 406)

A dialog ensues about how the servants can "see and hear things that others can't"(for "others" read GPU). The nanny notes that some people have friends over and close their doors to make sure their maids can't hear them, which is very suspicious. Those are the kinds of situations the nannies and other servants have now been instructed to pay close attention to – to listen for names and other useful information. (p. 406)

"But, Davydovna, some people might want to talk about personal things, or just simply gossip, and not want strangers to hear. Who would want a maid who eavesdrops? That would be terrible!"

"I didn't mean eavesdropping all the time; only when the talk was about politics. And besides, it's not 'eavesdropping,' it's just paying attention." (p. 407)

Indeed, the only "guidance" aimed at *domrabotnitsy* in etiquette manuals after 1930, confirms Catriona Kelly, was pep-talks encouraging them to report subversive activities on the part of their employers. By this time, domestic service was mentioned only in a negative context, for example, in the sardonic cartoons published in *Krokodil*.[105]

Davydovna tells Bogdan the story of a particularly "useful" maid who overheard talk of Trotsky, retrieved some half-burned incriminating letters, ratted on her employers, and received in reward their large apartment. When Bogdan remonstrates that they burn letters in their family too, the nanny tells her she knows they're loyal, and besides, she herself burns their letters. Davydovna could spy on them if she wanted to, "only of course I wouldn't do such a thing." (p. 407)

Bogdan's husband is not in the least surprised at this turn of events: "'Did you really doubt that they would turn such people as Davydovna into spies? It's not even called spying any more; it's "proletarian vigilance." I'm sure she feels proud that the state is asking her for help.' 'But she is a mature woman and should know what it means.' 'A lot of people do, but she used to be married to a policeman, so she doesn't find it strange. What is strange is that they were not warned not to say anything about it to their employers.' 'Perhaps they were, but in her mind we are still "one of us"'." (pp. 407-408)

The increasingly strict conformism of the 1930s caught up with Bogdan also. Her factory employers pestered her to send her daughter Natasha to the plant's kindergarten; she's told it doesn't "look good" that she, an *intelligent*, won't send her child to the place where the blue-collar workers send theirs – the workers "may think that our educated people don't trust our kindergarten." Her bosses also appeal to her sense of public duty: engineers like her will be more demanding than the workers about education and so raise the level of instruction at the factory kindergarten. She keeps demurring until she realizes they're so insistent not just for the reasons given: "Not trusting the parents, the party wanted to take over the raising of children as early as possible." They finally yield and put Natasha in the *iasli*, and it is potentially better for them. (pp. 414-415)

> Davydovna had probably encouraged [Natasha to read] because it must have been more convenient for her to have the child sitting in an armchair reading, but for Natasha it was a little early to spend hours bent over a book. Finally, there was one more consideration in favor of the kindergarten: we would no longer need a live-in nanny. Ever

since Davydovna told me that she had been asked to spy on us and had found nothing strange about it, I was afraid to have her around the house. If I did not need a permanent nanny, I could hire a more reliable person to do the cleaning – this time all of it...

Davydovna realized her services were no longer needed, and she came to me before I could work up the courage to talk to her. It was not easy for me to let Davydovna go: during the five years she had spent with us, she had become very attached to the child. (p. 415)

Bogdan's friend Tania lived in Leningrad with her husband, both also engineers. When they moved into a new apartment shortly before World War II, after a long wait, Bogdan asked her

"Did you hire a nanny for [their son] Yura?"
"No, nannies are very expensive in Leningrad, so Yura spends most of his time with his grandmother, and comes to see us on Sundays, but soon he'll start going to kindergarten, and then grade school, and he'll move in with us." (p. 413)

By this time too, nearly all the romanticism of the pre-revolutionary – and especially the pre-emancipation nanny – had been lost. Soviet reality permitted few to wear rose-colored lenses. In the childhood world of the St. Petersburg art historian Mikhail German (b.1933), there was little love lost between him and his caretaker. "The home was full of people. Nanny Tania was young and a bit of a thief [*vorovataia*] (according to rumor, she ate a chocolate pistol gifted to me, which I myself was saving to eat, and lied about it, [saying] the rats had eaten it). A threatening feeling emanated from her; I most likely irritated her."[106]

The Post-War Situation

Collective upbringing was played down from 1936 until the time of Khrushchev; in the mid-50s, it then had a slight revival.[107] Indeed, the idealism of the early Soviet decades was becoming an ever-more-distant memory in late Stalinist times. The Great Patriotic

War may have roused the Soviet peoples to heroic individual and national deeds, but it did little to alleviate the many material and social insufficiencies of the regime. Life was a struggle for many in the late 1940s; the divorce rate after the war skyrocketed.[108] Notices of marriage dissolutions plastered the back pages of local Soviet newspapers.

"In 1948 we became rich," Ruf Zernova (1919-2004) begins one of her best short stories, entitled "Elizabeth Arden."[109] As the story begins, the narrator's husband, an editor at a Leningrad publishing house, receives a supplementary half-time appointment at the Pedagogical Institute. Between his two salaries and her earnings of 300 rubles, their income now becomes close to 3000 rubles a year.

> Those same three hundred rubles which we paid our Simonovna, our granny Tasia – our nanny-cook-houseworker. In a word, a member of the family. As was once said of my own nanny. Only Simonovna did not live with us – she lived with her daughter, Shura-the-stoker, "at a dormatorry [sic] on Krestovskii." But occasionally she spent the night with us on a cot with netting that hung like a hammock, and when we returned home after visiting friends and, without turning on the light, we at once collapsed onto the already made up sofa-bed, into the cozy hollows between the balky springs, I would listen with indescribable pleasure for a few minutes more to her snoring, against the background of the children's quiet breathing. This snoring inspired calm: one could sleep, sleep; if one of the children should start to cry – she would get up; if they cried out – she'd respond; in the morning she would lift them up softly and carry them out to the kitchen...Marvelous, unforgettable nights.
>
> When we became rich, we began having Simonovna stay over one night a week – now we could allow ourselves this [luxury].

Post-war Soviet society still resembled the pre-war period in many respects. This is the situation reflected in literature of that era, according to Vera Dunham and Jerry Hough.[110] Good childcare was still hard to find, whether public or private. About 1950, still in her first marriage, the later-to-be Galina Zakhoder (b. ca. 1930?) had a decent enough job, two wonderful children, and "a surprisingly good nanny" which she was clearly fortunate to find.[111]

In 1957 a "landmark" Soviet household management book appeared which was destined to go through four editions by 1965. It was surprisingly similar to the "bestseller" of 1861, Elena Molokhovets's *Gift to Young Housewives*. In the 1957 work "there were no instructions on how to deal with servants (though there could have been: what were still euphemistically known as *domrabotnitsy*, 'house workers,' were beginning to disappear from Soviet families in the 1960s."[112]

The number of nannies was apparently declining, as a major source – peasant women coming to the city – dried up. These women looked for and found work other than as domestics in the 1950s and 1960s.[113] "In 1963, *Sem'ia i shkola* published a letter from a housewife who had one child and was expecting a second. The day care in her town had no openings, and she was unable to find a nanny..."[114] The state – "the public" – did not always trump the family – "the private" – in raising children in this period of Soviet history. Deborah Field presents the situation as follows. Parents were offered all kinds of official advice and heard admonitions aplenty about how to raise ideal Soviet citizens, yet they could still act as if all the rules and urgings were a kind of buffet-smorgasbord from which they could pick and choose only those things they wanted and reject what they didn't.[115]

In the last decades of Soviet Russia, childcare problems eased, as more government resources were spent on the problem. Still, grannies and other family members were often the key to relieving working mothers of the burden of tending their infants, and nothing like the pre-revolutionary situation with nannies re-emerged until the demise of the regime. With the advent of the "new Russians" and their great disposable income, a much more Western-like childcare system began to evolve. Newspapers of the 1990s and more recently – along with the internet – are once again full of want ads and advertising for nannies.

Conclusion

Despite mighty upheavals in Russia in the 1860s and after 1917, one is almost tempted – with respect to the job of nannying – to conclude that the more things changed, the more things stayed the same. True, it stopped being an occupation imposed on many women and became more a profession, often demanding formal training. The care of children, though, remained much as it had always been, whatever changes occurred in the thinking of family-life and childhood experts in the late nineteenth and early twentieth centuries. The women who became nannies still came mostly from the village throughout these years (though many also came from other middle-to-low social strata). What was expected of nannies evolved, in part due to their rising education levels and, later, to households' economic exigencies.

Having spent four chapters detailing the circumstances and lives of nannies, seeing the world mostly from the nanny's point of view, I turn in the following chapter to something like the child's point of view in considering what meaning a nanny had for a nurseling.

7

Significance of the Nanny in the Child's Life

The Nanny's Milieu: The World of the Child and Its Family

A nanny did not operate in a vacuum; she was an integral part (if not exactly a member) of a child's family. So the dynamics of that family and of parent-child relations in particular were of supreme importance to her. Clearly, a nanny's significance depended in large part on "her" family's internal situation and on the parents' views of child upbringing.

There is a widespread but mistaken view that a majority of noble families in Russia – especially of the low and middle ranks – from at least 1700 (or before) until the mid-nineteenth century exhibited poor internal dynamics. A few dysfunctional families and dubious source material have given rise to the erroneous view that most parents were distant and/or unloving toward their offspring, male and female, and mostly indifferent to their upbringing (*vospitanie*). These parents were allegedly more than happy to "dump" their children into the arms of caretakers, relieving themselves of an unpleasant and unwanted task.

If the hallmark of most gentry families was an absence of love and affection of parents for children, that fact alone would go a long way toward explaining the extraordinary hold of Russian nannies on the affections and memories of their (former) well-born charges. Such was not the case: by far the majority of noble families in the eighteenth and nineteenth centuries, low and high, featured one or two loving parents, usually closely involved in the *vospitanie* of their offspring.[1]

A nanny had, by definition, an influence on the early development of the child in her care, in nearly every way imaginable. The fundamental meaning of a Russian nanny is thus most likely to be found in the role(s) the nanny played in the emotional, moral, mental, and physical life of the child – in childhood but also later in life.[2] In the remainder of this chapter, therefore, I intend to examine the significance of the Russian nanny on a fairly modest scale. Grander issues about the nanny are examined in succeeding chapters.[3]

In answering the question posed implicitly by the title of this chapter, viewpoint certainly plays a role. The significance of the nanny from the parents' standpoint is not at all her significance from the child's perspective. I've spoken more than once in these pages about the ambivalence toward nannies of some parents. It is the second viewpoint (of the child) that is at the core of this chapter.[4] Few would doubt the cardinal importance of the nanny for the child. In countless memoirs and stories her "departure" or the author's separation from her is "the end of childhood."[5] As Tat'iana Passek eloquently put it: "All the poetry of my childhood life for a long time abandoned me along with my nanny."[6] But what specifically was it that made the nanny so indispensable and meaningful in the day-to-day lives of so many memoirists?

Nanny as Mother Substitute

Surrogate Mother? Many commentators are quick to conclude, based on a few famous memoir writers in particular, that the nannies of most Russian noble children in the eighteenth and nineteenth centuries were mother substitutes par excellence.[7] (I noted this proposition in Chapter 4 with respect to nanny stereotypes.) This image is largely derived from the fact that these few autobiographers tended to come from either dysfunctional families or families where the parents withheld their affections. Thus, for these children, the only love and tenderness they received in childhood came from a (typically peasant) woman who was totally devoted to her charge. Some historians have even drawn broader societal and political implications from these exceptional cases, a view I tend to reject.[8]

More extended reading of memoirs confirms a rather different conclusion about those early years in the family to which much is sometimes attributed. In the overwhelming majority of cases of Russian noble families, a peasant nanny was not a substitute for the child's birth mother but the *partner* of the mother. The two women were most often in a rather close relationship, usually quite friendly, with a rough division of labor – what Jonathan Gathorne-Hardy calls a "balance of power." As Ivan Goncharov writes in *Oblomov* (1859): "Then the careful rearing of the child began. The *mother set herself and the nanny* the task of raising a healthy child, of guarding him from colds, the evil eye, and other hostile influences. *They devoted themselves* to seeing that he was always happy and ate heartily."[9] The excellent second-rank novelist Evgeniia Tur (1815-1892) presents the relationship in similar terms:

> ...the nanny Ignat'evna, who assisted the mother to nanny both children, loved them equally, and if there arose disputes between her and [mother] Aleksandra Nikolaevna, they were, of course, more amusing than serious. These two women would reproach each other for excessive solicitude, would quarrel over which of them would pick the infant up in her arms, which of them was more able to cheer him up in the morning or sing him to sleep in the evening, which of them would notice in him before the other the first awakening of reason and understanding.[10]

More importantly, the birth mothers did not withhold their love in most cases. The two women shared the love of the child, and in turn bestowed their own love on the infant. Jealousy or other negative feelings were seemingly rare in these partnerships; few were the mothers who felt that their children did not love them or respond in kind to displays of affection from either parent. The phrasing that the nanny was a "second mother" is apt, but not in the sense one might infer – she was not a replacement, but a "dual" mother as it were.

This conclusion is strengthened, moreover, by similar findings about nannies in other countries.[11] On the lighter side, this is how the émigré novelist Mikhail Osorgin (1878-1942) presents it in *My Sister's Story* (1931). As the baby Kostia looks up from his crib, catching dark shapes in motion around him, he distinguishes neatly: "The most wonderful shadow of all, exclusively useful and pleasant, is Mother. Another, bearable, though somewhat coarse and unnecessary dark shadow, is Nurse." He doesn't know their names yet, but "the manifestations themselves interest him already in different, individual ways. The appearance of Mother provokes a passionate craving, a thirst to take speedy advantage of her useful qualities. The appearance of Nurse, accompanied by the gurgling of the bath and various other inconveniences, draws his attention away from the important problems of the world to the trifling facts of everyday life."[12]

To put it another way, although a nanny might eclipse the birth mother for some part of a child's early life, the norm would seem to have been that – for the bulk of families – there was a caring mother (and/or father), and her presence was not completely lost on a child, even one doted on by a peasant nanny. Importantly, and contrary to some commentators, I believe such mothers were in abundance not just in the second half of the nineteenth century but much earlier, in the preceding century and before.

An illuminating insight into the question of substitute mothering is provided by the psychoanalyst Erik Erikson. In his *Childhood and Society*, Erikson discusses "mother substitutes," in this case the nanny of a young boy named Peter. His foreign nursemaid was "a soft-spoken Oriental girl with a gentle touch" named Myrtle who "had been his main comfort for years because his parents were out often..." The nursemaid was dismissed by the mother, in part from jealousy.

> Whether she left or was sent away hardly mattered to the child. What mattered was that he lived in a social class which provides paid mother substitutes from a different race or class. Seen from the children's point of view this poses a number of problems. If you like your ersatz mother, your [birth] mother will leave you more often and with a better conscience. If you mildly dislike her, your mother will leave you with mild regret. If you dislike her very much and can provoke convincing incidents, your mother will send her away – only to hire somebody like her or worse. *And if you*

*happen to like her very much in your own way or in her own way, your mother will surely send her away sooner or later.*¹³

The crux of the matter comes down to that last statement, making the situation inapplicable for the majority of Russian nannies. They were in it for the long haul, and there is little evidence in the hundreds of memoirs I've read of any kind of jealousy in Russian mothers that would have led to their sending a nanny away. The exception is Natal'ia Trukhanova (1885-ca. 1960?), a ballerina.¹⁴ "Memories of childhood for some happy people are as of an incomparable paradise," she writes. "For others, these memories are linked with the memory of tender images of parents, with the cult of the family. Such happiness did not fall to my lot. I grew up in a broken home [*u razbitogo ochaga*]. And my childhood was without joy."

> Mama's dominant character trait was jealousy [*revnost'*]. She would go on and on about everything and everyone. Mama's jealousy even caused me my first sorrow: she took away from me my nanny, to whom I was "too attached." Giving away her own heart, mama demanded in return the absolute possession of the hearts of her chosen ones.¹⁵

Naturally, in the absence of a birth mother (through death, divorce, physical separation, or some other cause) a nanny would be considered a true surrogate for her. Thus, a Soviet scholar claims that Mstislav Dobuzhinskii's nanny M.O. Beliakova was "in some measure" a substitute for his mother because he lived with his father, quite apart from his mother.¹⁶ Such instances are not rare throughout Russian history, given historical mortality rates and the vagaries of married life. But the cases which stand out in the memoir literature of such a situation are not striking for a consequent greater focus on the nanny. Just the opposite: the memoirists who make a special point or plea for their nannies' being something like a mother substitute nearly all seem to be individuals whose mothers were alive and "in place" within the family. More importantly, these few writers appear deliberately to magnify the importance of the nanny in their lives, as if out of spite or revenge for real or imagined maternal neglect. The best examples of this phenomenon are probably Vera Figner, Natal'ia Durova, and Nikolai Berdiaev. (Pushkin might fit this mold as well; if only he'd finished his planned autobiography to allow us a hint as to what he thought his relationship as a child was to his nanny.)

The nanny was, most often I believe, both the mother's helpmate and even her confidante. A fine example of the kind of mothering joint enterprise between birth mother and nanny is that in Ol'ga Kornilova's family of the mid-nineteenth century. The two women would take turns tending the sick children through stressful nights.[17] Another example of the principle of partnership appears to be that of the nanny and mother of Tat'iana Shchepkina-Kupernik (1874-1952).[18] The émigré author Ol'ga Zhigalova – who calls herself "Tania" in most of her autobiographical writings – reveals how mother and nanny could be co-conspirators in childcare. The little girl has a well-known love of beer, often begging her papa for a swig. One morning "Taniusha" awakens with a coated tongue. "*Exchanging glances with mama*, nanny went out and returned with a tray – on the tray is a glass and in the glass, beer." Naturally, Tania readily downs the drink, shocked to discover the pair's secret: there is castor oil in the beer![19]

A trained psychotherapist with a Russian childhood, Elisaveta Fen (a pseudonym for Lydia Jackson; née Zhiburtovich;1899-1983), illustrates this point better than I can: "The person who carried me about and sang to me until I fell asleep was not my mother. I knew that, although at that time I knew them apart more through contact than by sight. They were distinct presences, which I never confused." Although her nanny Masha sat with her and turned away the monsters lurking in the corner until she could fall asleep, giving her a feeling of complete security, when she had bad dreams or nightmares, or awoke in fright during the night, she called out not for Masha but for "Mamma!" Her mother would come and calm her; mama's cool hand dispelled the pillow's heat. Her mother "never failed to come when I called in the night, or in the daytime. Although I was in [the] charge of a nurse, [mother] never seemed to be very far off when I badly needed her."[20]

Very rarely does one get a truly introspective look at a nanny, much less at the real relationship between a nanny and mistress-mother, unfiltered through any sentimental-Romantic prism or other distorting lens. Particularly valuable then is the following diary entry of Lidiia Avilova (1864-1943). In the 1890s, a young Anna (Aniuta) Pavlovna Pavlova (d. 1957), then about 17 years old, came to replace Avilova's old nanny in caring for her children. Looking back a quarter century later at how her relationship with Aniuta had developed, Avilova came to some revealing conclusions about both the nanny and herself.

> I will write about Aniuta. Ah, what a surprising, golden soul! How much she eased for me in my life! What a friend and comrade in sorrow! But if anyone heard our conversations, they'd laugh! Why, Aniuta is remarkable in that she is always in agreement with everything, and agrees with great conviction. This is natural, because she has no opinion of her own; she accepts on faith that of another, and mine is the last word [*avtoritetno*] for her. What's worse is that even my health is authoritative for her. Inevitably she is sick with whatever I have and absolutely in the same way as I. Hers will pass when mine passes. So we're always sick together, which is very inconvenient for me. In general, this is my mirror, and I have to say that I laugh till I cry at my own reflection [*smeius' nad svoim otrazheniem priamo do slez*]. And nevertheless I love to spend a little time talking with Aniuta. I listen to excerpts of what I was saying the day before, two days, a week ago and I think: can it be that I was saying this? My own words stun me with their intolerable self-assurance and their indisputable stupidity. I look in my mirror and chuckle [*khokhochu*]...[21]

The picture is both touching and slightly off-putting; it almost feels like she's describing a faithful dog, one selflessly devoted but also rather mindless.

There may be one excellent example of a Russian searching precisely for a mother substitute in his early years, and finding it in various women, including his nanny. That individual is the satirical novelist and short-story writer Nikolai Leskov (1831-1895), who will be discussed at length in different contexts in Chapters 8 and 9. One searches in vain in Leskov's autobiographical sketches for mention of his mother.[22] In his magisterial biography of the author, Hugh McLean says that Leskov held ambivalent feelings about both his father and his mother. The latter had many admirable qualities but was overly strict and far from loving. His image of both parents was an amalgam of the good and the bad.[23]

Two facts seem very telling in his early years. First, he claims in a late "note on myself" that he was orphaned at 16. Whereas his father did indeed die in 1848 when he was that age, his mother survived until the mid- to late 1880s, dying less than a decade before he did.[24] Second, his family lived for the first eight years of his life with an aunt (mother's sister) in the household of a brutal, tyrannical landowner named Strakhov who was a contrast to his own meek but distant father. With these facts to go on, McLean finds it fruitful to employ a Freudian – or at least heavily psychological – approach in speaking of Leskov's first years. McLean stresses the void in the writer's life at this time:

> Difficult as it is to reconstruct the emotional relationships of Leskov's early life, we can arrive at a reasonably plausible hypothesis of what they must have been. The central fact of Leskov's childhood is the deep emotional ache left by his parents – the deterioration, withdrawal, and death of his father, and the harshness of his mother. He tried to compensate for these losses in various ways, *by seeking substitute parents* among his near relations and endowing them with, or recognizing in them, qualities he felt his parents lacked. But the compensations never made up for the original loss; the ache remained in him for life, reappearing in many guises both in reality and in art.[25]

More to our point, McLean says Leskov "seems to have consolidated into an ideal image the impressions left in him by various surrogate mothers – his grandmother, *his nurse*, aunts – plus, no doubt, the positive feelings he had about his real mother."[26]

Significance of the Nanny in the Child's Life 195

Nanny as Servant

One of the most frequent observations found in literature and autobiographies is that servants and children have much in common. Among the best commentators on their similar predicament is Aleksandr Herzen. After discussing at length the alleged and real peccadilloes and foibles of servants, he continues:

> In all this there is more of childlike simpleheartedness than immorality...On this similarity of children with servants also rests their mutual attraction. Children hate the upper-crust bearing [*aristokratiia*] of adults and their charitably condescending manner because they [the children] are bright and understand that for them [the adults] they are children but for servants [they are] people. As a consequence of this, they much prefer to play cards and lotto with the maids than with the guests. The guests play for *them*, out of condescension; they give in to them, tease them and abandon the game at their own sweet will; maids usually play as much for themselves as for the children; from this the game becomes interesting.
> Servants are exceptionally attached to children, and this is not at all a slavish attachment, this is the mutual love of the *weak and innocent* [*prostye*].[27]

Elizaveta Vodovozova makes the same comparison: "Children were beings just as lacking in rights as serfs." "They punished children exactly like serfs for every transgression: gave [them] cuffs, pulled [them] by the hair, by the ears, pushed, drubbed, whipped, caned them, and in a great many families, beat and flogged [them] mercilessly."[28] What they shared, in the view of one astute observer, was not enough to make them identical. Their similar situations were highlighted when – and perhaps only when – the parent-child relationship was not close, no closer than that between the parent-master and servant. The father-master most often felt a duty to exercise "'fatherly care over his servants as if they were his children'."[29] This is, of course, a feeling of paternalism, on which not just the Russian old regime rested.

As well, servants and children – thrown together willy-nilly in an atmosphere sometimes rife with mistrust or at least apprehension on the part of other adults in the household (including, sadly, the young ones' parents) – frequently tend to become "co-conspirators": they share each others' secrets, learn to trust one another, and even reciprocate the distrust they often feel emanating from those other adults. As Pëtr Kropotkin (1842-1921) put it: "We never would have betrayed any one of the servants, nor would they have betrayed us."[30] Even more to the point are remarks of the author and *narodnik* activist Mariia Tsebrikova (1835-1917), who noted that "the consciousness of a common lack of rights linked the servants to the masters' children. Obedience for the sake of obedience was considered the mother of all virtues; the young were always at fault before their elders; a general feeling of humiliation allied the children with the servants in a close comradeship [*v tesnoe tovarishchestvo*]."[31]

At the same time, however, there could never be a true equality in the nanny-child relationship. The mutuality could go only so far and no further. Whether a serf or merely a nonnoble, the nanny was still beneath the masters, and the masters perforce included the youngest masters/ mistresses. Obedience was both owed to and due from nanny and child; each side was aware of the complexities in the relationship from a fairly early stage. Life histories are full of more or less spoiled children, more or less servile nanny-servants.

Nanny as Center and Anchor of the Child's World

For many memoirists, the nanny takes pride of place in their childhood, often seeming to displace the parents. Quite apart from the analysis offered in a previous subsection, explanations for this phenomenon are many, starting with the simplest and most obvious: in its earliest years, the time the child spent with the nanny was far greater than with any other person. Its nanny was the child's closest confidante in most cases. ("Good children must never keep secrets from their parents and nanny," as one early nineteenth-century fictional youngster announced rather smugly.[32]) We've already looked at a second reason: the nanny was a "second mother," occasionally even a replacement mother. There is also a further psychological reason for this, I believe. The sheer self-centeredness of the child makes the nanny paramount. There is no one so egoistic, self-centered, and solipsistic as a child, even one not particularly spoiled. Children are all the center of their own universe; everything revolves around them. How can the external embodiment of this feeling – the nanny – not be the most central "other" thing in the child's life? The nanny is perhaps the only one who comes close to looking upon the child as the child sees itself. In the extreme, nannies might seem to dissolve into or become one with their charges.

The most forceful presentation of this idea I've seen is in the autobiography of Princess Elizaveta L'vova (b. 1853). Her nanny, "baba Afrosin'ia," she considered "a part of myself as it were."

> I recall that I would rarely speak of myself in the singular person. As nanny would say: "We're going to bed," when I had to say goodnight to mama and my sisters; "Now we're going to take a bath," when she got me ready to bathe; and I would say about nanny's husband: "Something has upset our husband!" [*U nas muzh chto-to stal plokho videt'!*] or "Now we're going to write to Grisha." Grigorii was nanny's son who lived in Moscow; he died young from tuberculosis. With this notion [*predstavlenie*] that I have everything in common with nanny, I didn't even take into consideration that I love nanny; nanny and I were one![33]

Something similar can be found in fiction: eight-year-old Shurka (Aleksandr) Luzgin is the charge of the nearly saintly "nanny" Fedos Chizhik, an ordinary seaman. A month after the sailor's employment as nanny, Shurka has become besotted with him. The boy even wants to become a seaman and tries "in everything to imitate Chizhik, who by that time was his ideal." "*From a purely child's egoism he would not let Chizhik leave him*, in order to be together at all times, even forgetting about his mother, who, from the time of Chizhik's appearance, had somehow moved off to a secondary plane."[34]

Few have captured the self-absorption of the infant as well as Mikhail Osorgin. His tiny protagonist Kostia thinks of himself as "Old Boss."

> Mother, Nurse and the little girl [sister Katia] behave towards Old Boss in a patronizing and indulgent way, and yet they are mere objects of study, mere material for his growing consciousness. Their being is just as fantastic as the rest of the world – from the bars of his cot to the boundlessness of the ceiling. He has only to close his eyes and they are no longer. Their existence and nonexistence alternate to the will of Old Boss himself who calls them into being by the mere movement of an eyelid. Sometimes he prefers to any sight the sound of his own voice, and listens to the rise and fall of his wailing filling the world. Mother is quite wrong in thinking that he is in pain or uncomfortable: he is listening to the music and realizes for the first time that it is a symphony – a composition of his own creating – and that he himself is not only the orchestra, but both conductor and composer. Unwilling is his return to the seductions of daily life, bribed by a gentle voice or the promise of warmth and satiety. Sometimes the music breaks off unexpectedly and that is very painful. But then, life in general is an uncomfortable affair – Old Boss has felt that from the first.[35]

Osorgin's comically sardonic conclusion is that "It will end by the interests of the world conquering Old Boss, who, abandoning philosophy, will plunge head foremost into the mundane. Such is man's fate: simultaneously with the growth of the body, comes a lowering of the mind."

As a corollary to this point, however, I note that nannies – unlike parents, who often tend to (re-) live their own lives, vicariously, through their children – rarely fall into this psychological trap. On the one hand, it would be absurd on the surface, given the usual gap in social position and most other respects between the nanny and her employers. On the other hand, nearly all nannies understood a truth that sometimes eluded their nurselings' parents: children have an autonomous life of their own, quite apart from their parents' lives.

Nanny as Moral Compass

The complement of nanny piety and religiousness discussed in Chapter 4 was frequently a strong moral sense and high ethical standards. While this may be an overworked trope in some cases, there is for me at least an irreducible kernel of truth in the notion. As Tat'iana Kuzminskaia (1846-1925) succinctly said of her own nanny, Vera Ivanovna: "She was the spiritual barometer of the household. She enjoyed universal respect in the house."[36] An even more striking example is that of Kuzminskaia's niece, Tat'iana Tolstaia (1864-1950). Count Leo's oldest daughter, growing up with one of the great moral preachers of the nineteenth century, nonetheless also singles out her British nanny Hannah Tersey/Tarsey as instilling basic tenets of right and wrong in her:

> To three people I am especially grateful for my childhood:
> To my father, who guided our life and placed us in those circumstances in which we grew up.
> To my mother, who, in these circumstances, enhanced [*ukrasivshei*] life for us by all the means at her disposal, and –
> To Hannah, our British nanny [*vospitatel'nitsa*], who lived six years in our family and gave us so much love, care, and firm moral principles.[37]

While nannies may have played this role of moral teacher throughout Russian history, the most intriguing examples appear to show up in the Soviet period. I hesitate to argue a direct causal link, but still wonder if it can be only by chance that, between the Revolution and the end of the USSR, among the most prominent voices of humanity in Russian society – among those who more or less publicly resisted the moral degradations of Lenin, Stalin, and their epigones – many if not most speak of their nannies as an important part of their childhoods. I have in mind such figures as Elena Bonner, Boris Pasternak, Lidiia Chukovskaia, Lev Kopelev, Vera Panova, Ol'ga Berggol'ts (Bergholts), and Dmitrii Likhachev.[38] The case should not be overstated: clearly family must have played a large role in the moral upbringing of most of these individuals. Grandmothers and grandfathers – as in both Bonner's and Andrei Sakharov's cases – parents, even siblings all exerted an influence.

The temptation to make a bit more out of the nannies is great, but any generalization should be resisted. Still, there are those fascinating individual cases worth discussing.

- At times of greatest moral crisis for Pasternak, it was his nanny he seemed to recall first and foremost.

- Panova, a secret believer all her life, tried to help "undesirables" like Ruf Zernova in the 1950s. She notes that her nanny Mar'ia Alekseevna Kolesnikova was the *only* truly religious person in her immediate family circle and describes or implies a strong moral component in the nanny's sense of religion.

- Bonner assigns much greater moral status to her grandmother Batania than to her clearly flawed nanny Niura, yet spends most of her time with the latter. With Niura, as in many other cases, it may be the actions and behavior of the nanny – rather than any precepts or religious beliefs – that had some lasting impact.

- This is the case as well with Katerinushka, within the extended Likhachev family: "Should the need for anything arise, Katerinushka would appear in the household: if someone fell seriously ill and needed tending, if a baby was due and there was a need to prepare for its appearance in this world...if a girl got engaged and it was necessary to prepare a dowry for her – in all these cases Katerinushka would appear." This nanny would work tirelessly for other families as well; "she was always doing something." In sum, says Likhachev, Katerinushka "was accustomed all her life to helping those who were in need of her help."[39]

No one who's read Berggol'ts's autobiography could doubt either her affection for her nanny Dunia or, more significantly, the latter's being a kind of role model of inner fortitude. Dunia's indomitable spirit of resistance and constant striving to improve herself could well have inspired the author in the 1950s, when she was one of the first voices to question the pillars of Stalinist literature. The dissident Kopelev's case is more ambiguous and harder to argue: his favorite nanny, Polina Maksimovna, was religious but a pure anti-Semite. She tried to "subvert" his own Jewish faith, and succeeded fairly well. He prayed alongside her, went to Orthodox mass with her, and hoped to be baptized and get into Christian heaven thereby. "I hoped that when I grew up I would talk my parents into being baptized and then everything would be fine." As well, her strong monarchist and rabid anti-Bolshevik views clearly did not take hold of the young Kopelev. He fairly early became a true communist believer. But the fact that it is of Polina that he speaks more than of his parents in discussing his earliest ethical stirrings may signify.[40]

As tempting as it is to argue for a common moral loftiness in peasant nannies, I will not attempt to make that case. Suffice it to say that the examples adduced illuminate one possible role that a nanny might play in her young charge's life. For a "deconstruction" of the moral female/nanny archetype, see my discussion toward the end of Chapter 10.

Nanny as Family Chronicler, Oral Historian, Griot

Russian historians and genealogists owe a debt of gratitude to the Russian nanny. Dozens of memoirists testify to the fact that, without the input of their nanny, they would likely be unable to recount much of their family's and their own pasts. Indeed, Aleksandr Herzen chose to begin his glorious autobiography with a plea to his nanny Vera Artamonovna to tell him once more the tale of what happened to him and the family in 1812 when the French came to Moscow. Helen Reeve, introducing a collection of stories by a Soviet woman writer, says they recall "Boris Eikhenbaum's idea that it is a woman's task to preserve memory and to pass it on, to forge a link between generations."[41]

Descendants of the Decembrist Vasilii Ivashev remembered one "family member" for her memory as well as for her character. Ivashev had married Camille Ledantu in Siberia; the pair left three young children behind on their untimely deaths in 1840 and 1839 respectively. All three were nannied by a woman named Praskov'ia Dmitrievna. The children and nanny returned to European Russia; the latter moved in with oldest daughter Mariia when she married and nannied all Mariia's children. Ivashev's granddaughter – Mariia's daughter – recalled: "Nanny was a walking chronicle, and we passionately loved to hear her tales of our beautiful grandmother [Camille] with tresses down to her feet, [and] about the other wives of the Decembrists, whom she knew and remembered."[42] Nikolai Morozov's (1854-1946) nanny Tat'iana was a similar font of information about his grandfather, who had been killed by his own serfs in an affair of the heart and of honor.[43]

But how trustworthy are these oral traditions? Are they not of a piece with all the other fairy tales spun by nannies to entertain and occupy their nurselings? Here is what Mar'ia Kamenskaia (1817-1898) thought:

> About that which transpired before I was born, I will speak in the words of my father, mother, uncles, aunts, and my father's dear nanny [*nianiushka*], Matrena Efremovna...
>
> You must not think that I could get confused by the words of a simple nanny [*nian'ka*] and speak of things that never were [*nagovorit' nebyval'shchinu*] – no! Literary people of my time listened to this Matrena Efremovna with pleasure and, leaving her room [sic], would say: "This is not an old woman, but a living book." And of course she knew this family of her masters like the back of her hand, and therefore will be a great help [*podspor'e*] for my memoirs.[44]

Nannies, wet-nurses – in fact most servants – could play the same role of clan griot. One key to this role early on, quite naturally, was the general illiteracy of female serfs. We are speaking, moreover, of a phenomenon just one small step removed from a less positive image – that of the inveterate gossip. Men would have it that women excel at this foible; higher classes attribute it to lower ones.[45] Prejudices die hard; both of these are long overdue for demise. A second key to this role: nannies often lived to a ripe old age. Their longevity thus conferred the ability to play this role of historian. As the critic Boris Eikhenbaum reminds us, it's "the dust of time" that makes the most commonplace things into "museum pieces."[46]

Litterateurs loved to cover the same ground in their fiction as they did in their memoirs. A case in point: Leonid Obolenskii (1845-

1906), an author, philosopher, and critic, whose 1903 "Shadows and Specters" includes the following exposition, which poses the same question as Kamenskaia above:

> But I loved [even] more, at that time, the stories of one very ancient woman [named] Akimovna, who lived with us. She was at one time the wet-nurse of my grandfather on my father's side, and you can imagine how old she must have been if grandfather reckoned himself to be almost seventy! This very Akimovna would recount to me repeatedly [*ne odin raz*] always one and the same story about how my great-grandfather lost his princely rank. Her telling of the tale had in it so many romantic details that in later years I often wondered if this were not the fruit of fantasy, if not of Akimovna herself, then perhaps of those authors of the 20s whom the daughters and young wives of *pomeshchiki* read in her time in their estates? Did she not hear this story from her mistress and did her aged [*starcheskaia*] memory not mix up such a fictional tale with real events? However, the verisimilitude [*vernost'*] and preciseness of the real-life and especially the psychological details force me to dismiss this supposition. Beyond that, if Akimovna had almost completely lost memory regarding the latest events, on the other hand in the distant past she remembered all the smallest details of any occurrence, all the names of its participants, so that to presume a mixing up of an actual event with a tale she'd heard was hardly possible with her. And she was not yet so decrepit, despite her nearly century-mark age, that one could suspect the loss of her mental capacities.[47]

To get her stories started, all the narrator needs to do is ask Akimovna a question and she's off. "She would begin by answering the question, but after this the story would unwind all by itself, like a ball [rolling along]. I already said that, having preserved the clearest memory of the distant past, she had almost none regarding the present, and therefore, recounting for me one and the same thing for the tenth time, she was sure that she was speaking about this for the first time."

Nanny as "Bridge to 'the People'"

So many well-born memoirists speak about their connections to the peasantry as embodied in or facilitated through their nanny, not to speak of the claims made in this regard for Arina Rodionovna, that this topic has to be addressed.[48] It is tempting to take at face value the heartfelt protestations of a Herzen or a Zasulich that their democratic feelings were engendered in some part by their nannies. In fact, I have no great qualms about accepting most of these avowals. Close daily contact with household serfs, especially nannies and particularly before 1861, undoubtedly produced sentiments that intra-class associations could and did not.

The key to this phenomenon, of course, is in the amount of social distance that existed between masters and servants at any given time. In the seventeenth and early eighteenth centuries, when serfdom was becoming ever more deeply entrenched, the distance between social strata was growing but had not yet reached the proportions it did later. Whether 1762, when Peter III freed the gentry from compulsory state service, is the main watershed in this regard is a matter of some debate among historians. Some would argue that this was the major impetus for the separation of peasants and nobles that became more like a chasm in the course of the late eighteenth and early nineteenth centuries. Others would say that this was only one of many causes for the growing rift between social groups.

Be that as it may, we have already noted the continual exhortations by even enlightened social commentators that parents should "protect" their children from being in extended close proximity to people of "lower" standing. While socio-economic strata were clearly a large part of what defined "upper" and "lower" groups, we can be certain that another component of standing was general morals. This as much as anything was probably a saving grace for nannies – the perception (and reality?) that by and large they were good, devout women. Parents could usually convince themselves that, whatever the weaknesses of many peasants, a religious peasant woman was not a real threat to their beloved offspring.

Whatever goodwill the parents had toward the caretaker, the child generally had more. The best qualities of the nanny and her temperament were appreciated by both nurseling and parent, but the child much more than the adult was likely to project those qualities onto the social group from which the nanny came – this due to their more limited perspective and experience. Closest to the child's heart were probably those qualities which, for adults, might be seen in a more ambivalent light. Vaunted simplicity, meekness, probity, and directness would recommend themselves to young and old masters, but the young would see something more in these than their parents: these were qualities that often set the nanny and her fellow peasants alongside the child in outlook and behavior. The feeling of fellowship, of common humanity learned by nurselings from their nannies is, I would argue, not just a myth or a stereotype. Children absorbed a great deal from their caretakers, good and bad, but they almost inevitably would have been able to grasp the differences, good and bad, between adults in their own social circle and other adults around them. Until and unless prejudice arose, children should have been able to see aspects of peasant life that might escape even well-meaning parents.[49]

Nanny as "Antidote," Intercessor, and Mediator

There are several ways in which this phrase applies, most having to do with family dynamics and with the relationship between children and adults. It has already been discussed in a previous subsection of this chapter about how servants and children are in some ways much alike. Those remarks hold for nannies as for other servants. And in Chapter 4 I noted the ability of good nannies to empathize with their charges. Usually sincere and somewhat naive ("childlike"), the good nanny was generally "on the same wavelength" as the children she tended; she was their companion as well as their supervisor. She entered into their world almost completely. All of these factors played a major part in a function performed by many if not most nannies: that of intermediary and shield between parent and child – even between parent and parent – and between child and the surrounding world.

Nanny as antidote to everyday life. I have taken this phrasing not from the memoir literature but from a work of fictionalized autobiography. The characters are reportedly based on real figures in the life of the author, the poetess Poliksena Solov'ëva (1867-1924). The title character, Alena Petrovna, is not the nanny of the little boy Alësha (the surrogate of Solov'ëva) but the former nanny of Alësha's untimely deceased brother Serëzha. She is a gifted storyteller, who makes the past come more alive than even the present. She laughs as hard as the children during the telling. When she's busy up in the nursery regaling the children with her tales, spinning fantastic figures in their imaginations, the (other) grownups are an unwelcome intrusion. The children "felt in the adults an absence of that joy with which they themselves regarded Petrovna's fairy tales, and therefore the adults hindered them."

> They shrank from the indifferent tone of voice, from the unsympathetic [bezuchastnyi] question; the fairytale figures drooped and sagged like the petals of bright, tender flowers; and through them there began to show through the boring walls of the nursery, and simple, everyday life looked out from all the corners of the room.[50]

The parents simply don't understand who the real Alësha is; he's the hero of Petrovna's tales – he's big, handsome, powerful, and wise. Waking every morning, "he would look around with a surprised revulsion at the walls of the nursery" and with gloom at what he saw of himself. Everything around him seemed "monstrous" and "unreal." In almost Kierkegaardian terms, Solov'ëva describes her young protagonist's feelings about ordinary life:

> The melancholy [toska] of waking up, the unbearable melancholy of the return to everyday life – in which it was necessary to begin anew everything that had been the day before and that threatened to be tomorrow and so on and so on – this unbearable melancholy Alësha had known from earliest childhood. And for this reason he loved Petrovna so fervently, that she was for him a lively and bold antidote [protivorechie] to everyday life. She had lived so long on this earth...but this long, hard, and boring life had not conquered her; she had not submitted to it.[51]

This is the point of the fairy tales and storytelling discussed in Chapter 5. This is "the secret truth of the wondrous fairy tales" recounted by countless generations of nannies. It is a major reason why children tend to dote on their caretakers.

Nanny as family "glue," protectress, and harmonizer. One of the most direct statements of this aspect of the nanny's role can be found in the memoirs of Liudmila Vrangel' (1877-1969). She says that Nanny Vera Andreevna "was a kind of cement which held the fragile bond between my parents together. When she left, the family fell apart."[52] Not much different was the situation in the family of the educator Elizaveta Vodovozova (1844-1923). Her father and mother had frequent "small domestic scenes and quarrels, arising in the majority of cases from the upbringing of the children." He did not approve of her open coolness toward them. After her father died in the cholera of 1848, the family moved from town to permanent residence in the countryside; her mother entrusted the children's care almost entirely to nanny Mariia Vasil'evna (Masha). When her papa was still alive, he was mainly what held them all together. In the absence both of the father and of attention from the mother, that bond was quickly destroyed. Now each member of the family gradually began to live his own life. " ...only the burning devotion to us of nanny and our common love for her supported the bond between us." And when her older sister Anna is being forced by her increasingly destitute mother to marry an older man she doesn't love, it's to the nanny that Anna turns for succor: "Save me, nanny dear! . . Only you and you alone can save [me]!..." Vodovozova more than once calls Masha the family's or her own "guardian angel."[53]

In Anna Chertkova's family, when she was growing up, the situation was similar. The wife of Vladimir Chertkov, Tolstoi's prominent disciple, and a children's book author, Chertkova (1859-1927) remembered that although her mama would sometimes get angry, her nanny never did. Dar'ia Kuz'minishna, the nanny, always played the role of intermediary in others' (i.e., kids') fights and when they got upset or irate. She was the consummate reconciler and peacemaker in the family.[54]

The ways in which nannies tried to defend their charges were many and varied. I've already spoken at somewhat greater length about protective actions by nannies in the early post-October era. Frequently, protection was from the unwelcome intruder, a governess; for Herzen's "cousin" Tat'iana Passek and countless others, it was from physical punishment (usually from a father, sometimes a mother); for Tat'iana Aksakova-Sivers in 1898 it was from an unpleasant experience with a gang of Kronstadt sailors.[55] Two decades later, a graver threat from the same quarter came for Prince Andrei Kurakin (b. 1903). In 1919 his nanny "wanted to protect me at sixteen as [she did] at two." A sailor (from the Aurora) and a soldier came to arrest his mother, probably just because of her class origins. When she failed to appear, they moved to arrest him. But "nanny bristles, defending me and saying that I was sick. [The soldier] took no account of this objection and the poor woman, bathed in tears, had just enough time to make up a small packet containing a towel, a bar of soap, a pillow, and to give it to me." Then they hauled him off. "As I expected, nanny didn't forget me; she brought a good meal and a blanket. Of course, I didn't see her, but the fact of receiving something from the house gave me courage." Finally he's freed, but sent away to Moscow, whence he later headed south and finally emigrated.[56]

Nanny as Ongoing Presence

The lifelong helpmate and consoler. Over and over again one finds in memoirs and literature images of nannies who continue to care for their former charges long after they have stopped being assigned that duty. Their role of nanny ended, they remain a presence in the former charges' lives long beyond the nurselings' early years.[57] A few days after giving birth to the future impresario Sergei Diagilev (1872-1929), his mother died, reportedly due to injuries suffered because of his overlarge head. Diagilev left no autobiography or memoirs, but many of his closest friends wrote about him and his nanny. At one period in his teens, he went to live with his eldest sister, Anna Filosofova (1837-1912), a leading feminist, and her husband.

> When, as an undergraduate, Diaghilev moved from the Filosofovs' apartment to his own flat in Galernaya Street,

it was nanny Dunia who came from Perm to look after him. When, founding *The World of Art*, Diaghilev took a large apartment at 45 Liteiny Prospect, two of the rooms of which were reserved as editorial offices, nanny Dunia followed him there. All Seriozha's friends and collaborators knew her well. In his well-known portrait by Bakst, she is there to be seen in the background: and, at the gatherings of the editorial staff, and the famous *World of Art* Mondays that were held during the winter, nanny Dunia, wearing a black lace cap, would preside over the samovar in the big dining room; no light task, when thirty to forty guests were assembled for tea.[58]

Another intimate, Mstislav Dobuzhinskii, observed Diagilev perhaps more closely, or at least more penetratingly. His insight into Diagilev's character may shed some light on why the nanny remained with him to the end. Dobuzhinskii remembers him as always having the manners of a "grand seigneur," with the laziness of a pre-emancipation lord. But at the same time, "in all of his appearance [*oblik*], in his puffy face and soft lips, there was – however strange – something childlike (I remember his amusing manner of wiping his eyes 'with his little fist,' exactly like a child)."[59] All too many individuals, like Diagilev, grow older but perhaps fail to grow up. The "inner child" may be a truer reflection of the adult than most of us would care to admit.

Mikhail Osorgin the second (b. 1861), the journalist Serge Schmemann's great-grandfather, was governor of Grodno province in 1903. "…when overcome by the burdens of office, [he] would seek refuge in old Nyunichka's room." "Nyunichka" (it should more likely have been "nianechka") was Anne Tomi, the Swiss nanny who had come "when Mikhail Mikhailovich was born and stayed until her death 37 years later." "She grew fully into the family," writes Schmemann, "serving as confidante, comforter, chaperone, and friend to three generations of Osorgins." Osorgin, in unpublished memoirs, wrote: "I would lie down on her couch, and in her calm, level voice, her spectacles perched on the end of her nose, darning something for my parents, she would talk about the past, about my childhood or adolescence, when there were no worries." These therapeutic sessions were never to be interrupted.[60]

This aspect of a nanny's role in the child's life – the continuing presence – seems to me critical in the evolution of the mythology surrounding Pushkin's Arina Rodionovna and, by extension, other nannies. All (or most of us) have a lifelong desire, that never diminishes, to feel loved and to be cared for. The need for people in our lives who are concerned for us – deeply interested in our well-being, appreciate us for who we are, understand and love us almost unconditionally – doesn't end with childhood. Parents and siblings, other relatives, even close friends fulfill this role in most of our lives. Yet for noble Russians in the past, that one extra person – the former nanny – was an additional presence that often outshone the others and earned their heartfelt gratitude.

Nanny as Lifelong Inspiration

The preceding section dealt with a physical presence; there were frequent cases of a different sort. Ariadna Tyrkova-Vil'iams (1869-1962) noted, some 70 years after being in her nanny's care and 40-odd years after the nanny's death: "Simply and without thinking, I acquired [*nabiralas'*] from nanny's vitalizing juices [*fliuidy*] a love which even today still supports me."[61] Allusions in two different works set me thinking about this "lifelong" aspect to the nanny and its meaning.

The first is from Iurii Miroliubov's essay "The Role of Old Nannies in the Family."[62] His interlocutor, a Madame N[echkina], recounts an incident from her childhood:

> Nanny calls me:
> 'Thread my needle, I can't see with my glasses on.'
> I threaded it and tied the knot.
> 'What have you done? Untie it at once! Don't you see I'm making myself a *funeral blouse*? I've already prepared the stockings, slippers, dress, and now I'm making the blouse. You don't make a single *knot* in the thread for this! I'll have *plenty to untie in the Other World*! I've sinned enough during my life.'
> Hearing these words, the little girl grew frightened and ran to her mother, told her nanny's words. "But why are

you afraid?" she asked. "Nanny is doing it *right*!" and right then she told her that each person has a duty not only to live on this earth but in living, to think also about death, and to prepare for it in a Christian manner.

Miroliubov pondered this story and came to some conclusions about this incident that not all will agree with but are apropos to my line of argument:

> Here we can direct the attention of those studying peasant folklore and its mythology to the fact that in the people's consciousness *there was no boundary* between *life* and *death*. For a person of advanced age, his first duty was to prepare for death ...Nannies in homes, even those of the gentry, had great authority, and they instilled in the children the old-time Russian ideas of life and death. Thus...at first the idea of death – for which "nanny is preparing" – frightened [N], and at first she would all the time run to see "has nanny died or not!" Then, she became accustomed to this idea. When nanny all the same did finally die, this seemed to her *already completely natural*! Thus, the nanny, preparing herself for her own life's end, psychologically prepared the child for it as well. The child did not feel a shock as the result of her death. And the question about "knots" also etched itself deeply into the little girl's memory. She has not forgotten about it to this day. In this way Russian nannies have influenced the younger generation, instilling in them a correct idea about life and death. Nannies, having nannied children almost until their marriage, have passed on to them *all* peasant [*narodnye*] traditions.

The second allusion, in the memoirs of Anna Chertkova, a very religious person, brought a small frisson late in my investigations. After devoting almost the entire first part of her memoirs to her nanny, Dar'ia Kuz'minishna, Chertkova at the end tries to explain why her nanny has been so central in her life. The attempt is not particularly successful, but she comes close to capturing the most salient point, which I take to be the following. Her nanny was always there for her; she has been a comfort all her life and even when she is long gone, her memory and inspiration still help. Sounding very Daphne du Maurier-like, Chertkova writes that she has had a dream, in which she went back to Dubovka, her childhood estate home, and there talked with Dar'ia Kuz'minishna once again. At first she wants to hear all nanny's old stories and to recapture the happy moods of childhood. She wants to tell nanny all about her life, especially its great disappointments. "I feel so powerless, good-for-nothing... Life with all its terrors of the final years frightens me... The future is so terrifying, complicated, and dark. And the past is so clear, simple, and so dear."

Overwhelmed with nostalgia for the past, which will never return, for her happy childhood which she cannot retrieve, she despairs that she can't start life all over again. But then she "hears" the quiet voice of nanny, bending over her, not so much speaking as singing:[63]

> "Be careful, don't break the thread [*nitku ne porvi*]! Be patient, wait a while. Don't cry, my own dear child [*rodnaia detochka moia*]!"
>
> And how sweetly this voice sounds to me. It's been so very long since anyone called me: "*detochka*" [dear child]. And now I feel that I'm somehow lying in her lap, pressing my cheek to her breast. And she, silently caressing my hair with her hand, almost noiselessly says:
>
> "There's no reason to cry and grumble, my own dear child [*moe rodnoe, miloe ditia*]. Everything is all right – both that which has been and has passed, and it's all right [*khorosho*], *it must be all right* – and everything that is and will be..."
>
> And I awoke: in tears, hugging the pillow, I felt the presence of my dear, sweet nanny so vividly that for the first few minutes I couldn't believe that this was only a dream.

Chertkova and Miroliubov inadvertently suggested to me a potent image of the real-life Russian nanny, one that seems especially apropos given the constant references in the memoir literature to a nanny's frequent occupation: knitting. In Greek mythology, the

Significance of the Nanny in the Child's Life

Three Fates spun, measured, and cut the threads of each individual's life. In some small way, a nanny might be likened to Lachesis, the middle of the Fates. Lachesis held the threads, measured an individual's life, and to some extent may have been responsible for the quality of that life. A nanny's role, sometimes till the end of her days, was often to try to make sure that the child's life-thread remained secure and unbroken, without too many "knots," in caring hands.

Conclusion

Nannies played a variety of roles in children's lives, all of them important. Some, if not all, of the lessons learned in childhood would remain with these nurselings into adulthood. Because the nanny loomed so large in childhood, it is an easy assumption, difficult to demonstrate, that she probably exerted a strong influence on the child's later life. Having essayed explanations of how the nanny fit into young Russians' world, I turn in the next two chapters to investigations into some examples of ways in which nannies appeared in literature and how often the myth played out in lives other than Pushkin's.

8

The Long Literary Career of the Nanny

Nannies in World Literature

The story of nannies in literature is an old one. Nannies have populated not only popular/oral ("low") culture – in fairy tales, lullabies, and so on – but also high, written culture since earliest times. As Vladimir Nabokov has noted, a "story-telling old nurse is of course an ancient thematic device."[1] European literature provides many early examples of a nanny or nursemaid as a major character. She is there in tragedies about Phaedra written by Sophocles, Euripides, Seneca, and – much later – Racine. In Shakespeare's *Romeo and Juliet*, the heroine's nurse is her confidante and trusted messenger, while in his *Pericles* the nursemaid Lychorida is Marina's link with her own family's history.

The character evolves over time, in part following changing literary styles from Classicism to Romanticism to realism, in part mirroring changing socio-economic conditions, benefitting always from occasional and unpredictable epiphanies of genius. What could a fictional nanny (or wet-nurse) represent among Europe's reading or playgoing publics?[2]

Nannies were often part of a *chronotope*.[3] One aspect of chronotopes and genres has particular appeal, given the strong religious sensitivities ascribed to many nannies: For critics like Gary Saul Morson and Natalia Reed, "a sense of genre grows out of a sense of ethics." So genres and chronotopes often come down to how they display/reveal human character, especially its moral side.

Much of the best writing about nannies tries to accomplish just such a fleshing out of character and an illumination of the ethics of a situation.[4] The nanny character fits so nicely into this scheme that – with apologies to Bakhtin – I should like to propose a neologism, or at least a new meaning for a term already used in medicine. Such characters as a nanny should be called *chronotropes*, adding the letter "r" to the Russian critic's term. They represent an effort to capture – all at once – a sense of time and place, and some sort of symbolic meaning. My term has the added nicety of suggesting how easily such figures can slip into caricature or banality.

The Russian Case

Most of my readers will have long been aware – if only unconsciously – how often a character known as a nanny crops up in (modern) Russian poetry and literature. I can trace her Russian "high" roots back to about the late seventeenth century, but it is possible that a nanny appeared in some Kievan or Muscovite work even before that era. In Russia, about the time writing for enjoyment turned secular, nannies became more interesting characters. Beginning as a stock figure, like evil stepmothers and fairy godmothers, the nanny took on greater substance after 1700. Yet she long remained either a comic or tragic stereotype.

When Russian fairy tales began appearing in print in the late eighteenth century, they had evolved from oral stories to literary works authored by specific writers – a shift from low to high culture. Fairy tales collected and published in the 1780s often include the characters "*mamushki i nianiushki*" ("mammies and nannies").[5] This pat phrase shows up, for example, in the two 1786 collections, *A Cure for Melancholia* and *Grandfather's Strolls or The Continuation of Real Russian Fairy Tales*.[6] Together these anthologies contain some of the most famous Russian folktales, most of which speak of nannies as *de rigeur* at royal palaces.

It is ironic that a figure usually portrayed as pious and moral by the mid-nineteenth century should enter Russian high literature as a thoroughly venal, unlovable, and amoral/immoral character. In the well-known "Tale of the Rogue Frol Skobeev" (ca. 1690-1720), a nanny (*mamka*) plays a crucial but not sympathetic role.[7] Bribed by the conniving and upwardly mobile Frol, a member of the lesser Novgorod gentry, the nanny becomes a procuress. Not once, but on two separate occasions, she panders Annushka, the teenage girl she is supposed to look after. On both occasions, the nanny compounds the offense by lying, first to her young mistress, then to the girl's highly situated father. Still, Frol succeeds completely in his schemes, thanks in large measure to the pimping nanny's assistance; he marries Annushka and inherits all her wealthy father's estates. What is the perfidious nanny's punishment for her dereliction of duty, flaunting of prevailing social customs, and betrayal of the religious strictures by which she must have been raised? "Annushka's nanny remained living with Annushka and her husband in great honor to the end of her days."[8] The world had been turned partly upside-down.

Nannies Ere Pushkin: Expected, Unexceptional, Ambiguous. Matter-of-fact, Classicism-style treatments of nannies abound in works of major eighteenth-century authors like Mikhail Lomonosov, the fabulists Ivan Khemnitser and Ivan Krylov, and Gavrila Derzhavin. Aleksandr Sumarokov (1717-1777) cast a nanny in a pivotal role in his "The Tragedy of Khorev" (early 1750), giving advice, offering solace, even preventing the heroine's suicide.[9] At the same time, however, other authors depicted caretakers who are either unsympathetic or nearly peripheral to their charge's emotional life. In Nikolai Karamzin's 1792 story "Natal'ia, the Boiar's Daughter" the nanny is a rather ignorant, somewhat venal, altogether ordinary old woman – but still sympathetic to her nurseling.[10] (He doubtless borrowed much of his character from the earlier "Tale of the Rogue Frol Skobeev," which had appeared almost exactly a hundred years earlier.)

Whereas in real life peasant nannies evoked mixed feelings, they were rarely portrayed *in literature* as paragons of child caretaking.[11] In fact, the two main ingredients missing in most portrayals of nannies before Pushkin can be summed up in two words: goodness and nostalgia. Nostalgia first became important in portrayals of nannies in poetry rather than prose and plays, and only after sentimentalism and pre-Romanticism began to vie with the Classicism of earlier times.[12] Pushkin's friend Baron Del'vig

(1798-1831) was composing tender lines directed at his nanny by 1819-20, and he was not alone. The problem was that these figures tended to blur together with all other images of childhood: the same loving sentiments might be addressed to the birth mother, and the reader would have been hard pressed to distinguish between the two female figures. Mood was more important than character; the nanny did not stand out in any unusual way.

Fonvizin. The nanny truly comes into her own in a play by Denis Fonvizin (1745-1792); this masterpiece, known usually as "The Minor" (1760s?), was first staged in 1782.[13] Virtually the first words uttered are directed at the nanny. After playing a prominent part in the first two acts, however, she nearly disappears in the last three acts, at one point taking a position to one side, folding her arms, and standing "in slavish servility." We know immediately that the family at the center of this play are, as their name (Prostakov) conveys, "simpletons." But more than that, we know that they're not very good people from the way they mistreat their faithful servant, the nanny. The young man for whom the play is named, Mitrofan, is the callow teenage son in this petty gentry family, spoiled rotten by his overweening mother. His erstwhile nanny (*mama*) is Eremeevna (in typical fashion, called only by her patronymic), a paragon of (some) virtue.[14] Eremeevna is much abused by her masters, physically and especially verbally.[15] Eremeevna grumbles hyperbolically in Act II that she has to put up with a lot for just "five rubles a year and five slaps a day."[16] (Fonvizin interchangeably uses "*mama*" and "*mamka*" for "nanny" elsewhere.)

The overall comic effect of the exchanges is enhanced by the fact that Eremeevna – like most older female parts – would have been played by a male actor.[17] Thus, no matter how demeaning and insulting the abuse directed toward – heaped on – the nanny, one can still see in this kind of banter something more lighthearted than the words imply. We have little difficulty in construing it as typical of the give-and-take between master and servant in the literature of the day. (Beaumarchais handled relations of master and man quite similarly in *The Marriage of Figaro*.)[18]

In this play and especially in his better-wrought but less famous play "The Brigadier," Fonvizin was taking up the cudgels against excessive worship of everything foreign, especially French.¹⁹ The thoroughly Russian peasant Eremeevna is a foil for foreign tutors. Fonvizin's works in many ways culminate in a play by Ivan Krylov.

Krylov. Ivan Krylov (1768-1844), the greatest of Russia's fabulists-in-verse, was adept in other literary genres as well. His one-act play "A Lesson for Daughters" was first staged in St. Petersburg on 18 June 1807.²⁰ In the words of one scholar, "Krylov's comedy, directed against the cosmopolitan attitudes characteristic of a part of the Russian gentry, and mocking an excessive bowing before everything foreign, had great success on the stage."²¹ A major character in this frothy comedy of manners is Nanny Vasilisa, as is a family maid named Dasha. Nanny is a watchdog, set to stand guard over his daughters Fekla and Luker'ia by the country squire Vel'karov, who sees them indiscriminately in love with all things French and foreign. He forbids them to speak French and asks the nanny to make sure they do not. As the maid Dasha explains to another servant, Semën, who is also a complete Gallomane:

> So that they [the daughters] don't converse other than in Russian, [the squire's] appointed for them an old nanny, Vasilisa, who is supposed [*dolzhna*] to control this strictly, dogging their heels; and if they persist, to report it to him. At first they joked about this, but when nanny Vasilisa reported them, they saw that the old man is not joking; and now, wherever they go, nanny Vasilisa is after them; that is, they say one word not in Russian, nanny Vasilisa is right there to sniff it out [*tut s nosom*], and nanny Vasilisa can just about string 'em up [*ot niani Vasilisy prikhodit khot' v petliu*].²²

Vasilisa's classic line, repeated in variations throughout the play, is: "Little mother Luker'ia [or Fekla] Ivanovna, be so kind as to speak Russian." ["*Matushka, Luker'ia Ivanovna, izvol'te govorit' po-russki.*"] The girls are asked constantly to speak, to get angry (*gnevat'sia*), be sad (*pechalit'sia*), be happy (*radovat'sia*) – to do just about anything – exclusively in their native tongue.²³ By play's end, the girls are being punished for their monomaniacal pursuit of things French – and their concomitant indifference to modesty, caring, and meekness – by being forbidden to speak other than Russian until they improve on all counts. Nanny is again set on them, and they bemoan their fate, instinctively in French. Nanny Vasilisa brings down the curtain (and usually the house) with the play's final line: "*Matushki baryshni, izvol'te kruchinit'sia po-russki.*" [Little mother-mistresses, grieve in Russian, if you please.][24]

Radishchev. Peasants, usually sentimentalized (cf. Karamzin's story "Poor Liza"), became important in Russian literature toward the end of the eighteenth century, and peasant nannies naturally shared the spotlight. Not yet seen – as they would be by the later intelligentsia – as the epitome of what is worthy and good in Russia, the peasantry as portrayed in fiction still conveyed considerable power.[25] When Aleksandr Radishchev (1749-1802)[26] published his famous abolitionist novel *A Journey from St. Petersburg to Moscow* in 1790, one of the images he conjured with was that of a Russian peasant nanny.

The section of the *Journey* that mentions a nanny consists of a tale within the tale:[27] a traveler-companion of the narrator gives the reader an account of a public serf auction. A wastrel young lord, addicted to carousing and gambling, is being forced to sell off his serfs. Among the peasants being sold is an old man, the former *diad'ka* of the young master, his wife, and two other women. Listed like a bill of goods for sale, the females are described thus:

> The old woman of 80...had been the wet-nurse of the mother of their young master; had been his nanny [*nian'ka*] and had oversight of the home until that very hour when she was led out to the auction block. In all her time of service she had wasted [*utratila*] nothing of her masters, had acted out of self-interest in nothing [*nichem ne polorystvovalas'*], never lied, and if at times she irritated them it was only with her forthrightness.
>
> — A woman of 40, a widow, the wet-nurse of their young master. And to this day she still feels a certain tenderness toward him. In his veins flows her blood. She is a second mother to him, and he is more indebted to her for his life than to his own birth-mother. The latter conceived him

in lust, ignored him in his infancy. His wet-nurse and his nanny were the ones who reared him. They are parting with him as with a son.[28]

The story of the women is related with such passion and intensity that the (noble) reader must have been expected to blush with shame, repent, and reform.[29]

The Pushkin Factor

The reader will recall that at the end of Chapter 1 I posed a question whether Pushkin had an impact on literature similar to that which he had on memoir-writing. We have seen that nannies were stock figures in Russian literature before the 1820s. One might be tempted to argue that Pushkin's influence was not comparable here. But I would argue that he led other authors to look upon a nanny in a somewhat different light, and that made all the difference for the nanny in literature.

What did Pushkin do? He successfully combined nostalgia, Romanticism, aspects of serfdom and family life in a new way.[30] How did he manage this? I would say by doing three things. First, nearly all nannies in literature up until Pushkin wrote *Eugene Onegin* appear as fully developed adult actors. They are not mere abstractions; Fonvizin's Eremeevna and Krylov's Vasilisa, to take just two of many instances, are individualized characters that clearly anticipate Filippovna in *Onegin* in their recognizable humanity. But audiences were unlikely to be touched by strong sentiment (other than laughter) about them or their lives. Having served a purpose, they exited the stage, and few observers leaving their seats would likely have pondered their further fates or their "prehistory." Pushkin personalized a nanny as never before. He gave her a life before becoming a nanny: marriage at a very young age, a difficult time living with her in-laws, and finally an implied separation or termination of the marriage. A nanny with a past – this was novel.

Second, when *Onegin*'s central nanny character preceded in print by just a couple years Iazykov's poem on the death of Arina Rodionovna, the connection between life and literature no doubt struck readers much more forcefully than any literary character had in the past. Fonvizin and Krylov may have written about nannies, but few would associate their characters with the authors' private lives and their childhood nannies. Pushkin's own few poems about Arina would certainly have reinforced the connection between his characters and his personal biography. He had even written in a letter that Arina was the model for his creation Filippovna.[31] These factors may have brought her closer to readers than any earlier incarnation of a nanny. If nothing else, they probably helped fix a nanny as an ineluctable component of nineteenth-century Russian literature.

Third, and perhaps most important, the position that Pushkin quickly came to occupy within Russian literature was unique; he was the *nation*'s poet to a much larger extent than any predecessor, no matter how popular, had ever been. All that he created came to be seen – in true Romantic and idealistic fashion – as an expression of a unique Russian temperament, style, and tradition. The very mode of expression was key: he was, above all others, seen as the main creator of the modern Russian language. The aspirations for national greatness that he inspired and embodied placed characters

Nikolai Ge, *Pushchin Visiting Pushkin at Mikhailovskoe* (1875) oil on canvas

like Onegin, Tat'iana, and Tat'iana's nanny in a new and powerful light; they were expressions of the nation's "soul" in ways that the government's officially sponsored nationalism could never be.

Timing is all, in literature as in history. Pushkin's writings about nannies, beginning with the third chapter of *Onegin* in 1827, appear just about one year after the execution of five men and the forced Siberian exile of many more in the failed Decembrist uprising. Many of these conspirators from the nobility represented the "best and brightest" of their generation; many had participated in the campaigns of 1812-1815 – a defining time for Russia as a country and Russians' consciousness of themselves as a nation and a people. Pëtr Chaadaev's famous "First Philosophical Letter" was less than a decade away. Strong feelings became attached to people and things associated specifically, sometimes uniquely, to Russia. Already or within a short time, rightly or wrongly, a *sui generis* stamp would be applied to institutions like the peasant commune, Russian Orthodoxy, the tsarist autocracy. One "beneficiary" in literature of this ardent upsurge of nationalistic feeling was the peasant nanny.

Closer attention to nannies was almost certainly an inadvertent or unintended byproduct of his artistic endeavor for Pushkin. However, it was far from so for most of his followers. Pushkin devotees had promoted the image, the symbol, of Arina and her kind for all of Russian literature. (Unlike in ego-documents and quasi-autobiographical writings, the one thing Pushkin did *not* accomplish in literature was to fix the nanny firmly to childhood. Fictional nannies remained as much associated with their grown charges as with tiny ones.) It was left for the poet's epigones to pursue the theme in their writings.

Banality and Originality in the Nanny Theme

The Example of Chekhov. With tongue only partly in cheek, I suggest a litmus test – we could call it "the nanny index" – for literature in the modern period: the more often an author puts a nanny into his or her works, the more the writing tends to be unoriginal and routine. By the same rule of thumb, only when authors reach a level of high artistic maturity are they able to put a nanny into their works and avoid the pitfall of banality. I owe this insight to Anton Chekhov, who, in an early work, mocked the triteness of many of his fellow authors. Unoriginal writers populate their works with: "A count, a countess with traces of a kind of former beauty, a neighboring baron, a liberal litterateur, an impoverished nobleman, a foreign musician, blockheaded lackeys, *nannies*, governesses, a German estate overseer, an esquire and heir from America. Personages not pretty but sympathetic and attractive."[32]

Over the next few years Chekhov demonstrated that he was himself not immune to this kind of artistic laziness. Nanny characters in his short stories of 1880-85 – and there are many – are almost invariably stick figures. However, he could still display his talents by playing with such characters and stock situations, as in the beautifully executed story "Life in Questions and Exclamations" (1882), which seems, in part, to be a parody of Tolstoi's trilogy on childhood, adolescence, and young manhood (youth). The lengthy "Unnecessary Victory" (1882) has a nanny mostly undistinguished, but who at least was "an excellent pedagog" – she "did not lie even in her fairy tales." In the late 1880s and 1990s he was still writing many trite nanny minor characters into stories.[33]

It's noteworthy that, among the female "archetypes" in his mature works,[34] there was "the elderly female servant, a type for which Chekhov seems to have had considerable sentimental attachment." Bakhtin would recognize such characters as part of a chronotope. "Slow in motion and response and rather useless for most of their masters' service needs, these superannuated, kindly women are usually presented as guardians of the domestic everyday routine. As such, they provide a background of living scenery that gives any Chekhovian locale its special stamp of lifelike authenticity."[35]

Chekhov, however, was too great a genius not to dispense occasionally with all the usual claptrap and produce something much better. In his mature works he came up with several nannies that are unforgettable. Two recognized Chekhov masterpieces rendering aspects of childhood prominently feature nannies that are anything but typical. In "The Cook Marries" (1885), with a seven-year-old little boy named Grisha as the protagonist, there is a not especially pleasant nanny named Aksin'ia Stepanovna; she wears a "most malicious smile" at times, connives and manipulates to achieve her aims, and is in general far removed from the sweet and kindly nannies of most authors. "Grisha" (1886) features a nanny who allows her under-three-year-old charge a sip of strong drink.[36] In one of his most famous tales, "Sleepy" (1888), Chekhov's main character is a thirteen-year-old nanny, Var'ka. This young girl-nanny is totally original. In order to get the sleep she desperately needs but is deprived of by her charge's crying, she kills the infant. She then goes blissfully to sleep.[37]

Another masterful creation is the old nanny Anfisa in the *Three Sisters* (1900). She is an obvious candidate to be called by my neologism of *chronotrope*, but, though stereotypical, she is also a poignant reminder of what old age could mean for former serfs. Considered useless by the grasping, cruel Natasha, the nanny is a symbol of all that can go wrong in capitalism and a reminder of what was supposedly "right" in the old regime.[38] As one critic puts it, Anfisa "is already more of an ornament from the past than a functioning domestic servant. Like an old cat by the stove, she drowsily idles her time away in between token attempts to be useful and the traditional helpings of tea, until the fury of Natasha finally packs her off together with the sisters." At play's end Anfisa almost alone is content, with her own room, staying with Ol'ga.[39]

The Stereotype after Pushkin

Unlike Chekhov, however, most litterateurs were unable to rise to the challenge of treating a nanny in an original way. The evolution of nanny figures in literature parallels developments in educated society more generally. Uninformed idealization (or condemnation) of peasants early in the nineteenth century had gradually given way to more realistic thinking, as zemstvo workers and ethnographer-anthropologists studied rural life in the 1860s and 70s. Earlier seen as passive and submissive (and mainly, not Western), peasants – including some nannies – began to emerge belatedly as conscious actors, embracing or rejecting change.[40]

The "Literary Lullaby."[41] As we saw in Chapter 5, nannies often sing their nurselings to sleep. Litterateurs found the lullaby form conducive for audiences not so small as well. Iuliia Zhadovskaia

(1824-1883), the poet and novelist, wrote the lullaby-like poem "A Thought" (*Duma*) in 1847.[42] Unlike most such efforts, Zhadovskaia's lullaby is directed toward a female infant and discusses the difficulties a girl could expect in those days, yet be rewarded with a family. A nanny highlights the moral choices a wife and mother must make.

Chtoby deti tebe ne meshali,	So that the children not interfere for you,
Ty ikh v detskuiu s nian'koi zapresh'...	You'll shut them away in a nursery with a nanny...
I ne znaia serdechnoi pechali,	And feeling no sadness of the heart,
Preschastlivo svoi vek prozhivesh'.	You'll live out your life in great joy.

The nanny in Nekrasov's sentimental, even schmaltzy 1858 "Song for Eremushka" (*Pesnia Eremushke*) is, absurdly, well up on French Revolutionary slogans, hardly typical for women who were mostly archconservatives in their socio-political views. She sings to her charge:

S nimi ty rozhden prirodoiu –	These are your nature-given birthright –
Vozlelei ikh, sokhrani!	Nourish [and] preserve them!
Bratstvom, Ravenstvom, Svobodoiu	Fraternity, Equality, Liberty
Nazyvaiutsia oni.	Are they called.

The writer and radical activist Mikhail Mikhailov's poem "Nanny" (1847) is at least a pseudo-lullaby, written from the nanny's point of view, as she urges her young charge to drop off to sleep quickly so the child's guardian angel (*angel tvoi sviatoi*) will come down from heaven and show him all God's wonders.[43] In Fëdor Sologub's "Terrible Lullaby" (*Zhutkaia kolybel'naia*, 1913), the nanny is the "last line of defense for the child against the grim intruder, death."[44] This lullaby confounds the ordinary cradle song, which includes various "scares" for the infant but after each has a calming, reassuring chorus to soothe the babe. Sologub's verses avoid that common refrain (*"baiushki-baiu"*) and instead uses his own formula, *"bai-bai."* According to Valentin Golovin, this can be taken as anticipation of "absolute rest"– the ultimate "calm" of death.

Purple Prose. Sergei Pobedonostsev (1816-1850), older brother of the conservative *eminence grise* of the Alexander II and III and Nicholas II eras, Konstantin Pobedonostsev, made his name in the field of literature and publicistics. Sergei too was a staunch supporter of the pre-reform system in which he spent his entire life. Sergei's short story "The Nanny" (1845) is an overwrought, cliché-ridden tale.[45] As a forerunner of things to come, it is a kind of template of banality and might be said to establish a basic tenet of nanny literature: if an author wants to add a little pathos to a story, s/he can always throw in a suffering nanny. Just as in Radishchev and earlier prose, so it remained in mid- to late-nineteenth century, and even the best writers could barely escape the temptation.[46]

The story begins – in a framing *skaz* – with the funeral of a nanny, as sentimentalized as Pobedonostsev can make it. The nanny was the epitome of caring devotion and self-sacrifice. All loved her and are in tears as her service is said and the coffin sealed and lowered. Then comes a sort of flashback from the narrator, one Nadia Stepanovna. Her childhood was marred by a hostile stepmother. The nanny, Marfa Artamonovna, is the children's "guardian-angel" and "preceptor" (*nastavnitsa*). Marfa has all the usual traits of nannies, good and bad – ignorant, full of "superstitions" and kindly folkways. Marfa's life story is sorrowful, losing husband and baby to the pox. She becomes the nanny of Nadia's father, then housekeeper-manager of the manor, but later raises her first charge's children. Her final service to the family is to salvage the reputation of Nadia's sweetheart so the young lovers can marry. Thus, Nadia owes all her happiness to the self-sacrificing nanny. All her happiest memories of life, in both childhood and adulthood, are tied only to Marfa.[47]

Another, later exercise in cloying excess is Mariia Sakharova's tale entitled "Nanny. An Étude" (1883),[48] which establishes a second basic tenet: if one wants to show what's best about Russia, bring in a nanny. Sakharova's melange of turgid sentimentalism, Slavophilism, and Dostoevskii-Danilevskii *pochvennichestvo* ("nativism") is a tear-jerking tale of a noble family that falls on hard times and has to desert their ancestral homestead. When nanny learns her former nurseling Ol'ga has died, she follows suit.[49]

Sakharova's nanny is again the quintessential self-sacrificing woman, devoted and loving; she has virtually lived only for her charge and the family. But the story's coda extends this clichéd image of the nanny beyond the family to the whole country, to the Russian nation:

> A no-longer-needed life has burned itself out; an old heart has found its rest. For a long time – in a simple, peasant breast – it beat for the happiness of another's child and was extinguished without a grumble, tears, or curses for the suffering it experienced; quietly, like a forgotten lamp goes out – without a crackle or a flame – Wherever did you learn, who taught you how to love so, to forgive and to die, simple Russian woman? Is not your own people a giant, your Russian folk, the meek infant of the universe? Left behind by its older brother, the civilized man – despite all the physical and moral adversities brought on by itself and others – having nourished within itself, along with common sense, a profound feeling of love for man and mankind, concealing which from time to time in the inmost recesses of its soul, does it [Russia] not manifest it [love of mankind] by its constant readiness to sacrifice itself both for the common cause and for the good of individual persons? Will it not share with this brother at some time its spiritual wealth and not convey to him that view of life which it has been in possession of itself for such a long time and exclusively?

The Moral Watchdog. This stereotype recurs frequently in the post-emancipation period. A first-rate example is "The Truth" (*Pravda*, 1893) by Kapitolina Nazer'eva (1847-1900), a "comedic" take on Hamlet.[50] Nazer'eva – primarily a novelist and short story writer – had a "flair for ingenious plotting," according to one expert. She was good at developing complex, rounded characters. The nanny Pelageia Vlas'evna is a stickler for honesty but understands all the nuances of what "truth" can mean. She wants her former charge Alësha, just returned to his remarried mother's estate, to learn "the real truth" of what is wrong there. We think we know where the playwright is heading, but it turns out that Vlas'evna's main task is to put the honesty-demanding Alësha straight. She berates him for demanding too much "truth" from his mother and her wayward new spouse. Nazer'eva knows people sometimes need their illusions; if the truth removes the last comfort in life, it would be best not to reveal such truths. The nanny it is who imparts this last hard "truth."

Another fine example of a moral nanny, Fedos Chizhik in Konstantin Staniukovich's story "Nian'ka," is treated further on.

The Satiric Icon Disappears. After the glorious masterpieces of the satirists Fonvizin and Krylov, it is sad to report a dearth of comic nannies in the nineteenth century. Perhaps this was one more legacy of Pushkin's writings: he may have made it almost impossible, for much of the century, to laugh at nannies. Instead of the biting variety of satire involving nannies, the mid-century produced only the mildly humorous kind. A good example is a playlet by the radical Mikhail Mikhailov entitled "Nanny Dear (Satirical Scenes)" (*Nianiushka. [Satiricheskiia stseny]*) which could appear only after a reworking for the censors.[51] In the second of two acts, which takes place in the nursery, the 60-year-old Alena Ievlevna must deal with her 5-year-old charge Sasha, who is resisting going to bed, demanding sweets, and behaving like any small boy.[52] The high point of the satire comes when nanny Alena basically teaches little Sasha how to blackmail his mother into getting candy and other things he wants from her – all because, as he's told nanny, he saw his mother sitting on a divan and kissing an officer (with papa nowhere in sight).[53]

By the time we reach the late tsarist era, an original humorist like Arkadii Averchenko (1881-1925) is no longer using the nanny as a primary object of fun. Instead, in the little gem "A Woman's Tail" [sic], his gentle darts fly toward the opposite sex in general ("women are like hand grenades at rest" he assures his readers) and a little girl's nanny is just one more unexpected burden for a newlywed husband to bear.[54]

Gender-Bending and Backward-Looking Nannies. In looking for something new to say about – or *through* – nannies, two authors hit upon the idea of making a nanny male (not as a *diad'ka*, but as a true nanny). One of them was a writer of genius, Nikolai Leskov (1831-1895). In perhaps his best-known work, the comic masterpiece "The Enchanted Wanderer" or "Enchanted Pilgrim" (1873 or 1874), Leskov artfully employs the *skaz* technique.[55] In this novella we learn from the narrator Fliagin, born a serf, that he ran away from his master to the "free city" of Nikolaev, only to be accosted by a nobleman who recognizes his fugitive status. But instead of threatening Fliagin with arrest or his forced return to his master, the nobleman proposes something quite different and extraordinary.

> "You're just the man I want, just the man I want! ...you'll be able to look after my child: I'm engaging you as her nanny."
> I was horrified.
> "How do you mean as a nursemaid, sir? I'm quite unequal to such a task."
> "Oh, that's nothing," he said, "nothing at all. I can see that you'll make an excellent nanny. For I don't mind telling you," he said, "that I'm in an awful fix: my wife got tired of me and ran off with a cavalry officer...and she left her baby girl with me and I can't feed her, for I have neither the time nor the food, so you'll have to nurse her and I'll give you two silver roubles a month as your wages."
> "But, Lord, sir," I said, "it isn't a question of the two roubles! How shall I cope with such a job?"
> "Why," he said, "that's just nothing. You're a Russian, aren't you? Well, a Russian can cope with anything!"
> "Well, sir," I said, "it is quite true that I am a Russian, but I am a man and I haven't been gifted by nature with the things that are necessary for the nursing of a suckling babe."
> "Don't you worry about that," he said. "I'm going to buy you a goat from a Jew to help you out in this matter. All you'll have to do is milk the goat and feed my child on her milk."

I thought it over and said:

"Of course, sir, one could nurse a child with the help of a goat, but all the same," I said, "you really ought to get a woman for such a job."

"No," he said, "don't you ever mention women to me: they're the cause of all the trouble in the world. Besides, you can't get them, anyway..."

So I debated with myself and I decided: ...I agreed to stay on as a nurse.[56]

In the upshot, the nobleman's judgment is born out; Fliagin makes an excellent, if quite short-term, nanny.

The other author who played with gender was Konstantin Staniukovich (1843-1903), whose story "Nian'ka" – set in the late 1850s – was published in 1895.[57] His male nanny is Fedos Chizhik, batman for a naval officer named Luzgin. Chizhik is honorable, modest, conscientious, and kind, but little Shura's mother still dislikes him. She has him whipped for no good reason, the injustice of which causes Shura to hate his mother. Chizhik realizes that it's up to him to make things right between his charge and his mistress. He tells Shura that his mother is not a bad person, she just doesn't understand; men and women reason about many things differently, he adds.[58] Told without Leskov's sharp wit, virtually the same tale of a male nanny comes across as too sentimental, its saving grace the transmutation of gender.[59]

By the time Prince Vladimir Volkonskii (b.1846) wrote "The Family Chronicle of the Valdaiskii Princes" (1903), the idea and the persona of the nanny had both grown rather old and tired. Volkonskii wrote at length and in warm, loving tones of this stock figure. It is one of the most complete portraits of a pre-1861 nanny to be found in Russian literature. He added little that was new except some diverting details. He notes, for instance, a duty of nannies few others bothered to mention. His nanny character, Anfisa Vasil'evna, carried her nurselings' handkerchiefs around with her in a "hated" handbag. Whenever she saw the handbag, "willy-nilly she would remember her most important obligation [sic!], which consisted of blowing and wiping our noses," the narrator informs. "This solemn performance [of duty], sometimes even without any necessity, was repeated every half hour...In such cases, Anfisa Vasil'evna's fingers, under cover of the handkerchief, positively became a weapon of Inquisitional torture, which brought us to tears."[60] Another detail which makes Volkonskii's Anfisa more memorable than most run-of-the-mill nannies: she changes her storytelling with the seasons.[61]

Trying to Escape Stereotypes Toward the End of Tsarism

Along with Chekhov, by the 1880s there were other authors – excellent if second-rank – who found ways to move away from (beyond?) stereotypes of earlier times and present more rounded, full-blooded, and interesting characterizations of nannies in their fiction. The tendency became to make nannies touching but not maudlin figures. The treatment often was, or was close to, matter-of-fact. As befits the religious revival in the country as a whole in the second half of the nineteenth century, nannies' faith and religion were frequently highlighted.

I will discuss just three such writers here. One of the few authors who, like Chekhov, performed better than most in this respect was Mariia Krestovskaia (1862-1910), a novelist and short story writer. Also like Chekhov, she was an acute psychologist. In her novella *Early Storms* (1886) a somewhat selfish young daughter learns a great lesson from her mother, Mar'ia Sergeevna, and the family nanny.[62] The portrait of the (unnamed) nanny – a decent but flawed child caretaker[63] – is well-handled throughout, in a naturalistic and realistic way. The selfish mother has had a baby – Kolia – as a result of an affair, and her teenage daughter Natal'ia is hostile to Kolia, the obvious cause of her parents' breakup. After her mother's death, Natasha, who's never tended her half-brother, is forced by the nanny to care for him – and thereby has an epiphany. She and her father must take care of Kolia if they are to survive as a family, for, as her mother continually reminded her, Kolia "is not to blame." The nanny's role, while secondary to Mar'ia Sergeevna's, is complementary and crucial. Like a true double of the mother, she is not without fault but still gives the most important thing to Kolia, unconditional love, and helps Natasha see that she must do the same.

Elizaveta Militsyna (1869-1930) wrote well about peasants,

especially peasant women. Her short story "Nanny" fits into the body of her *oeuvre*; it is well-crafted, has some original elements, but is still somewhat derivative.[64] One reason to include it here is its extended delving into the religious mentality that we have come to associate with most nannies (Chapter 4). Another, that it recapitulates the presumed life-history of many a nanny from the mid- through the late nineteenth century. Third, it foreshadows a more brilliant effort by Ivan Shmelëv by supposedly telling her story in the nanny's own words (but in the language of the upper class). The nanny is preoccupied with one gloomy thought, her impending death, and the fear that her entire life of caring for three generations of a family has been wasted. "It's been three days now that the children haven't been to see me; it means that they weren't told to. It's obvious – however you devote yourself, with the masters you remain all the same a stranger." In the end, her two little charges do come to see her; calmed by their presence, she now sees only their young lives, not her own near death. "…and this life in her mind's eye has changed into an eternal life beyond the grave."

Yet another author who tended to avoid stereotypes was the engineer-writer N. Garin-Mikhailovskii (1852-1906).[65] In his acknowledged masterpiece, *Detstvo Tëmy* (Tëma's Childhood; 1892), the first part of a quasi-autobiographical tetralogy, the author includes a nanny and a *bonne* for the family's children and nothing much is made of them. But in some of his stories that was not the case. For example, the long conversation about heaven between five-year-old Petia and his stern old nanny – in "At the Estate of the Pomeshchitsa Iaryshcheva"– is unforced, not too precious, and altogether satisfying.[66] As with Militsyna, religion and the nanny's own viewpoint come into play prominently. The climax of the tale is unexpected. In bed nanny's thoughts turn to the past, when she was married and beautiful, and the master came and raped her – but she had ambiguous feelings toward him! – and left her alone "with her sin." He's long since died; she has to try to forget. "But what will happen to her? And how does she look on her mistress, his widow? But worst of all, to this day she's unrepentant in her soul!" She should go to a monastery, "to pray for her mortal sins before God and the people, before her husband and the mistress."

"A Father's Confession" features an angry father, too full of himself by half, who continually berates his sons' Russian nanny, calling her a "stupid woman." "My authority is so far established that once, passing by, I hear nanny's voice: 'Or I'll call papa!' 'Nanny, I do not at all want to be a bugbear for my own children: I forbid you to frighten the child with my name'," he admonishes her. This "new kind of father" eventually strikes the older son, who wants to run away with his little brother and nanny. He repents of his mistaken ideas of childrearing after the older boy dies; he behaves differently with the remaining boy – he is more loving.[67] Slightly over the top at the end, Garin-Mikhailovskii nonetheless captures in this one fine story the nuances and changing understanding of childhood and childcare in turn-of-the-century Russia. Russian nannies, for him, are no longer to be sentimentalized, are not merely figures of nostalgia.[68]

Post-Revolutionary and Anti-Revolution Synecdoche and Metaphor

Not surprisingly, the figure of a nanny remains powerful – in some ways becomes more powerful – after 1917, when she's the symbol not just of the "good old days" under serfdom but now even of the entire tsarist system. Soviet writers could hardly evoke this symbol, of course, at least not in support of tsarism; it was left for Russian émigrés to do so. In them, nostalgia for the old ways blends with nostalgia for Russia itself.

Lappo-Danilevskaia and Aldanov. In Nadezhda Lappo-Danilevskaia's potboiler *At the Estate* (1928), the housekeeper-companion – but former nanny – Alena Karpovna is a symbol of the past. Most particularly she represents what both the radical intelligentsia and the gentry ignored and neglected in their own ways, to the great detriment of each: the decent, Christian values of peasant Russia.[69] Almost too late does the protagonist, Georgii Petrovich Gangeblov, come to realize what he's lost in not marrying Alena when he had the chance. Alena and the local priest, Fr. Pëtr, help Gangeblov realize for the first time that he's concentrated all his life only on the material side of it. (He doesn't go to church and his muzhiks see him as non- or unchristian [*nekhrist*].) (pp. 43-45, 159-64) Alena also makes him see the only hope for the future lies in his grandson Vasilen'ka – Villi – an almost saintly boy of 7, preternaturally wise about what's truly important in life. (pp. 119-20) Having lost Alena to death, Gangeblov can still share his "revelation" about life and himself with Fr. Pëtr: as the nanny and his grandson have shown him, love for one's neighbor – selfless love – is uppermost in life. One must simply love God. One's natural response in finishing this sermon-like novel is to whisper "Amen."

Just the opposite to the over-earnest style of Lappo-Danilevskaia is the lighthearted, or at least ironic, approach of Mark Aldanov (pseudonym of Landau; 1886-1957) in his large novel *The Sources* (*Istoki*; 1950), set at the time of Alexander II's assassination. At one point, Professor Mikhail Cherniakov pays a call on Dostoevskii.

> At the bell the doors were not opened for a long time. Then rapid steps could be heard. A woman's voice said – unexpectedly very *cozily* (in a voice in which *could be heard a smile*):
>
> "Right away, right away, hold on a second" (although Cherniakov had pulled the cord just once and rather meekly). A woman with a simple, kindhearted [*milovidnoe*] face opened the door, dressed so simply that Mikhail Iakovlevich could not even make out whether this was a wife, maid, or nanny. "Most likely a nanny [*Skoree vsego niania*]. There are women who are by nature *nannyshaped* [*n ia n e o b r a zn y e*]"...
>
> "You've come to see Fëdor Mikhailovich? Please wait in the study...You can lay your things right here," said the woman with a pleasant smile, pointing to an ancient trunk, covered with grey cloth.
>
> "The trunk is also *nianeobraznyi*," thought Mikhail Iakovlevich, smiling amiably.[70]

Shmelëv. Ivan Shmelëv (1873-1950)[71] wrote *A Nanny from Moscow* (*Niania iz Moskvy*) in 1932-1933, but it was published only in 1937.[72] Shmelëv's genius reveals itself in three ways in this novella. First, he allows a nanny character equal footing with his gentry heroine;

this is almost unprecedented. In fact, she is the narrator of the tale. Second, he has the nanny speak – as best he could reproduce it – in "her own" language. Third, unlike the great majority who wrote about nannies post-1917 but focused on pre-1917 days, he dealt with the post-revolutionary period as well. While not unique, this temporal span was certainly unusual.

Let's take a very brief look at some of these elements before turning to the plot.[73] Making his nanny, Dar'ia Stepanovna, the narrator, Shmelëv employs the *skaz* technique of storytelling. Dar'ia is given peasant dialect and folk patterns of speech. Shmelëv, who, though born into a merchant family, lived among peasants when young, had a wonderful ear for peasant intonations, vocabulary, and phrasing. Though far from the first nonpeasant author to affect peasant speech in the mouth of a nanny, Shmelëv was still one of the very best, if not the best, at doing so. Not atypical of most peasants in Russian literature, nanny "reformulates" many words, saying, for instance, "*alistokraty*" instead of "*aristokraty*," "*trakhmalyi*" instead of "*krakhmal'nyi*," "*kolidor*" instead of "*koridor*." She draws out many vowels, gives words extra syllables. And it's stressed several times throughout that the nanny is illiterate. In fact, Shmelëv adds to the subtlety and irony of the book by deliberately taking this "post-emancipation" nanny and giving her nearly all the attributes of the typical *serf* (pre-emancipation) nanny.

When telling her life story to a nun in Paris in 1927, Dar'ia Stepanovna is over 70, with a bad heart. Before the revolution she worked for a feckless doctor, Konstantin Arkadych (Kostia), and his wife, both "pinko-liberals." The faithful nanny is poorly treated and taken for granted by "her family," even by their daughter Katia. She's not been paid her wages, as her bosses waste their money and await a nice inheritance from an aunt. When the nanny gets a few rubles she's told: "Why do you, *nianichka*, need money?..." and "You, *nian'*, just have to be patient, and we'll soon receive a large sum [*kush*], and we'll give you [your back wages] at once." The family is not bad; they have great plans – to build an almshouse – for nanny and other old working folks. "Just wait," big changes are coming; Kostia will be put in charge of all hospitals "when the revolution comes." They are, pre-1917, obviously "radical chic" *avant le mot*.

Shmelëv has written a brilliant refutation of the guiding ideas of the oppositional, rationalistic intelligentsia of the 1860s and 70s. This, for him, is the "reply" the vast majority of the peasants would have given the radicals if only they'd had the chance and could find their "voice" as he has provided it here. It's not just their politics that makes the family unworthy in Shmelëv's eyes; it's also – perhaps mostly – their attitude toward religion.[74] The parents call church rites stupid; they want their daughter to grow up to be "independent-minded" and so not rely on supernatural forces in her life. But, nanny objects, where will she find comfort when trouble comes, if not in God? Nanny decides the parents are spoiling Katia, not just in the usual sense but spiritually as well. The spoiled girl mistreats nanny after her early church training is stopped. At one point Dar'ia Stepanovna is resolved to leave them all, but when they refuse to give her a passport and the back wages she's due, and when Katia throws a huge tantrum, she relents and stays. She "got used to them"and found a measure of happiness, but still believes it's shameful that they don't take others' feelings into account.

Shmelëv allows himself the pleasure of playing off the saintly image of the nanny. When the mother, whom nanny has known since she was 7, confesses "We're guilty before you, *nianichka*! You're so good, and we...we're scoundrels before you!", nanny mildly upbraids her, telling her that they don't have God in their house (no icons) and so they have no rest, that things are bad in their house. Nanny recounts for her Paris interlocutor what would come next in those days: "'*Nianichka*,' she'd say, 'you work so hard for us...you're our most dear, you're just simple folk, you're from Tula, with work-calloused hands...' – and she'd pat my hand the whole time, God's truth. But then she'd go on, God forgive her: – 'Yes, we pray to you, like to an icon, we have to...why, you're ho-o-ly!...' – but there was no icon hung in their house, and they never prayed."[75] (pp. 256-57)

Nanny demurs to her interlocutor: "I'm not worthy of this." Indeed, while nanny is obviously quite "noble," she's an awful gossip. She tells her Paris interlocutor all sorts of tales "out of school" about her mistress, master, even Katia. A key passage comes when the father, dying, bids nanny "Don't leave Katichka, nanny; soon she'll be left all alone" and adds "Forgive us, nanny, for everything." He confesses that he expects no mercy in the afterlife; "you're happy, Dar'iushka, you have a God, but I have nothing; I've even forgotten how to pray." The mother suddenly dies before him; he lives on briefly. When he feels his end near, he calls Katia in and bids her farewell: "Only nanny will remain with you...She is your own kin; you must obey [*pochitai*] her...she won't abandon you, I've asked her."⁷⁶ "Don't forget nanny; she has been more right than we, she has pity for everyone..."

A particularly nice touch in the book is Shmelëv's use of folklore and fairy tales to show how "rooted" the old nanny is in the Russian nation. In several places in the novel the folktale of Ivan the Tsarevich and the Grey Wolf is invoked as a kind of model for the relationship between the nanny and Katia.⁷⁷ We learn nanny's full name only on the last few pages of the novel: Dar'ia Stepanovna Sinitsyna, but her first name and patronymic are there in the first few pages. She herself pronounces the phrase of the title, telling her Paris interlocutor that she's "a nanny from Moscow." Picaresque in its sweep and plot, the novel has Katia and nanny visit Turkey (where Dar'ia nannies Turkish – i.e., non-Christian – children), India, France, and America. They have memorable adventures everywhere, especially in Hollywood, where Katia becomes an actress and a movie star. Each place they find themselves, nanny's all-embracing love and compassion (even for non-Christians) reflects the universal appeal of Russian Orthodoxy. And even as Katia seems to become more and more secular and worldly, nanny's prayers save her and the man she loves from a sad end.⁷⁸

Tèffi. In the case of Nadezhda Tèffi (née Lokhvitskaia; 1872-1952) also, there is too much talent for her to use a nanny merely as instant "context" for the lost pre-revolutionary world. She simultaneously evokes that world and tweaks its nose, poking gentle fun at all the sentimentalized nannies of pre-revolutionary literature. In fact, one sees a sure sign of her breaking with the mold by writing about both present and former child caretakers. Like Shmelëv, she places many of her nannies in the post-1917 world. Nannies show up in too many of her works to enumerate here; one student of her *opus* even calls a group of them her "nanny stories."⁷⁹ If, in the prerevolutionary period, Tèffi was happy to debunk the "sugary image" (*susal'nyi obraz*) of the dear, kind nanny, she later became more of an admirer.

While she included many nanny figures in her pre-1917 work,[80] it seemed to take the revolution for her to realize the full potential of the character – and of folk motifs generally – in her stories.[81] In her "Nostalgia," for example, an old nanny, imported to France from Moscow, is the mouthpiece for all those who "feared a Bolshevik death" but died a different kind of death in exile, the embodiment of what all the émigrés feel for their lost homeland.[82] One reason why nannies are prominent in so many of Tèffi's stories is the centrality of children and the theme of childhood in her work, especially the later stories.[83] This choice probably reflects an evolution in her worldview. According to Edythe Haber, by the 1930s Tèffi was writing more and more about compassion and "a new kind of love." Earlier, "love" for Tèffi was "comical"and "false," bringing "bitter disillusion and pain" in its wake. The external show of passion concealed an inner indifference or even hostility, in Haber's analysis. The usually humorous satirist often treated "love" seriously; love was egoistic, the "assertion of one person over another," and "devouring." Tèffi's new love took the form of "tenderness" (*nezhnost'*), which was in fact the title of a 1938 book she published. This new love, says Haber, is "self-denying and instinctive," based on pity and akin to Christianity. It is "the most humble, divine face of love." This feeling is always irrational; "often its object is unworthy of it."[84] The coincidence with Ivan Shmelëv's themes is striking.

How powerful this turn in direction became can be seen in one of Tèffi's best post-emigration stories, "The Monster," the nominal focus of which is a nanny. In a long dialog, Valentina Sergeevna and her boyfriend Shparagov argue about whether she should be spending so much time and energy caring for her eighty-year-old former nanny. He insists that "You have to be rational about all this. You have to recognize that for your old nanny it would be best of all not to let slip the chance to end her earthly existence, which is joyless for her and very burdensome for you." Valentina accuses him of lack of understanding and grows angry: "Can't you understand with that magnificent reason of yours that I love my old nanny dear. Do you understand – lo-ve! That I'd give up all the cinema and other joys to prolong even for an hour her little, helpless life." Suppressing a laugh, he retorts that "that's the whole point. 'I love' is the main unhappiness of our human life!...How happy, contented, and satisfied we'll all be when we eradicate enemy number one: love for another human."[85] "You're a monster!" cries Valentina Sergeevna. "Yes!" Shparagov assents, "with honor." Tèffi then reveals her most important message, when Valentina Sergeevna next speaks: "It's horrible without love. All these old, and sick, and poor, and defenseless ones – they don't need us, but we them. Glory to God that they exist. For our sake, thank God. We would perish if not for them."

Soviet Writers. Aside from memoirists, authors of the Soviet Union did not often include a nanny in their works. One of the few who did, but only early on, was the sly satirist Mikhail Zoshchenko (1895-1958), who, in 1931, produced a small gem entitled "A Tale about a Nanny, or the Added Value of this Profession."[86] Set toward the end of or after NEP, the story still smacks of the 20s and its enterprising Ostap Benders. The Farforovs line up childcare even before the birth of their child. "They could not themselves provide their baby with care and affection. The two of them worked at the factory."

> So here they had a baby for real [*kak takovoi*] and, of course, they had to hire a nanny for him. Were it not so, of course, they wouldn't have done the hiring.
>
> The more so in that they were not in the habit of hiring nannies for themselves. They had no understanding of such grandness [*barstvo*].
>
> But now it was more advantageous for them to have a nanny than for Madame Farforov to leave her place of work and retire from manufacturing.
>
> And so here, of course, a nanny found employment with them. (p. 198)

The repeated interjection "of course" [*konechno*] serves notice to the reader, of course, that there is nothing about this situation that will follow the natural course of (expected) events. The nanny "was not so very old nor yet so very young. In a word, getting on in years and rather terrifying to behold.

But underneath that hideous exterior the Farforovs soon caught sight of a kind heart within her. And they could never have foreseen what sort of asp they had warmed in their bosom."

> But they, of course, had intentionally hired themselves such an ugly woman, so that she wouldn't gad about nor have any happiness of her own, and so that she would exclusively look after their little infant.
> Especially as they hired her on [good] recommendation. They were told this was a teetotaling, ugly old woman. And were told she loved children and really didn't let them out of her sight. And although she was an old woman, that she was an old woman completely worthy of becoming part of the new, classless society...
> And so they hire this nanny and they see that in truth she is pure gold, and not a [mere] nanny. Especially as she immediately fell in love with the infant. She's constantly on the go with him, doesn't let go of him, and strolls with him until nighttime. (p. 198)

One day, a member of the Farforovs' house committee named Tsaplin sees "a shabby old woman is standing on the corner. She is holding an infant in her arms." It's the nanny – and she's begging money for the baby! When Tsaplin tells the Farforovs that evening what he's seen, the couple confront the nanny.

> The nanny says:
> "There's no sin in this. Am I right simply to stand, or if tenderhearted passers-by put a little something in my hand. I," she says, "simply don't understand what the fuss is about. The infant doesn't suffer by it. And perhaps it even amuses him seeing the flow of people around himself."
> Farforov says:
> "Yes, but I don't want my baby to absorb such views in childhood. I will not allow you to behave in this way."
> Madame Farforova, clutching her infant to her bosom, says:
> "This is most highly offensive to us. We're firing you from your position." (pp. 199-200)

The house committee man approves this termination; the nanny has no one to blame but herself. But the unrepentant woman retorts rather defiantly: "Nannies are in short supply nowadays – they'll probably snap me right up. While with your whelp I barely cleared three rubles, and all the reproaches to put up with. I'll quit you myself, as you're unfeeling, disreputable people and not good bosses."[87] The old woman leaves "without a recommendation, and it's unknown whither she went. But it's likely she's off somewhere nannying an infant and earning a good income with him," concludes Zoshchenko. (p. 200)

This brilliant little vignette, dripping with irony, seems to indicate that "the new Soviet man" was unused to pre-revolutionary practices that were far from limited to aristocrats alone. Aside from this one divergence, however, Zoshchenko was clearly on the same wavelength as the émigré Tèffi.[88]

Village Prose." While introducing an old peasant character for color or emotional resonance had been a commonplace for decades, there seemed no place for that kind of backward-looking sentimentalism in the bumptious and forward-looking, class-conscious *proletarian* 1920s. And then events occurred of such horrific magnitude – forced collectivization and genocidal famine – that there was little desire or space for such characters in works of the 1930s and 1940s.[89] The new Soviet man and woman had to take the place of older literary figures. Industrialization and war and reconstruction focused almost all the nation's attention on other themes, mostly urban, and child caretakers probably seemed an afterthought among such weighty subjects.

By the 1950s and 60s, however, tastes were changing, and a kind of nostalgia for old times and ways emerged in the so-called "village prose" group of writers who produced work that felt suspiciously Slavophile-like. The pastoral had once again come into its own. For stories and novels set in the village, however, a nonfamily nanny would have been a *rara avis*. The natural counterpart to the nanny in the peasant world was the grandmother. So it is *ne sluchaino* (not by accident) that in place of a hired caretaker for children, there is a grandmother character in a large number of works that fit wholly or partly under the rubric of "village prose."[90] Important village-prose authors who highlight a major grandmother/nanny-like figure include Iurii Kazakov in "Pomorka" ("The Old Woman by the Sea," 1957); Nikolai Rylenkov in "Skazka moego detstva" ("A fairy tale of my childhood"; 1960s); and Valentin Rasputin in "Vasilii and Vasilisa" (*baba* Avdot'ia; 1966) and his *Farewell to Matyora* (Dar'ia Pinigina; 1976).

The focal point of the entire collection of Viktor Astaf'ev's stories called *The Final Bow* (1968, with enlarged editions)[91] is his grandmother, Katerina Petrovna, extremely reminiscent of most pre-emancipation nannies. A kind of epigone of the earlier "school" of village writers, Lidiia Aref'eva (b.ca. 1940), includes a long tale about her grandmother Katia's brief tenure as nanny for a wealthy merchant (before 1917) in a collection of quasi-autobiographical stories.[92]

Among the most memorable characters created by people associated wholly or in part with this new "going to the people" movement was Matrëna, the protagonist of Aleksandr Solzhenitsyn's poignant story "At Matrëna's Place" (1963). The narrator comes one late summer to a village to teach and finds living quarters in the hut of a middle-aged woman named Matrëna. She is longsuffering, her life a struggle, but she is never dour. Matrëna and the narrator hit it off rather well but he finds her a bit of a loner, with few close friends, nearly an outsider in her own village.

> She did not invite guests to her place in the evening, respecting my studies. Only for Twelfth Night [*Kreshchen'e*], returning from school, did I find dancing and became acquainted with Matrëna's three sisters, *who referred to Matrëna like an old woman – a godmother [lël'ka] or nanny [nian'ka]*. Until this day little was heard in our hut about the sisters – were they afraid Matrëna would ask them for help?[93]

Matrëna's relatives are all nearly her opposite: where she is almost ascetic and unconcerned with worldly goods, they are all-too-worldly and grasping. Their greed inadvertently brings down Matrëna's death and grave misfortune on themselves. At her wake, virtually all the villagers and her own relations are disapproving of her. Her sincerity and simplicity – which the narrator admired – are deemed bad by some; her sister-in-law scorns her for her "faults." From all they say the narrator becomes aware of the meaning of Matrëna's life. No, she did not accumulate things. She had no fine clothes. Her husband hadn't understood and abandoned her. She did not possess a congenial temperament. She was alien to her own kin; they laughed at her and thought her simpleminded, "working for others without pay." She had not even bothered to save up money for her own death.

> All of us lived alongside her and did not understand that she is that very person of righteousness without whom, according to the proverb, a village does not remain standing.
> Nor a city.
> Nor our entire world. (p. 56)

Conclusion

So many authors have invested so much in nanny figures over the centuries that no short summary of the phenomenon can do it justice. As I've tried to show, such characters evolved through time from fairly cardboard stereotypes to more full-blooded, realistic personae. Nonetheless, the temptation always remained to treat them as more than, say, simple peasant women. Whether in literary tropes or ideological representations, with all her connotations and connections with many writers' lives, a Russian nanny evoked strong emotions. Through cataclysms like the Great Reforms and the 1917 revolutions, just like real-life nannies, literary nannies persisted, even flourished.

What authors found so appealing in a nanny character, readers found equally appealing. The longevity of the figure in literature is ample testimony of the reading public's receptivity. Authors continually found ways to reinvent the nanny character so as to maintain their audience's interest and belief in nannies. As Chapter 10 will demonstrate more fully, the symbol of the nanny touched a variety of chords in readers (and citizens) Europe-wide. Literature was just one, but the main, sphere in which that symbol played out. The next chapter explores additional ways in which nannies, real and imagined, showed up in Russian culture and history.

9

To Mythologize or Not? Nanny's Role in Creative Lives

Connections Between Real-Life Nanny and Artistic Creativity

As the first chapter explored, there are several alleged links between Pushkin's writing and his having had a Russian peasant nanny as a child. Nearly all these (ideologically inspired) claims were shown to be exaggerated – some much more than others – but not all are entirely ungrounded. Nonetheless, these links between his nanny and the poet's writings had a demonstrable influence on many public figures who came after Pushkin. In this chapter I will examine other examples of these links – the nanny as part of the life of a child who later became prominent culturally, and the nanny as subject matter and/or inspiration in her charge's later work.[1]

The questions underlying this chapter's discussion are simply: (1) was there a strong connection between a person's having had a nanny in childhood and that person's adult life (later career or character); and (2) how (and why) did an author's real-life nanny become transmuted into art? Given the hoopla surrounding far too many nannies, I see a clear pattern in the connections discussed below. In some cases, the attention given a nanny by the person or those writing about the person seems just about right. In other cases, either the creative artist or some biographers make a great deal more out of the connection than I believe is justified – as in the case of Pushkin. At the heart of this latter problem is often the autobiographical fallacy. For purposes of analysis, let us call each case a "paradigm": the commensurate and the incommensurate (more informally, the "Goldilocks" and "anomalous" models).

Just as for literature, the two paradigms for "nanny as inspiration" fit well with other areas of culture – in music, art, and other spheres where she might instill values and ideas. In the spheres of both music and art, it would appear that the culture critic Vladimir Stasov (1824-1906) may have played a role advancing the "cause of the nanny" very similar to that of Pëtr Bartenev in developing the myth of Arina Rodionovna.

Two Paradigms. The Goldilocks model, wherein a real-life nanny appears to play a role entirely *commensurate* with her treatment by the writer or memoirist, is the simpler of the two. In this paradigm, there is no real "disconnect" between whatever role the real-life nanny played in the life of her nurseling when young and the role this nanny plays – or more often, the role others claim for her – in the life and works of her grown charge.[2]

Incommensurateness can show up in various ways. For one, we find authors who barely note the existence of their own nannies in writing about their childhood or in their lives more generally. Typically in such cases, while the writer tends to ignore or play down the place of a nanny in his (or her) own life, others – critics or biographers – want to impute a great deal to the existence of the nanny.[3] In other cases of incommensurateness, we find those who give a fulsome treatment to their nannies in their memoirs or other writings but whose post-childhood lives seem to offer little reason for such an exaggerated display of emotion.[4]

The question naturally arises: which paradigm outweighed the other? Were there more cases of commensurate treatments of nannies than incommensurate, or vice versa? For some time I was inclined to think the latter. Of late, however, I've come to the conclusion that – while more noteworthy or, often, more egregious – the fully incommensurate cases bow to the commensurate in numbers.

Excluded Cases. For nearly all the great Russian writers of the modern era there is some story that might be told about their nanny and how she relates to their writing; all fall within my first paradigm. Most of these stories would, however, be of no great moment. We are told, for example, that Dostoevskii's nanny, Alena

Frolovna, was apparently the prototype for nannies that appear in *The Idiot* (1868), *The Possessed* (1871-72), and elsewhere in his works.[5] (This nanny receives skewed attention in popular biographies of Dostoevskii.[6]) Tolstoi's peasant nannies, old Annushka and young Tat'iana Filippovna, about both of whom he writes in his unfinished memoirs, were *not* the model for Natal'ia Savishna, the nanny-cum-housekeeper who plays such a large role in his highly fictionalized work *Childhood*.[7] Turgenev, although he almost certainly had a peasant nanny as a child – and despite his inclusion of such figures in many of his novels (e.g., Liza's nanny Agaf'ia Vlas'evna in *Nest of Gentlefolk*, 1859) – was apparently never tempted to document her existence in any autobiographical writing. Aleksei Remizov (1877-1957) populates most of his quasi-autobiographical fiction with nannies (and wet-nurses), some of whom were possibly modeled on his own and his wife's childhood caretakers. His nanny was Praskov'ia Semenovna Mirskaia, nicknamed Praskov'ia Piskun'ia (Praskov'ia the Squeaker or Whiner).[8] There are also examples I've chosen to omit due mostly to intentional or nondeliberate obfuscation on the subject's part. The poets Adelaida Gertsyk (Gertsyk-Liubi; 1874-1925) and Semën Nadson (1862-1887) are prime examples (as is Nekrasov).[9] Deliberate obfuscation was seemingly a fond technique of many Silver Age poets and novelists.

Commensurate Cases

Aleksei Venetsianov (1780—1847)

When does the first depiction of a peasant nanny show up in Russian art? Not with some spurious "portrait" or bas-relief of Arina Rodionovna, nor with any other overblown rendering full of pretended moment or symbolism.[10]

The first portrayal of a peasant nanny of which I'm aware is a painting by Aleksei Venetsianov, and the nanny is his own (or at least his family's).[11] Since Venetsianov tended to leave nearly all his works undated (out of forgetfulness mostly), the dating of this work depends on the testimony of someone other than the artist. Although various dates have been assigned to it, the best source pegs its creation to the year 1829.[12] In any case, Venetsianov painted the picture after 1827, the landmark year of *Onegin*'s third chapter's

Aleksei Venetsianov, *Old Nanny in Peasant Head-dress* (1829?) oil on canvas

appearance, so the "magic" of Arina Rodionovna may have had some bearing on its creation.

The inspiration for this painting was simple: a family gathering at which some servants, including the nanny, were present. Venetsianov painted portraits of not only the nanny, Matrëna, but also the *dvornik* (groundskeeper) Prokhor or Fëdor. Neither the painter nor any biographers tried to make something special out of the work's existence. No mythologizing has surrounded Venetsianov and this nanny.[13]

The painter must have found the theme of nanny congenial, as he returned to it about a decade later, with his 1841 "Portrait of the Panaev Children with Their Nanny" (*Portret detei Panaevykh s nianei*), another oil on canvas.[14] It might also be noted that, at about the same time Venetsianov portrayed his old nanny, he painted another picture, "Wet-nurse with Child" (*Kormilitsa s rebenkom*), at present in the Tret'iakov Gallery, Moscow.[15]

Ivan Goncharov (1812-1891)

Goncharov's Works. The man whom many consider to be one of the main co-inventors – along with Sergei Aksakov and Lev Tolstoi – of the idyllic noble childhood replete with country estate and loving nanny (in the novel *Oblomov*) was, ironically, not of the gentry. Ivan Goncharov was born into a well-to-do merchant family in the Volga city of Simbirsk. In his sketchy autobiography (he actually produced three versions between 1859 and his death), written in the third person, he deliberately withheld information about his early years that might be of great interest for us: "I'll pass over in silence certain details of my childhood and adolescent years which I have in mind to use in one of my future works, if fate decrees it."[16] There is certainly no nanny mentioned, and one begins to suspect that Goncharov belongs to my second paradigm. But that conclusion would be premature.

In the second part of his fictionalized reminiscences, called "In my home parts," Goncharov says that on a return trip home, they "don't allow me to want for anything: all had long-since been got ready, anticipated. Beside the family, the old servants, with nanny at their head, fall all over me." The servants "remember my tastes, habits, where my writing desk stood, in which armchair I always sat, how to make my bed. The cook remembers my favorite dishes – and all can't get enough of me [*ne nagliadiatsia na menia*]."[17]

The Word of Others. In the reminiscences of the writer Gavriil Potanin, we have testimony that Goncharov did indeed have a loving nanny when he was young. This nanny, Anna Mikhailovna (called Annushka) had vision problems in old age and lost her sight. Although unreliable in many respects, Potanin's recollections serve to confirm what Goncharov himself spoke of in his fiction. Thus, Potanin recalled Goncharov's visit home in 1849, flush with his first literary successes, "and the captivating memories of childhood, and the shining face of his mother...and the billing and cooing [*vorkovanie*] of the blind nanny..."

> Touching were his conversations with the blind nanny. It seems to me he sometimes couldn't find words tender enough to call her. "My beloved dove! Do you remember what magical fairy tales you would coo to me?..." And he would kiss his dove and pet her on the head. "If you want,

Ivan Goncharov's nanny Annushka, ca. 1867

I'll shower you with gold for them?" The old woman would be offended [*obidetsia*] and whisper reproachfully: "Eh, Vania, foolish Vania! Of what use to me is your money in the grave? Dearer to me than anything in the world is your love!" – and she'd burst into tears to the point of hysteria.[18]

Perhaps more reliable and equally confirming are the memories of Goncharov's great-nephew, Mikhail Kirmalov (1863-1920). He writes of his great-uncle: "Ivan Aleksandrovich loved his own nanny Annushka tenderly. I well remember this old woman, who nannied me as well and lived at the time at leisure at my grandmother Aleksandra Aleksandrovna's in Khukhorevo. In her weak, dried-up body there lived the crystal pure soul of a child, full to the brim with love for children and for all the family..."[19]

So we should probably conclude that Goncharov's artistic creation of the nanny in *Oblomov* and the fictive rendering of his return home as an adult were both commensurate with his own life and nanny.[20]

Modest Musorgskii (1839-1881)

What Musorgskii Says and Created. In an autobiographical sketch, written in the third person, the composer states: "Under the direct influence of [his] nanny he became closely acquainted with Russian folk and fairy tales [*skazki*]. This acquaintance with the spirit of the Rus[sian] peop[le's] lif[e] was the main impulse of [his] musical improvisation until the beginning of [his] acquaintance with the most elementary rules of playing the piano."[21] It would be hard to find a more unambiguous statement of the link between a nanny and an artist's first impulses to create. (The nanny's tales so fired his imagination that they even kept him awake at nights, Musorgskii added.) Not immediately, but in later years, it would appear inescapable that the composer had not forgotten his nanny – although he never mentions her name – or at least the memory of what it was like for a child to have a nanny, as he had had, growing up on a country estate called Karevo.

To understand the context of Musorgskii's musical achievements, some personal and historical background is essential.[22] Romantic and peasant-sympathetic notions had permeated Russian society in the first half of the nineteenth century, as noted previously in these pages. The surge of interest in the folk (*narod*) surrounding emancipation and its implementation heightened these sentiments among many, especially the young, in higher strata of society. The youthful activism and idealism of the 1860s, culminating in the "going to the people," "populist" ("*narodnik*") and more revolutionary movements of the 1870s, presumably all had some impact on the impressionable young Musorgskii.[23] That, at least, is the view of David Brown, who argues that "the sentimental concept of the peasantry as the very heart and hope of Russian society for the future infected Musorgsky, as it did many other Russians, in the wave of euphoria that followed the Emancipation." Musorgskii, according to Brown, "joined in the broad wave of idealization of the former serfs – an idealization engaged in all the more easily" in the urban environment he inhabited than at Karevo with its "sharper reality" of real rural life.[24]

More directly, however, his acquaintance and quick bonding with Milii Balakirev (1836-1910) in the late 1850s seemed to reinforce or re-energize any longstanding interests in the peasantry which could have stemmed from his country-estate childhood and possibly from his own grandmother's being a former serf. Balakirev was one of the earliest first-rate musical minds to collect and study not just the words but also the music of the Russian *narod*. His sensibilities may have influenced Musorgskii, but the latter always remained a man more interested in individual people (*liudi*) rather than "the people" (*narod*).[25] In any case, two distinct currents in the fledgling composer's life came together in the late 1850s and 1860s: his peasant-folklore interest with his delight in and empathy for children. At the beginning of perhaps the single greatest creative period of his life, in 1868, Musorgskii produced the first of his children's song cycle, *The Nursery* (or *Scenes from Childhood*) entitled "With Nanny":

Come and tell me, Nannie dear,
all about the Boogie-man, once again,
the ogre Boogie-man!
How he sneaks around the woods at night;

how he catches little children there;
how he chews their little bones and swallows them!
and the children cry and shriek in agony.
Nannie dear! Is the reason the ogre eats them up
that they did not mind what their
mother said, or their father, and they
did not do what their Nannie told them?
    Nannie dear?
But I'd rather you would tell me
all about the king and queen
in the lovely palace far across the ocean;
how the king was lame and every time
that he tumbled down up a mushroom grew,
and the queen forever had a cold.
When she sneezed all the windows rattled.
Listen Nanna, dear, do not tell me
of the horrid Boogie-man!
I don't like him.
Better tell the other.
Come, the funny one.[26]

Of the seven total songs in the cycle, four are addressed to the nanny – the first, second, third, and fifth. The second is the beautifully realized psychological piece "In the Corner," in which the child "gets even" with his nanny for punishing him. To her accusation of wrongdoing, which starts the song, the child responds with denial, then self-justification, and finally anger:

My, but you're naughty!
you unrolled the yarn!
the knitting needles are lost! Naughty!
all the loops are undone!
and ink is all over the stockings.
Go now! Stand there!
in the corner! Bad Michael!
But I really did not do anything!
I did not touch the stockings or the yarn,
the kitten did it all, the kitty cat

lost the needles, spilled the ink and everything.
Your little boy has not been a naughty boy,
no, not at all.
But Nanna is a mean old thing:
and Nanna has a nasty, dirty nose.
Michael's hair is brushed and clean and neat;
Nanna's bonnet isn't neat at all!
Nanna was not fair to punish him,
and make him stand in the corner here.
So now Michael does not love his
Nannie nurse any more. So there!"[27]

The third song is very "natural," in Oskar von Riesemann's words, being literally about nature but also unforced and realistic. It is a simple recounting to the nanny of an adventure the child has had with a beetle while playing outdoors. The fifth is a long recitation of a bedtime prayer by a little girl who invariably forgets the last line after endless "God blesses" of parents, siblings, aunts and uncles. The nanny scolds her: "'You naughty girl to have forgotten! How often have I told you: and to me a sinner, be, O Lord, merciful!'" The child repeats the line and asks: "Is that right, nanny dear?"[28]

In matters musical I confess kinship to Lady Catherine de Bourgh in *Pride and Prejudice*: If I had ever learnt, I *might* have been a great proficient. Since that is not the case, I can rely gratefully on those more knowledgeable to provide the reader some idea of the inventiveness and expressiveness of Musorgskii's *Nursery* cycle. To Caryl Emerson, the songs are very "realistic"; "With Nanny" is a "spontaneous...illustration of the eagerly communicating psyche." In all the songs, Musorgskii uses "pitch intervals, amplifying the intonation curve into a melodic line and registering doubts, anxieties, and sudden pleasure in phrasing and pauses." "With Nanny" is not so much "performed" as "*enacted.*"[29] For David Brown, "With Nurse [Nanny]" is "a radically new song": frequent change of meter went with this tale of a child who "pesters his nurse for a story, constantly changing his mind about which one it shall be." Brown calls it "a bubbling stream of childish prattle, turning this way and that through humours, questions, and entreaties – the

To Mythologize or Not? Nanny's Role in Creative Lives 255

most ingenuous, uncoordinated chatter, demanding constant shifts of musical mood, tone, and intonation." "The result is a miniature, virtuoso dramatic monologue." The whole is so seamless that it appears that the music and text were created together, so closely do they fit together.[30] The song is also a "graphic projection of... terrors."[31]

At the same time he was completing the first of his *Nursery* songs, Musorgskii was deeply into another, much more elaborate undertaking: his only completed opera, what most critics consider his masterpiece, an adaptation of Pushkin's drama *Boris Godunov*. Just as Pushkin produced strikingly different variants of his original play (one lighter than the other), so too did the libretto by Musorgskii evolve from the first, "hyper realist" version of 1869 to the more lyrical, "operatic" 1872 version, finally performed (with drastic cuts) in 1874.[32] Of particular interest to us is the fact that in the original version, the part of Godunov's daughter Kseniia's nanny (*mamka*) is circumscribed; it grew in succeeding reworkings. From merely comforting Kseniia she gained a duet of folksongs with the tsarevna's brother Fëdor and a brief exchange with Boris. In addition, the diversion of the other nannies and the parrot in the side room was added.[33] It is clear that work on the opera and the song cycle affected each other; in both, Musorgskii was exploring ever more deeply the world of children.

To sum up, by his own direct testimony in his brief autobiography and from his masterpieces of the mid- to late 1860s, it appears that his nanny and her intense tales that had kept him awake nights when a child had a profound effect on the composer and his work. With Musorgskii there is some validity in saying his nanny inspired his later creativity.

The Views of Others. More than one biographer has accepted the "nanny-demotic-inspiration" argument at face value. One early example is Oskar von Riesemann, a very knowledgeable musical scholar with a specialization in Russian composers. His life of Musorgskii, first published in German in 1926, pays homage to the nanny and to the child Modest's "abnormal sensibility" which "made him so extraordinarily receptive of artistic impressions," as from her folktales. Riesemann shows some restraint:

Moussorgsky, however, unlike Pushkin, has made little direct artistic use of the varied and many-coloured scenes in the Russian fairyland that his nurse unveiled before him. The story told by the nurse in *Boris Godounov*, and the fantastic figures that the child in the song "Child and Nurse" sees pass before him, are the only artistic result of those childish recollections that in other ways bore such fruit in the boy's imagination. Moussorgsky made no use in his operas either of the fairy-tales, or of the *biliny*, the legends and popular epics of his country...[34]

Another musical scholar, however, called into question the basis on which Riesemann wrote the preceding lines – Musorgskii's self-assessment of the impact of those "fantastic figures" conjured by his nanny. Michel Calvocoressi first quotes another biographer's attempt to judge the ways in which the child Modest's exposure to fairy-tales might affect his thoughts:

In the homes of the Russian gentry, children lived in a supernatural world which they loved and in which they believed. For them the Baba-Yaga, the witch who lived in a hut standing on hens' legs, Koshchei, the cruel, deathless giant, and Prince Ivan, the young hero who could raise boulders weighing a ton, were beings whose aspect and character stood definite and well known, who were always present and inspired love, friendship, terror, and hatred.[35]

He then offers his own judgment. Maintaining that, while "pantomimic and graphic evocations...play a big part in Mussorgsky's music," Calvocoressi avers that the "picturesque and fantastic elements brilliantly put to use by Glinka and other Russians, especially Rimsky-Korsakof" did not.[36] Yet Calvocoressi is dubious not so much about the peasant-sympathetic element in Musorgskii's music, just the attribution of these feelings specifically to the nanny. "Apart from the delightful first number of his song-set *The Nursery*, which evokes a child delighted with the impressive tales told by his nurse," he writes, "the only things of his inspired by fantastic subjects are a couple of piano pieces in the *Pictures*

To Mythologize or Not? Nanny's Role in Creative Lives 257

from an Exhibition and the tone-poem *A Night on the Bare Mountain*. The speech, and also the songs, of the people around him may have created, even at that early time, stronger, far more lasting impressions." The either/or of Calvocoressi, however, seems forced. Of course, Musorgskii listened to many more peasants and their music than just his nanny. But the two sources of inspiration are not mutually exclusive. If anything, they would have been mutually reinforcing.

It is only in recent years that more judicious scholars have offered assessments that can help us resolve this issue of the nanny's – and serf grandmother's – "influence" on Musorgskii. Emerson in particular offers excellent judgments: "The Musorgsky nanny myth is complicated by his own peasant-origin grandmother, and the sense that the stories he heard in childhood were wickedly 'his' in the way that fully noble *bariny* had no right to claim." She believes that he "came to his stylized view of the 'folk' only after outgrowing his adolescent identity" and only later in life "resurrected...familiar tunes" of childhood.[37] David Brown offers what may be a definitive view of the "nanny" influence, one to which I fully subscribe. It seems that later, more contemporaneous "influences" were far more important to Musorgskii than any lingering impact of his childhood nanny.

> Though Vladimir Stasov believed that it was cherished memories from Musorgsky's own childhood that accounted for his preoccupation with the nurse/child relationship...it seems that his *Nursery* cycle was prompted by this present environment [in summer-fall 1870, spending much time with the Stasov family] – and perhaps not only by the Stasov brood but by his own niece and nephew...to whom he dedicated 'With the Doll'...[38]

It was Vladimir Stasov who patched together the several different sketches which Musorgskii wrote – probably in June 1880, shortly before his death – about his life into what we now think of as his "autobiography." This fact raises an issue we'll visit again shortly with the autobiographies of Glinka and Ge: How much of Stasov's own hobbyhorses (like peasant nannies) crept into this patchwork of Musorgskii essays?[39] Almost – but not quite – enough to move this composer to the second paradigm.

Andrei Belyi (1880-1934)

Nannies and governesses permeate the childhood memoirs of the symbolist Belyi (pseudonym of Bugaev). They came and went with regularity and frequency, some for cause, others due to illness. Many were called *bonnes* and were foreign; his wet-nurse and first nanny were both Russian. The list of these women and their tenures is easily established from Belyi's writings.[40] On the back of a photo of his wet-nurse, Afim'ia Ivanovna Lavrova, there is a rather puzzling inscription: "...my friend, companion of my childhood games. To her I first read my verses."[41]

Several of these women played a crucial role for him within a family almost literally at war. His loving, suffocating mother, who nicknamed him "Little Puss" (Kotik), was determined that he not grow up to be an intellectual ("a mathematician" in her scornful nomenclature) like his father. The arguments and fights were endless. He sought refuge in his own little world, the nursery with his nanny. Some nannies, like Raisa Ivanovna, knew how to shroud him in a protective cover of fairy tales to escape the constant battling of his parents; others, like the "dumb/mute" Henrietta Martynovna, did not. (p.104) (Calling her "dumb" [*nemaia*] is a pun on the Russian word for a German woman, *nemka*.) Her silence left him vulnerable.

From the "outer world" beyond his four walls his parents and various visitors "fly into my room, where I'm with nanny [*pod nianiu*], now papa, now mama; and, abandoning me again [throw themselves into discussions in the other room]."

> I don't trust them but I trust nanny.
>
> Life under nanny's care comprises...the end of October, November, part of December 1883; this short period stretches out in my consciousness into a year; during this period the very line of time forms and there's a thread of uninterrupted memories...
>
> The period being described, experienced as a year but

> encompassing no more than sixty days, stands under a device: of a child's room, a rug, a nanny...I would compare this period with the period of ancient Cretan civilization (before the Dorian invasion); and the cult of matriarchy is well-known to me; nanny, sitting in front of her little forged trunk is, in my eyes, both mother and temple goddess; all flows forth from her; and everything is safe when I'm with her [*pod nei*]; leave her and the hole of the dark corridor will swallow you up...and I'd be gobbled up. (pp. 181-82)

A bit later he adds: "The period with nanny stands under a heraldic device: she is holding together a world globe; should she disappear – everything will collapse..." (p. 184)

At this early period, he avers, first in prayer and then in fairy tales, he discovered the power and efficacy of symbols. (pp. 186, 192)

> In song, in the fairy tale and in the sounds of music I am given a way out of a joyless life; the world for me is now an esthetic phenomenon; there's neither delirium nor fear in the face of the empirics of our life; life is joy; and this joy – is a fairy tale; from the fairy tale begins my play [*moia igra*] in life; but the game is the purest symbolism.[42]
>
> There is the problem with me and Raisa Ivanovna of the consciously constructed third world beyond the worlds of prose and delirium; the third world is play, the symbolic, the "what if," suggested by the sounds of a flowing musical roulade; were it not for the fairy tale, bestowed on me by Raisa Ivanovna just in time, either I would have become an idiot, sunk in delirium, or I would have become a little old man before my time, prosaically peeping at father and mother's life; following these paths, I would have perished. (p. 186)

The parallels between his autobiography and his fiction about his childhood are overwhelming. Nearly all the significant nannies and governesses of his early years show up in either *Kotik Letaev* (1922) or *A Baptized Chinaman* (1927) or both. All wrapped in Steinerian mysticism (formally called anthroposophy), ancient mythology, and stream-of-consciousness musings, here is one of the most imaginative recreations of infancy and early childhood ever put on paper.[43] Nanny Aleksandra and Raisa Ivanovna are central figures in *Kotik Letaev*, fulfilling the exact roles as spelled out later in Belyi's memoirs. Nanny Aleksandra brings order to his chaotic life; she is "the regulator of experiences."[44]

Raisa Ivanovna is almost always called "dearest." A section of Chapter 4 is devoted entirely to her and the mediating role she played in his young life:

> I am a sinner: with mama I sin against Papa; with Papa against Mama. How can I exist and not sin?
>
> I must begin to live alone: I am not Papa's, not Mama's; but to live – is lonely...
> Dearest Raisa Ivanovna!   (KL 1971, p. 157)

The culmination and then release of the building tensions in the family occurs in chapters five and six. The concept of sin enters in Chapter 5; guilt and sexuality are leitmotifs. In Chapter 6, his nanny "is banished because of his mother's jealousy." The first section of Chapter 6, entitled "The Tree of Knowledge," carries an undercurrent of guilty feelings about "good and evil," Adam, Eve, paradise, the Tree... (KL 1999, pp. 160-62) Central to these ideas is Raisa Ivanovna. The first line of the section is about her (she's sewing). Later she takes him into her bed to sleep. (KL 1999, pp. 164-65) They "embrace" and hug each other. His description of the scene is close to evoking physical eroticism, even though he's only four. It almost sounds like they are enjoying sex. He sleeps in in the morning – past nine, till ten. Then "Raisa Ivanovna would often start making waves with her sheer nightgown; her bare white legs would glisten; she would steal over with a black stocking and a flannel underbodice..." (KL 1999, p. 171) None of this erotic subtext, however, is as explicit in the memoirs. Yet the connection between life and art is so strong here as to be among the best examples of paradigm one.

Vladislav Khodasevich (1886-1939)

The Background. The poet Khodasevich has left us no autobiography or memoirs as such. Had we better information about the realities of his childhood, we might be able to place him somewhere within the second paradigm. Certainly there are hints that that is where he might belong. But for now we will leave him in the first. There are many (auto)biographical elements in his poetry; as always, extreme care is required in using the poetry to reconstruct the life. Which "facts" do we extract from the verses, and with what degree of confidence? I offer only the one example: his treatment of his wet-nurse-nanny, Elena Aleksandrovna Kuzina, a peasant woman from Tula province.[45]

There is no doubt of the signal significance of Elena Aleksandrovna in Khodasevich's life. It appears incontrovertible that without her he would have had no life. A very weak baby, Khodasevich had difficulty sucking, and various wet-nurses refused his mother's offer of employment. Elena accepted, but in order to feed the future poet she had to turn her own newborn son over to a foundling hospital. This sacrifice was, as David Bethea indicates, tantamount to a death sentence for her own son, who did indeed succumb. "The debt that the future poet owed his nurse, therefore, was incalculable, and it is not curious that her example, which reads like fiction become life, should provide an important clue to the portrait of an artist *in statu nascendi.*"[46] This is the hint that I alluded to just above that Khodasevich may have been more "inventive" in speaking of his nanny than might otherwise appear to be the case. He might have greatly romanticized her in the mistaken notion that in doing so he could pay off this "debt."

Khodasevich's father was the son of a Polish nobleman, his mother a Russian Jewess who had converted to Catholicism. The home was suffused with Polish culture. The son had the task of moving from this cultural nest to the broader one of his homeland. His "irrevocable russification," as Bethea calls it, began in his kindergarten years but "might have begun even earlier with the appearance of a third very important adult influence on his childhood life." That influence, that "Russian presence" to offset his parents' bent, was his wet-nurse, Elena Kuzina.[47]

Tribute to a Nanny. Like his idol Pushkin, Khodasevich chose to "immortalize" this woman – in one of the most important poems he ever wrote. In the collection *The Heavy Lyre* (*Tiazhëlaia lira*; 1st ed.: Moscow, 1922) an untitled poem stresses her significance in his own development. I will simply quote Bethea's first-rate translation here.[48]

> Not by my mother, but by the Tula peasant woman
> Yelena Kuzina was I reared. She would
> warm my swaddling-clothes above the stove-bench,
> ward off bad dreams at bedtime with the sign of the cross.
>
> She knew no fairy tales and did not sing,
> and yet she always kept for me
> in a cherished trunk covered in white tin-plate
> either a Vyazemsky gingerbread or a mint gingerbread horse.
>
> She did not teach me prayers,
> but gave me absolutely everything she had:
> both her bitter motherhood
> and simply all that was dear to her.
>
> Only once, when I fell from a window,
> but rose alive (how I remember that day!),
> she placed a penny candle
> for the wondrous saving at the icon of the Iversk Virgin.
>
> And so Russia, you "renowned power,"
> by pulling at her teats with my lips,
> I sucked out the agonizing right
> to love and curse you...
>
> The years rush by. I need no future,
> the past is burned up in my soul,
> yet still alive is the secret joy
> that I too have one refuge:

> There in a heart eaten by worms,
> cherishing a love for me that is imperishable,
> sleeping next to tsarist, Khodynka guests
> is Yelena Kuzina, my nurse [*kormilitsa*].[49]

Bethea's lengthy analysis of this poem – stressing that the early stanzas are very autobiographical, focusing on the poet's supposed home situation as a child – notes that it was begun in 1917. Khodasevich then developed a sort of writer's block which unfroze only in the early 1920s, while he was engaged in writing about Pushkin. Bethea says that Khodasevich at that time made a critical discovery about Pushkin and Arina Rodionovna that inspired him to complete his own poem dedicated to his nanny *and to his alleged poetic Muse*. Khodasevich's "discovery" was, not surprisingly, related to the Pushkin poems "Dream" and "Confidante of Magical Antiquity."[50] The Arina myth proves its lasting power, for this error affects both the life of Khodasevich and the consequent biography by Bethea.[51]

This poem is pivotal in Khodasevich's artistic development:

> The actual milk with which Elena Kuzina nursed the infant becomes in the last five stanzas the psychic milk, the Russian language, that still nourishes Khodasevich, but in another way. In fact the poet, no longer an infant, has taken on the attributes of a solicitous and loving parent. And the miracle that saved Khodasevich...is transformed into the miracle of poetic speech, with its *chudotvornyi genii* (wonder-working genius). Of course, the source of inspiration, the embodiment of Khodasevich's Muse, remains the nurse, but the identification is left unsaid, below the surface. The reader must cast his own bridge between the physical act of giving milk and the metaphorical act of blowing on the shepherd's reed or handing the poet his lyre.[52]

Khodasevich – and Bethea – thus make the most explicit, the most rigorous argument about a nanny as muse that I've come across. With no evidence to the contrary available, we will have to take Khodasevich at his (poetical) word and accept his claims about his nanny (even though he took further inspiration from mistaken notions about Pushkin). After all, there's no denying that Khodasevich's error is still a reality for him – nothing's so but thinking makes it so. It matters not that he was wrong about Pushkin; it "worked" for him to think that Arina Rodionovna was his predecessor's muse and that his nanny Elena was his own.

Incommensurate Cases

Mikhail Glinka (1804-1857)

A case might be made that Glinka is the "father of Russian opera" and the first great Russian nationalist composer of the nineteenth century. Can the case be made that his nanny had a hand in his musical development?

What Others Have to Say: Russian Sources. Biographers and musicologists like to impute a "nanny influence" on a budding musical genius. The music scholar Vera Vasina-Grossman, in typical Soviet style, argues that the influence of one of Glinka's two nannies on his artistic development was enormous:

> Everything that Avdot'ia [Ivanovna] did was done by her quickly, easily, and somehow gaily. This serf woman was one of those peasant talents who, despite the harsh conditions of an unfree life found joy in art and conveyed this joy to others. To many Russian artists befell the true happiness of spending their childhood years, when consciousness especially thirstily imbibes all new impressions, not with foreign governors but with simple, heartfelt Russian nannies – talespinners and singers. Thus passed the childhood of Pushkin, who preserved a profound attachment to nanny Arina Rodionovna to the end of his life, thus passed the childhood of Glinka also.[53]

Placing herself deftly within the Glinka household, Vasina-Grossman is able to affirm: "To his family, in particular the grandmother, nanny Avdot'ia's songs seemed to be only a means to soothe and entertain the little boy. But for the future composer himself, they became the first musical impressions on which his ear was trained and a still unconscious but profound love for native Russian song was strengthened." Avdot'ia "sang about simple things the child could grasp." The sounds of these songs – sad, gay, what have you – "were as intimate and comprehensible as the sounds of his native language."

Another Soviet Glinka expert, Elizaveta Kann-Novikova, makes the strongest possible case for the musical influence of Avdot'ia Ivanovna. She stresses that the most important fact about his living with his grandmother was his total isolation, even from his parents and younger sisters, until the age of 6. The doors of his nursery were kept closed. She argues that almost the only musical sounds he heard in this period were the bells and church singing when his grandmother allowed him to go to church. But

> on the other hand, peasant song in all its pristine [*pervorodnaia*] purity penetrated the nursery of Mikhail Glinka in a broad flow, in its unique [*samobytnoe*] folk execution. This was in the songs the "under-nanny" Avdot'ia Ivanovna sang to Glinka. Only when the "grandmother's seclusion" ended did Glinka become acquainted with professional music of a way of thinking different in principle. Thus, life itself as it were created for Glinka laboratory-like conditions for his subsequent [*posledovatel'noe*] and relative "assimilation" ["*osvoenie*"] of two musical worlds in all their contradistinction [*protivopolozhnost'*].[54]

This scholar adds some colorful details, as did the first. It seems that the "'under-nanny,' and later nanny Avdot'ia Ivanovna was famed in the Novospassk district as a songstress [*pesel'nitsa*] and storyteller." "About Avdot'ia Ivanovna in addition it is known that her son was in later years an oboeist in the Novospassk orchestra... With this ends all our information about this Russian songstress, who stood by the cradle of Mikhail Glinka." (pp. 40-41)

Can Kann-Novikova and Vasina-Grossman be correct in their assessment of Avdot'ia's major contribution to Glinka's (and thus Russian) music? Is this just another case of misplaced ideological pleading? If it is, the fault is not the Soviet writers' alone. The documentation for Kann-Novikova's and Vasina-Grossman's views comes not from Glinka himself but from his much younger sister, Liudmila Shestakova (1816-1906). In her book *M.I. Glinka's Past and His Parents* (*Byloe M. I. Glinka i ego roditelei*) she says (p. 32) that the under-nanny Avdot'ia, "a merry, young woman" who "knew many different tales and songs," "was the first person who made the future composer acquainted with [*priobshchivshim k*] the creativity of the people."[55]

Unfortunately for the mythmakers, it is most probable that the sister had no direct evidence for her claims. Avdot'ia was likely long gone by the time Liudmila was born (some dozen years after her brother), and Glinka left the home about a year after her birth. Kann-Novikova acknowledges as much when she writes: "It remains to lament sadly the fact that this image was not imprinted on the basis of stories and memories of contemporaries who knew well the childhood period of Glinka's life." (p. 41) But she may reveal much more than she intended when she adds: "In any case, to forget about Avdot'ia Ivanovna would mean for biographers of Glinka about the same thing as for biographers of Pushkin to pass over the fairy tales and songs of the poet's celebrated nanny Arina Rodionovna." That is my point entirely: the cases are similar, and for good reason.

What Others Have to Say: Western Sources. David Brown, who, in his life of the composer, is rightly cautious about Glinka's autobiography and other assertions about musical influence on the child, nonetheless seems to ignore his own warning by ascribing to Avdot'ia more than is her due. Quoting Shestakova also, he maintains that Avdot'ia "knew many different tales and songs" and says that when little Misha was "bored or off colour," his grandmother would quickly yell for Avdot'ia to tell him a tale and to sing. He concludes, based on this suspect evidence, that Avdot'ia "fed his fancy with fairy stories, and nourished his musical needs on folk-song. Apart from bell music and the music heard in church, folk-song was the only other contact Glinka had with music for the first six years of his life."

If this all is to be believed, then the nanny's influence was enormous. As Brown notes: "From his nurse he could, of course, hear only folk melodies, but these he experienced in abundance, absorbing their characteristic shapes, rhythms and modes, and laying up that store of knowledge and understanding upon which he was able to draw many years later in his own compositions."[56]

It would have been prudent of Brown, and will be for us, to maintain his announced skepticism when it came to Avdot'ia. An excellent example of restraint in this regard is Richard Stites, who notes in passing the alleged influence of Avdot'ia but focuses immediately on the more natural and plausible connection between Glinka and folk-song. The mature composer absorbed what he wanted, deliberately and intentionally, when older, not subconsciously when a mere lad. There is good evidence of this borrowing process from serfs who knew Glinka well and remained alive after to testify about this link.[57]

What Glinka Has to Say. In his memoirs the composer writes: "Shortly after my birth, my mother Evgeniia Andreevna, née Glinka, was forced to turn my early *vospitanie* over to my grandma [*babka*], Fekla Aleksandrovna (my father's mother), who, having taken control of me, transferred me to her own room. I spent about three or four years with her, the wet-nurse, and nanny, seeing my parents very rarely." As already noted, Glinka actually had not one nanny but two: an older woman named Tat'iana Karpovna and an "under-nanny" [*podnian'ka*] named Avdot'ia Ivanovna. He reports that "My grandmother [*babushka*] coddled [*balovala*] me to an incredible degree; I was refused nothing; in spite of this, I was a sweet and well-behaved [*dobronravnyi*] child ..."[58]

In an effort to capture any and all influences on his musical development,[59] Glinka writes that "I was very religious [*nabozhen*] and church service rituals, in particular on festive holidays, filled my soul with the most vivid poetic joy." He attributes much, thus, to the "externals" of religion:

"Having learned to read very early, I often moved my grandma and her friends by reading the holy books [to them]. My musical ability at this time found expression in a passion for the sound of bells (pealing); I thirstily drank in these sharp sounds, and knew how to imitate the bell-ringers adeptly on two copper bowls. When I was ill, they brought small bells into the room for my amusement."

(p. 383) These preliminary self-observations are important for our purposes because one assumes that if a nanny had played any role at all in his earliest musical inclinations he would mention her in this context. He does not.[60]

If the two Soviet women scholars cited earlier are justified in their claims, why the passing, almost negligible reference to the nanny Avdot'ia – not even by name – in his autobiography? (He does refer to her by name in his adult correspondence, but not in connection with folk music.) Yet perhaps it's not his first two nannies we should scrutinize but his third:

> After the death of my grandma, the shape of my life changed a little...Besides my sister [NB: not Liudmila], a year younger than me, and my nanny, they soon took on another nanny, the widow of a surveyor, by the name of Irina Fedorovna Meshkova... This nanny was a simple and extraordinarily good woman, but mamma, although she didn't spoil [us] still loved us, and we had it good. Later, they added to Irina Fedorovna the French woman Roza Ivanovna. (p. 384)

Glinka calls Meshkova, hired to assist Avdot'ia Ivanovna, "my nanny of blessed memory" in a letter written to Konstantin Bulgakov in 1856. Although this sounds promising for her having some profound influence on the child, he mentions her again in his memoirs only in passing (in connection with her daughter) and but twice in his later correspondence.[61] Meantime, his feelings for music remained inchoate.

> Musical sensibility [*chuvstvo*] all the same [*vse eshche*] remained in an undeveloped and crude state in me. Even at 8 years old, when we were delivered from the invasion of Orel by the French, I listened with my former avidity to the ringing of the bells; I distinguished the peal of each church, and earnestly imitated it on copper bowls.
> Always surrounded by women, playing only with my sister and the nanny's daughter, I was in no way like [other] boys of my age. (pp. 384-85)

His father often held celebrations at the home for which he invited over the orchestra of his brother-in-law, Glinka's uncle and his mother's brother, who lived just eight versts away. The musicians would often remain at the Glinka residence for several days. After they had played dance tunes for the invited guests and the latter had left, they would play other pieces. Glinka recalls a time ca. 1814-15, when he was 10 or 11, and they played a quartet of Bernhard Crusell (1775-1838, born in Finland; in Russian, *Kruzel'*); "this music produced in me an incomprehensible new and enthralling impression; I remained the whole day after in a sort of feverish condition, plunged into an inexplicable, agonizingly sweet state, and the following day during drawing lesson was distracted ..." When his tutor notes that all he's thinking about is music, Glinka responds: "What's to be done? Music is my soul." Indeed, from that time on, he "passionately loved music"; his uncle's orchestra was the source of his greatest joy.

But just when it seems that high (mostly Western) culture only, and not a peasant nanny's vocalizations, was his sole musical inspiration, Glinka throws out a hint that low (peasant) music did influence his tastes. "During supper they [who?] usually played Russian songs... I liked these tender-sad – but completely accessible for me – sounds...and perhaps these songs, which I heard in childhood, were the primary reason that I later began primarily to elaborate Russian folk [*narodnaia*] music. (pp. 385-86) Glinka had first written "*otechestvennaia* (native) music" but then crossed the first word out and wrote "*narodnaia*" instead.

This kind of claim for nannies or peasant servants more generally would appear to be rather common, perhaps pro forma for Glinka's generation or half-generation.[62]

An Attempt to Solve the Puzzle of Glinka's Nanny. It may be either the imagination, faulty memory, or conscious distortion of Liudmila Shestakova that ascribes so much influence to her brother's nanny. Perhaps both Glinka (slightly) and his sister were influenced – consciously or unconsciously – to speak of nannies by Pushkin, as others seem to have been.[63] More likely, she felt the impact of others' thinking.

I do not mean to imply the presence of a "smoking gun," but the following facts satisfy me that Glinka and Shestakova were, in all likelihood, swayed by the peasant-sympathetic, nationalist views of Vladimir Stasov.

The evidence is as follows. Stasov first met Glinka in 1842; in 1847 the critic published his study of Glinka's use of folk motifs in his music. Stasov at this point became the foremost advocate of promoting "Russianness" in music in place of "Europeanness," however vaguely each term was defined. His conversations with Glinka helped convince Stasov of the fact that "traditional Russian art forms could be 'modernized' and brought to the 'European level.'"[64] (In 1849 or 1850, Stasov – now quite close to Glinka – also became well acquainted with the composer's sister Liudmila.)

In late 1854 Glinka wrote a *Biographical Note* for a new edition of the *Biographie universelle des musiciens* put out by the Belgian musicologist François-Joseph Fétis. He showed his draft to Stasov, who told him it was not good enough. Glinka did not send it to Fétis, and it was never published. In this first attempt at an autobiography, in the third person, there is no mention whatever of Avdot'ia, Meshkova, or even of his grandmother.[65] By 1855, after Glinka's return from a trip to France, it was the Stasovs (either Vladimir or his brother Dmitrii or both) and Shestakova who importuned the composer to write his memoirs.[66] The fact that Stasov and Shestakova had a direct hand in the writing of her brother's memoirs – seemingly a directing hand – is hard to ignore. It would not be much of an exaggeration to say that Glinka's memoirs were pretty much dictated to, and partly written by, Stasov and Shestakova.[67]

For one more reason I suspect Stasov as being most responsible for insinuating into Glinka's memoirs a peasant-nanny figure as an early musical influence. In an unpublished section of his own memoirs, Stasov wrote the following:

> Up to this time [1830] *only* one event had left on my soul a profound impression [*provela...glubokuiu chertu*] and left an extraordinary memory, not comparable to anything else. This was the moment when for the first time I entered the room of my mother after the birth of my younger brother, Boris. This occurred a full six years before school; I was then all of six years old, however I remember everything to the

last detail. Nanny Avdot'ia Ivanovna came into the nursery to me and said: "Come quickly into the bedroom, mamá is calling you."[68]

The coincidence of the nannies' names is highly suggestive. Did Stasov's own memories, so clearly etched, prompt him to get Glinka to include his peasant nanny in his autobiography? A third of a century later, in the 1890s, it was again Stasov and the music scholar-critic Nikolai Findeizen who urged Shestakova to write down her recollections of her brother and their family.[69] The problem is, as was noted, that she had no memories of Glinka's early years. It's a good guess that Stasov's "support" for her efforts included more than a small interjection of his own thinking about the importance of *narodnost'* in Glinka's life. If that is so, she was a willing, even eager "accomplice."

Nikolai Ge (1831-1894)

The Pushkin-Glinka-Stasov Connection. One of the most famous depictions of Aleksandr Pushkin was rendered in 1875 by the artist Nikolai Ge. His oil on canvas, entitled "Pushchin visiting Pushkin at Mikhailovskoe," was painted at a time when some critics (e.g., Dmitrii Pisarev) were attacking Pushkin's *oeuvre* and before the poet's great resurgence from the 1880s. It might almost be seen as an attempt to shore up the poet's image. The work includes three figures: the two of its title and a third, the nanny Arina Rodionovna.[70] What makes all this of interest for us is the painter's own "nanny" background and its possible link to this work.

The Ge family, French in origin, emigrated to Russia at the time of the 1789 revolution. Ge's childhood was spent in the village, among women. In the best source we have on this childhood, much is made of the similarities between the upbringing of Ge and that of the composer Mikhail Glinka, born over a quarter century before. There is a very good reason for this regular juxtaposition: it was the nationalistic critic Vladimir Stasov who was responsible for gathering Ge's autobiography, manuscripts, and others' memories about him and then publishing all the material in 1904. (introduction, 6-7) As we've seen, he had played a similar supportive role in the genesis of Glinka's autobiography (as well as Musorgskii's). In the case of Ge, if not also in the other two, the more one reads this life of the painter, the more one feels the spirit and hand of the critic. It is like the unfolding of Vladimir Nabokov's brilliant novel *Pale Fire*; the editor gradually seems to usurp the subject. Not Ge but Stasov thus tells us that

> Ge's father was rarely at home, his mother was no longer alive, and as with Glinka, two women – his grandmother and nanny – had care of the little boy. Perhaps, precisely because of this, the character of both, Glinka and Ge, to a significant degree obtained that soft, delicate, meek, in considerable part feminine cast [*sklad*] which so sharply distinguished them from many contemporaries who were subjected to completely different influences in childhood. Both Glinka and Ge speak with joy about their grandmother and nanny (Grig[orii] Nik[olaevich] calls the latter Natasha, but N.N. Ge himself, neither in speaking nor in his letters ever in his entire life called her anything other than simply "nanny"). (pp. 11-12)

An aunt, the father's sister, lived in the Ge household in the early 1830s and all three boys were at this time "in the hands of auntie Aleksandra Osipovna." But Ge himself never mentions her, not one word, and she had absolutely no influence on the fate of her nephew. So Stasov's focus is entirely on the grandmother, Dar'ia Iakovlevna, who by the early 1830s was "an old, feeble, good and pious woman of weak character," and on the nanny Natasha, "who had a powerful influence on N.N. Ge's entire spiritual makeup." (p. 12) After setting the stage as he thought proper, Stasov then and only then allows the painter to speak in his own words: "My infancy [*mladenchestvo*] began. It's difficult to talk about it, like about the light in the morning before sunrise, but everyone knows very well and recalls that which I'm remembering: it's as if I see these best years of life." But wait – Stasov feels the need for an interjection. He recounts scenes and conversations of the boy with the nanny, with the grandmother, presumably relying on Ge's autobiography, that "fly past his imagination."

Nikolai Ge, *My Nanny* (1867) oil on canvas

When little Kolia was just four (says the critic), "Dear nanny sat down on the floor; the little boy hugged nanny; he laughs with nanny; he sees the familiar big blue eyes, kisses them, [and] cries. Nanny began to feel sorry for both herself and her nurseling. "It's nothing, nothing; I'm just that way." (p. 14)   All that follows is a mix of Stasov and Ge, and although it's difficult to determine at times whose voice is being heard, it seems to me at least that the dominant one is always the critic's.

> Describing this scene which was etched so powerfully in the imagination of the young boy had to do with the fact that in the Ge family in the 1830s the main estate manager was the retired soldier Ogurtsov [a Simon Legree-like figure]. Everyone in the household trembled before him. He particularly hated the young, kind, good nanny, maybe mostly because she enjoyed the fullest sympathy of the grandmother and her grandchildren. He once stood watch as the young teacher Vostokov (who later married her) kissed her in the garden. Ogurtsov for this meted out a barbaric punishment, and there couldn't be any kind of justification for this. The grandmother and her grandchildren could only weep, wail bitterly, and nothing more. But Ogurtsov's monstrosities only increased the love, empathy, and profound heartfelt sympathy of the children for their dear nanny.

Stasov then separates himself from the narrative a bit by saying that at this point in the story he's retailing, "N. N. Ge exclaims": "Good, sweet nanny, I never again encountered your equal; for your heart, for your love I will never forget you, my teacher of truth, teacher of life! By your pure, humble common-folk love [sic! – *narodnaia liubov'*] you shielded [*osenila*] my childhood and bequeathed to me sensitivity for the sorrow of others." (p. 15)

It seems clear that his nanny was in no large way an inspiration for the painter's art, even though he did paint a portrait of her, in 1867. "My Nanny" (Moia niania) is a fairly small oil on canvas (35.8 x 28.5 cm).[71] (It's his grandmother who encourages him when, at a young age, Ge begins drawing pictures on the floor. She gives him paper so he can continue his drawing unrestrainedly. [p. 17])

Yet Stasov and Ge seem to make the nanny into a model of patient suffering and Christlike meek and humble behavior. From this it might even be possible for an overzealous biographer to trace a connection to the subject matter of his works. Early and late, the themes that he made most his own were religious. *The Last Supper*, executed in 1861, made his reputation, secured him an Academy professorship, and was purchased by the tsar, Alexander II. After a period of producing mostly historical works – and the Pushkin painting with the somewhat gratuitous inclusion of Arina Rodionovna – and becoming a Tolstoyan, he returned in the1880s to paintings on religious subjects, inspired by motifs from the New Testament and the life of Christ.

Mikhail Lermontov (1814-1841)

Students of Russian literature are aware of the odd parallels between the lives of Aleksandr Pushkin and Mikhail Lermontov. It will not surprise then that what biographers and hagiographers did for Pushkin and his childhood caretakers they have usually repeated for Lermontov. In fact, it is almost eerie the extent to which the same mythologizing has crept into most biographies of the second poet.

This mythopoeic work is made the easier by each poet's relations with his parents: in Pushkin's case, an unloving mother (and father), in Lermontov's, a dead mother and absent father. The future poet's mother died when he was just 3 and he was raised, at the dying mother's behest, by his wealthy grandmother, Elizaveta Arsen'eva (née Stolypina; 1760-1845) on her estate of Tarkhany.[72]

What Would-Be Mythmakers Have to Say. Like Glinka, Lermontov actually had two nannies, one a Russian peasant whose name cannot be established, the second a German *bonne*. Various Lermontov biographers have celebrated the Russian woman's role as comparable to Arina Rodionovna's in Pushkin's life. A certain Marfa Konovalova falsely claimed to be the Russian nanny, and that the young Lermontov was a friend and defender of the common folk. But P. Vyrypaev destroyed that myth in the early 1950s.[73] An anonymous source reporting "the nannies took a lot from his caprices" likewise fails the sniff test.[74]

Exaggeration and distortion surround the nanny whose name we do know, the *bonne*: Kristina (Khristina) Remer. The literature about Remer is extensive; yet nearly every account of her uses as its primary source one ur-narrative, the poet's life written by Derpt University professor Pavel Viskovatov (or Viskovatyi), born a year after the poet's death, who made Lermontov and his poetry his life's work. Here's the complete original:

> The German nanny [*bonna*], Khristina Osipovna Remer, appointed to look after Misha from the day of his birth, now remained inseparable from him. This was a woman of strict rules [*strogikh pravil*], religious. She instilled in her nursling a feeling of love for those close [to him], even for those who were in bondage to him. God forbid if he should address anyone of the household serfs with a coarse word or insult [them]. Khristina Osipovna would not like this, would shame the boy, make him ask forgiveness of the insulted party. All the household serfs respected this woman highly, but for the boy her influence was positive. The universal spoiling and love [for him in the household of his grandmother] had made him a spoiled child, in whom, despite the innate goodness, there was developing a spirit of willfulness and stubbornness, easily, with inattention, turning into cruelty in children.[75]

Viskovatov thus gives credit to Remer for saving Lermontov from an otherwise faulty upbringing.[76]

Too many of those seeking information about Lermontov's childhood ignore the dangers of the autobiographical fallacy and base their treatments on a fictional treatment of his childhood by the poet (and other dubious sources). Thus one author, Sergei Ivanov, states: "For all her love and wishes, grandmother couldn't take the place of his mother... 'His nanny, Khristina Osipovna Remer...encircled the boy with constant care and attention, but she didn't know how [*ne umela*] to be affectionate, to pet the child, to sing him a song.'" Ivanov claims Remer "was very attached to the child and had a good influence on him (she was a kind, responsive [*otzyvchivyi*] person, who sympathized with the serfs)."[77]

The same biographer says the poet's early years, spent in loneliness, without playmates, taught Lermontov to dream and fantasize. The documentation of the assertion is again Lermontov's

To Mythologize or Not? Nanny's Role in Creative Lives 277

quasi-autobiographical story, which manifestly exaggerates the "loneliness" of the boy – he had any number of playmates his own age brought in especially by his grandmother. Ivanov even goes so far as to affirm: "The tales of Khristina Osipovna – who was a devotee of medieval romanticism with knightly tourneys, legendary deeds – and the songs and tales of the household maids – fostered the development of [Lermontov's] childhood fantasies" (p. 20). No factual sources confirm this second claim – which even seems to contradict the first – and he offers no support. One Western biographer, however, has swallowed the bait and retails this unsubstantiated claim in his rendering of the poet's life.[78]

What Lermontov Has to Say. In 1830, ruminating about the poetry of the Russian *narod*, Lermontov wrote the following note:

> Our literature is so impoverished that I cannot borrow anything from it; and at 15 the mind does not take in impressions as swiftly as in childhood; but in those days I read almost nothing. – However, if I'd like to give myself up to poetry of the people [*vdat'sia v poeziiu narodnuiu*], then, most likely, I'd search for it no further than in Russian songs. – How sad that I had a German and not a Russian woman as a nanny – I didn't hear folktales...[*Kak zhalko, chto u menia byla mamushkoi nemka, a ne russkaia – ia ne slykhal skazok narodnykh...*] – in them, probably, there's more poetry than in all of French literature.[79]

It is tempting to make much of these words, as various biographers have. However, this appears to me to be more of a "pronouncement" or contrived thought than a real self-revelation or unselfconscious musing.[80] It probably occurred to Lermontov that it might be regrettable not to share a particular link with the great Pushkin. Surely, though, he absorbed enough of Russian folk culture from others surrounding him. *Not as proof*, but simply as an illustration of how likely this was to happen, one can refer to the poet's works. In his "autobiographical" story "I want to tell you...," in which Lermontov's alter-ego is given his typical name of Sasha Arbenin, the poet may or may not have been inspired by his real-life nannies or other servants. Here he writes:

> In winter the maids came into the nursery to sew and knit... Sasha was very gay with them. They petted him and kissed him ...recounted fairy tales about the Volga bandits to him, and filled his imagination with wonders of daring-do and gloomy pictures and antisocial ideas [*poniatiami protivuobshchestvennymi*]. He ceased loving toys and began to dream...He wanted someone to love him, kiss and caress him, but the old nanny had such firm [*zhestkie*] hands![81]

Nikolai Leskov (1831-1895)

The great satirist's nanny was Anna Stepanovna Kalandina. Stepanovna – her honorific among all family members – had been a serf of Leskov's mother (née Mar'ia Alfer'eva). She lived just short of a hundred years (1812-1911). In three different autobiographical sketches he produced, Leskov makes no mention of her at all.

What Others Say. The omission in his autobiographies has not prevented later Russian and Western biographers from expatiating anomalously on the place of Stepanovna in the writer's life. The dubious distinction of getting this legend started goes almost certainly to Rostislav Sementkovskii (1846-1918), the author and journalist, who contributed an introduction to Leskov's collected works in 1902. Sementkovskii, relying on the satirist's own words, rightly notes the absence of a strong parent-child relationship in Leskov's childhood:[82]

> As is evident from the personal reminiscences of Leskov himself... he was a loving son, but neither his father nor his mother were the individuals who had the most powerful effect on his worldview. He was deprived of his father early... As concerns his mother, the son portrays her as a woman who stood out in no particular... That means that not on this hand must we seek for the most decisive factors which influenced Leskov in childhood.

But then Sementkovskii commits the cardinal sin of equating Leskov's fiction with his life: "In his reminiscences [sic – meaning

To Mythologize or Not? Nanny's Role in Creative Lives 279

not his three autobiographies but all of his other literary works], other personalities stand out in much greater relief: the nannies, household servants, teachers, priests, relatives." Elucidating how the greatest influences on the young Leskov in real life all show up as characters in his stories, Sementkovskii seems to be insisting that all the details of Leskov's stories are autobiographical. "In order to characterize the influence which these various people had on Leskov, it is sufficient to recall the most typical figures. Let us take, for example, the nanny Liubov' Onisimovna ...," a character in Leskov's excellent story "The Toupee Artist" (*Tupeinyi khudozhnik*, 1883).[83]

Through an all-too-common carelessness, many later scholars have unthinkingly borrowed from Sementkovskii what they took to be factual matter. Thus, the Soviet critic P. Pustovoito, in his commentary to the story "The Toupee Artist," completes the vicious circle by claiming that "At the base of the story is set a true incident: Leskov's nanny Liubov' Onisimovna [sic!] fell in love with a serf makeup artist [*grimirovshchik*] in the Orël theater of Count Kamenskii. She ran away with her lover but was caught by the count's servants and cruelly punished."[84]

What Leskov Says. The writer's failure to talk about his nanny in his autobiographical sketches does not mean that he forgot about her completely or did not on occasion think of her. In fact, in his letters of the early 1890s (and probably earlier), he did not neglect to pass on his greetings to the old woman. "I send my greetings and respects to my nieces, and also to Stepanovna. How is she?" he wrote his sister (19 April 1891). Or: "Stepanovna evidently is not yet ready [presumably, to die], like a still-untempered horseshoe that the smith keeps throwing back into the forge to temper more thoroughly" (30 January 1893).[85]

The Key to Leskov and His Nanny. Since Leskov is mostly silent about Stepanovna, we must turn to other sources to learn much about her. Fortunately, his son Andrei knew her well in her later years and had many occasions to talk with her. The junior Leskov, refreshingly free of sentimentality and nostalgia in discussing his father's nanny's position in society and the family, offers a very full portrait of the (older) woman, warts and all.[86] He's particularly candid about a creature often nearly beatified by other writers: "I well remember Anna Stepanovna as a heavily wrinkled, withered old lady with lips respectfully shut tight in the presence of 'the masters,' which eagerly opened up for tireless reproaches and sermonizing addressed to all the younger servants who knew no respite [*spasenie*] or mercy from her, who didn't want to live in the same house with her."[87]

Andrei, like his father, seems a born storyteller, but he also offers invaluable testimony about the nanny's relationship to his father's writings. Unlike the too eagerly credulous Sementkovskii, the younger Leskov discusses with a critical and probing eye several of his father's works that parallel the latter's life. Of the many examples he gives, all of them illuminating, I'll confine myself to just a couple. In his story "Immortal Golovan" (*Nesmertel'nyi Golovan*, 1880), "taken from the diary of his grandmother Akilina Vasil'evna Alfer'eva," Nikolai Leskov describes how a mad dog named Riabka snapped its chain and attacked Anna Stepanovna when she was carrying him ("Nikolushka"). Leskov's son questions whether we can lend credence to the incident: Did the writer's grandmother really keep such a diary, when she had trouble even composing a letter to her son?[88] In reality, a rat severely bit Stepanovna while holding her tiny nursling; Leskov senior transmogrified the rodent into a rabid dog.[89]

In all of the relationships between writers and nannies, we almost invariably see the link from one side only. That's why it's good to have the dictated letters of Arina Rodionovna to Pushkin. And though they come second-hand and therefore without complete authenticity, it's also very satisfying to have Stepanovna's reported reactions to her quondam charge's work.

> Irreproachably restrained with respect to the older members of the Leskov clan, Stepanovna would get visibly upset before a youth [Andrei himself] over the inaccuracy of the events in their retelling by her former nursling: "What is he writing! Does he really think it was like that? Why, it was..." – and a merciless pointing out of one or another factual inaccuracy would follow. She would get indignant

"in her heart," would wring her hands [*vspleskivala rukami*], would reproachfully shake her grey head, always tied up in a kerchief. But to the creator of all these errors of protocol she uncovered she never dared to point out anything at all.[90]

At the same time, we can easily guess that Stepanovna's reproaches would have been nearly meaningless for Leskov. And that brings us neatly to a secondary question raised at the start of this chapter. What were Leskov's motivations for his frequent inclusion of characters that appear to be based on Stepanovna, on his memories of her?[91] As stated, I believe that psychological motivations played only a minor role in his "transmutations" of Stepanovna. However, for those desirous of having a good psychological explanation of how Leskov's relations with his parents and the lack of love he experienced as a child may have affected his later life – including his writing – I can recommend Hugh McLean's excellent discussion in his Leskov biography.[92]

Anton Chekhov (1860-1904)

If Nikolai Leskov was taciturn about his own life, Anton Chekhov was virtually silent.

Sibling Sources – One. From Anton Pavlovich himself we would never know that his was a family engaged in trade and that the children enjoyed the services of a nanny.[93] However, thanks to his younger brother Mikhail we know that little Antosha and his siblings did indeed have such a caretaker. In fact, Mikhail Pavlovich never seemed to tire of talking about this woman. He repeated his stories about her in almost everything he wrote about the family.

> To our good fortune, there fell to our lot the excellent nanny Agaf'ia Aleksandrovna Kumskaia, who knew how to tell a story marvelously [*udivitel'no*]. Our mother was also a master at telling a story. Nanny most of all would tell tales about the mysterious, the terrifying, the unusual, but mother – about the past, how as a girl she traveled in a tarantass throughout all of Russia from Vladimir province

to Taganrog, how the French and English bombarded us in the Sevastopol' [i.e., Crimean] war, and how poorly the peasants lived under serfdom. Reading my brother's works, I continually find in them traces of these two influences. And the poetic "Happiness" was written by him unquestionably under the impression of nanny's tales.[94]

All that Chekhov Offers. We have just two letters from him in which he reluctantly wrote a few lines about himself. In response to a request from his publisher – the playwright and belletrist Vladimir Tikhonov (1857-1914) – Chekhov supplied, on 22 February 1892, a very brief, offhand vita. Into this first "autobiography" he put a comment reminiscent of Leskov's (and those of many others): "You need my biography? Here it is...However, all this is nonsense [*vzdor*]. Write whatever you want. If there are no facts, then replace them with something lyrical."[95]

His fuller, better-known "autobiography" appears in an appendix to a letter from Yalta to Grigorii Rossolimo, a former classmate and lifelong friend, dated 11 October 1899. Here he states: "I have no doubt that [my] studies of the medical sciences have had a serious influence on my literary activity; they have significantly expanded [*razdvinuli*] the sphere of my observations, enriched me with knowledge the true value of which for me, as a writer, can be understood only by someone himself a doctor; they also have had a directing influence..."[96] He gives no information whatever about his early childhood, in either version, and says nothing of his nanny.

Sibling Sources – Two. On one occasion, oldest brother Aleksandr Pavlovich in Taganrog wrote a letter (31 July-2 August 1882) to his younger brothers Anton and Nikolai in Moscow. He observed in passing: "...brothers, childhood and maturity [*vozmuzhalost'*] are two different things." This thought must have prompted a free association to their shared childhood.

> From our former nanny [Kumskaia], thanks to time, has emerged [*poluchilas'*] a meek, humpbacked [*krokhotnaia, sgorblennaia*] little old lady with a very sweet, ugly little mug [*s predobroi rozhitsei*] and a whistle in her toothless mouth.

She sends you her abundant greetings [*massa poklonov*] and is firmly convinced that each of you [will be] at least a state minister or precinct supervisor [*kvartal'nyi nadziratel'*].⁹⁷

This letter may help explain why Anton had no good reason to recall the nanny Kumskaia fondly. Her changed disposition surely implies that she was nothing like this in her younger days tending the Chekhov children – and likely not the person glorified by brother Mikhail.

Aleksandr's (fictionalized) account of Chekhov's "childhood," moreover, differs considerably from Mikhail's with respect to Kumskaia. He barely mentions the *niania*, though she is called by her first name and patronymic, Agaf'ia Aleksandrovna. She is merely invoked to "show" her waking up the young Antosha when he's very sleepy. Absolutely nothing in Aleksandr's rendering makes the nanny seem unusual or highly loved by Anton. Since he wrote before 1917, that's completely understandable; hagiographic hues typically come in after the revolution.⁹⁸

Nanny's "Influence." There remains the question of his nanny's supposed influence on Anton's works. Mikhail's assertions are difficult to disprove, but no one else corroborates his assertions, least of all the author himself. In fact, in his correspondence Chekhov may have indicated the opposite. Take for instance the one specific example cited by Mikhail as to Kumskaia's alleged inspiration, the short story "Happiness," finished in early 1888. In his correspondence of that spring concerning this tale, "which I consider the best of all my stories," there is not a hint of his nanny's influence or memory. He merely asks Ia. P. Polonskii (in a letter of 25 March) "to allow me to dedicate it to you. In this you'll be doing my muse a great favor [*Etim Vy premnogo obiazhete moiu muzu*]." And in letters to and from his brother Aleksandr (14 and 21 June) neither of them says a word about the story's being inspired by Kumskaia.⁹⁹ Whether or not this was all a figment of Mikhail's democratizing imagination I cannot say. But it must in any case remain an open question about any influence exerted by Chekhov's nanny.

Elizaveta Vodovozova (1844-1923)

This is an example of the second kind of incommensurateness. Vodovozova (née Tsevlovskaia), a well-known nineteenth-century pedagog, makes an incredible show of love and affection for her nanny in her memoirs.[100] But she may protest too much: in her serious pedagogic works, she treats nannies almost as pariahs. To be fair, what she is really criticizing is serfdom. Yet there is more to it than that:

> Although among the numerous complement of serf nannies, wet-nurses [*mamki*] and *diad'ki* one could find not a few good natures self-sacrificingly devoted to their charges; still all that they could do for them [was] to instill trust, devotion, [and] awaken [*vozbudit'*] love for themselves. This, of course, was a not unimportant service for an epoch when Russian reality awakened only bad feelings. In this, many mammies [*mamushki*] and nannies, with their fairy tales, stories, and songs, supported knowledge of living Russian speech and interest in peasant poetry, which were being squeezed out ever more by the fashionable French language and passion for everything French. But being ignorant and superstitious, they could not broaden the mental horizon of their charges. At the same time [*K tomu zhe*] the life of gentry landowners took shape such that amidst the all too many maids, lackeys, and numerous playmates from among the serfs, the bad [*durnye*] elements undoubtedly outweighed the good.[101]

While this indictment pertains to pre-emancipation days, Vodovozova was not much less scathing toward child caretakers in the 1870s and 80s. "In the majority of cases they [parents] give the children up completely into the hands of nannies. A nanny is sweet and obliging, toys are alluring; but in two or three days she will have succeeded in passing on her entire store of stories and the games she's invented, and begin to repeat herself."[102]

The point is one emphasized throughout these pages: Vodovozova, an observant childhood expert, was ambivalent toward nannies. Unlike herself as a child, she could, as an adult, see the good and bad sides of a peasant nanny. The ambivalence appears clear when one compares Chapter 13 of her book – where she seems clearly to want to be able to eliminate the role of nannies and leave all the upbringing of a child of 3 or 4 to an active mother and no one else – with her very next chapter on 4-6-year-olds – where, in one of her math word problems she treats a nanny as the most expected, natural thing to have around children.[103]

A Unique Author-Nanny Relationship

Marina Tsvetaeva (1892-1941)

Rather unusual among Russian authors is the case of the poet Marina Tsvetaeva, which does not exactly fit either of my two paradigms, yet cries out to be included in this chapter. The poet famously had no nanny (as a child) but her sister Asia (Anastas'ia) did – a nanny who repulsed young Musia (Marina) by her nasty behavior toward herself ("she didn't love me but on occasion bragged about me") and by her name (Pushkin's Arina was "a dove" in his poetry; Asia's nanny's surname links her to a housefly). This nanny, Aleksandra Mukhina, is almost a parody of Arina Rodionovna: Marina would recite to the nanny instead of vice versa, and the unpleasant nanny objected to or rejected what she was being told.[104]

In her private notebooks, in an entry she titled "Dream of Pushkin" – dated about 20 July 1931, in Meudon France – Tsvetaeva had earlier mused about the various women in Pushkin's life and concluded: "I wouldn't want to be [Anna] Kern, nor [Amalia] Riznich [two of the poet's early dalliances], nor even Mariia Raevskaia. [I'd want to be Ekaterina] Karamzina [wife of the historian]. Or better still – the nanny. For [Pushkin treated] no one, no one, never, with such *aching* tenderness [*s takoi* shchemiashchei *nezhnost'iu*]...."[105]

But it's not the sister's nanny nor her interpretive conjectures and musings about Pushkin and Arina Rodionovna that make Tsvetaeva so curious a specimen for inclusion here. Rather, it's because her private life was so full of children and nannies for a half dozen of her most productive and yet difficult years. With first one and then a second young daughter to raise in the years from 1913-1919 – Ariadna (known as Alia), born in 1912, and Irina, born in 1917 – Tsvetaeva found herself constantly in need of good childcare, which she found hard to find. In these years she ran through as many as eight or nine nannies in rapid succession, and her notebooks are full of references to all of them: Grusha (in Moscow; August 1913) seems feckless or just plain dumb; Marfusha (in Yalta; late 1913) is called "the awful" or "the horrible"; Anneta (winter of 1913-1914) – the *"ocherednaia niania"* ("next-in-turn nanny") in the poet's felicitous phrase – was fired for cause; Klavdiia (February-May 1914) "the giraffe," left to nanny her sister's son; Kseniia Gavvá (April1914) was the "third nanny in Feodosiia," by Tsvetaeva's own calculation – she toilet-trained Alia; Nadia (ca. May 1914-ca. late summer 1915) also left to care for her sister's son Andriusha; Natasha (September 1915); Liuba (for much of 1917) who parts ways with the family because she doesn't want to leave Moscow after the Revolution; Nadia *redux* (August 1918) who was supposed to take over the care of Irina before the child died.

By a stroke of good fortune, we have not only Marina's musings about many of these women[106] but also Alia's. They coincide to a remarkable degree.

> Marina's influence on me, a tot, was enormous, interrupted by no one and nothing and – always at the zenith. Meanwhile, she did not spend so much time with me, did not go walking so often, did not indulge [me] in anything, did not pamper; occupied with all of this, to one degree or another, were the nannies, who left in memory no trustworthy trace, perhaps because they replaced one another frequently without getting accustomed to the house.
>
> From one of them it was necessary to part because instead of a little public garden on Dogs Square [*Sobach'aia ploshchadka*] she would lead me every time to the Nikolo-Peskovskaia Church – to endure the requiems and to kiss the deceased...
>
> A second one they let go because she turned out to be a pilferer and defective in her speech: instead of "bear" and "trousers," for example, she pronounced them – and I following her – "bar" and "truesers"; the third and the following ones left, it seems, on their own.

> Not one of these, or any of the others who cast intermittent shadows [could] overshadow for me Marina, who constantly as it were shone a light through all and everything: I was continuously drawn to and along behind her, like a heliotrope, and felt her presence constantly within myself, like the voice of conscience – so great was the convincing, demanding, subduing power radiating from her. The power of love.[107]

What does Tsvetaeva's home situation, hectic as it was, have to do with her art? She populated many of her great poems and autobiographical essays of the coming years with nannies and wet-nurses. One could speculate that her consciousness of caretakers was likely raised in the course of many years and that she therefore probably had good cause to recall their presence later and thus perhaps to include them in her poetry and prose. But there is no need to go that far. It is enough for me to establish the two sets of facts; whether they merely ran parallel, without ever touching, or they intersected in creative ways cannot be fully established.

Conclusion

At times there occur instances in which a more or less direct link between a nanny and artistic creation can be asserted and defended.[108] One finds evidence of the enduring power of nannies – not exaggerated – to inspire and stimulate their nurselings. Perhaps that is just as it should be: a child's imagination, once stirred, by whatever caretaker when young, is bound to be reflected in later creativity. If that imagination in turn, on occasion, runs away with itself, loses a sense of proportion, that is only to be expected (and forgiven).

The Pushkin-Arina model proved so seductive for so long, however, that its force can be seen in biographies and autobiographies of creative Russians for the rest of the nineteenth century and into the twentieth. The urge to mythologize was almost irresistible in the immediate post-Pushkin years. Hence the stories associated with, among others, Lermontov and Glinka. The claim of a nanny's influence on her grown charge's artistic endeavors – sometimes by the former charges, more often by their biographers – does not always withstand closer scrutiny.

In the next, final chapter I take another look at the larger-than-life figure of the nanny, not just in literature and other spheres of culture but in the broader life and consciousness of the Russian nation.

10

Nanny as Symbol

For all the importance of a caretaker in a child's life, of equal or greater interest is the significance of such a figure in the life of a nation. In Chapter 1 I explained that one Russian nanny became much more than a child's caretaker. In this chapter I try to explain, first, why some members of the gentry and intelligentsia tried to create a symbol out of nannies generically, and second, what the content of this symbol reveals about peasants, women, and Russians as a whole.

Development of the Symbol in Russia

A child's nanny became a symbol – in both Western Europe and Russia – in the eighteenth and nineteenth centuries, when times were highly unstable. In this period, nationalism was on the rise; the concept of motherhood/maternity became politicized.[1] In Russia more specifically, many factors contributed to the making of this nanny symbol. The most important were Romantic nationalism, nostalgia, and changing socio-economic relations. Ideas – including the symbol of the wet-nurse and nanny – gained in importance in direct proportion to the degree of physical-material instability and psychological insecurity felt by so many, at various levels of society.[2]

Romantic nationalism. This phenomenon arose, in Russia as

elsewhere, largely in response to a dominant French culture (somewhat "disguised" as cosmopolitanism),[3] the rationalism of the Enlightenment, and then the French Revolution. Spurred by German idealists, notably Johann Gottfried von Herder (much read and discussed in Russia),[4] Russian Romantic nationalists sought a unique, authentic identity for their country.[5] Unlike later, more virulent forms of nationalism, this proto-nationalism was couched mostly in positive terms. It praised what was best in one's country. It was not constantly expressed in negative, highly chauvinistic, or even racist terms. This search for true identity led Russians, as most other Romantic nationalists, to their "rural roots" – the peasantry – and to their language, extolling all the virtues of each. In turn, the nexus between peasant caretakers, language learning, and upbringing more generally led almost inevitably to a focus on wet-nurses and nannies.[6]

From 1800-1830, as composers strained to define "Russianness" in their music and critics called for a "national school of art," poets and writers kept trying to come up with a Russian "national hero."[7] It was not difficult for Romantic nationalists like the Slavophiles to settle on Pushkin as one such hero because of his great gift with the Russian language. It was then a simple step to connect Pushkin's gift with his peasant nanny.[8]

When the philosopher and social thinker Pëtr Chaadaev published his first Philosophical Letter in 1836, launching the Slavophile-Westernizer debates, he very nearly laid out a road map for the Romantic nationalists who, in his wake, mythologized or hagiographized Arina Rodionovna and so many other Russian nannies and wet-nurses. Chaadaev twice made brief mention of a wet-nurse or nanny [*nourrice*]. The sensation-producing first letter noted the figure in passing. Then in the "Fifth Letter" (unpublished but read and circulated in salon society in the early 1830s), he wrote: "*Is there in* [a newborn baby]...*any kind of thought which did not flow from the small circle of concepts deposited in its head by its mother, wet-nurse, or other human being in the first days of its life?*"[9]

Chaadaev took his readers/auditors in their thoughts back to mankind's childhood – but also to their own. It's almost as if he were laying down a signpost to all the nanny idolators who would follow, especially in the Slavophile camp: look to your wet-nurses and nannies, your infancy, for a sign of what's to come.[10] In a nation seeking both its roots and a brighter future, with people looking for comfort, reassurance, and a sense of identity, "the golden age" of childhood held a natural appeal, an almost irresistible attraction. Providers of comfort and security in childhood were symbols of that appeal.

Nostalgia increases in times of uncertainty, when people tend to look backward seeking inner peace – to earlier times for a people/nation, to childhood for an individual.[11] When people become nostalgic, they yearn not always *for* something so much as *from* something.[12] They want to know "Whence have we come" and "Whither are we going?" These questions – tied directly to a sense of identity – invariably, simultaneously, look both backward and forward. Most eighteenth- and nineteenth-century thinkers in Russia, as in Europe, were *both backward- and forward-looking*. A nanny or wet-nurse fit well into this dichotomy: she was both backward-looking, as the carrier of traditions and beliefs almost from time immemorial, but in a way also forward-looking, as the person nourishing and bringing up countless members of the future generation. To complicate the matter, "The Enlightenment emphasize[d] social and intellectual progress at the expense of cultural replication" and thus had "a deeply divided view" of the nanny.[13] As we have seen, in Russia, as elsewhere in Europe, self-appointed experts on childcare, social critics, and cultural arbiters all shared this ambivalence about nannies. It was only in overcoming some aspects of the Enlightenment, in particular its rationalism and its cosmopolitanism – often in the throes of nostalgia – that the allegory of the nanny could flourish.

The Cult of Maternity. In this same period, family relations often took on a new coloring. I would argue this was not so much from a different intrafamily dynamic as from changing functions and ideas about the nature of women and children. Thanks in large part to Rousseau and similar writers, several of what have been called "cults" emerged amid society's higher levels: the "cult of maternity or motherhood," the "cult of domesticity," and the "cult of the child."[14]

Rousseau's main contribution – and that of the poets William Wordsworth and William Blake after him – was to enable many who had not seen the very first years as a qualitatively distinct period of life to appreciate this view. What stirred Europeans of both the Age of Enlightenment and especially of the Romantic era was the dual nature of the motif of childhood. As Reinhard Kuhn has put it: "It is possible to see in this theme the expression of a combination of nostalgia for the past, as in Wordsworth, and a longing for a new and transcendental future, as in Novalis."[15] This powerful concept caught the imagination of Russian thinkers and writers as much as any in Western Europe.

The "cults" of maternity and domesticity were a potential double-edged sword for all women, including nannies. While on the surface affording greater prestige and status to women in society, with nannies no exception, they nonetheless tended to denigrate any participation of women in public activity or work outside the home. While placing strong value on the mothering of children, breastfeeding one's own young, and the display of love and affection to offspring, these cults nonetheless made narrow gender demands and placed severe limitations on women that many were simply not ready to acquiesce in.[16] So making a symbol of nannies both elevated and put them down at the same time.

Emancipation. Until serfdom ended in Russia (decades after most of Western Europe), there was little likelihood of wealthy nobles living apart from large domestic staffs.[17] After 1861 the dynamic between "master and man" inevitably, if only slowly, changed. Emancipation was part of unevenly evolving socio-economic relations that would eventually put most business dealings on a contractual and money basis. What interests me most in these unstable times was not the material aspects of this change but the attitudes of the people involved, especially the changing psychology of those in power. The serfowners might, in many cases, successfully rid themselves of patriarchal ideas and "sentimentality about serfdom" but not of a certain "nostalgia for serfdom," the desire to exercise control, and the belief that peasants require "perpetual tutelage."[18]

Freeing the serfs in Russia was, in many ways, a conscious act of renunciation and self-sacrifice for some (if not most) of the gentry. "Penitent nobles"[19] might be full of pity for their freed serfs; many nobles, penitent or not, were equally sorry for themselves. It may not be too big a stretch to suggest that the repentant nobles' own sense of self-sacrifice reminded some of their childhood peasant caretakers, who often seemed so self-sacrificing. One expression of this sympathy likely was to paint their former caretakers in overly positive and sentimental hues in ego-documents and fiction.

Strangely, a nearly opposite set of serfowner attitudes probably helped to feed the nanny symbol also. The paternalistic relationship between former master and serf was carried over in new but similar ways; concern and solicitude was as much a matter of self-interest as of compassion for the *pomeshchik*. He doubtless had no difficulty projecting backward in time his current feelings, again enfolding a childhood caretaker in a rosy-hued symbol.[20] Thus, I believe a mix of condescension, generosity, guilt, and empathy surrounding emancipation played a major role in the emergence and endurance of nanny symbolism.

Ideologies. Beyond Slavophilism, two other major ideological developments encouraged and sustained the prominent place afforded the nanny in Russian consciousness and culture. The first of these ideologies arose with the dying away of an old regime: it was profoundly conservative, even backward-looking, in much more than a merely political sense. It was patriarchal, nostalgic, sentimental, and aristocratic.[21] It was inspired by a way of life that flourished for roughly a hundred years – between about 1762 and 1861 – the period that saw at one end the emancipation of the Russian noble service class and at the other end the long-delayed emancipation of their serfs. In various forms this ideology survived long beyond the presumed watershed of 1861. It bears more than a passing resemblance to what in America would be called a slaveholding mentality, a defense of "the peculiar institution" and the way of life of the ante-bellum plantation.[22] We can call this the *krepostnichestvo* mentality, and it outlived the legal institution of serfdom.[23]

The second ideological development was also inspired by the old *krepostnoe* regime but was the near antithesis of the first way of thinking. This ideology was liberal (even radical), progressive and forward-looking; often egalitarian, rationalistic, and if not plebeian, certainly demotic.[24] While both currents of thought emanated largely from the top of the old-regime social structure, at least in the beginning, they had quite distinct concerns. The first reflected the needs, desires, and mentality of (most of) those in the upper echelons of the social structure; the second current reflected the needs, desires, and possibly the thinking of (presumably the majority of) those at the base of that structure – the peasantry. The first ideology seemed to change little over more than a century. The second mentality evolved through several stages, over many decades, all the while retaining a fundamental sameness, and might be called at various times demophilic, *narodnik* ("populist"), and even Soviet or communist.[25]

For each of these last two ideological currents, as for Slavophilism, the peasant nanny became a potent symbol. For the adherents of the first mentality, a nanny frequently represented all that was good and praiseworthy in the system they espoused or for which they felt strong nostalgia. In their memories and in their cultural works, they depicted not so much the reality of the nanny as an idealized image of the nanny – an idyll from a beautified pastoral past that industrialization, modernization, and finally revolution would eventually sweep away. Adherents of the second ideology had equally compelling reasons to conjure with images of a nanny. She represented a direct link with the common people, the folk, in the name of whom their endeavors were undertaken. She was typically symbolic of an entire wronged class that cried out for justice. For higher social strata in particular, invoking the presence of a peasant nanny in one's life was tantamount to establishing one's democratic *bona fides*. Russians of the nobility, like Pushkin, could be made instantaneously more acceptable to even Soviet authorities with a peasant nanny in their childhoods.[26]

Growth of the Symbol to Cult Status

To this point, nothing would seem to differentiate the origins and promotion of a nanny symbol in Russia from the same phenomenon in other nations like Britain, Italy, and Spain. The factors at work in Russia were, *mutatis mutandis*, about the same as those elsewhere. Yet the nanny symbol seems more potent in Russia than elsewhere. Two factors in the Russian case seem crucial to me. First, the peasantry remained over half of the population as late as the mid-twentieth century.[27] Second, a revolutionary regime came to power in 1917 that destroyed much of the old order yet never found the legitimacy it craved among the (mostly peasant) population.

To me the lasting power of the nanny image and symbol, the necessity for maintaining the cult of Arina Rodionovna, lies mostly in that second factor. For much of its eighty-plus years of existence, the Bolshevik-Soviet regime was at least somewhat at odds with its population, the bulk of whom for decades were peasants. It frequently attacked its people in ways direct and subtle. During the period of War Communism (1918-21), in the collectivization and "dekulakization" drives of 1928-33 and the ensuing government-induced famines in Ukraine and elsewhere, and especially in the years of the Great Terror, the country's leaders were alienated from much of the populace. So the regime continually sought ways to try to reconcile high culture and low culture, town and countryside, rulers and ruled.[28] The nanny symbol and the cult of Arina in particular served this purpose well.[29]

Content of the Symbol

In this section I will discuss the main elements of the myth/cult of Russian nannies. What is most striking in the symbol is not what is intrinsic to the figure herself, but what is invested in or imposed upon the figure by intellectuals.

As peasant and woman, the Russian nanny stood apart from nearly all those who discussed her in works of autobiography and fiction.[30] Yet as both peasant and woman, she appealed strongly to many intellectuals whose identities seemed less grounded. Simultaneously, she aroused both ambivalence and concern.[31] It is to a few such intellectuals, as we saw in Chapter 1, that we owe the birth, growth, and obsession with the Arina cult.

Archetypal Peasant Figure

The theme of town versus country recurs in virtually all world literatures. The classic Russian nanny was a quintessentially rural figure. Two aspects of village life play a role in nanny symbolizing: language and imagined peasanthood – all that allegedly differentiates a village dweller from more educated, modern, possibly corrupt urban residents.

Kulturträger as "Kultursprecher." It's always about language. The idea is as old as the practice: that her native tongue is passed on from wet-nurse to nurseling, and – if the nurturer is from the peasantry – along with that linguistic legacy, a world of folk traditions, beliefs, music, and "knowledge."[32] It is a small step from this idea to the notion that the exact same thing happens between a child and nanny, whether or not the nanny was originally the infant's wet-nurse. There is, of course, a basis for the belief: a child *does* hear the sounds, words, stories of his wet-nurse or nanny and thereby becomes acquainted with and accustomed to those sounds, words, and tales. This is why ancient Romans wanted Greek wet-nurses for their offspring, Armenians and Jews under the Russian Empire wanted Russian nannies – for the language benefits.

In this context, it is easy to see why, in both literature and memoirs throughout the eighteenth and nineteenth centuries, there is the classic struggle between the nanny and the governess. Quite aside from all other factors – the demanding nature of the governess and the forgiving nature of (most) nannies primarily, social distinctions secondarily – the fact that most governesses were foreign was key. Even if not foreign, a governess in a Russian household still had the major responsibility of teaching a child one or more foreign languages. The counterpoint could not have been more perfect: the governess represented those alien tongues and cultures, the nanny the child's native tongue and culture.[33] Nothing could have better suited patriotic and nationalistic thinkers, social commentators and satirists, than to latch onto this dichotomy and exploit it to the hilt.

In eighteenth- and early nineteenth century Russian noble households with children, wealthy and middling, there was typically at least one or more nannies to help raise the scions. These caretakers imparted all that gets imparted in an oral/aural culture – in the absence of radio, television, and, often, many books. Here lies the first and most important anchor for all the legends and myths about Pushkin and other cultural figures discussed in Chapter 9. This connection has not been lost on most students of nationalism, Romantic or otherwise. Benedict Anderson, for example, considers linguistic differentiation to lie at the very heart of his "imagined communities."[34]

So despite the unsupportable claims made for Arina Rodionovna's influence on Pushkin, the language-conveying

Pskov Memorial to Pushkin and Arina (1983)

component of nanny symbolism has a fairly strong basis in fact. The idea mirrors reality if not taken to extremes.[35]

Peasant Reality vs. Peasant Image. The state of being a peasant – actual peasanthood – is far from what entered nanny symbolism. What we lack is a word to mean that combination of good (and bad) qualities of villagers – all of the values, ideals, and foibles that outsiders impute or attribute to rural folk.[36] What the image of the peasant brought to soul-searching and Romantic-nationalist Russian intellectuals of the 1830s and later was, in a word, authenticity. For those unclear or uncertain about Russian identity, inspiration came most often from the sturdy village masses.[37]

With almost half the peasantry literally bound to the soil as serfs until 1861, peasants evoked the earth and all its nurturing power. Peasant women and men tended to believe in a mythic earth-mother,[38] and peasant women in turn reflected or recalled this myth for nonpeasant intellectuals. As sentimental and Romantic Russians fell in love with nature in the eighteenth and nineteenth centuries, they typically ascribed a close connection between the peasant and nature. So getting closer to nature meant perforce an attempt to get closer to the peasantry.

Perhaps the best example of how one important Russian intellectual brought peasant folklore and peasant beliefs into his own highly positive interpretations of the Russian people as a whole – and deeply affected the mythology of Russian nannies in general and Arina Rodionovna in particular – is of course Dostoevskii.[39] As Cathy Frierson details, however, peasant women also embodied for late nineteenth-century writers and thinkers negative images of the *baba* – the perceived ignorance, avarice, and superstition of the folk. Many of these attributes, at different times, entered the nanny image of the eighteenth and nineteenth centuries.

When Russian high culture began to feel the need to address the "others" in their midst, it was the late eighteenth century. That is precisely when nanny symbolizing began as well. But it was not until nearly the middle of the following century that the need became imperative – with the approaching end of serfdom and the re-ordering of (higher) society-peasant relations. Then the nanny image/symbol became more fixed, more tied to idealized peasanthood, and very positive. The symbol less and less reflected a very diverse group of working women, with all their warts and halos.

Archetypal Female Figure

The matter of gender is ages old as well. But heightened consciousness has brought it to the fore since the eighteenth century. Postmodernity has only increased the attention paid to sexual difference and power relations between the sexes.[40] While it might seem anomalous to speak of power lying in the hands (and arms) of a peasant woman, that is precisely what we are discussing: the psychic power of female caretakers. Whatever the presence of the parents in a person's childhood, that additional woman generally loomed as large or larger in her nurseling's physical and emotional life.

Two alleged components of femininity figure in the nanny symbol: woman's supposed caring, loving nature and female moral superiority. Whatever their charges at the time may have thought of their nannies in these two regards, it was easy for them in hindsight to attribute these qualities to their childhood caretakers.

A Feminine Mystique? In a masterful work about gender issues in Russian culture, most specifically literature, Barbara Heldt argued that the accepted canon of Russian literature has been until recently defined by and inclusive of male writers only.[41] For my purposes, what is of most interest in Heldt's study are the characteristics she associates with many (though far from all) mature females in Russian literature (and culture). The writers assuming the characteristics, all men, are designated in parentheses after the trait named: "dignity in submission" (Nekrasov); passivity, living only for those she loves (Chekhov); virtue and moral superiority (Pushkin, Turgenev); and silent endurance-cum-defiance (Dostoevskii).[42] (pp. 12ff, 33ff, 52)

My readers will easily see how Heldt's conclusions relate to the image of the Russian nanny in memoirs in Chapter 7 (and literature in Chapter 8). No wonder the figure is so familiar to so many. We are not dealing with a Russian stereotype but a female stereotype – what Margaret Adams has called "the compassion trap." This is an archetype that is *imposed* and not innate. I too question "the pervasive belief...that woman's primary and most valuable social function is to provide the tender and compassionate components of life and that through the exercise of these particular traits, women have set themselves up as the exclusive model for protecting, nurturing, and fostering the growth of others." As Adams states, "This arbitrary social definition of woman's prime function (in value terms) has encouraged the hypertrophied growth of a single circumscribed area of the feminine psyche, while other qualities have been subjected to gradual but persistent attrition."[43]

Peasant nannies themselves, at least for most of their history, probably never had their consciousness raised.[44] They would have been oblivious *of* – and possibly even impervious *to* – the arguments of an Adams or a Betty Friedan. In hindsight we can call them victims of more than just serfdom, more even than a patriarchal society that kept women "in their place." Defining gender was not likely to be something a village woman gave much thought to, especially one raised in the tenets of a male-centered, male-dominated Orthodox Church.[45] I assume that the vast majority of peasant women, including those who became nannies, learned attributes of gender from their village community and society more generally; this was an imposition, not a genetic inheritance.[46]

Moral Superiority of Peasant Nannies. There seems to exist a widespread belief that the pre-1861 nanny was, in many or even most cases, somehow a better person than her noble master – merely by dint of being a *serf woman*. The temptation to believe this may well be a form of self-delusion, what Bertrand Russell calls, in one of his best short essays, a belief in the "superior virtue of the oppressed."[47] Whether it is in Marx's views of the proletariat, the idea of "the noble Red Man," the "Ethiopianism" of many black preachers and intellectuals, or even some ideas about gender differences, this concept has shown a remarkable appeal and tenacity. Still, as Russell shows well, it is fallacious to impute moral superiority to any group – be it socio-economic, ethnic, racial, or sexual – based solely on the fact that that group has suffered in some way. The mere fact of being oppressed sheds no light on an individual's character.

Were it not for Lord Acton's famous dictum, one would be

tempted to say that there may have been as many "evil" slaves as there were Simon Legrees, as many immoral factory hands as there were robber barons. So the farthest one might want to venture would be to agree with the novelist Aleksandra Studzinskaia, who thoughtfully wrote: "Perhaps [a woman's] very situation in society is somewhat similar to the position of the Negro vis-a-vis the plantation owner: it gives her strength for struggle and resolve in adversity."[48] In short, to ascribe moral superiority to any group is to make the exact same kind of untenable generalization that anti-Semites, white supremacists, and misogynists make. To do so runs counter to the underlying spirit of this book, which argues that the specific individual case, the unique detail, is nearly always more important than the indiscriminate generalization.

As in earlier centuries, the Orthodox Church abetted this stereotyping of women in the nineteenth century. Befitting the secular view of the latter time, Orthodox writing "had come to project a domestic and maternalist ideal of womanhood." Separate social spheres defined by gender were stressed. Mothers were "educators of their children and moral arbiters within the family." Such ideas combined with earlier Orthodox ideals "that stressed both the subordinate position of women in the family and their central role in managing the domestic affairs of the household. This mixture produced an ideal that included elements of patriarchy, equality, and complementarity."[49] (p. 122) Orthodox writers extolled "the virtues of obedience, submissiveness, and patience in women." Women were allegedly well-suited for their domestic and maternal "calling" due to their "modesty, humility, selflessness, self-denial, patience, tolerance, tactfulness, tenderness, compassion, industriousness, practicality, physical dexterity, intuitiveness, and piety." (pp. 123-24)

Archetypal Russian Figure

Adding together the first symbolic role (peasant associations) with the second (supposedly feminine characteristics) discussed second, produces a grand synthesis of the nanny symbol: the nationalistic allegory. Looking at traits often associated with Russia or Russians as a whole – namely, a penchant for sacrifice or suffering, a devout

Christian faith, a profound capacity for loving, the sense of humility, and an open, generous nature – it becomes even more obvious why a peasant (serf) woman should be such a powerful, resonant figure in Russian culture. The classic (serf) nanny fits almost perfectly with so many of these traits. She could hardly help but acquire near-mythological status at the very time when Russians – in the 1830s through 1850s – were beginning a great quest for self-identification, the meaning of their lives, and the "purpose" of Russia in the world.[50] Every exploration of the so-called "Russian soul" begins with some or all of these traits as well.[51]

Religious Elements of the National Symbol. The subject of Russian Christian faith raised early in the preceding paragraph demands further discussion. The literature on this topic is enormous and has grown almost exponentially in recent decades.[52] The importance of religion for real-life nannies was affirmed and discussed in earlier chapters. But the notion that a serf nanny reflects and embodies the Russian national faith, Orthodoxy, is more problematic. There is a longstanding debate in the literature about the substance of ordinary Russians' faith. Some question whether there was any "there" there, or, to put it in the words of Simon Dixon, "how holy was Holy Russia?"[53]

Two particular features interest me most in this vast subject: the concepts of *dvoeverie* (literally, "dual faith") and the so-called *kenotic* element in Russian religion and culture. My sense of *dvoeverie* is of a popular/folk form of Christianity, frequently encouraged by Orthodox Church leaders, evident in earlier times and more recently, with all the limitations and strengths to which such forms of belief may be prone. As a *practice* it is not so much a combination of peasant paganism and Christianity but merely a variant of a faith held at various levels of Russian society.[54] Historically, however, *dvoeverie* has most often been used in a pejorative or accusatory sense. It now seems apparent that so-called *dvoeverie* is not necessarily the phenomenon it was taken to be for the better part of a century or more – part and parcel of peasant backwardness, superstition, and ignorance.[55] I would argue, then, that the nanny symbol, which deliberately excludes many traits and beliefs which might reflect poorly on a peasant woman, is on the mark in not bringing the idea of *dvoeverie* into the picture of nanny religiosity.

Russian *kenoticism* is also frequently misinterpreted.⁵⁶ Deriving from the Greek for "emptying," *kenotic* describes Christ's emptying his earthly self of divinity so that he might suffer and die as only humans can. Despite the best efforts of intellectuals like Dostoevskii and Tolstoi, it is certainly *not* a pillar of Orthodoxy that the Russian people are defined by a penchant for suffering.⁵⁷ Neither Russians in general, nor peasants in particular, seek out ways to suffer; they do not wallow in self-pity or self-flagellation.⁵⁸ The fact that both tsarist and communist regimes imposed heavy burdens and untold pain on their subject populations speaks to the character of the leaders, not the led. Countless peasant and nonpeasant revolts, uprisings, protests, and rebellions over several centuries indicate at least as strong a penchant not to put up with suffering as to endure it silently, even willingly.⁵⁹

Did either or both of these phenomena – *dvoeverie* and *kenoticism* – characterize peasant nannies? Some aspects of their behavior seem to fit into these notional categories. To the extent that humility was indeed a trait of some Russian nannies and to the extent, further, that the classic early nannies were most often serfs, there is a small kernel of truth in a *kenotic* image of the nanny. However, I've already argued in an earlier chapter that humility and submissiveness were as likely induced by the socio-economic and political circumstances of these women as to have been innate qualities.

Both concepts have been in part – even mostly – imposed on peasants from without. As part of the symbol of the nanny as long-suffering and full of humility, on one hand, and uniquely religious, on the other, they are misleading. *Some aspects* of these ideas are manifestations of *some aspects* of peasant and nanny thinking. However, they are as much or more a reflection of the thinking of outsiders who don't show true understanding of peasant thinking. These outsiders represent *from their own perspective* what they want peasants to believe.⁶⁰ There is no tendency toward humiliation or self-abasement in the nanny or the nation. To make of peasant nannies or the Russian people in general the kind of near-masochists that Dostoevskii and Daniel Rancour-Laferriere seem at times to have in mind is too large a stretch for the evidence to support. I have few reservations in agreeing with all those memoirists who viewed their own (and most?) Russian nannies as religiously devout, an example and inspiration to their charges. But to separate their faith in some fundamental way from that of their masters/employers is unnecessary.[61] To project this image of devout nannies further, beyond individual families, to a larger background and see in it a reflection of Orthodox Russia as a whole is a natural and probably defensible extension.

National Ideas More Generally. As for the more general thrust of this nationalistic symbol, it's crucial to note that Russia followed a broader global pattern in this respect.[62] Romantic nationalists like the proto-Slavophiles and Slavophiles of the 1840s and after, Pëtr Bartenev, Prince Vladimir Odoevskii, Dostoevskii and the *pochvenniki* – all develop some ideas of what national identity should be, usually assuming that these ideas emanate from the common people (*narod*). In this "imagined community" (Anderson's term), the qualities that the intellectuals and artists who assign themselves the role of national spokespeople emphasize are always idealized: the people are the embodiment of virtues and qualities that are highly desired by the spokespeople themselves. There begins "an age of national literary hero-worship in which the great authors of the past – masters of the native tongue, hence specially attuned, it is believed, to the national spirit – are revived, reappraised, and then presented as 'great figures which common opinion regards as embodying the soul or spirit of a given people'."[63] This is unmistakably what happens with Pushkin.

> ...the emergent national ideal, no matter in which country it is created and no matter what its specific attributes, is everywhere credited with general qualities of innocent simplicity and deep emotional responsiveness – moral qualities, essentially leveling ones, with built-in biases against existing manners and systems of education. The concept of national identity, a creation of frustrated writers, is an archetype of simple morality and humble social class; it subtly conveys not only the supposedly distinctive moral virtues of the citizen but the moral fraternity of all the nation's countrymen downtrodden and oppressed.[64]

Nanny as Symbol 305

The pious, self-sacrificing, infinitely loving, serf nanny of many memoirs and literature thus reaches her apotheosis as a symbol of the country. Not one of them, Arina Rodionovna included, could have foreseen the cult status that would be afforded them. Ironically, their alleged humbleness and innocence would have made it nearly impossible to identify with this vaunted figure.

Conclusion

It now becomes clear why Bartenev, Dostoevskii, and Aksakov elevated a single peasant woman to such a lofty position. This was a deliberate, Romantic, nationalistic effort to raise Russian self-worth and esteem. The fact that countless others followed suit and lifted their own nannies' status and value was a probably unforeseen consequence of this trio's efforts, just as the greater attention paid nannies was an unintended consequence of Pushkin's writings.

Nannies and wet-nurses became powerful symbols or allegories to suit the needs and desires of intellectuals and writers. In the purposive striving to remake one's self-image or the image of an entire nation, these thinkers gave birth to many ideas about Russians, especially the common folk. What could have been more natural than to place these "newborns" for nurture with an Orthodox peasant woman?

Concluding Thoughts

Is there a way to tie closer together the three distinct parts of this book? There may be, based on the largest role of Russian as well as other nannies, a role that brings me back to their significance on a worldwide scale. It also takes me to a level of generalization that I've eschewed, for the most part, throughout these pages. Here I will risk a generalization that I feel comfortable with. Given all that has been written in this book, it is clear that in addition to the flesh-and-blood person that a child might have known as a nanny in its earliest years, there was another figure that remained as a kind of shadow double to the real nanny in the child's consciousness as it grew. This twin was simply the idea of a nanny. Lived experience, much reading, and the surrounding culture all combined to help form this idea. The idea is not Russian in any sense; it is human.

Every human being seems to yearn in life for some things so basic that they are likely universal. These are not physical needs – food, water, shelter, and so on. I am thinking of psychic needs – the desire to be cared for. By "cared for" I mean both loved but also taken care of. We need to feel secure. Some people are fortunate enough to find most or all of these things in their earliest years. Others, less fortunate, do not. But even for the second group, the desires still exist. For many fortunate children, parents satisfy most of these desires. A child blessed with "good" parents enters the world feeling loved and secure. That feeling probably stays with such children all their lives.

With or without good parents, another caretaker in the life of a child cannot hurt. At the least, a nanny usually adds to the feeling of being taken care of and loved. In cases where parents are absent or "distant," the nanny can indeed play more of the role normally reserved for parents, in extreme instances, as a "substitute" parent. As noted in a previous chapter, moreover, Erik Erikson, Solzhenitsyn, and several memoirists even speak of the need for such "nannies" throughout life, people who help and care for others as they go through life. So powerful is the desire on the part of human beings both to offer and to receive assistance that Pëtr Kropotkin wrote a famous pamphlet about it, called *Mutual Aid: A Factor of Evolution* (1902), in part to refute "social Darwinists" and their ideas about "the struggle for existence." More importantly, in many cultures the idea of a special caretaker – *for both children and adults* – has become very popular in modern times. Indeed, the point of nannies in movies like *Mary Poppins* and *Nanny McPhee* is that they influence the attitude and behavior of the parents as much as – or more than – the children.

In short, nannies speak to that fundamental yearning described above. This seemingly lifelong desire is what I believe is behind the "idea of the nanny" that has become so appealing in Russian and other world cultures. Caring nannies, moreover, can hardly help but inspire their charges. It takes little imagination to turn the literal sense of inspiration to a more figurative one. Hence, a nanny who cares may inspire both good behavior and good work. If the work is not of a child but a mature former charge – and of a high creative nature – it may give rise to speculation that the work was somehow abetted directly by the nanny.

Whether Russia can claim any primacy in coming to some of these ideas is an interesting question. As one who grew up on fairy tales and folk songs of the Western variety, I cannot say that I ever came across the kind of references that Russian children grew up with – to *mamushki* and *nianushki* – as integral parts of popular songs and tales that date to the start of Russian culture. But then what are "fairy godmothers" if not a variation on this theme? Young and old, child and adult, nearly all hope to find in life the embodiment in real people of the idea of the nanny.

As for individuals, so too for communities. There is a reason why, when conscious effort was made to invest objects with symbolic significance for the nation as a whole, many writers and thinkers – in many countries – bethought themselves of wet-nurses and nannies. In Russia one special serf nanny took on special significance because of the stature achieved by one of her nurselings. Arina Rodionovna's legend became mythical, and she attained a kind of cult status not so much because of anything she herself did or might have done, but because she served a larger purpose for her country. She and her cohorts performed – *or were made to perform* – a very necessary task, that of bringing widely divided social strata closer together. They were asked to provide *or were said to provide* a kind of moral glue to bind closer together disparate socio-economic or political elements. The nanny was particularly well situated to perform these roles because she represented the nation's traditions, its shared language, its past. What was true before the 1917 revolution remained valid after that upheaval as well, except now the symbol was useful not just for social healing purposes: she was supposed somehow to bind the wounds the rulers were inflicting on the population.

The fact that a cult developed around one nanny in Russia is due to the convergence of many factors that reached a "critical mass." This nanny became the right idea, in the right place, at the right time to suit imaginations of the right sort. I once likened this development to "a perfect storm" in which peasant interest and sympathy conjoined with new thinking about maternity and concerns about family, including servants, to produce the remarkable attention paid to the serf nanny. But this interest in real-life nannies would have been insufficient to produce the mania I have detailed at great length here without the added force that came from Romantic and then increasingly self-assertive nationalism in the nineteenth century. When nationalism came under increased scrutiny in the early twentieth century, largely because the nation itself was disintegrating under self-inflicted pressures, the cult of the nanny (and *the* nanny, Arina) found its fullest expression.

To sum up what I've said about the nanny in real life and as image: What stands out most about Russian nannies in real life is that powerful image of a constant, nurturing, loving caretaker that remained with a myriad of children throughout their lives.

The universal need to feel loved and cared for – shared by not just children but adults as well – was satisfied by a large number of these nannies. Myriad nobles and other beneficiaries of a Russian nanny enjoyed the luxury of such continuous support, however little it may have inspired or contributed to cultural achievements. Yet for some writers, composers, and artists, the presence of a real-life nanny did indeed help spark creativity.

In culture and national consciousness, a Russian peasant woman became a potent symbol of the virtues of Russian life, especially pre-emancipation, then of "the world they had lost" for countless dispossessed families after the 1917 revolutions. She further became the supposed essential link between upper and lower social strata, "grounding" the otherwise too cosmopolitan and too privileged nobility. In Soviet times, she served almost the same purpose for those in charge – to bind the rulers to the ruled, town with country. The carefully nurtured symbol generated numerous myths that in turn have enriched Russian culture.

Endnotes

Introduction.

1. Throughout this study, the English word "nanny" is used to translate the Russian *niania* and its various diminutives (*nian'ka, nianiushka, nianechka*), which are always affectionate. An alternate translation would be "nursemaid." Both "nanny" and "nursemaid" have potentially misleading connotations for Western readers. Be that as it may, I prefer to use a term familiar in most English-speaking societies, especially Great Britain, which has given us such enormously popular literary characterizations of nannies as the dog Nana in J. M. Barrie's *Peter Pan* and Mary Poppins, the creation of P. L. Travers (pseud. of Helen Lyndon Goff).
See the discussion of terminology for children's caretakers and upbringers toward the end of this Introduction.

2. This is not to mention various Russian nannies' purported influence on tsars, radicals, and revolutionaries and even the work of Sigmund Freud.

3. While I will speak of all kinds of nannies, the one kind I will be ignoring for the most part is the family-member nanny. Siblings, grandmothers, aunts, uncles, and other near kin often cared for the infants and tots in their families, for shorter or longer periods. This was particularly true, however, for peasant families more than for the nobility, and I do not deal much with peasant families herein.

4. I have chosen to leave untranslated many Russian terms in these pages; for several of the most important ones, see the discussion of terminology toward the end of this introduction.

5. The brief discussion here centers on lived experience; for the philosophical/theoretical aspects of "alterity," see Chapter 10.

6. Vladimir Mikhnevich catches this phenomenon well in chapter 3 of his *Romany kukharki i kamelii. Rasskazy iz peterburgskoi zhizni* (St.Petersburg: M Nikolaev, [1881]), pp. 13-25.

7. I wrestle with this issue more fully in Chapter 4.

8. Biographies and autobiographies of women such as Iuliana Lazarevskaia, Princess Natal'ia Dolgorukaia, the boiarynia Feodosiia Morozova, Princess Ekaterina Dashkova, and, later, the Decembrist wives illustrate these qualities, severally or combined.

9. For all the writing about Russian women that has appeared in recent decades, I'm aware of no one short and succinct summary, in English, of gender issues in the 18th-20th centuries. Some come close but lack comprehensiveness. The most studied subjects, like intelligentsia women of the 19th century, often include brief overviews of some aspects of the topic. On Russian women's history, the bibliography is immense; among the best works are those of Richard Stites, Natal'ia Pushkareva, Barbara Evans Newman, Eve Levin, Barbara Alpern Engel, and Barbara Heldt (all cited in the bibliography).

10. See Chapter 10 for a closer examination of the female archetype.

11. This subject has been covered many times but among the very best treatments is one of the first: Hans Rogger, *National Consciousness in Eighteenth-Century Russia* (Cambridge, MA: Harvard University Press, 1960), Chapter IV, "The Discovery of the Folk," and Chapter V, "The Uses of History."

12. Naturally I cannot go into great detail on all or even most of these subjects, but not many of these 800-pound gorillas need be tackled head-on. In most cases I'm able to cite pertinent secondary sources which illuminate my subject or, more often, provide the proper context for my observations.

13. No single word conveys just the right tone of these terms; "sweet nanny" or "dear nanny" are close but not quite right. I had thought for a time to use the term "nannykins" for the various diminutives. While perfectly acceptable, I have decided against using a word that felt wrong when put into the mouth of a Russian child.

14. See Max Vasmer, *Etimologicheskii slovar' russkogo iazyka*, Vol. III (Moscow: Progress, 1987), p.94.

15. See Warner, *Monsters of Our Own Making: The Peculiar Pleasures of Fear* (Lexington: The University Press of Kentucky, 2007), p. 195.

Endnotes   313

16. *"Freilein"* also meant a lady-in-waiting at the Russian court.
17. See *Vecherniaia Moskva*, 3 Jan 1929, p. 4, where one want ad reads: "Needed – a *bonne* (Russian [perhaps Russian-speaking]) or lit[erate] nanny for 2 ch[ildren] " [*"Nuzhna bonna (russk.) ili niania gram. k 2 d."*].

Chapter One

1. Arina (Irina) is the subject of at least two monographs: A. I. Ul'ianskii, *Niania Pushkina* (Moscow-Leningrad: Izdatel'stvo AN SSSR, 1940) and Mikhail Filin, *Arina Rodionovna* (Moscow: Molodaia gvardiia , 2008). Had she lived in Soviet times, she would doubtless have been known as the All-Union Nanny.
2. Because *Onegin* and all its characters have been analyzed endlessly, I will forego any lengthy discussion. Suffice it to say that in this work Pushkin delivers, in just a handful of stanzas, a rounded, evocative, and appealing portrait of an old serf woman, a devoted and deeply loving family retainer named Filippovna.
3. There is a true cult surrounding Pushkin's nanny. An online search of Russian periodicals under the name "Arina Rodionovna" in 2009 came up with *more than 5,000 hits* for items published almost entirely in the past few years, most associated with Arina's 250th birth anniversary in 2008. Monuments to her spot the Russian landscape.
4. Soviet and Western biographers often begin with a fairy tale of the poet and his caretaker and are lucky to right themselves afterward. A large number succumb to the autobiographical fallacy – the temptation of equating the poet's literary works with autobiographical fact.
5. A good contemporary take on the life and legend of Arina can be found in Mikhail D. Filin's book cited previously and his article "Apologiia russkoi niani" in *Literaturnaia gazeta*, No. 5, 7 February 2007, p. 8. Each is a frustrating combination of sound scholarship and unsupported assertion. Filin, moreover, put out another volume commemorating Arina's sestercentennial: *Apologiia russkoi niani: K 250-letiiu Ariny Rodionovny* (Moscow: Russkii mir, 2009), a compilation of dozens of essays about Arina from the 1850s to the present.
6. One entire aspect of the myth concerns pictorial representations of Arina, as many "experts" have purported to find authentic images of her rendered by various artists. None of these arguments are, to my mind, very convincing. For further exploration, see, e.g., Nina I. Granovskaia, "Risunok Pushkina: Portrety Ariny Rodionovny," *Vremennik Pushkinskoi komissii*, 1971 (Leningrad: Nauka, Leningrad

Affiliate, 1973), pp. 27-30; Redmona G. Zhuikova, *Portretnye risunki Pushkina: katalog atributsii* (St. Petersburg: Dmitrii Bulanin, 1996); and M. Romm, "Skul'ptor Iakov Seriakov," *Neva*, No. 2 (February 1958), pp. 188-91. Not only are alleged drawings by Pushkin suspect, all other early attributions fail to satisfy. Later efforts are clearly not "from life." (See Chapter 9 for more about nannies in art more generally.)

Renderings of Arina, with or without the poet, are legion – in porcelain, bronze, oil, and other media. Among the best-known are those of Vasilii Maksimov (1844-1911), a pencil sketch of 1899 illustrating Pushkin's "K niane;" and more recent oils by Dmitrii Beliukin (b. 1962) – "The New Verse" (1995) and "Pushkin at Arina's in Mikhailovskoe" (1996) – all of which can be found easily online. Cf. http://www.liveinternet.ru/users/barucaba/post135036072/ and http://www.google.ru/search?q=%D0%B0%D1%80%D0%B8%D0%BD%D0%B0+%D1%80%D0%BE%D0%B4%D0%B8%D0%BE%D0%BD%D0%BE%D0%B2%D0%BD%D0%B0&hl=ru&newwindow=1&prmd=imvns&tbm=isch&tbo=u&source=univ&sa=X&ei=kyg5T4GCIL30gH99q3HAg&sqi=2&ved=0CEMQsAQ&biw=1920&bih=877 (both accessed Feb. 2012).

7. While she offers just a few judicious remarks about Arina in her trenchant analysis of various Pushkin myths, Stephanie Sandler explains why such myths adhere to Pushkin in *Commemorating Pushkin: Russia's Myth of a National Poet* (Stanford, Ca: Stanford University Press, 2004), especially, in the second chapter, pp. 71-72, and the introduction. Equally worthwhile but less germane for our purposes is her entry "The Pushkin Myth in Russia" in *The Pushkin Handbook* ed. by David M. Bethea (Madison: University of Wisconsin Press, 2005), pp. 403-23.

8. Ernest J. Simmons, *Pushkin* (New York: Vintage Books/Random House, 1964), p. 22. For most of these statements there is no contemporary supportive source whatever.

Cf. Tatiana Wolff: "Of these [childhood influences on Pushkin,] the nurse was the most remarkable....She had an inexhaustible store of Russian folk-tales and legends, songs and proverbs, from which Pushkin never ceased to draw inspiration. This was the balancing factor to the classical and French influences which Pushkin was subject in his early reading and in his formal education and provided the impetus he needed to establish Russian as a literary language, himself becoming, in the fullest sense of the words, Russia's poet. Pushkin expressed his gratitude to Arina Rodionovna many times in his poetry and lovingly drew her portrait as Tatiana's nurse in *Evgeny Onegin*." (*Pushkin on Literature*, comp., ed., and trans. by Wolff [London: Metheun & Co., Ltd., 1971], pp. 5-6.)

9. *Ibid.*, pp. 6-7, 22-23. More recent Western biographies make similar assertions. See, for example, Elaine Feinstein, *Pushkin: A Biography* (Hopewell, NJ: The Ecco Press, 1998), which, for the section on Pushkin's childhood at least, is very derivative. A more nuanced approach to a biography of the poet is David Bethea, "Kak pisat' biografiiu Pushkina v postlotmanovskuiu epokhu," *Lotmanovskii sbornik*, Issue 3 (Moscow: OGI, 2004), pp. 822-35.

10. Simmons, p. 100. Cf. similar claims in Janko Lavrin, *Pushkin and Russian Literature* (New York: The MacMillan Company,1948), p. 30.

11. Khodasevich, *O Pushkine* (Berlin: Petropolis, 1937), an enl. and rev. version of his *Poeticheskoe khoziaistvo Pushkina* of 1924. The relevant section is entitled "Iavleniia muzy," pp. 9-38.

12. A. Petrushov, "Ne boites' rytsarem proslyt'," *Pravda*, 21 December 1984, p. 6. Italics added.

13. As early as the 1950s, Vladimir Nabokov took several swipes at this myth, in his commentaries to his translation of *Evgenii Onegin* (Princeton: Princeton University Press, 1975) Vol. II, pp. 274, 361-62, 452-54. As sometimes happens with Nabokov, however, he overstates his case by trying to reduce Arina nearly to a nonentity. More recently, the émigré scholar Yuri Druzhnikov has punched many holes in the legend in an article in *Novyi zhurnal* ("Niania Pushkina v venchike iz roz," Bk. 201, 1995, pp. 226-56), reprinted in his collection of essays: *Vtoraia zhena Pushkina* (Moscow: Vagrius, 2000), pp. 396-428, and available online at www.druzhnikov.com/text/rass/duel/2.html (accessed December 2011). This essay (enlarged) is included in *Contemporary Russian Myths: A Skeptical View of the Literary Past* (Lewiston, NY: Edwin Mellen, 1999), which can also be found online at www.druzhnikov.com/english/text/vizit2.html. My own analysis was largely complete before I came across Druzhnikov's work.

14. Among those guilty of the autobiographical fallacy in their lives of Pushkin are Simmons, the dean of Pushkin biographers in the West, Wolff, the popular historian Henri Troyat, and David Magarshack.

15. Ul'ianskii's *Niania Pushkina*, pp. 8, 12. This book is replete with much useful information, many facts and figures, but also unfounded assertions. We should avoid calling her Iakovleva, as some scholars do, since unmarried peasant women rarely were called by their father's surnames. When she married Matveev, she and her sons could properly be called by his surname.

16. Pavlishcheva, "Vospominaniia o detstve A. S. Pushkina," *A. S.*

Pushkin v vospominaniiakh sovremennikov v dvukh tomakh (Moscow: Khudozhestvennaia literatura, 1985), Vol. I, pp. 29-30. She says that Arina was *her* nanny and Sasha's primary caretaker was a woman named Ul'iana. The latter's full name is unknown; she is indexed in most complete editions of Pushkin's works. Confused scholars have at times attached Arina's alleged surname Iakovleva to her, conflating the two.

Ul'iana is the woman Nabokov names as Pushkin's nanny. She is almost certainly the main character in a vignette into which the less careful have wrongly inserted Arina Rodionovna: the famous encounter of the future poet with Tsar Paul I. In a letter to his wife, Natal'ia Nikolaevna, dated 20-22 April 1834, Pushkin writes: "I don't intend to come to the heir [the future Aleksandr II] with congratulations and greetings – I have seen three tsars: the first [Paul] ordered my cap removed and berated my nanny for me – ." Pushkin, *Polnoe sobranie sochinenii v 17 tomakh*, Vol. XV (Moscow: Voskresen'e, 1996 – a reprint of the Academia ed. published in 1937-59), pp. 129-30. This multivolume set will hereafter be cited as *PSS*.

17. As Khodasevich notes in his brief essay "Arina Rodionovna," we have no early letters of Pushkin to his parents and sister, but there are 14 letters extant to his brother Lev during his time away from Arina "and in not one of them is there even a word about the nanny, not a query about her, not a greeting – nothing. This is hardly by chance. Pushkin attained a personal love for the nanny later." See his *Pushkin i poety ego vremeni*, Vol. II, ed. by Robert P. Hughes (Berkeley, CA: Berkeley Slavic Specialties, 2001), p. 177. Nabokov states in his commentaries to *Evgenii Onegin* that in mid-1824 Pushkin "had not seen his sister's old nurse [i.e., Arina] since his last visit to Mikhaylovskoe in the summer of 1819 (*if* she was there at the time) and was unaware in the summer of 1824 that in a month or so he was going to meet her again in the role of housekeeper (and *his* nurse)." See his *Eugene Onegin*, II, p. 362.

18. Cited in *Poet, Rossiia i tsari*, comp. by V. Naumov and S. Shokarev (Moscow: Fond Sergeia Dubova, 1999), p. 15.

19. *PSS*, XIII (1996), p. 127.

20. *PSS*, XIII, p. 129.

21. Mikhail Filin believes it's "hardly possible to doubt" that both Pushkin and his sister Ol'ga attended both the church service and the burial service (*Arina Rodionovna*, p. 138) but offers no evidence for his assertion. Ul'ianskii makes no such claim in his biography of Arina. N.O. Lerner, in his exhaustive compilation *A. S. Pushkin. Trudy i dni* (2nd rev. and

enl. ed.; St. Peterburg: Tipografiia Imperatorskoi akademii nauk, 1910) does not mention Arina's funeral. "Boris" (no surname) insists in a mythbusting online piece about Arina that Pushkin did not attend the funeral – http://funeralspb.narod.ru/necropols/smolenskoep/tombs/yakovleva/yakovleva.html (accessed Dec. 2011).

22. V. E. Vatsuro et al., eds., *A. S. Pushkin: stikhotvoreniia litseiskikh let 1813-1817* (St. Peterburg: Nauka, 1994), pp. 83, 562, 621, note to p. 173. Cf. Nina I. Granovskaia, *Esli ekhat' vam sluchitsia: ocherk-putevoditel'* (Leningrad : Lenizdat, 1989).

23. Cf. William Mills Todd's *The Familiar Letter as a Literary Genre in the Age of Pushkin* (Evanston, IL: Northwestern University Press, 1999).

24. *PSS*, II, bk. 1, pp. 439-40; *Muzykal'naia entsiklopediia v shesti tomakh,* ed. by Iu.V. Keldysh et al. (Moscow: Sovetskaia entsiklopediia/Sovetskii kompozitor, 1982), Vol. 6, pp. 614-15.

25. *PSS*, Vol. III, bk. 1 (1995), p. 33, and bk. 2 (1995), p. 1131 endnotes.

It seems Pavel Annenkov, who first published the unfinished poem in 1855, gave it the title it's ever since been best known by – "To Nanny" (*K niane* or more simply, *Niane*), though it's also called by its first line, "*Podruga dnei moikh surovykh....*" It's possible that his failure to polish and publish these lines indicates that Pushkin was already losing interest in his boon companion by the end of his exile.

26. It should be added, however, that he found equal or greater comfort in the companionship of much younger and more attractive female serfs, at least at night. His friend I. I. Pushchin attested to his dalliance with one pretty girl whom he got pregnant.

27. *PSS*, III, bk. 1, pp. 399-400, and bk. 2, pp. 1262-63.

28. Iazykov actually called his verses a "letter" "To P ___'s Nanny." The poem was published shortly thereafter, in Pushkin's *Severnye tsvety (Northern Flowers)*.

29. N. M. Iazykov, *Sochineniia* (Leningrad: Khudozhestvennaia literatura, 1982), pp. 105-106. First published in *Severnye tsvety* in 1828.

30. Iazykov, *Polnoe sobranie stikhotvorenii,* ed. and annot. by K. K. Bukhmeier (Leningrad: Sovetskii pisatel', 1964), pp. 628-29 (endnotes). The clearly humorous poem to Arina and the one in her memory are of a piece with what members of the former Arzamas Society (like Pushkin) prided themselves on; though Iazykov had not himself been a member of the by-then defunct Arzamas, his poems of this time include many eulogies and satires typical of the Society.

31. Iazykov, *Sochineniia*, p. 132-33. First published in *Severnye tsvety* in 1830.

32. "Aleksandr Sergeevich Pushkin. (1799-1837)," *Sovremennik*, 1838, v. X, No. 1, pp. 21-52; the anonymous biographical note in the 1838 *Portretnaia i biograficheskaia gallereia slovesnosti, khudozhestv i iskusstv v Rossii* (which the scholar M. Tsiavlovskii attributes, with some assurance, to the work's general editor Osip-Iulian Senkovskii); and M. Makarov, "Aleksandr Sergeevich Pushkin v detstve. (Iz zapisok o moem znakomstve)," *Sovremennik*, 1843, Vol. 29, No. 3, pp. 375-385.

33. Pletnev, "Aleksandr Sergeevich Pushkin," in *Sochineniia i perepiska P. A. Pletneva*, Vol. 1 (St. Petersburg: Akademiia nauk, 1885), pp. 364-386 (originally in *Sovremennik*, 1838, No. 10, pp. 21-52); the quoted line is on p. 376. Pletnev's readers thus heard something about a real woman named Arina Rodionovna. But it was apparently Iazykov's poems that stuck in people's minds more than what Pushkin himself had written.

In the mid-1840s, Dmitrii Bantysh-Kamenskii included a lengthy piece on the poet in his *Dictionary of Eminent Russians*. He speaks briefly of Pushkin's boyhood, but as with Pletnev, there is not a word about Arina in Pushkin's childhood. The only brief reference to her, not by name, is in a section on the Mikhailovskoe exile. See Bantysh-Kamenskii, *Slovar' dostopamiatnykh liudei Russkoi zemli*, Part [Vol.] 2 (St. Petersburg: Shtab Otdel'nago Korpusa Vnutrennei Strazhi, 1847). The entry for Pushkin seems almost an afterthought, as it appears not in the main body of the volume but in an appendix, pp. 58-105.

34. Berg, "Sel'tso Zakharovo," *Moskvitianin*, May 1851, Nos. 9/10, Part 3, "Sovremennye izvestiia," pp. 29-32. Who knows just how famous Arina was when Berg wrote?

35. After graduation, Bartenev moved to the capital for two years and became close to then Petersburg University rector Pëtr Pletnev, Pushkin's friend and biographer. He spent most Saturdays with the Pletnevs, where lovers of literature and conversation gathered, most of them great admirers of Pushkin.

36. Bartenev, "Vospominaniia P. I. Barteneva," *Rossiiskii arkhiv: Istoriia Otechestva v svidetel'stvakh i dokumentakh XVIII-XX vv.*, Vol. I (Moscow: Trite Studiia/Rossiiskii arkhiv, 1991), pp. 47-95; here, pp. 62-67, 77, 83ff.

37. A more detailed explanation of why Bartenev and the Slavophiles should be fixated on a peasant nanny appears in the main argument of Chapter 10.

Among the most discerning works on Slavophilism are Andrzej

Walicki, *The Slavophile Controversy: History of a Conservative Utopia in Nineteenth-Century Russian Thought*, trans. by Hilda Andrews Rusiecka (Oxford: Clarendon Press, 1975); Abbott Gleason, *European and Muscovite; Ivan Kireevsky and the Origins of Slavophilism* (Cambridge, MA: Harvard University Press, 1972); Peter K. Christoff, *An Introduction to Nineteenth-Century Russian Slavophilism. A Study of Ideas*, 4 vols. (various publishers, 1961-91); Nicholas V. Riasanovsky, *Russia and the West in the Teaching of the Slavophiles: A Study of Romantic Ideology* (Gloucester, MA: Peter Smith, 1965); Iurii Iankovskii, *Patriarkhal'no-dvorianskaia utopiia: Stranitsa russkoi obshchestvenno-literaturnoi mysli 1840-1850s-kh godov* (Moscow: Khudozhestvennaia literatura, 1981).

38. The first of Turgenev's "sportsman's sketches" had already appeared in January 1847 and the floodgates of peasant sympathy were about to burst open – first in literature, then in the whole *narodnik* movement of the 1860s and 70s. Demophilism was on the rise, and Bartenev was very much in tune with these sentiments.

39. Bartenev, "Rod i detstvo Pushkina," *Otechestvennyia zapiski*, 1853, Vol. 91, No. 11, Section II, pp. 1-20.

40. Bartenev, *O Pushkine: stranitsy zhizni poeta. Vospominaniia sovremennikov*, comp., introd. and annot. by A. M. Gordin (Moscow: Sovetskaia Rossiia, 1992), pp. 55-128; the quotation is on pp. 56-57. His attention to the grandmother shows the myth had yet to reach its apogee.

41. Annenkov, *Sochineniia Pushkina s prilozheniem materialov dlia ego biografii*, reprint ed. of the self-published 1855 ed. (n.p., n.d. [but 1985?]), pp. 3-4.

42. *Ibid.*, p. 119. Contrary to what some biographers claim, Pushkin never "cursed" his "French education"; in a letter to his brother in early November 1824 he refers to his inadequate ("accursed") early (formal) education at home with tutors and governors. But its being French seems far from what Pushkin is referring to in this letter. See *The Letters of Alexander Pushkin*, trans. and annot. by J. Thomas Shaw (Madison: The University of Wisconsin Press, 1967), pp. 188-89.

43. At the time, those knowledgeable about Pushkin and Arina ridiculed the more outrageous claims about her. See M. A. Dmitriev's letter to M.P. Pogodin of 30 January 1856: "...from the latest biography of Pushkin...we've learned that, probably, Pushkin was obliged for the Russianness [*narodnost'iu*] of some of his works to his dear old nanny [*nianiushka*], about whom people are writing so much these days that I believe she must be reeling in the other world [*ei ikaetsia na tom svete*]. In a word: nowadays they don't trot Pushkin out in front of the public other than with his old nanny. Karamzin and I. I. Dmitriev...would

have a good laugh at this; but Pushkin would blush at what this group is making of him [*krasnel by, predstavliaia iz sebia etu gruppu*]...You glorify just two gods: Pushkin and Gogol' and one goddess: the nanny Radivonovna! [sic] ...." Cited in commentary by A. L. Ospovat and N. G. Okhotin to a facsimile reproduction of Annenkov's *Materialy dlia biografii Aleksandra Sergeevicha Pushkina* (Moscow: Kniga, 1985), pp. 65-66.

44. Dostoevskii, "Zimnie zametki o letnikh vpechatleniiakh" (originally published in *Vremia*), in *Polnoe sobranie sochinenii v tridtsati tomakh* [hereafter, *PSS*], Vol. 5 (Leningrad: Nauka, 1973), p. 51. He expresses similar thoughts in his *Diary of a Writer* (*Dnevnik pisatelia*) for 1876. See *ibid.*, Vol. 23 (1981), pp. 80-82.

45. Aksakov, *Literaturnaia kritika*, comp., introd. and annot. by A. S. Kurilov (Moscow: Sovremennik, 1981), taken from online at http://az.lib.ru/a/aksakow_i_s/text_01301.shtml (1880) – in the "Kritika" subsection (accessed December 2011). This speech first appeared in Bartenev's *Russkii arkhiv* [hereafter, *RA*], 1880, Bk. 2, pp. 467-484. The references to Pushkin's "Russian frame of mind and soul"; his profound sympathy with the people's song, fairy tales, and way of life; and his village impressions of childhood and the relationship with his nanny ("mamushka") are on p. 473, as is the slight dig at his mother. More dithyrambs about Arina, the quoting of the two early poems and then the late poems, which *are* about Arina, are on pp. 474-75.

46. Pavel Annenkov, "Aleksandr Sergeevich Pushkin v Aleksandrovskuiu epokhu. Po novym dokumentam," *Vestnik Evropy* [hereafter, *VE*], November 1873, Vol. 6, No. 11, pp. 15-23.

47. *Ibid.*, p. 24.

Similarly, in the following installment, Annenkov's most important point is that prior to 1820 Pushkin was already paying a great deal of attention to fairy and folktales (in his "Ruslan and Liudmila" and his take on the Bova legend) and once again he makes no connection whatever to Arina in this regard. *Ibid.*, December 1873, No. 12, p. 482. Parenthetically, I find his comments here about Pushkin's immature works bear, at least indirectly, on the issue of how heartfelt his feelings toward Arina were. Annenkov notes that these early pieces are full of jokes, witticisms, and epigrams, and that many are in the form of "elegies." These same elements seem to be exactly what come out later in his poems concerning Arina. Thus these later works seem almost formulaic and not as individualized as most interpreters would have them.

48. *Ibid.*, February 1874, Vol. 1, No. 2, p. 536.

49. *Ibid.*, p. 537

50. But even this point needs further clarification. First, and most important, what all commentators on this point seem to have overlooked is that attributing Pushkin's linguistic skill to his nanny is merely a variation of an ancient theme about wet-nurses. According to nearly all cultures in which wet-nurses are employed, a child who breastfeeds with a woman not his own mother imbibes with her milk a host of other physical and intangible things, *including dexterity with the wet-nurse's language*. Thus, the most ardent propagators of Arina's myth are merely transferring the attributes of a wet-nurse to a nanny, a point I return to in Chapter 10.

Second, these same Arina idolators are consciously or unconsciously weaving into the Arina story an actual historical phenomenon: the influence on the Russian spoken at court (and in many homes of high nobility) exerted by peasant wet-nurses and nannies employed therein. Edward L. Keenan has commented on this phenomenon in a series of lectures at Wellesley College. He argues that the evolution of a supple *spoken* Russian at court owes perhaps as much to these peasant women of early modern times as it does to the literati and scholars who get most of the credit for its development. Thus, there may be slightly more basis in fact for the Arina language claims than a skeptic might suspect. I am indebted to Prof. Nancy Shields Kollmann of Stanford University for providing me with scanned copies of these two unpublished lectures, given in about 1978. The title of the relevant talk was "Ivan the Terrible and His Women, part 2: Dowagers, Nannies, and Brides," pp. 15-23.

51. M[ark] Azadovski, "Pushkin and Folklore," in I. Luppol et al., *Pushkin: A Collection of Articles and Essays on the Great Russian Poet A. S. Pushkin* (Moscow: USSR Society for Cultural Relations with Foreign Countries, 1939), p. 126. See also his "Pushkin i fol'klor," in *Pushkin: Vremennik pushkinskoi komissii*, 3 (Moscow-Leningrad: AN SSSR, 1937), pp. 152-182; idem, *Literatura i fol'klor: Ocherki i etiudy* (Leningrad: Khudozhestvennaia literatura, 1938); and Vadim Smirnov, *Literatura i fol'klornaia traditsiia: Voprosy poetiki (arkhetipy "zhenskogo nachala" v russkoi literature XIX - nachala XX veka* (Ivanovo: Iunona, 2001), p. 13. Azadovskii succumbs a bit to the Arina myth in his "Skazki Ariny Rodionovny" in *Russkaia skazka. Izbrannye mastera*, which he edited and annotated (Academia, 1932), pp. 273-292.

Nadezhda Tèffi and Daniil Kharms skewer bloated claims for Arina and her tales (see her "Nanny's Fairy Tale About the Mare's Head," *Iumoristicheskie rasskazy; Iz "Vseobshchei istorii, obrabotannoi 'Satirikonom'"* [Moscow: Khudozhestvennaia literatura, 1990], p. 76, and his two brief jabs in *Iumor nachala XX veka*, ed. by Stanislav Rassadin et al. [Moscow: OLMA-Press, 2003], pp. 483-85.) Similarly, Mikhail Zoshchenko laughs at the myth and Pushkin's "ballyhooed nanny" (*preslovutaia nian'ka*): "In the Days of Pushkin," *Izbrannoe* (Ann Arbor: University of Michigan Press, 1960), pp. 259-64. An English version (*Nervous People and Other Satires*, trans. by Maria Gordon and Hugh McLean, with the help of Fruma Gottschalk, ed. and introd. by McLean (New York: Vintage Books, 1963), pp. 273-78, somewhat misses the point by mistranslating *preslovutaia* as "renowned."

52. M. P. Viktorova and V. A. Koshelev argue that one can't take Pushkin's own words about Arina being the original of the Larin nanny literally. The third chapter was "begun already in Odessa and completed at Mikhailovskoe...before the time of Pushkin's particular intimacy [*sblizhenie*] with the nanny." See their article "Niania" in N. I. Mikhailovna, et al., eds., *Oneginskaia entsiklopediia*, Vol. II (Moscow: Russkii put', 2004), p. 186-87. Cf. Nabokov, *Eugene Onegin*, II, p. 362.

53. L. N. Pavlishchev, "Vospominaniia ob A. S. Pushkine," in *Poet, Rossiia i tsari* (Moscow: Sergei Dubov Foundation, 1999), p. 217. There's more than a hint of sour grapes in the recollections of the son of his older sister Ol'ga, but they serve to let at least some of the (hot) air out of the balloon inflated around Arina.

54. M. I. Osipova, "Rasskazy o Pushkine, zapisannye M. I. Semevskim," in Vatsuro et al., *A. S. Pushkin: stikhotvoreniia*, p. 460. Cf. Simmons, *Pushkin*, p. 220. Despite the potential fallacy, Iazykov's poems and Pushkin's "Winter's Evening" seem to confirm her taste for drink.

55. Generic nannies appear in, e.g., "Arap Petra Velikogo" (begun in 1827 but published only posthumously in 1837), "Roman v pis'makh" (late 1829), "A Russian Pelham" (begun in 1834-35), and variant draft fragments of "Rusalka."

56. The hero's nanny is called Orina Egorovna and early in the novella she sends him a letter reminiscent of a letter Arina sent Pushkin in 1827, sufficient "evidence" for V. A. Manuilov and E. V. Kholshevnikova ("O romane 'Dubrovskii'" in A. S. Pushkin, *Dubrovskii: Roman*, [Moscow: Detskaia literatura, 1975], p. 90) to believe Dubrovskii's nanny, portrayed with "special love," was modeled closely on Arina.

57. Shortly after Pushkin left the estate and returned to St. Petersburg, Arina asked the Osipovs to write and send to the poet a letter she

dictated to them, effusive with gratitude and affection. Quoted in Simmons, *Pushkin*, p. 220n.

58. Certainly this is the view of Ol'ga Sergeevna's son, Lev. See Pavlishchev, "Vospominaniia ob A. S. Pushkine,"p. 223. But he is a far from unimpeachable source with regard to his mother.

59. Goncharov, *Sobranie sochinenii v vos'mi tomakh* (Moscow: Khudozhestvennaia literatura, 1955), Vol. 8, p. 268.

60. His remark is quoted by Mikhail Filin in the *Literaturnaia gazeta* piece cited previously.

61. Grevs, "[Detstvo (1860-1872)]," in *Chelovek s otkrytym serdtsem: Avtobiograficheskoe i epistoliarnoe nasledie Ivana Mikhailovicha Grevsa (1860-1941)*, comp. and ed. by Oksana Borisovna Vakhromeeva (St. Petersburg: n.p. [but RAN], 2004), p. 19.

How far this "cult of personality" with the poet's nanny went can be seen in the frequently hilarious stories of the Pushkin scholar Mstislav Tsiavlovskii about efforts of the Soviet government to promote all things Pushkin. A 1924 competition to design a Pushkin memorial produced a winning entry placing Pushkin on horseback (!). Tsiavlovskii sardonically comments that "realism seizes the [design] creator to the depths of his soul, and one can only regret greatly that he did not envision the old woman Arina Rodionovna somewhere in the bushes in the near vicinity gathering wild strawberries or mushrooms." See Tsiavlovskii and Tat'iana Tsiavlovskaia, *Vokrug Pushkina*, prepared by K. P. Bogaevskaia and S. I. Panov (Moscow: Novoe literaturnoe obozrenie, 2000), pp. 151-56, 283-86. Ironically, a memorial to Pushkin erected in Pskov in recent decades does indeed feature Arina as prominently as the poet. See the cover illustration of my book.

62. See Jonathan Gathorne-Hardy, *The Unnatural History of the Nanny* (New York: Dial Press, 1973), Chapter 1, pp. 17-32, and pp.129ff, 163ff, 282-85; Elaine Ostry, *Social Dreaming: Dickens and the Fairy Tale* (New York: Routledge, 2002), Chapter One: "Nurse's Stories: Fairy Tales as Cultural Voices": "The young Charles Dickens did not know how lucky he was to have a nursemaid who scared him silly with her stories. But the older Dickens did know, and acknowledged his debt to his nurse, Mary Weller, in his article 'Nurse's Stories' (1860)"; Leonard Shengold, M.D., "Dickens, Little Dorrit, and Soul Murder," *Psychoanalytic Quarterly* Vol. 57, No. 3 (1988), pp. 390-421, but especially pp. 392-98; Frank McLynn, *Robert Louis Stevenson: A Biography* (New York: Random House, 1993) – re the tremendous influence of Alison Cunningham, "Cummy," pp. 13-20, 26, 28-29 and passim; anonymous

review of the McLynn biography in *The Economist*, 19 June 1993, p. 95, in which the reviewer, unlike McLynn, places the germination of *Dr. Jekyll and Mr. Hyde* with the nanny; Marie Campbell, *Strange World of the Brontës* (Wilmslow, England: Sigma Leisure, 2001), "Those Who Served," pp. 85-86 (re Tabitha Aykroyd, nicknamed "Old Tabby Brontë," and her "appearances" – transmuted – in both *Jane Eyre* and *Wuthering Heights*).

Katie Trumpener feels "that in Britain, the dispatch of upperclass kids to boarding school solidifies an obsession with the nanny in retrospect" (email of 11/11/2009 to the author). This would indeed be a close parallel to the Russian experience, where boys as young as 7-8 but usually a few years older were sent away from home to cadet corps and similar military or government institutions to complete their educations.

63. The pernicious practice of incorporating lines from the poet's *oeuvre* as factual material for his biography has been noted more than once. Lack of information and primary sources is not the basic issue. There are almost too many sources, each voice straining to be heard, to get in their word in their own way. The primary sources, while abundant, are far from consistent, and their reliability is always subject to double- and even triple-checking against other sources.

64. It is unsurprising that in a recent book devoted to Soviet mythmaking about Pushkin, there is not a word about Arina Rodionovna. Instead the author tackles various other myths, all of them of some interest: for example, that "Pushkin was a 'friend of the Decembrists,' an enemy of 'tsarism,' a disillusioned liberal, a pagan [*iazychnik*], a confirmed [*zakorenelyi*] atheist, a firm Voltairean and admirer of Pugachëv etc. etc." See Viktor M. Esipov, *Pushkin v zerkale mifov* (Moscow: Iazyki slavianskoi kul'tury, 2006).

Similarly reticent about Arina – because the focus lies elsewhere – is a collection of Western scholars' essays about Pushkin and mythmaking: *Cultural Mythologies of Russian Modernism: From the Golden Age to the Silver Age*, ed. by Boris Gasparov, Robert P. Hughes, and Irina Paperno (Berkeley: University of California Press, 1992).

65. Wachtel, *The Battle for Childhood: Creation of a Russian Myth* (Stanford, CA: Stanford University Press, 1990).

66. See Chapters 8 and 9 in particular.

67. I.e., works of fiction that contain strong autobiographical elements but do not purport to tell the author's life-story. I avoid the term "pseudo-

autobiography," a different literary device, defined mostly by the "authorial voice," according to Wachtel in his *Battle for Childhood*. It can be stated, however, that in this one respect – the treatment of nannies – "pseudo-autobiographies" are more or less identical to both true autobiographies and belles-lettres.

68. In the case of three others, editors or compilers noted the existence of a nanny in the subject's childhood, although the authors themselves were silent on the subject. Both Admiral Pavel Chichagov (17651849) and the poet Vasilii Zhukovskii (1783-1852) mention nannies generically, merely in passing, but not their own particular nannies.

69. For more details about these memoirists, see Chapter 2.

70. Without question, the proportions I've given would be higher had I not included nonnobles in my lists. Peasants, workers, priests, and nonupper-class intellectuals (often *raznochintsy*, or those not easily pegged to any specific social group) – all of whom are represented in my readings – tended either not to have nonfamily nannies or to fail to note them in their autobiographies.

71. I would say that in two cases there was an even more direct connection. The autobiographies of Pushkin's very close friend Pavel Nashchokin (1801?-1854) and of the "maiden cavalry trooper" Nadezhda Durova (1783-1866) were both (re)written with direct input from the poet. Both record the (obligatory?) presence of nannies in childhood – *after* discussions with Pushkin. Nashchokin's draft and Pushkin's reworked versions are all in the poet's complete works: "Zapiski P. V. N.[ashchokina], im diktovannye v Moskve, 1830," in Pushkin, *PSS*, Vol. 11, pp. 189-192; and Vol. 12 (both Moscow: AN SSSR, 1949), pp. 287-92. A much fuller version of his autobiography, with commentary by L. B. Modzalevskii, can be found in *Rukoiu Pushkina: Nesobrannye i neopublikovannye teksty*, comp. and ed. by M. A. Tsiavlovskii, Modzalevskii, and T. G. Zenger (Moscow-Leningrad: Academia, 1935), pp. 116-27. See also N. Ia. Eidel'man, "Vospominaniia Pavla Voinovicha Nashchokina, napisannye v forme pis'ma k A. S. Pushkinu," *Prometei*, 1974, Bk. 10, pp. 275-292. The relevant sections of Durova's autobiography, entitled "My Childhood Years" (*Detskie leta moi*) and "Several features from my childhood years" (*Nekotorye cherty iz detskikh let*), are both contained in the enlarged version of her memoirs, retitled *Zapiski Aleksandrova (Durovoi). Dobavlenie k "Devitse-kavalerist"* (1839). They are included in the edition of the *Zapiski* published as *Izbrannoe* (Moscow: Sovetskaia Rossiia, 1984), pp. 31-63 and 64-104 respectively.

72. For more on both Khodasevich and Tsvetaeva, see Chapter 9.

73. Heldt, *Terrible Perfection: Women and Russian Literature* (Bloomington: Indiana University Press, 1987), Chapter 1.

Chapter Two

1. See Chapter 8 for a discussion of nannies in literature.

2. My less-than-unimpeachable source for this story is a letter to a newspaper in Bishkek, Kyrgyzstan, from one I. Savelov ("O dvuglavom orle," *Vechernii Bishkek*, 23 June 1993, p. 3).

3. *Slovar' russkogo iazyka XI-XVII vv.*, ed. by S.G. Barkhudarov et al., Vol. 7 (Moscow: Nauka, 1980), pp. 318-20 for *kormilitsa, kormil'nitsa, kormitel'nitsa*, and the adjectival *kormilitsyn*; Vol. 11 (Moscow: Nauka, 1986), p. 454 for *niania, nian'ka, nianiushka*, and the adjectival *nian'kin*; see also Vol. 9 (Moscow: Nauka, 1982), pp. 24-25 for *mamka, mamushka, mama*$^{1-2}$, and the adjectival *mamkin*. Cf. Vadim V. Dolgov, *Byt i nravy drevnei Rusi: miry povsednevnosti XI-XIII vv.* (Moscow: Iauza/Eksmo, 2007), pp. 44-65.

The creative lexicographer Vladimir Dal' (1801-1872) notes in his dictionary – without supporting evidence – the following custom: "In olden times [*vstar'*], a nanny was appointed to look after girls, right up to [their] marriage, and she kept this honorific title forever." See Dal', *Tolkovyi slovar' zhivogo velikorusskogo iazyka*, Vol. 2 (Moscow: Russkii iazyk, 1979; a reprint of the 1881 ed.), p. 564 ("*niania*").

4. See Nancy Shields Kollmann, *Kinship and Politics: The Making of the Muscovite Political System, 1345-1547* (Stanford: Stanford University Press, 1987), especially pp. 57-59, 159-87; Marshall T. Poe et al., *The Russian Elite in the Seventeenth Century*, 2 vols. (Helsinki: FASL, 2004), especially I, pp. 26ff concerning clans, and I, Appendix 4, plus II, pp. 385-469, concerning individuals; and Edward L. Keenan, Jr., "Muscovite Political Folkways," *Russian Review*, April 1986, Vol. 45, No. 2, pp. 115-81.

5. V. Beneshevich, "Cheliadnina, Agrippina (Agrafena) Fedorovna," in *Russkii biograficheskii slovar'*, Vol. 22 (St. Petersburg: I.N. Skorokhodov, 1905), p. 132, 133-34; see also, for Telepnev-Obolenskii, *ibid.*, Vol. 20 (1912), pp. 447-49. Cf. Natal'ia Pushkareva, *Women in Russian History from the Tenth to the Twentieth Century*, trans. and ed. by Eve Levin (Armonk, NY: M. E. Sharpe, 1997), pp. 67-68, 90.

6. This painting was preliminary to Makovskii's larger rendering of "The Death of Ivan the Terrible" (1888). The nanny painting can be viewed

in color online at: http://2photo.ru/ru/post/26230 (accessed Feb. 2012) and many other sites.

7. *Ivan Groznyi* (Moscow: Nauka, 1975), p. 207. The book is available in English as well: Ruslan G. Skrynnikov, *Ivan the Terrible*, ed. and trans. by Hugh F. Graham (Gulf Breeze, FL: Academic International Press, 1981), where this anecdote is related on p. 172.

8. Thyret, " 'Blessed is the Tsaritsa's Womb': The Myth of Miraculous Birth and Royal Motherhood in Muscovite Russia," *Russian Review*, October 1994, Vol. 53, No. 4, p. 491 n65.

9. Aleksei Suvorin, *O Dmitrii Samozvanetse; kriticheskie ocherki, s prilozheniem novago spiska sledstvennago dela o smerti tsarevicha Dmitriia* (St.Petersburg: A. S. Suvorin, 1906), pp. 189, 191-192.

10. As many readers will know, however, two rumors about this death – mutually contradictory – sprang up very shortly after the heir's demise, spread by enemies of the regent Boris Godunov and by interested neighbors in Poland. The first was that Godunov himself had the young boy killed, to put himself and his family on the throne. The second was that the boy had not been killed at all but had escaped and would return to save his people from the illegitimate and unjust rule of the usurper Godunov.

Literature about the consequences of Dmitrii's death (the *Smuta*, or Time of Troubles; Godunov; and especially the various "False Dmitriis" who appeared to claim their "rightful inheritance") is too voluminous to cite here. A recent study of the tsarevich's death is by Liudmila Taimasova: *Tragediia v Ugliche: Chto proizoshlo 15 maia 1591 goda?* (Moscow: Omega, 2006).

11. See letter 134 (no date, but ca. 1680), in G.G. Luk'ianov, "Chastnaia perepiska kniazia Petra Ivanovicha Khovanskago, ego sem'i i rodstvennikov," *Starina i novizna: Istoricheskii sbornik*, Bk. 9 (Moscow: Synod Press, 1905), p. 411.

12. Quoted in Natal'ia L. Pushkareva, *Chastnaia zhizn' russkoi zhenshchiny: nevesta, zhena, liubovnitsa (X-nachalo XIX v.)* (Moscow: "Ladomir," 1997), p. 89.

13. All of my information comes from S. Shubinskii, "Dlia biografii grafa Ioanna-Ernsta Minikha," *RA*, 1866, cols. 1545-1567.

14. Both historians and novelists take nannies in high-born families as a given. For instance, the historian I. Khrushchov writes, in a biographical sketch of the mother of the first Romanov tsar: "The

higher a young girl stood in social position...the more protected she was from the outside world. In the milieu of very wealthy people this life of the terem unfolded [*razvilas'*] amid a whole complement of nannies and maidservants." See Khrushchov, "Kseniia Ivanovna Romanova (Velikaia staritsa inokinia Marfa)," *Drevniaia i novaia Rossiia: Istoricheskii illiustrirovannyi ezhemesiachnyi sbornik*, December 1876, Vol. III, pp. 317-43; here, p. 317. Aleksandra Shchepkina, in her historical novel of the seventeenth century *Boiare Starodubskie: Istoricheskii roman iz vremën tsaria Alekseia Mikhailovicha* (Moscow: I. N. Kushnerev & Co., 1897), includes a nanny in a major role.

15. See the Moscow city censuses for the seventeenth and eighteenth centuries: *Perepisi moskovskikh dvorov semnadtsatago stoletiia* and *Perepisi moskovskikh dvorov vosemnadtsatago stoletiia*, both 1896.

16. He was the father of the famous diplomat and statesman Ivan Matveevich Murav'ev-Apostol' and grandfather of the Decembrists Sergei, Matvei and Ippolit Murav'ev-Apostol'.

17. *Rossiiskii arkhiv: Istoriia Otechestva v svidetel'stvakh i dokumentakh XVIII-XX vv.*, Vol. V (Moscow: Trite Studiia/Rossiiskii arkhiv, 1994), p. 8.

18. *Zhizn' i prikliucheniia Andreia Bolotova opisannye samim im dlia svoikh pitomkov* (Moscow: Academia, 1931; reprinted by Oriental Research Partners, Cambridge, England, 1973), I, p. 8. This passage comes from letter 4, ostensibly dated 1738, but in fact written much later, probably in the 1790s. (The entire 29 chapters of his autobiography were written between 1789 and 1816.)

19. This quotation comes from the same book – vol. 1 – but a different, online ed. without pagination, originally published in Tula in 1988 by the Priokskoe knizhnoe izdatel'stvo (no pagination).

20. *Avtobiograficheskiia zapiski Dmitriia Borisovicha Mertvago. 1760-1824* (Moscow: Russkii Arkhiv/T. Ris, 1867), pp. 8-10.

21. Dolgorukov, *Povest' o rozhdenii moem, proiskhozhdenii i vsei zhizni, pisannaia mnoi samim i nachataia v Moskve 1788-go goda v Avguste mesiatse, na 25-om godu ot rozhdeniia moego*, vol. I, ed. by N. V. Kuznetsova and M. O. Mel'tsin (St. Petersburg: Nauka, 2004), p. 29. The unabashed sexism would be typical of the day.

22. Dolgorukov, *Kapishche moego serdtsa, ili Slovar' vsekh tekh lits, s koimi ia byl v raznykh otnosheniiakh v techenie moei zhizni*, ed., annot., and with an introd. by V. I. Korovin (Moscow: Nauka, 1997), p. 71. Here he supplied her surname: Bromontova.

23. "Zapiski Fedora Panteleimonovicha Pecherina," *Russkaia starina* [hereafter, *RS*], December 1891, Vol. 72, p. 594.

24. *Ibid.*, n3.

25. While most Western historians seem to accept this autobiography as reasonably authentic, I am more persuaded by the view of the cultural historian Iurii Lotman, who says that "it is not possible to understand A. E. Labzina's memoirs as a naively 'photographic' reproduction of reality, as commentators on them frequently do." Lotman's incisive, persuasive analysis shows that Labzina's work is a great historical resource *not because of its historical accuracy* but precisely because it is almost totally subjective and ideological. See his "Dve zhenshchiny" in *Besedy o russkoi kul'ture: Byt i traditsii russkogo dvorianstva (XVIII–nachalo XIX veka)* (St. Petersburg: Iskusstvo–SPB, 1994), pp. 287-313. Further support for the ideological nature of the memoirs comes from V. M. Bokova in her introduction to *Istoriia zhizni blagorodnoi zhenshchiny* (Moscow: Novoe literaturnoe obozrenie, 1996), pp. 6-7. Among recent Western commentaries on the Labzina memoirs, see especially the introduction by Gary Marker to *Days of a Russian Noblewoman: The Memories of Anna Labzina 1758-1821*, trans. and ed. by Marker and Rachel May (DeKalb: Northern Illinois University Press, 2001) – Marker coming close to Lotman's interpretation on pp. xiii-xvii; Mary Zirin, entry on Labzina in *Dictionary of Russian Women Writers*, ed. by Marina Ledkovsky, Charlotte Rosenthal, and Zirin (Westport, CT: Greenwood Press, 1994), pp. 355-56; the introduction by Judith C. Zacek to the 1974 ORP reprint of the 1914 ed. of *Vospominaniia Anny Evdokimovny Labzinoi. 1758-1828*; and Barbara Heldt's treatment of the memoirs in *Terrible Perfection*, pp. 77-79.

26. Margaret Ziolkowski offers a first-rate analysis of the persistence of the hagiographic tradition in Russian literature in her *Hagiography and Modern Russian Literature* (Princeton: Princeton University Press, 1988).

27. Labzina, "Vospominaniia A. E. Labzina," *RS*, January 1903, Vol. 34, Appendix, footnote, pp. 15-16. The author "rehearsed" this scene thoroughly, seeking just the right tone and touch: she produced not one version but two, in the first of which the nanny is much more prominent in her father's last thoughts than in the second, published version. One more argument for the possible nonhistoricity of the memoirs is the resemblance this "preamble" bears to the fiction of Aleksandra Khvostova, a woman, like Labzina, intimate to the circles of both the writer Mikhail Kheraskov and the leading Masonic figure Aleksandr Labzin. Khvostova was Kheraskov's niece, Labzina his ward. Khvostova's "Excerpts. Hearth and Brook" (*Otryvki. Kamin i rucheek; 1796)* includes a deathbed scene with a dying father bestowing his blessing on his daughter. See Mary Zirin's entry for Khvostova in *Dictionary of Russian Women Writers*, p. 291.

28. It is more than a little suggestive that Labzina's nanny is not provided a name. Since in almost every autobiography or memoir published after 1830 the authors take care to name their nannies, this is one more small but potent argument that Labzina's nanny may be fictional or semifictional, of a piece with the work as a whole.

29. In almost all ways, Labzina's autobiography/autohagiography resembles Mikhail Bakhtin's concepts of the "everyday-life adventure" and of the folk or fairy tale. See Bakhtin, *The Dialogic Imagination: Four Essays*, ed. by Michael Holquist, trans. by Caryl Emerson and Holquist (Austin: the University of Texas Press, 1981), p. 112-19.

30. Other sources, including Labzina's diary and the recollections of her niece, show Labzina in an even less flattering, perhaps duplicitous light. Marker, introduction to *Days of a Russian Noblewoman*, pp. xviii-xxi; Sof'ia Laikevich, "Vospominaniia Sof'i Alekseevny Laikevich," *RS*, October 1905, Vol. 124, No. 10, pp. 172-74, 177, 183-84 as well as the introductory remarks by Boris L. Modzalevskii, *ibid.*, p. 169.

31. Throughout this book I will refer to rulers by their Westernized names once crowned but by their Russian names before ascending the throne.

32. The most important source about Nicholas's nanny and her purported influence on the young boy is Baron Modest Korf's *Materialy i cherty k biografii imperatora Nikolaia I* in *Sbornik imperatorskago istoricheskago obshchestva*, Vol. 98, ed. by N.F. Dubrovin (St. Petersburg, 1896), pp. 1-100. Two other informative works are Nikolai Shil'der, *Imperator Nikolai Pervyi, ego zhizn' i tsarstvovanie*, Vol. 1 (Moscow: Charli, 1997) and W. Bruce Lincoln, *Nicholas I: Emperor and Autocrat of All the Russias* (Bloomington: Indiana University Press, 1978). Both rely heavily on Korf.

For an interesting recent study of Nicholas – what can only be called a patriotic-revisionist view – see the online work by the contemporary (post-Soviet) historian Boris Tarasov at: http://gosudarstvo.voskres.ru/tarasov/index.htm (accessed August 2008).

33. Shil'der, *Imperator Nikolai Pervyi*, p. 8.

34. *Ibid.*, p. 9. We have additional personal information about Jane Lyon and her family. See Anthony G. Cross, *By the Banks of the Neva : Chapters from the Lives and Careers of the British in Eighteenth-Century Russia* (Cambridge; New York: Cambridge University Press, 1997), p. 246.

35. Shil'der, *Imperator Nikolai Pervyi*, p. 9. This same story is recounted in another major biography of Nicholas: Theodor Schiemann's 4-vol. *Geschichte Russlands unter Kaiser Nikolaus I* (Berlin, 1904-1919), I, p. 181.

Endnotes 331

One noted contemporary scholar seems to accept the decisive role of the nanny's stories in shaping Nicholas's Polish attitudes. See Lincoln, *Nicholas I*, p. 50. Recently also, the Russian historian Tat'iana Kapustina says that Lyon "exerted considerable influence on the grand duke's developing character" ("Nicholas I" in the *Emperors and Empresses of Russia: Rediscovering the Romanovs*, ed. by Donald J. Raleigh, comp. by A.A. Iskenderov [Armonk, NY: M. E. Sharpe, 1996], p. 259).

Among other things credited to Jane Lyon, she is also supposed to have taught the young Nikolai Pavlovich his Russian letters (shades of Pushkin). It is curious that while this story is retailed in the current, online *Encyclopedia Britannica*, it does not figure in the authoritative eleventh ed. of the *EB*.

36. A.N. Radishchev, *Izbrannye filosofskie sochineniia*, ed. by I. Ia. Shchipanov (Leningrad: Politicheskaia literatura,1949), p. 305. This is an eerie anticipation of Stalin's notorious dictum that "cadres decide everything."

During the Napoleonic wars, not just a good upbringing but a *Russian* upbringing (*russkoe vospitanie*) "was one of the favorite theories of Russian educators [literally, enlighteners – *prosvetiteli*]," according to Natal'ia N. Mazur ("K rannei biografii A.S. Khomiakova," *Lotmanovskii sbornik*, Issue 2 (Moscow: RGGU, 1997), p. 202.

37. Novikov, "O vospitanii i nastavlenii detei dlia rasprostraneniia obshchepoleznykh znanii i vseobshchego blagopoluchiia,"*Izbrannoe* (Moscow: Pravda, 1983), p. 384. Much more about nannies' "prejudices" and "superstitions" follows in Chapter 4.

38. *Ibid.*, p. 403.

39. E. N. Medynskii, "Traktat ottsa dekabristov A. F. Bestuzheva 'O vospitanii' (1798)," *Sovetskaia pedagogika*, November 1955, No. 11, p. 76. In 1800, a decade before his death, Bestuzhev the father was appointed administrator of the Imperial Academy of Arts, where he could perhaps try to implement his pedagogic ideas on an even broader scale.

40. *Ibid.*, p. 78.

41. Berezaiskii was born in 1762 in Iaroslavl' province, the son (or grandson) of a village cleric. Seminary educated, between 1783 and 1816 he was a teacher of literature and mathematics. In the mid- to late 1780s Berezaiskii contributed to various journals, including the Nikolai Novikov-published *Children's Reading* (Russia's first children's magazine). He published two major French translations and a textbook on math for noble girls. He died in 1821. See Dmitrii M. Moldavskii,

Russkaia narodnaia satira (Leningrad: "Prosveshchenie," 1967), pp. 212-218.

42. *Anekdoty drevnikh poshekhontsev* (St. Petersburg: Tipografiia godudarstvennoi meditsinskoi kollegii, 1798). Available online (accessed Jan. 2012): http://babel.hathitrust.org/cgi/pt?id=mdp.39015011918607;page=root;seq=12;view=1up;size=100;orient=0. The book was long very popular, reissued in 1821, on the occasion of Berezaiskii's death, and again in 1863. When Berezaiskii wrote, the word *"anekdot"* did not necessarily connote a funny story; it usually referred to a little-known or unknown happening, historical or curious, and might almost be rendered as "vignette."

43. Art follows life in this instance. The great collectors of folklore, folktales, proverbs and sayings, songs, and related material had already begun their work by the 1770s. In this they were part of a European-wide phenomenon, of course, beginning with Charles Perrault in France (*Histories ou Contes du Temps Passé*, 1697), but anticipating the brothers Grimm by some three decades or more. Among the most important Russian collectors were: the first, Professor Anton Barsov of Moscow University (*Sobranie 4291 drevnikh rossiiskikh poslovits*, 1770 – and two more editions by 1787); the poet Ippolit Bogdanovich (*Ruskiia poslovitsy*, 1785 – who gathered his examples at Catherine II's direct request); and Mikhail Chulkov (*Slovar' ruskikh sueverii*,1782).

44. Jessica Tovrov believes erroneously that "this concern was not common until the middle of the [nineteenth] century" (*The Russian Noble Family: Structure and Change* [New York: Garland Publishing, 1987], p. 153). Catriona Kelly shows that it persisted well into the twentieth century; see her *Children's World: Growing Up in Russia, 1890-1991* (New Haven: Yale University Press, 2007), pp. 367, 408.

45. Grum, *Rukovodstvo k vospitaniiu, obrazovaniiu i sokhraneniiu zdorov'ia detei*, 3 vols. (St. Petersburg: M. Ol'khin, 1843-45); here, Vol. II: *Vozrasty: detskii i otrocheskii. Vospitanie fizicheskoe* (1844), pp. 370-74.

46. Anonymous (but male, and likely Shalikov himself), "Mysli, kharaktery i portrety," *Damskii zhurnal*, October 1827, No. 19, p. 14.

47. Hammarberg, "Women, Critics, and Women Critics in Early Russian Women's Journals," Chapter 9 in *Women and Gender in 18th-Century Russia*, ed. by Wendy Rosslyn (Aldershot, Hampshire, England: Ashgate Publishing Ltd., 2003), pp. 187-207; here, pp. 189-93, 194-95, 200-201.

48. "Pis'mo k F. F. P__ii. (O metode vospitaniia)," *ibid*., May 1827, No. 11,

pp. 188-89 (the piece is signed V. Z. ...v," a pseudonym not known as one of Shalikov's and not deciphered by Ivan Masanov in his 4-vol. *Slovar'*). This installment was the first part of a two-part "letter," concluded in the following issue.

49. Anon., "Pis'mo k F.F. P__ii," *Damskii zhurnal*, June 1827, p. 232.

50. *Ibid.*, p. 233.

51. *Ibid.*, p. 234. Italics added.

Chapter Three

1. Pisemsky, *One Thousand Souls*, trans. by Ivy Litvinov (New York: Grove Press, Inc., 1959), p. 190.

2. Omitting here merchant, intelligentsia, clergy, and peasant households.

3. Pre-1861 our sources for serf numbers are the various (partial) censuses (*perepisi* and *revizii*) taken by the central government from the 1720s to 1858. Among many serious issues in using these sources: they do not distinguish – until very late – between peasants engaged in fieldwork on some master's estate and the household staff of that estate (*dvorovye liudi*).

4. See I. Ignatovich, *Pomeshchich'i krest'iane nakanune osvobozhdeniia*, third ed. (Moscow, 1925), cited in P.A. Zaionchkovskii, *Otmena krepostnogo prava v Rossii*, 2nd enl. and rev. ed. (Moscow: Ministerstvo prosveshcheniia RSFSR, 1960), p. 18. Cf. Aleksandr Troinitskii, *Krepostnoe naselenie v Rossii, po 10-i narodnoi perepisi* (St. Petersburg, 1861), pp. 369, 435 n6; Peter Kolchin, *Unfree Labor: American Slavery and Russian Serfdom* (Cambridge: Harvard University Press, 1987), pp. 161, 369.

5. Princess Tat'iana Golitsyna (b.1909) notes that, long after the demise of serfdom, in 1916, "we four children required the attention of seven people," to wit, a Russian and an English governess and a personal maid for her and her next oldest sister, a nanny and under-nanny each for youngest sister and baby brother. Galitzine, *The Russian Revolution: Childhood Recollections* (Princeton: Princeton University Press, 1972), pp. 8-9. Princess Mariia L'vova (ca. 1864-ca. 1930?) astonishes when she claims that she had neither nanny nor governess – but thereafter rather contradicts herself about a nanny. See her *"Vospominaniia,"* Appendix I of Prince G. E. L'vov, *Vospominaniia* (Moscow: Russkii put', 2002), pp. 320, 350. Cf. Priscilla Roosevelt, *Life on the Russian Country Estate: A Social and Cultural History* (New Haven: Yale University Press, 1995), pp. 102ff.

6. Cf. Vladimir M. Kabuzan, *Narodonaselenie Rossii v XVIII-pervoi polovine XIX v. (po materialm revizii)* (Moscow: AN SSSR, 1963), p. 154; Seymour Becker, *Nobility and Privilege in Late Imperial Russia* (DeKalb, IL: Northern Illinois University Press, 1985), pp. 182, 187 (Table C-2). A major hole in Becker's counts is the absence of personal nobles; he estimates their numbers to be between 4,000 and 5,000 in the early twentieth century. Cf. Arcadius Kahan, *The Plow, the Hammer, and the Knout: An Economic History of Eighteenth-Century Russia*, with Richard Hellie (Chicago: The University of Chicago Press, 1985), pp. 24-25, and Boris N. Mironov with Ben Eklof, *The Social History of Imperial Russia* (Boulder, CO: Westview Press), Vol. I, p. 254.

7. Kabuzan, *Narodonaselenie*, p.187.

His figures for numbers of *landowning* households are:

Estimated Number of Noble Landowning Families, 1861-1912

Year	No. of Families
1861	114,500-115,500
1877	98,000-100,000
1895	103,000-104,500
1905	86,500-88,000
1912	94,500-96,500

8. As the number of clerical and *raznochintsy* families combined was at least that of noble families, and the count of urban/merchant families far exceeded that for the nobility, my guess for the total number of nonfamily nannies (not just "classic" caretakers) exceeds 300,000.

9. It is unclear to me what criteria separated this subcategory from subcategory 9, "Domestic servants [*Prisluga domashniaia*]: chefs [*povara*], lackeys, cooks [*kukharki*], maids, etc." It is not certain, but likely, that *diad'ki* fell under subcategory 6, with nannies.

10. *Pervaia vseobshchaia perepis' naseleniia rossiiskoi imperii 1897 g.*, ed. by Nikolai A. Troinitskii, Vol. 24, Notebook [*Tetrad'*] 2 (Final), ([Moscow]: Central Statistical Committee of the Ministry of Interior, 1903-04), pp. 150-151 (for Moscow); Vol. 37, *tetrad'* 2 and final (1903), pp. 134-135 (for SPB); and Vol. 47 (1904), p. 112 (for Odessa). Some of these statistics, as well as for 1902 Moscow, are available online (accessed September 2008) at: http://www.hist.msu.ru/Labs/Ecohist/DBASES/Census/index.html.

These figures offer no basis to extrapolate to the total number of nannies in these urban areas, much less in all of Russia. (They do indicate, however, that the institution of the *diad'ka* was dying out by the turn of the twentieth century.) Of more interest is some ratios. The total populations of the three cities above in this census were, respectively, 1,038,600 residents; 1,264,900 residents; and 403,800 residents. There was, therefore, roughly 1 female domestic worker for every 470 inhabitants in Moscow, one per 411 inhabitants in the capital, and about one per 632 residents in Odessa.

11. *Glavneishiia predvaritel'nyia dannyia perepisi g. Moskvy 31 ianvaria 1902 g.*(Moscow: Gorodskaia uprava. Statisticheskii otdel, 1902-03), Vypusk 3, section III, Table II, part G, pp. 214, 246.

12. Parenthetically, one can note a seemingly silly claim made by the philosopher Nikolai Berdiaev (1874-1948) that nannies in Russia "had altogether a special position, which was distinct from, and in a sense above, all the established social classes" ([Nicolas Berdyaev, *Dream and Reality: An Essay in Autobiography* [New York: Collier Books, 1962], p. 20). While not to be taken literally, this remark appears to fail figuratively as well. Memoirists apart from Berdiaev all tend to stress the very specific and concrete social milieu from which their nannies came.

13. Buturlin, "Zapiski grafa Mikhaila Dmitrievicha Buturlina," *RA*, 1897, Bk. 1, No. 2, p. 242. He was seconded in this opinion by Baroness Sofiia Buksgevden (Sophie Buxhoeveden, *Before the Storm* [London: Macmillan and Co., 1938], p.4).

14. This propensity of the aristocrats to hire English nannies is deliciously satirized by Karolina Pavlova (1807-1893) in her 1848 novel *A Double Life* (trans. and introd. by Barbara Heldt Monter [Ann Arbor, MI: Ardis, 1978], p. 8: "As is well known, a girl of the highest circles cannot be without an English-woman. In our society we do not speak English, our ladies generally read English novels in French translations, and Shakespeare and Byron are completely beyond their reach, but if your sixteen-year-old daughter speaks otherwise than in English she is badly educated. It often follows that the mother, not as well-educated as her daughter, has trouble talking to her, but this inconvenience is of slight importance. A child needs an English nurse more than a mother." Pavlova could justly be called the "Jane Austen of Russia."

15. Mandel'shtam, "Otets" ("Father"), in *Tret'ia kniga*, comp. by Iu.L. Freidin (Moscow: Agraf, 2006), p. 456. This book contains material not in her first two autobiographies (*Hope Against Hope* and *Hope Abandoned*, 1970 and 1972 respectively), including material about her childhood.

16. Chertkova, *Iz moego detstva. Vospominaniia A. K. Chertkovoi* (Moscow: I. N. Kushnerev and Co., 1911), p. 161; Glinka, "Zapiski," *RS*, April 1870, Vol. I, No. 4, p. 384; Vodovozova, *Na zare zhizni*, ed. and annot. by E.S. Vilenskaia and L.I. Roitberg, 2nd ed. (Moscow: Khudozhestvennaia literatura,1964), I, pp. 89ff; Shklovskii, "Zhili-byli" in *Sobranie sochinenii v trekh tomakh*, Vol. I: *Povesti. Rasskazy* (Moscow: Khudozhestvennaia literatura, 1973), p. 22; Mariia Beketova, *Al. Blok i ego mat': vospominaniia i zametki* (Leningrad: "Petrograd," 1925), p. 29 (Beketova was Blok's aunt); Vera Panova, *O moei zhizni, knigakh i chitateliakh* (Leningrad: Lenizdat, 1975), chap. 4; L'vov, *Vospominaniia*, p. 90; Tat'iana Kuzminskaia (née Bers), *Moia zhizn' doma i v iasnoi poliane: Vospominaniia* (Moscow: Pravda, 1986), p. 53. There is an English translation: *Tolstoy as I Knew Him: My Life at Home and at Yasnaya Polyana* (New York: The Macmillan Company, 1948). Kuzminskaia was Leo Tolstoi's sister-in-law, the likely original of Natasha Rostova in *War and Peace*.

17. Vrangel', *Dalekoe proshloe: Otryvki iz rasskazov moei materi* (Paris, 1934), pp. 71-72.

18. Vishniakov, *Svedeniia o kupecheskom rode Vishniakovykh (1762-1847 gg.)* (Moscow: G. Lissner and A. Geshel', 1905), Part 2, pp. 148, 158. For Lazhechnikov and Volkova, see endnote 21 below.

19. Pushkareva, *Chastnaia zhizn'*, p. 229.

20. Konechnyi, "Byt peterburgskogo kupechestva," in *Peterburgskoe kupechestvo v XIX veke*, comp. and annot. by Konechnyi (St. Petersburg: Giperion, 2003), p. 14.

21. Cf. Ivan Lazhechnikov's autobiography quoted by S. Vengerov in his "Kritiko-biograficheskii ocherk," in Lazhechnikov, *Sobranie sochinenii*, Vol. I (Moscow: Mozhaisk-Terra, 1994), p. 17; Ekaterina Andreeva-Bal'mont, *Vospominaniia* (Moscow: Sabashnikov Publishing, 1997), pp. 15, 31ff; Valerii Briusov, *Iz moei zhizni: Moia iunost'. Pamiati* (Moscow: M. and S. Sabashnikov, 1927), p. 13; Mikhail Sabashnikov, *Vospominaniia* (Moscow: "Kniga," 1983), pp. 50ff; Pëtr Shchukin, *Vospominaniia P. I. Shchukina*, Moscow: Sinodal Press, 1911), p. 11; Dmitrii [Abrikosov], *Revelations of a Russian Diplomat: The Memoirs of Dmitrii I. Abrikossow* (Seattle: University of Washington Press, 1964), pp. 3ff; Anna Volkova (née Vishniakova), *Vospominaniia, dnevnik i stat'i* (Nizhnii Novogorod: Nizhegorodskoe Pechatnoe Delo, 1913), pp. 7-10; Andrei Belyi, *Na rubezhe dvukh stoletii*, prep. and annot. by A. V. Lavrov (Moscow: Khudozhestvennaia literatura, 1989), pp. 100, 181-85, 484 n1.

22. Ivan Goncharov, "Na rodine," (fictionalized autobiography) in *Sobranie sochinenii* 1980, p. 267; Nikolai Rusanov, *Iz moikh vospominanii*,

Book 1 (Berlin: Z.I. Grzhebin, 1923), pp. 9, 53; Nikolai Leikin, *Moi vospominaniia//Nikolai Aleksandrovich Leikin v ego vospominaniiakh i perepiske* (St. Petersburg: T-vo R. Golike and A. Vil'borg, 1907), pp. 10, 12; Dmitrii Likhachev, *Izbrannoe: Vospominaniia*, 2nd rev. ed. (St. Petersburg: Logos, 1997), p. 37; Panova, *O moei zhizni*, p. 10; Mikhail P. Chekhov,"Ob A. P. Chekhove. Vospominaniia M. P. Chekhova," *Rampa i zhizn'*, 1 July 1912, No. 27, p. 2, and idem., "Biograficheskii ocherk. (1860-1887)," in *Pis'ma A. P. Chekhova*. Vol. 1: 1876-1887 (Moscow: M. P. Chekhova/I. D. Sytin, 1912), p. xiii; Ivan Shmelëv, "Kak ia stal pisatelem," in *Sobranie sochinenii*, Vol. II: *V"ezd v Parizh: Rasskazy. Vospominaniia. Publitsistika* (Moscow: Russkaia kniga, 1998), p. 296; Osip Mandel'shtam, *Shum vremeni*, annot. by A. A. Morozov, prep. by S. V. Vaselenko and Morozov (Moscow: Vagrius, 2002), pp. 28-29.

23. Boris Pasternak, *Liudi i polozheniia: Avtobiograficheskii ocherk*, in *Polnoe sobranie sochinenii s prilozheniiami v odinnadtsati tomakh*, Vol. III (Moscow: Slovo, 2004), p. 296; Lev Deich, *Za polveka* (Cambridge, MA: Oriental Research Partners, 1975), pp. 11-12; Martov (Iulii Tsederbaum), *Zapiski sotsial-demokrata* (Cambridge, MA: Oriental Research Partners, 1975), pp. 13, 17; Leon Trotsky (Bronshtein), *My Life* (New York: Grosset & Dunlap, 1960), passim; Ben Wexler, *One Small Russian Jew: An Historical Autobiography* (Lauderdale-by-the-Sea, FL: Phantom Books, 1991), pp. 4, 17, 31, 70, 127-29. Manya Harari, the translator of Pasternak's most famous work and the daughter of a Russian-Jewish banker, talks about her own nannies as well (*Memoirs: 1906-1969* [London: Harvill Press, 1972], p. 13).

An 1820 regulation forbade the hiring of Christian servants in Jewish homes, a law apparently observed in the breach, as the Senate reiterated the ban in 1910. See ChaeRan Y. Freeze, *Jewish Marriage and Divorce in Imperial Russia* (Hanover, NH: Brandeis University Press/University Press of New England, 2002), pp. 67-68. Cf. Angela Rustemeyer, *Dienstboten in Petersburg und Moskau 1861-1917: Hintergrund, Alltag, Soziale Rolle* (Stuttgart, Germany: Franz Steiner Verlag, 1996), p. 60, who differs from Freeze, however, on whether the discriminatory articles were dropped in 1861.

Marietta Shaginian noted that the situation was similar for her own ethnic group, the Armenians, for whom Russian wet-nurses and nannies were a link to the Russian language and all things Russian. See both her "Avtobiografiia" in *Sem'ia Ul'ianovykh. Ocherki. Stat'i. Vospominaniia* (Moscow: Khudozhestvennaia literatura, 1959), p. 642, and *Chelovek i vremia: Istoriia chelovecheskogo stanovleniia* (Moscow: Khudozhestvennaia literatura, 1980), p. 67.

24. Thus, the offspring of doctors and dentists (Dostoevskii, Nikolai Astrov, the actor Igor' Il'inskii), professors (Ivan Snegirev, himself a professor), engineers (the historian Dmitrii Likhachev), priests (another historian, Sergei Solov'ëv; the zemstvo doctor Savvatii Sychugov; and the radical critic Nikolai Dobroliubov), theater people (the ballet superstar Galina Ulanova), and even factory workers (Aleksandr Miliukov) have all discussed their nannies. See Astrov, *Vospominaniia*, Vol. 1 (Paris: YMCA Press, 1941), pp. 20-22 and passim; Il'inskii, *Sam o sebe* (Moscow: Iskusstvo, 1973), pp. 11-12; "Vospominaniia I. M. Snegireva," *RA*, 1905, No. 5, pp. 10-11; Likhachev, *Izbrannoe*, pp. 37ff; Solov'ëv, *Izbrannye trudy. Zapiski*, ed. by A. A. Levandovskii and N. I. Tsimbaev (Moscow: Moscow University Press, 1983), pp. 229ff; Sychugov, *Zapiski bursaka*, ed. and annot. by S. Ia. Shtraikh (Moscow: Academia, 1933), pp. 34-36, 40-41; *Pervoe polnoe sobranie sochinenii N.A. Dobroliubova v chetyrekh tomakh* (St. Petersburg: A.S. Panafidina, 1911), Vol. I, pp. 54-55, 69, 79 and 79n1, 103, 128-29, 136, 138-39, and 353; Ulanova, *Ia ne khotela tantsevat'*, comp. by Saniia Davlekamova (Moscow: AST-Press SKD, 2005), p. 7; Miliukov, *Dobroe staroe vremia (ocherki bylago)* (St. Petersburg: A. F. Bazunov, 1872), pp. 22-23, 29, 82.

25. Nikolai Levakovskii, "Vospominaniia N. Levakovskago," *RS*, October 1907, No. 10, p. 128 (italics added); Skabichevskii, "Iz vospominanii o perezhitom," in *Literaturnye vospominaniia* (Moscow: Agraf, 2001), pp. 48-49.

26. Valentina Dmitrieva, *Tak bylo. Put' moei zhizni* (Moscow: Molodaia gvardiia, 1930), p. 24; I.I. Shangina, et al., eds., *Russkie deti: Osnovy narodnoi pedagogiki. Illiustrirovannaia entsiklopediia* (St. Petersburg: Iskusstvo-SPB, 2006), p. 8; cf. the articles "sister" (*sestra*), p. 338, and "caretaker" (*pestun'ia*), pp. 263-65.

On rarer occasions village boys were male nannies within their own families. The serf-born Aleksandr Nikitenko, who rose to become a professor and a government censor, is a good example. See "Povest' o samom sebe. Posmertnyia zapiski i dnevnik akademika i professora Aleksandra Vasil'evicha Nikitenko," *RS*, August 1888, Vol. 59, No. 8, pp. 305-341.

27. Tyrkova-Vil'iams, *To, chego bol'she ne budet: vospominaniia izvestnoi pisatel'nitsy i obshchestvenoi deiatel'nitsy A. V. Tyrkovoi-Vil'iams (1869-1962)*, ed. by Diana Tevekelian (Moscow: Slovo, 1998), pp. 63-64. Virtually the same dismal picture of peasant caretakers of their own children was painted by Ol'ga Semenova-Tian-Shanskaia in her classic "Zhizn' 'Ivana': Ocherki iz byta krest'ian odnoi iz chernozemnykh gubernii." See the excerpts in *"A se grekhi zlye, smertnye...: Russkaia*

semeinaia i seksual'naia kul'tura glazami istorikov, etnografov, literatorov, fol'kloristov, pravovedov i bogoslovov XIX-nachala XX veka, Vol. 1, comp. and ed. by N. L. Pushkareva and L. V. Bessmertnykh (Moscow: Ladomir, 2004), pp. 651, 653, 654.

28. Kanatchikov, *Iz istorii moego bytiia*, Vol. I (Moscow: "Zemlia i fabrika," 1929), p. 3. Italics added.

29. Dmitrieva, *Tak bylo*, pp. 14, 18, 22-24.

30. "Vospominaniia Ekateriny Ivanovny Raevskoi," *Istoricheskii vestnik* [hereafter, *IV*], December 1898, Vol. 74, No. 12, p. 944.

31. Vladimir Taneev, *Detstvo. Iunost'. Mysli o budushchem* (Moscow: Izdatel'stvo AN SSSR, 1959), p. 56.

32. Any male who still had a nanny beyond 7 was liable to be thought the equivalent of "a momma's boy." It is thus spot-on when, to insult a *gimnaziia* student, his classmates tease this "simpleton" (the title character in an Aleksei Pisemskii short story) by saying that he still sleeps with his nanny. See Pisemskii, "Tiufiak," in *Izbrannye proizvedeniia* (Leningrad-Moscow: Khudozhestvennaia literatura, 1932), pp. 40-41. An English language version exists: A. Pisemsky, *The Simpleton*, translator unnamed (Westport, CT: Hyperion Press, Inc., 1977; being a reprint of the 1959 Foreign Languages Publishing House, Moscow, ed.).

33. Among the few exceptions I have found to this nearly universal rule is Anna Zhukova (1869-1954), a doctor and pedologist. She and her two sisters slept in one room with their nanny, who happened to be their father's aunt. Finding their room filthy, the father exploded at the nanny, who packed her things to leave. "She was very querulous, and we watched her preparations without caring." See Anna Bek (née Zhukova), *The Life of a Russian Woman Doctor: A Siberian Memoir, 1869-1954*, trans. and ed. by Anne D. Rassweiler (Bloomington: Indiana University Press, 2004), p. 23.

34. This fact was not to the liking of some ultra-conservatives. As the publicist Iosif Kolyshko (1861-1938) wrote late in the nineteenth century: "to love someone else's children, to show them affection, to minister to their little hurts [*vrachevat' ikh boboshki*] – this is the business of nannies. But nannies in our schools is not the thing. What a pity!

"It seems to me that it would be much, much better in bringing up [*vospityvat'sia*] our children – and their world would be much purer – if their *vospitanie* were entrusted [only] to women up to a certain age (13-14)." See his "Utility of Love" in *Malen'kiia mysli. 1898-1899 g.g.* (St. Petersburg: Prince V. P. Meshcherskii, 1900), p. 252.

35. Charykov, *Glimpses of High Politics: Through War & Peace 1855-1929: The Autobiography of N. V. Tcharykow, Serf-Owner, Ambassador, Exile* (London: George Allen & Unwin Ltd., 1931), p. 29.

36. I'd read many autobiographies filled with such figures before reading Nikolai Leskov's 1864 novel *No Exit* (Nekuda) and having a small "Eureka!" moment. The fifth chapter of book three is entitled "Duenna."

37. Alliluyeva [Allilueva], *20 Letters to a Friend*, trans. by Priscilla Johnson (London: Hutchinson, 1967), pp. 234-35.

38. Likhachev, *Izbrannoe*, pp. 37ff; Avilova, "A.P. Chekhov v moei zhizni," in *A. P. Chekhov v vospominaniiakh sovremennikov* (Moscow: Khudozhestvennaia literatura, 1960), p. 202.

39. Figner, *Zapechatlennyi trud. Vospominaniia v dvukh tomakh*, Vol. I (Moscow: Mysl', 1964), p. 59; Miroliubov, *Sakral'noe Rusi* (Moscow: ADE "Zolotoi Vek," 1996), Vol. I, p. ii.

40. Eugenie Fraser, *The House by the Dvina: A Russian-Scottish Childhood* (New York: Walker and Company, 1984), p. 97.

41. "Vospominaniia Anny Koz'minichny Lelong," *RA*, 1913, No. 6, pp. 785-86.

42. Dobuzhinskii, *Vospominaniia*, Vol. 1, comp. and ed. by Evgenii Klimov with the aid of Dobuzhinskii's two sons (New York: Put' zhizni, St. Seraphim Foundation, Inc., 1976), p. 316.

43. Among memoirists whose family nannies moved on to become housekeepers: Natal'ia Tuchkova-Ogareva (1829-1913), Ariadna Tyrkova-Vil'iams (1869-1962), Vsevolod Rozhdestvenskii (1895-1977), and Irina Malina (1906-1995?). In literature one finds this the case with Pelageia Evgrafovna in Pisemskii's *Thousand Souls*.

44. Findeizen, *Iz moikh vospominanii* (St. Petersburg:Rossiiskaia natsional'naia biblioteka, 2004), p. 67. This volume is issue 8 of *Rukopisnye pamiatniki*.

45. Orlitskii [pseud. of Okreits], *Dalekie gody: Avtobiograficheskaia khronika* (St. Petersburg: Glavnoe upravlenie udelov, 1899), p. 22.

46. Miroliubov, *Sakral'noe Rusi*, I, p. ii.

47. Unkovskaia, *Vospominaniia* (Petrograd: B.M. Vol'f, 1917), pp. 201-202.

48. Cf. N.A. Ivanovo, "Sotsial'no-demograficheskaia situatsiia," in A.N. Sakharov et al., *Rossiia v nachale XX veka* (Moscow: Novyi khronograf, 2002), pp. 76-78. In the nineteenth and early twentieth centuries, Russia had one of the highest birthrates in the world, higher in the countryside

than in the city. Up to the age of 40, the mortality rate for women exceeded that for men, whereas at older ages the situation for the genders was the reverse. For more information on female mortality in the nineteenth century, see Ludvig B. Besser and K. Ballod, *Smertnost', vozrastnoi sostav i dolgovechnost' pravoslavnago narodonaseleniia oboego pola v Rossii za 1851-1890 gody* (St. Petersburg: Academy of Sciences, 1897), p. 57 and large Table 2 at end of book.

It is a matter of minor interest that rural birthrates should be higher than urban ones; village women would have practically all breastfed their own children and thus should have reduced their fertility compared to gentry women, who overwhelmingly employed wet-nurses. Clearly other factors outweighed the contraceptive effects of nursing. Cf. P.W. Howie and A.S. McNeilly, "Effect of breastfeeding patterns on human birth intervals," *Journal of Reproduction and Fertility*, July 1982, Vol. 65, No. 2, pp. 545-57.

49. See Simon Szreter, *Fertility, Class and Gender in Britain, 1860-1940* (Cambridge: Cambridge University Press, 1996), pp. 294-96; Hans-Georg Müller et al., "Fertility and Life Span: Late Children Enhance Female Longevity," *Journal of Gerontology*, 2002, Vol. 57A, No. 5, pp. B202-B206.

50. See S. W. Jackman with Berangere Steel, eds., *Romanov Relations: the Private Correspondence of Tsars Alexander I, Nicholas I and The Grand Dukes Constantine and Michael with their Sister Queen Anna Pavlovna 1817-1855* (London: Macmillan and Co., Ltd., 1969), pp. 193-94, 249-51.

51. Nikolai Davydov, *Iz proshlago*, Vol. II (Moscow: Pechatnik Press, 1917), p. 16.

    The best-known example of the plight of an older nanny is probably the elderly Anfisa in Chekhov's *Three Sisters*. Still loved and protected by eldest sister Ol'ga, the poor old woman is hounded by the grasping *parvenu* Natasha. See Chapter 8.

52. Z. D. "Vospominanie iz detstva A. S. Pushkina," in *Kniga vospominanii o Pushkine*, ed. by Mstislav Tsiavlovskii (Moscow: Mir, 1931), p. 24; Malevskii-Malevich, "Iz vospominanii," *RA*, May 1908, Bk. 2, No. 5, p. 98; "Iz vospominanii Baronessy M. P. Frederiksa," *IV*, January 1898, Vol. 71, No. 1, p. 67n5. Frederiks's nanny received a pension.

53. See Shchepkina-Kupernik, *Nezametnye liudi* (Unnoticed People – a felicitous title), 2nd ed. (Moscow: D. P. Efimov, 1901), "Eyewitnesses of life: Efimych, A Drama with a Nanny" (*Svideteli zhizni: Efimych, Nian'kina drama*], pp. 278-351; Militsyna,"Nian'ka" in *Razskazy* (Moscow: A.I. Snegireva, 1905), pp. 191-200.

To see the difference between mere competent storytelling and a master psychologist, compare both of these authors with Nadezhda Tèffi's treatments of the same theme (what to do with old servants when the nanny's nurseling has grown or they can no longer serve) in "And Time Ran Out..." (*I vremeni ne stalo...*) in *Zemnaia raduga* (New York: Chekhov Publishing House, 1952), p. 76 especially; and in such stories as "The Quiet Factory" (*Tikhaia zavod'*) and "A Serf Soul" (*Krepostnaia dusha*) in *Tikhaia zavod'* (Paris: Zemgor, 1921), pp. 5-13 and pp. 49-55 respectively. Tèffi never reaches for bathos; she is more matter-of-fact – but still touching – about old people in general, not just former servants.

54. *Dnevnik pisatelia za 1876*, p. 20.

55. Nathalie Majolier [Mamontova], *Step-Daughter of Imperial Russia* (London: Stanley Paul & Co., Ltd., 1940), pp. 14-15, 123-24.

56. Dobuzhinskii, *Vospominaniia*, ed. by G. I. Chugunov (Moscow: Nauka, 1987), pp. 368-69, n5; Dobuzhinskii, *Pis'ma*, comp. and annot. by Chugunov (Moscow: "Dmitrii Bulanin," 2001), pp. 114 (letter of May 1911), 215, 221, 227 (letters of 1928-29), and 330, letter 28, n2; *Literaturnoe nasledstvo: Gertsen i Ogarev I*, Vol. 61 (Moscow: AN SSSR, 1953), p. 326 (letter of 1852) and 326, n1 to letter 26; A. N. Dubovikov, "Pis'ma E. I. Gertsena," *Literaturnoe nasledstvo*, Vol. 63 (Moscow: AN SSSR, 1956), pp. 422, 427-28; Blok, "Avtobiografiia," *Sobranie sochinenii v vos'mi tomakh*, Vol. 7 (Leningrad: Khudozhestvennaia literatura, 1963), pp. 80; 476 nn 25, 27; 162; and 246 (diary entries for 1911-1913; Beketova, *Al. Blok i ego mat'*, pp. 28-29; L'vov, *Vospominaniia*, p. 90.

Yet even a beloved nanny like Blok's could end up poorly. After his death, widowed, she went completely blind; she had no children. One of Blok's aunts "placed her in an almshouse." "At present [early 1920s] she is in an almshouse near Smolny. Her life, of course, was very sad, the more so that people rarely visit her due to the great distance," wrote another aunt (Beketova, *ibid.*).

57. Vrangel', *Dalekoe proshloe*, p. 36. Do all the details reveal a guilty conscience?

58. Zhelikhovskaia, *Kak ia byla malen'koi. Iz vospominanii ranniago detstva V. P. Zhelikhovskoi*, 2nd rev. and enl. ed. (St. Petersburg: A. F. Devrien, 1894), pp. 47-48.

59. Andreev[a], *Cold Spring in Russia*, trans. by Michael Carlisle (Ann Arbor, MI: Ardis, 1978), p. 27.

60. As A. O. Konstantinov and M. V. Stroganov note in their commentary

on the term *"starushka"* in *Evgenii Onegin*, a woman not even 40 but occupied with running a household, who lived in the country, was a widow, and with a daughter of marriageable age could easily be called a *"starushka."* Onegin talks of Tat'iana's mother thus in Chapter 3, IV, 11-12. The term has a nuance of kindly irony. As opposed to the word *"starukha"* (which is not used at all in *EO*), *"starushka"* carries no indication of the age of someone like Praskov'ia Larina. Stroganov, ed., *Roman A. S. Pushkina «Evgenii Onegin»: Materialy k entsiklopedii*, Vol. 2 (Tver: Tver State University, 2002), p. 160.

61. Dmitrii Obolenskii [Obolensky], *Bread of Exile: A Russian Family*, trans. by Harry Willetts (London: Harvill Press, 1999), p. 197; Figner, *Zapechatlennyi trud*, Vol. I, p. 55; Russell interview in Anna Horsbrugh-Porter, ed., *Memories of Revolution: Russian Women Remember*, interviews by Frances Welch and Elena Snow (London: Routledge, 1993), p. 41.

62. Ossorgin [sic], *My Sister's Story* (New York: The Dial Press, 1931), p. 38.

63. Gippius, "Avtobiograficheskaia zametka," in S.A. Vengerov, ed., *Russkaia literatura XX veka*, Vol. I (Moscow: Mir, 1914) as reprinted in *Slavische Propyläen*, Vol. 115 (Munich: Wilhelm Fink Verlag, 1972), p. 174.

64. Cf. the analysis of Bakhtin's view of peasant (or "folkloric") time in *The Dialogic Imagination*, pp. 207-210; also, Eviatar Zerubavel, *Time Maps: Collective Memory and the Social Shape of the Past* (Chicago: University of Chicago Press, 2003), Chapter 1 and passim; Chris J. Chulos, *Converging Worlds: Religion and Community in Peasant Russia, 1861-1917* (DeKalb: Northern Illinois University Press, 2003), Chapter 2: "Telling Time."

65. Dolgorukov, *Kapishche moego serdtsa*, p. 63.

66. I've looked for some note of this in, e.g., Geroid T. Robinson, *Rural Russia Under the Old Regime* (New York: Macmillan, 1949); Jerome Blum, *Lord and Peasant in Russia* (Princeton, NJ: Princeton University Press, 1961), who does say, however, that some masters made periodic distributions of clothing, food, and small amounts of cash to their *dvorovye liudi* [p. 457]; Kolchin, *Unfree Labor*, though he does discuss wages for runaway serfs assigned to Urals factories on pp. 310-312; and Richard Stites, *Serfdom, Society, and the Arts in Imperial Russia: The Pleasure and the Power* (New Haven: Yale University Press, 2005). It is not to be found either in Mironov's magnum opus: *Sotsial'naia istoriia Rossii*, but he, like Blum, does make passing reference to *dvorovye* receiving monthly money payments (not calling them wages) in his more recent *Blagosostoianie naseleniia i revoliutsii v imperskoi Rossii: XVIII-nachalo XX veka* (Moscow: Novyi Khronograf, 2010), p. 276. It's telling that the latter work's index

has no subheading for *dvorovye* under the topic of wages (*zarplaty*).

The best sources by far on the subject of wages and salaries for serfs – employed outside the manorial estate ("off-campus" as it were) – are Kahan, *The Plow*, pp. 59-61, 68-69, 79, 124-28, 138-41, 290-93, and especially 144-55; and Mironov, *Blagosostoianie*, Chapter 10. Kahan says nothing about salaried *dvorovye* (and in fact may misuse this word by referring to household members of field-peasant families by the term).

Serfs on *obrok* (quitrent) but others as well were hired out to work in transportation, the textile industry (mostly women), construction, mining, crop harvesting, and many other industries. Serfowners eager to have skilled and literate workers available for their own use or for outside hire encouraged their peasants to improve themselves in many ways.

67. See, for example, "Vospominaniia Eleny Iur'evny Khvoshchinskoi. (Rozhdennoi Kniazhny Golitsynoi)," *RS*, May 1897, No. 5, p. 369. She notes that this was not the rule among *pomeshchiki*. It might well have been the case that the practice occurred mostly on the wealthier estates, but it could be found among the middling gentry as well.

I.M. Kabeshtov says that in the 1840s the *dvorovye liudi* (household serfs) of Prince Sergei Volkonskii – like his mother and he – received the following compensation monthly: two poods of rye flour, one pood of groats, and one ruble cash. See his *Moia zhizn' i vospominaniia* (Sumy: K.M. Pashkov, 1906), p. 15.

Evidence of salaried serfs in a less wealthy gentry family may be found in Katherine Pickering Antonova, *Importance of the Woman of the House: Portrait of a Russian Gentry Family, 1830-1866* (forthcoming from Oxford, fall 2012), chapter 3; and Sergei Antonov has found several references to serfs being paid cash wages in the Tsentral'nyi istoricheskii arkhiv Mosvkvy (TsIAM) fonds 49 and 50 (personal communication, 26 November 2011).

68. N.A. Leikin, *Moi vospominaniia*, pp.10, 12.

69. *Zapiski N. F. Bunakova. Moia zhizn', v sviazi s obshcherusskoi zhizn'iu, preimushchestvenno provintsial'noi. 1837-1905* (St. Petersburg: Obshchestvennaia pol'za, 1909), p. 5.

70. See Taneev, *Detstvo*, p. 56; Novoselova, "Vospominaniia 50-kh godov. Pamiati ottsa," *RS*, October 1911, Vol. 148, No. 10, p. 99.

71. Andrei Dostoevskii, "Iz 'Vospominanii'," in *F. M. Dostoevskii v vospominaniiakh sovremennikov*, vol. I (Moscow: Khudozhestvennaia literatura, 1964), p. 42 ; Bibikov, "Niania," *Russkaia beseda*, 1856, II, p. 72.

72. Figner, *Zapechatlennyi trud.* I, pp. 61-62; Liudmila Shelgunova, *Iz dalekogo proshlogo,* in vol. II of N.V. Shelgunov, M.I. Mikhailov, and Shelgunova, *Vospominaniia v dvukh tomakh* (Moscow: Khudozhestvennaia literatura, 1967), p. 184.

73. Assignat rubles were issued from 1769 until 1843. Their value fell continuously throughout this period, from being equal to the silver coin ruble when they first appeared to a third of a coin ruble in 1810 (and not much more than a quarter silver ruble from 1811-1842). See Thomas C. Owen, "A Standard Ruble of Account for Russian Business History, 1769-1914: A Note," *The Journal of Economic History,* Vol. 49, No. 3 (Sept. 1989), Table 2, p. 704.

74. Berggol'ts, *Dnevnye zvezdy* (Moscow: Sovremennik, 1975), pp. 80-81.

75. Astrov, *Vospominaniia,* I, p. 36. Astrov (1868-1934), a political activist and member of the Russian Duma before World War I, died in emigration, in Prague.

76. Cf. A. N. Kupreianova, "Iz semeinykh vospominanii," *Bogoslovskii vestnik* [hereafter, *BV*], April 1914, Vol. 1, No. 4, pp. 661-62; Vrangel', *Dalekoe proshloe,* p. 36.

77. Cf. Wachtel, *Battle for Childhood,* pp. 111-14.

78. "Vospominaniia Grigoriia Ivanovicha Filipsona," *RA,* 1883, Bk. 3, No. 5, p. 77.

79. Tolstoi, *Polnoe sobranie sochinenii* [hereafter, *PSS*], Vol. 5 (M-L: Khudozhestvennaia literatura, 1931), pp. 241-58, but especially p. 255 (letter to Count Sergei Bludov).

80. Tsebrikova, "Stranitsa k istorii nashego zhenskago domashniago vospitaniia v nedavniuiu starinu," *Russkaia shkola,* July/August 1893, Nos. 7/8, p. 37.

81. *Na zare zhizni,* I, p. 92.

82. Ziloti, *V dome Tret'iakova* (New York, 1954), p. 17. In later years, the nanny returned to visit the family and brought her daughter Sasha with her; perhaps to compensate for the past and somehow soothe her conscience, Vera Ziloti's mother paid for Sasha to attend high school.

83. Bibikov, "Niania," p. 69. This sketch may be fictionalized.

84. Olitskaia, *Moi vospominaniia* (Frankfurt/Main: Possev-Verlag, 1971), Vol. I, pp. 15-16. She grew up just at the turn of the century.

85. Bal'mont, *Avtobiograficheskaia proza* (Moscow: Algoritm, 2001), p. 80; the preceding quote is from p. 38.

86. On post-emancipation nannies, see Chapter 6.

Chapter Four

1. These limits force me to exclude more ink spilt on nannies in the royal household, about many of whom there are fascinating stories to tell, but who, after 1800, were overwhelmingly foreign-born. We know many details, for instance, about the nannies of Alexander II, Alexander III, and Aleksei Nikolaevich (who survived the family massacre in 1918, but whose *diad'ka* did not). Cf. Charlotte Zeepvat, *From Cradle to Crown: British Nannies and Governesses at the World's Royal Courts* (Phoenix Mill, England: Sutton Publishing Ltd., 2006).

2. Since this chapter deals with "real-life" nannies for the most part, I postpone detailed discussion of literary and cultural stereotypes and symbolism for a later time.

3. Tovrov, *The Russian Noble Family*, pp. 82-83, 152-57, 167, 193-99, 206, 303, 362f; Rustemeyer, *Dienstboten*, passim; Pushkareva, "Mat' i ditia v russkoi sem'e XVIII-nachala XIX veka," *Sotsial'naia istoriia: Ezhegodnik 1997* (Moscow: ROSSPEN, 1998), pp. 227-39; eadem, "Materinstvo i materinskoe vospitanie v Rossiiskikh sem'iakh XVIII-nachala XIX v.," in *Rasy i narody: Ezhegodnik*, 1998, vol. 25, p. 112; eadem, *Chastnaia zhizn'*, pp. 89, 200-229; Roosevelt, *Life*, pp. 102-04, 178-79, 278; Figes, *Natasha's Dance: A Cultural History of Russia* (New York: Henry Holt and Company, 2002), pp. 118-129.

Rustemeyer (p. 39) says "The nanny is an absolutely mythical figure among Russian servants, a target for sentimentality of many generations of gentry masters.... It would be incautious to draw conclusions about reality from the glorified picture of nannies in memoirs." I disagree; she has not looked at enough memoirs.

Figes (p. 125) rightly calls his nanny portrait a stereotype, but then seems to endorse much of it, and concludes with the mildly erroneous assertion: "More than a surrogate mother, the nanny was the child's main source of love and emotional security."

My disagreements with Rustemeyer and Figes are not great, however. She is objecting to anyone's trying to prove the validity of the mythical, sentimental image of the nanny from the writings of the masters. He does not fully subscribe to the stereotype.

Another author who gets it partly wrong – through generalization and simplification – about nannies is Wachtel in his *Battle for Childhood*, p. 106.

4. Irina Elenevskaia, *Vospominaniia* (Belgium: A. Rosseels Printing Co., [1968]), p. 8; Evgenii Trubetskoi, *Iz proshlago* (Vienna, 1920), pp. 24, 61. Still a different picture of a typical nanny is presented in a literary sketch (by an unknown author) in the early 1840s. In this view, virtually all nannies were serfs and older than forty (not true), thin (far from true!), wore only calico dresses, rarely got away from the house, were models of love and devotion, and so on. See "Niania" in *Russkii ocherk: 40–50-e gody XIX veka*, comp., ed., and annot. by V.I. Kuleshov (Moscow: Izdatel'stvo moskovskogo universiteta, 1986), pp. 61-70; here, pp. 60, 66.

5. A good illustration of a family's mixed feelings about pre-1861 nannies *but from a nonnoble milieu* is the correspondence between Nikolai Dobroliubov (1836-1861), the "radical democrat," and his parents in the early 1850s. See *Pervoe polnoe sobranie*, I, pp. 54-55, 79n1, 128-29, 136, 138-39.

6. [Toll'], "O nian'kakh," *Zhurnal dlia vospitaniia*, March 1858, No. 3, pp. 443-63. Page references appear in parentheses in the body of the text. Toll's life was remarkably parallel to Dostoevskii's.

7. An anonymous reviewer was in close agreement with all Toll's major arguments and the indictment of most peasant nannies. This issue of nannies, he says, "has for us still a special, national significance: our nannies, taken for the most part from the serf estate, comprise a purely Russian phenomenon, a Russian type, having nothing in common with the *bonnes* and *Wärterinn* found abroad," a patently absurd claim. "Our nannies bring to *vospitanie* their own particular element: ...they look on their nurselings with servility, as on their future masters, and thus the nanny's relationships with the small lord, with his parents, with the servants are made still more complicated, ill-defined, and senseless." The "undefined" nature of nanny-nurseling relations "has a fatal effect on the moral sense of the child: he learns to order the nanny about and from the youngest years is nourished with the spirit of *barstvo* [lording it over others]..." (unsigned review, *Razsvet, zhurnal nauk, iskusstv i literatury dlia vzroslykh devits*, Vol. III, July 1859, No. 7, pp. 37-39; here, p. 39).

8. *Poslovitsy russkogo naroda. Sbornik V. Dalia v dvukh tomakh*, Vol. 2 (Moscow: Khudozhestvennaia literatura, 1984), p. 75.

9. Cf. I. I. Illiustrov, *Zhizn' russkogo naroda v ego poslovitsakh i pogovorkakh*, 3rd rev. and enl. ed. (Moscow, 1915), p. 195, endnote 12.

10. Cf. Z. E. Mordvinova's hagiography of Mariia Leont'eva (b. 1792) with its paean to the "patriarchal" intimacy of eighteenth-century

families: "Among the huge household staff which filled the lord's manor house, each person was known and close to the child, and the numerous mammies and nannies [*mamushki i nianiushki*] were held to be like members of the family [*derzhalis' kak chleny sem'i*], which was not at all considered a disgrace in boiar clans. The excellent types of these friends of the children [sic] have now quite disappeared, but a hundred years ago [i.e., ca. 1800] every Russian child reckoned [his] nanny to be a relative [*rodnym chelovekom*] and mothers did not fear to entrust their children to the care of experienced and devoted servants." Mordvinova, *Stats-dama Mariia Pavlovna Leont'eva, Nachal'nitsa Vospitatel'nago Obshchestva Blagorodnykh Devits: Biograficheskii ocherk* (St. Petersburg: Ministry of Internal Affairs, 1902), p. 11.

11. As Nikolai Pomialovskii says in his 1861 novella "Bourgeois Happiness": "...do you not love your old nanny, but does she dare to think about being your equal?" Pomialovskii, "Meshchanskoe schast'e," in *Sochineniia v dvukh tomakh*, Vol. I (Moscow-Leningrad: Khudozhestvennaia literatura, 1965), p. 184.

12. Jessica Tovrov says "few adult noblemen seem to have considered their houseserfs to be part of the family in any important sense" but also believes the Russian nobility became much more intimate with their household staffs than the English did with theirs (*The Russian Noble Family*, pp. 2, 70-73, 78-81, 82-86). She would doubtless agree with Bruce Robbins (*The Servant's Hand: English Fiction from Below* [New York: Columbia University Press, 1986], p. 185) that from about 1800-1850 in England, the servant is not "a member of the family" but is merely "connected" with it.

13. Goncharov, "Slugi starogo veka," *Sobranie sochinenii* 1980, Vol. 7, p. 182.

14. Tolstoi, *PSS*, Vol. 34 (Moscow: Khudozhestvennaia literatura, 1952), p. 374.

15. In a more perfect world, this part of Chapter 4 might have been combined with parts of Chapters 9 and 10. There is no doubt that the "idea" or symbol of the nanny affected how memoirists viewed their nannies.

16. In notes for his *Diary of a Writer*, Dostoevskii mused to himself: "There are absolutely holy people, are these individual cases ([his own] nanny Alena Frolovna) or a quality common to all the people?" *PSS*, Vol. 24: *Dnevnik pisatelia za 1876 god noiabr'-dekabr'* (1982), p. 181.

17. Solov'ëv, *Izbrannye trudy*, p. 229.

Two generations later, another memorable nanny with religious sensibilities – the young peasant woman Tania – came to replace the historian's grandson Sergei's (1885-1942) "fat old nanny." The poet-thinker writes: "She and I even used to have philosophical disputes and misunderstandings. Once I asked her whether God sits, stands, or lies. Firm in her theology, Tania replied that he neither sits, nor stands, nor lies." This response gave him pause; he soon came to the conclusion that God probably "hangs." "…but just how – neither standing nor sitting – would he [i.e., was he able to] hang himself up? Another time I affirmed that my papa was without sin, to which Tania objected: "God knows of your papa's sins, my dear [*moi milyi*]." Solov'ëv, *Vospominaniia* (Moscow: Novoe literaturnoe obozrenie, 2003), p. 81.

18. Passek, *Iz dal'nykh let: Vospominaniia*, Vol. I (Moscow: Khudozhestvennaia literatura, 1963), p. 56. Italics added.

19. Mamaev, "Zapiski," *IV*, January 1901, Vol. 83, No. 1, p. 76.

20. Ekaterina Sushkova (1812-1868), *Zapiski 1812-1841* (Leningrad: Academia, 1928), p. 28.

21. A later example purportedly applicable to the pre-1861 era: "Nanny Annushka was one of those old-time [*starinnye*] servants, who, having no personal life, lived for the interests of their masters and watched over their interests like they were her own. Annushka…would chide mother for not knowing how to keep house and, in her opinion, not looking after her husband well." See Zinaida Zhemchuzhnaia, *Puti izgnaniia: Ural, Kuban', Moskva, Kharbin, Tian'tszin* (Tenafly, NJ: Ermitazh/Hermitage, 1987), p. 8.

22. See, however, Nikolai Astrov, *Vospominaniia*, I, pp. 48f, and F[eliks] T[ol]l', "O nian'kakh," pp. 443-44. Unsurprisingly, the vast majority of memoirists – female and male – paint their mothers in similar colors, as more serious and less fun-loving than their fathers. In a patriarchal society, where women had limited rights and even wife-beating sometimes extended beyond the peasantry and petit bourgeoisie, one would be astonished to find parents portrayed otherwise.

23. The smiling-faced nanny was that of Dmitrii Likhachev (*Izbrannoe*, p. 37). His Katerinushka may still not be a good counter-example, however; this photo is from 1936, not during her years of nannying little Mitia.

For an excellent photo collection of nannies and wet-nurses – all from a late period – see Elena Lavrent'eva and Vladimir Shtul'man, *Detstvo moe…: Deti v russkoi fotografii vtoroi poloviny XIX-nachala XX vv.* (Moscow: Belyi gorod, 2008), pp. 136-49. I'm greatly indebted to Katharina Kucher for sending me scans of these pages.

24. *Zapiski N. F. Bunakova.* p. 5.

25. Rusanov, *Iz moikh vospominanii,* pp. 101-102.

26. Sechenov, *Avtobiograficheskie zapiski Ivana Mikhailovicha Sechenova* (Moscow: Academy of Sciences, 1945), p. 9.

27. During the prolonged emancipation process, one hyperbolically observed: "The women make wonderful nurses [i.e., nursemaids], and I don't suppose any child gets more undivided attention than the little charge of a Russian nurse." Herbert Barry, *Ivan at Home; or, Pictures of Russian Life* (London: The Publishing Company, Ltd., 1872), p. 280.

28. Bunakov, *Zapiski N. F. Bunakova,* p. 5; Vodovozova, *Na zare zhizni,* I, pp. 92f, 131. Cf. the quasi-autobiographical fiction of Bibikov, "Niania," p. 69.

29. Skabichevskii, "Iz vospominanii o perezhitom," in *Literaturnye vospominaniia* (Moscow: Agraf, 2001), pp. 45-47; the quotation is on pp. 48-49. Written almost certainly after 1891, as an autobiographical letter of that date makes it unlikely this account was available then.

30. Vil'gel'm Kiukhel'beker, *Puteshestvie. Dnevnik. Stat'i* (Leningrad: Nauka, 1979), p. 38; Prince S. M. Volkonskii and B. L. Modzalevskii, eds., *Arkhiv dekabrista S. G. Volkonskago,* Vol. I: *Do Sibiri,* part 1 (Petrograd: R. Golike and A. Vil'borg, 1918), pp. xxvii-xxviii; Ol'ga Bulanova-Trubnikova, *Tri pokoleniia* (Moscow-Leningrad, 1928), pp. 5-67 (especially 45-46), 145.

"I was a month and a half old when mother carried me in her arms from Chita, where I was born, to Petrovskii, and 6 years old when the family left the Petrovskii factory; and here is where the best memories of my childhood end," recalls Ol'ga Ivanova (1830-1891), daughter of the Decembrist Ivan Annenkov. "I never had a nanny [*nian'ka*]. The Decembrists rocked, nannied, taught, and raised me [*Menia kachali, nianchili, uchili i vospityvali dekabristy*]." See "Vospominaniia Ol'gi Ivanovny Ivanovoi," in *Vospominaniia Poliny Annenkovoi* (Krasnoiarsk: Krasnoiarsk Book Publishing, 1977), p. 198.

31. Herzen [Gertsen], *Byloe i dumy,* Vol. I (Moscow: Khudozhestvennaia literatura, 1962), p. 59. He may, unconsciously, have tried for the remainder of his life to prove his nanny wrong.

32. *Vospominaniia* (Moscow: Gosizdat Khudozhestvennoi literatury, 1959), pp. 87-95. One suspects almost a slight case of cowardice or at least

moral failure on the part of these upper-class revolutionaries in having the devoted family servant do the dirty work here. But the police would certainly have looked beyond her and arrested the masters had she been found out.

33. M.S. Uglichaninova (ca. 1830-after 1900) is a prime example. Her nanny "almost never showed me any love and treated me coarsely [*grubo*]. In general, this was an unkind woman, or, to put it better, a bad [*vrednyi*] product of serfdom, and her bitterness vented itself on me." When the girl tried to show her nanny affection, "she always pushed me away rudely, calling [me] the masters' spawn." She took pleasure in discussing her own death, to cause her nurseling pain. Uglichaninova, "Vospominaniia vospitannitsy Smol'nago monastyria sorokovykh godov," *Russkii vestnik*, [hereafter, *RV*] September 1900, Vol. 269, No. 9, pp. 144-45. At a much later time, the nanny of Kornei Chukovskii's second son, Boris (b. 1910) was also apparently a "devil." See Chukovskii, *Dnevnik 1901-1969*. Vol. I: 1901-1929 (Moscow: OLMA-PRESS, 2003), p. 57.

34. Natal'ia L. Pushkareva, "Russian Noblewomen's Education in the Home as Revealed in Late 18th- and Early 19th-Century Memoirs," in Rosslyn, ed. *Women and Gender*, p. 113 and p. 125 endnote 18.

35. *Uchrezhdeniia i ustavy kasaiushchiesia do vospitaniia i obucheniia v Rossii iunoshestva oboego pola, vo udovol'stvie Obshchestva*, 2 vols. (St. Petersburg: n.p., 1774); here, Vol. I, pp. 92-94.

36. This is not to say, however, that all peasant serf girls and women were illiterate. There are contrary examples, most often among the serf populations of the largest estates, where males and females were often given extensive vocational training to become artists, artisans, actors, musicians, and so forth. The Stroganovs, Demidovs, and other magnates doubtless had many literate serf girls on their estates. Another classic example, not from among the greatest grandees, is the famous serf harem of Pëtr Alekseevich Koshkarov. Many of these young girls, who serviced the master's sexual and physical needs, were trained to read and write. Most of the serfs in Varvara Turgeneva's household were also literate. On Koshkarov, see "Zapiski Ianuariia Mikhailovicha Neverova. 1810-1826 gg.," *RS*, 1883, Vol. 40, pp. 432ff; on the Turgenevs, Varvara Zhitova, *Vospominaniia o sem'e I. S. Turgeneva* (Tula: Tul'skoe knizhnoe izdatel'stvo, 1961), pp. 41, 63f.

37. Among the few exceptions to the rule: Efimovna, the nanny of A. N. Kupreianova's mother ("Iz semeinykh vospominanii," p. 650; Anna

Lelong's nanny ("Vospominaniia Anny Koz'minichny Lelong," p. 786; and Sergei Solov'ëv's Tania (*Vospominaniia*, p. 81).

38. See Chapter 10.

39. One delightful consequence, for the children, of the nanny's belonging so completely to an oral culture, was her acquired skill as a storyteller, as will be seen in the following chapter.

40. The few examples I've found come from post-1861 autobiographies.

41. "Vospominaniia Grigoriia Ivanovicha Filipsona," p. 80.

42. Aleksandr Ritter, (1790?-1851), *Otzvuki minuvshago (vospominaniia starago pomeshchika)*, 3rd ed. (Moscow: Universitetskaia Tipografiia, 1899), p. 22.

Similar post-1900 scenes show up in Irina Malina, *Ia vspominaiu... (1906-1920)* (St. Peterburg: Petropol', 1995), p. 36 (with a wet-nurse); Horsbrugh-Porter, ed., *Memories of Revolution*, interview of Tatiana Toporkova, p. 14: "I still remember going with my mother to the kitchen to take part in the letter-writing ceremony. Our old nurse was completely illiterate and other neighbouring servants came with their own requests...several women stood in the shadows and dictated in a monotonous voice. It seemed to me that all they did was send endless greetings to all the members of the village commune, each of whom had to be mentioned fully with name and patronymic. I asked my mother why such a dull letter had to be sent, and she explained that it was most important not to forget anyone, otherwise an ignored villager would be terribly hurt and feel insulted." Cf. nearly identical vignettes in Agniia Barto, *Zapiski detskogo poeta* (Moscow: Omega, 2006), p. 125, and Berggol'ts's *Dnevnye zvezdy*, p. 82. But the *pièce de résistance* is the beautifully rendered, hilarious extended scene in a Nadezha Tèffi short story (called "The Wet-nurse" (*Mamka*), in *Chernyi iris: Razskazy* (Stockholm: Severnye ogni, 1921), pp. 59-63, but entitled "The Letter" (*Pis'mo*) in an earlier collection, *Dym bez ognia* (St. Petersburg: Novyi Satirikon, 1914), pp. 21-24.

43. *Melochi iz zapasa moei pamiati*, 2nd enl. ed. (Moscow: Grachev and Company, 1869), p. 17.

44. Nadezhda Ioffe notes that she "never saw such superstitious people as in [Soviet] prison and in the camp" – in exile in the late 1920s; even members of the intelligentsia and some highly educated women started believing completely in omens, fortune telling, and dreams. See Ioffe, *Vremia nazad. Moia zhizn', moia sud'ba, moia epokha* (Moscow: T.O.O. "Biologicheskie nauki," 1992), p.126.

45. On the subject of "superstition" and religion, Vera Shevzov offers valuable insights in *Russian Orthodoxy on the Eve of Revolution* (New York: Oxford University Press, 2004), pp. 19-20, 122, and passim. See also my Chapter 10.

46. Bronislaw Malinowski's *Magic, Science, and Religion* argues that human creativity/self-expression is distinguished by the degree of control man exercises in various activities. Anthropologists like Clifford Geertz and Marshall Sahlins have little use for Malinowski's functionalist approach, but, for all its flaws, it may still offer insights into peasant life, where control is often lacking. For a recent exploration of the problem of "mentalities" in social sciences, see G.E.R. Lloyd, *Demystifying Mentalities* (Cambridge: Cambridge University Press, 1990), in particular the conclusion, pp.135-45. In general, Lloyd sees more difficulties than insights in the work of those trying to ascribe deep, underlying, even determining mindsets to various communities, societies, or peoples.

47. One first-rate recent source on this subject is Marina Vlasova, *Russkie sueveriia: entsiklopedicheskii slovar'* (St. Petersburg: Azbuka, 1998), with an excellent bibliography. But at least a half dozen such works have appeared since 1995, including Linda J. Ivanits's uneven *Russian Folk Belief* (Armonk NY: M.E. Sharpe, Inc., 1989). Of earlier works, I have consulted Ivan Sakharov, *Skazaniia russkogo naroda*, part 1 (1836; re-issued in 1837), parts 1-4 issued as new Vol. 1, 3rd ed. (1841); Vol. 2 (1849); N. Ia. Nikiforovskii, *Prostonarodnyia primety i pover'ia* (1897) and *Predaniia o narodnykh russkikh sueveriiakh, poveriakh i nekotorykh obychaiakh* (Moscow: Sergei Orlov, 1861). Most of the last book was "borrowed" from *Slovar' russkikh sueverii* (1782).

The gathering of folklore and folkways of all kinds was a great cottage industry throughout Europe after about 1700 and well into the 1800s. As in any enterprise of this nature, there must have been a fair amount of "invention" as well as "discovery" in these pioneering works. Not always completely sympathetic toward the peasants, these students of the folk nonetheless took a deep and abiding interest in their way of life, culture, and thinking. Among many works treating this subject, see Rudolf Newhäuser, *Towards the Romantic Age. Essays on Sentimental and Preromantic Literature in Russia* (The Hague: Martinus Nijhoff, 1974), pp. 127-42; and Rogger, *National Consciousness*, Chap. IV. It is clear that the compilers of folk ways and beliefs (including Pushkin) were essentially talking to the same women (and sometimes men) who were or might become nannies.

48. *My Literary and Moral Wanderings and Other Autobiographical Material,*

trans. by Ralph E. Matlaw (New York: E. P. Dutton & Co., Inc., 1962), pp. 17-18.

49. Sabaneeva, *Vospominaniia o bylom 1770-1828 gg.*, in V. M. Bokova, comp., *Istoriia zhizni blagorodnoi zhenshchiny* (Moscow: Novoe literaturnoe obozrenie, 1996), p. 386.

50. Sychugov, *Zapiski bursaka*, pp. 40-41. The daughter-in-law of the great actor Mikhail Shchepkin, Aleksandra Shchepkina (1824-1917) became afraid of the dark/night because of the nannies' deliberate efforts to scare them with stories of dangerous creatures under the bed. *Vospominaniia Aleksandry Vladimirovny Shchepkinoi* (Sergiev Posad: I. I. Ivanov, 1915), p. 3.

51. Kornilova, *Byl' iz vremen krepostnichestva. (Vospominaniia o moei materi i eia okruzhaiushchem)* (St. Petersburg: "Obshchestvennaia Pol'za" Society, 1890), p.133.

52. *Povesti moei zhizni: memuary*, Vol. I (Moscow: Academy of Sciences Press, 1962), pp. 32-35. He notes, however, a more positive aspect to this phenomenon: "To all of my child's fears there adhered a significant portion of curiosity also. Everything out of the ordinary, alien to our real world was thereby of interest and the danger thus alluring!"

53. Passek, *Iz dal'nykh let*, I, pp. 99, 101f.

54. Morozov, *Povesti moei zhizni*, Vol. II, p. 589. Ever the seeker of truth, he later established that this had to be Donati's Comet and thus he was 4 years old at the time (i.e., it was a comet of 1850). Numerous memoirists note the 1812 comet's foreshadowing Napoleon's invasion.

55. Snegirev, "Vospominaniia I. M. Snegireva," *RA*, 1905, No. 5, pp. 10-11. He notes (p. 29) that this same prediction was recalled after the French invade and seize Moscow in 1812.

    Prince Mikhail Shakhovskoi (b. ca. 1847) had good reason to remember the ill omens of his nanny when she told him, in 1869, of a dream that portended bad things from a trip he planned. All she predicted came true. Shakhovskoi, "Original'nyi sluchai," *IV*, April 1900, Vol. 80, No. 4, pp. 156-166.

56. Passek, *Iz dal'nykh let*, I, pp. 99-102.

57. A few might occasionally suffer lapses of sloth (laziness) or wrath (getting angry), but I've come across none accused of lust, gluttony, greed, or envy.

58. Andrei Dostoevskii, "Iz 'Vospominanii'," in *F. M. Dostoevskii*, I, p. 42.

59. Fraser, *House by the Dvina,* p. 97. Shalovchikha died the following spring, in 1906, at around age 104.
60. Mar'ia Kamenskaia, *Vospominaniia* (Moscow: Khudozhestvennaia literatura, 1991), pp. 21-22, 24-26, 98-99.
61. Trubetskoi, *Iz proshlago,* pp. 62, 64, 66.
62. Vereshchagin, *Ocherki, nabroski, vospominaniia V. V. Vereshchagina* (St. Petersburg: Ministry of Communications/A. Benke, 1883), p. 153. The constant thrashings of a hired nanny did not prove as ephemeral for Ekaterina Novoselova (b. 1837), who says "I believe that this left on my character a kind of reserve and keeping to myself." See her "Vospominaniia 50-kh godov," p. 99.
63. Davydov, *Iz proshlago,* Vol. I, 2nd ed. (Moscow: I. D. Sytin Press, 1914), p. 7; Shchepkina, *Vospominaniia,* p. 3.
64. Kovalevskaia, *Vospominaniia. Povesti* (Moscow: Nauka, 1974), p. 13.
65. Vasil'eva, "Pod roditel'skim krovom," *IV,* November 1901, Vol. 86, No. 11, pp. 477, 492-94. Even though this work appears in the Zaionchkovskii et al. multivolume guide to memoirs, there is a strong possibility it is semi- or total fiction.
66. Kupreianova, "Iz semeinykh vospominanii," pp. 652-53.
67. "Avtobiograficheskiia zapiski A. D. Borovkova," *RS,* September 1898, Vol. 95, No. 9, p. 556. One is reminded of the British admiral shot, in Voltaire's wry quip, "to encourage the others."
68. Passek, *Iz dal'nykh let,* I, pp. 120-21. This nanny is not even mentioned in Herzen's own memoirs. Ever the "democrat," perhaps he deliberately overlooked her.

    The writer Anastasiia Verbitskaia's (1861-1928) nanny was equally unkind; she appeared to take pleasure in inflicting mental pain on her nurseling. See Verbitskaia, *Moemu chitateliu!* 2nd rev. ed. (Moscow: I. N. Kushnerev and Co., 1911), pp. 70-71. A remarkably nasty nanny can be found not in the memoir literature but in a short story entitled "Mill'flër" by Shchepkina-Kupernik. This angry nanny baselessly accuses a little girl of theft and perjury. But as the core of this story comes from her own childhood, it's possible the nanny is also based on fact.
69. Pirogov, *Voprosy zhizni: dnevnik starago vracha, pisannyi iskliuchitel'no dlia samogo sebia, no ne bez zadnei mysli, chto, mozhet byt', kogda-nibud' prochtet i kto drugoi;* comprising vol. 1 of his *Sochineniia* (St. Petersburg: M. M. Stasiulevich, 1887), pp. 210-12.

70. Buxhoeveden, *Before the Storm*, pp. 11-12.

71. Likhachev, *Izbrannoe*, pp. 37-38. In her autobiographical *Veter vetku klonit* (Paris: Beresniak Press, 1948), Ol'ga Zhigalova says that Little Tania (her fictionalized self) finds herself at one point alongside nanny's skirt and apron, holding nanny's hand. "With the apron nanny comes to an end and all the rest of nanny is unclear, flat" (p. 11).

72. Buxhoeveden, *Before the Storm*, p. 7.

73. Sabaneeva, *Vospominaniia o bylom*, pp. 342-46, 349, 413, 432.

74. Head gear was extremely important for peasant women – indeed for almost all women – in Russia. Numerous folk beliefs centered on the power of uncovered hair to affect lives, generally not favorably.

75. "Krepostnaia dusha," *Tikhaia zavod'*, p. 49. Among real-life counterparts to this fictional nanny, with their burial outfits, were those of Vera Panova (see her *O moei zhizni*, p. 11) and – in great detail – Ol'ga Zhigalova (*Veter vetku klonit*, pp. 93-94).

76. See Lavrent'eva and Shtul'man, *Detstvo moe*, pp. 137-39, 142-49; also Andreev, *Cold Spring*, photo at the bottom of p. 99a.

77. Trunks generally contain a record of – are a symbol of – a person's entire life. But for one author, they are a symbol of even more: the lives of everyone, the entire nation. After 1917 "the Russian Empire – huge, immovable, like grandmother's trunk – burst apart and drifted sideways, and heeled over...The all-Russian grandmother's trunk burst into fire and the flames swallowed up the thousands of never-seen things in it, one more beautiful than another, preserved for ages. And someone dipped an enormous towel into the blood, and shook it, and wrote in the heavens in fiery letters: 'fratricide, crime...in the year one thousand nine hundred and eighteen ...'." See Iurii Miroliubov, *Babushkin sunduk: Sbornik rasskazov* (Madrid: [Galina Miroluboff], 1974), pp. 7-11.

78. I hasten to add, however, that not just nannies employed trunks; all peasant – and perhaps the bulk of higher-born – women stored their possessions in them. One of my anonymous reviewers acutely suggests that "nannies may have been even more attached to their trunks because the trunk became the one piece of furniture in the masters' houses that belonged to them and that linked them to their past in the village."

79. See Kamenskaia, *Vospominaniia*, p. 94.

80. Taneev, *Detstvo*, p. 57.

81. Coe, *When the Grass was Taller: Autobiography and the Experience of Childhood* (New Haven: Yale University Press, 1984), p. 113. The philosopher of spaces and physical objects, Gaston Bachelard, has paid particular attention to boxes, drawers, chests, and caskets. Noting that a "lock is a psychological threshold," he says that chests and trunks "are objects *that may be opened*" and when they open "a new dimension – the dimension of intimacy" opens; "this dimension can be an infinite one." See his *The Poetics of Space*, trans. by Maria Jolas (Boston: Beacon Press, 1994), pp. 81, 85-86. Cf. Taneev, *Detstvo*, p. 57: "Under each little cover I expected every time something unexpected and secret, and it soothed my soul when nanny raised one or another lid, even though I well knew what was to be found under each lid [of compartments in the top drawer of her bureau]. It seemed to me all the same that something completely unexpected would appear thence."

82. Bachelard, *Poetics of Space*, p. 84.

83. Vrangel', *Dalekoe proshloe*, p. 71; Khodasevich, *Tiazhelaia lira: Chetvertaia kniga stikhov 1920-1922* (Moscow-Leningrad: Gosudarstvennoe izdatel'stvo, 1922), pp. 21-22; Tikhomirov, *Teni proshlogo* (Moscow: "Moscow," 2000), p. 46.

84. Olitskaia, *Moi vospominaniia*, I, p. 15; Taneev, *Detstvo*, p. 146; it was the same with the trunk of Tat'iana Passek's nanny (*Iz dal'nykh let*, I, p. 101).

85. Tikhonov, "Byloe. (Iz semeinoi khroniki)," *IV*, February 1900, Vol. 79, No. 2, pp. 535-36.

86. *Ibid.*, pp. 536-38. Zhigalova has an almost identical scene, in the same exquisite detail, in her autobiography (*Veter vetku klonit*, pp. 93-94).

87. Prince Vladimir Volkonskii, "Semeinaia khronika kniazei Valdaiskikh," *RV*, April 1903, Vol. 284, No. 4, pp. 600-603 (in Chapter 4, "Nanny Anfisa Vasil'evna").

Vera Panova's nanny slept on the family's "antideluvian" trunk in the days after the October Revolution, while they all survived for a year by selling off its contents (Panova, *O moei zhizni*, pp. 61-62, 78).

Chapter Five

1. Priscilla Roosevelt's elegant work on country estates marks the same phenomenon; in a nice turn of phrase, Elizaveta Vodovozova likens this semi-annual travel, with a train of up to twenty carts and carriages, to the "Great *Völkerwanderung*" of history. See Roosevelt's *Life*, pp. 119-20; Vodovozova, *Na zare zhizni*, I, p. 115. Cf. Elena Guro's evocation

of the almost unbearable excitement attending these trips in her story "Priezd v derevniu" (*Sochineniia*, comp. by G.K. Perkins [Oakland, CA; Berkeley Slavic Specialties, 1996], pp. 62-67).

Yuri Slezkine has written, concerning twentieth-century émigré autobiographies of women: "The childhood's sacred center is the country estate, *where the protagonist enjoys a special relationship with the sprawling house*, the overgrown park, the lily-covered pond, *the peasant nanny who is as innocent as the young author*, and the peasant children who may or may not be as innocent." See Slezkine, "Lives as Tales," in Sheila Fitzpatrick and Slezkine, eds., *In the Shadow of Revolution: Life Stories of Russian Women from 1917 to the Second World War*, trans. by Slezkine (Princeton: Princeton University Press, 2000), p. 18. Italics added.

Andrew Wachtel treats this motif as part of a set of myths in his *Battle for Childhood*.

2. Bachelard, *Poetics of Space*, p. 6. His discussion of these poetics (first two chapters) is classic. His definition of the term "topoanalysis" is "the systematic psychological study of sites of our intimate lives... space contains compressed time. That is what space is for" (p. 8). The philosopher-literary scholar Mikhail Bakhtin has enunciated similar views in his theory of the "chronotope." See Bakhtin, *The Dialogic Imagination*.

3. "Vospominaniia Anny Koz'minichny Lelong," p. 794. The pattern remained intact after emancipation, as Anastasiia Tsvetaeva (1894-1993) (*Vospominaniia*, 3rd enl. ed. [Moscow: Sovetskii pisatel', 1984], p.44); Lidiia Avilova (1864-1943) (*Rasskazy, vospominaniia* [Moscow: Sovetskaia Rossiia, 1984], p. 193); and Baroness Sophie Buxhoeveden (1883-1956) (*Before the Storm*, pp. 2, 37, 55) bear witness.

Not surprisingly, this pattern held true for the royal family also. The Grand Duchess Marie comments that "Dmitrii [her younger brother] and I lived with our nurses [nannies] and attendants in a series of rooms on the second floor. This nursery suite, the domain of our infancy, was entirely isolated from the rest of the palace. It was a little world of its own..."(Marie, Grand Duchess of Russia [Mariia Pavlovna Romanova], *Education of a Princess* [New York: The Viking Press, 1931], pp. 10-11). Her cousins, Ol'ga and Tat'iana, daughters of Nicholas II, occupied the entire second floor of a wing of the Alexander Palace.

4. M. Tsvetaeva, *Izbrannaia proza v dvukh tomakh*, Vol. 2 (New York: Russica Publishers, 1979), p. 227. There are, however, many other examples of this "topsy-turvy" separation. Cf. Kovalevskaia, *Vospominaniia*, p. 28.

Endnotes   359

5. E. Gertsyk, *Vospominaniia: Memuary, zapisnye knizhki, dnevniki, pis'ma* (Moscow: Moskovskii rabochii, 1996), p. 49. Cf. Vera Kharuzina, *Proshloe. Vospominaniia detskikh i otrocheskikh let* (Moscow: Novoe literaturnoe obozrenie, 1999), pp. 20, 186, 199. Boris Zaitsev refers to this separate world as "the realm of women"or "women's kingdom" (*zhenskoe tsarstvo*), Chekhov – more condescendingly – the Crones' Kingdom ("Bab'ego tsarstvo") in an 1894 story.

6. Bakhtin, *The Dialogic Imagination*, p. 248. Cf. Bachelard, *Poetics of Space*, pp. 25-26.

7. Nadezhda Tèffi, *Razskazy* (Letchworth-Herts, England: Prideaux Press, 1980), p. 170; Helene Iswolsky, *No Time to Grieve...An Autobiographical Journey* (Philadelphia: The Winchell Company, 1985), p. 9; Adelaida Gertsyk, *Stikhi i proza*, Vol. I, comp. by T. N. Zhukovskaia (Moscow: Vozvrashchenie/Dom Mariny Tsvetaevoi, 1993), pp. 52-53, 69 ("a path to God"); Nikolai Antsiferov, *Iz dum o bylom: Vospominaniia*, comp. and annot. by A.I. Dobkin (Moscow: Feniks/ Kul'turnaia initsiativa, 1992), p. 29 ("the symbol of life"); Anastasiia Tsvetaeva, *Vospominaniia*, p. 44 ("companion of childhood, its joys and sorrows").

8. M. Tsvetaeva, *Stikhotvoreniia i poemy v piati tomakh*, Vol. 4: *Poemy* (New York: Russica Publishers, Inc., 1983), pp. 260-272; 378-79. This poem can be found in English in Catriona Kelly, ed., *An Anthology of Russian Women's Writing, 1777-1992*, trans. by Kelly et al. (Oxford: Clarendon Press, 1994), pp. 260-75, and in Russian in the same volume, pp. 446-61. Kelly's penetrating commentary on the poem's meaning and language is in her *A History of Russian Women's Writing 1820-1992* (Oxford: Clarendon Press, 1994), pp. 312-17.

9. Kupreianova, "Iz semeinykh vospominanii," p. 651; Antsiferov, *Iz dum o bylom*, p. 46; Andreev, *Detstvo: Povest'* (Moscow: Sovetskii pisatel', 1966), pp. 51ff.

10. Morozov, *Povesti moei zhizni*, I, pp. 29-30.

11. Kropotkin, *Memoirs of a Revolutionist* (Boston: Houghton Mifflin Company, 1930), p. 7.

12. *Ibid.*, pp. 45-46.

13. "Zapiski Ianuariia Mikhailovicha Neverova. 1810-1826 gg.," *RS*, 1883, XL, pp. 429-446; these have been excerpted in N. N. Rusov, comp., *Pomeshchich'ia Rossiia po zapiskam sovremennikov* (Moscow: Obrazovanie, 1911), pp. 136ff.

14. Tsebrikova, "Stranitsa k istorii," pp. 33-35. Tsebrikova was a prolific publicist, author of fiction, translator, pedagog, and journal editor.

Nikolai Vrangel' (1847-1923), a noble entrepreneur, recalls a nursery similar to Tsebrikova's, but notes that parents placed their children in such poor rooms not out of some animus but simply out of ignorance or inattention. See his *Ot krepostnichestva do bol'shevikov* (Moscow: Novoe literaturnoe obozrenie, 2003), pp. 33-34.

15. Horsbrugh-Porter, ed., *Memories of Revolution*, p. 57.

16. Magdalen King-Hall, *The Story of the Nursery* (London: Routledge & Kegan Paul, 1958), p. 207. This fine little book has much of interest to say not only about the nursery but about nannies as well, from early modern times to the twentieth century.

17. Guro, "Priezd v derevniu," pp. 63, 64. The wallpaper (*oboi*) was *nadoevshie*.

18. Kovalevskaia, *Vospominaniia*, pp. 10-11. Others with strong "olfactory memories" of childhood are Il'ia Tolstoi (see *Tolstoy, My Father: Reminiscences* [Chicago: Cowles Book Co., Inc., 1971], p. 19); Alexandre Benois (Benua, *Moi vospominaniia*, 2nd enl. ed. [Moscow: Nauka, 1990], Vol. I, pp. 199, 351); Mikhail Lind ("Moi zapiski," *Rossiiskii arkhiv: Istoriia Otechestva v svidetel'stvakh i dokumentakh XVIII-XX vv.* [Vol. XII], New Series [Moscow: Trite Studiia/Rossiiskii arkhiv, 2003], Appendix, p. 618 [everyone in his family, including the nannies, had their own smell]); and Natal'ia Krandievskaia-Tolstaia (*Vospominaniia* [Leningrad: Lenizdat, 1977], p. 16).

19. Kovalevskaia, *Vospominaniia*, pp. 10, 28.

The memory of the nursery stayed with the majority of these memoirists, a more or less permanent fixture of their recollected pasts. It was, of course, a common symbol for childhood, an evocation of "the golden age" that beckons most of us back to a happier time. By the early twentieth century, the image had become such a cliché that Chekhov comes close to mocking this icon of infancy in the gushing sentiments expressed by the *pomeshchitsa* Ranevskaia (*The Cherry Orchard*, Act One). But the attitude was not one of derision for most memoirists. As a child, the poet and novelist Andrei Belyi tells us, he was truly comfortable only within the confines of this space (*Na rubezhe*, p. 176).

20. Trubetskoi, *Iz proshlago*, pp. 5-6. In her article "Anton Chekhov and English Nostalgia" (*Orbis Litterarum*, April 2001, Vol. 56, No. 2, p. 125), Svetlana O. Klimenko offers a fine counterpoint to Trubetskoi: "In all his plays, Chekhov's nostalgic characters do not simply reminisce, they *look forward to the past*. They invoke the past in order to fantasize a different future from the one they are actually having. Or they portray a future in order to imagine how they themselves will be remembered."

21. Aksakov, *Years of Childhood*, trans. by Alec Brown (New York: Vintage Books, 1960), p. 90.

22. Grigoryev, *My Literary and Moral Wanderings*, pp. 19, 23-24. A. A. Fet "knew nothing more gratifying than both the maids rooms...you could sit and listen for a lifetime!" (*Rannie gody moei zhizni* [Munich: Wilhelm Fink Verlag, 1971], pp. 10-11, 12) For the author Vladimir Korolenko, the kitchen – one of the warmest spots in the house during long winter evenings – served exactly the same purpose as the maids room for others. When his parents were out on visits, he would spend hours there listening to the women's stories. See *Istoriia moego sovremennika* (Moscow: Khudozhestvennaia literatura, 1965), p. 33.

The realist painter Vasilii Vereshchagin (1842-1904) may be unique in the memoir literature in confirming some of a parent's reservations about the servants' quarters – he got an early sex education there. His mother thereafter ordered nanny "never to leave us in the maids room and particularly in the male servants' room..." (*Detstvo i otrochestvo khudozhnika V. V. Vereshchagina*. Vol. I: *Derevnia. – Korpus. – Risoval'naia shkola* [Moscow: I. N. Kushnerev and Co., 1895], p. 15).

23. Herzen, *Byloe i dumy*, I, p. 50.

A nearly identical, ringing endorsement of spending time in the company of the servants, in the servants' quarters, is that of Aleksei Galakhov (1807-1892) in his "Iz zapisok cheloveka: Pervye gody zhizni do postupleniia v shkolu," *RV*, May 1876, Vol. 123, No. 5, pp. 115-17 (signed "Sto-Odin").

24. "Vospominaniia Anny Koz'minichny Lelong," pp. 794, 792. Lelong thus aligns herself with Herzen in claiming a kind of moral uplift derived from the *devich'ia*. But it is equally likely that these authors chose to ascribe the shaping of their adult views to a time anterior to the actual period of development of those viewpoints.

25. L'vova, "Davno minuvshee. Otryvki iz vospominanii detstva," *RV*, October 1901, Vol. 275, No. 10, pp. 403-404.

26. Skalon, "Vospominaniia," in *Russkie memuary: Izbrannye stranitsy, XVIII vek* (Moscow: Pravda, 1988), p. 461.

27. Lev Uspenskii, *Zapiski starogo peterburzhtsa* (Leningrad: Lenizdat, 1970), p. 130.

28. In the allegedly autobiographical tale "I vremeni ne stalo..." Tèffi, *Zemnaia raduga*, p. 76.

29. Andrei Leskov, *Zhizn' Nikolaia Leskova po ego lichnym, semeinym*

i neseminym zapisiam i pamiatiam v dvukh tomakh, (Moscow: Khudozhestvennaia literatura, 1984), Vol. I, p. 92.

30. Kovalevskaia, *Vospominaniia*, pp. 16-26.

31. Russian children's games were thoroughly explored in the nineteenth century by two well-known pedagogs. See Egor Pokrovskii (1838-1895), *Detskie igry preimushchestvenno russkiia (v sviazi s istoriei, etnografiei, pedagogiei i gigienoi)*, 2nd rev. and enl. ed. (Moscow: V. F. Rikhter, 1895) and Elizaveta Vodovozova, *Umstvennoe i nravstvennoe razvitie detei ot pervago proiavleniia soznaniia do shkol'nago vozrasta. Kniga dlia vospitatelei*, 4th rev. ed. (St. Peterburg: V. S. Balashev, 1891), chapters 16 and 18. More recent works include Izabella I. Shangina's *Russkie deti i ikh igry* (St. Petersburg: Iskusstvo-SPB, 2000); her edited collection *Russkie deti: Osnovy narodnoi pedagogiki. Illiustrirovannaia entsiklopediia* (St. Petersburg: Iskusstvo-SPB, 2006), which incorporates parts of the earlier book; and Maina P. Cherednikova, *Golos detstva iz dal'nei doli –: igra, magiia, mif v detskoi kul'ture* (Moscow: Labirint, 2002).

32. Lavrent'eva, "Avtobiografiia malen'kago cheloveka," *RS*, October 1908, Vol. 136, No. 10, p. 201.

33. Benua, *Moi vospominaniia*, I, p. 393.

34. Sologub, "Hide and Seek" [Priatki] in *Best Russian Short Stories*, comp. and ed. by Thomas Seltzer (New York: Boni and Liveright, Inc., 1918), p. 166. I have made a few minor changes to improve the translation. In a macabre ending, the girl dies from obsessively playing the game.

35. "Vasia" was a common name for cats in Russia, much like "Tom" in the U.S.

36. Chekhov, "Zhizn' i vstrechi," *Literaturnoe nasledie*, Vol. I: *Vospominaniia. Pis'ma* (Moscow: Iskusstvo, 1995), pp. 131-32.

37. Fen, *A Russian Childhood* (London: Methuen & Co, Ltd, 1961), p. 101.

38. The first baby carriage appeared in England ca. 1730; but manufacture of carriages on a broad scale started only about 1840 (and were not called prams until ca. 1857). See Min Lewis, "Perambulators," in Arnold Haskell and Lewis, *Infantilia: The Archaeology of the Nursery* (London: Dennis Dobson, 1971), pp. 74 and 88, citing a 1923 paper by Samuel J. Sewell.

39. *Na zare zhizni*, I, pp. 123-24 (italics added). A foremost guide to raising children in the 1830s and 40s highly recommended fresh air and strolls for their health. See Grum, *Rukovodstvo*, II, pt. 1, sect. XIII.

40. Tat'iana Aksakova-Sivers (1892-1982), *Semeinaia khronika*, Vol. I (Paris: Atheneum, 1988), p. 28.

41. Berdiaev (*Dream and Reality*, p. 20) says: "My very first recollection of childhood is associated with [nanny]: I remember walking by her side, at the age of four or so, down an alley in the garden, in my father's family estate, Obukhovo." Sophie Kovalevskaia begins her memoirs with a similar recollection – though in general she says she was rarely taken out on walks when very young, and then only in very good weather or on holidays (*Vospominaniia*, pp. 9, 12) – as does the Soviet dissident Lev Kopelev: "Summer 1917. Nanny – my nurse, Polina Maksimovna, whom Mama called a *bonne* – strolls along the Kreshchatik [in Kiev] with me and my two-year-old brother, Sanya" (*The Education of a True Believer*, trans. by Gary Kern [New York: Harper & Row, 1980], p. 1).

42. Tat'iana Rozanova, "Vospominaniia ob ottse V. V. Rozanove i obo vsei sem'e," *Novyi zhurnal*, 1976, No. 124, p. 221.

43. Herzen, *Byloe i dumy*, I, p. 47; Tatiana Tchernavin (Tat'iana Chernavina), *My Childhood in Siberia* (London: Oxford University Press, 1972), p. 8.

44. Trubetskoi, *Iz proshlago*, p. 35; Anna Levitskaia, "Vospominaniia," *Rossiiskii arkhiv: Istoriia Otechestva v svidetel'stvakh i dokumentakh XVIII-XX vv.*, Vol. IX (Moscow: Trite Studiia/Rossiiskii arkhiv, 1999), p. 266.

45. Skalon, "Vospominaniia," pp. 461-62.

46. A. A. Kornilov, *Molodye gody Mikhaila Bakunina. Iz istorii russkago romantizma* (Moscow: M. and S. Shabashnikov, 1915), p. 34; Sychugov, *Zapiski bursaka*, p. 40; Kharuzina, *Proshloe*, pp. 53-71.

47. Chukovskaia, *Pamiati detstva* (St. Petersburg: Limbus Press, 2000), p. 17.

48. Shchepkina-Kupernik, *Vospominaniia* (Moscow: Zakharov, 2005), p. 10.

49. Fraser, *House by the Dvina*, p. 68.

50. *Shum vremeni*, pp. 28-32.

51. Rylov, *Vospominaniia* (Leningrad: Khudozhnik RSFSR, 1977), pp. 5-7. Something very similar occurred with Aleksandra Shchepkina and her nannies in the 1820s (*Vospominaniia*, p. 17).

52. Catherine De Hueck, *My Russian Yesterdays* (Milwaukee: The Bruce Publishing Company, 1951), p. 86; Vrangel', *Dalekoe proshloe*, p. 66; Sergei Mintslov, *Dalekie dni. Vospominaniia. 1870-90 gg.* (Berlin: Sibirskoe izdatel'stvo, n.d. [but 1925]), p. 7.

53. See, e.g., Anastasiia Tsvetaeva, *Vospominaniia*, pp. 15-16; Sabaneeva, *Vospominaniia o bylom*, p. 385. Eliseev's, on Tverskaia, known to all as the finest shop in Moscow to buy provisions, became the very pedestrian Gastronom No.1 during Soviet days.

54. [Boris Borisov], *Russian Boy* (Westminster, England: P. S. King & Staples Ltd., 1942), p. 15; Harari, *Memoirs*, p. 22; Vladimir Obolenskii, *Moia zhizn'. Moi sovremenniki* (Paris: YMCA Press, 1988), p.10; Buxhoeveden, *Before the Storm*, pp. 2-4, 13; and Rozanova, "Vospominaniia," p. 221. Cf. Al'bin M. Konechnyi, ed., comp. and annot., *Progulki po Nevskomu prospektu v pervoi polovine XIX veka* (St. Petersburg: Giperion, 2002); and Marina Burenina, *Progulki po Nevskomu prospektu* (St. Petersburg: Litera, 2002).

55. Beketova, *Al. Blok i ego mat'*, p. 15.

56. Koni, *Peterburg. Vospominaniia starozhila (Memuary)* (St. Petersburg: Atenei,1922), p. 39. He notes that the gallery was later turned into apartments.

57. Kropotkin, *Memoirs*, pp. 3-4.

Some of the most interesting Russian socio-cultural history of the past century has emanated from a handful of practitioners who have a wonderful "feel" for the places and spaces, houses and neighborhoods through which now dead women and men have passed. Superb examples of this genre have come, in earlier eras, from Ivan Grevs (1860-1941) and Nikolai Antsiferov (1889-1958). They appear to have found two worthy successors in more recent times. The work of the émigré scholar and culturologist Vasilii Shchukin evokes life on the nineteenth-century gentry estate [*usad'ba*] as well as any litterateur of the past. The journalist and historian Viacheslav Nedoshivin's *Strolls Through the Silver Age: Homes and Fates* discusses the residences and lives of nearly all the great poets of the late nineteenth and early twentieth centuries. See Shchukin, *Rossiiskii genii prosveshcheniia. Issledovaniia v oblasti mifopoetiki i istorii idei* (Moscow: Rossiiskaia politicheskaia entsiklopediia [ROSSPEN], 2007); Nedoshivin, *Progulki po serebrianomu veku: Doma i sud'by* (St. Petersburg: Litera, 2005).

58. Kornilova, *Byl' iz vremen*, p.99.

59. Libedinskii, *Sviaz' vremeni: Vospominaniia, povesti, ocherki, rasskazy* (Moscow: Sovetskii pisatel', 1962), p. 16.

60. Ivanova, *Vospominaniia: Kniga ob ottse* (Moscow: RIK Kul'tura, 1992), p. 53.

61. Kuzminskaia, *Moia zhizn'*, I, p. 91; III, p. 342.

62. *Povesti moei zhizni*, p. 40. Cf. A.A. Milne's marvelous poem "Explained" in *Now We Are Six*.

63. Pavel Viskovatyi/Viskovatov, *Zhizn' i tvorchestvo M. Iu. Lermontova*

(Moscow: Gelios ARV, 2004), p. 23. In this telling, Remer saves the "spoiled child" from turning into a cruel adult. As with Pushkin, the hagiography surrounding Lermontov's life is widespread, often carried to extremes, and nearly all spurious. See Chapter 9.

64. Sychugov, *Zapiski bursaka*, p. 36.

65. The title of this section borrows from a wonderful compendium of the same name about British nannies' little sayings: *Nanny Says*, as recalled by Sir Hugh Casson and Joyce Grenfell, ed. by Diana, Lady Avebury (London: Dobson Books Ltd., 1972).

66. "Zapiski P.N. Kostyleva," *RA*, No. 1, p. 124.

67. N, "Moe detstvo. (Iz moikh vospominanii)," *Russkaia shkola*, December 1903, Vol. 14, No. 12, pp. 75, 82. (at end: "N" in the Latin alphabet)

68. Valentin Krivich (pseud. of V.I. Annenskii), "Innokentii Annenskii po semeinym vospominaniiam i rukopisnym materialam," *Literaturnaia mysl'*, No. 3 (Leningrad, 1925), p. 218. Krivich says his father would reminisce often about this nanny and her expressions; his biographical sketch is, however, far from always reliable.

69. Libedinskii, *Sviaz' vremen*, pp. 17-18, 21.

70. Bunin, *Stories and Poems*, trans. by Olga Shartse (Moscow: Progress Publishers, 1979), p. 196.

71. Andreev, *Cold Spring*, p. 28. Italics added.

72. I have borrowed this phrase directly from Gathorne-Hardy, in his *Unnatural History*, pp. 60, 129, and 282.

73. *The Republic of Plato*, ed. and trans. by Benjamin Jowett (New York, P. F. Collier & Son, n.d.), Part II: The Individual, the State, and Education; here, pp. 57-59. Italics added. I am indebted to Patrick Cooke for this reference. Socrates, of course, often played "devil's advocate."

74. One of Kornei Chukovskii's most poignant essays is his description of the battle over fairy tales in the Soviet Union. The utilitarian "realists" hoped to do away with any fantasies that drew young people away from the tasks at hand in contemporary society; fairy tale defenders like Maxim Gorky and Chukovskii argued for the essentiality of fairy tales and what stirs the imagination, preparing children to cope with work and life. The battle raged, on and off, from the 1920s through the 1950s. See Chapter 5 of *Ot dvukh do piati* (Moscow: Detskaia literatura, 1968), available in English (abridged) as *From Two to Five* (Berkeley: University of California Press, 1971).

A particular worry of well-born Russian parents pre-1917 was the language their offspring might hear from their village-born caretakers – foul language, superstition, ignorant speculation, and other claptrap. The irony is that it is precisely language which is at the heart of the mythology and cult of nannies like Arina Rodionovna, as noted in Chapter 1 and analyzed in Chapter 10.

75. There is almost no end of academic exegeses of the content and meaning of these stories. See Bruno Bettelheim's landmark *The Uses of Enchantment: The Meaning and Importance of Fairy Tales* (New York: Alfred a. Knopf, 1976), which took a Freudian view of the tales' meaning and argued strongly for the benefits to children of hearing such stories. Earlier studies still worth reading include the works of Marie-Louise von Franz and Robert Darnton's "The Meaning of Mother Goose" in *The New York Review of Books* (February 2, 1984), pp. 41-47. More recent significant works on the value and meaning of fairy tales have come from Maria Tatar (*The Annotated Brothers Grimm* [2004], *The Annotated Classic Fairy Tales* [2002], and *Off with Their Heads! Fairy Tales and the Culture of Childhood* [1992]); Jan M. Ziolkowski (*Fairy Tales from Before Fairy Tales: The Medieval Latin Past of Wonderful Lies* [2007]); Jack Zipes (*When Dreams Came True: Classical Fairy Tales and Their Tradition* [2nd ed., 2007], *Breaking the Magic Spell: Radical Theories of Folk and Fairy Tales* [rev. and exp. ed., 2002], *Why Fairy Tales Stick: The Evolution and Relevance of a Genre* [2006], and, as editor, *Spells of Enchantment: the Wondrous Fairy Tales of Western Culture* [1991] and *The Oxford Companion to Fairy Tales* [2000]); Marina Warner (*From the Beast to the Blonde: On Fairy Tales and Their Tellers* [1995]and *No Go the Bogeyman : Scaring, Lulling, and Making Mock* [1999]); and Fernando Savater (*Childhood Regained: The Art of the Storyteller* [1982]).

For those interested more in Russian folk and fairy tales, there are the classic collections of A.N. Afanas'ev (widely available in both Russian and English) and many other eighteenth- and nineteenth-century collectors – all in Russian, some in English – and the multivolume compendium in English of Jack V. Haney: *The Complete Russian Folktale* (Armonk, NY: M. E. Sharpe, 1999-2006). Other English-language collections include those of Arthur Ransome *Old Peter's Russian tales* (New York: Dover Publications [1969], an unabridged republication of the 1916 ed.), *The Firebird and Other Russian Fairy Tales*, ed. and with an introd. by Jacqueline Onassis (New York: Viking Press, 1978); Irina Zheleznova, comp. and trans., *Folk Tales from Russian Lands* (New York: Dover Publications, 1969); and the very pointed *Politicizing Magic: An Anthology of Russian and Soviet Fairy Tales*, ed. by Marina Balina, Helena

Goscilo, and Mark Lipovetsky (Evanston, IL: Northwestern University Press, 2005). Analysis of the content, meaning, and storytelling circumstances of these tales can be found in Vladimir Propp, *Morfologiia skazki*, in English as *Morphology of the Folktale*, trans. by Laurence Scott, 2d ed., rev. and ed. with a preface by Louis A. Wagner (Austin: University of Texas Press, 1968); Haney's first volume, *An Introduction to the Russian Folktale* and his introduction to vol. 3 (repeated for vol. 4); see also Maria Kravchenko, *The World of the Russian Fairy Tale* (Bern, Switzerland: Peter Lang, 1987).

76. "Cool" media require the active participation of the audience; they are usually associated with the sense of hearing rather than vision. To be successful, the storyteller must not just recite to a passive audience; she or he must elicit a response. Content alone might be sufficient, in many cases, to secure the desired, the necessary reaction. But when that was not enough, the skills of the reciter were crucial. See McLuhan, *The Medium is the Massage* (New York:); Bettelheim, *Uses of Enchantment*, pp. 143, 150-51. Cf. Gathorne-Hardy, *Unnatural History*, p. 282, who claims nothing is "more powerfully impressing than the spoken word, particularly that invented by the narrator and directed personally at a small audience, except perhaps television."

77. Thus, for example, on the estate where the future Slavophile brothers Ivan and Pëtr Kireevskii grew up, in the village of Dolbino, "there were no male and female jesters, fools, or storytellers." See A. Peterson, "K rasskazam i anekdotam g-zhi Tolychevoi o V. I. Kireevskom," *RA*, August 1877, Bk. 2, No. 8, p. 479.

78. In Russia as in other countries, a kind of professionalization of this art of storytelling occurred over time. By the end of the nineteenth and beginning of the twentieth century, several memoirists note, there were many well-known "bards" ["*skaziteli*"] who gave performances both in public venues and in private homes. Cf. Kirill V. Chistov, "Severnorusskie skaziteli i osoznanie bylin obshcheetnicheskim naslediem russkikh," *Narodnye traditsii i fol'klor: Ocherki teorii* (Leningrad: Nauka, 1986), pp. 83-106; and *Russkaia skazka. Izbrannye mastera*, ed. and annot. by Mark Azadovskii (Moscow-Leningrad: Academia, 1932).

79. For why fairy tales have to have happy endings, as being close in kind to myths, see Yuri M. Lotman, *Universe of the Mind: A Semiotic Theory of Culture*, trans. by Ann Shukman (Bloomington: Indiana University Press,1990), p. 159. Lotman argues that originally there was "no alternative form in the shape of tragedy" so that "the eschatological

end by definition [could] only be the final triumph of good and the condemnation and punishment of evil."

79a. Pushkarev, *Stikhotvoreniia* (St. Petersburg: S. Stepanov, 1869), pp. 80-82.

80. Chukovskii's trenchant observations on this subject are found in *From Two to Five*, pp. 61-64. The music critic Nikolai Findeizen (1868-1928) says that he "delighted" in listening to the fairy tales of his brother's nanny, Matresha, who "would recite them expressively, at times in a sing-song voice, often miming with her eyes" (*Iz moikh vospominanii*, p. 67).

81. See her *Izbrannaia proza*, II, p. 310.

82. Figner, *Zapechatlennyi trud*, I, pp. 56-57.

83. Shchukin, *Rossiiskii genii*, p. ii. The remainder of the discussion of his ideas comes from pp. 272-96, especially pp. 285-86.

84. Bulgakov, *Avtobiograficheskie zametki. Dnevniki. Stat'i* (Orel: Izdatel'stvo Orlovskoi gosudarstvennoi teleradioveshchatel'noi kompanii, 1998), pp. 23-24. The quote from Struve is in his brief Foreword, p. 3.

85. Aksakov, *Years of Childhood*, pp. 309-12; Buxhoeveden, *Before the Storm*, pp. 6-10. Cf. Kopelev, *Education of a True Believer*, p. 6; Alliluyeva, *20 Letters*, p. 237; *Vospominaniia Iuriia Arnol'da*, Vol. I (Moscow: E. Lissner and Iu. Roman, 1892), p. 2.

86. Chertkova, *Iz moego detstva*, p. 166.

87. Alexander Verestchagin [Vereshchagin], *At Home and in War 1853-1881: Reminiscences and Anecdotes*, trans. by Isabel F. Hapgood (New York: Thomas Y. Crowell and Co., 1888), p. 8. *Doma i na voine* originally appeared in print in 1885.

88. The examples that follow come from N.A. Ursov, ed. and annot., *Russkie pesni* (Gor'kii: OGIZ, 1940), pp. 134-38. All came from nineteenth-century collections of the Nizhnii Novgorod region or from transcriptions of songs remembered by a woman born in 1851.

89. Cf. Shchepkina, *Vospominaniia*, pp. 10-11.

90. Dal', *Tolkovyi slovar'*, II, p. 296. Dostoevskii attests to what nannies have, "from time immemorial, hummed and sung endlessly as they rock their babies": You'll dress all in gold, my pet,/And wear a gen'ral's epaulet (*The Idiot*, tr. by Constance Garnett (New York: The Modern Library, n.d. [ca. 1935]), p. 310 (my rephrasing from the Russian).

91. Marina Warner, *Monsters of Our Own Making: The Peculiar Pleasures of*

Fear (Lexington: The University Press of Kentucky, 2007), p. 193. (This is a re-issue of her earlier book *No Go the Bogeyman*.)

92. *Ibid..*, pp. 194, 196, 199-200 (italics added).

93. Sheryl A. Spitz speaks of the "frustration" felt by mothers, nannies, and sisters who are "tied to the cradle by a helpless infant" and stresses these women's "ambivalent attitude toward the child – half love, half hate" which is revealed in the lullaby. See her "Social and Psychological Themes in East Slavic Folk Lullabies," *The Slavic and East European Journal*, Vol. 23, No. 1 (Spring, 1979), pp. 18-21.

94. See Brown, *Musorgsky: His Life and Works* (New York: Oxford University Press, 2002), pp. 69-70. Brown says that his later "Eremushka's Lullaby" (a song from 1868) is "a fully lyrical piece...returning to the theme of peasant infancy in a world of hardship...in direct line from Musorgsky's earlier *Cradle Song*." The inspiration for the new composition was another giant of Russian literature, the poet Nekrasov. "But while Ostrovsky's nurse had offered her grandson a prospect of survival through unremitting toil, Nekrasov's nurse can only counsel submission and then, in the gentle F sharp major final stanza, which varies music that had soundly [sic – sounded?] so bleakly in the first, fantasize on escape for her orphan charge" (p. 98).

95. *Ibid.*, p. 205.

96. *Ibid.*, p. 223, 228ff.

97. For those interested in the subject, see, *inter alia*, *Russian Folk Lyrics*, trans. and ed. by Roberta Reeder, with an introductory essay by V. Ja. Propp (Bloomington: Indiana University Press, 1993) [a rev. and enl. ed. of her *Down Along the Mother Volga: An Anthology of Russian Folk Lyrics* (1975)]; Milii Balakirev, *Sbornik russkikh narodnykh pesen* (Moscow: Muzgiz, 1936); and *Liubimye russkie narodnye pesni: dlia golosa v soprovozhdenii fortepiano*, comp. by V. Zharov (Moscow: Muzyka, 1989). The literature about Russian folk songs, while not as great perhaps as that for folk and fairy tales, is still substantial, yet very little has been written on the subject in English. One translated work is Vadim Prokhorov's *Russian Folk Songs: Musical Genres and History* (Lanham, MD: Scarecrow Press, 2002).

98. Miroliubov, *Sakral'noe Rusi*, Vol. II, bk. 4: *Russkaia mifologiia. Ocherki i materialy*, p. 203.

99. N, "Moe detstvo," p. 88ff.

100. Blok's aunt details his fitful nights with his "tormented" nanny

Avdot'ia "who wore herself out, now singing him songs, now muttering some nonsense about the dogs..." Beketova, *Al. Blok i ego mat'*, p. 18.

101. *Veter vetku klonit*, p. 86.

102. Even late into the twentieth century, one universally recognized channel of communication, for news and current events, for affairs domestic and foreign, was the *OBSDD* network: *Odna baba skazala, drugaia dobavila*...(One old woman said, to which another added...). No tsarist or even Soviet censor ever succeeded in fully interdicting this system of free expression.

103. Fen, *Russian Childhood*, p. 234. Evidently Aniuta was not illiterate.

104. Astrov, *Vospominaniia*, I, pp. 37-38. One of the favorite subjects of their people-watching was the young Anastas'ia Ziablova, who went on to great fame as the author of such books as *The Keys to Happiness* and many other racy bestsellers.

105. Berggol'ts, *Dnevnye zvezdy*, p. 80.

Of course, the children did not really leave their nannies to themselves at such times; the possessions of the nanny were too fascinating to ignore.

106. I'm grateful to Christine Worobec for stimulating these thoughts in conversations and personal emails during 2007-2008.

107. For example, Kate Pickering Antonova has found records of a noble family's payments for their nanny's travel. See her PhD dissertation, *'The importance of the woman of the house': Gender, property and ideas in a Russian provincial gentry family, 1820-1875* (Columbia University, 2007), p. 280 (to be published in revised form by Oxford University Press in late 2012).

No memoirists, however, speak of direct financial support from the family for the nannies' travel.

108. Solov'ëv, *Izbrannye trudy*, p. 229.

109. N, "Moe detstvo," p. 75. Cf. Lou Andreas-Salomé, *Looking Back: Memoirs*, ed. by Ernst Pfeiffer; trans. by Breon Mitchell (New York: Paragon House, 1991), p. 34, and Zhigalova, *Veter vetku klonit*, p. 91.

110. Shmelëv, *Bogomol'e*, in *Sochineniia v dvukh tomakh* (Moscow: Khudozhestvennaia literatura, 1989), Vol. 2, pp. 47-63.

111. Two of Ivan Shmelëv's quasi-autobiographical works bear religious titles. It's in the second work, *The Year of Our Lord* (*Leto Gospodne*, 1933), that we learn of the nanny-nurseling relationship between Vania and

"Domnushka" (*Sochineniia*, II, p. 177). For more, see my Chapter 8. On the huge religious subtext of Shmelëv's writings, see especially L. N. Kiiashko, "Obraz detstva v avtobiograficheskoi proze I. S. Shmeleva," in *I. S. Shmelev v kontekste slavianskoi kul'tury*, Vol. VIII of *Krymskie Mezhdunarodnye Shmelevskie chteniia: Sbornik materialov mezhdunarodnoi nauchnoi konferentsii*, ed. by V. P. Tsygannik (Alushta: no Publisher, 2000 [1999]), pp. 16-19. Among factors influencing Shmelëv's portrayals of characters from his childhood were the loss of his only son, killed by the Bolsheviks in 1921, and his idolization of the *carpenter* "Gorkin," a father figure both earthly and divine.

112. Panaeva, *Roman v peterburgskom polusvete. Sochinenie N. Stanitskago* (St. Petersburg: K. Vul'f, 1863), p. 69.

113. Zhemchuzhnaia, *Puti izgnaniia*, p. 16.

114. Passek, *Iz dal'nykh let*, I, pp. 91 and 120n. Not entirely incongruously, this same woman, Iudina, treated her nurseling poorly. See Chapter 4. Nearly the opposite occurred, however, in the family of Liudmila Vrangel', whose father invited a sick pilgrim (*bogomolka*) to come to their home as nanny. See her *Dalekoe proshloe*, pp. 69-70.

115. Pylin [Pavlov], *Pervye chetyrnadtsat' let 1906-1920* (n.p., [California], 1972), p. 8.

116. This is quite unlike the situation with, say, British nannies. There is, however, one great exception to this generalization. The very special case of "the Wolf Man" is discussed later in this chapter.

117. This account (see following endnote) is one of just a handful by a nanny herself; the autobiographical story was allegedly dictated to one of the nanny's former charges. Suspiciously more like fiction than memoir, and certainly as much reworked and written by the scribe as by the nanny, the autobiography nonetheless appears in the Zaionchkovskii guide to nonfiction memoirs.

118. Avdot'ia G. Khrushcheva (1786-1872), "Vospominaniia krepostnoi starushki A. G. Khrushchovoi (Zapisannyia V. N. Volotskoiu)," *RA*, April 1901, Vol. 39, Bk. I, No. 4, pp. 531-32.

119. *M.A. Balakirev i V. V. Stasov: Perepiska*, Vol. I (Moscow: Muzyka, 1970), pp. 187 and 412, n8.

120. "Avtobiograficheskiia zapiski A. D. Borovkova," p. 556. As for the sinfulness, that was discussed in a previous section of this chapter.

121. *Iz proshlago*, II, p. 14.

122. Kelly, *Children's World*, p.575.

123. See, *inter alia*, Peter Gay, introduction to "From the History of an Infantile Neurosis ('Wolf Man')," in *The Freud Reader*, ed. by Gay (New York: W.W. Norton & Co., 1989) and his *Freud: A Life for Our Time* (New York: W.W. Norton & Co., 1988), pp. 287-88; Sergius Pankejeff, *The Wolf-Man by the Wolf-Man, with The Case of the Wolf-Man, by Sigmund Freud and A Supplement by Ruth Mack Brunswick*, ed., with notes, an introduction, and chapters by Muriel Gardiner, and a foreword by Anna Freud (New York: Hill and Wang/Noonday Press, 1991); James L. Rice, *Freud's Russia: National Identity in the Evolution of Psychoanalysis* (New Brunswick, NJ: Transaction Publishers, 1993), pp. 1-2; Alexander Etkind, *Eros of the Impossible: The History of Psychoanalysis in Russia*, tr. by Noah and Maria Rubins (Boulder, CO: Westview Press, 1997), ch. 3; and Catriona Kelly, "A Wolf in the Nursery: Freud, Ethnography, and the History of Russian Childhood," accessed online in March 2011 at http://childcult.rsuh.ru/article.html?id=67313. The literature on Pankeev is extensive.

Chapter Six

1. Just a reminder that "unfree" did not necessarily mean uncompensated. See Chapter 4.

2. At both the top and bottom of society, there was little sense of change. As Ivan Aksakov wrote to Herzen in June 1861: "You tell yourself constantly that one of the greatest of social revolutions is being accomplished, but you don't feel it" (quoted by Mikhail Dragomanov in his forward to *Pis'ma K.Dm. Kavelina i Iv.S. Turgeneva k Al.Iv. Gertsenu* [Geneva: H. Georg, 1892], p. x). More than one serfowner who spoke with his serfs upon their returning from church the day the emancipation proclamation was read out during services would report hearing no word of excitement. Instead, peasants were prone to say that, according to what they had heard, they would "have to obey some more" – that, and nothing else.

3. Aleksandr Nikitenko, *Dnevnik v trekh tomakh* (Leningrad: Khudozhestvennaia literatura, 1955), II, pp.179-180.

4. *Istoriia moego sovremennika*, p. 60.

5. N. Shatilov, "Iz nedavniago proshlago," *Golos minuvshago*, January 1916, No. 1, p. 193. Italics added.

6. Zaionchkovskii, *Otmena*, pp. 139-40.

7. L'vov, *Vospominaniia*, p. 95.

8. Glinskii, "Iz letopisi usad'by Sergeevki," *IV*, October 1894, Vol. 58, pp. 70-72, 83.

9. Lev Tolstoi's plans for his field and household serfs were a model of rational planning; his peasants were preternaturally cautious, likely suspicious, and very self-interested. See Tolstoi, *PSS*, Vol. 5 (1931), pp. 241-58.

    It's not clear whether live-in nannies were the norm from 1861-1917. On gentry estates in the country, it almost certainly was; in cities there may have been more nannies spending only their days with young children.

10. Kharuzina, *Proshloe*, pp. 19-20. By the turn of the century, some nannies probably got involved in the labor movement. See Rebecca Spagnolo, "Serving the household, asserting the self: urban domestic servant activism, 1900-1917," in *The Human Tradition in Imperial Russia*, ed. by Christine D. Worobec (Lanham: Rowman & Littlefield Publishers, 2009).

11. This was the post-emancipation world for other than nannies as well: in 1865 the first congress of governesses and home teachers convened in Moscow "with the aim of founding a society of mutual aid."

12. Mandel'shtam, *Shum vremeni*, pp. 27 and 230 n.

    The bulk of employment offices in both capitals before the turn of the century were apparently privately run. Among the some two dozen in Petersburg were the Finland Mediatory Office, "Usluga" ("Service"), Moscow Recommendatory Office, Labor Intermediary on Goncharnaia Street, the M. Bravina Bureau on Grafskii Lane, and a labor exchange near the Moscow Gate. Each city had established a municipal employment office by early in the century. The St. Petersburg Bureau for the Hire of Servants sat at Simeonovskaia Street 5 (present-day Belinskii Street).

    One supposed difference between private and city offices was that the former vetted their hires and offered recommendations, while the latter sent out less qualified people – a rule often observed in the breach. Another – that the profits went to entrepreneurs and not city coffers. See Vladimir Ruga and Andrei Kokorev, *Moskva povsednevnaia: ocherki gorodskoi zhizni nachala XX veka* (Moscow: Olma Mediagrupp, 2005), p. 335; Sergei Glezerov, "I earnestly request a position as lackey..." at http://nvspb.ru/stories/ubeditelmzno_proshu_mesto_lake (accessed January 2012).

13. *Ibid.*

14. Leskov, "O 'kvakereiakh'. (Post-scriptum k 'Iudoli')," in *Polnoe sobranie sochinenii*, 3rd ed., Vol. 33 (St. Petersburg: A.F. Marks, 1903), p. 99 (hereafter, *PSS*).

15. Kharuzina, *Proshloe. Vospominaniia*, p. 32.

16. Andreev, *Cold Spring*, p. 26.

17. *Ibid.*, p. 27.

18. Pëtr A. Piskarev and L. L. Urlab, *Milyi Staryi Peterburg: Vospominaniia o byte starogo Peterburga nachala XX veka* (St. Petersburg: Giperion, 2007), pp. 251f.

19. Trubetskoi, *Iz proshlago*, p. 61.

20. Solov'ëv, *Vospominaniia*, p. 81.

21. *Knizhka nianek. Nastavleniia, kak kholit' i vospityvat' malen'kikh detei.* (page references in the text) The booklet was first published as an appendix to the progressive journal *Uchitel'* (The Teacher) late that year. Published from 1861 to 1870, *Uchitel'* was a St. Petersburg bimonthly for teachers, parents, and everyone occupied with the raising and training of children. It championed equal education for girls and boys, and fully equal rights for women (including political rights). See A.G. Dement'eva et al., eds., *Russkaia periodicheskaia pechat' (1702-1894): Spravochnik* (Moscow: Gosizdat politicheskoi literatury, 1959), pp. 420-21.

22. See Chapter 2.

23. Leskov, "Domashniaia cheliad'. Istoricheskiia spravki po sovremennomu voprosu (1887)," *PSS*, vol. 22 (1903), pp. 150-163.

24. Pushkin's nanny, Arina, was perhaps the "gold standard" for beloved caretakers by this time, her mythologizing having begun in the early 1850s. See Chapters 1 and 10.

25. V.A. Veremenko, *Dvorianskaia sem'ia i gosudarstvennaia politika Rossii (vtoraia polovina XIX-nachala XX v.)* (St. Petersburg: Evropeiskii dom, 2007), pp. 65ff.

26. *Ibid.* p. 60.

27. Cf. Catriona Kelly's description of the "child-centered family" and new notions of childhood which had emerged by the 1890s to early 1900s in *Children's World*, Part I.

28. *Dnevnik pisatelia za 1876 god*, p. 246.

29. *Ibid.*

30. This and much of the following information comes from the excellent monograph by Angela Rustemeyer, *Dienstboten*; here, pp. 197ff. Some of the quotations which follow are from the original sources Rustemeyer cites, others are Rustemeyer's own words.

31. See Hedwig Wegmann's "Entwicklung des mutter- und geschichte sauglingsschutzes in russland der padiatrie," trans. by Iu.M. Bogdanov (accessed January 2009 at: http://medafarm.ru/php/content.php?id=5883). Wegmann (1908-1985) was a prominent German pediatrician.

32. Hutton, *Russian and West European Women, 1860-1939* (Lanham, MD: Rowman & Littlefield Publishers, Inc., 2001) p. 216.

33. André Kourakine, *De l'aigle imperiale a l'étoile rouge* (Paris: La table ronde, 1970), p. 31.

34. How does one characterize this remarkable person – easily one of the most fascinating and influential cultural figures of the late nineteenth and early twentieth centuries – feminist? muse? psychoanalytic pioneer? friend of philosophers, poets, and composers? It is all too common – and too facile – to view her always through the prism of the extraordinary men – Nietzsche, Rilke, Freud – in whose lives she occupied a prominent position. One attempt to do her justice is Rudolph Binion's *Frau Lou: Nietzsche's Wayward Disciple* (Princeton: Princeton University Press, 1968).

35. Andreas-Salomé, *Looking Back*, p. 34.

36. Kolyshko, *Malen'kiia mysli*, p. 450.

37. *Zapiski kniazia Dmitriia Aleksandrovicha Obolenskogo: 1855-1879* (St. Petersburg: SpvII RAN/"Nestor-Istoriia," 2005), p. 39 (italics added); cf. Morozov, *Povesti moei zhizni*, Vol. II, p. 600.

38. Lifar, *Serge Diaghilev: His Life, His Work, His Legend: An Intimate Biography* (New York: G. P. Putnam's Sons, 1940), p. 11.

39. Leskov, "Domashniaia cheliad'", pp. 151-52.

40. Cf. Nikolai Arsen'ev (b. 1888), *Dary i vstrechi zhiznennogo puti* (Frankfurt-am-Main, Germany: Posev, 1974), p. 86.

41. So say the actor Mikhail A. Chekhov (b. 1891), Irina Elenevskaia (b. 1897), and Prince Andrei Kurakin (b. 1903). See Chekhov, *Literaturnoe nasledie*, I (1995), pp. 131-33; Elenevskaia, *Vospominaniia*, pp. 8-10; and Kourakine, *De l'aigle imperiale*, pp. 21, 31ff.

42. Rozhdestvenskii, *Stranitsy zhizni*, 2nd enl. ed. (Moscow: Sovremennik, 1974), p. 25.

43. Libedinskii, *Sviaz' vremen*, pp. 21-22. "Yawning, she would make the sign of the cross on her lips so that the unclean one wouldn't jump into it..." She goes to church and "performs" as expected, but in the kitchen she tells "funny stories, sometimes a little indecent, about people of the spiritual calling." Sometimes in the nursery she'd comfort Iurochka and his sister by mimicking parts of the church services: "Resurrection, resurrection, the dogs have torn into the priest! And if not for the deacons, they'd have torn him to bits!"

44. Vera Panova says her nanny was "the most religious person in the family," actually "the only religious person" among her near ones. Nanny comprehended in her belief "the kingdom of heaven – the afterlife, beyond the grave; every minute she had in mind that life on the other side , took joy only in it." Nanny "was forever fasting...like a nun, wearing herself out" to the point that she often got sick. She taught little Vera, in the name of that better life, "to fear sin and observe God's commandments." See *O moei zhizni*, p. 10.

45. Andreev, *Detstvo*, p.45.

46. Caretakers of Aleksandr Blok and Vera Kharuzina.

47. Shchepkina-Kupernik, *Vospominaniia*, pp. 24-25; Andreev (b. 1903), *Cold Spring in Russia*, p. 28; S. B. Shmerling, comp., *Traditsii sem'i* (Sverdlovsk: Sredne-Ural'skoe knizhnoe izdatel'stvo, 1988), p. 45; Panova, *O moei zhizni*, p. 53. Sergei Mintslov (1870-1933), left untended, once suckled a Borzoi bitch. "Afterwards, whenever I'd explode in anger, [nanny] Masha would say: 'There, there, why so angry? it's the canine blood at work!'" (*Dalekie dni*, p. 6)

48. Both Aleksandr Blok and Andrei Belyi (each born in 1880) had nannies with this failing (Beketova, *Al. Blok i ego mat'*, pp. 20-21; Belyi, *Na rubezhe*, p. 184) as did nannies of Tat'iana Shchepkina-Kupernik (b. 1874) and Irina Malina (b. 1906). Vladimir Posse's (1864) fifteen-year-old nanny Mar'iushka, smelling of "bad vodka and onions," made him fearful (*Perezhitoe i produmannoe*, Vol. I: *Molodost' (1864-1894)* (Leningrad: Izdatel'stvo pisatelei v Leningrade, 1933), p. 11.

49. These kinds of problems continued right into the Soviet period, as evidenced by the complaints received at the labor dispute arbitration boards of the domestic workers union *Napit* in the 1920s. See Z. A. Bogomazova, *Domashniaia rabotnitsa* (Moscow: VTsSPS, 1928), pp. 70-72.

50. Andreev, *Cold Spring*, pp. 28-29, 38-39. The mother of the author Lev Uspenskii (b. 1900) got involved with revolutionaries which in turn affected all members of the family, including the servants. "Of course,

it was impossible to hide anything from nanny; I don't know what sort of negotiations mama had with her, but nanny pretended that she knew nothing." (Uspenskii, *Zapiski*, p. 51)

51. Rustemeyer, *Dienstboten*, p. 174.
52. Quoted by Rustemeyer, *Dienstboten*, p. 167. Italics added.
53. *Ibid.*, p. 78. Nikol'skaia Square was the location of an employment office. On prostitutes in the capital at the turn of the century, see Piskarev and Urlab, *Milyi Staryi Peterburg*, pp. 83f.
54. The author's essay on the institution of – plus literature and myths about– the *diad'ka* had to be cut from this book to economize space but may be requested by email: salangrant@verizon.net.
55. Ekaterina Foteeva's succinct but devastating picture of what happened to some 155,000 landowners and most of the wealthy merchants of Russia is an excellent starting point for those interested in the fates of the pre-1917 upper classes. She tries to account for roughly 23 million wealthier or upper-class tsarist subjects from before the revolutions. See her "Sotsial'naia adaptatsiia posle 1917 goda: zhiznennyi opyt sostoiatel'nykh semei," in V. V. Semenova and Foteeva, eds., *Sud'by liudei: Rossiia XX vek. Biografii semei kak ob"ekt sotsiologicheskogo issledovaniia* (Moscow: Institut sotsiologii RAN, 1996), pp. 240-75.

    She concludes that, while the revolutions brought immediate, catastrophic consequences for nearly all of these families, the impact was usually limited in time and that, more importantly, their "cultural capital" (i.e., higher education) often permitted former well-off families to restore their lost status positions and occupy rather high positions in socialist society. By "adapting," such people achieved a surprising distinction: "we believe that the relative position of our families in the Soviet social hierarchy corresponds to their status in pre-revolutionary society" (p. 273).

56. Alla Andreeva, *Plavanie k nebesnomu kremliu* (Moscow: "Uraniia," 1998), pp. 10, 25, 35 (for the quotation and all other information in the next paragraph).
57. Cf. Ol'ga Il'ina-Lail', "Vostochnaia nit'. Iz vospominanii," *Zvezda*, 5 January 2001, p. 172: the nanny saves the life of a little girl named Musia by hiding the child at her own home in the village.
58. See Tsvetaeva, *Neizdannoe: Sem'ia: Istoriia v pis'makh* (Moscow: Ellis Lak, 1999), pp. 251-56; eadem, *Izbrannaia proza*, II, p. 67; eadem, *Neizdannoe: Zapisnye knizhki v dvukh tomakh*, Vol. II: 1919-1939 (Moscow: Ellis Lak, 2001), pp. 84-85; and Simon Karlinsky, *Marina Tsvetaeva: The Woman,*

her World and her Poetry (Cambridge: Cambridge University Press, 1985), pp. 81-82.

59. Skriabina, *Stranitsy zhizni* (Moscow: Progress-Akademiia, 1994), p. 70. Clearly, NEP made for a breathing space not just for higher echelons of society.

60. See Horsbrugh-Porter, ed., *Memories of Revolution*, pp. 27-37. For Irina Sergeevna Tidmarsh (née Konkevicha; b. 1903), not a nanny but a former maid, Masha, came to Moscow from the countryside with food to help her family survive the post-revolution famine. (*Ibid.*, pp. 60-61).

61. The story is available online at http://english.pravda.ru/main/2002/04/11/27546.html (accessed November 2008).

62. Kourakine, *De l'aigle imperiale*, pp. 21-22, 173-80.

63. Michael Budberg, *Russian Seesaw* (London: Martin Hopkinson, Ltd., 1934), pp. 20, 40-48. In a beautifully rendered, nonautobiographical story called "Three Lives," Nadezhda Tèffi recounts a tale of a gentry family and their nanny that could have been a composite of several of the autobiographical stories just presented ("Tri zhizni" in *Zemnaia raduga*).

64. It goes without saying, perhaps, that the nobility suffered most of all as a class between 1918 and the early 1930s. In Barbara Alpern Engel's estimate, by "the end of the civil war, about 11 to 12 percent of the pre-revolutionary nobility remained in the Soviet Union – approximately 10,000 noble families, or about 50,000 people in all" (*A Revolution of Their Own: Voices of Women in Soviet History*, ed. by Engel and Anastasiia Posadskaya-Vanderbeck, trans. by Sona Hoisington (Boulder, CO: Westview Press, 1998), p. 102.

65. Radical Bolsheviks' philosophy at its more irrationally exuberant might well be likened to that of Prof. Henry Higgins in *My Fair Lady*: a woman should be "more like a man" – a wage earner outside the home.

66. Pipes, *Russia under the Bolshevik Regime* (New York: Alfred A. Knopf, 1993), p. 187.

67. Wendy Z. Goldman, *Women, the State and Revolution: Soviet Family Policy and Social Life, 1917-1936* (New York: Cambridge University Press, 1993), pp. 1-13. Goldman describes the "utopian" phase of Bolshevik thinking on the family and childrearing. Barbara Evans Newman, however, differs with Goldman on Kollontai; Newman says Kollontai did not want the state to take over childrearing but for adults in communal living to share this responsibility (personal communication to the author, 2008).

68. Berlin, "Political Ideas in the Twentieth Century," in Isaiah Berlin, *Four Essays on Liberty* (Oxford and New York: Oxford University Press, 1969), p. 17, cited in Nina L. Khrushcheva, *Cultural Contradictions of Post-Communism: Why Liberal Reforms Did Not Succeed in Russia* (A Paper from the Project on Development, Trade, and International Finance) (New York: Council on Foreign Relations, 2000), p. 7.

69. Goldman, *Women, the State and Revolution*, pp. 11-12.

70. The most recent account of this phenomenon of the "waifs" is Kelly *Children's World*, where it occupies the entire second part of the volume.

71. On the need but lack of funding for state childcare and literature about the problem, see especially Hutton, *Russian and West European Women*, pp. 192, 198, 208, 211ff, 227, 355; Goldman, *Women, the State and Revolution*, chapter 2, pp. 59-100, and 126-28, 248-49; Gail Lapidus, *Women in Soviet Society: Equality, Development, and Social Change* (Berkeley: University of California Press, 1978), pp. 100-103, 128-35; and Pipes, *Russia under the Bolshevik Regime*, p. 331.

72. Dolgikh, "[Autobiographical Q&A]," in *A Revolution of Their Own*, ed. by Engel and Posadskaya-Vanderbeck, pp. 156, 164.

73. Priemskii, *Vospominaniia iz zhizni inzhenera* (Sarov: RFIaTs-VNIIEF, 2006), p. 10.

74. Many of those who used the system to their advantage in the straitened 1920s later paid a heavy price. During the purges of the 1930s, current or former "privileges" were a most inviting and convenient point of attack against any and all "enemies of the revolution."

75. Katukova, *Tak bylo* (Moscow: ACT, 2005), p. 22.

76. Cf. Orlando Figes, *The Whisperers: Private Life in Stalin's Russia* (New York: Metropolitan Books/Henry Holt and Company, 2007), pp. 47-48.

77. Bonner, *Dochki – Materi* (New York: Chekhov, 1991), pp. 33, 49, 51ff.

78. Goldman, *My Disillusionment in Russia* (Mineola, NY: Dover Publications, 2003), pp. 16, 20.

79. It's hard to pin down an exact year of origin for this term. I've not come across it in any pre-revolutionary sources. Judging by the want ads in *Vecherniaia Moskva*, the expression passed from being a two-word phrase to a single word some time in the mid-1930s.

80. *Materialy po statistike Leningrada i Leningradskoi gubernii*, Issue 6 (Leningrad: Central Statistical Administration, 1925), tables, pp. 240-57. I am indebted to Jussi Wacklin for this reference.

81. *Ibid.*, pp. 248-49 (line 191). Under the category *prisluga* (servants), there is a subcategory for "personal servitors" [*lichnaia prisluga*], which is in turn broken down into "those living as a single servant," "nannies and wet-nurses," and "other personal servants."

82. Hutton, *Russian and West European Women*, p. 230 n40.

83. Alliluyeva, *20 Letters*, p. 135.

84. Spagnolo, "When Private Home Meets Public Workplace: Service, Space, and the Urban Domestic in 1920s Russia," in Christina Kiaer and Eric Naiman, eds., *Everyday Life in Early Soviet Russia: Taking the Revolution Inside* (Bloomington: Indiana University Press, 2006), pp. 230-55; here, pp. 242-43.

85. Kelly, *Refining Russia: Advice Literature, Polite Culture, and Gender from 1760* (Oxford: Oxford University Press, 2001), p. 292.

86. See the absorbing and insightful discussion of Timasheff's "classic" by several authors in *Kritika: Explorations in Russian and Eurasian History*, Fall 2004, Vol. 5, No. 4.

87. *Ibid.*

88. Goldman, *Women, the State and Revolution*, pp. 297, 312-14.

89. Figes, *The Whisperers*, pp. 47-48.

90. "My borolis' za ideiu," *Zhenskaia sud'ba v Rossii: Dokumenty i vospominaniia*, ed. by B.S. Ilizarov, comp. by T.M. Goriaeva et al. (Moscow: Rossiia molodaia, 1994), p. 90.

91. *Ibid.*, pp. 90-91.

92. Priemskii, *Vospominaniia*, pp. 18-19.

93. Entry for 16 June 1942 cited in Kazimiera J. Cottam, ed. and trans., *Defending Leningrad: Women Behind Enemy Lines*, 2nd rev. ed. (Nepean, CAN: New Military Publishing, 1998), p. 40. I am indebted to Anita Kondoyanidi for this reference.

94. Bogomazova, *Domashniaia rabotnitsa*, pp. 71-72. I owe the knowledge of this little book to Catriona Kelly's *Children's World*.

95. *Spirit to Survive: The Memoirs of Princess Nicholas Galitzine* (London: William Kimber, 1976), p. 161.

96. Sakharov, *Memoirs*, trans. by Richard Lourie (New York: Alfred A. Knopf, 1990), p. 20.

97. Rein interview with Slava Sergeev, *Novoe vremia*, 24 October 2004, No. 43, pp. 42-43. We should be mildly skeptical of the coincidence with Arina's birthplace; Rein may be embellishing the tale.

98. *Ibid.*

99. Hutton, *Russian and West European Women*, p. 284. Cf. Kelly, *Children's World*, Chapter 10, especially pages 403-409.

100. See the extended discussion of this story in Chapter 8.

101. Mikhail German, *Slozhnoe proshedshee (Passé composé)* (St. Petersburg: Iskusstvo, 2000), p. 20.

102. Hutton, *Russian and West European Women*, pp. 340 and 340n, 355. The Great Depression made some difference for domestic employment in Europe, perhaps less so in the USSR (pp. 341f). The figures for both periods are likely under-reported. Not only was the information hard to come by, but it was in most people's interests, materially and ideologically, to lie about servants.

103. Goldman, *Women, the State and Revolution.*, pp. 291, 296, 331ff, 340-41; Pipes, *Russia Under the Bolshevik Regime*, p. 200.

104. Her memoirs – *Mimikriia v SSSR: Vospominaniia inzhenera 1935-1942 gody* (Frankfurt/Main: Polyglott-Druck GmbH, n.d.) – are an invaluable social document. An English translation of part of the book is available as "Memoirs of an Engineer," pp. 394-418 in Sheila Fitzpatrick and Yuri Slezkine, eds., *In the Shadow of Revolution: Life Stories of Russian Women from 1917 to the Second World War*, trans. by Slezkine (Princeton: Princeton University Press, 2000). All of the account that follows in the text is drawn from this English version, with page number references shown in parentheses.

105. Kelly, *Refining Russia*, p. 292 n191.

106. German, *Slozhnoe proshedshee*, p. 20.

107. Lapidus, *Women in Soviet Society*, pp. 240-43. But that brief flowering of 1920s thinking soon faded, and the family as caretaker was once again emphasized in the 1970s.

108. See http://19411945.net/2009/02/25/demograficheskaja_situacija_v_period_vojjny.html (accessed Dec. 2010); also, Dmitrii M. Chechot, *Sotsiologiia braka i razvoda* (Leningrad: Znanie, 1973), p. 10.

109. *Zhenskie rasskazy* (Ann Arbor, MI: Hermitage/Ermitazh, 1981), pp. 9-10. Strong autobiographical elements reportedly show up in this work of fiction by a journalist, translator, and camp survivor.

Three of the stories in this collection, along with several others, have been published in English: Ruth Zernova, *Mute Phone Calls and Other Stories*, trans. by Ann Harleman, Martha Kitchen, and Helen Reeve;

selected, ed., and with an introd. by Reeve (New Brunswick, NJ: Rutgers University Press, 1991).

110. See Vera Dunham, *In Stalin's Time: Middleclass Values in Soviet Fiction*, enl. and rev. ed. (Durham: Duke University Press, 1990) and Hough's introduction to the first edition in which he argues that all that Dunham says about the later time holds true for the 30s as well. The literature that Dunham chose to examine, says Hough, merely reflected and elaborated on the social "deal" made earlier, that "its ratification in middlebrow literature lagged behind its actual enactment" (p. xxviii). Dunham's section on childrearing practices unfortunately does not discuss caretakers or nannies (pp. 91-96).

111. Galina Zakhoder, *Zakhoder i vse-vse-vse . . .: Vospominaniia* (Moscow: Zakharov, 2003), p. 17. She became the second wife of the poet and children's author Boris Zakhoder.

112. Kelly, *Refining Russia,* p. 324.

113. Kelly, *Children's World*, p. 415. One poor substitute: a Soviet program of the 1950s or 60s called *Radio Nanny* (anticipatory of twenty-first-century Western television programming). The children's poet Agniia Barto (1906-1981) describes with subtle humor how she was invited to appear on it, to receive their "medal for smiles" and to read some of her poems (*Zapiski*, pp. 59-60).

114. Deborah A. Field, *Private Life and Communist Morality in Khrushchev's Russia* (New York: Peter Lang Publishing, Inc., 2007), p. 87. She devotes an entire chapter (Chapter 6, "Child Rearing and the Problem of Selfishness," pp. 83-97) to this subject and mentions a nanny just this once.

115. *Ibid.*, Chapter 6 and the Conclusion, pp. 99-103.

Chapter Seven

1. See my "The Russian Gentry Family: A Contrarian View," *Jahrbücher für Geschichte Osteuropas*, Vol./Bd. 60, No./Heft 1 (March 2012).

2. In the final analysis, whether a nanny might possibly have "inspired" her charge in some way to accomplish something creatively *in later life* may be an important but secondary issue. For more on this issue, see Chapter 9.

3. Lacking in this book is any pretension of an anthropological (or sociological) examination of nannies. For those interested in this aspect of nannies, I would suggest works such as Sarah Blaffer Hrdy's

Mothers and Others: The Evolutionary Origins of Mutual Understanding (Cambridge: Harvard University Press, 2009) with its analysis of "alloparents"; John Bowlby's 3-volume *Attachment and Loss* (NY: Basic Books [19691980]); and the research of Beatrice Whiting. Cf. Melvin Konner, "It Does Take a Village," *The New York Review of Books*, Vol. LVIII, No. 19 (December 8, 2011), pp. 37f.

4. One viewpoint I will avoid devoting much space to is the Freudian. While I don't deny the possible validity of some of the ideas of psychoanalysis – and therefore occasionally incorporate or quote ones that I find pertinent – I'm not eager to attempt a Freudian explanation of matters. More importantly, I do not believe it possible to put deceased persons "on the couch" as it were and attempt the *requisite* dialog with them.

5. Examples from sources mostly already cited in preceding chapters are Baron Nikolai Vrangel', Liudmila Vrangel', Tat'iana Passek, Tat'iana Tolstaia, and Nikolai Mamaev. Cf. Andrew Wachtel's discussion (in his *Battle for Childhood*) of the double loss for Leo Tolstoi's "alter ego" Nikol'enka of both his mother and his nanny Savishna.

6. Passek, *Iz dal'nykh let*, p. 106.

7. Three of the most notable autobiographers decrying an emotionally depriving mother (or both parents) are Vera Figner, Elizaveta Vodovozova and Natal'ia Durova. Given the prominence they achieved historically, and in today's women's studies, it is easy to fathom why they have unduly colored the views of researchers on intra-family dynamics. Richard Coe is one investigator whose skewed views of Russian mothers in general and of those in autobiographies in particular are striking.

8. E.g., claiming generational change – from passiveness to more assertiveness/ rebelliousness – or even revolutionary change, based on childrearing practices. See Grant, "Russian Gentry Family."

9. Goncharov, *Oblomov*, the Ann Dunnigan trans., slightly altered (New York: Signet/New American Library, 1963), p. 145. Italics added.

10. *Tri pory zhizni, Roman Evgenii Tur* (Moscow: V. Got'e, 1854), p. 5. Tur was the pseudonym of Elizaveta Vasil'evna Salias de Turnemir [Sailhas de Tournemire]; née Sukhovo-Kobylina.

11. See in particular Gathorne-Hardy, *Unnatural History*, Chapter 4: "The Nanny as Mother; the Nanny-Mother Partnership," especially pp. 126-48; also pp. 30, 109. Gathorne-Hardy might disagree with my take on his views, however; he says that "on the whole the most common"

mother-nanny relationship he found [in Britain] was one in which the mother plays a subservient role to the nanny, at least for the first few years. It may be a partnership, he adds, though one in which the mother's "presence is no doubt felt during infancy," but she "does not fully enter into until later on." Still, at its best, he acknowledges, "the Nanny situation was a particular form of multiple mothering."

12. Os[s]orgin, *My Sister's Story*, p. 15.

13. *Childhood and Society*, 2nd rev. and enl. ed. (New York: W. W. Norton & Co., 1963), pp. 56-57. Italics added.

   In a 1972 essay ("Play and Actuality") Erikson discussed how a "maternal caretaker" helps a child develop a sense of wholeness and thus of identity. There must always be interplay between the subject child and some other object(s). If the child depends for its "basic education" on "a mothering supported by a family and a community, so will it, all through life, depend on *equivalents* (and not on *substitutes*) of the constituents of that early mutuality."

   I conclude that a nanny is just one of many possible maternal "equivalents" that a person encounters and enjoys the benefits of in life and that it would be a mistake to exaggerate the significance of most nannies as mother "substitutes." Erikson says that "the early mother's equivalent in each later stage [of life] must always be the sum of all the persons and institutions which are significant for his wholeness in an expanding arena of interplay. As the radius of physical reach and of cognitive comprehension, of libidinal attachment and of responsible action – as all these expand, there will, of course, always be persons who are substitutes for the original mother." See *Explorations in Psychohistory: The Wellfleet Papers*, ed. by Robert Jay Lifton with Eric Olson (New York: Simon and Schuster, 1974), p. 116.

14. Almost everything about Natal'ia's childhood was exceptional. Her father was a Kievan singer-actor, the son of a Gypsy father and a half-Polish, half-German mother, who failed as a businessman and a husband, finally abandoning his wife and daughter. Her mother was a Frenchwoman, orphaned early, for whom everything in life turned out badly. A black cloud hung over her. The only thing she "accomplished" in life was the physical and moral *vospitanie* of her own daughter, for whom she sacrificed herself completely. It is no wonder that Trukhanova experienced nearly everything the opposite of most Russian children of her time.

15. Trukhanova, *Na stsene i za kulisami: vospominaniia* (Moscow: Zakharov, 2003), pp. 5-8.

16. See G. I. Chugunov, endnote to Dobuzhinskii's *Vospominaniia* (1987), pp. 368-69, n5.

17. Kornilova, *Byl' iz vremen*, p. 76. Tyrkova-Vil'iams (1869-1962) is another excellent example; see her *To, chego bol'she ne budet*, pp. 37-39.

18. Shchepkina-Kupernik, *Vospominaniia*, pp. 25-26.

19. *Veter vetku klonit*, pp. 25-26 (italics added). The book has been rendered into English as *Across the Green Past* (Chicago: Henry Regnery Co., 1952), with minor differences between the two versions.

20. Fen, *Russian Childhood*, pp. 49-51

21. Avilova, diary entry for 15 December 1918 in *Rasskazy*, pp. 291-92.

22. His "Avtobiograficheskaia zametka" and "Zametka o sebe samom" and a third brief sketch given to the bibliographer P. V. Bykov are all in his son Andrei's biography of his father: *Zhizn' Nikolaia Leskova*, I, pp. 39-47, 49-50, and 50-51 respectively.

23. McLean, *Nikolai Leskov: The Man and His Art* (Cambridge, MA: Harvard University Press, 1977), pp. 16-18.

24. It was common Russian usage to call a child who had lost his mother an orphan or even a "complete orphan." It was not a term often (ever?) used for children who had lost only their father.

25. McLean, *Nikolai Leskov*, p. 24. Italics added.

26. *Ibid.*, p. 20. Italics added.

27. Herzen, *Byloe i dumy*, I, pp. 52-53.

28. *Na zare zhizni*, I, p. 126.

29. Robbins, *Servant's Hand*, p. 150, quoting Lawrence Stone.

30. Kropotkin, *Memoirs*, p. 19. Cf. Ekaterina Raevskaia (née Bibikova; a writer and *pomeshchitsa*), "Vospominaniia Ekateriny Ivanovny Raevskoi," *IV*, November 1898, Vol. 74, No. 11, pp. 527-28.

31. Tsebrikova, "Dvadtsatipiatiletie zhenskogo voprosa 1861-1886 gg.," p. 194, in V. A. Manuilov, "M. K. Tsebrikova i ee vospominaniia," *Zvezda*, June 1935, No. 6.

32. In the story "Ditia i niania," *Detskaia biblioteka*, cited by Jessica Tovrov in *The Russian Noble Family*, p. 167.

33. L'vova, "Davno minuvshee. Otryvki iz vospominanii detstva," *RV*, October 1901, Vol. 275, No. 10, p. 410. By the same token, L'vova has to know from her nanny that her wet-nurse is "special" – she can't be like any other wet-nurse; otherwise, she would not be what the egoistic child needs and wants!

34. Staniukovich, "Nian'ka," in *Morskie rasskazy* (Minsk: Iunatstva, 1981), accessed online at http://orel.rsl.ru/nettext/russian/stanykowich/njnj.htm, p. 13 (of 31).
35. Os[s]orgin, *My Sister's Story*, p. 16.
36. Kuzminskaia, *Moia zhizn'*, p. 53.

    Of his nanny Mar'iushka the historian Sergei Solov'ëv would say: "...I cannot fail to acknowledge her religious-moral influence"; she "had no small influence on the formation of my character" (*Izbrannye trudy*, pp. 229-31). Anna Chertkova's beloved nanny Dar'ia, "a woman of integrity [*poriadka*] and firm moral views," was "a woman rare in the high [moral] qualities of her soul" (*Iz moego detstva*. pp. 11, 160, 167).

37. *Vospominaniia* (Moscow: Khudozhestvennaia literatura, 1976), pp. 38-39. She learned to abhor lying from Hannah (p. 44). "All of us children soon submitted ourselves completely to her influence and believed that everything she told us, without any doubt, was good for us...." (p. 43). Il'ia Tolstoi says virtually the same thing in his memoirs; see *Tolstoy*, pp. 16-17.
38. I note that Lisa A. Kirschenbaum, in her study *Small Comrades: Revolutionizing Childhood in Soviet Russia, 1917-1932* (New York: RoutledgeFalmer, 2001), singles out in her "Postscript: Three Childhoods" (pp. 165-180) precisely three of these individuals to discuss: Berggol'ts, Kopelev, and Bonner, noting the nannies of each.
39. On Pasternak and his nanny, see Chapter 9; on Panova, *O moei zhizni*, pp. 10, 22, 31, 53f; for Bonner's Batania, see her *Dochki – Materi*, pp. 37, 157-58 especially, and for her nanny Niura, pp. 64, 70-79, 89, 117; on Likhachev, *Izbrannoe*, pp. 38-40.

    Panova's autobiography and its various redactions make for an especially interesting bit of socio-cultural history. The "final," post-Soviet, and posthumous version that came out in 2005 (St. Petersburg: Zvezda) placed in front of this 1975 title the almost defiant words "*Moe i tol'ko moe*" – as if demonstrating how much the Soviet censors had made her cut from two earlier versions. See the discerning analysis of this and other "official" memoirs by Catriona Kelly, "The Authorised Version: The Auto/Biographies of Vera Panova," in *Models of Self: Russian Women's Autobiographical Texts*, ed. by Marianne Liljeström, Arja Rosenholm, and Irina Savkina (Helsinki: Kikimora Publications, 2000), pp. 63-80.

40. Berggol'ts devotes many pages to Dunia in *Dnevnye zvezdy*, but in particular pp. 78-86, 94-96; on Kopelev's Polina Maksimovna, see *Education of a True Believer*, pp. 2-7.

41. Introduction to Zernova, *Mute Phone Calls*, p. xv (Reeve gives no citation for Eikhenbaum; I've been unable to locate this thought in his writings). If this is the case, what then of blind Homer and all the other male bards of antiquity? Are they the exceptions that prove Eikhenbaum's "rule"? Hardly; even today storytellers in Ireland and many other countries are typically male.

   John Randolph ('"That Historical Family": The Bakunin Archive and the Intimate Theater of History in Imperial Russia, 1780-1925,' *The Russian Review*, October 2004, Vol. 63, No. 4, p. 587) notes that noble women like the Bakunin sisters might be family historians as well, based on family records, mostly religious. This was "a gendered role that grew out of estate management."

42. Bulanova-Trubnikova, *Tri pokoleniia*, p. 145. Svetlana Allilueva (*20 Letters to a Friend*, p. 239) uses the exact same phrase ("a walking chronicle of her age") about her own nanny of the 1930s, adding "What a lot she carried with her to the grave!" This nanny knew *all* the Kremlin gossip.

43. Morozov, *Povesti moei zhizni*, I, pp. 26-27.

44. *Vospominaniia* (Moscow: Khudozhestvennaia literatura, 1991), pp. 18-19.

   Just a few more good examples from autobiographies: Shchepkina, *Vospominaniia*, p. 123; Kharuzina, *Proshloe*, pp. 19-20; Lind, "Moi zapiski," p. 603. Tellingly, it is one of the great regrets of Nikolai Leskov's son that he did not in good time tap into the wealth of memories preserved by his father's aged nanny Stepanovna. See Andrei Leskov, *Zhizn' Nikolaia Leskova*, I, p. 94. Leonid Obolenskii (1845-1906) also notes this phenomenon in his fictionalized memoirs: "Tipy nedavniago proshlago," *IV*, April 1900, Vol. 79, No. 4, pp. 94-95.

45. To quote the country singer Randy Travis, in his "Forever and ever, amen," in evoking an image of love everlasting: "as long as old men sit and talk about the weather, as long as old women sit and talk about old men . . . ." "Servants talk about people, gentlefolk discuss things" is the humorous epigram for Penelope Lively's *Nothing Missing but the Samovar and other stories* (London: Heinemann, 1978).

46. Eikhenbaum, *Moi vremennik. Marshrut v bessmertie* (Moscow: Agraf, 2001), p. 21.

47. "Teni i prizraki," *Russkaia mysl'*, April 1903, Vol. 23, No. 4, second section, pp. 3-5 (for this and the following quote). Akimovna employs all the usual tropes of a fairy-tale teller (p. 53): e.g., "*dolgo li, korotko,*

i skol'ko tomu vremeni proshlo uzh skazat' tebe ne mogu, a tol'ko byla eto zima..." ("Has it been a long or a short time, just how much time I can't tell you, just that it was winter").

48. This topic obviously borders on the issue of nanny as symbol, which I treat later; here I discuss her role in nonsymbolic terms.

49. One author who stressed this aspect of "the nursery" and nannies was the popularizing writer-historian Vladimir Mikhnevich (1841-1899) in his *Russkaia zhenshchina XVIII stoletiia* (Moscow: Kuchkovo pole/ Giperboreia, 2007), pp. 30f.

50. "Petrovna," in *Tainaia pravda i drugie razskazy* (St. Petersburg: M. O. Vol'f, 1912), p. 80.

Very similar is the theme of Fëdor Sologub's "fairy tale" entitled "Who Art Thou?" – in which the twelve-year-old Grishka, son of a cook, is an inveterate dreamer. In the "dull northern metropolis" where he lives, things are not as they are in his fantasies; none of the people is as he feels they should be. He even hates his own name and thus comes to dream that he's under an enchantment, that his real name and identity – that of a prince – have been taken away from him. If only he could recall them, all would be different! See *The Sweet-Scented Name and Other Fairy Tales, Fables and Stories* (New York: G.P. Putnam's Sons, 1915), pp. 67-86.

51. Solov'ëva, "Petrovna," p. 81.

In very similar terms, the memoirist-revolutionary Vera Figner says that only with nanny "did we feel like our true selves" (*Zapechatlennyi trud*, I, pp. 57, 59).

52. Vrangel', *Dalekoe proshloe*, p. 72.

53. *Na zare zhizni*, I, pp. 93, 131, 292.

54. Chertkova, *Iz moego detstva*, p. 172.

55. Cf. Figner, *Zapechatlennyi trud*, pp. 78-79, and Trubetskoi, *Iz proshlago*, pp. 62-63; Passek, *Iz dal'nykh let*, I, pp. 105-06; Aksakova-Sivers, *Semeinaia khronika*, I, p. 36.

56. Kourakine, *De l'aigle imperiale*, pp. 21-22, 166. His memoirs are dedicated to this nanny, "with all my love."

57. Not surprisingly, as we will see in Chapter 8, this is the way the nanny has often been portrayed throughout world – and Russian – literature. Chekhov speaks to what I have in mind in the second act of *Uncle Vania*, when the retired professor Serebriakov and the old nanny Marina Timofeevna are consoling each other.

58. Lifar, *Serge Diaghilev*, p. 11.

59. Dobuzhinskii, *Vospominaniia* (1976), p. 294.

60. Schmemann, *Echoes of a Native Land: Two Centuries of a Russian Village* (New York: Alfred A. Knopf, 1997), pp. 92-93.

61. See Tyrkova-Vil'iams, *To, chego bol'she ne budet*, p. 36.

62. Miroliubov, *Sakral'noe Rusi*, II, bk. 4: *Russkaia mifologiia. Ocherki i materialy*, pp. 203-204.

63. Chertkova, *Iz moego detstva*, pp. 176-78.

Chapter Eight

1. See *Eugene Onegin, A Novel in Verse*, by Aleksandr Pushkin; trans. from the Russian, with a commentary, by Vladimir Nabokov, 4 vols., rev. ed. (Princeton: Princeton University Press, 1975); here, Vol. II, p. 274. For more about Edgeworth's *Ennui* and its significance concerning nannies and wet-nurses, see Chapter 10.

2. In Russia before 1861, the nanny most often had a triune identity – of woman, peasant, and servant, all of them potent for engaging authors' attention. One of the first novelists in Russia, Mikhail Chulkov (ca. 1742-1792), epitomizes the trendiness of these identities in *The Mocker* (1766-68 and 1789) and *The Comely Cook* (1770). See J.G. Garrard, *Mixail Čulkov: An Introduction to his Prose and Verse* (The Hague: Mouton, 1970).

3. See Bakhtin, *Dialogic Imagination*, p. 250. Although it may be a distortion of his idea to employ the term with reference to a character rather than a place and time, I find it a fitting and almost indispensable usage. In a chronotope, says Bakhtin, "time becomes in effect, palpable and visible; the chronotope makes narrative events concrete, makes them take on flesh, causes blood to flow in their veins."

Jay Ladin, in his stimulating essay "Fleshing Out the Chronotope," acknowledges the contradictions and circularity of thought in Bakhtin's concept of the chronotope. But Ladin gets bogged down in overfine analysis, trying to systematize Bakhtin. This seems the antithesis of what Bakhtin, a major anti-systematizer, would want. See Caryl Emerson, ed., *Critical Essays on Mikhail Bakhtin* (New York: G.K. Hall & Co., 1999), pp. 212-36. Emerson's own introduction, pp. 1-26, is very worthwhile reading. Emerson senses "an ethical component to [Bakhtin's] chronotopic progressions, a Hegelian faith in the growth of meaning over time" (p. 12). Nanny literary figures would tend to support her argument of such a progression, as they are associated with earlier chronotopes, and generally represented superstition, ignorance, irrationalism, or plain silliness. Yet there is an element of complexity even here, as nannies were so often invested with heightened moral and ethical feelings that gave deeper meaning to life.

4. Emerson's introduction to *Critical Essays*, p. 10, and Ladin's essay, p. 223.

5. The same phrase recurs constantly in folk lullabies also. See, e.g., *Poeziia detstva: russkoe narodnoe tvorchestvo dlia detei*, comp. and annot. by Valeriia Eremina (St. Petersburg: Aleteiia, 2004), songs 4, 5, 37.

6. *Lekarstvo ot zadumchivosti* and *Dedushkiny progulki ili prodolzhenie nastoiashchikh russkikh skazok. Russkaia skazka v izdaniiakh 80-kh godov 18 veka* (St. Petersburg: Tropa Troianova, 2001), prepared and annot. by K.E. Korepova. This is Vol. 5 of the *Polnoe sobranie russkikh skazok*, subtitled *Rannie sobraniia*.

Peasant songs on historical themes, dating to the seventeenth century but put down on paper only later, also contain the ubiquitous rhyming couple "nannies and mammies." See the songs about "The Birth of the Tsarevich Peter" (i.e., Peter I) and the boiar Skopin-Shuiskii in *Istoricheskie pesni XVII veka*, ed. by B.N. Putilov et al. (Leningrad: Nauka, 1966), pp. 78, 145-46.

7. Mikhail Skripil', *Russkaia povest' XVII veka* (Leningrad: Khudozhestvennaia literatura, 1954), pp. 155-166. An adequate English translation can be found in Serge A. Zenkovsky, ed. and trans., *Medieval Russia's Epics, Chronicles, and Tales* (New York: E. P. Dutton & Co., 1963). Because the nanny is actually an older girl's companion, not linked intimately and symbolically to a very young nursling, she is viewed much as any other servant. The character is little differentiated and presented mostly as loyal or perfidious – classic *servant* traits – and in nonsymbolic terms.

This story (and similar tales) is a literary landmark, beginning the partial supplantation of hagiographic and religious writings by more secular works that foreshadow a deeper and more rapid change of mores and manners in the century that followed. No longer is God or the Devil a real presence in this story. (In fact, Frol rather offhandedly dismisses his own sins of rape and unsanctioned marriage of a minor by saying it's all God's will.) From about 1700 or so the hitherto dominant and virtually unchallenged church-based reading matter of earlier centuries would increasingly yield pride of place in readers' leisure-time reading to stories and novels that had an entirely different purpose.

8. Skripil', *Russkaia povest'* , p. 166. For an excellent analysis of the tale,

see Marcia A. Morris, *The Literature of Roguery in Seventeenth- and Eighteenth-century Russia* (Evanston, IL: Northwestern University Press, 2000), Chapter 3 especially.

This tale is replicated in works of the eighteenth century, most notably in Ivan Novikov's "The Novgorod Girls' Christmas Party," a story in his 1785-86 collection *The Adventures of Ivan the Rich Merchant's Son and Other Stories and Tales*. This work includes the same betrayal of her charge by the nanny. And in a second story in this collection, "The Misadventures of Annushka, the Merchant's Daughter" another corrupt nanny connives with a more aggressively sexual young girl and her lover to evade parental oversight. The nanny almost revels in the young pair's enjoyment of illicit sex. See Morris, *ibid.*, pp. 54-62, 96-99. Also helpful is Gitta Hammarberg, "Eighteenth Century Narrative Variations on 'Frol Skobeev'," *Slavic Review*, Autumn-Winter, 1987, Vol. 46, No. 3/4, pp. 529-39.

9. Aleksandr Sumarokov, *Polnoe sobranie vsekh sochinenii, v stikhakh i proze*, in 10 vols. (Moscow: Moscow University press of N. Novikov, 1787); here, part III, pp. 1-57. The play was written, perhaps, with the tale of Frol Skobeev in mind, more likely with all of Classical literature in view.

10. "Natal'ia, boiarskaia doch'," *Izbrannye sochineniia* (Moscow-Leningrad: Khudozhestvennaia literatura, 1964), Vol. II, p. 630. Did the issue of *Moskovskii zhurnal* with Karamzin's story end up in the library of Pushkin's father? In the early pages of the tale, we find a young girl, unable to sleep. "Natal'ia sat, head in hand – she felt a little sadness, a little languor in her heart; everything seemed not quite right to her, everything was uncomfortable; she got up and sat down again; finally, having roused her nanny [*mama*], she told her that her heart was heavy."

11. That the gentry longed for higher-quality nannies is perhaps indicated by the ongoing practice of hiring foreign nannies.

12. For more on sentimentalism in Russian literature, see the standard work of Rudolf Neuhäuser, *Towards the Romantic Age: Essays on Sentimental and Preromantic Literature in Russia* (The Hague: Martinus Nijhoff, 1974); *Landshaft moikh voobrazhenii: stranitsy prozy russkogo sentimentalizma*, comp., introd., and annot. by Valentin I. Korovin (Moscow: Sovremennik, 1990); K. Skipina, "O chuvstvitel'noi povesti," *Russkaia proza*, ed. by B.M. Eikhenbaum and Iu. Tynianov (The Hague: Mouton, 1963 – reprint of 1926 edition), pp. 13-41; on Karamzin in particular, see Gitta Hamarberg, *From the idyll to the novel: Karamzin's*

Sentimentalist Prose (Cambridge: Cambridge University Press, 1991).

13. Two adequate English versions exist: F. D. Reeve, comp. and trans., *An Anthology of Russian Plays*, Vol. I (New York: Vintage, 1961); George Z. Patrick and George Rapall Noyes, trans., in Noyes, ed. and trans., *Masterpieces of the Russian Drama*, Vol. I (New York: Dover Publications, Inc., 1961).

14. We see, however, that the nanny is no saint herself. She has, for instance, clearly spoiled Mitrofan, albeit willy-nilly; and it hardly seems her place to be "damning" a smoker for his bad habit, which Mrs. Prostakova – probably rightly for the age – calls no sin (Act II, Scene 5).

15. Mrs. Prostakova several times calls her an "ogress," "hussy," or "wretch" (*bestiia*) as well as an "old witch" ("*staraia ved'ma*") and even a "bitch" or "slut" ("*sobach'ia doch'* ") with a "nasty muzzle" or "filthy mug" ("*skvernaia khara*"). Mitrofan addresses her as "an old bag" ("*stara khrychovka*"). The end of Act II is a fine illustration of the mistress's poor treatment of the nanny.

16. That a serf receives wages might seem strange to some. See my discussion in Chapter 3.

    To make sure the audience can't miss the point, a tutor says: "Your life, Eremeevna, is like hell], to which she replies, in tears: "What an ill wind has brought me to. Forty years I've been in service and all the thanks I get...."

17. The actor Ia. D. Shumskii, for example, "brilliantly played the role"in the 1780s. See V. A. Kovalev et al., eds. and comps., "*Minuvshee menia ob"emlet zhivo...*": *Vospominaniia russkikh pisatelei XVIII-nachala XX v. i ikh sovremennikov. Rekomendatel'naia bibliograficheskaia entsiklopediia* (Moscow: "Knizhnaia palata," 1989), p. 16.

18. Oddly, the scholar Pavel Berkov insists that Eremeevna must be treated as a tragic figure, with "the psychology of a slave." See his *Istoriia russkoi komedii XVIII v.* (Leningrad: Nauka, 1977), pp. 230, 251.

19. Seen as early as 1729 in Prince Antiokh Kantemir's first satire "To My Mind," this theme came into its own in comedies of Aleksandr Sumarokov, such as "Monstrosities" (*Chudovishchi*, 1750), "A Quarrel Over Nothing" (*Pustaia ssora*, 1750), and other of his works of mid-century. See Vol. 5 of his *Polnoe sobranie sochinenii v stikhakh i proze* (Moscow: N. I. Novikov – Moscow University Press, 1781). Cf. Harold B. Segel, ed., trans., and annot., *The Literature of Eighteenth-Century Russia: A History and Anthology* (New York: E. P. Dutton & Co., 1967),

vol. II, pp. 318-320.

20. Krylov, *Sochineniia v dvukh tomakh*, II (Moscow: Khudozhestvennaia literatura, 1969), with commentary by L.N. Stepanov. Its link with Karamzin's "A Knight of Our Time" and many eighteenth-century satires is clear and direct, but – as Stepanov notes – the true inspiration was Molière's *Precieuses ridicules* (1659).

21. *Ibid.*, p. 470. See also the analysis by Valentin Korovin, *Poet i mudrets: Kniga ob Ivane Krylove* (Moscow: TERRA, 1996), pp. 263-271.

22. Krylov, *Sochineniia*, II, p. 395.

23. *Ibid.*, pp. 396-399.

24. *Ibid.*, p. 434. Pushkin was well-acquainted with this play and its nanny. See his letter to P. A. Viazemskii of August 14-15, 1825, in which he writes: "Your native tongue is poetry so who's to blame that you so rarely speak it...there's not anyone like a[n Admiral] Shishkov or a Sergei Glinka, or another nanny Vasilisa, [standing] over you, so as to shout at you: be so kind as to swear in rhymes, be so kind as to complain in verse."

25. Cathy Frierson's account of peasant images takes a later date as starting point, but what she says applies rather well to earlier decades. See her *Peasant Icons: Representations of Rural People in Late Nineteenth-Century Russia* (New York: Oxford University Press, 1993).

26. A thoroughgoing political radical, Radishchev probably remains a *homo unius libri* for many students of Russian history and literature. Steeped in the ideas of the Enlightenment and sentimentalism, Europeanized yet extremely patriotic, Radishchev challenged both his sovereign and his fellow nobles with his fictionalized account of travels about the Russian countryside.

An older biography of Radishchev is that of David Marshall Lang, *The First Russian Radical: Alexander Radishchev 1749-1802* (London: George Allen & Unwin Ltd., 1959); more recently he has been the subject of works by Allen McConnell (*A Russian Philosophe: Alexander Radishchev 1749-1802* [Westport, CN: Hyperion Press, 1981; a reprint of the 1964 ed.]) and especially Dmitrii Babkin (*A. N. Radishchev: Literaturno-obshchestvennaia deiatel'nost'* [Moscow: Nauka, 1966]).

27. A literary device which found wide favor among Russian writers of the golden and silver ages, the *skaz*, or framing story, permits the introduction of a narrator separate from the author himself, who recounts – usually in first person – his own adventures.

28. A. N. Radishchev, *Puteshestvie iz Peterburga v Moskvu*, pp. 37-199 in

his *Izbrannye filosofskie sochineniia*, ed. by I. Ia. Shchipanov (Leningrad: Politicheskaia literatura,1949). An excellent English translation by Leo Wiener, with a thoughtful introduction by Roderick Page Thaler, is available (Cambridge, MA: Harvard University Press, 1966) which includes Catherine II's vehement and increasingly almost hysterical commentary on the book.

29. Most "travel literature" of the eighteenth century – such as Montesquieu's *Persian letters* (1721), Voltaire's *Letters Concerning the English Nation* (1732), Laurence Sterne's *A Sentimental Journey Through France and Italy* (1768), and Charles Dupaty's *Lettres sur l'Italie en 1785* (1789) – typically had a dual purpose. They not only described and commented on the situation in countries visited (in fact or in fancy) but also, and especially, critiqued affairs in one's own country. Perhaps the most famous example of all, Swift's *Gulliver's Travels* (1726), did not even need the fig leaf of a journey to a real geographic locale. A recent discussion of travel literature in Russia is Andreas Schönle, *Authenticity and Fiction in the Russian Literary Journey, 1790-1840* (Cambridge, MA: Harvard University Press, 2000). See also T. Roboli, "Literatura puteshestviia," in *Russkaia proza*, ed. by Eikhenbaum and Tynianov, pp. 42-73.

30. See Chapter 10 for an analysis of these various forces at work in literature and in Russian life.

31. The letter's contents were not common knowledge until the 1870s, but the cognoscenti probably knew the gist of the letter long before that.

32. Chekhov, *Polnoe sobranie sochinenii i pisem*, Vol. I, ed. by A. M. Egolin and N. S. Tikhonov (Moscow: Khudozhestvennaia literatura, 1944), p. 60. Italics added. Hereafter, *PSSiP*. Cf. Carolina De Maegd-Soëp, *Chekhov and Women: Women in the Life and Work of Chekhov* (Columbus, OH: Slavica Publishers, 1987), p. 205, who makes the same point, but cites governesses rather than nannies as her prime example.

33. Countless stories include a nanny minor character, though, to his credit, not usually sentimentalized. They were sometimes "silly" or "stupid." See, e.g., "Three Years," "The Investigator," "The Wedding," "The Neighbors,""In the Dark," "The Cripple," "About Love," "The Lady with the Lapdog," "A Living Good," and "The Literature Teacher."

34. In discussing possible misogyny in Chekhov's plays, the critic Nicholas Morav'evich identifies four such archetypes. In addition to the old female servant noted in the text, they are the *jeune fille;* the dominant and assertive woman; and the "humble and understated toiler." See

his "Women in Chekhov's Plays" in *Chekhov's Great Plays: A Critical Anthology*, ed. and introd. by Jean-Pierre Barricelli (New York: New York University Press, 1981), pp. 210-13.

35. *Ibid.*, pp. 213-14.
36. Chekhov, *PSSiP*, IV (1946), pp. 49-53; V (1946), pp. 7-10.
37. *Ibid*, VII (1947), pp. 12-17.
38. Does the character offer a sly critique of Marxian thought also? As she is no longer able to work, of what value is she? Does the so-called "labor theory of value" deny or diminish her value in some way? "The right to keep your job, no matter how shoddy your work or how unnecessary the job itself, was the essence first of Russian communal security and then Soviet socialist security," observes Nina Khrushcheva. "In Chekhov's *Three Sisters* the old peasant nanny is too old to work as she once did. The sisters, however, insist that she stay in the house and help as much or as little as she can, pretending that everything remains the same. Having a job was rarely a matter of money, but rather a matter of personal belonging to a group, being like everyone else [*kak vse*]." See *Cultural Contradictions*, p. 23.
39. Morav'evich, "Women in Chekhov's Plays," p. 214.
40. Cf. Stephen P. Frank, "'Simple Folk, Savage Customs?' Youth, Sociability, and the Dynamics of Culture in Rural Russia, 1856-1914," *Journal of Social History*, Vol. 25, No. 4 (Summer 1992), pp. 711-36; Frierson, *Peasant Icons*, Chapter 2 and Conclusion; Steven A. Grant, "The Peasant Commune in Russian Thought 1861-1905" (PhD dissertation, Harvard, 1973), *passim*. Andrew Donskov, *The Changing Image of the Peasant in Nineteenth Century Russian Drama* (Helsinki: Suomalainen Tiedeadatemia, 1972), p. 35, cites Donald Fanger to the effect that, in early "peasant literature," it's not the characters that are of interest but the situations in which they find themselves.
41. In Russia, this form dates to the appearance of Admiral Aleksandr S. Shishkov's translated lullabies (*Detskaia biblioteka, izdannaia na nemetskom iazyke gospodinom Kampe, a s onogo perepechatannaia g.****, Part 1 [SPB, 1773]). According to the scholar Valentin Golovin, no fewer than 500 authored lullabies have appeared since then. See his *Russkaia kolybel'naia pesnia v fol'klore i literature* (Åbo, Finland: Åbo Akademi University Press, 2000), pp. 277, 292, 311-14, 327, 329-31.

Among the earliest authors to venture their own versions of lullabies were Vasilii Zhukovskii (in 1813), Pushkin, Aleksandr Polezhaev (1835), and Mikhail Lermontov, whose celebrated Cossack lullaby of

1838 was inspired by Sir Walter Scott's "Lullaby of an Infant Chief" (1815). They were followed shortly by the likes of Nikolai Nekrasov, Afanasii Fet (Shenshin), and Taras Shevchenko.

42. Zhadovskaia, *Polnoe sobranie sochinenii Iu. V. Zhadovskoi v chetyrekh tomakh*, ed. by P.V. Bykov, 2nd posthumous ed., enl. and rev.; Vol. I (St. Petersburg: I.P. Perevoznikov, 1894), pp. 85-86.

43. Mikhailov, *Polnoe sobranie stikhotvorenii* (Leningrad: Academia, 1934), p. 572; 738 n to 443.

44. Golovin, *Russkaia kolybel'naia pesnia*, pp. 315-17. Cf. Semën Nadson's 1883 poem "Upali volnistye kudri na plechi," where death is an "old nanny" (*niania staraia*), in *Stikhotvoreniia S. Ia. Nadsona s portretom, faksimile i biograficheskim ocherkom*, 27th ed. (St. Petersburg: M.A. Aleksandrov, 1913), p. 235 (but the poem was published only posthumously).

45. "Niania," *Otechestvennye zapiski*, November 1845, Vol. 43, No. 11, pp. 1-73.

He borrows from Pushkin and every other well-known trope about nannies. His work would hold little interest (apart from who his brother was) but for its early appearance (and its utter unoriginality).

In a similar situation to Pobedonostsev's in being the less talented and less well-known of two siblings, the poet and memoirist Pavel Zhadovskii (1825-1891) wins no prize for originality in his work, but might qualify for some kind of longevity award: he invokes banal nanny images in poems from the mid-1850s through the mid-1880s. Adopting a wistful and often almost maudlin sensibility, he constantly invoked a "painful heart" or "painful soul."

46. E.g., in the Leskov short story "Administrative Grace," where a slandered professor is buried and only "his old nanny and two elderly colleagues" show up for the funeral.

47. American contemporaries will recognize shades of the "magic Negro" motif in such renderings of Russian nannies.

48. "Niania. Etiud," *Drug zhenshchin*, April 1883, No. 4, pp. 18-34. The lengthy quotation is on pp. 33-34. I cannot find any biographical data for Sakharova.

49. This literary creation seems to have inspired Vera Figner when writing of her own nanny's death in *Zapechatlennyi trud*, I, p. 63.

50. Nazer'eva, *Dramy i komedii* (St. Petersburg: S. Dobrodeev, 1895), pp. 274-319. This play is a "comedy" in the same sense that many of Chekhov's dramas are comedies.

51. Published in *Moskvitianin*, 1851, July, No. 13, Sect. III, Bk. 1, pp. 65-80. See Pëtr Fateev, *Mikhail Mikhailov – revoliutsioner, pisatel', publitsist* (Moscow: Mysl', 1969), pp. 110ff. His first play had been a comedy "Auntie" (*Tetushka*) – an attack on serfdom and serfowners. But it couldn't be published until 1860. "Nanny Dear" is one of many of his works which are, for Soviet hack critics, "ardent sermons of the ideas of good, light, freedom, and love for the downtrodden and injured" – thus, an examplar of not just a literary stereotype but a political-ideological one as well. See Shelgunovs and Mikhailov, *Vospominaniia*, II, pp. 465, 572-73nn.

52. *Moskvitianin*, *ibid.*, pp. 65-76. Clearly the ideological stereotype enters the literary here.

53. *Ibid.*, pp. 79-80.

54. *Iumor nachala XX veka*, ed. by Stanislav Rassadin et al. (Moscow: OLMA-Press, 2003), pp. 373-76. He couldn't resist the temptation altogether; see "Nanny" ("*Nian'ka*") in the collection *O khoroshikh, v sushchnosti, liudiakh!* 4th ed. (St. Petersburg: Novyi Satirikon, 1914).

Like Nadezhda Tèffi, Averchenko loved to play with the fairy tale genre; see his anthologies of short stories: *A Dozen Knives in the Revolution's Back* and *Dreams About the Past* (both 1921). (Trotskii and Lenin are frequent targets of his barbs.)

55. Readers are made aware at the start that they may be treated to a tall tale – the narrator calls himself Fliagin, literally "a man of the flask" – and Leskov/Fliagin does not disappoint.

56. Leskov, *Selected Tales*, trans. by David Magarshack (New York: Farrar, Straus and Cudahy/The Noonday Press, 1961), p. 81. I've taken the liberty of amending Magarshack's generally excellent translation in order to bring out my theme better.

Leskov included female nannies in many of his stories, including also *The Enchanted Pilgrim*, but most were unmemorable. They were typically "scene-setters" and background decoration in such works as *Laughter and Sorrow* (1871); *A Ruined Clan* (1874); "Will-o'-the-Wisps" (1875); "The Toupee Artist. A Graveside Tale" (1883); and "The Bugbear" (1885).

57. Staniukovich, *Sobranie sochinenii v shesti tomakh*, Vol. 1 (Moscow: Khudozhestvennaia literatura, 1958), pp. 15-81. Page references appear in the body of the text in parentheses.

58. Through the rather trite expedient of Shura's falling gravely ill and Chizhik's staying at his side day and night to nurse him, Luzgina

finally recognizes his true character and great love for the boy. The doctor tells her what a wonderful caregiver she has.

59. By rights, this story should probably have been discussed in a chapter on *diad'ki*, not here, especially given Shura's somewhat "advanced" age of 7-8. But I have deferred to the author's insistence on using the feminine term.

60. Volkonskii, "Semeinaia khronika," p. 594. Presumably he took his title from Sergei Aksakov's masterpiece. As the inveterate borrower that he was, Volkonskii may well have taken this detail from the memoirs of Erazm Stogov (1797-1880), who notes of his own nanny that from her belt "hung a handkerchief, of thick blue linen with white spots, with which she frequently wiped my nose; but the handkerchief was of such coarse material that after a wiping I saw stars for quite a while...." See "Zapiski E. I. Stogova," *RS*, January 1903, vol. 113, no. 1, p. 142.

Mar'ia Kamenskaia (1817-1898) tells a variation of this theme in her memoirs. She once lived near the Grigorovich family with five children. "Their children had a strange peculiarity," she writes; "every other one was either very long in the nose or snub-nosed." "And Vasilii Ivanovich [the father] would often say, laughing, that people's profiles depend on their nannies, that their nanny Nasten'ka, into whose arms fell their first son Kolia, would blow his nose lifting the nose upward with the handkerchief, while nanny Marfa, to whom in turn was given their second daughter Aniuta, blew her nose downward, would finish blowing and pull powerfully on the nose twice more...." Sure enough, the Grigorovichs' first-born, Nikolai (Kolia) had a snub nose, the second, "long-nosed Niuta," was followed by "the snub-nosed Sonichka," in whose wake came "the long-nosed Kosten'ka," and after him "the delightful infant Vasia with a little button instead of a nose." See Kamenskaia, *Vospominaniia*, pp. 148-49.

61. This idiosyncracy is not mentioned by any other author (of fiction or autobiography) that I can recall. What was the difference between her "summer" and her "winter" stories? "The first breathed of sincerity and the unamusing poetry [*nezateilivaia poeziia*] of the common folk, so closely acquainted with nature and popular beliefs." Summer tales would usually evoke a smile, joy, laughter, but sometimes sadness as well. The winter tales, "fear, tears" and "sometimes at night produced anxious dreams." Volkonskii, "Semeinaia khronika," p. 597.

62. Krestovskaia, *Rannyia grozy. Ispytanie* (St. Petersburg: A. S. Suvorin, 1889). She was the daughter of the well-known writer Vsevolod Krestovskii.

63. "This nanny always irritated [Mar'ia Sergeevna] with her incompetence [*neumelost'*], but at this moment she could not even bear the sight of her...." In one incident of slight and unintended negligence, the nanny leaves her charge alone briefly; he falls to the floor and sustains a bloody nose. Yet in time of later crisis, this nanny is a rock of dependability and support.

64. Militsyna, *Razskazy*, pp. 191-200.

65. Nikolai Mikhailovskii used the pseudonym N. Garin. Concerning the relationship between his life and his writing, see John McNair, "Childhood and the Quest for Self: Nikolai Garin-Mikhailovsky and the Uses of Autobiography," in *New Zealand Slavonic Journal*, 2001, Vol. 35, pp. 49-60.

66. Garin-Mikhailovskii, "V usad'be pomeshchitsy Iaryshchevoi," *Rasskazy i ocherki* (Moscow: Pravda, 1984), pp. 283-84

67. "He has a foreign nanny [*bonna*] – a German woman . . . quite young, loving, quiet, he fell in love with [her] and in two months had begun speaking with her in German. Now he is thinking in this language.

"I infer this from the fact that with the dog, for example, he speaks in German.

"And one has to see what friends he is with his German nanny!

"They have their own conversations, their own secrets, and the most sensitive, tender love for each other: they're comrades.

"But all the same he loves me most of all." (*Ibid.*, p. 311)

68. See Kelly, *Children's World*, Part I.

69. Lappo-Danilevskaia, *V usad'be: Roman* (Paris: Concorde, 1928); page references appear in the text.

70. *Istoki*, Vol. I (Paris: YMCA-Press, 1950), pp. 254-55. Aldanov's treatment in this novel of the morganatic marriage of Alexander II and Princess Dolgorukova – and their nanny – is also worth noting.

71. In Ol'ga Sorokina's biography-cum-critique of Ivan Shmelëv and his works, the eleventh chapter is devoted to *Nanny from Moscow*. She says: "The idea for Shmelyov's newest work had originated during the winter of 1926-27, when the author and his wife [shared a large apartment in Sèvres with another Russian family]...the propinquity of a Moscow family must have seemed the friendly nudge of some muse-*concierge* to a favored writer-tenant, for the Karpov family had brought their old nanny with them from France....when the doors were ajar, [the

Shmelyovs] could overhear the racy, colloquial conversations between the Karpovs' nanny and her special young friend. The parlance of the family servant became the aural prototype for Shmelyov's fictional nanny – the narrator of his novel." See Sorokin (sic), *Moscoviana: The Life and Art of Ivan Shmelyov* (Oakland, CA: Barbary Coast Books, 1987), p. 196. On p. 311 (n1) she cites two sources for this information: an A. V. Kartashov article in *Sbornik*, Munich, 1956; and a Shmelëv letter of 19 November 1926. [This monograph has been translated into Russian, with the author's name "Russianized": Ol'ga Nikolaevna Sorokina, *Moskoviana: Zhizn' i tvorchestvo Ivana Shmeleva* (Moscow: Moskovskii rabochii/ Skify, 1994).]

The only cautionary note that must be sounded here is that Sorokina derives much of what she says about Shmelëv's childhood from his quasi-autobiographical novels from the 1930s *Leto Gospodne* (*The Year of our Lord* – also called *Anno Domini*) and *Bogomol'e* (*Pilgrimage*). This is always very risky. But the information she adduces for the author's "revelation" concerning using a Russian nanny is to me convincing.

72. Mar'ia Tsebrikova (1835-1917), the author and pedagog, published a small book (30 pp.) entitled *Rasskaz niani* in 1911 that almost seems to anticipate Shmelëv's opus, even to the point of using the *skaz* technique. However, her small effort is quite dissimilar; it is a moralistic little tale designed, as the title of the series in which it appears proclaims, "for the family and school." The title character is a well-rounded, if somewhat stereotypical figure, a former serf, with well-developed "moral antennae."

73. Shmelëv, *Niania iz Moskvy* (published together with *Istoriia liubovnaia*) in *Istoriia liubovnaia* (Moscow: Moskva, 1995), pp. 243-405. Page references to the edition used appear in the body of the text.

74. They would not even have baptized Katia were it not for the aunt whose money they covet. They refuse to let nanny teach Katia her prayers or have Katia wear a cross.

75. Icons and the concept of "conciliarity" (*sobornost'*) play a large role in what happens in this novel. For example, on pp. 259-60, where not just the icon of St. Nicholas (*Nikolai-Ugodnik*) but also the icons of the Mother of God of Iversk and of Kazan are noted. See S.V. Sheshunova, "Roman I. S. Shmeleva *Niania iz Moskvy* v svete kategorii sobornosti," in *I. S. Shmelev v kontekste slavianskoi kul'tury*, Vol. VIII of *Krymskie Mezhdunarodnye Shmelevskie chteniia: Sbornik materialov mezhdunarodnoi nauchnoi konferentsii*, ed. by V. P. Tsygannik (Alushta: no Publisher, 2000 [1999]), pp. 24-28. Cf. Sorokin, *Moscoviana*, passim, for an excellent

discussion of Shmelëv's religiosity. Alexandra Smith's "I.S. Shmelev," in *Twentieth-Century Russian Émigré Writers* (Vol. 317 of *Dictionary of Literary Biography*), ed. by Maria Rubins (Detroit, MI: Thomson Gale, 2005), pp. 293-300, is also useful but appears disturbingly close to Sorokin's work (uncredited).

76. This scene is reminiscent of the father-daughter farewell in Labzina's memoirs (Chapter 2).

77. See especially the poignant ending, p. 405, where the dying nanny wants only to be buried, like the Grey Wolf, at her mistress's side. Cf. Sorokin, *Moscoviana*, pp. 207-208.

78. This novel is far from Shmelëv's only mystical-religious work. His 1926 story "The Blessed" (*Blazhennye*) in his *Sobranie sochinenii*, Vol. II: *V"ezd v Parizh: Rasskazy. Vospominaniia. Publitsistika* (Moscow: Russkaia kniga, 1998), pp. 99-106, is a near-perfect picture of what he saw in the aftermath of the 1917 revolution (he emigrated in December 1922) that made him a sad, old man before his time. Full of spiritualism and God, it is an elegy and perhaps even a panegyric for the "old Russia" of his youth. The 9th and 11th volumes of *Krymskie Mezhdunarodnye Shmelevskie chteniia* (endnote 683), ed. by Lidiia Spiridonova (Evstigneeva) discuss Shmelëv and Slavic/Orthodox spiritual traditions and culture.

79. See Elizabeth B. Neatrour, *Miniatures of Russian Life at Home and in Emigration: The Life and Works of N. A. Tèffi* (PhD dissertation, Indiana University, 1972), pp. 185, 226.

80. Her story "Golden Childhood" (*Dym bez ognia*, pp. 175-181) is pointedly deflating about both the ideal of its title and the nanny-child relationship.

81. According to L.A. Spiridonova (Evstigneeva), in Paris one day Tèffi encountered an old Russian nanny and her masters/employers on the Eiffel Tower – an incident which may have affected the writer somewhat like Shmelëv's nanny epiphany. This woman was asking her employers for some hempseed oil and fishheads, declaring to them that she has in mind to raise fowl. "You've gone too far!" the nanny would tell them. "No stove-couch, no felt boots (*valenki*) [await her in a dreary retirement]." Tèffi was touched by this meeting with the nanny and, says Spiridonova, this had an effect on her future writing. Spiridonova, "Teffi," in *Russkaia satiricheskaia literatura nachala XX veka* (Moscow: Nauka, 1977), pp. 156-70.

82. Tèffi, "Nostal'giia," in *Nostal'giia. Rasskazy. Vospominaniia* (Leningrad: Khudozhestvennaia literatura, 1989), pp. 161-164.

83. Many of her best, most playful, and biting satires involve fairy tales. The delightful "A Little Fairy Tale" (1920s) details the unenviable fates of fairy tale monsters under the Soviet regime (*Sobranie sochinenii*, Vol. 3, *Gorodok* [Moscow: Lakom, 1999]); her droll "Nanny's Tale About the Mare's Head" (1910) pokes fun at idealized nannies (*Iumoristicheskie rasskazy; Iz "Vseobshchei istorii, obrabotannoi 'Satirikonom'*," comp. and annot. by D. D. Nikolaev [Moscow: Khudozhestvennaia literatura, 1990]); and "The Terrifying Fairy Tale" (*Sobranie sochinenii*, Vol. I: *I stalo tak* . . . [Moscow: "Lakom," 1998]) scares children not with monsters but a stock-market crash.

84. Haber, Foreword to Tèffi, *Gorodok* (NY: Russica Publishers, Inc., 1982), pp. ix-x.

85. Although written before the true extent of Nazi atrocities became fully apparent, Tèffi's story is almost prescient in having Shparagov anticipate some of Nazism's worst ideas. Equally, he is reminiscent of Dostoevskii's Underground Man. "Love makes us maintain the life of those specimens who are completely unneeded and even harmful for mankind. Some tubercular gentleman, who eats up the ration which could sustain a needed, working man. Moreover, the one with TB could infect others with his sickness. And he also depletes the strength of those who are looking after him. Mankind bears all of this unnecessary burden, and for what?" Shparagov's plan is to get rid of only the incurably ill at first, but then gradually get rid of all superfluous people.

In the end, Shparagov lovingly helps Valentina with the nanny and leaves us wondering if he was only playing devil's advocate. Tèffi's viewpoint seems to be that, despite his protestations and perhaps even his own preferences, Shparagov – like most of us – can be irrational, and love persists, no matter what.

86. Zoshchenko, *Izbrannye proizvedeniia v dvukh tomakh* (Leningrad: Khudozhestvennaia literatura, 1968), pp. 197-200. Page references appear in the body of the text. An English version of this story, "The Nursemaid," appears in Zoshchenko, *Nervous People and Other Satires*, trans. by Maria Gordon and Hugh McLean, with the help of Fruma Gottschalk, ed. and introd. by McLean (New York: Vintage Books, 1963), pp. 181-184 (but in a variant reading).

87. Zoshchenko puts a nice Soviet gloss on the situation in his conclusion: "She [the nanny] was probably in desperate need of money; otherwise it's just very hard to explain her behavior. But I simply can't grasp what she needs the money for. The old woman is fed, clothed, has

nice felt boots [*valenki*], receives a nice salary. This is just some sort of caprice on her part and, mainly, most likely, [due to] her former petty-bourgeois upbringing, a senseless craving for money, and an incorrect worldview." (p. 200)

88. The great comic Arkadii Raikin picked up on similar themes – of a nanny "using" her would-be employers – in his classic TV routine "Ah, nanny, nanny" in the 1950s, available online at http://rutube.ru/tracks/1384358.html?v=34ccce5c74bedb8567492e0033c8f1f0 and – an extended radio version – http://www.staroeradio.ru/audio/16668 (accessed November 2011). My thanks to Alissa Klots for these references.

89. Some historians consider the destruction of the Russian village in the twentieth century as the single most important historical event for that country, notwithstanding the devastation of World War II.

90. See the excellent discussion in Kathleen Parthé, *Russian Village Prose: The Radiant Past* (Princeton: Princeton University Press, 1992), Chapters 2 and 3 passim, and eadem, "The Rural Writer's Imagined Childhood: Poetry and Politics," in *a/b: Auto/Biography Studies* Fall 1996, Vol. 11, No. 2. *Special Issue: Rethinking Russian Autobiography*, ed. by Marina Balina, pp. 87-104 – here, pp. 95-97 – where grannies (and grampas) are shown typically to evoke nanny-like sentiments – i.e., nostalgia for the past, family bonds, childhood memories of happy times. Almost to clinch the comparison, most have trunks.

91. Astaf'ev, *Poslednyi poklon: Povest'* [sic] (Perm: Permskoe knizhnoe izdatel'stvo, 1968). Stories like "Predchuvstvie ledokhoda" ("A Harbinger of Spring"; 1988) and various pieces in his collection *The Steed with the Rose-Colored Mane* (first published 1964) also feature grandmother/nanny figures.

92. See Aref'eva, *Ispoved' bez dukhovnika* (Moscow: RIO GPNTB SSSR, 1990), pp. 27-29. This story purports to show something of what a post-emancipation nanny might have felt for unsympathetic employers and charges, especially an older, capricious nurseling.

93. Solzhenitsyn, *Matrenin dvor* (London: Flegdon Press, 1965), pp. 25-26; italics added. Further page references are in the text.

Chapter Nine

1. In all cases, I will be speaking only of people who themselves documented and spoke of their having had a nanny or whose nannies were documented by others close to them, usually a sibling or offspring.

In the absence of more direct testimony, I cannot judge the merits of such second-hand claims as V.L. Velichko's about the nanny of the philosopher Vladimir Solov'ëv and his siblings: "In the period from 6 to 10 years of age, occupied with [Vladimir's] *vospitanie* was – besides his parents – Anna Kuz'minishna Kolerova, whom he jokingly called Anna-the-Prophet [*Anna-prorochitsa*] because she would occasionally see things in dreams, predictions of that which more than once occurred and *produced on her young nurseling a powerful impression.*" (This quotation from Velichko's *Vladimir Solov'ev. Zhizn' i tvoreniia*, 2nd ed. [St. Petersburg, 1903], p. 11, is in Sergei Luk'ianov, "O Vl. S. Solov'ev v ego molodye gody. Materialy k biografii," in *Zhurnal ministerstva narodnago prosveshcheniia*, March 1915, N.S. Part 56, Section 2, p. 36.) (Italics added)

2. Limitations of space alone prohibit inclusion of many interesting examples of these paradigms. E.g., the writer Vsevolod Garshin (1855-1888) [sources: Garshin, *Polnoe sobranie sochinenii V. M. Garshina* (St. Petersburg: A. F. Marks, 1910) – "Avtobiograficheskaia zametka," pp. 5-9 compared to his brother's "Vospominaniia brata, Evgeniia Mikhailovicha," *ibid.*, pp. 9-15]; the composers Peter Tchaikovsky (1840-1892) [Modest Chaikovskii, *The Life and Letters of Peter Ilich Tchaikovsky*, ed. by Rosa Newmarch, 2 vols. (New York: Vienna House, 1973); here, Vol. I, pp. 5-15; *Vospominaniia o P.I. Chaikovskom*, comp. and ed. E.E. Bortnikova et al. (Moscow: Gosudarstvennoe muzykal'noe izdatel'stvo, 1962), appendix; David Brown, *Tchaikovsky: A Biographical and Critical Study*. Vol. I: *The Early Years (1840-1874)* (London: Victor Gollancz Ltd., 1978), pp. 27-28]; Sergei Rakhmaninov (1873-1943) [*Rachmaninoff's recollections, told to Oskar von Riesemann* (New York, The Macmillan Company, 1934); Vera Briantseva, *Detstvo i iunost' Sergeia Rakhmaninova*, 2nd ed. (Moscow: Sovetskii kompozitor, 1973), pp. 10, 27ff; Sergei Bertensson and Jay Leyda, *Sergei Rachmaninoff: A Lifetime in Music* with Sophia Satina (New York: New York University Press, 1956), pp. 1-3]; Sergei Prokof'ev (1891-1953) [Prokof'ev, *Avtobiografiia*, 2nd enl. ed. (Moscow: Sovetskii kompozitor, 1982), p. 39; Vladimir Blok, *Muzyka Prokof'eva dlia detei* (Moscow: Muzyka, 1969), p. 27; *S.S. Prokof'ev: Materialy. Dokumenty. Vospominaniia*, 2nd enl. ed., comp. and ed. S.I. Shlifshtein (Moscow: Gosudarstvennoe muzykal'noe izdatel'tstvo, 1961), pp. 71, 627 n17]; and Aleksandr Grechaninov (1864-1956) [Grechaninov, *Moia zhizn'*, 2nd enl. ed. (New York: Raausen Brothers/Novyi zhurnal, [1951]), pp. 18-19]; the opera singer Antonina Nezhdanova (1873-1950) ["Vospominaniia," in *Antonina Vasil'evna Nezhdanova: Materialy i issledovaniia*, ed. by V.A. Vasina-Grossman

(Moscow: Iskusstvo, 1967), pp. 9-10; V.M. Bogdanov-Berezovskii, "Velikaia russkaia pevitsa," *ibid.*, p. 207]; and the actor Igor' Il'inskii (1901-1987) [Il'inskii, *Sam o sebe*, 2nd rev. and enl. ed. (Moscow: Iskusstvo, 1973), p. 11].

3. Despite the authors' (sometimes relative) lack of attention to their real-life nannies, nanny characters frequently figure in their writings or other creative works, sometimes as major characters, usually not as mere conventions or symbols. In every case, the literary treatment of a nanny or nannies is not merely *pro forma*, run-of-the-mill. A question naturally arises for the anomalous model: why and in what ways did the nanny become an inspiration beyond what might be otherwise expected? The answer to this question is, in virtually all cases: use of a nanny character satisfied the artistic-esthetic needs of the author. It may be that the author would have included nanny characters in his/her writing regardless of the existence of a real-life nanny in childhood.

4. In this second subset of the paradigm, a somewhat different question might be asked: why should adult men and women exaggerate the place of their childhood nannies in their own lives? The answer here appears to be that a nanny character satisfies primarily some psychological (e.g., emotional or political) needs of the adult.

5. This, according to his brother, Andrei, not Fëdor himself. She even bears her own name in *The Possessed*. See Andrei M. Dostoevskii, "Iz 'Vospominanii'," in *F. M. Dostoevskii v vospominaniiakh*, I, p. 390.

6. See, e.g., Iurii Seleznev, *Dostoevskii*, 4th ed. (Moscow: Molodaia gvardiia, 2004), p. 13.

7. Tolstoi, "Vospominaniia," *PSS*, Vol. 34 (1952), pp. 373-74. Instead, the housekeeper Praskov'ia Isaevna is rendered as Savishna. See commentary to "Moia zhizn'," *PSS*, Vol. 23 (1957), p. 563n22.

8. Cf. his "Podstrizhennymi glazami: iz knigi vospominanii, in Remizov, *Neuemnyi buben: roman, povesti, rasskazy, skazki, vospominaniia*, comp. and annot. by V.A. Chalmaev (Kishinev: Lit. Artistike, 1988), pp. 459-64, 475-76, 479; and *V rozovom bleske* (Letchworth, England: Bradda Books, 1969), pp. 395-97.

9. Gertsyk offers contradictory evidence in "Iz mira detskikh igr," in her *Stikhi i proza*, I, pp. 40, 66 (was there no nanny or just no devout nanny?), as does Nadson – probably the most popular Russian poet of the 1880s-90s – in his "Avtobiografiia S. Ia. Nadsona,"*VE*, March 1887, Vol. 22, Bk. 2, p. 437 *vice* notes in *Stikhotvoreniia S. Ia. Nadsona*, p. viii, not to mention his poetry (*ibid.*, pp. 103, 111, 229-31), which doesn't

seem to be about his own mother and childhood.

10. Peasants appear in Russian art as part of genre painting in the middle to late eighteenth century; this is a recognizable trend throughout Europe at the time. Early examples in Russia of artists portraying peasants are A. Vishniakov, M. Shibanov, and I. Ermenev. But their subjects are the peasantry – in groups – more than individual peasants.

11. On Venetsianov and the beginnings of nationalism in Russian art, see Rosalind Polly Gray, "The Real and the Ideal in the Work of Aleksei Venetsianov," *Russian Review*, Vol. 58, No. 4 (Oct., 1999), pp. 655-675; Tat'iana Alekseeva, "Venetsianov i razvitie bytovogo zhanra," in *Istoriia russkogo iskusstva*, Vol. 8, bk. 1 (Moscow: Nauka, 1963, pp. 546-98; and *Venetsianov and his School*, comp. and introd. by Tat'iana Alekseeva; trans. by Carolyn Justice and Yuri Kleiner (Leningrad: Aurora Art Publishers, 1984).

Pavel Fedotov's (1815-1852) pencil drawing of Domnushka, a serf nanny in the Zhdanovich family (c. 1847), and another drawing from 1848-49 are other early pictorial representations. In the second, a young boy named Vasilii (Vasia) asks an older woman stroking a cat on her lap: "Nanny, which Vasia do you love more, me or kit[ty]?" ("Vasia" was a common feline name, the equivalent of "Tom" in the U.S.). Print reproductions are in Iakov D. Leshchinskii, *Pavel Andreevich Fedotov: Khudozhnik i poet* (Leningrad-Moscow: Iskusstvo, 1946), pp. 112-13; *Pavel Fedotov: Katalog* (St. Petersburg: Seda-S, 1993), item 165, and in Igor' E. Grabar' et al., *Istoriia russkogo iskusstva*, Vol. 8, Bk. 2 (Moscow: Nauka, 1964), p. 326.

12. Nikolai Venetsianov, in *Aleksei Gavrilovich Venetsianov: Stat'i. Pis'ma. Sovremenniki o khudozhnike*, comp., annot. and introd. by A. V. Kornilova (Leningrad: Iskusstvo, 1980), pp. 210, 212, and endnote, p. 337.

13. Aleksandr Benois is said to have (re)discovered Venetsianov in the 1890s and sung his praises – and that of the nanny portrait – to his protegé-artist Zinaida Serebriakova (1884—1967). She reportedly copied it as a form of training. See http://biopeoples.ru/women/page,2,733-zinaida-evgenevna-serebrjakova.html (accessed Jan. 2012).

In some histories of Russian art or biographies of the painter, this work is entitled "Old Nanny in a Head-Dress" (*Staraia niania v shlychke*). See Galina Leont'eva, *Aleksei Gavrilovich Venetsianov* (Leningrad: Iskusstvo, 1988), eighteenth (unnumbered) page following p. 288. But in other studies, equally authoritative, the painting bears a different title: "Old Woman in Head-Dress" (*Starukha v shlychke*). Grabar' et al., *Istoriia russkogo iskusstva*, Vol. 8, Bk. 1 (Moscow: Nauka, 1963), p. 583. The testimony of the artist's "nephew" Nikolai, cited above, would seem to resolve the issue in favor of the first title.

This oil on canvas, now in the State Russian Museum in St. Petersburg, can be found in color online (accessed Feb. 2012) at: http://artru.info/il/3973/.

14. *Zhivopis' pervoi poloviny XIX veka*, ed. by Ia.V. Bruk and L.I. Iovleva, Vol. 3 (Moscow: Skanrus/State Tretiakov Gallery, 2005), pp. 78-79. The painting depicts the children of Vladimir Ivanovich Panaev (1792-1853), privy councillor and state secretary, with their nanny (almost invisible, on the far left of the canvas). The children are in two separate groupings, supposedly "joined" by the figure of the nanny. See this oil in color online (accessed Jan. 2012) at: http://www.artcyclopedia.ru/portret_detej_panaevyh_s_nyanej_1841venecianov_aleksej_gavrilovich.htm.

15. A date of late 1820s is given in *Aleksei Venetsianov*, with text by Tamara Kozhevnikova, ed. by N. Nadol'skaia et al. (Moscow: Belyi gorod, 2001), p. 38 (with reproduction); an early 1830s date is found in *Zhivopis' pervoi poloviny XIX veka*, p. 76.

"Wet-nurse with Child" may be viewed in color online (accessed Feb. 2012) at: http://www.artcyclopedia.ru/kormilica_s_rebenkom_nachalo_1830hvenecianov_aleksej_gavrilovich.htm.

16. The three versions are in Goncharov, *Sobranie sochinenii* (1955), I, pp. 221-230; the quote here is from p. 221.

17. Goncharov, "Na rodine," *Sobranie sochinenii* (1980), VII, pp. 258-349; here, p. 267.

His relations with nanny Annushka are made to seem all the sweeter in that "Mother loved us not with that sentimental, animal-like love which spills out in heated shows of affection, in a weak pandering to and satisfying of children's whims and which spoils the children." *Ibid.*, p. 269.

18. Potanin, "Vospominaniia ob I.A. Goncharove," in *I.A. Goncharov v vospominaniiakh sovremennikov* (Leningrad: Khudozhestvennaia literatura, 1969), pp. 29, 40-41. Potanin was briefly the home tutor of the children of Goncharov's sister, A.A. Kirmalova.

19. Kirmalov, "Vospominaniia ob I.A. Goncharove," *ibid.*, p. 113. His memoirs are published here for the first time, abridged, from a ms. in TsGALI, f. 488, op. 1, No. 51.

20. This does not mean, however, that attempts to mythologize Goncharov's

nanny are not extant. See, for example, the short essay by V.I. Mel'nik, "I.A. Goncharov's Nanny" posted online: http://www.portalslovo.ru/philology/37111.php (accessed January 2012); originally, *Literaturnaia Rossiia*, No. 14, 7 April 2006 (also available online).

21. Musorgskii, *Literaturnoe nasledie: Pis'ma, biograficheskie materialy i dokumenty*, comp. by A. A. Orlova and M. S. Pekelis (Moscow: Muzyka, 1971), p. 267. There were actually several different sketches, in Russian and French, written shortly before the composer's death (i.e., ca. June 1880). V. V. Stasov, Musorgskii's long-time friend, patched them together into a "standard" text. See the discussion in Musorgskii, *Pis'ma i dokumenty*, comp. by A. N. Rimskii-Korsakov with V. D. Komarova-Stasova (Moscow-Leningrad, 1932), pp. 416-21, concerning the various drafts of the autobiography. One always worries at the involvement of the heavy-handed nationalist Stasov in the editing of memoirs like Musorgskii's and Ge's – or Mikhail Glinka's, as we will see shortly.

22. Readers interested in more detail and analysis than can be offered here are referred to two excellent biographies of the composer: D. Brown, *Musorgsky* (2002) and Caryl Emerson, *The Life of Musorgsky* (Cambridge: Cambridge University Press, 1999). Other valuable Western studies include *Musorgsky: In Memoriam 1881-1981*, ed. by Malcolm Hamrick Brown (Ann Arbor, MI: UMI Research Press, 1982); Richard Taruskin, *Musorgsky: Eight Essays and an Epilogue* (Princeton: Princeton University Press, 1993).

23. The standard and in most respects still unsurpassed study of "populism" is Franco Venturi, *Roots of Revolution: A History of the Populist and Socialist Movements in Nineteenth Century Russia*, trans. by Francis Haskell (New York: Knopf, 1960).

24. D. Brown, *Musorgsky*, pp. 30f, 68.

25. See M. Brown, "Native Song and National Consciousness in Nineteenth-Century Russian Music," *Art and Culture in Nineteenth-Century Russia*, ed. Theofanis George Stavrou (Bloomington: Indiana University Press, 1983); Richard Hoops, "Musorgsky and the Populist Age," in M. Brown, *Musorgsky: In Memoriam*, pp. 271-306; Edward Garden, "Balakirev's Influence on Musorgsky," in M. Brown, *Musorgsky: In Memoriam*, pp. 11-27; Emerson, *Life of Musorgsky*, pp. xviii-xx, 3, 7-15; Taruskin, *Musorgsky*, p. 385.

26. Henry S. Drinker, *English Texts for the Songs of Modeste Moussorgsky (1835-1881)* ([PA: self-published, 1951?]), p. xiv. See Oskar von Riesemann, *Moussorgsky*, trans. by Paul England (New York: Tudor Publishing Co., 1935), pp. 10, 142-44. Musorgskii wrote the first song in

the series *Scenes from Childhood* two years before adding the next four. In 1872 he wrote the last two, the earlier five having been renamed by that time *The Nursery*, a suggestion of the composer's friend and "mentor" Stasov.

27. Drinker, *English Texts*, p. xv.

28. *Ibid.*, p. xv-xvi. Cf. Riesemann, *Moussorgsky*, pp. 144-45.

29. Emerson, *Musorgsky*, pp. 71-75. For additional musical insights of the song "With Nanny," see Michael Russ, *Music Analysis,* Vol. 9, No. 1 (*A Musorgsky Symposium*), March 1990), pp. 47-65.

30. D. Brown, *Musorgsky*, p. 104.

31. *Ibid.*, p. 200. A more detailed musical description of the piece is on pp. 105 and 113.

32. The recent Chester Dunning (and others) work *The Uncensored* Boris Godunov: *The Case for Pushkin's Original* Comedy, *with Annotated Text and Translation* (Madison: The University of Wisconsin Press, 2006) appears a model of scholarship; see in particular Caryl Emerson, "The Ebb and Flow of Influence: Muffling the Comedic in the Move toward Print," pp. 192-232. Emerson's earlier *Boris Godunov: Transpositions of a Russian Theme* (Bloomington, IN: Indiana U Press, 1986) is still of value as well. For the opera alone, see Richard Taruskin's superb "Musorgsky vs. Musorgsky: The Versions of 'Boris Godunov' (II)," *19th-Century Music*, Vol. 8, No. 3 (Spring, 1985), pp. 245-72.

33. Cf. Musorgskii, *Boris Godunov: Opera v chetyrekh deistviiakh s prologom* (Moscow: Gosizdat, Muzykal'nyi sektor, 1928), pp. 40ff.

34. Riesemann, *Moussorgsky*, pp. 9-10.

35. Cited in Michel D. Calvocoressi, *Modest Mussorgsky: His Life and Works* (London: Rockliff Publishing Corp., 1956), p. 14. The biographer quoted is Pierre d'Alheim, husband of the noted Russian-French singer and Musorgskii "popularizer" Mariia Olenina-d'Alheim (1869-1970).

36. *Ibid.*

37. Personal communication to the author, June 2005.

38. D. Brown, *Musorgsky*, p. 197.

39. See Musorgskii, *Literaturnoe nasledie*, p. 267, and the enlightening discussion of the various drafts in Musorgskii, *Pis'ma i dokumenty*, pp. 416-21.

40. The caretaker next after Afim'ia his wet-nurse was named Aleksandra and she was with the child from his first year, 1880, until late in 1883.

A German *bonna*, Karolina Karlovna came after Aleksandra (end of December 1883 or early January 1884-February 1884). Her successors were: Fanny Andreevna (ca. February 1884-spring 1884), Raisa Ivanovna Rapoport (German or Swiss; spring 1884-fall 1885), Henrietta Martynovna (German; fall 1885-fall 1886), Fraulein Nokkert (German; fall 1886-spring 1887), Mlle. Matilda (French; May 1887), Koenig and Becker (German; both April 1887 or a little later), Mlle. Mary (French; January-March 1888), Madame Theresa (French *bonna*; April-fall 1888), Madame Fumichon (French; fall 1888-spring 1889), and Mlle. Belle Radin (French; May 1889-fall 1892). It's interesting that many noted public figures appear in these pages under pseudonyms (e.g., I. I. Ianzhul the statistician is called Pompul', the lawyer-historian of the Great Reforms Grigorii Avetovich Dzhanshiev becomes Mrktich Avetovich), but the nannies are given their real names.

41. Belyi, *Na rubezhe*, second page (unnumbered) following p. 224. Further page references to this volume are in parentheses in the body of the text. This work is part of an autobiographical trilogy written in the 1920s and 30s.

    It is odd that she would be a "companion" in childhood, unless she remained within the household in a capacity other than wet-nurse, and even odder that she would be the first audience for his early versifying. Neither Belyi nor the editor-annotator of his autobiography offers an explanation for this puzzle.

42. One is reminded of Johan Huizinga's magnificent study of culture as play, *Homo Ludens* (1938).

43. J. D. Elsworth notes that the Platonic idea of anamnesis (recollection of Ideas which the soul had known in a previous existence) appears clearly in Belyi's novel *The Third Symphony* (also, *The Return*; 1905) and plays a "prominent" role in *Kotik Letaev*. Memory and reminiscence are major components of the system of anthroposophy. See his excellent *Andrey Bely: A Critical Study of the Novels* (Cambridge: Cambridge University Press, 1983), p. 59. Another first-rate study of *Kotik Letaev* can be found in Coe, *When the Grass was Taller*, pp. 83, 101-102.

44. Belyi, *Kotik Letaev*, trans. by Gerald Janecek (Evanston, IL: Northwestern University Press, 1999), p. 38. This edition is much to be preferred to Janecek's 1971 Ardis edition which had many errors and lacks the rich annotations of the later version. Further references are in the text, designated KL 1971 or KL 1999.

45. Instead of relying mostly on Khodasevich's own writings, I want to take as the basis of my investigations a first-rate biography of the poet

by David M. Bethea. Bethea, however, may at times rely overmuch on Khodasevich's poetry and literary studies as biographical facts.

46. Bethea, *Khodasevich: His Life and Art* (Princeton, NJ: Princeton University Press, 1983), pp. 9-10.

47. *Ibid.*, p. 9.

48. *Ibid.*, pp. 218-219. Quoted by permission. I've made one minor change in his translation which might be misleading to some.

49. In their travels through Russia in the early 1900s, Rainer Maria Rilke and Lou Andreas-Salomé encountered a Russian "peasant poet" named Spiridon Drozhzhin (1848-1930) who inspired Rilke. In turn, Rilke translated and published the Russian's works. One of Drozhzhin's works is called "My Muse" and it bears a more than passing resemblance to Khodasevich's paean to his nanny. See Anna A. Tavis, *Rilke's Russia: A Cultural Encounter* (Evanston, IL: Northwestern University Press, 1994), pp. 52-55.

50. Bethea, *Khodasevich*, pp. 219-223. Khodasevich's detailed analysis of Pushkin's poems and his reasoning for why Arina was Pushkin's muse can be found in his *O Pushkine* (Berlin: Petropolis [Speer and Schmidt], 1937), an enl. and rev. version of his "Iavleniia muzy," *Poeticheskoe khoziaistvo Pushkina* of 1924, pp. 9-38.

    Unfortunately, Bethea's analytic efforts regarding how these two poems tie in to Pushkin's nanny – not to speak of Khodasevich's own would-be revelation about his idol Pushkin – appear to be for nought, as the reader will recall from Chapter 1.

51. I won't argue that the myth's impact on Khodasevich was necessarily negative; it might be seen as just the reverse. But I think that the second impact, on his biographer, may be deleterious. Bethea's comments about Khodasevich's comparison of the two nannies, his own and Pushkin's, reliably report what Khodasevich himself was thinking and saying but they are based on a few dubious assumptions.

52. Bethea, *Khodasevich*, pp. 224-25.

53. Vasina-Grossman, *Mikhail Ivanovich Glinka* (Moscow: Muzyka, 1979), pp. 7-8. She ignores Glinka's "favorite nanny," a nonpeasant woman named Meshkova, discussed below.

54. Kann-Novikova, "Narodno-pesennyi mir v detskoi M.I. Glinki; niania Avdot'ia Ivanovna," Chapter 3, section 1, of her *M.I. Glinka: novye materialy i dokumenty*, Issue I (Moscow-Leningrad: Muzgiz, 1950), p. 40. Additional page references are in the text in parentheses.

55. Quoted in Glinka, *Literaturnye proizvedeniia i perepiska* (Moscow: Muzyka, 1973), Vol. I, p. 365 notes 2, 6.

56. D. Brown, *Mikhail Glinka: A Biographical and Critical Study* (reprint: New York: Da Capo Press, 1985), pp. 7-8, 12-13.

57. Stites, *Serfdom*, pp. 85-86, 392.

58. "Zapiski Mikhaila Ivanovicha Glinki. 1804-1854," *RS*, April 1870, Vol. I, No. 4, pp. 382-83. Further page references appear in the text in parentheses.

The memoirs were issued as a book a year later; a third time, ed. by V.V. Stasov, in 1887, and a fourth (ed. by A.N. Rimskii-Korsakov) in 1930. More recent editions are cited hereafter as well.

The greatest family influence on the child Glinka was this extremely over-protective grandmother. An older brother had been lost in infancy, and she was probably determined to see that he survived. It was she who chose the babe's wet-nurse and his nannies and looked after his rearing. He lived in her room until she died; only then did he transfer to a nursery and have the company of others his own age.

59. He told his friend Nestor Kukol'nik in a letter about the composition of the autobiography that he was "excluding everything that did not have a direct or indirect relationship to my artistic life" (quoted by Brown, *Mikhail Glinka*, p. 7).

60. Of minor interest, perhaps, is the fact that the English Wikipedia biography of Glinka mentions both the church bells and the nanny's folksongs but the Russian Wikipedia version does not. The former, however, says that peasant choirs' vocal technique of *podgolosnaia* (literally, "under the voice") use of dissonant harmonies beneath a melody was a more significant long-term influence than either of the other two.

61. Glinka, *Literaturnye proizvedeniia*, Vol. IIB, pp. 179 and 180n; *Mikhail Ivanovich Glinka: Literaturnoe nasledie*, Vol. 2 (Leningrad-Moscow: Gosudarstvennoe muzykal'noe izdatel'stvo, 1953), pp. 635-36.

62. The composer, musician and music theorist-scholar Iurii Arnol'd (1811-1898), for example, says in his own autobiography that "...we had serf household staff from the Great Russian provinces. Mama nursed me herself; but I had assigned to me in addition a nanny and a young girl 'under-nanny' [*"pod-niania"*], whose responsibility consisted of amusing the child. From these two personal servants of mine I first heard various Russian folktales and songs, and I grew up on them."

Vospominaniia Iuriia Arnol'da, I, p. 2.

In rapid succession, meanwhile, young Misha Glinka progressed through "a governess from St. Petersburg, Varvara Fedorovna Kliammer, a girl of 20 from the Smolnyi Institute who taught him many subjects, including music (i.e., to play the piano and to read music); then his uncle's first violinist "to teach me to play the violin."

63. That Liudmila had her own agenda in her biography of her brother is more than likely, as we will see shortly, though Serge Bertensson, who knew her slightly and might have shed some light on the issue with a little critical thinking, ignores all such questions in his loving tribute to her ("Ludmila Ivanovna Shestakova – Handmaid to Russian Music," *The Musical Quarterly*, Vol. 31, No. 3 [July 1945], pp. 331-338).

64. Yuri Olkhovsky, *Vladimir Stasov and Russian National Culture* (Ann Arbor, MI: UMI Research Press, 1983), p. 28.

65. Brown, *Mikhail Glinka*, includes an English translation of this note in an appendix, pp. 305-309.

66. *Ibid.*, p. 290.

67. Varvara Komarova-Stasova ["Vlad. Karenin"], *Vladimir Stasov: Ocherk ego zhizni i deiatel'nosti*, 2 vols. (Leningrad: Mysl', 1927), I, pp. 348-49 and especially p. 349n2; cf. II, pp. 430, 485, 593. His biographer was his niece.

68. Quoted, *ibid.*, I, p. 85.

69. See Z. M. Perepelkina, "L.I. Shestakova – sister, friend, and preserver of the legacy of M.I. Glinka," in Russian, at http://nasledie.smolensk.ru/pkns/index.php?option=com_content&task=view&id=585&Itemid=96 (accessed October 2008).

70. *Nikolai Nikolaevich Ge, ego zhizn', proizvedeniia i perepiska*, comp. by V. Stasov (Moscow: I.N. Kushnerev and Co., 1904), pp. 248-51, 343. Page references hereafter are in the text, parenthesized.

Ge had made every effort to get the spirit of the painting right; he had seen a death mask of Pushkin owned by Pëtr Kochubei, had even visited Mikhailovskoe and the neighboring Kern estate. Yet many critics heartily disliked Ge's oil.

71. A gift to the Tret'iakov Gallery in 1897 by N.N. Ge, the artist's son, the work is apparently not available online.

Besides Ge and Venetsianov, numerous other artists have depicted their own or others' nannies. Well-known are Igor' Grabar's oil

"Nanny with Child" (1892), Iakov Polonskii's pencil sketch of his nanny Matrëna (ca. 1851?), and illustrations in this book.

72. P. E. Shchegolev, *Lermontov: Vospominaniia. Pis'ma. Dnevniki...* (Moscow: Agraf, 1999), pp. 15, 19, and passim. The grandmother practically extorted from the boy's father Misha's continued stay with her. (The two adults remained hostile to one another until the father's death in late 1831 or 1832.) The toddler slept in his grandmother's bedroom, not with his nanny.

Walter Vickery is rightly dismissive of claims that Lermontov's great-grandmother nannied little Misha. See his *M. Iu. Lermontov: His Life and Work*, ed. by Ellen Rosenbaum Langer (Munich: Otto Sagner, 2001), p. 394.

73. Vyrypaev, "Lermontov i krest'iane (po materialam arkhivov penzenskoi oblasti)," in *Literaturnoe nasledstvo*, Vol. 58: *Pushkin. Lermontov. Gogol'* (Moscow: AN SSSR, 1952), p. 446. He cited the biographers V. A. Manuilov and N. L. Brodskii for making this mistake. This and other spurious Lermontov testimony regularly shows up in Soviet hagiographies of the writer extolling his closeness to the people.

74. N. Rybkin article (*IV*,1881) cited in Shchegolev, *Lermontov*, p. 23.

75. Viskovatyi, *Zhizn' i tvorchestvo*, pp. 17-19. Viskovatov's sources were the testimony of a few intimate friends of the poet, like Sviatoslav (Sviatopolk) Raevskii (1808-1876), his grandmother's godson, and Lermontov's relation Akim Shan-Girei (1818-1883), both of whom were Misha's childhood playmates. Whatever Viskovatov thought they had said about Remer, their own words convey little of what he relates in his biography.

The recollections of Shan-Girei about young Lermontov appear in the collection *M. Iu. Lermontov v vospominaniiakh sovremennikov*, comp., ed., and annot. by M. I. Gillel'son and O. V. Miller (Moscow: Khudozhestvennaia literatura, 1989), pp. 33-55. (This compendium is more complete than the 1964 edition with the same title.) Raevskii's reminiscences are merely quoted/cited and were apparently never written down (p. 6).

The most one can find in Shan-Girei's recollections is the statement, remembering Lermontov in about 1825: "I recall still, as if in a dream, the face of the kind old German woman, Kristina Osipovna, Michel's nanny...." Quoted by Shchegolev, *Lermontov*, p. 29, from Shan-Girei's memoirs, pp. 725-26.

The only other "original" source about Remer is the list of people who accompanied Lermontov on a trip to the Caucasus in 1825 to seek a "cure" for the sickly lad: "Spisok..." *Otechestvennye zapiski*, 1825, part 23, No. 64, Aug., p. 260. Among the many sources quoting just these two original accounts, often with unwarranted embellishments and distortions, are: A. Mikhailova, "Detskii uchebnik Lermontova," *Khochu vsë znat': Nauchno-populiarnyi al'manakh*, 1957, No. 1, p. 269; V. A. Manuilov, *Lermontov v Tarkhanakh* (Penza, 1949), p. 36; Manuilov, *Letopis' zhizni i tvorchestva M. Iu. Lermontova* (Leningrad: Nauka, 1964), p. 19; Sergei Ivanov, *M. Iu. Lermontov: Zhizn' i tvorchestvo* (Moscow: Prosveshchenie, 1964), pp. 19-20, 20n1, 22; A. D. Zhizhina, "Lermontov i ego nastavniki," *Nauchnye Doklady Vysshei Shkoly. Filologicheskie Nauki*, 1972, No. 4, pp. 21-30, here: p. 26.

76. Virtually the only other information about Remer one can find is the estimate by A. Mikhailova that she "left the home of Lermontov's grandmother, most likely, in 1827, when they took the thirteen-year-old Misha to Moscow to enroll [him] in the boarding school at Moscow University, and there remained with him only the French governor Capet." Mikhailova, "Detskii uchebnik Lermontova," pp. 264-69.

To add to the confusion and dearth of good information about Remer, the seemingly definitive encyclopedia devoted to the poet calls her his "governess," not nanny. See V. A. Manuilov et al. eds., *Lermontovskaia entsiklopediia* (Moscow: Sovetskaia entsiklopediia, 1981), p. 465.

77. Sergei Ivanov, *M. Iu. Lermontov*, pp. 19-20. Ivanov's questionable sources include some of the poet's creative works – to be cited shortly – and possibly Raevskii or Shan-Girei's imperfect memories.

78. See Paul N. Paganuzzi (P.N. Paganutstsi), *Lermontov (Avtobiograficheskie cherty v tvorcherstve poeta)* (Montreal: Monastery Press, 1967), p. 22, who has it that Remer, "raised on the ideas of German Romantic literature," promoted the development of fantasy in Lermontov. He is equally credulous about the child Lermontov's relations with local peasants.

Another biographer, Tat'iana Ivanova, is equally undeterred by the minefield of the quasi-autobiographical fiction. She claims, following almost word-for-word Lermontov's fictive re-creation, that the maids and servants – including the nanny? – talked a lot about the Tarkhany peasants and their affairs in front of young Misha; that he learned of the abuses of serfdom from them. See her *Iunost' Lermontova* (Moscow: Sovetskii pisatel', 1957), p. 12.

79. See Lermontov, *Sochineniia v shesti tomakh*, Vol. VI, ed. by B. V. Tomashevskii (M-L: AN SSSR, 1957), p. 387.

80. As a guess, I'd say it was likely occasioned by the publication of Iazykov's poem dedicated to Pushkin's nanny (published in 1828) and by Pushkin's poem "Winter's Evening," which first saw print in 1829 and was republished in 1830.

81. Quoted by Shchegolev, *Lermontov*, p. 22. The date of this fragment is unknown, but it probably dates from 1837 or 1838; *ibid.*, p. 23 n1.

82. Sementkovskii, "Nikolai Semenovich Leskov," in Leskov, *Polnoe sobranie sochinenii*, I, p. 11.

83. *Ibid.*, p. 12.

84. Leskov, *Izbrannye sochineniia* (Moscow: Khudozhestvennaia literatura, 1979), p. 552.

This commentator basically repeats not Leskov's childhood nanny's experiences but Leskov's story of man's inhumanity to man under serfdom.

A much better performance in this regard comes from the American scholar Hugh McLean. He does not conflate Leskov's life and fiction, as does Sementkovskii. Instead, McLean makes such judicious observations as: "There are in Leskov's writings…not only bitterness and resentment but also many warm feelings associated with the women of his childhood. He seems to have consolidated into an ideal image the impressions left in him by various surrogate mothers – his grandmother, his nurse, aunts – plus, no doubt, the positive feelings he had about his real mother." And: "Since the beginning of his career as a writer of fiction, Leskov had often used his putative memories as a means of defictionalizing that fiction, giving his readers the illusion of having been led from literature into life…In the age of realism, however, the word 'real' must be regarded with suspicion, and this rule applies to Leskov as much as any other writer of that era. But suspicion should not lead to wholesale denial of Leskov's 'real' claims." See McLean, *Nikolai Leskov*, pp. 20 and 436.

McLean's monumental biography cum explication of nearly all Leskov's writings is so well-balanced that it's a surprise to see him make the following questionable statement: "Perhaps the most unusual, and most characteristic, feature of [Leskov's] memoirs [sic – there are none in any real sense] is ambiguity. *His formula for combining remembered fact with invented fiction was unique.*" *Ibid.*, p. 436; italics added. As nearly every Russian writer from Pushkin through Tolstoi to Marina Tsvetaeva has done the same thing (and acknowledged the same) – as have most non-Russian writers as well – it's hard to agree with McLean's position here.

85. See Leskov, *Zhizn' Nikolaia Leskova*, I, p. 95 and 95 footnotes.
86. See *ibid.*, pp. 90-91, 94-95.
87. *Ibid.*, p. 92. Katherine Pickering Antonova notes a similar situation with a family nanny (being heartily disliked by the other female servants) in her dissertation "'The Importance of the Woman of the House'" (Columbia, 2007 – soon to be a book), p. 281.
88. Leskov, *Zhizn' Nikolaia Leskova*, I, pp. 91-92.
89. Not done with spinning real-life straw into fictive gold, five years later Nikolai Leskov put Stepanovna into another story as Annushka "the hurler." This was the children's tale "The Bugbear" (*Pugalo*, 1885) – partly based again on the incident with the rat, which the terrified young nanny had vehemently thrown from the finger he'd clamped down upon. *Ibid.*, p. 93.

   Unhappily, the son muddies the water by suggesting that another character in this tale of "The Bugbear" – the soldier's wife Marina Borisovna – might also be an avatar of Stepanovna. Perhaps rightly, Andrei doesn't even feel the need to discuss the relationship between "The Toupee Artist" and the reality of Leskov's nanny.

90. *Ibid.*, p. 94.
91. While not a full explanation in any sense, the following nugget from a letter to K. A. Greve dated 5 December 1888 is of interest. Citing Tolstoi, Leskov writes that "what is true is not that which is and has been, but that which could be, in accord with the qualities of the human soul." Quoted, *ibid.*, p. 92.
92. After a Freudian examination of the author's difficulties with each parent – the distant or absent father and the ambiguous or even cold mother – McLean sums up the situation:

   > Difficult as it is to reconstruct the emotional relationships of Leskov's early life, we can arrive at a reasonably plausible hypothesis of what they must have been. The central fact of Leskov's childhood is the deep emotional ache left by his parents – the deterioration, withdrawal, and death of his father, and the harshness of his mother. He tried to compensate for these losses in various ways, by seeking substitute parents among his near relations and endowing them with, or recognizing in them, qualities he felt his parents lacked. But the compensations never made up for the original loss; the ache remained in him for life, reappearing in many guises both in reality and in art.

See McLean, *Nikolai Leskov*, pp. 8-24 (quotation from p. 24).

93. Two nannies actually: the younger Agaf'ia Kumskaia and an old nanny named Aksin'ia Stepanovna. See N. I. Gitovich and Lidiia D. Gromova-Opul'skaia, comps., *Letopis' zhizni i tvorchestva A. P. Chekhova*, Vol. I (Moscow: Nasledie, 2000), p. 39. Gitovich had died before this second edition appeared; her first, single-volume edition came out in 1955 and is inferior in scope and detail.

94. Chekhov, "Ob A. P. Chekhove," *Rampa i zhizn'*, p. 2. Cf. his almost identical "Biograficheskii ocherk," *Pis'ma A. P. Chekhova*, I, p. xiii. These words appear almost verbatim in Mikhail's *Vokrug Chekhova* (Moscow: Academia, 1933), a book reprinted many times since.

    In 1933, not long before his death and possibly with the encouragement of his Soviet editors, Mikhail recalled one more detail about the Chekhovs' nanny. See *Vokrug Chekhova: Vstrechi i vpechatleniia*, 4th rev. and enl. ed., comp. and annot. by S. M. Chekhov, with a foreword by E. Z. Balabanovich (Moscow: Moskovskii rabochii, 1964), p. 54.

95. Chekhov, *PSSiP*, Vol. XV overall/*Pis'ma* Vol. 3: *1890-1892* (1949), p. 322.

96. *PSSiP*, XVIII/6: *Pis'ma, 1899-1900* (1949), pp. 243-244.

97. See Gitovich and Gromova-Opul'skaia, p. 96.

98. A. Sedoi (Chekhov), *Iz detstva Antona Pavlovicha Chekhova* (St. Petersburg: Pechat' graficheskogo instituta, 1912), pp. 90-91. "Childhood" is somewhat misleading here; given allusions in the book (pp. 6, 120), Anton would have been about 12-13 years old in the period Aleksandr describes.

99. *PSSiP*, XIV/2: *Pis'ma, 1888-1889* (1949), p. 58; *PSSiP*, VI (1946), endnotes, p. 510.

100. Vodovozova, *Na zare zhizni*, I, pp. 89, 93, 121, 131.

101. Vodovozova, *Umstvennoe i nravstvennoe razvitie*, p. 32. (The first edition appeared in 1871.)

102. *Ibid.*, p. 239.

103. *Ibid.*, pp. 280-307, 320.

104. Tsvetaeva, "Moi Pushkin," *Izbrannaia proza*, Vol. II, pp. 249-79; here, pp. 257-70. "Moi Pushkin" was written in 1937. See also the essay called "The Devil," pp. 151-66. Most – but not all – of the autobiographical essays in this second volume are included in English translation in *A Captive Spirit: Selected Prose*, trans. and ed. by J. Marin King (Ann Arbor, MI: Ardis Publishers, 1994); missing are "Mother's Fairy Tale" and "The Khlysty Women."

105. Tsvetaeva, *Neizdannoe: Svodnye tetradi*, prepared, annot. and introd. by E. B. Korkina and I. D. Shevelenko (Moscow: Ellis Lak, 1997), Notebook 3, p. 451.

106. *Ibid.*, passim; *Neizdannoe: Sem'ia: Istoriia v pis'makh*, comp. and annot. by E. B. Korkina (Moscow: Ellis Lak, 1999), pp. 155-77 passim, 251-60, 274; *Neizdannoe: Zapisnye knizhki v dvukh tomakh*. Vol. I: 1913-1919, comp. and prepared by E. B. Korkina and M. G. Krutikova (Moscow: Ellis Lak, 2000), pp. 18-33, 49-51, 76-77.

107. Ariadna Efron, *Stranitsy vospominanii* (Paris: LEV, 1979), pp. 29-30.

108. For those interested in the equally compelling stories of the poet-novelist Boris Pasternak, composer Igor' Stravinskii, actors Konstantin Raikin and Igor' Il'inskii, and artists Vasilii Vereshchagin and Mstislav Dobuzhinskii – all fine examples of the Goldilocks model for nannies – please request information from the author at salangrant@verizon.net.

Chapter 10

1. Unlike in real life, the nanny cannot easily be separated from the wet-nurse in this discussion. *Symbolically*, the two figures serve a very similar purpose. The nanny/wet-nurse symbol arose in various countries, at roughly the same time, for similar *generic* reasons. The figure became more of a cult in Russia for quite *specific* reasons.

    Two astute treatments of the wet-nurse symbol in British literature deserve mention: Katie Trumpener's *Bardic Nationalism: The Romantic Novel and the British Empire* (Princeton: Princeton University Press, 1997), Chapter 5, where the wet-nurse Elinor Donoghoe in Maria Edgeworth's *Ennui* is discussed as part of Irish reaction to British colonialism, and Julie Kipp, *Romanticism, Maternity, and the Body Politic* (Cambridge: Cambridge University Press, 2003), where the same wet-nurse is examined as a symbol of maternity.

2. This line of reasoning is similar to Liah Greenfeld's argument that loss of status and resentment are prime causes for the rise of modern nationalism. See her *Nationalism: Five Roads to Modernity* (Cambridge, MA: Harvard University Press, 1992).

3. My emphasis on the opposition to French culture draws on Gerald Newman's *The Rise of English Nationalism: A Cultural History 1740-1830* (New York: St. Martin's, 1987). An argument similar to Newman's – that nationalism defines itself mostly as opposition to another culture – can be found in Gerald Porter's contribution to *Imagined States: Nationalism, Utopia, and Longing in Oral Cultures* (Logan, UT: Utah State

University Press, 2001), ed. by Luisa Del Giudice and Porter. His essay "'Who Talks of My Nation?' The Role of Wales, Scotland, and Ireland in Constructing 'Englishness'" (pp. 101-35) places the rise of English proto-nationalism a century earlier than Newman, closer to home, and in a locus of low culture (oral and broadside ballad traditions) rather than high culture. As Porter neatly puts it at the end of his piece: "Stereotypes of the other...are not given but constructed, in gestalt terms, as the reverse mirror of the ideal, which gains in complexity from their simplicity. Ultimately, Englishness was the negation of a negation. Identity was confirmed by the discovery of reverse selves." (p. 131).

Another contributor to the Del Giudice and Porter volume argues that "the identification of a generalized *Auslander* or foreign enemy is rooted in a sense of one's own identity," and "representations of that outsider will change according to how precarious that self-sense is." The process of "enemy-making" often reflects a nation's "crisis of identity" (p. 6; also, pp. 136-63 [Tom Cheesman essay]).

Jacques Barzun discusses this same phenomenon in his "Cultural Nationalism and the Makings of Fame," in *Nationalism and Internationalism: Essays Inscribed to Carlton J. H. Hayes*, ed. by Edward M. Earle (New York: Octagon Books/Farrar, Strauss and Giroux, 1974 [reprint of the 1950 ed.]), pp. 3-17. He unfortunately limits his concern to just England, Germany, and Italy (pp. 3-5), whereas Russia would have served at least as well.

4. Herder was well-acquainted with the Russian Empire, working as a teacher in Riga for many years; he wrote essays on Peter the Great and about Ukraine and predicted a great future for the Slavic nations. In 1772 Herder published his *Treatise on the Origin of Language* and later that decade brought out his collection of folk songs. His *Ideas on a Philosophy of the History of Mankind* (1784-91) was translated into Russian and published in abridged form in 1829. He is the man who wrote that "A poet is the creator of the nation around him..." Whether Pëtr Bartenev studied Herder I cannot say; it seems more than likely, however, that he became familiar with Herder's ideas and sentiments while at university, as nearly all the bright young men of his generation did.

Cf. Anthony D. Smith, *Theories of Nationalism*, 2nd ed. (New York: Holmes & Meier Publishers, 1983), pp. 180-85. Ekaterina Zhukova's *Gerder v Rossii: bibliograficheskii ukazatel'* (Moscow: Universitetskaia kniga, 2007; 51 pp.) is a useful guide to the literature. Her dissertation and book on Herder (*Gerder i filosofsko-kul'turologicheskaia mysl' v Rossii: monografiia* [Moscow: Universitetskaia kniga, 2007]) were unavailable to me. However, Arsenii Gulyga's excellent essay on Herder's *Idee zur Philosophie* ...is available online (accessed November 2009): http://marsexx.narod.ru/lit/gerder-prilojenia.html.

5. Edward C. Thaden, "The Beginnings of Romantic Nationalism in Russia," *American Slavic and East European Review*, Vol. 13, No. 4 (December 1954), pp. 500-521. See also the useful discussion of *narodnost'* ("nationalism"), national consciousness, and Romanticism in Peter K. Christoff, *The Third Heart: Some Intellectual-Ideological Currents and Cross Currents in Russia 1800-1830* (The Hague: Mouton, 1970), the first two chapters especially.

On Romanticism and nationalism more generally, see Anthony D. Smith, *The Antiquity of Nations* (Cambridge, England: Polity Press, 2004), Chapter 9, pp. 236-54.

The literature on nationalism alone is staggeringly large. Among the best treatments I've found are several books by Smith, including his early *Theories of Nationalism* (1st ed. 1971); his excellent short summary *Nationalism: Theory, Ideology, History* (Cambridge, England: Polity Press, 2001); the partially overlapping readers ed. by Smith and John Hutchinson: *Nationalism* (Oxford/New York: Oxford University Press, 1994) and the more comprehensive five-volume *Nationalism: Critical Concepts in Political Science* (London and New York: Routledge, 2002). See also Greenfeld, *Nationalism*; Aviel Roshwald, *The Endurance of Nationalism* (Cambridge, England: Cambridge University Press, 2006); and *History and National Destiny: Ethnosymbolism and its Critics*, ed. by Montserrat Guibernau and John Hutchinson (Oxford: Blackwell, 2004).

I'm grateful to Melissa Stockdale and Marjorie Mandelstam Balzer for pointing me to Smith and Roshwald.

6. Linguistic battles of the mid-eighteenth- through the early decades of the nineteenth century – culminating in the apotheosis of Pushkin – helped determine whether French or more nativist style and content would dominate written and spoken Russian. Admiral Shishkov, President of the Russian Academy and then Minister of Public Education, is a pivotal figure. His "Meditation on Old and New Style of the Russian Language" (*Razsuzhdenie o starom i novom sloge rossiiskogo iazyka*, 1803) was a landmark in educated Russians' consciousness of their own language and its centrality for defining Russian nationality (*narodnost'*). See, inter alia, V.M. Zhivov, *Iazyk i kul'tura v Rossii XVIII veka* (Moscow: Shkola "Iazyki russkoi kul'tury, 1996), especially Chapter 4 (available

in English as Victor Zhivov, *Language and Culture in Eighteenth-Century Russia*, trans. by Marcus Levitt [Boston: Academic Studies Press, 2009]); *The Emergence of National Languages*, ed. by Aldo Scaglione (Ravenna: Longo, 1984), pp. 146-49; *Aspects of the Slavic Language Question*, ed. by Riccardo Picchio and Harvey Goldblatt, Vol. 2 (New Haven: Yale Concilium, 1984), pp. 187-233, 235-96; and P. Garde, "A propos du premier mouvement slavophile," *Cahiers du Monde russe et soviétique*, Vol. 5, No. 3 (July-September 1964), pp. 261-69.

Equally important was the critique of all things foreign in Russian *vospitanie*. Cf. the anonymous *Izobrazhenie nyneshnikh nravov i nyneshniago vospitaniia* (Moscow: A. Reshetnikov, 1816) with its heartfelt diatribe against all the foreign tutors, governors and governesses in Russia.

7. See Marina Frolova-Walker, *Russian Music and Nationalism: From Glinka to Stalin* (New Haven: Yale University Press, 2007), pp. 1-5; Richard Taruskin, *Defining Russia Musically: Historical and Hermeneutical Essays* (Princeton, NJ: Princeton University Press, 1997), part 1, especially chapters 1, 2, and 8; Liubov' Kiseleva, "K formirovaniiu kontsepta natsional'nogo geroia v russkoi kul'ture pervoi treti XIX v.," *Lotmanovskii sbornik*, Issue 3 (Moscow: OGI, 2004), pp. 69-92, and her related article "Stanovlenie russkoi natsional'noi mifologii v nikolaevskuiu epokhu (susaninskii siuzhet)," *Lotmanovskii sbornik*, Issue 2 (Moscow: OGI, 1997), pp. 279-302.

8. Orest Somov's pathbreaking lecture-essay "On Romantic poetry"(1823) stressing folklore, peasant speech, and the concept of *narodnost'* in great poets' works doubtless helped Bartenev and others to connect Pushkin closer to Arina.

9. Chaadaev, *Polnoe sobranie sochinenii i izbrannye pis'ma*, Vol. I (Moscow: Nauka, 1991), pp. 91 (Letter 1) and 150 (Letter 5). The letters are in Russian in this same volume, with the relevant passages appearing on pp. 325 and 384 (the term used is "*kormilitsa*"). The letters are available in two English translations: *The Major Works of Peter Chaadaev: A Translation and Commentary* by Raymond T. McNally (Notre Dame: University of Notre Dame Press, 1969), where the relevant passages are on pp. 30 and 115-16; and *Philosophical letters & Apology of a Madman*, trans. with an introd. by Mary-Barbara Zeldin (Knoxville: University of Tennessee Press (1969).

Malcolm Hamrick Brown calls the year 1836 a cultural watershed nonpareil, marked by the appearance of Pushkin's *Captain's Daughter*, Glinka's *Life for the Tsar*, Gogol's *Revizor*, and Chaadaev's first

"Philosophical Letter" ("Native Song," in Stavrou, ed. *Art and Culture*, 79f).

10. An early biographer notes that Chaadaev and his brother Mikhail, who lost their parents young, were looked after by nannies and a *diad'ka*, under the guardianship of relatives, until the age of seven. See Stepan Zhikharev, "Pëtr Iakovlevich Chaadaev. Iz vospominanii sovremennika," *VE*, July 1871, Bk. 7, pp. 176-77.

11. Katie Trumpener argues that the function of nostalgia "is to restore innocence by covering over other memories." Trumpener, "The Time of the Gypsies: A 'People Without History' in the Narratives of the West," in *Critical Inquiry*, Vol. 18, No. 4 (Summer 1992), pp. 843-84; here, p. 853. Reprinted in *Identities*, ed. by Kwame Anthony Appiah and Henry Louis Gates, Jr. (Chicago: University of Chicago Press, 1995), pp. 338-379.

There is little doubt that the nostalgia attached to nannies and wet-nurses throughout Europe must have often served this purpose. This was particularly true of Russian noble culture in the nineteenth century: serfowners and their offspring, in all the autobiographical works I've read, found it almost impossible to admit to any sins with respect to their serfs and with regard to their nannies in particular.

12. See Fred Davis, *Yearning for Yesterday: A Sociology of Nostalgia* (Great Britain: Macmillan, 1979), Chapter 5, "Nostalgia and Society," especially pp. 103-104, 108-110, 115-16. Cf. Klimenko, "Anton Chekhov," *Orbis Litterarum*, pp. 136-37, and Freud's *angst vor etwas*.

13. Trumpener, *Bardic Nationalism*, pp. 202, 203.

14. Julie Kipp points out that all manner of writers "utilized the mother-child bond as a figure for other forms of social relationship." See her *Romanticism, Maternity*, p. 54.

On the cult of domesticity, see Diana Greene, "Mid-Nineteenth Century Domestic Ideology in Russia," in *Women and Russian Culture*, ed. Rosalind Marsh (New York: Berghahn, 1998).

15. Kuhn, *Corruption in Paradise: The Child in Western Literature* (Hanover, NH: University Press of New England, 1982), p. 4.

16. Kipp's *Romanticism, Maternity* provides an excellent discussion of all these gender issues.

17. Recent scholarship suggests that what formerly seemed like a great divide between eastern and western Europe based on the existence and growth of serfdom in the former was not all that big. In this respect, as

with the evolution of the nobility into an estate defined not so much by birth as by landownership and service to the state, Russia by the first half of the eighteenth century was looking more and more like most other European states, less and less like a country unique in its social structures. Cf. H.M. Scott, "Introduction: Serfdom and Service Nobility," Chapter 1 of *The European Nobilities in the Seventeenth and Eighteenth Centuries*, ed. by Scott, Vol. 2: *Northern, Central and Eastern Europe* (London: Longman, 1995), pp. 1-10, but especially pp. 6-8.

18. Cf. Daniel Field, *The End of Serfdom: Nobility and Bureaucracy in Russia, 1855-1861* (Cambridge, MA: Harvard University Press, 1976), pp. 134-36, 294f, 342-43.

19. "Penitent nobles" (*kaiushchiesia dvoriane*), a well-turned phrase of the journalist and social critic Nikolai Mikhailovskii, who originally applied it precisely to "the men of the 1860s," saw themselves as peasants' benefactors, both before *and after* emancipation.

20. Jerome Blum believed that in general in Europe lords disliked emancipation legislation and peasants liked it. See *The End of the Old Order in Rural Europe* (Princeton, NJ: Princeton University Press, 1978), pp. 401, 403. Cf. Paul [Pavel] Miliukov, *Outlines of Russian Culture. Part III: Literature* trans. by Valentine Ughet and Eleanor Davis, ed. by Michael Karpovich (Philadelphia: University of Pennsylvania Press, 1942), p. 38: "The moral incentive of the nobility played a large part in the emancipation of the serfs and in the work preparatory thereto."

21. The nanny as a fixture in nearly all works of fiction which one way or another idealized or celebrated the "good old days" in pre-emancipation Russia was probably set once and for all with Pushkin but also with his near-contemporaries, the pair of fine historical novelists Mikhail Zagoskin (1789-1852) and Ivan Lazhechnikov (1792-1869). Later, the somewhat inferior historical novelist Pavel Mel'nikov-Pecherskii (1818-1883) also employed nanny characters to provide colorful background. The poet Vsevolod Dolgorukov (pseud. Sibirskii; d. 1912) defends and exalts the age of serfdom in "The Golden Age (a grandfather's tale)." He claims that people "slander" those times "now" (in the 1880s and 90s), arguing that there was no oppression then, and all were happy in "the good old days." In other poems he frequently invokes nannies as symbolic of those better times. See *Ne ot skuki. Stikhotvoreniia* (Tomsk: Sibirskii vestnik, 1890), pp. 26, 46, 273-75.

22. The written preamble to David O. Selznick's 1939 film *Gone With the Wind* catches this mindset's aura almost perfectly: "There was a land of Cavaliers and Cotton Fields called the Old South...Here in this pretty

world Gallantry took its last bow...Here was the last ever to be seen of Knights and their Ladies Fair, of Master and of Slave...Look for it only in books, for it is no more than a dream remembered. A Civilization gone with the wind..."

23. It is my impression that ideologies sometimes (usually?) acquire names and formulations not from their adherents but from those inimical to them, and generally rather later than earlier in the game. This appears to be the case with terms such as *krepostnichestvo* and *narodnichestvo*. The first term was not, so far as I can determine, in use before the nineteenth century, although the institution of serfdom had been developing rapidly in Russia since the late sixteenth century and especially after 1649. (The adjective *"krepostnoe,"* on the other hand, was well-known in the eighteenth century. It referred to the legally bound peasants of a serfowner.) But when important social strata became increasingly abolitionist in sentiment, they needed a label for all they held in abhorrence.

Similarly, cultural and political elements of demophilism began to exhibit themselves long before peasant-sympathetic activists thought to label them, positively (or Marxists and conservatives – pejoratively), as *narodnik*. On the latter term, see Richard Pipes, *"Narodnichestvo* – A Semantic Inquiry," *The Slavic Review*, September 1964, Vol. 23, pp. 441-58.

24. Two examples of the nanny symbol in progressive literature: Avdot'ia Panaeva's anti-serfdom novel *Romance in the Petersburg Demimonde – Roman v peterburgskom polusvete (1863);"* and Nikolai Ogarëv's radical-democratic "Song of a Russian Nanny by the Bed of a Master's Child" ("An Imitation of Lermontov") (1871) in S. A. Reiser, comp., ed., and annot., *Vol'naia russkaia poeziia XVIII-XIX vekov: Sbornik stikhotvorenii* (Moscow: Khudozhestvennaia literatura, 1975), 206-207, 558n. This poem also appears in N. P. Ogarëv, *Izbrannoe proizvedeniia*, Vol. I: *Stikhotvoreniia* (Moscow: Khudozhestvennaia literatura, 1956), pp. 411-412.

25. On liberal-progressive-radical demophilism, Westernizers, and "populism" the literature is voluminous; see, inter alia, Martin Malia, *Alexander Herzen and the Birth of Russian Socialism* (New York: Grosset & Dunlap, 1961); Vasilii Shchukin, *Russkoe zapadnichestvo: genezis, sushchnost', istoricheskaia rol'* (Łódź : Ibidem, 2001); idem, "Russkoe zapadnichestvo sorokovykh godov XIX veka kak obshchestvenno-literaturnoe iavlenie," in *Rossiiskii genii*, pp. 5-154; D.I. Oleinikov, *Klassicheskoe rossiiskoe zapadnichestvo* (Moscow: Mekhanik, 1996); Venturi, *Roots of Revolution*;

Arthur P. Mendel, *Dilemmas of Progress in Tsarist Russia* (Cambridge: Harvard University Press, 1961); James H. Billington, *Mikhailovsky and Russian Populism* (Oxford: Clarendon Press, 1958); Philip Pomper, *Peter Lavrov and the Russian Revolutionary Movement* (Chicago: University of Chicago Press, 1972).

26. These ideological currents wind their way through and inform both autobiographies and memoirs, on the one hand, and works of fiction, art, and music, on the other. Despite all kinds of modernization within Russian society, strong links to the past – especially among the peasantry but for other social strata as well – remained a given during the entire period from Peter the Great through Lenin and Stalin to their successors. The ongoing tension between old and new was one source of sharply varying perceptions of and attitudes toward "backward" common folk: peasants, servants, nannies.

    The literature on "modernization" is large and continually growing, too voluminous to do justice here. For a concise statement of the current state of the debate vis-à-vis Russian history, see Michael David-Fox, "Multiple Modernities vs. Neo-Traditionalism: On Recent Debates in Russian and Soviet History," *Jahrbücher für Geschichte Osteuropas*, 2006, Vol. 54, No. 4, pp. 535-55.

    An excellent example of how a nanny can figure in these processes of change is the case of Anna Labzina, discussed in Chapter 2, where Anna and her nanny – representing the religious old ways – stand in sharp contrast to her husband – a symbol of modernizing, rationalistic new ways.

27. See Nicholas P. Vakar's *The Taproot of Soviet Society* (New York: Harper, 1962).

28. The one division it paid little heed to was that between workers and peasants on the one hand, and nobles on the other. On paper at least, there was no place for the well-born in the Soviet Union and there was some attention paid to try to eradicate the pre-revolutionary elites.

29. Ironically, attempts to mythologize Lenin's own nanny failed miserably. There is some useful information about this woman, Varvara Grigor'evna Sarbatova (1820-1890), some of which might prove interesting to would-be Freudians. See, for example, Dmitrii Ul'ianov and Anna Ul'ianova-Elizarova, *O V. I. Lenine i sem'e Ul'ianovykh: Vospominaniia. Ocherki. Pis'ma. Stat'i* (Moscow: Politizdat, 1988), p. 27 (where his mother "tore a bawling Volodia from her breast" and tossed him to the nanny); S. B. Shmerling, comp., *Traditsii sem'i* (Sverdlovsk: Sredne-Ural'sksoe knizhnoe izdatel'stvo, 1988), p. 41 (where the mother and

nanny enforce some strict toilet-training); and *Vospominaniia rodnykh*, vol. 1 of 5 (Moscow: Politizdat, 1969), pp. 84-85, 92, 131 n2. However, when the daughter of this nanny published accounts of Lenin's boyhood purportedly based on her mother's recollections, Dmitrii and Mariia Ul'ianov(a) tore the work to shreds: "Detskie i iunosheskie gody Il'icha (Vospominaniia o V. I. Lenine)," in D. I. Ul'ianov, *Vospominaniia o Vladimire Il'iche*, 4th enl. ed. (Moscow: Politizdat, 1971), pp. 117-18.

30. The term "alterity"("otherness") – currently fashionable in philosophy, literary and cultural studies, and some other social sciences – springs to mind when discussing the tripartite identity of the classic Russian nanny. I will not discuss the third component – nanny as servant – in this chapter.

Cheyney Ryan points out that there are major philosophical differences between (and practical consequences of) "Difference" and "Otherness" – the first celebrating pluralism and leading to inclusiveness, the second fearing alterity and leading to exclusiveness. His discussion of the ideology of "modernity" as an ideology of "progress" and the two basic "metanarratives" of progress "at the heart of modernity" is especially apropos. The "master-and-slave narrative" has been critiqued ("attacked") by Nietzsche (and Hegel), Ryan affirms, with the goal of promoting liberation and equality. The "civilized-and-savage" narrative is critiqued/attacked by those urging recognition and acceptance. Not liberation but peace and reconciliation is the ultimate goal of this second critique. See Ryan, "The Two Faces of Postmodernism, or the Difference between Difference and Otherness," *Who, Exactly, is the Other? Western and Transcultural Perspectives*, ed. by Steven Shankman and Massimo Lollini (Eugene OR: Oregon Humanities Center/University of Oregon, 2002), pp. 15-22.

31. As Paul Freedman observes, humans constantly apply a concept of "the Other" to "more or less familiar strangers, the exotic, or those standing in the way of progress." These "others" are represented as "inferior, primitive, degenerate, or even alluring." Typically, their "otherness" is not based on strict objective circumstances; it is subjective, invented "by being structured as radically different from an unexamined but anxiously defended 'normalcy'." Freedman finds that discourse about peasants (and women) in his period "oscillated violently among three poles: unfavorable alterity ('otherness'), similarity, and favorable dissimilarity." Thus, peasants could be painted as bestial or with childlike simplicity, as stupid or clever, intractable or pliant and patient. But these were not just either/or images – peasants could also be seen, simultaneously, as both of these sets of opposites. Freedman,

Images of the Medieval Peasant (Stanford: Stanford University Press, 1999), pp. 301f.

32. See, for example, Valerie Fildes, *Wet Nursing: A History from Antiquity to the Present* (Oxford, England: Basil Blackwell, 1998), pp. 20 (in antiquity, "There was a universal belief that the physical and mental characteristics of the nurse were imbibed by the child through her milk"), 33f, 42, 73, 91, 111-13, 128, 141, 162, 194; eadem, *Breasts, Bottles, and Babies: A History of Infant Feeding* (Edinburgh: Edinburgh University Press, 1986), pp. 15, 30, 189-90; Kipp, *Romanticism, Maternity*, pp. 39-45.

33. Perhaps more important, however, were differences in religion. If a governess came from abroad (or even the Baltics) her faith was likely to be Catholic or Protestant. A peasant nanny might easily conclude that her (former) charge's immortal soul was endangered from constant contact with a non-Orthodox caretaker. I admit the memoir literature rarely if ever discusses this aspect of the nanny-governess tension, but that it played a role seems inescapable, given the well-documented, strong religious feelings of most Russian nannies.

34. Anderson, *Imagined Communities: Reflections on the Origin and Spread of Nationalism* (London: Verso, 1983), Chapter 5. Cf. Pavel Miliukov, *Ocherki po istorii russkoi kul'tury. Chast' tret'ia. Natsionalizm i obshchestvennoe mnenie*, Vyp. 1, third ed. (St. Petersburg: M.A. Aleksandrov, 1909), p. 7: "A nationality is a social group disposing of such a single and necessary means for uninterrupted psychic interaction as a language and which has worked out for itself a constant store of *odnoobraznye* psychic habits [*navyky*] which regulate the correctness and repeatability of the phenomena of this interaction." He continues: "From this definition there flows on its own the importance of language for nationality. One can even say that language and nationality are, if not identical concepts, completely overlapping one another. The limits/bounds of one are the same as the bounds of the other."

35. There is perhaps little need to remind the reader that this link continues to the present. Cf. Tat'iana Bek's interview with the Russian-Jewish émigré writer David Markish: "Kto on takoi – evrei? David Markish: 'V Rossii – moi glavnyi chitatel'," *NG [Novaia gazeta?]. Ex Libris*, No. 16 (266), 29 April 2004, p. 1.

36. "Peasantness" fails; perhaps we need a neologism like "peasanticity." See, e.g., Frierson, *Peasant Icons*, especially Chapter 8; Freedman, *Images*; Amy S. Wyngaard, *From Savage to Citizen: The Invention of the Peasant in the French Enlightenment* (Newark: University of Delaware Press, 2004); Donskov, *Changing Image*; Stephen P. Frank, "Confronting

the Domestic Other: Rural Popular Culture and Its Enemies in Fin-de-Siècle Russia," *Cultures in Flux: Lower-Class Values, Practices, and Resistance in Late Imperial Russia*, ed. by Frank and Mark D. Steinberg (Princeton NJ: Princeton University Press, 1994), especially pp. 76-82, 91-93; and Donald Fanger, "The peasant in literature," in *The Peasant in Nineteenth-Century Russia*, ed. by Wayne S. Vucinich (Stanford, CA: Stanford University Press, 1968), pp. 231-62.

37. Not for Russians alone, of course. For the central role of the idea of peasants in ideologies of nationalism, see, inter alia, Anthony D. Smith, *Chosen Peoples* (Oxford: Oxford University Press, 2003), Chapter 2, especially pp. 33-40, and pp. 213ff; and Roshwald, *Endurance of Nationalism*, pp. 68-73. On peasants=authenticity see Smith, pp. 37-40.

38. Cf. Joanna Hubbs, *Mother Russia: The Feminine Myth in Russian Culture* (Bloomington IN: Indiana University Press, 1988), especially Chapter 3 and the Conclusion.

39. See, e.g., Linda J. Ivanits, *Dostoevsky and the Russian People* (Cambridge, UK: Cambridge University Press, 2008).

40. Women as much as peasants were long considered "others," as Paul Freedman argues (*Images, loc. cit.*). Females have, in the dominant (male) discourse of most ages, been portrayed as both "slave" and "savage," according to Cheyney Ryan (*Who, Exactly, is the Other?*, pp. 15ff).

A book ed. by Peter I. Barta, *Gender and Sexuality in Russian Civilisation* (Routledge, 2001), which contains an essay on "Gender and National Identity," was unfortunately unavailable to me.

41. It is men, Heldt says, who have told us what is and is not good literature as well as how to view literary characters. Gender has influenced their views in any number of ways, both implicitly and explicitly. The result, intended or not, has been to consign female writers to a secondary position at best, to oblivion at worst. Males have similarly shortchanged female characters, typically exalting or denigrating them, but either way diminishing them as human beings. See *Terrible Perfection*. (Additional page references in the text.)

Joe Andrew also traces images of women as they evolved (or better, mutated) in the works of successive male authors, from Fonvizin, Radishchev, and Karamzin in the eighteenth century to Pushkin, Lermontov, Gogol', Turgenev, and Chernyshevskii in the nineteenth. See his *Women in Russian Literature, 1780-1863* (New York: St. Martin's Press, 1988).

42. The qualifier "mature" is deliberate; Heldt holds that "Russian heroines incarnate perfection in youth or in extreme old age" (*Terrible Perfection*, p. 28).

43. "The Compassion Trap," in *Woman in Sexist Society: Studies in Power and Powerlessness*, ed. by Vivian Gornick and Barbara K. Moran (New York: Signet/New American Library, 1972), p. 556.

   The ultraconservative, misogynistic Russian novelist, playwright, and publicist Iosif Kolyshko (1861-1938) captures the view Adams is fighting almost perfectly in his essay "The Utility of Love" (*"Ispol'zovanie liubvi"*): "What's important is the principle that a woman is more full of love than a man, more patient than he, more tidy, purer in soul, that children feel more trust for her, for she reminds them of their mother, their nanny. It's important to make use of all this still-inexpensive material of female charm for children, of female affection." Outside of family duties, just three spheres of life, according to Kolyshko, would "exhaust the woman's question" – namely, charity work, the *vospitanie* of children, and, anomalously, agriculture. See his *Malen'kiia mysli*, pp. 243, 245f, 252.

   Equally misogynistic but making a wholly different argument about women as nannies was the philosopher Arthur Schopenhauer, who wrote (in his essay "On Women"): "Women are suited to being the nurses [i.e., nannies] and teachers of our earliest childhood precisely because they themselves are childish, silly and shortsighted, in a word big children, their whole lives long: a kind of intermediate stage between the child and the man, who is the actual human being, 'man'." See his *Sämtliche Werke*, Vol. 6: *Essays and Aphorisms* (Wiesbaden: Eberhard Brockhaus, 1947), p. 651.

   Two recent discussions of the female archetype are, from the historical perspective – Cissie Fairchilds, *Women in Early Modern Europe, 1500-1700* (Harlow, England: Pearson/Longman, 2007), Chapter 1: "Inferiors or Equals? Ideas about the Nature of Women," pp. 9-31, stressing Bible and Church teachings; and, as found in the work of Carl Jung – David Tacey, *How to Read Jung* (New York: W.W. Norton & Company, 2007); see especially pp. 54-65, 69-72.

44. Cf. Christine D. Worobec, *Peasant Russia: Family and Community in the Post-Emancipation Period* (DeKalb: Northern Illinois University Press, 1995), especially Chapter 6 ("The Culture of Patriarchy"), but also passim. While nominally concerned only with the peasantry after 1861 (relying on the wealth of source material generated by the zemstvos and courts), most of what Worobec writes about customs and beliefs can safely be applied to peasants before emancipation as well.

45. Despite a great deal of attention in Russian religious thought to Mariology and sophiology, I believe this characterization is valid. On Russian Mariology, see Shevzov, *Russian Orthodoxy*, Chapter 5; Paul Valliere, *Modern Russian Theology: Bukharev Soloviev Bulgakov: Orthodox Theology in a New Key* (Grand Rapids, MI: William B. Eerdmans Publishing Company, 2000); Alexander Schmemann, *The Celebration of Faith: Sermons*, 3 vols., trans. by John A. Jillions (Crestwood, NY: St. Vladimir's Seminary Press, 1991-2001) – here, vol. 3, pp. 60f; and Sergei Bulgakov, *The Orthodox Church*, rev. trans. by Lydia Kesich (Crestwood, NY: St. Vladimir's Seminary Press, 1988), p. 67. About sophiology in Vladimir Solov'ëv's and Sergei Bulgakov's thinking see essays by Bernice Glatzer Rosenthal and Valliere in *Russian Religious Thought*, ed. by Judith Deutsch Kornblatt and Richard F. Gustafson (Madison: University of Wisconsin Press, 1996).

46. The literature on peasant women and peasants more generally is so voluminous as virtually to defy citation, but in addition to the Worobec book cited above, one can benefit from a reading of the essays by Moshe Lewin, Michael Confino, George Yaney, and Worobec in *The Russian Review*, Vol. 44, No. 1 (January 1985); cf. Vadim Aleksandrov, *Obychnoe pravo krepostnoi derevni Rossii XVIII-nachalo XIX v.* (Moscow: Nauka, 1984).

David Rancour-Laferriere's discussion of Russian mothers and children ("Is the Slave Soul of Russia a Gendered Object?") in *The Slave Soul of Russia: Moral Masochism and the Cult of Suffering* (New York: New York University Press, 1995), pp. 134-80, presumably applies to peasant mothers and nannies. I disagree with most of his arguments on these women's replicating a "slave" mentality in their upbringing of children.

The crucial distinction between "nature" and "nurture" escaped even the most enlightened admirers and supporters of women in nineteenth-century Russia. For example, the pedagog and would-be psychologist Pëtr Kapterev (1849-1922) elaborated at some length, in a series of public lectures that became journal articles and a separate book, on the differences between men and women. In upholding the "modern" view that there are differences but that these differences imply no value judgments (about what is "better" or "worse"), Kapterev was at the cutting edge on this issue. However, his explanation of the causes of differences seems to come down, more or less, to the idea that "anatomy is destiny" and he appears hard-pressed to dig himself out of a serious stereotyping hole. See Kapterev, *Dushevnyia svoistva zhenshchin: Publichnyia lektsii P.F. Kaptereva* (St. Petersburg: School for

Deaf-Mutes Press, 1895); this was originally published as a series of articles in *Obrazovanie* in 1894.

47. See his *Unpopular Essays* (New York: Simon and Schuster, 1950), pp. 58-64. His comments about the situation of women are on pp. 60-61.

48. Studzinskaia, "Avtobiografiia," in "Smes'" section (sect. 3), *Russkoe slovo*, July 1860, No. 7, p. 13.

49. See William G. Wagner, "'Orthodox Domesticity': Creating a Social Role for Women," *Sacred Stories: Religion and Spirituality in Modern Russia*, ed. by Mark D. Steinberg and Heather J. Coleman (Bloomington IN: Indiana University Press, 2007), pp. 119-45. Page citations are in the text.

    Cf. Isolde Thyrêt, "Women and the Orthodox Faith in Muscovite Russia: Spiritual Experience and Practice," *Orthodox Russia: Belief and Practice Under the Tsars*, ed. by Valerie A. Kivelson and Robert H. Greene (University Park PA: Pennsylvania State University Press, 2003), pp. 159-75, especially pp. 166, 174.

50. Abbott Gleason offers a succinct summary of the milieu of late eighteenth-century ideas – especially the religious frame of mind – from which the concept of the idealized nanny emerged, in his "Ideological structures," in Nicholas Rzhevsky, ed., *The Cambridge Companion to Russian Culture* (Cambridge, UK: Cambridge University Press, 1998), pp. 103-124. On Russia's "particular spiritual vocation" see especially pp. 105-108. One of Russia's greatest historians frequently examined aspects of Russian "morality" in history in his occasional writings and lectures. See the pieces collected in Vasilii Kliuchevskii, *O nravstvennosti i russkoi kul'ture* (Moscow: Institut rossiiskoi istorii RAN, 1998).

51. Cf. Wladimir Weidlé, *Russia: Absent and Present*, trans. by A. Gordon Smith (New York: Vintage/Random House, 1961), especially Chapter 6.

52. I would recommend three collections of essays: the Kivelson-Greene *Orthodox Russia* – with an excellent annotated bibliography on pp. 277-82, *Seeking God: the Recovery of Religious Identity in Orthodox Russia, Ukraine, and Georgia*, ed. by Stephen K. Batalden (DeKalb: Northern Illinois University Press, 1993), and *Russian Religious Thought*, ed. by Judith Deutsch Kornblatt and Richard F. Gustafson (Madison: University of Wisconsin Press, 1996); Laura Engelstein, "Holy Russia in Modern Times: An Essay on Orthodoxy and Cultural Change," *Past & Present*, No. 173 (November 2001), pp. 129-56; Gregory L. Freeze's review article "Recent Scholarship on Russian Orthodoxy: A Critique," in *Kritika: Explorations in Russian and Eurasian History*, Vol. 2, No. 2

(Spring 2001), pp. 269-78; Scott M. Kenworthy, "To Save the World or to Renounce It: Modes of Moral Action in Russian Orthodoxy," in *Religion, Morality, and Community in Post-Soviet Societies*, ed. by Mark D. Steinberg and Catherine Wanner (Bloomington, IN and Washington DC: Indiana University Press/Woodrow Wilson Center Press, 2008), pp. 21-54; Kenworthy, *The Revival of Monasticism in Modern Russia: The Trinity-Sergius Lavra, 1825-1921*, unpublished PhD dissertation, Brandeis University, 2002 (his book based on the dissertation was unavailable to me); Valliere, *Modern Russian Theology*; and Shevzov, *Russian Orthodoxy*.

53. Dixon, "How holy was Holy Russia? Rediscovering Russian religion," in *Reinterpreting Russia*, ed. by Geoffrey Hosking and Robert Service (London: Arnold, 1999), pp. 21-39.

54. Marjorie Mandelstam Balzer and Richard Stites have both coined formulations that stress peasants' somewhat eclectic sense of religion. See Marjorie Mandelstam Balzer, *The Tenacity of Ethnicity: A Siberian Saga in Global Perspective* (Princeton NJ: Princeton University Press, 1999), pp. 61-66 (the phrase "multifaceted faith" appears on p. 64); and Richard Stites, *Revolutionary Dreams: Utopian Vision and Experimental Life in the Russian Revolution* (New York: Oxford University Press, 1989), p. 122, who calls typical folk belief "*mnogoverie*" or multiple faith (cited by Chulos, "Myths of the Pious or Pagan Peasant in Post-Emancipation Central Russia (Voronezh Province)," *Russian History/Histoire Russe*, Vol. 22, No. 2 (Spring 1995), p. 199n70.

55. Stella Rock sees the *concept* as largely a twentieth century construct. See her *Popular Religion in Russia: 'Double Belief' and the Making of an Academic Myth* (London/New York: Routledge, 2007) and "What's in a Word?: A Historical Study of the Concept *Dvoeverie*," *Canadian-American Slavic Studies*, Vol. 35, No. 1 (Spring 2001), pp. 19-28.

Eve Levin makes a similar point and argues that religious scholars, historians, and other intellectuals – not to mention politically motivated Soviet academics – using the *term* have continually sought to criticize and devalue folk beliefs, the better to control or even eliminate them. See her "*Dvoeverie* and Popular Religion" in *Seeking God*, Batalden ed., pp. 31-52.

56. The so-called kenotic aspect of Russian Orthodox faith has been emphasized by G.P. Fedotov in such books as *The Russian Religious Mind*, 2 vols. (Cambridge: Harvard University Press, 1946-66), especially Vol. 1, Chapter 4; and *A Treasury of Russian Spirituality* (New York: Sheed & Ward, 1948); but also by previous theologians and thinkers like Sergei

Bulgakov and Vladimir Solov'ëv. Cf. Steven Cassedy, "P.A. Florensky and the Celebration of Matter," in *Russian Religious Thought*, ed. by Kornblatt and Gustafson, pp. 95-97.

57. Cf. *Sviataia Rus': Bol'shaia entsiklopediia russkogo naroda. Russkoe pravoslavie*, ed. by O.A. Platonov et al., 5 vols. (Moscow: Institut russkoi tsivilizatsii, 2009-); here, Vol. 3 (2009), pp. 299-300, the entry for *"stradanie"* (suffering) by Platonov himself.

58. One thinks of Rancour-Laferriere's *Slave Soul of Russia*, a highly provocative and, in the end, unsatisfying examination of what he calls the phenomenon of "moral masochism" in Russian history. While able to array a vast number of examples of such "masochism," the author states that by all of these he does "not so much mean to characterize Russians as to offer a characteristic of many, perhaps most Russians," seemingly a distinction without a difference. He apophatically (disingenuously?) says: "Perhaps masochism is even the essence of the Russian soul, but such a claim would really have to be the topic of another book. A psychological trait, not national character, has been my focus here." (p. 245)

    A similarly misguided set of generalizations suffuses Anna Feldman Leibovich's *The Russian Concept of Work: Suffering, Drama, and Tradition in Pre- and Post-Revolutionary Russia* (Westport CT: Praeger, 1995). She claims, for example, that "the Russian...glorified the pain of suffering" (p. 5).

59. It might surprise some to learn that one leading interpreter of the Russian faith, Pavel Novgorodtsev, in his classic essay on the essence of Orthodox consciousness, does not even mention the idea of suffering. For Novgorodtsev, the basic principle of Orthodoxy is neither Catholicism's discipline nor Protestantism's freedom. The main qualities and special features of Orthodoxy are contemplativeness (with an implied passivity), humility, spiritual simplicity, joy in God, a need to manifest religious feeling in outward signs, and the expectation of the Kingdom of God beyond this earth. See his "Sushchestvo russkago pravoslavnago soznaniia," *Pravoslavie i kul'tura: Sbornik religiozno-filosofskikh statei*, ed. by V.V. Zenkovskii (Berlin: Russkaia kniga, 1923), pp. 7-23 (also in Novgorodtsev, *Sochineniia* [Moscow: Raritet, 1995].

60. My understanding of these matters is not universally held. For mostly supportive views on *dvoeverie*, see in particular the Rock and Levin works cited previously; Chulos, *Converging Worlds*, pp. 7-8, Chapter 1, and passim; Chulos, "Myths of the Pious," pp. 181-216, especially pp. 199-202, but also 182-83n5, and 207-213; Dixon, "How holy was Holy

Russia?," pp. 23-26, 33-34; and Nicholas Riasanovsky, *Russian Identities: A Historical Survey* (New York: Oxford University Press, 2005), pp. 28-29. Much different is the interpretation of Linda Ivanits, *Russian Folk Belief*, Part 1, Chapter 1, and pp. 36-37. A useful short bibliography is in Kivelson and Greene, *Orthodox Russia*, p.278.

61. Indeed, Vera Shevzov has analyzed the nearly opposite phenomenon: the impact of peasant belief in building a community of believers in the late nineteenth century, bringing together the Orthodox hierarchy, village folk, and the well-born. See her "Letting the People into Church: Reflections on Orthodoxy and Community in Late Imperial Russia," in Kivelson-Greene, *Orthodox Russia*, pp. 59-77; here, pp. 60-61; and *Russian Orthodoxy*, pp. 3-11, 19-20, 122.

62. Cf. Newman, *The Rise of English Nationalism*, Chapter Six, "The Moral Elevation of the English National Identity," pp. 123-56, from whom I am borrowing. Similar arguments can be found in Prasenjit Duara, "Historicizing National Identity, or Who Imagines What and When," in *Becoming National: A Reader*, ed. by Geoff Eley and Ronald Grigor Suny (New York: Oxford University Press, 1996), pp. 151-77.

There are symbolism and myths attached to the ante-bellum black mammy in America and the British nanny, though neither became a national allegory in quite the way Arina and her fellow caretakers did. *Ayahs* in India, *otsuki* and *komori* in Japan, as well as nursemaids in Italy, Spain, Germany and elsewhere in Europe also all seem to fall short of the attention paid Russian nannies. For a brief comparative essay on nannies in various countries, please apply to the author at salangrant@verizon.net.

63. Newman, *Rise of English Nationalism*, p. 126.

64. *Ibid.*, p. 127.

Bibliography

Archival Sources

Nikolai Maryshev papers, Bakhmeteff Archive, Columbia University

Vladimir Vladimirovich Nabokov papers, 1918-1974, Manuscript Division, Library of Congress

Sergius Pankejeff [Sergei Pankeev] papers, 1901-1979, Manuscript Division, Library of Congress

Ekaterina Roshchina-Insarova papers, Bakhmeteff Archive, Columbia University

Pavel Shatilov papers, Bakhmeteff Archive, Columbia University

G.A. Tal' (Thal) papers, Bakhmeteff Archive, Columbia University

G[eorgii] G[ustavovich] Tel'berg papers, 1915-1940, Manuscript Division, Library of Congress

Vladimir Unkovskii papers, Bakhmeteff Archive, Columbia University

Nikolai Zhigulev papers, Bakhmeteff Archive, Columbia University

Primary Sources: Autobiographies, Memoirs, Other Ego-Documents

NB: Primary and secondary sources that appeared only in Russian periodicals have almost all been excluded from this bibliography, even though cited in endnotes, to conserve space. All these periodicals are listed at the end of the bibliography.

A. P. Chekhov v vospominaniiakh sovremennikov (Moscow: Khudozhestvennaia literatura, 1960)

Bibliography 437

A. S. Pushkin v vospominaniiakh sovremennikov v dvukh tomakh, 2 vols. (Moscow: Khudozhestvennaia literatura, 1985)

F. M. Dostoevskii v vospominaniiakh sovremennikov, 2 vols. (Moscow: Khudozhestvennaia literatura, 1964)

I.A. Goncharov v vospominaniiakh sovremennikov (Leningrad: Khudozhestvennaia literatura, 1969)

Vospominaniia rodnykh [o Lenine], vol. 1 of 5 (Moscow: Politizdat, 1969)

Abrikosov, Dmitrii. *Revelations of a Russian Diplomat: The Memoirs of Dmitrii I. Abrikossow* (Seattle: University of Washington Press, 1964)

Aksakova-Sivers, Tat'iana. *Semeinaia khronika*, Vol. I (Paris: Atheneum, 1988)

Allilueva, Svetlana [Alliluyeva]. *20 Letters to a Friend*, trans. by Priscilla Johnson (London: Hutchinson, 1967)

Andreas-Salomé, Lou. *Looking Back: Memoirs*, ed. by Ernst Pfeiffer; trans. by Breon Mitchell (New York: Paragon House, 1991)

Andreev, Vadim. *Detstvo: Povest'* (Moscow: Sovetskii pisatel', 1966)

Andreeva, Alla. *Plavanie k nebesnomu kremliu* (Moscow: "Uraniia", 1998)

Andreeva-Bal'mont, Ekaterina. *Vospominaniia* (Moscow: Sabashnikov Publishing, 1997)

Annenkov, Pavel. *Materialy dlia biografii Aleksandra Sergeevicha Pushkina*, annot. by A. L. Ospovat and N. G. Okhotin, facsimile reproduction (Moscow: Kniga, 1985)

___. *Sochineniia Pushkina s prilozheniem materialov dlia ego biografii*, reprint ed. of the self-published 1855 ed. (n.p., n.d. [but 1985?])

Antsiferov, Nikolai. *Iz dum o bylom: Vospominaniia*, comp. and annot. by A.I. Dobkin (Moscow: Feniks/ Kul'turnaia initsiativa, 1992)

Arnol'd, Iurii. *Vospominaniia Iuriia Arnol'da*, 3 vols. (Moscow: E. Lissner and Iu. Roman, 1892-93)

Arsen'ev, Nikolai. *Dary i vstrechi zhiznennogo puti* (Frankfurt-am-Main, Germany: Posev, 1974)

Astrov, Nikolai. *Vospominaniia*, Vol. 1 (Paris: YMCA Press, 1941)

Avilova, Lidiia. *Rasskazy, vospominaniia* (Moscow: Sovetskaia Rossiia, 1984)

Bal'mont, Konstantin. *Avtobiograficheskaia proza* (Moscow: Algoritm, 2001)

Bartenev, Pëtr. *O Pushkine: stranitsy zhizni poeta. Vospominaniia sovremennikov,* comp., introd. and annot. by A. M. Gordin (Moscow: Sovetskaia Rossiia, 1992)

___. "Vospominaniia P. I. Barteneva," *Rossiiskii arkhiv: Istoriia Otechestva v svidetel'stvakh i dokumentakh XVIII-XX vv.*, Vol. I (Moscow: Trite Studiia/ Rossiiskii arkhiv, 1991)

Barto, Agniia. *Zapiski detskogo poeta* (Moscow: Omega, 2006)

Bek, Anna. *The Life of a Russian Woman Doctor: A Siberian Memoir, 1869-1954,* trans. and ed. by Anne D. Rassweiler (Bloomington: Indiana University Press, 2004)

Beketova, Mariia. *Al. Blok i ego mat': vospominaniia i zametki* (Leningrad: "Petrograd", 1925)

Belyi, Andrei. *Na rubezhe dvukh stoletii,* prep. and annot. by A. V. Lavrov (Moscow: Khudozhestvennaia literatura, 1989)

Benois, Alexandre [Benua]. *Moi vospominaniia,* 2nd enl. ed., 2 vols. (Moscow: Nauka, 1990)

Berdiaev, Nikolai [Nicolas Berdyaev]. *Dream and Reality: An Essay in Autobiography* (New York: Collier Books, 1962)

Berggol'ts, Ol'ga. *Dnevnye zvezdy* (Moscow: Sovremennik, 1975)

Bertensson, Sergei and Jay Leyda, *Sergei Rachmaninoff: A Lifetime in Music,* with Sophia Satina (New York: New York University Press, 1956)

Blok, Aleksandr. *Sobranie sochinenii v vos'mi tomakh,* Vol. 7 (Leningrad: Khudozhestvennaia literatura, 1963)

Bogdan, Valentina. *Mimikriia v SSSR: Vospominaniia inzhenera 1935-1942 gody* (Frankfurt/Main: Polyglott-Druck GmbH, n.d.) English partial trans. available as "Memoirs of an Engineer," in Sheila Fitzpatrick and Yuri Slezkine, eds., *In the Shadow of Revolution: Life Stories of Russian Women from 1917 to the Second World War,* trans. by Slezkine (Princeton: Princeton University Press, 2000), pp. 394-418

Bolotov, Andrei. *Zhizn' i prikliucheniia Andreia Bolotova opisannye samim im dlia svoikh pitomkov* (Moscow: Academia, 1931; reprinted by Oriental Research Partners, Cambridge, England, 1973)

Bonner, Elena. *Dochki – Materi* (New York: Chekhov, 1991)

[Borisov, Boris]. *Russian Boy* (Westminster, England: P. S. King & Staples Ltd., 1942)

Bortnikova, E.E. et al., comp. and eds. *Vospominaniia o P.I. Chaikovskom* (Moscow: Gosudarstvennoe muzykal'noe izdatel'stvo, 1962)

Briusov, Valerii. *Iz moei zhizni: Moia iunost'. Pamiati* (Moscow: M. and S. Sabashnikov, 1927)

Budberg, Mikhail [Michael]. *Russian Seesaw* (London: Martin Hopkinson, Ltd., 1934)

Buksgevden, Baroness Sofiia (Sophie Buxhoeveden). *Before the Storm* (London: Macmillan and Co., 1938)

Bulanova-Trubnikova, Ol'ga. *Tri pokoleniia* (Moscow-Leningrad, 1928)

Bulgakov, Sergei. *Avtobiograficheskie zametki. Dnevniki. Stat'i* (Orel: Izdatel'stvo Orlovskoi gosudarstvennoi teleradioveshchatel'noi kompanii, 1998)

Bunakov, Nikolai F. *Zapiski N. F. Bunakova. Moia zhizn', v sviazi s obshcherusskoi zhizn'iu, preimushchestvenno provintsial'noi. 1837-1905* (St. Petersburg: Obshchestvennaia pol'za, 1909)

Chaikovskii, Modest. *The Life and Letters of Peter Ilich Tchaikovsky*, ed. by Rosa Newmarch, 2 vols. (New York: Vienna House, 1973)

Charykov, Nikolai. *Glimpses of High Politics: Through War & Peace 1855*1929: The Autobiography of N. V. Tcharykow, Serf-Owner, Ambassador, Exile* (London: George Allen & Unwin Ltd., 1931)

Chekhov, Mikhail A. *Literaturnoe nasledie*, Vol. I: *Vospominaniia. Pis'ma* (Moscow: Iskusstvo, 1995)

Chekhov, Mikhail P. "Biograficheskii ocherk. (1860-1887)," in *Pis'ma A. P. Chekhova*. Vol. 1: 1876-1887 (Moscow: M. P. Chekhova/I. D. Sytin, 1912)

___. "Ob A. P. Chekhove. Vospominaniia M. P. Chekhova," *Rampa i zhizn'*, 1 July 1912, No. 27

Chernavina, Tat'iana [Tatiana Tchernavin]. *My Childhood in Siberia* (London: Oxford University Press, 1972)

Chertkova, Anna. *Iz moego detstva. Vospominaniia A. K. Chertkovoi* (Moscow: I. N. Kushnerev and Co., 1911)

Chukovskaia, Lidiia. *Pamiati detstva* (St. Petersburg: Limbus Press, 2000)

Chukovskii, Kornei. *Dnevnik 1901-1969*, 2 vols. (Moscow: OLMA-PRESS, 2003)

Cottam, Kazimiera J., ed. and trans. *Defending Leningrad: Women Behind Enemy Lines*, 2nd rev. ed. (Nepean, CAN: New Military Publishing, 1998)

Davydov, Nikolai. *Iz proshlago*, Vol. I, 2nd ed. (Moscow: I. D. Sytin Press, 1914); Vol. 2 (Moscow: Pechatnik Press, 1917)

De Hueck, Catherine. *My Russian Yesterdays* (Milwaukee: The Bruce Publishing Company, 1951)

Deich, Lev. *Za polveka* (Cambridge, MA: Oriental Research Partners, 1975)

Dmitriev, Mikhail. *Melochi iz zapasa moei pamiati*, 2nd enl. ed. (Moscow: Grachev and Company, 1869)

Dmitrieva, Valentina. *Tak bylo. Put' moei zhizni* (Moscow: Molodaia gvardiia, 1930)

Dobroliubov, Nikolai. *Pervoe polnoe sobranie sochinenii N.A. Dobroliubova v chetyrekh tomakh*, 4 vols. (St. Petersburg: A.S. Panafidina, 1911)

Dobuzhinskii, Mstislav. *Pis'ma*, comp. and annot. by G.I. Chugunov (Moscow: "Dmitrii Bulanin", 2001)

___. *Vospominaniia*, Vol. 1, comp. and ed. by Evgenii Klimov with the aid of Dobuzhinskii's two sons (New York: Put' zhizni, St. Seraphim Foundation, Inc., 1976)

___. *Vospominaniia*, ed. by G.I. Chugunov (Moscow: Nauka, 1987)

Dolgorukov, Prince Ivan. *Kapishche moego serdtsa, ili Slovar' vsekh tekh lits, s koimi ia byl v raznykh otnosheniiakh v techenie moei zhizni*, ed., annotated, and with an introduction by V. I. Korovin (Moscow: Nauka, 1997)

___. *Povest' o rozhdenii moem, proiskhozhdenii i vsei zhizni, pisannaia mnoi samim i nachataia v Moskve 1788-go goda v Avguste mesiatse, na 25-om godu ot rozhdeniia moego*, vol. I, ed. by N. V. Kuznetsova and M. O. Mel'tsin (St. Petersburg: Nauka, 2004)

Dostoevskii, Fëdor. *Polnoe sobranie sochinenii v tridtsati tomakh* (Leningrad: Nauka, 1972-1990)

Durova, Nadezhda. *Izbrannoe* (Moscow: Sovetskaia Rossiia, 1984)

Efron, Ariadna. *Stranitsy vospominanii* (Paris: LEV, 1979)

Eikhenbaum, Boris. *Moi vremennik. Marshrut v bessmertie* (Moscow: Agraf, 2001)

Elenevskaia, Irina. *Vospominaniia* (Belgium: A. Rosseels Printing Co., [1968])

Engel, Barbara Alpern, and Anastasiia Posadskaya-Vanderbeck, eds. *A Revolution of Their Own: Voices of Women in Soviet History* (Boulder, CO: Westview Press, 1998)

Fen, Elizaveta. *A Russian Childhood* (London: Methuen & Co, Ltd, 1961)

Fet, Afanasii. *Rannie gody moei zhizni* (Munich: Wilhelm Fink Verlag, 1971) reprint of 1893 edition

Figner, Vera. *Zapechatlennyi trud. Vospominaniia v dvukh tomakh*, 2 vols. (Moscow: Mysl', 1964)

Findeizen, Nikolai. *Iz moikh vospominanii* (St. Petersburg: Rossiiskaia natsional'naia biblioteka, 2004) *Rukopisnye pamiatniki* 8

Fitzpatrick, Sheila, and Yuri Slezkine, eds., *In the Shadow of Revolution: Life Stories of Russian Women from 1917 to the Second World War*, trans. by Slezkine (Princeton: Princeton University Press, 2000)

Fraser, Evgeniia [Eugenie]. *The House by the Dvina: A Russian-Scottish Childhood* (New York: Walker and Company, 1984)

Garshin, Vsevolod. *Polnoe sobranie sochinenii V. M. Garshina* (St. Petersburg: A. F. Marks, 1910)

Ge, Nikolai. *Nikolai Nikolaevich Ge, ego zhizn', proizvedeniia i perepiska*, comp. by V. Stasov (Moscow: I.N. Kushnerev and Co., 1904)

German, Mikhail. *Slozhnoe proshedshee (Passé composé)* (St. Petersburg: Iskusstvo, 2000)

Gertsyk, Evgeniia. *Vospominaniia: Memuary, zapisnye knizhki, dnevniki, pis'ma* (Moscow: Moskovskii rabochii, 1996)

Gillel'son, M.I. and O. V. Miller, eds., comps. and annot. *M. Iu. Lermontov v vospominaniiakh sovremennikov* (Moscow: Khudozhestvennaia literatura, 1989)

Glinka, Mikhail. *Literaturnye proizvedeniia i perepiska* (Moscow: Muzyka, 1973-), Vol. I of his *Polnoe sobranie sochinenii* ed.by Tamara N. Livanova et al.

___. *Mikhail Ivanovich Glinka: Literaturnoe nasledie*, Vol. 2 (Leningrad-Moscow: Gosudarstvennoe muzykal'noe izdatel'stvo, 1953)

Goldman, Emma. *My Disillusionment in Russia* (Mineola, NY: Dover Publications, 2003)

Golitsyna [Galitzine], Irina. *Spirit to Survive: The Memoirs of Princess Nicholas Galitzine* (London: William Kimber, 1976)

Golitsyna [Galitzine], Princess Tat'iana. *The Russian Revolution: Childhood Recollections* (Princeton: Princeton University Press, 1972)

Goncharov, Ivan. *Sobranie sochinenii v vos'mi tomakh*, vol. 1 (Moscow: Khudozhestvennaia literatura, 1955)

Grechaninov, Aleksandr. *Moia zhizn'*, 2nd enl. ed. (New York: Raausen Brothers/Novyi zhurnal, 1951)

Grigor'ev [Grigoryev], Prince Apollon. *My Literary and Moral Wanderings and Other Autobiographical Material*, trans. by Ralph E. Matlaw (New York: E. P. Dutton & Co., Inc., 1962)

Guro, Elena. *Sochineniia*, comp. by G.K. Perkins (Oakland, CA; Berkeley Slavic Specialties, 1996)

Harari, Manya. *Memoirs: 1906-1969* (London: Harvill Press, 1972)

Herzen [Gertsen], Aleksandr. *Byloe i dumy*, 2 vols. (Moscow: Khudozhestvennaia literatura, 1962)

Horsbrugh-Porter, Anna, ed. *Memories of Revolution: Russian Women Remember* (London: Routledge, 1993)

Il'inskii, Igor'. *Sam o sebe*, 2nd rev. and enl. ed. (Moscow: Iskusstvo, 1973)

Ilizarov, B.S., ed., and comp. by T.M. Goriaeva et al. *Zhenskaia sud'ba v Rossii: Dokumenty i vospominaniia* (Moscow: Rossiia molodaia, 1994)

Ioffe, Nadezhda. *Vremia nazad. Moia zhizn', moia sud'ba, moia epokha* (Moscow: T.O.O. "Biologicheskie nauki", 1992) English version: *Back in Time: My Life, My Fate, My Epoch – The Memoirs of Nadezhda A. Joffe*, trans. by Frederick S. Choate (Oak Park, MI: Labor Publications, Inc., 1995)

Ivanova, Lidiia. *Vospominaniia: Kniga ob ottse* (Moscow: RIK Kul'tura, 1992)

Ivanova, Ol'ga. "Vospominaniia Ol'gi Ivanovny Ivanovoi," *Vospominaniia Poliny Annenkovoi* (Krasnoiarsk: Krasnoiarsk Book Publishing, 1977)

Izvolskaia, Elena [Helene Iswolsky]. *No Time to Grieve...An Autobiographical Journey* (Philadelphia: The Winchell Company, 1985)

Jackman, S.W. with Berangere Steel, eds. *Romanov Relations: the Private Correspondence of Tsars Alexander I, Nicholas I and The Grand Dukes Constantine and Michael with their Sister Queen Anna Pavlovna 1817-1855* (London: Macmillan and Co., Ltd., 1969)

Kabeshtov, I.M. *Moia zhizn' i vospominaniia* (Sumy: K.M. Pashkov, 1906)

Kamenskaia, Mar'ia. *Vospominaniia* (Moscow: Khudozhestvennaia literatura, 1991)

Kanatchikov, Semën. *Iz istorii moego bytiia*, Vol. I (Moscow: "Zemlia i fabrika", 1929)

Katukova, Ekaterina. *Tak bylo* (Moscow: ACT, 2005)

Kavelin, Konstantin, and Ivan Turgenev. *Pis'ma K.Dm. Kavelina i Iv.S. Turgeneva k Al.Iv. Gertsenu* (Geneva: H. Georg, 1892)

Kharuzina, Vera. *Proshloe. Vospominaniia detskikh i otrocheskikh let* (Moscow: Novoe literaturnoe obozrenie, 1999)

Bibliography 443

Khodasevich, Vladislav. *O Pushkine* (Berlin: Petropolis, 1937)

___. *Pushkin i poety ego vremeni*, Vol. II, ed. by Robert P. Hughes (Berkeley, CA: Berkeley Slavic Specialties, 2001)

Kiukhel'beker, Vil'gel'm. *Puteshestvie. Dnevnik. Stat'i* (Leningrad: Nauka, 1979)

Komarova-Stasova, Varvara [Vlad. Karenin], *Vladimir Stasov: Ocherk ego zhizni i deiatel'nosti*, 2 vols. (Leningrad: Mysl', 1927)

Koni, Anatolii. *Peterburg. Vospominaniia starozhila (Memuary)* (St. Petersburg: Atenei, 1922)

Kopelev, Lev. *The Education of a True Believer*, trans. by Gary Kern (New York: Harper & Row, 1980)

Kornilova, Ol'ga. *Byl' iz vremen krepostnichestva. (Vospominaniia o moei materi i eia okruzhaiushchem)* (St. Petersburg: "Obshchestvennaia Pol'za" Society, 1890)

Korolenko, Vladimir. *Istoriia moego sovremennika* (Moscow: Khudozhestvennaia literatura, 1965)

Kovalev, V.A. et al., eds. and comps. *"Minuvshee menia ob"emlet zhivo...": Vospominaniia russkikh pisatelei XVIII-nachala XX v. i ikh sovremennikov. Rekomendatel'naia bibliograficheskaia entsiklopediia* (Moscow: "Knizhnaia palata", 1989)

Krandievskaia-Tolstaia, Natal'ia. *Vospominaniia* (Leningrad: Lenizdat, 1977)

Krivich [Annenskii], Valentin. "Innokentii Annenskii po semeinym vospominaniiam i rukopisnym materialam," *Literaturnaia mysl'*, No. 3 (Leningrad, 1925), pp. 208-255

Kurakin, Andrei [André Kourakine]. *De l'aigle imperiale a l'étoile rouge* (Paris: La table ronde, 1970)

Kuzminskaia, Tat'iana. *Moia zhizn' doma i v iasnoi poliane: Vospominaniia* (Moscow: Pravda, 1986) English trans.: *Tolstoy as I Knew Him: My Life at Home and at Yasnaya Polyana* (New York: The Macmillan Company, 1948)

L'vov, Prince Georgii E. *Vospominaniia* (Moscow: Russkii put', 2002)

L'vova, Princess Mariia. *"Vospominaniia"*, App. I in Prince G. E. L'vov, *Vospominaniia* (Moscow: Russkii put', 2002)

Lazhechnikov, Ivan. *Sobranie sochinenii*, Vol. I (Moscow: Mozhaisk-Terra, 1994)

Leikin, N.A. *Moi vospominaniia//Nikolai Aleksandrovich Leikin v ego vospominaniiakh i perepiske* (St. Petersburg: R. Golike and A. Vil'borg Company, 1907)

Leskov, Andrei. *Zhizn' Nikolaia Leskova po ego lichnym, semeinym i neseminym zapisiam i pamiatiam v dvukh tomakh*, 2 vols. (Moscow: Khudozhestvennaia literatura, 1984)

Levitskaia, Anna. "Vospominaniia," *Rossiiskii arkhiv: Istoriia Otechestva v svidetel'stvakh i dokumentakh XVIII-XX vv.*, Vol. IX (Moscow: Trite Studiia/Rossiiskii arkhiv, 1999), pp. 251-85

Libedinskii, Iurii. *Sviaz' vremeni: Vospominaniia, povesti, ocherki, rasskazy* (Moscow: Sovetskii pisatel', 1962)

Likhachev, Dmitrii. *Izbrannoe: Vospominaniia*, 2nd rev. ed. (St. Petersburg: Logos, 1997)

Lind, Mikhail. "Moi zapiski," *Rossiiskii arkhiv: Istoriia Otechestva v svidetel'stvakh i dokumentakh XVIII-XX vv.*, Vol. XII, New Series (Moscow: Trite Studiia/Rossiiskii arkhiv, 2003), Appendix

M.A. Balakirev i V. V. Stasov: Perepiska, 2 vols. (Moscow: Muzyka, 1970)

Majolier, Nathalie [Mamontova]. *Step-Daughter of Imperial Russia* (London: Stanley Paul & Co., Ltd., 1940)

Malina, Irina. *Ia vspominaiu...(1906-1920)* (St. Petersburg: Petropol', 1995)

Mandel'shtam, Nadezhda. *Tret'ia kniga*, comp. by Iu.L. Freidin (Moscow: Agraf, 2006)

Mandel'shtam, Osip. *Shum vremeni*, annot. by A. A. Morozov, prep. by S. V. Vaselenko and Morozov (Moscow: Vagrius, 2002) English version: *The Noise of Time: Selected Prose* trans. and with critical essays by Clarence Brown (Evanston, IL: Northwestern University Press, 2002)

Martov, L. (Iulii Tsederbaum), *Zapiski sotsial-demokrata* (Cambridge, MA: Oriental Research Partners, 1975)

Mertvago, Dmitrii. *Avtobiograficheskiia zapiski Dmitriia Borisovicha Mertvago. 1760-1824* (Moscow: Russkii Arkhiv/T. Ris, 1867)

Miliukov, Aleksandr. *Dobroe staroe vremia (ocherki bylago)* (St. Petersburg: A. F. Bazunov, 1872)

Mintslov, Sergei. *Dalekie dni. Vospominaniia. 1870-90 gg.* (Berlin: Sibirskoe izdatel'stvo, n.d. [but 1925])

Morozov, Nikolai. *Povesti moei zhizni: memuary*, 2 vols. (Moscow: Academy of Sciences Press, 1962)

Musorgskii, Modest. *Literaturnoe nasledie: Pis'ma, biograficheskie materialy i dokumenty*, comp. by A. A. Orlova and M. S. Pekelis (Moscow: Muzyka, 1971)

___. *Pis'ma i dokumenty*, comp. by A. N. Rimskii-Korsakov with V. D. Komarova-Stasova (Moscow-Leningrad, 1932)

Nikitenko, Aleksandr. *Dnevnik v trekh tomakh* (Leningrad: Khudozhestvennaia literatura, 1955)

Novikov, Nikolai. *Izbrannoe* (Moscow: Pravda, 1983)

Obolenskii, Dmitrii [Obolensky] *Bread of Exile: A Russian Family*, trans. by Harry Willetts (London: Harvill Press, 1999)

Obolenskii, Prince Dmitrii. *Zapiski kniazia Dmitriia Aleksandrovicha Obolenskogo: 1855-1879* (St. Petersburg: SpvII RAN/"Nestor-Istoriia", 2005)

Obolenskii, Vladimir. *Moia zhizn'. Moi sovremenniki* (Paris: YMCA Press, 1988)

Okreits, Stanislav [Orlitskii, pseud.], *Dalekie gody: Avtobiograficheskaia khronika* (St. Petersburg: Glavnoe upravlenie udelov, 1899)

Olitskaia, Ekaterina. *Moi vospominaniia* (Frankfurt/Main: Possev-Verlag, 1971)

Pankeev, Sergei [Sergius Pankejeff]. *The Wolf-Man by the Wolf-Man, with The Case of the Wolf-Man, by Sigmund Freud and A Supplement by Ruth Mack Brunswick*, ed., annot. and introd. by Muriel Gardiner (New York: Hill and Wang/Noonday Press, 1991)

Panova, Vera. *O moei zhizni, knigakh i chitateliakh* (Leningrad: Lenizdat, 1975)

Passek, Tat'iana. *Iz dal'nykh let: Vospominaniia*, 2 vols. (Moscow: Khudozhestvennaia literatura, 1963)

Pasternak, Boris. *Liudi i polozheniia: Avtobiograficheskii ocherk*, in *Polnoe sobranie sochinenii s prilozheniiami v odinnadtsati tomakh*, Vol. III (Moscow: Slovo, 2004)

Pavlov [Pylin], Boris. *Pervye chetyrnadtsat' let 1906-1920* ([California]: n.p., 1972)

Perepisi moskovskikh dvorov semnadtsatago stoletiia and *Perepisi moskovskikh dvorov vosemnadtsatago stoletiia*, both 1896

Pervaia vseobshchaia perepis' naseleniia rossiiskoi imperii 1897 g., ed. by Nikolai A. Troinitskii, Vols. 24, 37, and Vol. 47 (Moscow: Central Statistical Committee of the Ministry of Interior, 1903-04)

Pirogov, Nikolai. *Voprosy zhizni: dnevnik starago vracha, pisannyi iskliuchitel'no dlia samogo sebia, no ne bez zadnei mysli, chto, mozhet byt', kogda-nibud' prochtet i kto drugoi*; comprising vol. 1 of his *Sochineniia* (St. Petersburg: M. M. Stasiulevich, 1887)

Pletnev, Pëtr. "Aleksandr Sergeevich Pushkin," *Sochineniia i perepiska P. A. Pletneva*, Vol. 1 (St. Petersburg: Akademiia nauk, 1885), pp. 364-386

Posse, Vladimir Posse. *Perezhitoe i produmannoe*, Vol. I: *Molodost' (1864-1894)* (Leningrad: Izdatel'stvo pisatelei v Leningrade, 1933)

Priemskii, Dmitrii. *Vospominaniia iz zhizni inzhenera* (Sarov: RFIaTs-VNIIEF, 2006)

Prokof'ev, Sergei. *Avtobiografiia*, 2nd enl. ed. (Moscow: Sovetskii kompozitor, 1982)

Pushkin, Aleksandr. *The Letters of Alexander Pushkin*, trans. and annot. by J. Thomas Shaw (Madison: The University of Wisconsin Press, 1967)

___. *Polnoe sobranie sochinenii v 17 tomakh* (Moscow: Voskresen'e, 1996)

___. *Rukoiu Pushkina: Nesobrannye i neopublikovannye teksty*, comments by L. B. Modzalevskii; M. A. Tsiavlovskii, Modzalevskii, and T. G. Zenger comps. and eds. (Moscow-Leningrad: Academia, 1935)

Radishchev, Aleksandr. *Izbrannye filosofskie sochineniia*, ed. by I. Ia. Shchipanov (Leningrad: Politicheskaia literatura,1949)

Rakhmaninov, Sergei. *Rachmaninoff's recollections, told to Oskar von Riesemann* (New York, The Macmillan Company, 1934)

Ritter, Aleksandr. *Otzvuki minuvshago (vospominaniia starago pomeshchika)*, 3rd ed. (Moscow: Universitetskaia Tipografiia, 1899)

Romanova, Mariia [Grand Duchess Marie]. *Education of a Princess* (New York: The Viking Press, 1931)

Rozhdestvenskii, Vsevolod. *Stranitsy zhizni*, 2nd enl. ed. (Moscow: Sovremennik, 1974)

Rusanov, Nikolai. *Iz moikh vospominanii*, Bk. 1 (Berlin: Z.I. Grzhebin, 1923)

Rusov, N.N., comp. *Pomeshchich'ia Rossiia po zapiskam sovremennikov* (Moscow: Obrazovanie, 1911)

Rylov, Arkadii. *Vospominaniia* (Leningrad: Khudozhnik RSFSR, 1977)

Sabaneeva, Ekaterina. *Vospominaniia o bylom 1770-1828 gg.*, in V. M. Bokova, comp., *Istoriia zhizni blagorodnoi zhenshchiny* (Moscow: Novoe literaturnoe obozrenie, 1996)

Sabashnikov, Mikhail. *Vospominaniia* (Moscow: "Kniga", 1983)

Sakharov, Andrei. *Memoirs*, trans. by Richard Lourie (New York: Alfred A. Knopf, 1990)

Sechenov, Ivan. *Avtobiograficheskie zapiski Ivana Mikhailovicha Sechenova* (Moscow: Academy of Sciences, 1945)

Shaginian, Marietta. *Chelovek i vremia: Istoriia chelovecheskogo stanovleniia* (Moscow: Khudozhestvennaia literatura, 1980)

___. *Sem'ia Ul'ianovykh. Ocherki. Stat'i. Vospominaniia* (Moscow: Khudozhestvennaia literatura, 1959)

Shchegolev, Pavel E. *Lermontov: Vospominaniia. Pis'ma. Dnevniki...* (Moscow: Agraf, 1999)

Shchepkina, Aleksandra. *Vospominaniia Aleksandry Vladimirovny Shchepkinoi* (Sergiev Posad: I. I. Ivanov, 1915)

Shchepkina-Kupernik, Tat'iana. *Vospominaniia* (Moscow: Zakharov, 2005)

Shchukin, Pëtr. *Vospominaniia P. I. Shchukina* (Moscow: Sinodal Press, 1911)

Shelgunova, Liudmila. *Iz dalekogo proshlogo*, in vol. II of N.V. Shelgunov, M.I. Mikhailov, and Shelgunova. *Vospominaniia v dvukh tomakh* (Moscow: Khudozhestvennaia literatura, 1967)

Shklovskii, Viktor. *Sobranie sochinenii v trekh tomakh*, Vol. I: *Povesti. Rasskazy* (Moscow: Khudozhestvennaia literatura, 1973)

Shlifshtein, S.I., ed. *S.S. Prokof'ev: Materialy. Dokumenty. Vospominaniia*, 2nd enl. ed. (Moscow: Gosudarstvennoe muzykal'noe izdatel'tstvo, 1961)

Shmelëv, Ivan. *Sobranie sochinenii*, <8>vols. (Moscow: Russkaia kniga, 1998-<2001>)

Skabichevskii, Aleksandr. *Literaturnye vospominaniia* (Moscow: Agraf, 2001)

Skabichevskii, Mikhail. "Iz vospominanii o perezhitom," *Literaturnye vospominaniia* (Moscow: Agraf, 2001)

Skalon, Sof'ia. "Vospominaniia," *Russkie memuary: Izbrannye stranitsy, XVIII vek* (Moscow: Pravda, 1988)

Skriabina, Elena. *Stranitsy zhizni* (Moscow: Progress-Akademiia, 1994)

Solov'ëv, Sergei [1820-1879]. *Izbrannye trudy. Zapiski*, ed. by A. A. Levandovskii and N. I. Tsimbaev (Moscow: Moscow University Press, 1983)

Solov'ëv, Sergei [1885-1942]. *Vospominaniia* (Moscow: Novoe literaturnoe obozrenie, 2003)

Sushkova, Ekaterina. *Zapiski 1812-1841* (Leningrad: Academia, 1928)

Sychugov, Savvatii. *Zapiski bursaka*, ed. and annot. by S. Ia. Shtraikh (Moscow: Academia, 1933)

Taneev, Vladimir. *Detstvo. Iunost'. Mysli o budushchem* (Moscow: Izdatel'stvo AN SSSR, 1959)

Tikhomirov, Lev. *Teni proshlogo* (Moscow: "Moscow", 2000)

Tolstaia, Tat'iana. *Vospominaniia* (Moscow: Khudozhestvennaia literatura, 1976)

Tolstoi, Il'ia [Ilya Tolstoy]. *Tolstoy, My Father: Reminiscences* (Chicago: Cowles Book Co., Inc., 1971)

Tolstoi, Lev [Count Leo]. *Polnoe sobranie sochinenii* 90 vol. in 78 (M-L: Khudozhestvennaia literatura, 1928-58)

Trotskii, Lev (Bronshtein) [Leon Trotsky]. *My Life* (New York: Grosset & Dunlap, 1960)

Trubetskoi, Evgenii. *Iz proshlago* (Vienna, 1920)

Trukhanova, Natal'ia. *Na stsene i za kulisami: vospominaniia* (Moscow: Zakharov, 2003)

Tsiavlovskii, Mstislav, ed. *Kniga vospominanii o Pushkine* (Moscow: Mir, 1931)

Tsvetaeva, Marina. *A Captive Spirit: Selected Prose*, trans. and ed. by J. Marin King (Ann Arbor, MI: Ardis Publishers, 1994)

___. *Izbrannaia proza v dvukh tomakh*, 2 vols. (New York: Russica Publishers, 1979)

___. *Neizdannoe: Sem'ia: Istoriia v pis'makh* (Moscow: Ellis Lak, 1999)

___. *Neizdannoe: Svodnye tetradi*, prepared, annot. and introd. by E. B. Korkina and I. D. Shevelenko (Moscow: Ellis Lak, 1997)

___. *Neizdannoe: Zapisnye knizhki v dvukh tomakh*, 2 vols. (Moscow: Ellis Lak, 2001)

Tsvetaeva, Anastasiia. *Vospominaniia*, 3rd enl. ed. (Moscow: Sovetskii pisatel', 1984)

Tuchkova-Ogareva, Natal'ia. *Vospominaniia* (Moscow: Gosizdat Khudozhestvennoi literatury, 1959)

Tyrkova-Vil'iams, Ariadna. *To, chego bol'she ne budet: vospominaniia*

Bibliography 449

izvestnoi pisatel'nitsy i obshchestvenoi deiatel'nitsy A. V. Tyrkovoi-Vil'iams (1869-1962), ed. by Diana Tevekelian (Moscow: Slovo, 1998)

Ul'ianov, Dmitrii and Anna Ulianova-Elizarova, *O V. I. Lenine i sem'e Ul'ianovykh: Vospominaniia. Ocherki. Pis'ma. Stat'i* (Moscow: Politizdat, 1988)

Ulanova, Galina. *Ia ne khotela tantsevat'*, comp. by Saniia Davlekamova (Moscow: AST-Press SKD, 2005)

Unkovskaia, Aleksandra. *Vospominaniia* (Petrograd: B.M. Vol'f, 1917)

Uspenskii, Lev. *Zapiski starogo peterburzhtsa* (Leningrad: Lenizdat, 1970)

Vasina-Grossman, V.A., ed. *Antonina Vasil'evna Nezhdanova: Materialy i issledovaniia* (Moscow: Iskusstvo, 1967)

Venetsianov, Nikolai. "Moi zapiski. 1845-1850 (?)" and "Moi vospominaniia detstva 1845 goda, genvaria 15 d[nia]. g. Stavr[opol']," *Aleksei Gavrilovich Venetsianov: Stat'i. Pis'ma. Sovremenniki o khudozhnike*, comp., annot. and introd. by A. V. Kornilova (Leningrad: Iskusstvo, 1980), pp. 207-214

Vengerov, S.A., ed. *Russkaia literatura XX veka*, Vol. I (Moscow: Mir, 1914) Reprint: *Slavische Propyläen*, Vol. 115 (Munich: Wilhelm Fink Verlag, 1972)

Verbitskaia, Anastasiia. *Moemu chitateliu!* 2nd rev. ed. (Moscow: I. N. Kushnerev and Co., 1911)

Vereshchagin, Aleksandr [Alexander Verestchagin]. *At Home and in War 1853-1881: Reminiscences and Anecdotes*, trans. by Isabel F. Hapgood (New York: Thomas Y. Crowell and Co., 1888) *Doma i na voine* originally appeared in 1885.

Vereshchagin, Vasilii. *Detstvo i otrochestvo khudozhnika V. V. Vereshchagina.* Vol. I: *Derevnia. – Korpus. – Risoval'naia shkola* (Moscow: I. N. Kushnerev and Co., 1895)

___. *Ocherki, nabroski, vospominaniia V. V. Vereshchagina* (St. Petersburg: Ministry of Communications/A. Benke, 1883)

Vishniakov, Nikolai. *Svedeniia o kupecheskom rode Vishniakovykh (1762-1847 gg.)* (Moscow: G. Lissner and A. Geshel', 1905)

Vodovozova, Elizaveta. *Na zare zhizni*, 2 vols., ed. and annot. by E.S. Vilenskaia and L.I. Roitberg, 2nd ed. (Moscow: Khudozhestvennaia literatura,1964) Rev. and abr. for children, the early part of these memoirs was published as *Istoriia odnogo detstva* and, in English, as *A Russian childhood*, trans. by Anthony Brode and Olga Lane (London, Faber and Faber, 1961)

Volkonskii, Prince S. M. and B. L. Modzalevskii, eds., *Arkhiv dekabrista S. G. Volkonskago*, Vol. I (Petrograd: R. Golike and A. Vil'borg, 1918)

Volkova, Anna. *Vospominaniia, dnevnik i stat'i* (Nizhnii Novgorod: Nizhegorodskoe Pechatnoe Delo, 1913)

Vrangel', Baron Nikolai. *Ot krepostnichestva do bol'shevikov* (Moscow: Novoe literaturnoe obozrenie, 2003) English version: *The Memoirs of Baron N. Wrangel 1847-1920: From Serfdom to Bolshevism*, trans. by Brian and Beatrix Lunn (Philadelphia: J.B. Lippincott Company, 1927) [republished: New York: Haskell House, 1971]

Vrangel', Liudmila. *Dalekoe proshloe: Otryvki iz rasskazov moei materi* (Paris, 1934)

Wexler, Ben. *One Small Russian Jew: An Historical Autobiography* (Lauderdale-by-the-Sea, FL: Phantom Books, 1991)

Zakhoder, Galina. *Zakhoder i vse-vse-vse . . .: Vospominaniia* (Moscow: Zakharov, 2003)

Zhelikhovskaia, Vera. *Kak ia byla malen'koi. Iz vospominanii ranniago detstva V. P. Zhelikhovskoi*, 2nd rev. and enl. ed. (St. Petersburg: A. F. Devrien, 1894)

Zhemchuzhnaia, Zinaida. *Puti izgnaniia: Ural, Kuban', Moskva, Kharbin, Tian'tszin* (Tenafly, NJ: Ermitazh/Hermitage, 1987)

Zhigalova, Ol'ga. *Veter vetku klonit* (Paris: Beresniak Press, 1948) English version: *Across the Green Past* (Chicago: Henry Regnery Co., 1952)

Zhitova, Varvara. *Vospominaniia o sem'e I. S. Turgeneva* (Tula: Tul'skoe knizhnoe izdatel'stvo, 1961)

Ziloti, Vera. *V dome Tret'iakova* (New York, 1954)

Primary Sources - Literary Works, Publicistics, Essays, Other

Afanas'ev, Aleksandr N. *Narodnye russkie skazki* in numerous editions and translations, some including the erotic tales, some – for children – not

Aksakov, Ivan. *Literaturnaia kritika* comp., introd. and annot. by A. S. Kurilov (Moscow: Sovremennik, 1981)

Aksakov, Sergei. *Years of Childhood*, trans. by Alec Brown (New York: Vintage Books, 1960) – though some would place this with autobiographies

Aldanov [pseud. of Landau], Mark. *Istoki*, Vol. I (Paris: YMCA-Press, 1950)

Anonymous. "Niania", *Russkii ocherk: 40–50-e gody XIX veka*, comp., ed.,

Bibliography 451

and annot. by V.I. Kuleshov (Moscow: Izdatel'stvo moskovskogo universiteta, 1986)

Anonymous. *Izobrazhenie nyneshnikh nravov i nyneshniago vospitaniia* (Moscow: A. Reshetnikov, 1816)

Aref'eva, Lidiia. *Ispoved' bez dukhovnika* (Moscow: RIO GPNTB SSSR, 1990)

Astaf'ev, Viktor. *Poslednyi poklon: Povest'* [sic] (Perm: Permskoe knizhnoe izdatel'stvo, 1968)

Balakirev, Milii. *Sbornik russkikh narodnykh pesen* (Moscow: Muzgiz, 1936)

Balina, Marina, Helena Goscilo, and Mark Lipovetsky, eds. *Politicizing Magic: An Anthology of Russian and Soviet Fairy Tales* (Evanston, IL: Northwestern University Press, 2005)

Belyi, Andrei. *Kotik Letaev*, trans. by Gerald Janecek, rev. ed. (Evanston, IL: Northwestern University Press, 1999) and 1st ed. (Ann Arbor, MI: Ardis, 1971).

Berezaiskii, Vasilii. *Anekdoty drevnikh poshekhontsev* (St. Petersburg: Tipografiia godudarstvennoi meditsinskoi kollegii, 1798). Available online (accessed Jan. 2012): http://babel.hathitrust.org/cgi/pt?id=mdp.39015011918607;page=root;seq=12;view=1up;size=100;orient=0

Bunin, Ivan. *Stories and Poems*, trans. by Olga Shartse (Moscow: Progress Publishers, 1979)

Chaadaev, Pëtr. *The Major Works of Peter Chaadaev: A Translation and Commentary* by Raymond T. McNally (Notre Dame: University of Notre Dame Press, 1969)

___. *Philosophical Letters & Apology of a Madman*, trans. and introd. by Mary-Barbara Zeldin (Knoxville: University of Tennessee Press, 1969)

___. *Polnoe sobranie sochinenii i izbrannye pis'ma*, Vol. I (Moscow: Nauka, 1991)

Chekhov, Aleksandr [Sedoi]. *Iz detstva Antona Pavlovicha Chekhova* (St. Petersburg: Pechat' graficheskogo instituta, 1912)

Chekhov, Anton. *Polnoe sobranie sochinenii i pisem*, multivolume, ed. by S. D. Balukhatyi et al. (Moscow: Khudozhestvennaia literatura, 1944-)

Chukovskii, Kornei. *Ot dvukh do piati* (Moscow: Detskaia literatura, 1968) English (abridged) version: *From Two to Five*, trans. and ed. by Miriam Morton (Berkeley: University of California Press, 1971)

Dal', Vladimir, comp. *Poslovitsy russkogo naroda. Sbornik V. Dalia v dvukh tomakh*, 2 vols. (Moscow: Khudozhestvennaia literatura, 1984)

Dolgorukov, Vsevolod. *Ne ot skuki. Stikhotvoreniia* (Tomsk: Sibirskii vestnik, 1890)

Drinker, Henry S. *English Texts for the Songs of Modeste Moussorgsky (1835-1881)* ([PA: self-published, 1951?])

Eremina, Valeriia, comp. and annot. *Poeziia detstva: russkoe narodnoe tvorchestvo dlia detei* (St. Petersburg: Aleteiia, 2004)

Filin, Mikhail, comp. *Apologiia russkoi niani: K 250-letiiu Ariny Rodionovny* (Moscow: Russkii mir, 2009)

Garin-Mikhailovskii, Nikolai. *Rasskazy i ocherki* (Moscow: Pravda, 1984)

Gertsyk, Adelaida. *Stikhi i proza*, Vol. I, comp. by T. N. Zhukovskaia (Moscow: Vozvrashchenie/Dom Mariny Tsvetaevoi, 1993)

Goncharov, Ivan. *Oblomov*, trans. by Ann Dunnigan (New York: Signet/ New American Library, 1963)

___. *Sobranie sochinenii v vos'mi tomakh* (Moscow: Khudozhestvennaia literatura, 1952-1955) 2nd ed. 1980

Grum, Kondratii. *Rukovodstvo k vospitaniiu, obrazovaniiu i sokhraneniiu zdorov'ia detei*, 3 vols. (St. Petersburg: M. Ol'khin, 1843-45)

Haney, Jack V. *The Complete Russian Folktale* (Armonk, NY: M. E. Sharpe, 1999-2006)

Iazykov, Nikolai. *Polnoe sobranie stikhvorenii*, ed. and annot. by K. K. Bukhmeier (Leningrad: Sovetskii pisatel', 1964)

___. *Sochineniia* (Leningrad: Khudozhestvennaia literatura, 1982)

Illiustrov, I.I. *Zhizn' russkogo naroda v ego poslovitsakh i pogovorkakh*, 3rd rev. and enl. ed. (Moscow, 1915)

Kapterev, Pëtr. *Dushevnyia svoistva zhenshchin: Publichnyia lektsii P.F. Kaptereva* (St. Petersburg: School for Deaf-Mutes Press, 1895)

Karamzin, Nikolai. *Izbrannye sochineniia*, 2 vols. (Moscow-Leningrad: Khudozhestvennaia literatura, 1964)

Kelly, Catriona, ed. *An Anthology of Russian Women's Writing, 1777-1992*, trans. by Kelly et al. (Oxford: Clarendon Press, 1994)

Khodasevich, Vladislav. *O Pushkine* (Berlin: Petropolis [Speer and Schmidt], 1937)

___. *Tiazhelaia lira: Chetvertaia kniga stikhov 1920-1922* (Moscow-Leningrad: Gosudarstvennoe izdatel'stvo, 1922)

Kliuchevskii, Vasilii. *O nravstvennosti i russkoi kul'ture* (Moscow: Institut rossiiskoi istorii RAN, 1998)

Knizhka nianek. Nastavleniia, kak kholit' i vospityvat' malen'kikh detei, appendix to *Uchitel'* (1863)

Kolyshko, Iosif. *Malen'kiia mysli. 1898-1899 g.g.* (St. Petersburg: Prince V. P. Meshcherskii, 1900)

Korepova, K.E., prep. and annot. *Lekarstvo ot zadumchivosti* and *Dedushkiny progulki ili prodolzhenie nastoiashchikh russkikh skazok. Russkaia skazka v izdaniiakh 80-kh godov 18 veka* (St. Petersburg: Tropa Troianova, 2001) Vol. 5 of *Polnoe sobranie russkikh skazok*, subtitled *Rannie sobraniia*

Korovin, Valentin, comp. and annot. *Landshaft moikh voobrazhenii: stranitsy prozy russkogo sentimentalizma* (Moscow: Sovremennik, 1990)

Kravchenko, Maria. *The World of the Russian Fairy Tale* (Bern, Switzerland: Peter Lang, 1987)

Krestovskaia, Mariia. *Rannyia grozy. Ispytanie* (St. Petersburg: A. S. Suvorin, 1889)

Krylov, Ivan. *Sochineniia v dvukh tomakh*, 2 vols. (Moscow: Khudozhestvennaia literatura, 1969)

Lappo-Danilevskaia, Nadezhda. *V usad'be: Roman* (Paris: Concorde, 1928)

Lermontov, Mikhail. *Sochineniia v shesti tomakh*, Vol. VI, ed. by B. V. Tomashevskii (Moscow-Leningrad: AN SSSR, 1957)

Leskov, Nikolai. *Izbrannye sochineniia* (Moscow: Khudozhestvennaia literatura, 1979)

___. *Polnoe sobranie sochinenii*, 3rd ed., 36 vols. (St. Petersburg: A.F. Marks, 1902-03)

___. *Selected Tales*, trans. by David Magarshack (New York: Farrar, Straus and Cudahy/The Noonday Press, 1961)

Materialy po statistike Leningrada i Leningradskoi gubernii, Issue 6 (Leningrad: Central Statistical Administration, 1925)

Mikhailov, Mikhail. *Polnoe sobranie stikhotvorenii* (Leningrad: Academia, 1934)

Militsyna, Elizaveta. *Razskazy* (Moscow: A.I. Snegireva, 1905)

Miroliubov, Iurii. *Babushkin sunduk: Sbornik rasskazov* (Madrid: [Galina Miroluboff], 1974)

Musorgskii, Modest. *Boris Godunov: Opera v chetyrekh deistviiakh s prologom* (Moscow: Gosizdat, Muzykal'nyi sektor, 1928)

Nadson, Semën. *Stikhotvoreniia S. Ia. Nadsona s portretom, faksimile i biograficheskim ocherkom*, 27th ed. (St. Petersburg: M.A. Aleksandrov, 1913)

Nazer'eva, Kapitolina. *Dramy i komedii* (St. Petersburg: S. Dobrodeev, 1895)

Nikolaev, D.D., comp. and annot. *Iumoristicheskie rasskazy; Iz "Vseobshchei istorii, obrabotannoi 'Satirikonom'"* (Moscow: Khudozhestvennaia literatura, 1990)

Novgorodtsev, Pavel. *Sochineniia* (Moscow: Raritet, 1995)

Noyes, George Rapall, ed. and trans. *Masterpieces of the Russian Drama*, 2 vols. (New York: Dover Publications, Inc., 1961)

Ogarëv, Nikolai. *Izbrannye proizvedeniia*, Vol. I: *Stikhotvoreniia* (Moscow: Khudozhestvennaia literatura, 1956)

Onassis, Jacqueline, ed. and introd. *The Firebird and Other Russian Fairy Tales* (New York: Viking Press, 1978)

Osorgin, Mikhail [Michael Ossorgin], *My Sister's Story* (New York: The Dial Press, 1931)

Panaeva, Avdot'ia. *Roman v peterburgskom polusvete. Sochinenie N. Stanitskago* (St. Petersburg: K. Vul'f, 1863)

Pavlova, Karolina. *A Double Life*, trans. and introd. by Barbara Heldt Monter (Ann Arbor, MI: Ardis, 1978)

Pisemskii, Aleksei. *Izbrannye proizvedeniia* (Leningrad-Moscow: Khudozhestvennaia literatura, 1932) English version: Pisemsky, *The Simpleton* (Westport, CT: Hyperion Press, Inc., 1977)

___ [Alexei Pisemsky]. *One Thousand Souls*, trans. by Ivy Litvinov (New York: Grove Press, Inc., 1959)

Plato. *The Republic of Plato*, ed. and trans. by Benjamin Jowett (New York, P. F. Collier & Son, n.d.)

Pokrovskii, Egor. *Detskie igry preimushchestvenno russkiia (v sviazi s istoriei, etnografiei, pedagogiei i gigienoi)*, 2nd rev. and enl. ed. (Moscow: V. F. Rikhter, 1895)

Pomialovskii, Nikolai. *Sochineniia v dvukh tomakh*, 2 vols. (Moscow-Leningrad: Khudozhestvennaia literatura, 1965)

Propp, Vladimir. *Morfologiia skazki*, 2nd ed. (Moscow: Nauka, 1969). English: *Morphology of the Folktale*, trans. by Laurence Scott, 2nd ed., rev. with a preface by Louis A. Wagner (Austin: University of Texas Press, 1968)

Pushkin, Aleksandr. *A. S. Pushkin: stikhotvoreniia litseiskikh let 1813-1817* V.E. Vatsuro et al., eds. (St. Peterburg: Nauka, 1994)

___. *Eugene Onegin, A Novel in Verse*, trans. and annot. by Vladimir Nabokov, 4 vols., rev. ed. (Princeton: Princeton University Press, 1975)

Putilov, B.N. et al., eds. *Istoricheskie pesni XVII veka* (Leningrad: Nauka, 1966)

Radishchev, Aleksandr. *Puteshestvie iz Peterburga v Moskvu* in *Izbrannye filosofskie sochineniia*, ed. by I. Ia. Shchipanov (Leningrad: Politicheskaia literatura,1949) English tr. by Leo Wiener, *A Journey from St. Petersburg to Moscow* (Cambridge, MA: Harvard University Press, 1966)

Ransome, Arthur. *Old Peter's Russian tales* (New York: Dover Publications [1969], an unabridged republication of the 1916 ed.)

Rassadin, Stanislav et al., eds. *Iumor nachala XX veka* (Moscow: OLMA-Press, 2003)

Reeder, Roberta, ed. and trans. *Russian Folk Lyrics*, with introd. by V. Ja. Propp (Bloomington: Indiana University Press, 1993) – rev. and enl. ed. of her *Down Along the Mother Volga: An Anthology of Russian Folk Lyrics* (1975)

Reeve, F.D., comp. and trans. *An Anthology of Russian Plays*, 2 vols. (New York: Vintage, 1961-63)

Reiser, S.A., comp., ed., and annot. *Vol'naia russkaia poeziia XVIII-XIX vekov: Sbornik stikhotvorenii* (Moscow: Khudozhestvennaia literatura, 1975)

Remizov, Aleksei. *Neuemnyi buben: roman, povesti, rasskazy, skazki, vospominaniia*, comp. and annot. by V.A. Chalmaev (Kishinev: Lit. Artistike, 1988)

___. *V rozovom bleske* (Letchworth, England: Bradda Books, 1969)

Schopenhauer, Arthur. *Sämtliche Werke*, Vol. 6: *Essays and Aphorisms* (Wiesbaden: Eberhard Brockhaus, 1947)

Segel, Harold B., ed., trans., and annot. *The Literature of Eighteenth-Century Russia: A History and Anthology*, 2 vols. (New York: E. P. Dutton & Co., 1967)

Seltzer, Thomas, ed. *Best Russian Short Stories* (New York: Boni and Liveright, 1918)

Shchepkina, Aleksandra. *Boiare Starodubskie: Istoricheskii roman iz vremën tsaria Alekseia Mikhailovicha* (Moscow: I. N. Kushnerev & Co., 1897)

Shchepkina-Kupernik, Tat'iana. *Nezametnye liudi*, 2nd ed. (Moscow: D. P. Efimov, 1901)

Shmelëv, Ivan. *Niania iz Moskvy*, in *Istoriia liubovnaia* (Moscow: Moskva, 1995)

___. *Sochineniia v dvukh tomakh*, 2 vols. (Moscow: Khudozhestvennaia literatura, 1989)

Skripil', Mikhail. *Russkaia povest' XVII veka* (Leningrad: Khudozhestvennaia literatura, 1954)

Sologub, Fëdor. *The Sweet-Scented Name and Other Fairy Tales, Fables and Stories* (New York: G.P. Putnam's Sons, 1915)

Solov'ëva, Poliksena. *Tainaia pravda i drugie razskazy* (St. Petersburg: M. O. Vol'f, 1912)

Solzhenitsyn, Aleksandr. *Matrenin dvor* (London: Flegdon Press, 1965)

Staniukovich, Konstantin. *Morskie rasskazy* (Minsk: Iunatstva, 1981)

___. *Sobranie sochinenii v shesti tomakh*, Vol. 1 (Moscow: Khudozhestvennaia literatura, 1958)

Sumarokov, Aleksandr. *Polnoe sobranie vsekh sochinenii, v stikhakh i proze*, 10 vols. (Moscow: Moscow University press of N. Novikov, 1781-87)

Tèffi, Nadezha. *Chernyi iris: Razskazy* (Stockholm: Severnye ogni, 1921)

___. *Dym bez ognia* (SPB, 1914)

___. *Gorodok* (NY: Russica Publishers, Inc., 1982)

___. *Nostal'giia. Rasskazy. Vospominaniia* (Leningrad: Khudozhestvennaia literatura, 1989)

___. *Razskazy* (Letchworth-Herts, England: Prideaux Press, 1980)

___. *Sobranie sochinenii*, 3 vols. (Moscow: Lakom, 1998-99)

___. *Tikhaia zavod'* (Paris: Zemgor, 1921)

___. *Zemnaia raduga* (New York: Chekhov Publishing House, 1952)

Toll', Feliks. "O nian'kakh," *Zhurnal dlia vospitaniia*, March 1858, No. 3, pp. 443-63

Tsebrikova, Mar'ia. *Rasskaz niani* (Moscow: Red. "Iunaia Rossiia", 1911)

Tsvetaeva, Marina. *Stikhotvoreniia i poemy v piati tomakh*, Vol. 4: *Poemy* (New York: Russica Publishers, Inc., 1983) At least 3 of planned 5 vols. appeared, 1980-83.

Tur, Evgeniia. *Tri pory zhizni, Roman Evgenii Tur* (Moscow: V. Got'e, 1854)

Uchrezhdeniia i ustavy kasaiushchiesia do vospitaniia i obucheniia v Rossii iunoshestva oboego pola, vo udovol'stvie Obshchestva, 2 vols. (St. Petersburg: n.p., 1774)

Ursov, N.A. ed. and annot. *Russkie pesni* (Gor'kii: OGIZ, 1940)

Vodovozova, Elizaveta. *Umstvennoe i nravstvennoe razvitie detei ot pervago proiavleniia soznaniia do shkol'nago vozrasta. Kniga dlia vospitatelei*, 4th rev. ed. (St. Peterburg: V. S. Balashev, 1891)

Zenkovsky, Serge A., ed. and trans. *Medieval Russia's Epics, Chronicles, and Tales* (New York: E. P. Dutton & Co., 1963)

Zernova, Ruf [Ruth]. *Mute Phone Calls and Other Stories*, trans. by Ann Harleman, Martha Kitchen, and Helen Reeve; selected, ed., and with an introd. by Reeve (New Brunswick, NJ: Rutgers University Press, 1991)

___. *Zhenskie rasskazy* (Ann Arbor, MI: Hermitage/Ermitazh, 1981)

Zhadovskaia, Iuliia. *Polnoe sobranie sochinenii Iu. V. Zhadovskoi v chetyrekh tomakh*, ed. by P.V. Bykov, 2nd posthumous ed., enl. and rev., 4 vols. (St. Petersburg: I.P. Perevoznikov, 1894)

Zharov, V., comp. *Liubimye russkie narodnye pesni: dlia golosa v soprovozhdenii fortepiano* (Moscow: Muzyka, 1989)

Zheleznova, Irina, comp. and trans. *Folk Tales from Russian Lands* (New York: Dover Publications, 1969)

Zoshchenko, Mikhail. *Izbrannoe* (Ann Arbor: University of Michigan Press, 1960)

___. *Izbrannye proizvedeniia v dvukh tomakh* (Leningrad: Khudozhestvennaia literatura, 1968)

___. *Nervous People and Other Satires*, trans. by Maria Gordon and Hugh McLean, with the help of Fruma Gottschalk, ed. and introd. by McLean (New York: Vintage Books, 1963)

Secondary Sources, Published

Aleksandrov, Vadim. *Obychnoe pravo krepostnoi derevni Rossii XVIII-nachalo XIX v.* (Moscow: Nauka, 1984)

Alekseeva, Tat'iana, comp. *Venetsianov and his School*, trans. by Carolyn Justice and Yuri Kleiner (Leningrad: Aurora Art Publishers, 1984)

___. "Venetsianov i razvitie bytovogo zhanra," *Istoriia russkogo iskusstva*, Vol. 8, bk. 1 (Moscow: Nauka, 1963, pp. 546-98

Anderson, Benedict. *Imagined Communities: Reflections on the Origin and Spread of Nationalism* (London: Verso, 1983)

Andrew, Joe. *Women in Russian Literature, 1780-1863* (New York: St. Martin's Press, 1988)

Appiah, Kwame Anthony and Henry Louis Gates, Jr., eds. *Identities* (Chicago: University of Chicago Press, 1995)

Azadovskii, Mark. *Literatura i fol'klor: Ocherki i etiudy* (Leningrad: Khudozhestvennaia literatura, 1938)

___. "Pushkin and Folklore," I. Luppol et al., eds. *Pushkin: A Collection of Articles and Essays on the Great Russian Poet A. S. Pushkin* (Moscow: USSR Society for Cultural Relations with Foreign Countries, 1939)

___. "Pushkin i fol'klor," *Pushkin: Vremennik pushkinskoi komissii*, 3 (Moscow-Leningrad: AN SSSR, 1937), pp. 152-82

___. "Skazki Ariny Rodionovny" in *Russkaia skazka. Izbrannye mastera*, ed. and annot. by Azadovskii (Academia, 1932), pp. 273-292.

Babkin, Dmitrii. *A. N. Radishchev: Literaturno-obshchestvennaia deiatel'nost'* (Moscow: Nauka, 1966)

Bakhtin, Mikhail. *The Dialogic Imagination: Four Essays*, ed. by Michael Holquist, trans. by Caryl Emerson and Holquist (Austin: the University of Texas Press, 1981)

Balzer, Marjorie Mandelstam. *The Tenacity of Ethnicity: A Siberian Saga in Global Perspective* (Princeton NJ: Princeton University Press, 1999)

Bantysh-Kamenskii, Dmitrii. *Slovar' dostopamiatnykh liudei Russkoi zemli*, Part [Vol.] 2 (St. Petersburg: Shtab Otdel'nago Korpusa Vnutrennei Strazhi, 1847), appendix

Barricelli, Jean-Pierre, ed. and introd. *Chekhov's Great Plays: A Critical Anthology* (New York: New York University Press, 1981)

Barry, Herbert. *Ivan at Home; or, Pictures of Russian Life* (London: The Publishing Company, Ltd., 1872)

Batalden, Stephen K., ed. *Seeking God: the Recovery of Religious Identity in Orthodox Russia, Ukraine, and Georgia* (DeKalb: Northern Illinois University Press, 1993)

Becker, Seymour. *Nobility and Privilege in Late Imperial Russia* (DeKalb, IL: Northern Illinois University Press, 1985)

Berkov, Pavel. *Istoriia russkoi komedii XVIII v.* (Leningrad: Nauka, 1977)

Besser, Ludvig B. and K. Ballod, *Smertnost', vozrastnoi sostav i dolgovechnost' pravoslavnago narodonaseleniia oboego pola v Rossii za 1851-1890 gody* (St. Petersburg: Academy of Sciences, 1897)

Bethea, David. "Kak pisat' biografiiu Pushkina v postlotmanovskuiu epokhu," *Lotmanovskii sbornik*, Issue 3 (Moscow: OGI, 2004), pp. 822-35

___. *Khodasevich: His Life and Art* (Princeton, NJ: Princeton University Press, 1983)

Bettelheim, Bruno. *The Uses of Enchantment: The Meaning and Importance of Fairy Tales* (New York: Alfred a. Knopf, 1976)

Billington, James H. *Mikhailovsky and Russian Populism* (Oxford: Clarendon Press, 1958)

Binion, Rudolph. *Frau Lou: Nietzsche's Wayward Disciple* (Princeton: Princeton University Press, 1968)

Blok, Vladimir. *Muzyka Prokof'eva dlia detei* (Moscow: Muzyka, 1969)

Blum, Jerome. *The End of the Old Order in Rural Europe* (Princeton, NJ: Princeton University Press, 1978)

___. *Lord and Peasant in Russia* (Princeton, NJ: Princeton University Press, 1961)

Bogomazova, Z.A. *Domashniaia rabotnitsa* (Moscow: VTsSPS, 1928)

Bokova, V.M. comp., *Istoriia zhizni blagorodnoi zhenshchiny* (Moscow: Novoe literaturnoe obozrenie, 1996), introduction

Briantseva, Vera. *Detstvo i iunost' Sergeia Rakhmaninova*, 2nd ed. (Moscow: Sovetskii kompozitor, 1973)

Brown, David. *Mikhail Glinka: A Biographical and Critical Study* (reprint: New York: Da Capo Press, 1985)

___. *Musorgsky: His Life and Works* (New York: Oxford University Press, 2002)

___. *Tchaikovsky: A Biographical and Critical Study*. Vol. I: *The Early Years (1840-1874)* (London: Victor Gollancz Ltd., 1978)

Brown, Malcolm Hamrick, ed. *Musorgsky: In Memoriam 1881-1981* (Ann Arbor, MI: UMI Research Press, 1982)

Bruk, Ia.V. and L.I. Iovleva, eds. *Zhivopis' pervoi poloviny XIX veka*, Vol. 3 (Moscow: Skanrus/ State Tretiakov Gallery, 2005)

Bulgakov, Sergei. *The Orthodox Church*, rev. trans. by Lydia Kesich (Crestwood, NY: St. Vladimir's Seminary Press, 1988)

Burenina, Marina. *Progulki po Nevskomu prospektu* (St. Petersburg: Litera, 2002)

Calvocoressi, Michel D. *Modest Mussorgsky: His Life and Works* (London: Rockliff Publishing Corp., 1956)

Campbell, Marie. *Strange World of the Brontës* (Wilmslow, England: Sigma Leisure, 2001)

Casson, Sir Hugh and Joyce Grenfell *Nanny Says*, ed. by Diana, Lady Avebury (London: Dobson Books Ltd., 1972)

Chekhov, Mikhail P. *Vokrug Chekhova* (Moscow: Academia, 1933)

Chekhov, S.M., ed., comp. and annot. *Vokrug Chekhova: Vstrechi i vpechatleniia*, 4th rev. and enl. ed. (Moscow: Moskovskii rabochii, 1964)

Cherednikova, Maina P. *Golos detstva iz dal'nei doli –: igra, magiia, mif v detskoi kul'ture* (Moscow: Labirint, 2002)

Chistov, Kirill V. *Narodnye traditsii i fol'klor: Ocherki teorii* (Leningrad: Nauka, 1986)

Christoff, Peter K. *An Introduction to Nineteenth-Century Russian Slavophilism. A Study of Ideas*, 4 vols. (various publishers, 1961-91)

___. *The Third Heart: Some Intellectual-Ideological Currents and Cross Currents in Russia 1800-1830* (The Hague: Mouton, 1970)

Chulos, Chris J. *Converging Worlds: Religion and Community in Peasant Russia, 1861-1917* (DeKalb: Northern Illinois University Press, 2003)

Cross, Anthony G. *By the Banks of the Neva: Chapters from the Lives and Careers of the British in Eighteenth-Century Russia* (Cambridge; New York: Cambridge University Press, 1997)

Dal', Vladimir. *Tolkovyi slovar' zhivogo velikorusskogo iazyka*, 4 vols. (Moscow: Russkii iazyk, 1979; a reprint of the 1881 ed.)

Davis, Fred. *Yearning for Yesterday: A Sociology of Nostalgia* (Great Britain: Macmillan, 1979)

Del Giudice, Luisa and Gerald Porter, eds. *Imagined States: Nationalism, Utopia, and Longing in Oral Cultures* (Logan, UT: Utah State University Press, 2001)

Dement'eva, A.G. et al., eds. *Russkaia periodicheskaia pechat' (1702-1894): Spravochnik* (Moscow: Gosizdat politicheskoi literatury, 1959)

Dolgov, Vadim V. *Byt i nravy drevnei Rusi: miry povsednevnosti XI-XIII vv.* (Moscow: Iauza/Eksmo, 2007)

Druzhnikov, Yuri. *Contemporary Russian Myths: A Skeptical View of the Literary Past* (Lewiston, NY: Edwin Mellen, 1999)

Dunham, Vera. *In Stalin's Time: Middleclass Values in Soviet Fiction*, enl. and rev. ed. (Durham: Duke University Press, 1990)

Dunning, Chester et al. *The Uncensored Boris Godunov: The Case for Pushkin's Original Comedy, with Annotated Text and Translation* (Madison: The University of Wisconsin Press, 2006)

Earle, Edward M., ed. *Nationalism and Internationalism: Essays Inscribed to Carlton J. H. Hayes* (New York: Octagon Books/Farrar, Strauss and Giroux, 1974 [reprint of the 1950 ed.])

Eikhenbaum, Boris M. and Iurii Tynianov, eds. *Russkaia proza* (reprint: The Hague: Mouton, 1963)

Eley, Geoff and Ronald Grigor Suny, eds. *Becoming National: A Reader* (New York: Oxford University Press, 1996)

Elsworth, J.D. *Andrey Bely: A Critical Study of the Novels* (Cambridge: Cambridge University Press, 1983)

Emerson, Caryl. *Boris Godunov: Transpositions of a Russian Theme* (Bloomington, IN: Indiana U Press, 1986)

___, ed. *Critical Essays on Mikhail Bakhtin* (New York: G.K. Hall & Co., 1999)

___. *The Life of Musorgsky* (Cambridge: Cambridge University Press, 1999)

Erikson, Erik. *Childhood and Society*, 2nd rev. and enl. ed. (New York: W. W. Norton & Co., 1963)

Esipov, Viktor M. *Pushkin v zerkale mifov* (Moscow: Iazyki slavianskoi kul'tury, 2006)

Etkind, Alexander. *Eros of the Impossible: The History of Psychoanalysis in Russia*, tran. by Noah and Maria Rubins (Boulder, CO: Westview Press, 1997)

Evstigneeva [Spiridonova], Lidiia. *Russkaia satiricheskaia literatura nachala XX veka* (Moscow: Nauka, 1977)

Fairchilds, Cissie. *Women in Early Modern Europe, 1500-1700* (Harlow, England: Pearson/Longman, 2007)

Fateev, Pëtr. *Mikhail Mikhailov – revoliutsioner, pisatel', publitsist* (Moscow: Mysl', 1969)

Fedotov, Georgii P. *The Russian Religious Mind*, 2 vols. (Cambridge: Harvard University Press, 1946-66)

___. *A Treasury of Russian Spirituality* (New York: Sheed & Ward, 1948)

Feinstein, Elaine. *Pushkin: A Biography* (Hopewell, NJ: The Ecco Press, 1998)

Field, Deborah A. *Private Life and Communist Morality in Khrushchev's Russia* (New York: Peter Lang Publishing, Inc., 2007)

Field, Daniel. *The End of Serfdom: Nobility and Bureaucracy in Russia, 1855-1861* (Cambridge, MA: Harvard University Press, 1976)

Figes, Orlando. *Natasha's Dance: A Cultural History of Russia* (New York: Henry Holt and Company, 2002)

___. *The Whisperers: Private Life in Stalin's Russia* (New York: Metropolitan Books/Henry Holt and Company, 2007)

Fildes, Valerie. *Breasts, Bottles, and Babies: A History of Infant Feeding* (Edinburgh: Edinburgh University Press, 1986)

___. *Wet Nursing: A History from Antiquity to the Present* (Oxford, England: Basil Blackwell, 1998)

Filin, Mikhail. *Arina Rodionovna* (Moscow: Molodaia gvardiia, 2008)

Foteeva, Ekaterina. "Sotsial'naia adaptatsiia posle 1917 goda: zhiznennyi opyt sostoiatel'nykh semei," *Sud'by liudei: Rossiia XX vek. Biografii semei kak ob"ekt sotsiologicheskogo issledovaniia*, V. V. Semenova and Foteeva, eds. (Moscow: Institut sotsiologii RAN, 1996), pp. 240-75

Frank, Stephen P. and Mark D. Steinberg, eds. *Cultures in Flux: Lower-Class Values, Practices, and Resistance in Late Imperial Russia* (Princeton NJ: Princeton University Press, 1994)

Freedman, Paul. *Images of the Medieval Peasant* (Stanford: Stanford University Press, 1999)

Freeze, ChaeRan Y. *Jewish Marriage and Divorce in Imperial Russia* (Hanover, NH: Brandeis University Press/University Press of New England, 2002)

Freud, Sigmund. *The Freud Reader*, ed. by Peter Gay (New York: W.W. Norton & Co., 1989)

Frierson, Cathy. *Peasant Icons: Representations of Rural People in Late Nineteenth-Century Russia* (New York: Oxford University Press, 1993)

Frolova-Walker, Marina. *Russian Music and Nationalism: From Glinka to Stalin* (New Haven: Yale University Press, 2007)

Garrard, J.G. *Mixail Čulkov: An Introduction to his Prose and Verse* (The Hague: Mouton, 1970)

Gasparov, Boris, Robert P. Hughes, and Irina Paperno, eds. *Cultural Mythologies of Russian Modernism: From the Golden Age to the Silver Age* (Berkeley: University of California Press, 1992)

Gathorne-Hardy, Jonathan. *The Unnatural History of the Nanny* (New York: Dial Press, 1973)

Gay, Peter. *Freud: A Life for Our Time* (New York: W.W. Norton & Co., 1988)

Gitovich, N.I. and Lidiia D. Gromova-Opul'skaia, comps., *Letopis' zhizni i tvorchestva A. P. Chekhova*, 2 vols. (Moscow: Nasledie, 2000-04)

Bibliography 463

Gleason, Abbott. *European and Muscovite; Ivan Kireevsky and the Origins of Slavophilism* (Cambridge, MA: Harvard University Press, 1972)

Goldman, Wendy Z. *Women, the State and Revolution: Soviet Family Policy and Social Life, 1917-1936* (New York: Cambridge University Press, 1993)

Golovin, Valentin. *Russkaia kolybel'naia pesnia v fol'klore i literature* (Åbo, Finland: Åbo Akademi University Press, 2000)

Gornick, Vivian and Barbara K. Moran, eds. *Woman in Sexist Society: Studies in Power and Powerlessness* (New York: Signet/New American Library, 1972)

Grabar, Igor' E. et al., *Istoriia russkogo iskusstva*, Vol. 8, 2 bks. (Moscow: Nauka, 1963-64)

Granovskaia, Nina I. *Esli ekhat' vam sluchitsia: ocherkputevoditel'* (Leningrad: Lenizdat, 1989)

Greenfeld, Liah. *Nationalism: Five Roads to Modernity* (Cambridge, MA: Harvard University Press, 1992)

Guibernau, Montserrat and John Hutchinson, eds. *History and National Destiny: Ethnosymbolism and its Critics* (Oxford: Blackwell, 2004)

Hamarberg, Gitta. *From the idyll to the novel: Karamzin's Sentimentalist Prose* (Cambridge: Cambridge University Press, 1991)

Haskell, Arnold and Min Lewis, *Infantilia: The Archaeology of the Nursery* (London: Dennis Dobson, 1971)

Heldt, Barbara. *Terrible Perfection: Women and Russian Literature* (Bloomington: Indiana University Press, 1987)

Hellbeck, Jochen and Klaus Heller, eds. *Autobiographical Practices in Russia - Autobiographische Praktiken in Russland* (Göttingen: V&R unipress, 2004)

Hosking, Geoffrey and Robert Service, eds. *Reinterpreting Russia* (London: Arnold, 1999)

Howie, P.W. and A.S. McNeilly, "Effect of breastfeeding patterns on human birth intervals," *Journal of Reproduction and Fertility*, July 1982, Vol. 65, No. 2

Hubbs, Joanna. *Mother Russia: The Feminine Myth in Russian Culture* (Bloomington IN: Indiana University Press, 1988)

Hutton, Marcelline. *Russian and West European Women, 1860-1939* (Lanham, MD: Rowman & Littlefield Publishers, Inc., 2001)

Iankovskii, Iurii. *Patriarkhal'no-dvorianskaia utopiia: Stranitsa russkoi obshchestvenno-literaturnoi mysli 1840-1850s-kh godov* (Moscow: Khudozhestvennaia literatura, 1981)

Iumor nachala XX veka, ed. by Stanislav Rassadin et al. (Moscow: OLMA-Press, 2003)

Iumoristicheskie rasskazy; Iz "Vseobshchei istorii, obrabotannoi 'Satirikonom'" (Moscow: Khudozhestvennaia literatura, 1990)

Ivanits, Linda J. *Dostoevsky and the Russian People* (Cambrige, UK: Cambridge University Press, 2008)

___. *Russian Folk Belief* (Armonk NY: M.E. Sharpe, Inc., 1989)

Ivanov, Sergei. *M. Iu. Lermontov: Zhizn' i tvorchestvo* (Moscow: Prosveshchenie, 1964)

Ivanova, Liudmila V. and Iurii A. Tikhonov, eds. *Mir russkoi usad'by: Ocherki* (Moscow: Nauka, 1995)

Ivanova, Tat'iana. *Iunost' Lermontova* (Moscow: Sovetskii pisatel', 1957)

Kabuzan, Vladimir. *Narodonaselenie Rossii v XVIII-pervoi polovine XIX v. (po materialam revizii)* (Moscow: AN SSSR, 1963)

Kahan, Arcadius. *The Plow, the Hammer, and the Knout: An Economic History of Eighteenth-Century Russia*, with Richard Hellie (Chicago: The University of Chicago Press, 1985)

Kann-Novikova, Elizaveta. *M.I. Glinka: novye materialy i dokumenty*, Issue I (Moscow-Leningrad: Muzgiz, 1950)

Kapustina, Tat'iana. "Nicholas I," *Emperors and Empresses of Russia: Rediscovering the Romanovs*, ed. by Donald J. Raleigh, comp. by A.A. Iskenderov (Armonk, NY: M. E. Sharpe, 1996)

Karlinsky, Simon. *Marina Tsvetaeva: The Woman, her World and her Poetry* (Cambridge: Cambridge University Press, 1985)

Keldysh, Iu.V. et al., eds. *Muzykal'naia entsiklopediia v shesti tomakh* (Moscow: Sovetskaia entsiklopediia/Sovetskii kompozitor, 1982)

Kelly, Catriona. *Children's World: Growing Up in Russia, 1890-1991* (New Haven: Yale University Press, 2007)

___. *A History of Russian Women's Writing 1820-1992* (Oxford: Clarendon Press, 1994)

___. *Refining Russia: Advice Literature, Polite Culture, and Gender from 1760* (Oxford: Oxford University Press, 2001)

Khrushcheva, Nina L. *Cultural Contradictions of Post-Communism: Why Liberal Reforms Did Not Succeed in Russia* (A Paper from the Project on

Development, Trade, and International Finance) (New York: Council on Foreign Relations, 2000)

Kiiashko, L.N. "Obraz detstva v avtobiograficheskoi proze I. S. Shmeleva", *I. S. Shmelev v kontekste slavianskoi kul'tury*, Vol. VIII of *Krymskie Mezhdunarodnye Shmelevskie chteniia: Sbornik materialov mezhdunarodnoi nauchnoi konferentsii*, ed. by V. P. Tsygannik (Alushta: n.p., 2000 [1999]), pp. 16-19

King-Hall, Magdalen. *The Story of the Nursery* (London: Routledge & Kegan Paul, 1958)

Kipp, Julie. *Romanticism, Maternity, and the Body Politic* (Cambridge: Cambridge University Press, 2003)

Kirschenbaum, Lisa A. *Small Comrades: Revolutionizing Childhood in Soviet Russia, 1917-1932* (New York: RoutledgeFalmer, 2001)

Kivelson, Valerie A. and Robert H. Greene, eds. *Orthodox Russia: Belief and Practice Under the Tsars* (University Park PA: Pennsylvania State University Press, 2003)

Klimenko, Svetlana O. "Anton Chekhov and English Nostalgia", *Orbis Litterarum*, April 2001, Vol. 56, No. 2, pp. 121-37

Kolchin, Peter. *Unfree Labor: American Slavery and Russian Serfdom* (Cambridge: Harvard University Press, 1987)

Kollmann, Nancy Shields. *Kinship and Politics: The Making of the Muscovite Political System, 1345-1547* (Stanford: Stanford University Press, 1987)

Konechnyi, Al'bin M. "Byt peterburgskogo kupechestva," in *Peterburgskoe kupechestvo v XIX veke*, comp. and annot. by Konechnyi (St. Petersburg: Giperion, 2003)

___, ed., comp. and annot. *Progulki po Nevskomu prospektu v pervoi polovine XIX veka* (St. Petersburg: Giperion, 2002)

Korf, Baron Modest. *Materialy i cherty k biografii imperatora Nikolaia I*, in *Sbornik imperatorskago istoricheskago obshchestva*, Vol. 98, ed. by N.F. Dubrovin (St. Petersburg, 1896)

Kornblatt, Judith Deutsch and Richard F. Gustafson, eds. *Russian Religious Thought* (Madison: University of Wisconsin Press, 1996)

Kornilov, A.A. *Molodye gody Mikhaila Bakunina. Iz istorii russkago romantizma* (Moscow: M. and S. Shabashnikov, 1915)

Korovin, Valentin. *Poet i mudrets: Kniga ob Ivane Krylove* (Moscow: TERRA, 1996)

Kuhn, Reinhard. *Corruption in Paradise: The Child in Western Literature* (Hanover, NH: University Press of New England, 1982)

Lang, David Marshall. *The First Russian Radical: Alexander Radishchev 1749-1802* (London: George Allen & Unwin Ltd., 1959)

Lapidus, Gail. *Women in Soviet Society: Equality, Development, and Social Change* (Berkeley: University of California Press, 1978)

Lavrent'eva, Elena and Vladimir Shtul'man, *Detstvo moe ...: Deti v russkoi fotografii vtoroi poloviny XIX-nachala XX vv.* (Moscow: Belyi gorod, 2008)

Lavrin, Janko. *Pushkin and Russian Literature* (New York: The MacMillan Company,1948)

Ledkovsky, Marina, Charlotte Rosenthal, and Mary Zirin, eds. *Dictionary of Russian Women Writers* (Westport, CT: Greenwood Press, 1994)

Leibovich, Anna Feldman. *The Russian Concept of Work: Suffering, Drama, and Tradition in Pre- and Post-Revolutionary Russia* (Westport CT: Praeger, 1995)

Leont'eva, Galina. *Aleksei Gavrilovich Venetsianov* (Leningrad: Iskusstvo, 1988)

Lerner, N.O. *A. S. Pushkin. Trudy i dni*, 2nd rev. and enl. ed. (St. Peterburg: Tipografiia Imperatorskoi akademii nauk, 1910)

Leshchinskii, Iakov D. *Pavel Andreevich Fedotov: Khudozhnik i poet* (Leningrad-Moscow: Iskusstvo, 1946)

Lifar', Sergei [Serge Lifar]. *Serge Diaghilev: His Life, His Work, His Legend: An Intimate Biography* (New York: G. P. Putnam's Sons, 1940)

Lifton, Robert Jay with Eric Olson, eds. *Explorations in Psychohistory: The Wellfleet Papers* (New York: Simon and Schuster, 1974)

Liljeström, Marianne, Arja Rosenholm, and Irina Savkina, eds. *Models of Self: Russian Women's Autobiographical Texts* (Helsinki: Kikimora Publications, 2000)

Lincoln, W. Bruce. *Nicholas I: Emperor and Autocrat of All the Russias* (Bloomington: Indiana University Press, 1978)

Lively, Penelope. *Nothing Missing but the Samovar and other stories* (London: Heinemann, 1978)

Lloyd, G.E.R. *Demystifying Mentalities* (Cambridge: Cambridge University Press,1990)

Lotman, Iurii. *Besedy o russkoi kul'ture: Byt i traditsii russkogo dvorianstva (XVIII–nachalo XIX veka)* (St. Petersburg: Iskusstvo–SPB, 1994)

Bibliography 467

___ [Yuri]. *Universe of the Mind: A Semiotic Theory of Culture*, trans. by Ann Shukman (Bloomington: Indiana University Press,1990)

Maegd-Soëp, Carolina de. *Chekhov and Women: Women in the Life and Work of Chekhov* (Columbus, OH: Slavica Publishers, 1987)

Malia, Martin. *Alexander Herzen and the Birth of Russian Socialism* (New York: Grosset & Dunlap, 1961)

Malinowski, Bronislaw. *Magic, Science and Religion, and Other Essays*, sel. and introd. by Robert Redfield (Boston, Beacon Press, 1948)

Manuilov, V.A. *Lermontov v Tarkhanakh* (Penza, 1949)

___, et al. eds. *Lermontovskaia entsiklopediia* (Moscow: Sovetskaia entsiklopediia, 1981)

___. *Letopis' zhizni i tvorchestva M. Iu. Lermontova* (Leningrad: Nauka, 1964)

Marker, Gary. *Days of a Russian Noblewoman: The Memories of Anna Labzina 1758-1821*, trans. and ed. by Marker and Rachel May (DeKalb: Northern Illinois University Press, 2001), introduction

Marsh, Rosalind, ed. *Women and Russian Culture* (New York: Berghahn, 1998)

McConnell, Allen. *A Russian Philosophe: Alexander Radishchev 1749-1802* (Westport, CN: Hyperion Press, 1981; a reprint of the 1964 ed.)

McLean, Hugh. *Nikolai Leskov: The Man and His Art* (Cambridge, MA: Harvard University Press, 1977)

McLynn, Frank. *Robert Louis Stevenson: A Biography* (New York: Random House, 1993)

Mendel, Arthur P. *Dilemmas of Progress in Tsarist Russia* (Cambridge: Harvard University Press, 1961)

Mikhnevich, Vladimir O. *Russkaia zhenshchina XVIII stoletiia* (Moscow: Kuchkovo pole/ Giperboreia, 2007)

Miliukov, Pavel. *Ocherki po istorii russkoi kul'tury. Chast' tret'ia. Natsionalizm i obshchestvennoe mnenie*, Vyp. 1, 3rd ed. (St. Petersburg: M.A. Aleksandrov, 1909)

___ [Paul]. *Outlines of Russian Culture. Part III: Literature*, trans. by Valentine Ughet and Eleanor Davis, ed. by Michael Karpovich (Philadelphia: University of Pennsylvania Press, 1942)

Miroliubov, Iurii. *Sakral'noe Rusi,* 2 vols. (Moscow: ADE "Zolotoi Vek", 1996)

Mironov, Boris. *Sotsial'naia istoriia Rossii perioda imperii – XVIII-nachalo XX v.: genezis lichnosti, demokraticheskoi sem'i, grazhdanskogo obshchestva i pravovogo gosudarstva*, 2 vols., 2nd rev. and exp. ed. (St.-Petersburg: D. Bulanin, 2003). English version, with Ben Eklof, also 2 vols. *The Social History of Imperial Russia* (Boulder, CO: Westview Press, 2000)

___. *Blagosostoianie naseleniia i revoliutsii v imperskoi Rossii: XVIII-nachalo XX veka* (Moscow: Novyi Khronograf, 2010)

Moldavskii, Dmitrii M. *Russkaia narodnaia satira* (Leningrad: "Prosveshchenie", 1967)

Mordvinova, Z.E. *Stats-dama Mariia Pavlovna Leont'eva, Nachal'nitsa Vospitatel'nago Obshchestva Blagorodnykh Devits: Biograficheskii ocherk* (St. Petersburg: Ministry of Internal Affairs, 1902)

Morris, Marcia A. *The Literature of Roguery in Seventeenth- and Eighteenth-century Russia* (Evanston, IL: Northwestern University Press, 2000)

Müller, Hans-Georg et al. "Fertility and Life Span: Late Children Enhance Female Longevity," *Journal of Gerontology*, 2002, Vol. 57A, No. 5

Nabokov, Vladimir, tr. and annot. *Evgenii Onegin*, 4 vols. (Princeton: Princeton University Press, 1975)

Nadol'skaia, N. et al., eds. *Aleksei Venetsianov*, with text by Tamara Kozhevnikova (Moscow: Belyi gorod, 2001)

Naumov, V. and S. Shokarev, comp. *Poet, Rossiia i tsari* (Moscow: Fond Sergeia Dubova, 1999)

Nedoshivin, Viacheslav. *Progulki po serebrianomu veku: Doma i sud'by* (St. Petersburg: Litera, 2005)

Neuhäuser, Rudolf. *Towards the Romantic Age: Essays on Sentimental and Preromantic Literature in Russia* (The Hague: Martinus Nijhoff, 1974)

Newman, Gerald. *The Rise of English Nationalism: A Cultural History 1740-1830* (New York: St. Martin's, 1987)

Nikiforovskii, N.Ia. *Predaniia o narodnykh russkikh sueveriiakh, poveriakh i nekotorykh obychaiakh* (Moscow: Sergei Orlov, 1861)

___. *Prostonarodnyia primiety i povier'ia* (1897)

Oleinikov, D.I. *Klassicheskoe rossiiskoe zapadnichestvo* (Moscow: Mekhanik, 1996)

Olkhovsky, Yuri. *Vladimir Stasov and Russian National Culture* (Ann Arbor, MI: UMI Research Press, 1983)

Ostry, Elaine. *Social Dreaming: Dickens and the Fairy Tale* (New York: Routledge, 2002)

Bibliography   469

Paganuzzi, Paul N. [P.N. Paganutstsi]. *Lermontov (Avtobiograficheskie cherty v tvorcherstve poeta)* (Montreal: Monastery Press, 1967)

Parthé, Kathleen. *Russian Village Prose: The Radiant Past* (Princeton: Princeton University Press, 1992)

Pavel Fedotov: Katalog (St. Petersburg: Seda-S, 1993)

Picchio, Riccardo and Harvey Goldblatt, eds. *Aspects of the Slavic Language Question*, Vol. 2 (New Haven: Yale Concilium, 1984)

Pipes, Richard. *Russia under the Bolshevik Regime* (New York: Alfred A. Knopf, 1993)

Platonov, O.A. et al., eds. *Sviataia Rus': Bol'shaia entsiklopediia russkogo naroda. Russkoe pravoslavie*, 5 vols. (Moscow: Institut russkoi tsivilizatsii, 2009-)

Poe, Marshall T. et al. *The Russian Elite in the Seventeenth Century*, 2 vols. (Helsinki: Academia Scientiarum Fennica, 2004)

Pomper, Philip. *Peter Lavrov and the Russian Revolutionary Movement* (Chicago: University of Chicago Press, 1972)

Prokhorov, Vadim. *Russian Folk Songs: Musical Genres and History* (Lanham, MD: Scarecrow Press, 2002)

Pushkarev, N.L. and L. V. Bessmertnykh, comps. and eds. *"A se grekhi zlye, smertnye...": Russkaia semeinaia i seksual'naia kul'tura glazami istorikov, etnografov, literatorov, fol'kloristov, pravovedov i bogoslovov XIX-nachala XX veka*, Vol. 1 (Moscow: Ladomir, 2004)

Pushkareva, Natal'ia. *Chastnaia zhizn' russkoi zhenshchiny: nevesta, zhena, liubovnitsa (X-nachalo XIX v.)* (Moscow: "Ladomir", 1997)

___. "Mat' i ditia v russkoi sem'e XVIII-nachala XIX veka," *Sotsial'naia istoriia: Ezhegodnik 1997* (Moscow: ROSSPEN, 1998), pp. 227-39

___. "Materinstvo i materinskoe vospitanie v Rossiiskikh sem'iakh XVIII-nachala XIX v.", in *Rasy i narody: Ezhegodnik*, 1998, vol. 25, pp. 105-124

___. "Russian Noblewomen's Education in the Home as Revealed in Late 18th- and Early 19th-Century Memoirs," in Rosslyn, ed. *Women and Gender* (q.v.)

___. *Women in Russian History from the Tenth to the Twentieth Century*, trans. and ed. by Eve Levin (Armonk, NY: M. E. Sharpe, 1997)

Rancour-Laferriere, David. *The Slave Soul of Russia: Moral Masochism and the Cult of Suffering* (New York: New York University Press, 1995)

Riasanovsky, Nicholas V. *Russia and the West in the Teaching of the Slavophiles: A Study of Romantic Ideology* (Gloucester, MA: Peter Smith, 1965)

___. *Russian Identities: A Historical Survey* (New York: Oxford University Press, 2005)

Rice, James L. *Freud's Russia: National Identity in the Evolution of Psychoanalysis* (New Brunswick, NJ: Transaction Publishers, 1993)

Riesemann, Oskar von. *Moussorgsky*, trans. by Paul England (New York: Tudor Publishing Co., 1935)

Robbins, Bruce. *The Servant's Hand: English Fiction from Below* (New York: Columbia University Press, 1986)

Robinson, Geroid T. *Rural Russia Under the Old Regime* (New York: Macmillan, 1949)

Rock, Stella. *Popular Religion in Russia: 'Double Belief' and the Making of an Academic Myth* (London/New York: Routledge, 2007)

Rogger, Hans. *National Consciousness in Eighteenth-Century Russia* (Cambridge, MA: Harvard University Press, 1960)

Roosevelt, Priscilla. *Life on the Russian Country Estate: A Social and Cultural History* (New Haven: Yale University Press, 1995)

Roshwald, Aviel. *The Endurance of Nationalism* (Cambridge, England: Cambridge University Press, 2006)

Rosslyn, Wendy, ed. *Women and Gender in 18th-Century Russia* (Aldershot, Hampshire, England: Ashgate Publishing Ltd., 2003)

Rubins, Maria, ed. *Twentieth-Century Russian Émigré Writers* (Vol. 317 of *Dictionary of Literary Biography*) (Detroit, MI: Thomson Gale, 2005)

Ruga, Vladimir and Andrei Kokorev. *Moskva povsednevnaia: ocherki gorodskoi zhizni nachala XX veka* (Moscow: Olma Mediagrupp, 2005)

Russell, Bertrand. *Unpopular Essays* (New York: Simon and Schuster, 1950)

Russkii biograficheskii slovar', Vols. 20 and 22 (St. Petersburg: I.N. Skorokhodov, 1905, 1912)

Rustemeyer, Angela. *Dienstboten in Petersburg und Moskau 1861-1917: Hintergrund, Alltag, Soziale Rolle* (Stuttgart, Germany: Franz Steiner Verlag, 1996)

Rzhevsky, Nicholas, ed. *The Cambridge Companion to Russian Culture* (Cambridge, UK: Cambridge University Press, 1998)

Sakharov, A.N. et al. *Rossiia v nachale XX veka* (Moscow: Novyi khronograf, 2002)

Sakharov, Ivan. *Skazaniia russkogo naroda*, part 1 (1836; re-issued in 1837), parts 1-4 issued as new Vol. 1, 3rd ed. (1841); Vol. 2 (1849)

Sandler, Stephanie. *Commemorating Pushkin: Russia's Myth of a National Poet* (Stanford, CA: Stanford University Press, 2004), introduction and Ch. 2

___. "The Pushkin Myth in Russia," *The Pushkin Handbook* ed. by David M. Bethea (Madison: University of Wisconsin Press, 2005), pp. 403-23

Savater, Fernando. *Childhood Regained: The Art of the Storyteller*, trans. by Frances M. López-Morillas (New York: Columbia University Press, 1982)

Scaglione, Aldo, ed. *The Emergence of National Languages* (Ravenna: Longo, 1984)

Schiemann, Theodor. *Geschichte Russlands unter Kaiser Nikolaus I* (Berlin, 1904-1919), Vol. I

Schmemann, Alexander. *The Celebration of Faith: Sermons*, 3 vols., trans. by John A. Jillions (Crestwood, NY: St. Vladimir's Seminary Press, 1991-2001)

Schmemann, Serge. *Echoes of a Native Land: Two Centuries of a Russian Village* (New York: Alfred A. Knopf, 1997)

Schönle, Andreas. *Authenticity and Fiction in the Russian Literary Journey, 1790-1840* (Cambridge, MA: Harvard University Press, 2000)

Scott, H.M. *The European Nobilities in the Seventeenth and Eighteenth Centuries* Vol. 2: *Northern, Central and Eastern Europe* (London: Longman, 1995)

Seleznev, Iurii. *Dostoevskii*, 4th ed. (Moscow: Molodaia gvardiia, 2004)

Shangina, Izabella I., ed. *Russkie deti: Osnovy narodnoi pedagogiki. Illiustrirovannaia entsiklopediia* (St. Petersburg: Iskusstvo-SPB, 2006)

___. *Russkie deti i ikh igry* (St. Petersburg: Iskusstvo-SPB, 2000)

___. *Russkii traditsionnyi byt: Entsiklopedicheskii slovar'* (St. Petersburg: Azbuka-klassika, 2003)

Shankman, Steven and Massimo Lollini, eds. *Who, Exactly, is the Other? Western and Transcultural Perspectives* (Eugene OR: Oregon Humanities Center/University of Oregon, 2002)

Shchukin, Vasilii. *Rossiiskii genii prosveshcheniia. Issledovaniia v oblasti mifopoetiki i istorii idei* (Moscow: Rossiiskaia politicheskaia entsiklopediia [ROSSPEN], 2007)

___. *Russkoe zapadnichestvo: genezis, sushchnost', istoricheskaia rol'* (Łódź: Ibidem, 2001)

Shevzov, Vera. *Russian Orthodoxy on the Eve of Revolution* (New York: Oxford University Press, 2004)

Shil'der, Nikolai. *Imperator Nikolai Pervyi, ego zhizn' i tsarstvovanie*, Vol. 1 (Moscow: Charli, 1997)

Shmerling, S.B., comp. *Traditsii sem'i* (Sverdlovsk: Sredne-Ural'sksoe knizhnoe izdatel'stvo, 1988)

Simmons, Ernest J. *Pushkin* (New York: Vintage Books/Random House, 1964)

Skrynnikov, Ruslan. *Ivan Groznyi* (Moscow: Nauka, 1975), available in English as *Ivan the Terrible*, ed. and trans. by Hugh F. Graham (Gulf Breeze, FL: Academic International Press, 1981)

Slezkine, Yuri. "Lives as Tales," in Sheila Fitzpatrick and Slezkine, eds., *In the Shadow of Revolution: Life Stories of Russian Women from 1917 to the Second World War*, trans. by Slezkine (Princeton: Princeton University Press, 2000)

Slovar' russkikh sueverii (1782)

Slovar' russkogo iazyka XI-XVII vv., ed. by S.G. Barkhudarov et al., Vols. 7, 9, and 11 (Moscow: Nauka, 1980-86)

Smirnov, Vadim. *Literatura i fol'klornaia traditsiia: Voprosy poetiki (arkhetipy "zhenskogo nachala" v russkoi literature XIX - nachala XX veka* (Ivanovo: Iunona, 2001)

Smith, Anthony D. *The Antiquity of Nations* (Cambridge, England: Polity Press, 2004)

___. *Chosen Peoples* (Oxford: Oxford University Press, 2003)

___. *Nationalism: Theory, Ideology, History* (Cambridge, England: Polity Press, 2001)

___. *Theories of Nationalism*, 2nd ed. (New York: Holmes & Meier Publishers, 1983 [1971])

Smith, Anthony D. and John Hutchinson, eds. *Nationalism* (Oxford/New York: Oxford University Press, 1994)

___. *Nationalism: Critical Concepts in Political Science* (London and New York: Routledge, 2002)

Sorokina [Sorokin], Ol'ga. *Moscoviana: The Life and Art of Ivan Shmelyov* (Oakland, CA: Barbary Coast Books, 1987) Russian tr. *Moskoviana: Zhizn' i tvorchestvo Ivana Shmeleva* (Moscow: Moskovskii rabochii/ Skify, 1994)

Spagnolo, Rebecca. "When Private Home Meets Public Workplace: Service, Space, and the Urban Domestic in 1920s Russia," in Christina Kiaer and Eric Naiman, eds., *Everyday Life in Early Soviet Russia: Taking the Revolution Inside* (Bloomington: Indiana University Press, 2006), pp. 230-55

Stavrou, Theofanis George. *Art and Culture in Nineteenth-Century Russia* (Bloomington: Indiana University Press, 1983)

Steinberg, Mark D. and Catherine Wanner, eds. *Religion, Morality, and Community in Post-Soviet Societies* (Bloomington, IN and Washington DC: Indiana University Press/Woodrow Wilson Center Press, 2008)

Stites, Richard. *Revolutionary Dreams: Utopian Vision and Experimental Life in the Russian Revolution* (New York: Oxford University Press, 1989)

___. *Serfdom, Society, and the Arts in Imperial Russia: The Pleasure and the Power* (New Haven: Yale University Press, 2005)

Stroganov, M.V. ed. *Roman A. S. Pushkina « Evgenii Onegin »: Materialy k entsiklopedii*, 2 vols. (Tver: Tver State University, 2002)

Suvorin, Aleksei. *O Dmitrii Samozvanetse; kriticheskie ocherki, s prilozheniem novago spiska sledstvennago dela o smerti tsarevicha Dmitriia* (St.Petersburg: A. S. Suvorin, 1906)

Szreter, Simon. *Fertility, Class and Gender in Britain, 1860-1940* (Cambridge: Cambridge University Press, 1996)

Tacey, David. *How to Read Jung* (New York: W.W. Norton & Company, 2007)

Taimasova, Liudmila. *Tragediia v Ugliche: Chto proizoshlo 15 maia 1591 goda?* (Moscow: Omega, 2006)

Taruskin, Richard. *Defining Russia Musically: Historical and Hermeneutical Essays* (Princeton, NJ: Princeton University Press, 1997)

___. *Musorgsky: Eight Essays and an Epilogue* (Princeton: Princeton University Press, 1993)

Tatar, Maria. *Off with Their Heads! Fairy Tales and the Culture of Childhood* (Princeton, NJ: Princeton University Press, 1992)

Tavis, Anna A. *Rilke's Russia: A Cultural Encounter* (Evanston, IL: Northwestern University Press, 1994)

Todd, William Mills. *The Familiar Letter as a Literary Genre in the Age of Pushkin* (Evanston, IL: Northwestern University Press, 1999)

Tovrov, Jessica. *The Russian Noble Family: Structure and Change* (New York: Garland Publishing, 1987)

Troinitskii, Aleksandr. *Krepostnoe naselenie v Rossii, po 10-i narodnoi perepisi* (St. Petersburg, 1861)

Trumpener, Katie. *Bardic Nationalism: The Romantic Novel and the British Empire* (Princeton: Princeton University Press, 1997)

Tsygannik, V.P., ed. *I. S. Shmelev v kontekste slavianskoi kul'tury*, Vol. VIII of *Krymskie Mezhdunarodnye Shmelevskie chteniia: Sbornik materialov mezhdunarodnoi nauchnoi konferentsii* (Alushta: n.p., 2000 [1999])

Ul'ianov, Dmitrii I. *Vospominaniia o Vladimire Il'iche*, 4th enl. ed. (Moscow: Politizdat, 1971)

Ul'ianskii, A.I. *Niania Pushkina* (Moscow-Leningrad: Izdatel'stvo AN SSSR, 1940)

Vakar, Nicholas P. *The Taproot of Soviet Society* (New York: Harper, 1962)

Valliere, Paul. *Modern Russian Theology: Bukharev Soloviev Bulgakov: Orthodox Theology in a New Key* (Grand Rapids, MI: William B. Eerdmans Publishing Company, 2000)

Vasina-Grossman, Vera. *Mikhail Ivanovich Glinka* (Moscow: Muzyka, 1979)

Venturi, Franco. *Roots of Revolution: A History of the Populist and Socialist Movements in Nineteenth Century Russia*, trans. by Francis Haskell (New York: Knopf, 1960)

Veremenko, V.A. *Dvorianskaia sem'ia i gosudarstvennaia politika Rossii (vtoraia polovina XIX-nachala XX v.)* (St. Petersburg: Evropeiskii dom, 2007)

Vickery, Walter. *M. Iu. Lermontov: His Life and Work*, ed. by Ellen Rosenbaum Langer (Munich: Otto Sagner, 2001)

Viktorova, M.P. and V. A. Koshelev. "Niania," *Oneginskaia entsiklopediia*, Vol. II, N. I. Mikhailovna, et al., eds. (Moscow: Russkii put', 2004)

Viskovatyi/Viskovatov, Pavel. *Zhizn' i tvorchestvo M. Iu. Lermontova* (Moscow: Gelios ARV, 2004)

Vlasova, Marina. *Russkie sueveriia: entsiklopedicheskii slovar'* (St. Petersburg: Azbuka, 1998)

Vokrug Pushkina, prep. by K. P. Bogaevskaia and S. I. Panov (Moscow: Novoe literaturnoe obozrenie, 2000)

Vucinich, Wayne S., ed. *The Peasant in Nineteenth-Century Russia* (Stanford, CA: Stanford University Press, 1968)

Wachtel, Andrew. *The Battle for Childhood: Creation of a Russian Myth* (Stanford, CA: Stanford University Press, 1990)

Walicki, Andrzej. *The Slavophile Controversy: History of a Conservative Utopia in Nineteenth-Century Russian Thought*, trans. by Hilda Andrews Rusiecka (Oxford: Clarendon Press, 1975)

Warner, Marina. *From the Beast to the Blonde: On Fairy Tales and Their Tellers* (New York: Farrar, Straus and Giroux, 1995)

___. *Monsters of Our Own Making: The Peculiar Pleasures of Fear* (Lexington: The University Press of Kentucky, 2007) Re-issue of *No Go the Bogeyman: Scaring, Lulling, and Making Mock* (New York: Farrar, Straus, and Giroux, 1999)

Weidlé, Wladimir. *Russia: Absent and Present*, trans. by A. Gordon Smith (New York: Vintage/Random House, 1961)

Wolff, Tatiana, comp., ed., and trans. *Pushkin on Literature* (London: Metheun & Co., Ltd., 1971)

Worobec, Christine D., ed. *The Human Tradition in Imperial Russia* (Lanham: Rowman & Littlefield Publishers, 2009)

___. *Peasant Russia: Family and Community in the Post-Emancipation Period* (DeKalb: Northern Illinois University Press, 1995)

Wyngaard, Amy S. *From Savage to Citizen: The Invention of the Peasant in the French Enlightenment* (Newark: University of Delaware Press, 2004)

Zacek, Judith C. *Vospominaniia Anny Evdokimovny Labzinoi. 1758-1828* (reprint of 1914 ed.—Cambridge, Eng.: Oriental Research Partners, 1974), introduction

Zaionchkovskii, Pëtr. *Otmena krepostnogo prava v Rossii*, 2nd enl. and rev. ed. (Moscow: Ministerstvo prosveshcheniia RSFSR, 1960)

Zeepvat, Charlotte. *From Cradle to Crown: British Nannies and Governesses at the World's Royal Courts* (Phoenix Mill, England: Sutton Publishing Ltd., 2006)

Zenkovskii, V.V., ed. *Pravoslavie i kul'tura: Sbornik religiozno-filosofskikh statei* (Berlin: Russkaia kniga, 1923)

Zerubavel, Eviatar. *Time Maps: Collective Memory and the Social Shape of the Past* (Chicago: University of Chicago Press, 2003)

Zhivopis' vtoroi poloviny XIX veka: Seriia zhivopis' XVIII-XX vekov. Vol. 4, Bk. 1: A-M (Moscow: Krasnaia ploshchad', 2001)

Zhivov, Viktor M. *Iazyk i kul'tura v Rossii XVIII veka* (Moscow: Shkola "Iazyki russkoi kul'tury", 1996) English version: Victor Zhivov, *Language and Culture in Eighteenth-Century Russia*, trans. by Marcus Levitt (Boston: Academic Studies Press, 2009)

Zhukova, Ekaterina. *Gerder v Rossii: bibliograficheskii ukazatel'* (Moscow: Universitetskaia kniga, 2007)

Ziolkowski, Margaret. *Hagiography and Modern Russian Literature* (Princeton: Princeton University Press, 1988)

Ziolkowski, Jan M. *Fairy Tales from Before Fairy Tales: The Medieval Latin Past of Wonderful Lies* (Ann Arbor: University of Michigan Press, 2007)

Zipes, Jack. *Breaking the Magic Spell: Radical Theories of Folk and Fairy Tales*, rev. and exp. ed. (Lexington: University Press of Kentucky, 2002)

___, ed. *The Oxford Companion to Fairy Tales* (New York: Oxford University Press, 2000)

___, ed. *Spells of Enchantment: the Wondrous Fairy Tales of Western Culture* (New York: Viking, 1991)

___. *When Dreams Came True: Classical Fairy Tales and Their Tradition*, 2nd ed. (New York: Routledge, 2007)

___. *Why Fairy Tales Stick: The Evolution and Relevance of a Genre* (New York: Routledge, 2006)

Secondary Sources, Unpublished

Antonova, Katherine Pickering. 'The importance of the woman of the house': Gender, property and ideas in a Russian provincial gentry family, 1820-1875 – Columbia University doctoral dissertation, 2007 (forthcoming from Oxford University Press, fall 2012, as *Importance of the Woman of the House: Portrait of a Russian Gentry Family, 1830-1866*)

Keenan, Edward L. "Ivan the Terrible and His Women, part 2: Dowagers, Nannies, and Brides," unpublished lecture, ca. 1978

Kenworthy, Scott M. The Revival of Monasticism in Modern Russia: The Trinity-Sergius Lavra, 1825-1921 – Brandeis University doctoral dissertation, 2002

Neatrour, Elizabeth B. Miniatures of Russian Life at Home and in Emigration: The Life and Works of N. A. Tèffi – Indiana University doctoral dissertation, 1972

Periodicals - Russian

Bogoslovskii vestnik

Damskii zhurnal

Drevniaia i novaia Rossiia: Istoricheskii illiustrirovannyi ezhemesiachnyi sbornik

Drug zhenshchin

Istoricheskii vestnik (IV)

Khochu vsë znat': Nauchno-populiarnyi al'manakh

Literaturnaia gazeta

Literaturnoe nasledstvo

Lotmanovskii sbornik

Moskvitianin

Nauchnye Doklady Vysshei Shkoly. Filologicheskie Nauki

Novyi zhurnal

Otechestvennyia/Otechestvennye zapiski

Pravda

Prometei

Rossiiskii arkhiv: Istoriia Otechestva v svidetel'stvakh i dokumentakh XVIII-XX vv.

Russkaia starina (RS)

Russkaia shkola

Russkaia beseda

Russkii arkhiv (RA)

Russkii vestnik (RV)

Sovetskaia pedagogika

Sovremennik

Starina i novizna: Istoricheskii sbornik

Vecherniaia Moskva

Vechernii Bishkek

Vestnik Evropy (VE)

Zhurnal ministerstva narodnago prosveshcheniia

Periodicals, Other

a/b: Auto/Biography Studies

American Slavic and East European Review
Cahiers du Monde russe et soviétique
Canadian-American Slavic Studies
Critical Inquiry
Jahrbücher für Geschichte Osteuropas
The Journal of Economic History
Journal of Social History
Kritika: Explorations in Russian and Eurasian History
The Musical Quarterly
The New York Review of Books
Past & Present
Psychoanalytic Quarterly
Russian History/Histoire Russe
Russian Review
Slavic Review

Index

Aksakov, Ivan, 10, 28-29, 38, 305, 320, 372
Aksakov, Sergei, 114-15, 133, 249; *Family Chronicle*, 7
Aksakova-Sivers, Tat'iana, 208
alcohol(ism), 22, 24, 102-103, 164, 192, 225, 322
Aldanov, Mark, 234-35; *The Sources*, 235, 399
Alexander II, 227, 235, 274, 346, 399
Alexander III, 227, 346
allegories/allegory, 291, 301, 305, 435 See also symbol(s)
Allilueva [Alliluyeva], Svetlana, 63, 387
almshouse(s), 68, 236, 342
alterity, favorable/unfavorable ("civilized-and-savage" narrative, familiar strangers, dissimilarity, otherness, the Other, outsider[s]), 96, 298, 303, 312, 420, 427
ambiguity/ambiguities, 34, 8, 51-52, 69, 83, 416
ambivalence, 3-4, 49-50, 83, 188, 194, 205, 284, 291, 295, 369
Anderson, Benedict, 297

Andreas-Salomé, Lou, 161, 375, 411
Andreev, Vadim, 111, 164
Andreev(a) [Andreyev], Olga Chernov, 70, 129, 154-55, 164
Annenkov, Pavel, 26-31, 317, 320
anthroposophy, 260, 410
anti-Semitism, 200, 301
Antsiferov, Nikolai, 111, 364
archetypes, 88, 201, 304; female, 224, 299, 394, 430; peasant, 296; Russian, 301 See also symbol; allegory
Arina Rodionovna, Chapter 1, 76, 94, 102, 221-22, 247, 280, 285, 313, 316-18, 322-23, 411; Arina cult/myth, Chapter 1, 158, 204, 210, 223, 246, 249, 263-64, 266, 271, 275, 287, 290, 295, 297-98, 305, 309, 313-15, 319-24, 366, 374, 422, 435
Arnol'd, Iurii, 134, 412-13
Astaf'ev, Viktor, 243
Astrov, Nikolai, 75, 142, 338, 345
Austen, Jane, 11, 254, 335
autobiographers/memoirists/ autobiographies, 2, 5, 8-9, 11, 36-37, 44-46, 47, 58, 91, 100,

106, 109, 144, 158, 162, 164, 188, 287, 325, 352, 383, 426; autohagiography, 47, 330; émigré autobiographies, 358
autobiographical fallacy, 2, 10, 245, 276, 313, 315, 322
Averchenko, Arkadii, 229, 397; "Nian'ka," 397; "A Woman's Tail," 229
Avilova, Lidiia, 63, 193, 358

baby carriage/pram/perambulator, 121, 362
Bachelard, Gaston, 106, 109, 111, 357-58
Bakhtin, Mikhail, 110, 216, 224, 330, 343, 358, 389
Bakunin, Mikhail, 123
Balakirev, Milii, 145, 252
Balzer, Marjorie Mandelstam, 421, 433
Bal'mont, Konstantin, 78; *Under a New Sickle*, 78
Barrie, J.M., 17, 311; *Peter Pan*, 311
Bartenev, Pëtr, 10, 26-28, 30-31, 38, 246, 304-305, 318-19, 420, 422
Barto, Agniia, 382
Beketova, Mariia, 336, 369-70
beliefs, peasant See peasants
Belyi, Andrei, 122, 165, 258-60, 336, 360, 410; *A Baptized Chinaman*, 259; *Kotik Letaev*, 122, 165, 259-60
Benois (Benua), Aleksandr, 120, 406
Berdiaev (Berdyaev), Nikolai, 192, 335, 363
Berezaiskii, Vasilii, 51-52, 156, 331-32; *Anecdotes of the Old Poshekhonians*, 51-52
Berggol'ts, Ol'ga, 75, 142, 159, 199-200, 386
besprizorniki/besprizornye, 171

Bestuzhev family, 50-51, 331
Bethea, David, 261-63, 315, 411
Bibikov, M.P., 73, 78
Blok, Aleksandr, 69, 125, 342, 369-70, 376
Blum, Jerome, 343, 424
Bogdan, Valentina, 179-82
Bolotov, Andrei, 45
bonne/bónna, 12, 111, 152, 155, 233, 258, 275, 313, 347, 363
Bonner, Elena, 156, 172, 176. 199-200, 386
Borovkov, Aleksandr, 102, 145
bourgeoisie See middle class
breastfeeding, 292, 321, 341 See also wet-nurse
British nannies, 48, 57-58, 70, 105, 121, 169, 199, 346, 365, 371, 435
Brown, David, 138, 251, 254, 257, 266-67, 369
Brown, Malcolm Hamrick, 422
Buksgevden See Buxhoeveden
Bulgakov, Sergei, 133, 431, 433-34
Bunakov, Nikolai, 73, 90, 92
Bunin, Ivan, 129
Buturlin, Prince Mikhail, 57
Buxhoeveden, Sophia, 103-104, 134, 335, 358
byvshie, 169

caretaker(s), 1-3, 8, 11-13, 17, 22, 25, 44, 52-53, 55-57, 60, 62, 69, 77, 79, 81-85, 88, 92-93, 106, 111, 117, 124, 144, 148-49, 152, 155, 157-59, 162, 167, 169, 171, 173, 176, 179, 182, 187, 204-205, 207, 217, 232, 238, 242, 247, 275, 281, 284, 287, 289-90, 293, 297, 299, 308-309, 313, 316, 334, 338, 366, 374, 381-82, 384, 428, 435
Catherine II ("the Great"), 48, 94, 332, 394

censuses, city, 44, 56, 173, 328, 334-35
Chaadaev, Pëtr, 223, 290, 422-23
Chaikovskii (Tchaikovsky), Pëtr, 404
change (and continuity), 9, 79, 146, 149-50, 152, 155, 161-62, 165-67, 173-74, 176-78, 185, 225, 292, 294, 372, 383, 390, 420, 426
Chekhov, Aleksandr, 282-83, 418
Chekhov, Anton, 223-25, 232, 281-83, 299, 359-60, 388, 394-95, 418; *The Cherry Orchard*, 360; "The Cook Marries," 224-25; "Grisha," 225; "Happiness," 281, 283; "Life in Questions and Exclamations," 224; "Sleepy," 225; *Three Sisters*, 225, 341, 395, 397; *Uncle Vania*, 388; "Unnecessary Victory," 224
Chekhov, Mikhail A., 120
Chekhov, Mikhail P., 281, 283, 418
Chertkova, Anna, 134, 207, 211-12, 386
chests See trunks
childcare/lack of childcare/childcare facilities (including communal nurseries, day care, kindergarten[s]), 3, 39, 79, 152, 170f, 175, 178-79, 183-84, 234, 379
childhood/infancy (generic), 17, 29, 36, 52, 97, 106, 158, 185, 188, 213, 234, 374; motif of childhood/cult of the child, 36, 47, 62, 90, 94, 109, 113, 122, 144, 148, 188, 191, 218, 224, 239, 249, 260, 291-92, 358, 360, 401
children's self-centeredness, 196
children's similarity with servants, 194-96 See also servants
childrearing See *vospitanie*

Christianity, Christian faith/values, 101, 200-201, 211, 234-35, 238-39, 302, 337 See also Orthodoxy
chronotope See literature
Chukovskaia, Lidiia, 123, 199
Chukovskii, Kornei, 123, 351, 365
Chulkov, Mikhail, 332, 389
clans and clan politics in Muscovy, 40, 348
class differences/distinctions/conflicts, 23, 6, 9, 32, 34, 49, 51, 59, 67, 73, 83, 85, 94, 96, 112, 114, 124, 158, 166-67, 169, 176-77, 190, 202, 204, 208, 233, 241-42, 293-94, 304, 324-25, 335, 351, 377-78, 382, 402-403
Classicism, 9, 215, 217
clergy, 6, 58-59, 81, 333-34
clothing/dress, 103-105, 157, 179, 343, 347; burial outfit, 105, 210
Coe, Richard, 106, 383, 410
collectivization/dekulakization, 175, 242, 295
commensurateness/incommensurateness, 245-84
common folk, 274-75, 305, 398, 426 See also *narod*; peasants
compensation See wages/salaries
conservativism, 88, 92, 161, 164, 226-27, 293-94, 339, 425, 430
conspiracy of silence, memoirists', 75, 94
continuity/continuities See change (and continuity)
cosmopolitanism, 219, 290-91, 310
costume See clothing
country (gentry) estate(s)/manor(s)/*usad'ba*, 3, 13, 19-20, 23, 45, 60, 62-63, 65, 73, 77, 96, 109, 111, 129-30, 132-33, 141, 145, 149-52, 154, 168, 203, 212, 217, 227, 249, 251-52, 275, 322,

333, 344, 348, 351, 357-58, 363-64, 367, 373, 387, 413
cradle song(s), 126, 137-38, 140, 226, 369
cultural relativism, 96
cultural replication by nannies, 291
Cure for Melancholia, A, 216

Dal', Vladimir, 326
Damskii zhurnal (Fine Ladies' Journal), 52-54
Davydov, Nikolai, 101, 145
day care See childcare
death and dying, 62, 67, 87, 97-99, 133, 171, 191, 211, 226-27, 239, 396
Decembrists/Decembrist uprising (1825), 50, 93, 201-202, 223, 312, 324, 328, 350
Del'vig, Baron Anton, 30, 217-18
demophilism, 28, 255, 294, 319, 425 See also *narodnichestvo/narodnik*
Derzhavin, Gavrila, 217
diad'ka, 57, 86, 121, 142, 166, 179, 220, 230, 284, 334-35, 346, 377, 398, 423
Diagilev, Sergei, 162-63, 208-209
Dickens, Charles, 35, 140, 323
disciplining See punishment
divorce, 145, 175, 183, 191
Dixon, Simon, 302
Dmitriev, Mikhail, 95-96, 319-20
Dmitrii Ivanovich (both sons of Ivan IV Groznyi), 42-43
Dobroliubov, Nikolai, 338, 347
Dobuzhinskii, Mstislav, 64, 69, 191, 209, 419
Dolgorukov, Prince Ivan, 45, 71
Dolgorukov, Vsevolod (pseud. Sibirskii), 424
domestic service/workers (*domashniaia rabotnitsa,* domestic workers union), 64, 161, 173-74, 176, 178, 180, 184, 376
domrabotnitsa/-y See domestic service
Dostoevskii, Fëdor (and his family), 7, 10, 28, 38, 68, 73, 100, 159, 228, 235, 246-47, 298-99, 303-305, 320, 338, 347-48, 368, 402; *Diary of a Writer,* 320, 348; *The Idiot,* 247; "Little Boy at Christ's New Year's Party," 68; *The Possessed,* 247; Underground Man, 402; "Winter Notes on Summer Impressions," 28
double/dual belief (multifaceted faith) See *dvoeverie*
dress See clothing
drinkers/drinking/tippling See alcohol(ism)
Druzhnikov, Yuri, 315
Durova, Nadezhda, 192, 325, 383
duties, nanny's other than childcare, 82, 117-18, 158; duenna/chaperone/companion, 22-23, 33, 47, 56, 63, 86, 205, 209, 234, 317, 340, 390, 410
dvoeverie, 302-303, 433-34
dvorovye liudi (serfs), 55, 62, 96, 149-52, 204, 276, 333, 343-44, 348, 373, 412

Edgeworth, Maria (and her novel *Ennui*), 389, 419
education/educators/pedagogy/ *obrazovanie,* 6, 9, 12, 26, 50-54, 77, 83, 94-95, 98, 102, 112, 135, 155, 158-60, 181, 185, 283-84, 304, 314, 319, 324, 331, 359, 362, 374, 377, 384, 400, 431
Efron, Ariadna (Alia; daughter of Marina Tsvetaeva), 285-86
ego-documents, 2, 7, 9, 223, 293

Eikhenbaum, Boris, 201-202, 387
ekonomka See housekeeper(s)
Elagina, Avdot'ia (salon of), 26
emancipation of the serfs, 2, 6, 56-57, 62, 64, 68, 149-52, 161, 252, 293, 350, 372, 424; abolitionist novel/abolitionist sentiment/"peasant question," 54, 85, 220, 425
Emerson, Caryl, 254, 257, 389
employment offices, 62, 153, 165, 373, 377
Engel, Barbara Alpern, 312, 378
Enlightenment, The, 9, 49-50, 290-92, 393
Eremeevna (character in Fonvizin's play *The Minor*), 218-19, 221, 392
Erikson, Erik, 190, 308, 384; *Childhood and Society*, 190
eroticism, 146, 260
ethical standards/ethics See morality
Ethiopianism, 300

fairy godmothers, 132, 216, 308
fairy tales, 17, 20, 26-27, 29, 31, 51-52, 54, 91, 106, 130-33, 140, 162, 202, 206-207, 215-16, 224, 238, 250-51, 256, 258-59, 262, 266, 277-78, 284, 308, 320, 322, 330, 365-69, 387-89, 397, 402; battle over, 365; for summer or winter, 232, 398
False Dmitrii(s), 327
family/families (generic), 6, 40, 43, 55, 59, 67-68, 120-21, 130, 153, 155-56, 160, 164, 166-67, 169-71, 173, 175, 177-79, 184-85, 187-89, 195, 199, 205, 207-208, 221, 228, 301, 304, 309, 374, 378, 384, 403; clerical, 58, 81, 334, 347; cult of, 191; dysfunctional, 187-88;

intrafamily dynamics/parent-child relations, 9, 157, 187, 205, 278, 291, 383; Jewish, 58-59, 337; lower-class, 167; merchant/bourgeois/urban, 6, 58-59, 167, 169-70, 175, 236, 249, 281, 334, 377; middle-class, 160, 167; noble/gentry, 2, 18-19, 40, 54-57, 67, 81-82, 109-10, 141-42, 157-58, 167-68, 172, 187-89, 218, 311, 327, 334, 344, 347-48, 370, 377-78; nongentry, 57, 59; peasant, 67, 154, 171, 311, 344; size, 56; soviet, 178-79, 184
family chronicler/griot, 201-203
famine, 171, 177, 242, 295, 378
Fedotov, Georgii P., 433
Fedotov, Pavel, 66, 119, 406
female See women
Fen, Elisaveta (pseud. of Lydia Jackson), 120, 141, 192
Fet, Afanasii (pseud. of Shenshin), 114, 133, 361, 396
Field, Deborah, 184, 382
Figes, Orlando, 82, 175, 346
Figner, Vera, 63, 70, 73, 132-33, 192, 383, 388, 396
Filin, Mikhail, 313, 316
Filippovna (Larin nanny in Pushkin's *Eugene Onegin*), 32, 37, 221-22, 313
Filipson, Grigorii, 76, 95
Findeizen, Nikolai, 64, 271, 368
foibles/weaknesses of nannies, 46, 82, 94-103, 135, 145, 164, 204 See also alcohol(ism)
folk (the) See *narod*
folk songs/music, 17, 30, 115, 134, 139, 255, 266-68, 369, 412, 420
folktales, 27, 32, 34, 51, 132, 216, 238, 255, 277, 314, 320, 332, 366-67, 413

folk ways/beliefs/culture/lore/
    wisdom, 3, 17-18, 26-27, 31, 51-
    52, 85, 126, 211, 227, 238, 252,
    277, 298, 332, 353, 356, 422, 433
Fonvizin, Denis, 7, 218-19, 221, 229,
    429; *The Brigadier*, 218-19; *The
    Minor*, 7, 218
fortune-telling, 52, 96-97, 141, 352
Foundling Home (*Vospitatel'nyi
    dom*), 159
framing story See *skaz*
Fraser, Evgenia, 64
Freedman, Paul, 427-29
fréilein (term), 12, 313
Freud, Sigmund/Freudianism, 144,
    146-47, 194, 311, 366, 375, 383,
    417, 423, 426
Frierson, Cathy, 298, 393
Fröbel Society (St. Petersburg), 160

Gallomania, 17, 27-28, 219-20, 284,
    290, 314, 335, 419, 421
Gannibal, Mariia Alekseevna, 19,
    22, 26-27, 30-31, 319
Garin-Mikhailovskii (Garin),
    Nikolai, 233-34, 399; "At the
    Estate of the Pomeshchitsa
    Iaryshcheva," 233; *Detstvo Tëmy*,
    233; "A Father's Confession,"
    234
Garshin, Vsevolod, 404
Gathorne-Hardy, Jonathan, 189,
    365, 367, 383-84
Ge, Nikolai, 222, 257, 271-75, 408,
    413; "My Nanny," 273-74;
    "Pushchin visiting Pushkin at
    Mikhailovskoe," 222, 271, 413
gender/gender issues, 5-7, 112, 164,
    230-32, 292, 299-301, 312, 341,
    387, 423, 429, 431
gender studies, 8 See also women's
    studies

generalization(s), 4, 10-11, 82, 199,
    301, 307, 346, 371, 434
generations/generational change,
    27, 63-64, 79, 105, 112, 121, 201,
    209, 211, 233, 269, 291, 346, 383
Gertsyk, Adelaida, 247, 405
Gertsyk, Evgeniia, 110
Gippius, Zinaida, 71
Gladkov, Fëdor (and his novel
    Cement), 171
Gleason, Abbott, 432
Glinka, Liudmila See Shestakova,
    Liudmila
Glinka, Mikhail, 256-57, 264-72,
    275, 287, 408, 411-13, 422
Glinskaia, Elena, 40
Godunov, Boris, 255, 327 See
    also Pushkin: *Boris Godunov*;
    Musorgskii: *Boris Godunov*
Gogol', Nikolai, 320, 422, 429
golden age See childhood
Goldilocks model, 245-46, 419
Goldman, Emma, 173
Golitsyna, Irina, 176
Golitsyna, Tat'iana, 333
Goncharov, Ivan, 34, 87, 133, 189,
    249-51, 407-408; *Oblomov*, 189,
    249, 251
gossip, 141, 164, 180, 202, 237, 387
governess(es), 12, 30, 45, 56-58, 67,
    71, 95, 101, 121, 123, 125-26, 144,
    153, 169, 208, 224, 258-59, 296,
    333, 373, 394, 413, 415, 422, 428
governor(s): for youths, 27, 57, 121,
    126, 133, 179, 264, 319, 415, 422
*Grandfather's Strolls or The
    Continuation of Real Russian Fair*,
    216
Great Patriotic War See World War
    II
Great Reforms of the 1860s, 25,
    149-51, 244, 410

Grevs, Ivan, 34, 364
Grigor'ev, Prince Apollon, 34, 97, 114-15
Grum, Kondratii, 52, 83, 362
Guro, Elena, 113, 357-58, 360

hagiography, 33, 36, 47, 90, 100, 275, 283, 290, 329-30, 347-48, 365, 390, 414
Hammarberg, Gita, 53, 391
Harari, Manya, 337
Hegel, Georg W.F., 389, 427
Heine, Heinrich, 35
Heldt (Monter), Barbara, 38, 299, 312, 329, 429-30
help wanted ads/advertising, 62, 158, 173, 175, 184
Herder, Johann Gottfried von, 290, 420-21; *Ideas on a Philosophy of the History of Mankind*, 420; *Treatise on the Origin of Language*, 420
Herzen, Aleksandr, 69, 93, 102, 114-15, 122, 143, 195, 201, 204, 350, 352, 355, 361, 372; *Byloe i dumy* (*My Past and Thoughts*), 11, 201, 355
high (written) and low (oral/popular) culture, 95-96, 130, 132, 141, 215-16, 295, 298, 420
hired caretaker(s)/nannies, 59-60, 62, 71-73, 88, 151-52, 155, 158, 171, 174, 176, 241-42, 268, 355
Home of the Kazan Mother of God for the Training of Russian Nannies/*Priiut vo imia Kazanskoi Materi dlia vospitaniia russkikh nianek*, 159-60
homeless children See *besprizorniki*
homes for single mothers, 171
house (including attics, halls, stairs, classrooms, *devich'ia*/ maids room, kitchen, *liudskaia*/ male servants' room), 109-17, 141-42, 144, 237, 352, 358, 361, 364, 376 See also nursery
house serfs See *dvorovye liudi*
household servants/staff, 56, 63-64, 71, 75, 79, 86, 89, 117, 151, 156, 161, 165, 173-78, 180, 184, 225, 278, 292, 334-35, 348, 376, 381 See also servants; *dvorovye liudi*
housekeeper(s)/*ekonomka/kliuchnitsa*, 46, 56, 63-65, 68, 162, 176, 227, 234, 247, 316, 340, 405
humility/humbleness: trait of nannies, 88, 90, 101, 164, 274, 301, 303, 305
Hutton, Marcelline, 161, 178, 379, 381

iasli (creches) See childcare
Iazykov, Nikolai, 23-27, 317-18; "On the Death of A. S. Pushkin's Nanny," 24, 221, 317-18, 322, 416; "To A.S. Pushkin's Nanny," 23-24, 317-18, 322
icon(s), 88, 107, 113, 117, 127, 164, 237, 262, 400
ideology/-ies, 26, 35, 169, 171, 244-45, 265, 293-94, 329, 381, 397, 425-27, 429 See also *narodnichestvo; krepostnichestvo*
ignorance, 4, 52-53, 94-96, 177, 298, 302, 360, 390
illiteracy, 12, 17, 23, 94-96, 141, 155, 159, 202, 236, 351-52, 370
Il'in, Mikhail See Osorgin [Ossorgin], Mikhail
Il'inskii, Igor', 338, 405
imagined community/-ies, 297, 304
incommensurateness See commensurateness
industrialization and capitalism, 152, 225, 242, 294

intellectual(s), 2, 54, 96, 108, 258, 295, 298, 300, 303-305, 325, 433
intelligentsia, 25, 59-60, 81, 132, 167, 179, 181, 220, 234, 237, 289, 312, 333, 352
intercessor/intermediary/protectress: nanny as, 27, 31, 168-69, 205-208
Ivan IV (Groznyi, "the Terrible"), 42-43
Ivanits, Linda, 353, 435
Ivanov, Sergei, 276, 415
Izmailov, Aleksandr, 145

Jung, Carl, 430

Kahan, Arcadius, 344
Kamenskaia, Mar'ia, 202, 398
Kann-Novikova, Elizaveta, 265-66
Kantemir, Prince Antiokh, 392
Kapterev, Pëtr, 431
Karamzin, Nikolai, 217, 285, 319-20, 391-92, 429; "A Knight of Our Time," 393; "Natal'ia, the Boiar's Daughter," 217, 391; "Poor Liza," 6, 220
Keenan, Edward L., 321
Kelly, Catriona, 146, 174, 180, 332, 359, 374, 379, 386
kenoticism, 302-303, 433
Kharms, Daniil, 321-22
Kharuzina, Vera, 123, 152, 154, 376
Khemnitser, Ivan, 217
Kheraskov, Mikhail, 329
Khodasevich, Vladislav, 18, 38, 106, 261-64, 316, 325, 410-11; *The Heavy Lyre*, 262-63
Khomiakov, Aleksei, 26
Khrushcheva, Nina, 395
kindergarten(s) See childcare
Kipp, Julie, 419, 423
Kireevskii brothers, Pëtr and Ivan, 26, 367
knitting, 22, 115, 141, 160, 213-14, 253
Knizhka nianek (Handbook for Nannies), 156-58, 374
Kollontai, Aleksandra, 170-71, 378
Kolyshko, Iosif, 161, 339, 430
Komarova-Stasova, Varvara, 413
Konechnyi, Al'bin, 59
Kopelev, Lev, 199-201, 363, 386
Korf, Baron Modest, 48, 330
kormilitsa See wet-nurse
Kornilova, Ol'ga, 98, 126, 192
Korolenko, Vladimir, 150, 361
Koshkarov, Pëtr, 112, 351
Kourakine, André See Kurakin, Prince Andrei
Kovalevskaia, Sof'ia (Sophie), 101, 113-14, 118, 363
krepostnichestvo, 293-94, 425
Krestovskaia, Mariia, 232, 398-99; *Early Storms*, 232
Krivich, Valentin (pseud. of V.I. Annenskii), 365
Kropotkin, Prince Pëtr, 111, 120, 126, 196, 308; *Mutual Aid: A Factor of Evolution*, 308
Krylov, Ivan, 217, 219-21, 229; "A Lesson for Daughters," 219-21, 393
Kupreianova, A.N., 111, 351
Kurakin, Prince Andrei, 161, 169, 208, 375
Kuzminskaia, Tat'iana, 199, 336

Labzina, Anna, 46-47, 329-30, 401, 426
Lachesis, 213
language (Russian), 1, 17, 37, 39, 58, 70, 131, 222, 233, 236, 263, 265, 290, 296-98, 309, 314, 321, 337, 366, 421; acquisition/

learning, 17, 39, 58, 139, 263, 290, 296-98, 321, 366; benefits of, 58-59, 337; and linguistic battles, 421-22; and literature, 1, 314; and nationality, 9, 222-23, 296-98, 309, 421, 428; qualities of, 131-32, 290 See also peasants: speech
Lappo-Danilevskaia, Nadezhda (and her novel *At the Estate*), 234-35
law(s) on marriage, the family, and guardianship, 170-71, 175, 178
Lazarevskaia, Iuliia, 312
Lazhechnikov, Ivan, 59, 424
Leikin, Nikolai, 73
Lelong, Anna, 64, 90, 110, 115, 351-52 361
Lenin (Ul'ianov), Vladimir, 169, 199, 397, 426-27; Leninism, 169
Lermontov, Mikhail, 34, 128, 275-78, 287, 364-65, 396, 414-16, 429; "I want to tell you...," 276-78; "Cossack Lullaby," 138, 396
Leskov, Andrei, 118, 387
Leskov, Nikolai, 118, 153-54, 156, 162, 193-94, 230, 278-82, 387, 416-17; "Administrative Grace," 396; "Domestic Help," 156, 162; *Enchanted Pilgrim/Wanderer*, 230-31, 397; "Immortal Golovan," 280; *Laughter and Sorrow*, 397; *No Exit*, 340; "Pugalo" ("The Bugbear"), 397, 417; *A Ruined Clan*, 397; "The Toupee Artist. A Graveside Tale," 397, 416-17; "Will-o'-the-Wisps," 397
letter-writing ceremony/rite/scene, 95, 352
Levin, Eve, 312, 433-34
Libedinskii, Iurii, 126, 162, 376
Lifar, Sergei, 162

life cycles, 60-71, 109
life expectancy/longevity, 65-67
Life of Avvakum written by himself, 47
Likhachev, Dmitrii, 63, 104, 199-200, 338, 349
literature (Russian, excluding memoir literature), 1-2, 4, 6, 9, 11, 15-16, 34, 37-39, 63, 67, 71, 95, 114, 146, 158, 183, 194-95, 200, 208, 213, Chapter 8, 246, 275, 277, 287, 296, 299, 305, 318-19, 326, 329, 340, 369, 377, 382, 388, 391-92, 425, 429; banality in, 223-25; chronotope, 110, 215, 224, 358, 389-90; European, 35, 215; "folkloric time," 343; genre(s), 36-38, 215-16, 219, 397; ideological stereotypes in, 397; literary (authored) lullaby, 138-39, 225-27; realism, 215, 232, 416; village prose, 242-44, 403 See also language and literature
Lomonosov, Mikhail, 217
Lotman, Iurii, 329, 367-68
low/popular/oral culture See high culture
lullabies See cradle song(s)
Lyon, Jane (nanny of future Nicholas I), 48, 330-31
L'vov, Prince Georgii, 69, 151
L'vova, Princess Elizaveta, 116, 197, 385
L'vova, Princess Mariia, 151, 333

magic, 17, 96, 106, 111, 130, 138, 250, 353
"magic Negro," 396
maid(s) See servant(s)
Malina, Irina, 340, 352, 376
Malinowski, Bronislav, 353
mámka/mammy/*mámushka* (term), 12

Mamontova, Natal'ia, 68
mamushki i nianiushki/"mammies and nannies" (phrase), 132, 216, 308, 348
Mandel'shtam, Nadezhda, 58, 335
Mandel'shtam, Osip, 59, 124, 153, 165; *Shum vremeni (The Noise of Time)*, 124, 153, 165 Mariology, 431
Marker, Gary, 329-30
Marlinskii (pseud.) See Bestuzhev brothers
Marx, Karl/Marxian thought, 9, 171, 300, 395, 425
Mary Poppins, 17, 308, 311
master and man, relations of See servants
maternity/maternal instinct/motherhood, 5, 161, 289, 309; cult of domesticity/maternity, 289, 291-92, 301, 419; mother substitute/replacement/second mother/multiple mothering, 47, 188-94, 308, 384, 417; maternal figures, 384; maternal neglect, 191-92
McLean, Hugh, 194, 281, 416-18
meekness/docility: trait of nannies, 33, 47, 88-90, 164, 205, 228, 274, 282 See also humility/humbleness
Mel'nikov-Pecherskii, Pavel, 139 *In the Forests* 139, 424
"member(s) of the family," 86-87, 130, 157, 183, 348
memoir literature/memoirs/memoirists See autobiographers
mentalities, 233, 293-94, 353, 431 See also ideologies
merchants/merchantry, 6-7, 58-59, 83, 100, 103, 109, 167, 333-34, 377

Mertvago, Dmitrii, 45
mesiachina See wages/salaries
middle class, 59, 67, 83, 85, 103, 160, 167-70, 349
Mikhailov, Mikhail, 226, 229, 397; "Nanny," 226; "Nanny Dear (Satirical Scenes)," 229, 397
Mikhailovskii, Nikolai (social activist), 424
Mikhailovskii, Nikolai (writer) See Garin-Mikhailovskii
Mikhailovskoe (Pushkin family estate, place of exile), 18-25, 27, 30, 32-34, 38, 222, 271, 314, 318, 322, 413
Militsyna, Elizaveta, 68, 232-33; "Nanny" ("*Nian'ka*"), 233
Miliukov, Pavel (Paul), 424, 428
Mintslov, Sergei, 376
Miroliubov, Iurii, 64, 139, 210-12, 356; *Babushkin sunduk: Sbornik rasskazov*, 356; "The Role of Old Nannies in the Family," 210-11
Mironov, Boris, 343-44
misogynists/misogyny, 301, 394-95, 430
modernization, 9, 294, 426
Monter, Barbara See Heldt, Barbara
morality/moral sense/values/virtues/views (including ethical standards/ethics, moral stories, moral influence, moral upbringing), 4, 13, 29, 31, 47, 51, 54, 84, 102, 115, 128-29, 131-32, 154, 157, 160, 162, 164, 170, 188, 198-201, 204, 215-16, 226, 228-29, 299-301, 304, 309, 347, 361, 384, 386, 389-90, 400, 424, 432
Morozov, Nikolai, 98-99, 111, 127-28, 162, 202, 354
mother(s) See maternity

Index 489

multigenerational nannies, 63-64
Murav'ev brothers, 328
Murav'ev, Matvei, 45-46
music, 1, 22, 64, 138-39, 198, 246, 251-59, 264-71, 290, 296, 351, 368-69, 409, 412-13, 426; of bells/pealing, 265-68, 412; dissonant harmonies, 412; heard in church, 265-66; musical influence/inspiration, 251, 257, 264-70, 412; peasant, 269
Musorgskii, Modest, 138, 251-58, 271, 369, 408-409; *Boris Godunov*, 255-56, 409; "Child and Nurse," 256; "Cradle Song," 138, 369; "In the Corner," 253-54; "A Night on Bare Mountain," 257; "The Nursery"/"Scenes from Childhood," 252, 254-56, 409; "Pictures from an Exhibition," 256-57; "With Nanny," 252-56, 409; "With the Doll," 257
mythmaking/mythologizing/mythopoeic work, 22, 29, 81, 128, 210, 245-46, 249, 266, 275, 287, 290, 324, 374, 408, 426
myth of Arina See Arina Rodionovna
myths/mythology (generic/non-Arina), 1-2, 10-11, 17, 35, 39, 130, 132, 205, 211-13, 257, 260, 275, 295, 297-98, 310, 324, 358, 366-67, 377, 435

Nabokov, Vladimir, 215, 315-16; *Pale Fire*, 271-72
Nadson, Semën, 247, 396, 405-406
"nannies and mammies" (phrase) See *mamushki i nianiushki*
Nanny McPhee, 17, 308
nanny stereotype See women: female stereotype

narod/common people, 29, 100, 115-16, 251-52, 277, 294, 304 See also peasants
narodnichestvo/narodnik, 15, 35, 98, 196, 252, 294, 319, 425 See also ideology
narodnost', 271, 319, 421-22
national identity See Russian identity
nature, 98-99, 123, 254, 298, 398
Nazer'eva, Kapitolina (and her play *The Truth*), 228-29
Nekrasov, Nikolai, 139, 226, 247, 299, 369, 396; "Song for Eremushka," 226, 369
Never-never-land, 132
Neverov, Ianuariia, 112
Newman, Barbara Evans, 312, 378
Newman, Gerald, 419-20
niánia/nián'ka/niániushka/niánechka (terms), 11, 173, 311, 326
Nicholas I, 48-49, 93, 330-31
Nicholas II, 227, 358
Nietzsche, Friedrich, 375, 427
nobility/noble culture, 9, 49, 57, 85, 112, 166, 169, 176, 179, 223, 294, 310-11, 321, 334, 348, 378, 424
Norland School for Nannies, 160
nostalgia, 86, 212, 217, 221, 234, 242, 289, 291-92, 294, 403, 423
Novalis (pseud. of Friedrich von Hardenberg), 292
Novgorodtsev, Pavel, 434
Novikov, Nikolai, 49-51, 83, 331
Novikov, Ivan, 391; "The Misadventures of Annushka the Merchant's Daughter," 391; "The Novgorod Girls' Christmas Party," 391
Novoselova, Ekaterina, 73, 355
nursery, 95, 112-14, 116, 122, 134
Nurse[maid] Matilda, 17

Obolenskii, Prince Dmitrii (b. 1822), 162
Obolenskii, Prince Dmitrii (b. 1918), 70
Obolenskii, Leonid, 202, 387
Obolenskii family, 57, 97, 125
obrazovanie See education
obrok (quitrent), 73, 151, 344
Odoevskii, Prince Vladimir, 304
Ogarëv, Nikolai, 93-94, 139, 425; "Song of a Russian Nanny by the Bed of a Master's Child," 425
Olitskaia, Ekaterina, 78, 106, 345
oral/aural culture, 95, 141, 297, 352
Orthodox Church/Orthodoxy, 5, 88, 142, 154, 159-60, 162, 200, 223, 238, 300-305, 401, 428, 432-35; community of believers, 435; *sobornost'*/conciliarity, 400
Osorgin, Mikhail Jr., 209
Osorgin [Ossorgin], Mikhail (pseud. of Il'in), 70, 189-90, 197-98; *My Sister's Story*, 70, 189-90, 197-98
Ostrovskii, A.N. (and his play *The Voevoda*), 138, 369

paganism, 302, 324
Palaeologa, Zoe (Sophia), 39
Panaeva, Avdot'ia (and her novel *Romance in the Petersburg Demimonde*), 143, 425
Pankeev, Sergei (the "Wolf-Man"), 146-47, 372
Panova, Vera, 199-200, 356-57, 376, 386
Passek, Tat'iana, 89, 98-99, 102, 143, 188, 208, 357, 383
Pasternak, Boris, 59, 199-200, 386, 419
patriarchy/paternalism, 5, 195, 292-93, 300-301, 347-49, 430

Paul I, 121, 316
Pavlishcheva, Ol'ga See Pushkina, Ol'ga
Pavlova, Karolina (and her novel *A Double Life*), 335
peasant sympathy/interest, 15-16, 26-27, 32, 35, 251-52, 256, 269, 309, 319, 353, 425 See also demophilism; *narodnichestvo/narodnik*
peasants/peasantry, 2-4, 6-8, 12, 15-17, 25-27, 32, 40, 43, 51-52, 54, 57, 60, 62, 67, 71, 76, 87, 94-96, 103, 105, 116, 131-32, 149-50, 167-68, 175, 177-78, 204-205, 211, 237, 251, 281, 289-90, 292, 294-96, 303, 325, 344, 349, 353, 424, 426, 430-31; art/*lubok*, 107; belief(s)/thinking/"backwardness," 51-52, 88, 96-99, 133, 175, 211, 234, 302, 426, 435; image(s) of, 220, 225, 232-33, 242-44, 247-49, 251, 298-99, 393, 406, 427-29; literature/poetry, 284, 395, 411; music/choirs/*podgolosnaia*, 134, 139, 252, 257, 265, 269, 390, 412; *poslovitsy*/proverbs/sayings, 85; song See folk song; speech/idioms/rhyming/rhythm, 31, 129, 139, 236, 252, 284, 290, 296-98, 422 See also superstition
pedagogy/pedagog(s) See education
penitent nobles See repentant nobles
Peter I "(the Great")", 43, 390, 420, 426
Peter III, 204
pilgrimages, 42, 142-43, 371
piety/devoutness: trait of nannies 45, 88, 198, 204, 301-304, 405
Pipes, Richard, 170, 179

Pisemskii, Aleksei, 55, 339; *A/One Thousand Souls*, 55, 340
Plato/Platonism, 129-30, 410
play/games, 70, 113, 118-20, 123, 135-36, 140, 195, 254, 258, 268, 276, 284, 362, 410
Pletnev, Pëtr, 25, 318
Pobedonostsev, Sergei, 227, 396; "The Nanny," 227
pochvennichestvo/pochvenniki (nativism), 228, 304
political exile(s), 18-20, 23, 25, 27, 30, 32, 43, 69, 73, 93, 164, 172, 176, 223, 239, 317-18, 352
political views of nannies, 92-94, 125, 164, 226
Pomialovskii, Nikolai (and his novella "Bourgeois Happiness"), 348
populism/populist See *narodnichestvo/narodnik*
postmodernism, 299, 427
pre-Romanticism, 217 See also sentimentalism
preparation/professionalization of nannies See training of nannies
Priemskii, Dmitrii, 171-72, 175
privileges, 5, 8, 34, 65, 82, 94, 114, 172, 175, 310, 379
progress, 291, 294, 427
Prokof'ev, Sergei, 404
prostitution/prostitutes, 144, 165-66, 173, 377
proto-nationalism, 290, 420 See also Romantic nationalism
psychoanalysis, 190, 375, 383 See also Freud, Sigmund
Pugachëv/Pugachëv revolt, 45, 324
punishment (including corporal/physical)/disciplining, 89, 101-102, 120-22, 129, 158, 164, 195, 208, 219, 253-54

Pushchin, Ivan, 222, 271, 317
Pushkarev, Nikolai, 130-31; "National fairy tales," 131
Pushkareva, Natal'ia, 59, 82, 312
Pushkin, Aleksandr, Chapter 1, 44, 46-47, 68, 73, 94, 121, 145, 158, 164, 192, 213, 217, 221-23, 225, 229, 245, 255-56, 262-64, 266, 269, 271, 275, 277, 280, 285, 287, 290, 294, 297, 299, 304-305, 313-25, 353, 391, 393, 395, 411, 413, 421-22, 424, 429; *Boris Godunov*/"Comedy about Tsar Boris," 30, 32, 255-56, 409; *The Captain's Daughter*, 422; "Confidante of Magical Antiquity," 263; "A Dream" ("*Son*"), 22, 29, 263; *Dubrovskii*, 33, 322; *Evgenii (Eugene) Onegin*, 6, 15-16, 32, 37, 103, 145, 221, 223, 247, 313-15, 316, 322, 343; "The Hamlet" ("*Gorodok*"), 22; "... Once Again I Visited" ("*... Vnov' ia posetil*"), 23; "To Nanny" ("*K niane*"), 157, 314, 317; "A Winter's Evening" ("*Zimnii vecher*"), 22, 322, 416
Pushkin, Lev, 19, 316
Pushkin family/Pushkins, 19, 25, 27, 32
Pushkina, Ol'ga, 19-20, 31, 33, 316, 322-23

quitrent See *obrok*

Radio Nanny, 382
Radishchev, Aleksandr, 49-50, 220-21, 227, 393, 429; *A Journey from St. Petersburg to Moscow*, 220-21
Raevskaia, Ekaterina, 60
Raikin, Arkadii (and his broadcast sketch "Ah nanny nanny"), 403

raising children See *vospitanie*
Rakhmaninov, Sergei, 404
rationalism, 47, 237, 290-91, 294, 426
raznochintsy, 325, 334
Rein, Evgenii, 38, 177-78, 380
religion/religiosity, 5, 47, 50, 87-90, 96, 133, 143, 154, 162-64, 176, 198, 200, 204, 211, 215, 217, 233, 237, 267, 274-76, 302-304, 353, 371, 376, 386-87, 390, 401, 426, 428, 431-34 See also Orthodox Church
Remizov, Aleksei, 247
repentant/penitent nobles (*kaiushchiesia dvoriane*), 293, 424
Revolution of 1905, 165
Revolution(s) of 1917 (February/March, October/November), 6, 114, 166, 168, 172, 199, 239, 244, 294-95, 310, 377, 401
revolutionary movements, 243, 252, 319
Riesemann, Oskar von, 254-56
Rilke, Rainer Maria, 375, 411
Rimskii-Korsakov, Nikolai, 256
Romanov family, 57, 166, 327-28, 346, 358
Romantic/Romanticism, 9, 32, 59, 108, 123, 132, 192, 215, 217, 221-22, 251-52, 292, 298, 415, 421
Romantic nationalism, 289-91, 297-98, 304-305, 309, 421
room and board See wages/salaries
Roosevelt, Priscilla, 82, 357
Rousseau, Jean-Jacques, 53, 291-92
Rozanov, Vasilii, 42
Rozhdestvennskii, Vsevolod, 162, 340
Rusanov, Nikolai, 91
Russell, Bertrand, 300
Russian folk See *narod*

Russian identity/soul/nationalism, 9, 223, 228, 290-91, 298, 302, 304, 420, 429, 434; Russianness/Russian nationality, 270, 290, 319; national consciousness, 8, 17, 34, 132, 223, 287, 293, 310, 421; nationalistic allegory, 301-305; "purpose" of Russia, 302
Russian school of art, 290
Russian soul See Russian identity
Russian stereotype See stereotypes
Rustemeyer, Angela, 82, 165-66, 337, 346, 375
Ryan, Cheyney, 427, 429

Sabaneeva, Ekaterina, 97, 104
Sakharov, Andrei, 172, 177, 199,
Sakharov, Ivan, 353
Sakharova, Mariia, 227-28, 396; "Nanny. An Étude," 227-28
Schmemann, Serge, 209
School for Children's Medical Nurses and the Home for Children, 160
Scott House, 154
Sechenov, Ivan, 91
secularism, 6, 9, 47, 141, 216, 301, 390
self-sacrificing trait of nannies, 5, 227-28, 284, 293, 305
Sementkovskii, Rostislav, 278-79, 416
sense of identity, 8, 291
sentimentalism, 68, 217, 220, 227, 234, 238, 242, 292, 346, 391-94
serfdom/serfage/serfs, 3, 9, 25, 44, 54-55, 57-58, 67, 71-73, 75-76, 86-89, 116, 133, 144-45, 152, 156, 165, 204, 221, 234, 281, 283-84, 292-93, 298, 300, 351, 397, 415-16, 423-25
servants/master-servant relationship, 3-4, 8-9, 44, 50,

53-54, 56, 59, 62-64, 67, 76, 82, 85-89, 97-98, 101, 112-18, 141, 145, 150-56, 158-59, 162, 165-66, 168-69, 172-73, 176-78, 180-81, 184, 194-96, 202, 204-205, 218-19, 224-25, 249, 269, 277-79, 284, 309, 333-34, 337, 342, 346-49, 351-52, 361, 373, 376, 378, 380-81, 387, 389-90, 394, 400, 412-13, 415, 417, 426-27
servants and children See children's similarity with servants
sewing/needlepoint/embroidery, 104, 107, 129, 160, 210-11, 260
sex/sexuality/sexual affairs/sex education/eroticism, 144-47, 165, 179, 260, 351, 361, 391 See also gender; prostitution
sexual differences/sexism, 5, 299, 328
Shakespeare, William, 30, 215, 335; *Romeo and Juliet*, 215
Shalikov, Pëtr, 52-53, 83, 333
Shan-Girei, Akim, 414-15
Shchepkina, Aleksandra, 101, 328, 354, 363, 387
Shchepkina-Kupernik, Tat'iana, 68, 124, 192, 355, 376
Shchukin, Vasilii, 132-33, 364, 425
Shelgunov, Nikolai, 73
Shelgunova, Liudmila, 73
Shenshin (pseud.) See Fet, Afanasii
Shestakova (Glinka), Liudmila, 266, 269-71, 413
Shevzov, Vera, 353, 431, 435
Shishkov, Admiral Aleksandr, 393, 395, 421; "Meditation on Old and New Style of the Russian Language," 421
Shmelëv, Ivan, 142-43, 233, 235-39, 370-71, 399-401; *Bogomol'e* (*Pilgrimage*), 142-43; "The Blessed," 401; *Niania iz Moskvy* (*Nanny From Moscow*), 235-38
Shvarts, Dmitrii, 20, 22, 32
Simmons, Ernest J., 18, 314-15
singers/singing, 116, 133-39, 160, 212, 264-65, 370, 384, 404-405, 409
Skabichevskii, Aleksandr, 59, 92, 350
Skalon, Sof'ia, 117, 123
skaz, 227, 230, 236, 393, 400
Slavophile(s)/Slavophilism, 15, 26, 28, 35, 38, 227, 242, 290, 293-94, 304, 318-19, 367
Slezkine, Yuri, 358
Smith, Anthony, 421, 429
Snegirev Ivan, 99, 338, 354
snoring, 140, 183
social Darwinists, 308
social mobility, 8, 64-65, 95, 217
social origins of nannies, 44, 57-58, 73, 167
Sologub, Fëdor, 118, 226-27, 362, 388; "Hide and Seek," 118, 362; "Terrible Lullaby," 226-27; "Who Art Thou?", 388
Solov'ëv, Sergei (historian b. 1820), 88, 142, 338, 386
Solov'ëv, Sergei (grandson of preceding, b. 1885), 155, 352
Solov'ëv, Vladimir, 404, 431, 433-34
Solov'ëva, Poliksena, 206
Solzhenitsyn, Aleksandr, 243-44, 308; "At Matrëna's Place," 243-44
Somov, Oleg, 422
song(s), 26, 29, 31, 133-37, 252-57, 259, 264-66, 269, 276-77, 308, 314, 322, 368, 370, 409 See also singing; folk songs
sophiology, 431

Sorokin[a], Ol'ga, 399-401
Spagnolo, Rebecca, 174, 373
staircase(s)/stairs/stairways See house
Stalin (Dzhugashvili), Iosif, 40, 63, 166, 172, 175, 177, 331, 426; Stalinism, 31, 166, 179, 182, 199-200
Staniukovich, Konstantin, 231; "Nian'ka," 229, 231
Stasov, Vladimir, 10, 145, 246, 257, 269-74, 408-409, 413
statute on marriage family and guardianship See law(s) on marriage the family and guardianship
Steiner, Rudolph, 260
stereotype(s)/stereotyping, 4-7, 57, 69, 71, 81-82, 88, 91, 166, 188, 205, 216, 225, 228, 232-33, 244, 299-301, 346, 397, 400, 431; cultural, 346, 420; Russian, 301-305 See also women: female stereotype
Stites, Richard, 267, 312, 343, 433
stock figure, 216, 221, 231 See also stereotype
Stogov, Erazm/Erast, 90, 398
stories and storytelling, 1, 8, 33, 49, 51, 54, 97-98, 111, 115-16, 129-32, 140, 188, 203, 207, 212, 216, 232, 257, 266, 284, 296, 331, 354, 361, 367, 376, 398 See also folktales; fairy tales
Stravinskii, Igor', 419
strolls/strolling See walks and strolls
Struve, Pëtr, 169
substitute parent(s), substitute/surrogate mother, 188-94, 308, 346, 384, 416 See also maternity
suffering, penchant for/masochism, 301, 303, 434

Sumarokov, Aleksandr, 217, 392; *Monstrosities*, 392; *A Quarrel Over Nothing*, 392; *The Tragedy of Khorev*, 217, 391
sunduk See trunks
superior virtue of the oppressed, 300-301
superstition, 4, 51-52, 88, 94-99, 126, 133, 227, 284, 298, 302, 331, 352-53, 366, 390
Sychugov, Savvatii, 97, 123, 128, 338,
symbol(s)/symbolism, 2, 17, 95, 216, 223, 225, 244, 247, 259, Chapter 10, 309-10, 346, 348, 356, 359-60, 388, 390, 405, 419, 424-26, 435; of maternity, 419; wet-nurse symbol, 419 See also allegories; archetypes
syphilis, 165 See also sex

Taneev, Vladimir, 62, 73, 357
Taruskin, Richard, 408-409
Tchaikovsky, Peter See Chaikovskii, Pëtr
Tèffi, Nadezhda, 105, 117, 238-40, 242, 321-22, 342, 352, 361, 378, 397, 401-402; "Golden Childhood," 401; "A Little Fairy Tale," 402; "The Monster," 239-40, 402; "Nanny's Tale About the Mare's Head," 322, 402; "Nostalgia," 239; "The Terrifying Fairy Tale," 402; "The Wet-nurse," 352
Thyrêt, Isolde, 42
Tikhonov, Vladimir, 106-108, 282
Toll', Feliks, 83-85, 347
Tolstaia,Tat'iana, 199, 383, 386
Tolstoi,Il'ia, 360, 386
Tolstoi, Count Lev (Leo), 36, 76, 87, 127, 133, 207, 247, 249, 303, 336, 373, 383, 405; *Childhood*, 224,

247, 383, 405, 416-17; *War and Peace*, 336
Tolstoi, Count Fëdor, 100
Tolstoi family, 57
Tovrov, Jessica, 82, 332, 348
town and/vs. country/urban-rural, 5, 58, 109, 295-96, 298, 310, 341
training of nannies, 85, 158-61, 185
travel/trips, 42-44, 64, 75-76, 102, 106, 142-44, 281, 354, 357-58, 370, 411 See also pilgrimages
travel literature, 394
Travers, P.L., 17, 311
Trotskii, Lev (Bronshtein; Leon Trotsky), 181, 397
Trubetskoi, Prince Evgenii, 100, 114, 155, 360
Trubetskoi family, 100
Trumpener, Katie, 324, 419, 423
trunks and chests, 105-108, 142, 235, 259, 262, 356-57, 403
Tsebrikova, Mariia/Mar'ia, 76-77, 112, 196, 359-60, 400; *Rasskaz niani*, 400
Tsiavlovskii, Mstislav, 318, 323
Tsvetaeva, Anastasiia, 358-59
Tsvetaeva, Marina, 38, 110-11, 132, 168, 285-87, 325, 416, 418; "The Devil," 418; "Moi Pushkin," 418; "Poem of the Staircase," 111
Tuchkova-Ogareva, Natal'ia, 93, 340
Tur, Evgeniia (pseud.), 189, 383
Turgenev, Ivan, 58, 81, 133, 159, 247, 299, 319, 351, 429; *Nest of Gentlefolk*, 247
Turnemir, Evgeniia See Tur, Evgeniia
tutors, home/foreign, 45, 57, 126, 133, 219, 269, 319, 392, 407, 422 See also governors

Tyrkova-Vil'iams, Ariadna, 60, 159, 210, 340, 385

Ul'iana (Pushkin's nanny), 31-32, 121, 316
Ul'ianov, Dmitrii, 426-27
Ul'ianskii, A.I., 313, 315-16
unions: domestic workers', 174, 176, 179-80, 376
upbringing See *vospitanie*
Uspenskii, Lev, 117, 376-77
ustavnye gramoty See emancipation
utopianism, 169-71, 378

Vasilisa (nanny character in Krylov play *Lesson for Daughters*), 219-21, 393
Vasina-Grossman, Vera, 264-65, 411
Venetsianov, Aleksei, 247-49, 406-407, 413-14; "Old Nanny in Peasant Head-dress," 247-49, 406-407; "Portrait of the Panaev Children with Their Nanny," 84, 249; "Wet-nurse with Child," 61, 249, 407
Veremenko, Valentina, 157-58
Vereshchagin [Verestchagin], Aleksandr, 134
Vereshchagin, Vasilii, 72, 101, 134, 361, 419
Viazemskii, Pëtr, 393
village life, 3, 96, 126, 296 See also peasants
village beliefs See peasant beliefs
village prose See literature
Viskovatov/Viskovatyi, Pavel, 275-76, 414
Vodovozova, Elizaveta, 77, 92, 121, 195, 207, 283-84, 357, 383
Volkonskii, Prince Vladimir, 231-32, 398; "The Family Chronicle

of the Valdaiskii Princes," 231-32, 398

vospitanie (childrearing/upbringing), 3, 12-13, 27-28, 45, 47, 48-51, 53-54, 94-95, 134, 158, 160, 162, 170-71, 175, 187, 199, 207, 234, 267, 271, 276, 284, 290, 331, 339, 347, 378, 382-84, 403-404, 422, 430-31; "nature" vs. "nurture," 431; upbringing, collective, 170-71, 182, 378

vospitatel'(i)/vospitatel'nitsa(y), 12, 26-27, 122, 154, 199

Vrangel', Liudmila, 58, 69, 106, 207, 342, 371, 383

Vrangel', Baron Nikolai, 360, 383

Wachtel, Andrew, 36, 324-25, 346, 358, 383

wages/salaries (including room and board), 71-74, 151-52, 157-58, 160, 162, 165, 171, 179, 183, 230, 236-37, 343-44, 392, 403

walks and strolls, 102, 121-26, 140, 286, 363

Warner, Marina, 12, 137-38

Westernizer(s), 290, 425-26

wet-nurse(s)/wet-nursing/*kormilitsa*, 12, 38-39, 43-44, 46, 51-53, 59-62, 73, 77, 82, 94, 97, 102-104, 134, 139, 142, 152, 159, 173, 202-203, 215, 220-21, 247, 249, 258, 261-64, 267, 284, 289-91, 296, 305, 309, 321, 337, 341, 349-50, 352, 380, 385, 389, 407, 409-410, 412, 419

Wolf-Man See Pankeev, Sergei

womanhood See women

women: alleged nature of, 291, 299, 430-31; educated, 352; female moral superiority, 299-301; female stereotype (including nanny stereotype), 5-7, 69, 81-82, 88, 91, 166-67, 188, 216, 225, 228, 232-33, 244, 299-300, 346; female writers (generic), 7, 53, 359, 429; female "archetypes," 88, 201, 224, 299-301, 312, 394-95, 430; feminism, 5-6, 9, 208, 375; fertility rates, 65, 340-41; in Chekhov, 224, 299, 341, 359, 394-95; in society, 292; violence against/rape, 6, 233, 390; working/career/professional, 6, 8, 38, 171, 174, 178-79, 299

women's "kingdom"/"*zhenskoe tsarstvo*," 359

women's studies, 8, 94, 312, 383

World War II, 177, 182, 403

Worobec, Christine, 370, 430-31

Zaionchkovskii, Pëtr, 151, 355, 371

Zakharovo (Pushkin family estate), 19, 25,

Zernova, Ruf, 183, 200, 381

Zhadovskaia, Iulia, 225-26, 396; "A Thought" (*Duma*), 226

Zhigalova, Ol'ga, 141, 192, 356-57

Zhukovskii, Vasilii, 26, 325, 395

Zinov'ev, Grigorii, 170, 172

Zoshchenko, Mikhail, 178, 240, 322, 402-403; "A Tale about a Nanny/The Nursemaid," 240-42, 402-403

www.ingramcontent.com/pod-product-compliance
Lightning Source LLC
Chambersburg PA
CBHW021824220426
43663CB00005B/127